STUDIES IN HOMOSEXUALITY

A GARLAND SERIES

Edited with
Introductions by

Wayne R. Dynes
Hunter College, City University
of New York

and Stephen Donaldson

Contents of Series

VOLUME X

Homosexuality and Government, Politics, and Prisons

Edited with Introductions by

Wayne R. Dynes

Hunter College, City University of New York

and Stephen Donaldson

Garland Publishing, Inc.

New York & London 1992

Library of Congress Cataloging-in-Publication Data

Homosexuality and government, politics and prisons / edited by Wayne R. Dynes and Stephen Donaldson.
p. cm. — (Studies in homosexuality ; v. 10)
ISBN 0-8153-0555-9
1. Homosexuality—Government policy—History. 2. Gays—Political activity—History. I. Dynes, Wayne R. II. Donaldson, Stephen. III. Title: Homosexuality and government, politics and prisons. IV. Series.
HQ76.25.H6746 1992
305.9'0664—dc20 92-13896
CIP

Printed on acid-free, 250-year-life paper
Manufactured in the United States of America

General Introduction

Over the past quarter century powerful currents of research and writing on homosexuality, lesbianism, and bisexuality have rippled through widening channels, finding outlets in scores of journals affiliated with more than a dozen disciplines. While this increase in the volume of publications signals a welcome lessening of the taboo on the subject and a growing sense of its importance, this profusion makes it difficult for even specialists to monitor the progress of scholarship in its many domains. Much of the key material in this area has appeared in hard-to-locate and often unlikely appearing academic periodicals, which have escaped even diligent indexers and bibliographers. Moreover, not a few of these journals appeared in very limited issues and cannot be found today even in the larger research libraries.

To make more accessible to the reader the classic, the pioneering, and the most recent outstanding articles of scholarly work in a wide variety of disciplines, this series gathers a selection of such articles, reprinting them in thirteen volumes organized by discipline. Sifting through thousands of journal articles, the editors have chosen for republication works of scholarly distinction without attempting to impose any uniform ideological perspective on a field still characterized by lively controversies. Dates of original publication of the selections included in these volumes span the twentieth century, from Erich Bethe's landmark 1907 article on Dorian pederasty in *Rheinisches Museum* to current articles embodying the latest techniques of archival research and conceptual analysis. In some cases, it has been impossible to obtain permission to reprint material we felt worth inclusion; Haworth Press, for example, declined to permit republication of any articles from the *Journal of Homosexuality*. Fortunately, that periodical is widely available so that its absence does not detract from our goal of furnishing important but hard-to-find research.

The earlier situation in which work on homosexuality typically found its home in the social sciences and in medicine has significantly broadened, with important work in history, the humanities, and the arts. Attention has also shifted from the isolated individual to the interaction of the gay/lesbian/bi person with his/her peers. Increased attention has also been devoted to cultural representations in novels and poetry, films and popular music.

Each individual volume brings together the best article-length scholarship on homosexuality from that discipline and will save the specialist a great deal of time and effort. Each volume is self-contained; at the same time, the entire series is designed so that the reader seeking a broad understanding of the phenomena of homosexualities and their cultural, literary, and historical manifestations can make profitable use of the volumes representing other disciplines.

The introduction to each volume examines the history of the discipline(s) represented and its approaches to the study of homosexuality, critiques the development of research in the field, notes milestones in the evolution of thought and research, raises methodological issues, discusses conceptual questions, and suggests directions for future investigation and developments in the field. These introductions allow the reader from outside the discipline to survey and appreciate the issues raised. At the same time specialists will find a constructive critique of the state of their discipline as well as an appreciation of its contributions to the overall development of gay, lesbian, and bisexual scholarship. Appended to each introduction is a survey bibliography of important book-length works in that field.

Introduction

In the long history of Western civilization, its governments have repeatedly succumbed to the temptation to regulate the most intimate details of human life. Sexuality, especially same-sex behavior, has been a recurrent though not universal preoccupation of governments from the most ancient times to the present.

Until the twentieth century, scholarly reflection on government emphasized abstract theorizing on the purpose, character, and organization of the body politic or state; empirical analyses such as that of Machiavelli were the exception. In more recent decades, grand normative theory has, however, largely yielded to scrutiny of the political process; this task in turn required a redefinition of the subject of inquiry so as to include public actors who influence political behavior, including interest groups. Addressing the functioning of these "pressure groups," the discipline overlaps with sociology. When academic inquiry organized as "political science" focused on the mechanics of state power, the question of purpose languished in scholarly backwaters, tainted by association with ideology and lack of scientific methodology. Neglected in political science departments, the question of the proper scope of state power has engaged the passionate concern of activists in the gay, lesbian, and bisexual movement. In this volume, functional analyses join normative essays in spotlighting the relationship between government and homosexuality.

Some aspects of that relationship, such as law, police activity, social work, governmental medicine, and its historical development, figure in other volumes of this series, to which the reader is referred.

Government-sponsored Pederasty

It is a truism that much of Western history has seen government in the role of antagonist to homosexual activity and those practicing it. Surprisingly, however, the history begins with government on the other side, promoting pederasty in ancient Crete from about 650 B.C. (in the belief of later Greeks in order to curb overpopulation and institutionalize the training of soldiers). The rulers of Sparta imported this system after 615 and incorporated it in the constitution of their state. At twelve the Spartan boy became the erotic companion of a twenty-two–year-old male, who trained him for the next eight years, until he was ready for full-time military duty. Two years later he got his own boy. At thirty he married, and then would leave the all-male barracks. A similar system existed for females, relatively privileged in Sparta compared to other Greek states.

Spartan pederasty was so successful that Solon introduced it to Athens as part of his new constitution in 594–93 B.C. The Athenians, however, focused more on intellect and character than on military training of the boys. Athens prohibited prostituting male citizens, though clients could purchase the services of noncitizen males. After Sparta had conquered Athens, it remained for Thebes to overthrow Spartan rule (371 B.C.) by forming its "Sacred Band," a military unit of three hundred pairs of lovers. The Macedonians wiped out the Sacred Band to the last man and youth in 338, thus ending the prominence, though not the role, of pederasty in Greek government.

While most Greek thinkers united in praising the institution of pederasty, Plato in his old age turned against it and denounced it in the *Laws*, but his call for its suppression found no response until the Christians emerged triumphant in the fourth century of our era.

Various forms of homosexuality, chiefly pederastic, flourished at the courts of ancient China, but the practice played no role in the structure of the state. In Japan the ruling samurai class honored pederastic (and later ephebophilic) traditions consistently, and the Ashikaga shoguns in particular brought homosexuality to great prominence at the court, but the tradition did not enjoy government sponsorship. Many of the rulers of India engaged in homosexual behavior, but with little effect on government policy. One exception was Tipu Sultan's reported policy of rape of English prisoners in the course of his wars against Britain. Likewise various Islamic potentates engaged in pederasty, but without a formal government role other than in the acquisition of boys for the court by the army and tax collectors.

In the late Roman republic, passive homosexuality became a political issue as Cicero defamed Mark Antony with accusations of having assumed that role. The sexual system in Rome reflected the political one, in that the adult Roman citizen could easily take the penetrative role—likened to Rome's conquests—but not the passive (subjugated) one, reserved for noncitizens, boys, and slaves under the law. As often as not, the Roman emperors of the first two centuries flaunted their homosexual amours, but they refrained from enshrining their tastes as government policy.

Homophobic Government and Enlightenment Reformers

The adoption of Christianity as the state religion in the Roman Empire resulted in the decree of capital punishment for sodomy, derived from Jewish law, in 342, inaugurating a long tradition of governmental hostility in Christian Europe and its colonial offshoots. The Jewish legal prohibition seems to stem from Persian antecedents based on Zoroastrian religion. After the fall of the Empire in the West, the criminal prohibitions passed for the most part out of the realm of secular government and into the religious sphere, culminating in the Inquisition, though the victims of the Inquisitors were formally turned over to the secular authorities just before burning.

In the later Middle Ages, European secular governments undertook to control homosexuality, following the lead of the Italian city-states beginning with Bologna in 1265. Campaigns against sodomites blighted various Italian centers, with vice squads active in Venice, Florence, and other municipalities. France and Norway also assumed secular jurisdiction in the thirteenth century. The Holy Roman Empire (despite its name a secular organization) adopted criminal legislation specifying capital punishment in 1532; Henry VIII imposed the death penalty for sodomy in England a year later. The English political theorist Thomas Hobbes defended this legislation as necessary to promote population growth.

Despite the general prohibition of sodomy, a number of European monarchs had reputations for homosexuality and the maintenance of court favorites or "minions," among them Edward II and James I of England and Henri III and Louis XIII of France. Often their political opponents wielded homophobia as a tool with which to attack them. Other monarchs, such as Frederick the Great of Prussia, William III of Holland and England, and Juan II of Castille, avoided such general clique formation notwithstanding their homosexual inclinations or liaisons with a single favored lover.

Criticism of the sodomy laws based on general principles of the legitimate purposes of government dates to Cesare Beccaria, who in 1764 published his influential treatise *Dei delitti e delle pene* (On Punishments and Crimes). Voltaire endorsed Beccaria's work, and this line of thought bore fruit in 1791 when the revolutionary French Assembly omitted sodomy from the list of sexual offenses; this exclusion was affirmed in the Code Napoleon of 1810, becoming normative for much of Europe and Latin America.

In England Jeremy Bentham (1748–1832), creator of utilitarian political theory, wrote over six hundred pages arguing against the sodomy law on various grounds, but none of these texts appeared in his lifetime, and most of them remain unpublished.

The establishment of modern military forces, with their strict organization and discipline, collided with homosexual behavior when governments viewed illegal sodomy as subversive in the ranks. During the Napoleonic wars, as Arthur N. Gilbert has shown, the British government conducted savage reprisals against "buggery" in the Navy, well-established as it may have been as a naval tradition (according to Winston Churchill). United States forces ignored homosexual behavior until a widespread naval investigation (first targeted at sexually passive sailors only and then widened to include civilians) arose at the Newport, Rhode Island, base shortly after the end of World War I. The ensuing scandal led to a condemnation of the witch-hunt by the Senate Naval Affairs Committee, after which the issue died. Backed by repressive psychiatric theories, American official action against gay and lesbian service personnel developed again in the last years of World War II, as profiled in studies by Alan Bérubé. Although homosexuality has ceased to be a military issue in most countries of the industrialized world, including Canada, American armed forces continue to attempt to exclude anyone involved in homosexual conduct or tendencies from their ranks.

Censorship

Another area in which government has long impacted on sexuality has been censorship, which Henry VIII introduced in England in 1538. French censorship ended with the Revolution, but Comstockery remained vigilant in England and the United States into the twentieth century. In Britain the government censored not only print but also theatrical presentations. A court declared the London periodical *Gay News* obscene for blasphemy (the House of Lords concurring) after publishing a poem by James Kirkup in 1976. Parliament's adoption of Clause 28 of the Local Government Act of 1988 banned British local councils from funding anything which "promotes" homosexuality.

In the nineteenth century the United States banned the importation of "obscene" works and prohibited homosexual materials from the mails (the Supreme Court overturned the latter ban in 1954), but censorship of domestic publishers faded after William Burroughs' *Naked Lunch* won a lengthy court battle, enabling Grove Press to publish the novel in 1964. Yet legal efforts to suppress what conservative officials considered homosexual pornography increased during the Reagan and Bush administrations. Local governments closed many gay porno theaters, allegedly in the interest of AIDS prevention.

In 1989 Senator Jesse Helms (Republican of North Carolina) mounted a campaign against sexuality in the arts in connection with the homoerotic photographs of the late Robert Mapplethorpe. In 1990 Dennis Barrie, director of the Contemporary Arts Center in Cincinnati, Ohio, was slapped with an indictment but then won an acquittal by jury trial of obscenity for displaying the Mapplethorpe exhibition. Despite this victory the National Endowment for the Arts came under repeated fire for sponsoring materials deemed prohomosexual and blasphemous.

Canada continues to censor the importation of homosexual publications, and the distinguished Toronto gay monthly *The Body Politic* had to endure several prosecutions in the 1980s which finally put it out of business. Censorship was general in the Communist world and persists in many Latin American, African, Asian, and Muslim countries today.

Rise and Fall of the First Homosexual Movement

The end of the nineteenth century saw the beginning of an organized attempt to influence German state policy on homosexuality, to wit, the repeal of Paragraph 175 of the Imperial penal code, which criminalized male homosexuality only. Founded by Magnus Hirschfeld in 1897, the Berlin Scientific-Humanitarian Committee heralded the entry of homosexuals as a group into the political process, with far-reaching if not immediately apparent or even desired consequences. The committee's first act was to draft a petition to the German legislature, obtaining some six thousand names for it from among the intellectual elite. A Dutch branch appeared in 1911 after passage of a law raising the age of consent for homosexual acts only. In Germany a rival group, the German Friendship Association, emerged in 1920, but renounced politics in 1923, turning to social activities and publishing. The committee remained an elitist organization and never tried to build a mass base. Its strategy of attacking the criminal law through the depiction of homosexuality as a medical matter was not only a dismal failure, but gave rise to far-reaching negative consequences, especially in the United States. The movement publicized the concept of the exclusive homosexual as a distinctive type of person, and Kurt Hiller in 1921 introduced the notion of homosexuals as a minority group. Despite book-length studies by John Lauritsen and David Thorstad, and by James Steakley, today's activists have largely ignored the precedent of the German movement, possibly because of its ghastly denouement.

The rise to power of the Nazis doomed the German movement: Hirschfeld presciently departed in 1929; the Committee disbanded under pressure in 1933, when the Nazis publicly burned its library and files. A year later the homosexuality of storm-trooper leader Ernst Röhm was used against him in a political struggle within the Nazi party, ending in his execution and that of other homosexuals in the leadership of the paramilitary SA organization. This event turned out to be a mere prelude to the worst persecution of homosexuality known to history. The historian must question the extent to which the conceptual innovations of the German movement helped pave the way for this holocaust. In 1935 the Nazis strengthened Paragraph 175, though continuing to ignore lesbianism, then began rounding up not only genuine male homosexuals but also occasional political enemies under its terms; eventually even the Chief of Staff of the armed forces, General von Fritsch, became a victim in a move to break the resistance of the Junkers in the Army. Convictions rose to nearly nine thousand in 1937.

Arrestees for homosexuality went to concentration camps where they had to wear a pink triangle rather than the black of other criminal convicts; the severity of the conditions under which they were held ensured that few survived. Executions began under the euthanasia program as early as 1933. While the army resisted the arrest policy, it commonly sent homosexual soldiers to the Eastern Front to die in combat. German allies such as Vichy France, Mussolini's Italy, and Horthy's Hungary also undertook persecutions of homosexuals, though without formally criminalizing homosexual acts (except for persons under twenty-one in France). The total number of deaths resulting from the Nazi persecution of homosexuals is disputed, estimates ranging from five thousand to one million.

In the Soviet Union, the revolutionary Bolshevik regime legalized homosexuality as part of a general abrogation of tsarist laws, but following the Nazi example, Stalin recriminalized male homosexuality in 1934, and this law remained in effect even after the formal dissolution of the Soviet Union in 1991. Thugs attacked the fledgling Soviet gay and lesbian movement which formed, with considerable help from western Europe, in the wake of Gorbachev's perestroika.

Communist homophobia drew little notice in the United States. In 1950 Republican Senator Joseph McCarthy unleashed a campaign against homosexuals on the grounds that they were Cold War security risks, then persuaded the Senate to mount an investigation into the employment of homosexuals in government. The political repercussions of this campaign lasted long after McCarthy himself met censure by the Senate in 1954.

The Second Homosexual Movement

After liberation from the Nazis, the Netherlands became the first country to revive a politically oriented homosexual movement at the end of 1946. In the United States, the continuous history of the movement begins with Henry (Harry) Hay's founding of the clandestine Mattachine Society in Los Angeles at the end of 1950. A lesbian movement appeared with the inception of the Daughters of Bilitis in San Francisco in 1955.

In England law reform came to the fore with the publication of a report favoring decriminalization from a parliamentary committee headed by Sir John Wolfenden in 1957. This committee arose at the urging of the Church of England and a number of prominent intellectuals. Lobbyists for repeal formed The Homosexual Law Reform Society, but Parliament did not act until 1967.

Law reform in the United States began with a model penal code drafted by the American Bar Association in 1961; the state of Illinois adopted it that very year. Eventually, through a combination of court action and legislative repeal, half of the American states decriminalized by the end of the 1980s, though the Supreme Court's *Hardwick* decision upholding the constitutionality of the Georgia sodomy law—for homosexuals only—was a major setback.

The Mattachine Society of Washington focused on the federal government throughout the 1960s, addressing such issues as federal employment, security clearances, and military service. Taking their cue from the black civil rights movement, "homophile" groups, rapidly growing but then still without a mass base, staged demonstrations starting in 1965. Finding that the classification of homosexuality as a mental illness blocked their way, the movement confronted the psychiatric establishment, winning a struggle within the American Psychiatric Association in 1973. Major efforts went into breaking the taboo against discussion of homosexuality in the mass media and forming coalitions with liberal religious groups and civil liberties lobbies. A national publication, a gay church, and a gay student movement helped to build a more effective political effort by the late 1960s.

In June 1965, the U.S. Court of Appeals, in the Bruce Scott case, reversed Scott's disqualification for federal employment; this set the stage for the Civil Service Commission's acceptance of homosexuals in the 1970s. Congress quietly eliminated one of the last McCarthy-era legacies, the barrier to immigration of homosexuals, in 1990, though restrictions on HIV-positive foreigners remain at issue.

The last of the questions involving the federal government left over from the sixties is that of the U.S. military's bar to homosexuals. Some progress has been made in that homosexual discharges are no longer of a less-than-honorable character, but the basic policy of refusing anyone with homosexual experience or inclinations has withstood all challenges. Federal criminal law and military law also continue to prohibit sodomy; federal gay civil rights bills have yet to reach the hearing stage in committee, though two openly gay congressmen from Massachusetts survived sexual scandals in the late 1980s with their seats and most of their influence intact, whereas previous members of Congress had been forced out of office upon exposure as homosexual.

On a local scale, homophile organizations and public-spirited lawyers often challenged, with general success, such repressive police practices as raids on gay bars and entrapment of homosexuals.

Coordination of lobbying efforts benefited from 1966 on from a continent-wide umbrella organization embracing nearly all the gay and lesbian groups, the North American Conference of Homophile Organizations (NACHO), but in 1970 NACHO fell victim to internal struggles; no comparable organization has since arisen to unite the steadily diversifying movement.

In June of 1969 the growing radicalism of the times, fueled by opposition to the Vietnam war and the militancy of the black and women's movements, found its catalyst in the Stonewall riots in New York City. Tens of thousands of homosexual men and women, inspired by news coverage of Stonewall, joined and formed politically active gay organizations, transforming the movement from an elite lobby to a mass movement.

Gay Liberation

Ideologically, the homosexual movement of the early 1970s reflected the inspiration of leftist radicalism, but before long diversity became apparent, and as more and more sectors of the gay community found voice in various organizations, a wide political spectrum became evident. A mass wave of "coming out" provided the new groups with a steady influx of willing workers, and politicians began to notice the growth of a significant "gay vote." National marches on Washington in 1979 and 1987 attracted tens of thousands of demonstrators, and politicians and commentators alike began to think of the homosexuals as an interest group or even an ethnic minority playing the political game like any other.

There was resistance, of course, mainly from fundamentalist Protestants and from the Roman Catholic hierarchy, and the struggle for gay civil rights laws (banning discrimination in employment, housing, and public accommodations) had its ups and downs throughout the decade, mostly played out at the local level, frequently with public referenda. Cities saw rights ordinances adopted, repealed, and readopted. Often a local gay rights law had to coexist with an unreformed state sodomy law, so that a homosexual could go to prison for his actions but his employer could not fire him for them. Wisconsin adopted a statewide gay rights law in 1981; Massachusetts followed in 1990; Connecticut, Hawaii, and New Jersey joined their ranks the following year.

Gay men and lesbians became visible actors in party politics in the United States, forcing battles over gay rights planks in the platforms of the Democratic party. Openly gay and lesbian legislators became effective spokespeople for gay interests in the political process. Occasionally in the big cities a sizable gay voting block was effective, but at other times, notably in presidential elections, the divisions among gay and lesbian voters were more obvious.

From the United States this wave of mass activism spread rapidly abroad. The Canadian movement, which dates from 1964, achieved decriminalization in 1969, and three provinces (Quebec, Ontario, and the Yukon) adopted gay rights laws. In Latin America, where the tradition of the Code Napoleon held sway, providing no criminal law against which reformers could mobilize, and where Mediterranean concepts of homosexuality served to hinder the emergence of a sense of gay community, progress was slower. In Europe, however, the new-style movement took off. West Germany repealed Article 175 in 1969. The International Gay [later Lesbian and Gay] Association appeared in 1978 as a coalition of independent groups and sponsored a series of annual conferences. The ILGA's base remained in Europe, but it made a sustained effort to reach out to the Third World and held its 1991 conference in Acapulco, Mexico. France, Norway, New Zealand, and even Israel adopted national gay rights laws, but Britain moved backward with Clause 28. First Denmark and then Sweden legalized same-sex marriage or its equivalent.

This trend, which increasingly turned government back into an ally of at least the politically mobilized segment of the gay, lesbian, and bisexual population, in the 1980s ran into the growing AIDS epidemic, diverting attention from criminal and rights laws to medical concerns. This shift also had the effect of making the gay movement more like conventional political interest groups, in that its primary focus became the allocation of national resources, where it competed with other groups with varying degrees of success. Towards the end of the decade, however, the pressure of ever-increasing fatalities fostered the emergence of new activist and even radical (in tactics if not ideology) groups such as ACT UP, signaling a growing militancy in the movement at large.

Major political struggles have taken place over issues of government-sponsored AIDS education, which has often seemed to have an unstated agenda of discouraging all homosexual activity rather than focusing on high-risk behavior. Large-scale closings of gay bath houses and cinemas by local governments, under the guise of AIDS prevention measures, encountered little or no protest from gay leaders.

A new political issue emerging at the end of the 1980s was the demand for familial rights, ranging from quasimarital status for "domestic partners" to parental rights.

A discussion of the movement would not be complete without mention of the bisexual movement, which originated on the two American coasts about 1971, influenced by the sexual freedom trend as well as by gay liberation, and quickly grew, riding a "bisexual chic" wave which crested in 1974 and then receded. Leaders of the "bisexual liberation" movement emphasized their dissatisfaction with dualistic concepts of sexual orientation and identity and their sense that bisexuals were victimized by discrimination from homosexuals as well as heterosexuals. Some spokespeople openly stated their feeling that bisexuality was superior to either form of "exclusivism." But these claims were rarely acknowledged. Skeptical of the concept of bisexuality, many homosexual leaders refused to accord legitimacy to this new element. The bisexual liberation movement virtually expired around the turn of the decade for a number of reasons, among them a new "biphobia" associated with the AIDS epidemic.

By the mid-1980s, however, a second-wave bisexual movement was springing up, fueled largely by women dissatisfied with the extremes of lesbian separatism. This new movement has continued to burgeon, accompanied by an upwelling of books and periodicals and a growth of the practice of including the term "bisexual" along with "lesbian and gay" in the names of groups, and by 1991 had formed not only a national organization, Bi-Net USA, but also held an international bisexual conference in Amsterdam. The precise relationship of the bisexual movement organizations to the gay and lesbian movements remains a matter of considerable debate.

The academic side of the gay and lesbian movement began in 1966 with the founding of the Student Homophile League at Columbia University. The student movement quickly spread to become a dense national network. In 1973 faculty and graduate students began to organize the Gay Academic Union in New York in order to promote gay studies across disciplines and to fight discrimination within academia. After several years of success, GAU faltered, leaving the field to a host of caucuses within the traditional academic disciplines. In 1987 scholars met at Yale for the first of a series of annual conferences; the 1991 event, held at Rutgers University, drew fifteen hundred to two thousand attendees and authorized the foundation of a pan-disciplinary Society for Lesbian, Gay, and Bisexual Studies.

A general tendency towards the proliferation of diverse organizational expressions of subgroups within the movement gained strength in the 1980s, giving birth to groups representing African Americans, Asian and Pacific Americans, American Indians, Hispanic Americans, and other ethnic identities.

Research Questions

For the political scientist, much research into the political behavior of gays and lesbians—whether as voters or as lobbyists—remains to be done. Political science theory must address the delicate question of the relationship between the organized movement (with its emphasis on exclusive, self-identified, and subculture-participant homosexuals and lesbians) on the one hand, and the homosexually involved general populace (for many if not most of whom same-sex eroticism is a part-time or occasional interest rather than a full-time defining identity) on the other. For the near future, it appears that gay political action will continue to follow the example of the traditional ethnic or national minority—the benefits of gay rights laws accruing only to those willing to accept the specified categories of sexual orientation, for example—but history suggests that this model may fade with time and greater integration in the wake of wider acceptance. Whether common interests in fighting discrimination or obtaining social benefits will continue to counteract the centrifugal pull of the various other political ties overlapping the "gay community" (class, ethnic background, gender, ideology, etc.) also remains to be seen. As the notion that the "natural home" of gay people lies on the radical left declines, the import of major political philosophies—liberalism, libertarianism, conservatism, anarchism, and socialism—needs to be studied in depth.

Prisons, Jails, and Reformatories

Prisons, jails, and reformatories are government-sponsored sex-segregated total institutions which confine people by order of a court. With a very few exceptions, sexual acts in such facilities necessarily involve members of the same sex. The number of males in particular who reside in these environments is staggering—well over a million in the United States alone—so that one may consider this walled-off but constantly intermingling archipelago far and away the largest "gay ghetto."

When one considers the aftermath of concentration in such places on the millions more who have lived in them but are then released to their communities, the significance of the patterns learned in them for the entire society looms large. Yet because the vast majority of prisoners function heterosexually outside confinement, these patterns differ markedly from those of the androphile model which characterizes the modern industrial-world gay subculture. Instead, these institutions offer the best-known and most concentrated example of situational homosexuality, mixed with strong elements of other non-androphilic models. They shed considerable light on the full range and potential for homosexual behavior by heterosexuals, hosting as they do social worlds in which not only sexual acts but also long-term sexual/emotional pair-bonding take place between people of the same sex, both of whom consider themselves and are considered by their peers to be heterosexual. These acts and couple relationships are not only common but receive support and validation from the prisoners' subculture, in sharp contrast with the attitudes of the general society.

Jailhouse sexual mores also interest the scholar in that they represent the survival in the Western industrialized world of non-androphilic conceptions of homosexuality. Some of these patterns were thought to have vanished with the buffalo herds of the Great Plains, but in fact they remain strongly rooted among the lower socio-economic classes which provide the bulk of prisoners, though producing few academics.

As yet, very little quality research on sexuality in confinement has appeared. Most of what has surfaced in scholarly format over the years has consisted of attempts to address the self-defined "problem" of homosexuality on the part of penologists who have generally reflected the values and assumptions of their employers. The administrators of these systems usually seek to obscure such behavior, nearly universally prohibiting it and insisting in public that its incidence is minimal, as they believe its presence reflects poorly on the management of the incarceration systems.

The researcher seeking to fathom the world of the prisoner faces numerous obstacles: he often appears to prisoners to be associated with the administration and hence is distrusted; he must try to obtain reliable data on behavior which violates the disciplinary codes and which tends to be secretive and shielded from the prying eyes of outsiders; he must work with a concept and terminology of homosexuality which is quite different from the one to which he has usually been accustomed. The sociologist Wayne Wooden found a way around these obstacles by collaborating with a prisoner, Jay Parker; their 1982 book *Men Behind Bars* continues to dominate the literature as the only major systematic survey of the entire sexual structure of a prison. Alan J. Davis' classic 1968 study of the Philadelphia jail system, included herein, remains the most thorough statistical study of local jails, though unfortunately limited to the topic of rape. Davis had the considerable investigative resources of the district attorney's office at his disposal. Other works tend to be anecdotal or based on very limited data (though Donald Tucker's "participant observer" approach, reprinted here from Anthony Scacco's *Male Rape* anthology, yields considerable theoretical insight), and one cannot yet point to either a developed body of empirical research or a commanding theoretical approach to sexuality in confinement.

In addition a great deal of variation occurs from one type of institution to another, with the most salient differences from all accounts being between those confining men (about 94 percent of the American total) and those incarcerating women (though the latter have inspired numerous studies, such as those by Rose Giallambardo and by Ward and Kassebaum herein). The security level of the prison (which roughly correlates with the length of sentences being served there, the experience level and the violence potential of the prisoners) is a major factor, with both consensual and forced sexuality rising with the level; big-city institutions differ from small rural facilities, and jails ("temporary" detention centers for those awaiting trial or sentencing or serving short sentences) in general show some differences from prisons, which hold convicted felons. Institutions for juveniles have not to date experienced a systematic survey, but by all accounts they are not only the most sexually active confinement facilities, but are also schools in which the sexual mores of the prisoner are commonly learned.

For students of general sexuality and homosexuality in particular, the very high incidence rates of same-sex behavior on the part of prisoners whose unconfined patterns are generally heterosexual pose major theoretical challenges, but these have gone largely unexamined. It seems clear that in the absence of the opposite sex and in the presence of a subcultural tradition which at least tolerates if not validates such behavior (the homophobic tradition of the larger society notwithstanding), a great majority of young males is not only capable of sexual arousal to the point of orgasm while in the penetrating role with another male, but will go to considerable lengths to realize this capability in action. Does this mean that most or all males are partially homosexual or bisexual and that this element in their sexuality awaits only the lifting of social oppression and sufficient sexual deprivation for its expression? Similar questions arise in connection with woman prisoners.

Or does this capacity for arousal perhaps point to flaws in the prevalent conception of homosexuality? The typical male prisoner, like most males in Mediterranean-influenced or Asian cultures, insists that the "active," penetrating, controlling role is not homosexual, only "masculine," and that whatever classification some scholar may attach to the act, his psychological reality remains a heterosexual one. He regards the passive, submissive partner as a quasi-female, not as another man (even the heterosexual forced into this role is universally thought to have "lost his manhood"), and sees him as the only member of the pair doing anything "abnormal." Pursuing this thought leads one to broader considerations regarding the accuracy or utility of applying androphilia-derived conceptual and theoretical schemes to the domains of other models of homosexuality, such as the gender-differentiated one which seems most influential here, though mixed with strong elements of the age-differentiated and Roman-type dominance-enforcement models. Because such situational homosexuality has little to do with "gay and lesbian identity" and the politics associated with it, it has commanded little theoretical attention from academics involved in gay studies, but examination of this phenomenon may shed considerable light on general issues of sexual orientation.

Other neglected issues are the role of dominance and submission in such behavior on the part of heterosexuals; the relationship between power, aggression, and eros; the influence of jailhouse mores on the sexual practices of the wider culture; the role of confinement sexuality in perpetuating rape (of both sexes) and other acts of violence after release; the stark differences between women's and men's prison cultures; the insufficiency of masturbation as a sexual outlet; the transfer of conceptual structures from one setting to another; the function of rape in these settings as a social ritual or rite de passage; and the historical phenomenon represented by the survival of earlier patterns of homosexuality in contemporary society. Clearly much work remains to be done in this area.

Bibliography

Adam, Barry D. *The Rise of a Gay and Lesbian Movement.* Boston: Twayne, 1987.

Barwasser, Karlheinz A. *Schwulenhetz im Knast: eine Dokumentation.* Bielefeld, Germany: Pusteblume, 1982.

Bayer, Ronald. *Private Acts, Social Consequences: AIDS and the Politics of Public Health.* New York: Free Press, 1989.

Bérubé, Allan. *Coming Out Under Fire: The History of Gay Men and Women in World War Two.* New York: Free Press, 1990.

Büssing, Sabine. *Of Captive Queens and Holy Panthers: Prison Fiction and Male Homoerotic Experience.* Frankfurt am Main: Peter Lang, 1990.

Consoli, Massimo. *Stonewall: Quando la rivoluzione è gay.* Rome: Napoleone, 1990.

Costello, John. *Mask of Treachery.* New York: William Morrow, 1988.

D'Emilio, John. *Sexual Politics, Sexual Communities: The Making of a Homosexual Minority in the United States, 1940–1970.* Chicago: University of Chicago Press, 1983.

Gay Left Collective. *Homosexuality: Power and Politics.* London: Allison and Busby, 1980.

Hafkamp, Hans, and Maurice van Lieshout, eds. *Pijlen van naamloze liefde: pioniers van de homo-emancipatie.* Amsterdam: Uitgeverij SUA, 1988.

Humphrey, Mary Ann. *My Country, My Right to Serve: Experiences of Gay Men and Women in the Military, World War II to the Present.* New York: Harper Collins, 1990.

Humphreys, Laud. *Out of the Closets: The Sociology of Homosexual Liberation.* Englewood Cliffs, N. J.: Prentice-Hall, 1972.

Jellonek, Burkhard. *Homosexuelle unter dem Hakenkreuz: Die Verfolgung von Homosexuellen im Dritten Reich.* Paderborn: Schöningh, 1990.

Lauritsen, John, and David Thorstad. *The Early Homosexual Rights Movement (1864–1935).* New York: Times Change Press, 1974.

Levin, Jim. *Reflections on the American Homosexual Rights Movement.* New York: Gay Academic Union, 1983.

Lockwood, Daniel. *Prison Sexual Violence.* New York: Elsevier, 1980.

Marotta, Toby. *The Politics of Homosexuality.* Boston: Houghton Mifflin, 1981.

Mitchell, Pam, ed. *Pink Triangles: Radical Perspectives on Gay Liberation.* Boston: Alyson, 1980.

Plant, Richard. *The Pink Triangle: The Nazi War Against Homosexuals.* New York: Holt, 1986.

Propper, Alice M. *Prison Homosexuality: Myth and Reality.* Lexington, Mass.: Lexington Books, 1981.

Salierno, Giulio. *La ripressione sessuale nelle carceri italiane.* Rome: Tattilo, 1973.

Scacco, Anthony M. Jr., *Rape in Prison.* Springfield, Ill.: Charles C. Thomas, 1975. Idem, ed. *Male Rape: A Casebook of Sexual Aggressions.* New York: AMS Press, 1982.

Shepherd, Simon, and Mick Wallis, eds. *Coming on Strong: Gay Politics and Culture.* London: Unwin Hyman, 1989.

Steakley, James. *The Homosexual Emancipation Movement in Germany.* New York: Arno Press, 1975.

Teal, Donn. *The Gay Militants.* New York: Stein and Day, 1971.

Timmons, Stuart. *The Trouble with Harry Hay: Founder of the American Gay Movement.* Boston: Alyson, 1990.

Williams, Colin J., and Martin S. Weinberg. *Homosexuals and the Military: A Study of Less than Honorable Discharge.* New York: Harper & Row, 1971.

Wooden, Wayne S., and Jay Parker. *Men Behind Bars: Sexual Exploitation in Prison.* New York: Plenum Press, 1982.

Contents

ERRATA

A Punk's Song: View from the Inside by Donald Tucker should appear in the section entitled "Prisons."

Government and Politics

CLOSETS OF POWER

BY TAYLOR BRANCH

As a high government official and a homosexual, Dan Bradley led a double life that is common among congressmen, White House aides, and others in the political world. Here is his story, and theirs.

POLITICS came naturally to Dan Bradley. Despite his handicap as a "children's-home boy," he was elected class president every year in high school. At Mercer University he beat out eleven candidates to become freshman class president, and served on nearly every board and society in the school—the classic popular student-activities zealot. "I knew their names, faces, majors, where they came from, and their activities at school. I made it my business to know." In his career as a leader of the movement to bring legal services to the poor, Bradley operated the same way. Perhaps unconsciously, he sought to become acquainted with a wide mass of people at a genuine though superficial level, and he sought their approval on the same plane. He was preoccupied with the general good and with the broader classes of human nature, as opposed to the quirks or depths of any individual. His knowledge of people was wide but thin, precise but not intimate.

Taylor Branch, a former Washington editor of Harper's, *is co-author of* Labyrinth, *a book about the murder of Orlando Letelier, published by Viking Press. He is at work on a biography of Martin Luther King, Jr.*

All this made Dan Bradley a good politician. It also helped guard his secret even before he knew he had one. The ability to live in a web of broad but shallow relationships, to design a public face and hide a private one, served Bradley well in both worlds of his adult life. The political personality, it seems, is tailor-made for life in the closet.

In March of this year, Bradley became the highest federal official in American history to declare publicly that he was a homosexual. Upon resigning as president of the government-funded Legal Services Corporation, he told *The New York Times* that he had survived in politics only by living a double life of "sheer, unmitigated fear." He also told the *Times* that he had many homosexual friends who were congressmen, congressional staff people, White House aides, bureaucrats, and lawyers throughout Washington. They all shared a clandestine life inside the closet.

As a powerful but frightened subculture, the closeted politicians in Washington have learned how to recognize, protect, communicate with, and seduce one another—all the while leading professional lives and keeping the "straights" largely unaware. In a capital where gossip, scandal, and political advantage are highly prized, this has been a remarkable collective feat.

Since "coming out," Bradley has traveled the country on a tour of celebration. He has met reinforcements—who are closeted mayors, city councilmen, clergymen, ordinary folk—and they have feted him as one who has done what they cannot bring themselves to do. He has also received moving testaments of acceptance from heterosexuals, strangers and old friends alike. Casting off practiced habits of deception, he has spoken and moved about freely for the first time in many years, like a newly released prisoner. In June, a woman friend asked him to be the "bridesmaid" at her wedding. Bradley agreed, laughing. He carried an enormous bouquet out of the church in the traditional recession alongside the best man, former Assistant Secretary of State Richard Holbrooke.

It has been a gay time for Bradley in the literal sense of that word, which homosexual activists appropriated for themselves from the police slang for prostitutes. The word itself is telling. Bradley hopes that this high will not be followed by a relapse into self-doubt and self-loathing, like all the others, but he knows that he has rejected his lies more than he has accepted himself. "I hated being in the closet more than I hated being gay," he says. Moreover, he knows that many of the closeted gays who applauded his declaration are also threatened by it. He is a challenge to them; his general acceptance by heterosexuals undercuts their argument that they must remain in the closet to avoid persecution. Some gay public officials in Washington have criticized Bradley for drawing attention to them at a time when closeted politicians are menaced on several fronts. Shortly after the *Times* article on Bradley, an incipient scandal broke out in Washington over charges that several congressmen had had homosexual relations with young pages. Meanwhile, political groups affiliated with the Moral Majority have stepped up their mass solicitations for a war against the "homosexual conspiracy" in Washington, and conservative scandal sheets have surfaced, naming the names of liberal gay congressmen.

These and other forces could bring the enormous, hidden homosexual subculture under public scrutiny for the first time, with results ranging from suicide to improved mental health. Most people of all sexual persuasions wish to avoid the ordeal. Bradley doesn't, for reasons that are somewhat cloudy. Partly for personal catharsis and partly out of conviction that it is politically astute, he is revealing the details of a personal and political life in the closet. Dan Bradley's story is unique, of course, like everyone's. But it is at least one true version of life as a closeted homosexual in the political world.

I.

A Straight Pill

DAN BRADLEY formally entered the closet in 1968. At that time he had accumulated a grand total of "no more than ten seconds" of sexual experience with another person in his twenty-eight years. Those ten seconds convinced him that his life was cursed, as he had always feared.

He trembled and prayed on a trip from Philadelphia back to his office in Belle Glade, Florida, where he was a pioneer lawyer for migrant laborers and an early leader in the effort to make legal services available to the poor. During the lunch hour, Bradley locked the door and became dizzy and nauseated. In a state of panic, he began calling the psychiatrists listed in West Palm Beach, begging for an emergency appointment.

The psychiatrist he found shared an office with a dentist. Even in the late 1960s, some Florida analysts discovered that more patients would walk through the door if they could maintain the pretext of a sore tooth. Bradley welcomed the ruse. Greatly agitated, he told the doctor that he did not know why he was there. He blurted out half-sentences about symptoms ranging from dizzy spells and fits of nausea to attacks of inexplicable depression.

"Mr. Bradley," interrupted the psychiatrist, "are you a homosexual?"

Bradley said nothing. After a long silence, he opened his mouth to reply, but he began crying instead. A great tide obliterated his reserve. He wept, shook, and sobbed for over an hour. When it was over, the psychiatrist said, "Tell me about yourself." Bradley droned on for hours, disgorging himself again in words, looking expectantly at the doctor now and then in the hope that some detail might explain the beast.

Born into Georgia's once prominent Bulloch family, he had been packed off to a Baptist orphanage at the age of five, along with five brothers and sisters. His mother had died unexpectedly; his father was physically disabled and hospitalized; nothing was left of the family prestige except for memories of entertaining FDR in Georgia.

The 500 boys and girls at the Georgia Baptist Children's Home led dreary, regimented lives. All the boys were bused regularly to the local barber college, where rookie barber students gave them patchy, telltale haircuts. All the orphans checked their clothes out of the general storage room, trading up as they grew. Each child lived in a cottage with twenty-three others, ruled by a married couple. For some reason, both the husband and the wife were called "the matron." Generally, the matrons were poor, devout, often illiterate Baptists, who received free room and board in return for meting out Old Testament discipline to their wards. Bradley, a seven-year-old bed wetter, was obliged to drink mixtures of turpentine and castor oil, and to take cold winter showers in front of his cottage mates.

Bradley pleaded with the psychiatrist to tell him that there was enough stigma in this background to explain a thousand cases of homosexuality. What tortured him was that no one else at the orphanage had turned out like him, though they had all grown up under the same conditions. And his brothers and sisters had inherited the same genetic pool. Why only Bradley?

And he had flourished at the orphanage. He embraced the church wholeheartedly. He learned the Bible almost by heart, and his devotion and quick wit made him something of a religious prodigy. When he was only twelve, preachers in the churches around Atlanta would call on Bradley to lead the entire congregation in prayer. By the time he was fourteen, preachers from all over Georgia would ask the children's home to send Bradley as a shining example of the church's good works. Bradley would stand, the worshipers would beam, and the preacher would announce that the young lad planned to become a minister.

From his earliest Bible classes, Bradley learned to banish the subject of sex to the distant recesses, along with other sins. He remembered hearing the bolder orphans, at puberty, bragging graphically of their conquests in the outside world, describing sex with girls pretty much the way they would talk of pulling the legs off grasshoppers. To Bradley, it was an alien world, devoid of the Christian spirit. He planned to cross the great gulf by a vague, mysterious route that had something to do with magic and marriage.

Bradley did not know exactly how females were supposed to make their entrance into his private world, but he became increasingly worried, over the years, when he detected no stirring at all. In Psychology 101, he felt a quickening when he read descriptions of sexual attraction among persons of the same sex. Soon he was in the college library reading treatises on homosexuality, careful to conceal them inside his regular textbooks.

Instinctively, he reread the Book of Job—many, many times. Logic, faith, and the beginnings of desperation convinced him beyond a doubt that his religious belief was being tested. Just as God had inflicted pestilence, personal bereavement, and all manner of physical suffering on Job, Bradley thought, He was now dangling an invitation to heathen despair in front of Bradley. Bradley had always been proud of his inner strength. With the Book of Job firmly in mind, he contained all thoughts of his fellow males while awaiting his deliverance. He abstained from sex during his teens and twenties, when his peers were coupling, reproducing, divorcing, and otherwise trying to match their genitals with their hopes.

THE CONFERENCE in Philadelphia was like many other gatherings of the "poverty bar" before and since. It ended on Friday. The next morning, several hours before his flight back to Florida, Bradley was reading the *Philadelphia Inquirer* and watching the skaters on an enclosed ice rink in an arcade beneath his hotel, when he sensed that others, also reading newspapers, were watching him. His fear told him that many were homosexuals congregated around the ice rink. Bradley walked quickly upstairs into the hotel bathroom. There, three urinals down, he was shocked to see a man standing casually waving an erect penis back and forth. Bradley had never seen another man's erection. He walked out, and paced the hotel floor in circles of confused fascination. Then he went back to the ice rink and posed nervously behind his *Inquirer*.

Presently, a blond young street urchin in blue jeans and a T-shirt walked up and said, "I'll let you suck me for five dollars." Bradley recoiled and fled without a word. He walked more circles and returned. When the young hustler repeated the proposition, Bradley nodded.

At Georgia Baptist Children's Home, the matrons had often punished Bradley by washing his mouth out with a lye-based soap. Now, after the hustler collected his money and left, Bradley rushed into the bathroom, lathered up a washcloth with octagonal soap, and scrubbed his mouth vigorously, feverishly. He told all this to the psychiatrist at West Palm Beach the following Monday, and on subsequent visits over the next several months. Bradley pressed the psychiatrist to reveal the accumulated wisdom of his profession on two questions: what causes homosexuality, and can it be cured? But nothing offered encouragement. He asked about the latest theories of behavior modification and shock therapy. He wanted a palliative, if not a complete, cure. "The words I used were a 'straight pill,'" he says. "I wanted to know if there was a 'straight pill' I could take to help me."

The doctor offered no pills. Gradually, Bradley abandoned his Job theory, though he would slide back to it many times. He could say to himself and the doctor that although he had never completed a sexual act with anyone, he was a homosexual. It was a permanent condition, not a divine test—or if it was a test, he had failed it. Bradley knew with greater clarity that he could never accept having sex with men; he would rather die. He realized that he could never be a lawyer, public servant, or politician and function as a homosexual. "I decided it was no big deal. I'd just be asexual, as I had been all my life."

II.

A Fraternity of Despair

WHEN THE Nixon administration came to power in 1969, Bradley managed to get himself assigned to the job of creating a new Legal Services program in the Virgin Islands, out of harm's way. He worked very hard and traveled constantly. During the six months he was based in the Virgin Islands, he took only one full day off—to wander on the white beaches of San Juan, Puerto Rico.

The quickening came to him in advance of the specific realization that one section of the beach was special. Several hundred men were packed together, surrounded closely on all sides by mixed couples. "They all had their slinky little bathing suits and their effeminate mannerisms," says Bradley. "I knew what it was."

Bradley stood by a hot-dog stand to watch.

A sunbather approached and introduced himself vaguely as Tom the sailor. Bradley called himself Dan the lawyer. After some evasive conversation, the sailor departed, but then returned. Bradley kept a rendezvous that night and managed to taste piña colada and smoke marijuana. Later that night, he took Tom the sailor back to his hotel room for what amounted to the first sexual experience of his life.

When the fear rushed in on him the next day, he resolved to think of the incident as an isolated blip of failure after a year of successful repression. It helped that he did not feel the slightest personal interest in Tom the sailor, whom Bradley took to be from the unsavory caste of those who had given in to their homosexuality.

In 1970, after a brief tour of duty in Mississippi helping victims of Hurricane Camille, Bradley was called to Washington as special assistant to Terry Lenzner, President Nixon's director of Legal Services. There Bradley used his growing political skills to stave off attacks on Legal Services by disgruntled conservatives. Consumed by the political war, Bradley lived for months in a small hotel room, surrounded by phone messages and legal tracts. His discipline held up, and he never ventured into the seedy downtown areas where he imagined the homosexuals to be. For safety's sake, he tried to limit his few social engagements to female company and to pick out women with whom he sensed a nonsexual, "buddy" rapport. This plan did not always work, however. After many convivial lunches, one woman lured Bradley into bed by telling him that her fiancé had just informed her that he was a homosexual, and demanding comfort. "It was horrible," Bradley recalls, but some days later, she wrote to say that she had fallen in love with him.

To fend off this woman's advances, Bradley began inventing fairy tales about his romantic passion for a woman named Barbara, Terry Lenzner's assistant. His violent nerves lent an air of authenticity to the stories. Bradley began seeing more of Barbara, who became one of his lifelong friends. Rumors soon were circulating in the Legal Services office about Bradley's love triangle, and about how he was conducting himself with admirable restraint.

The charade taxed Bradley's limited social prowess for several months, until fate rescued him in the form of a promotional transfer to Atlanta as director of Legal Services for the Southern states. The job required a civil-service background investigation, and Bradley imagined how brilliant sleuths might locate Tom the sailor; but they didn't, of course.

One day in Atlanta, a high-powered real-estate woman named Sally* walked into Bradley's office and sat down on his lap. "She was the most aggressive woman I've ever known," he says. Sally announced that she had heard about him from mutual acquaintances in Washington. She listed a number of her illustrious Washington lovers from the past and wondered out loud when and how she would get to know Bradley. She pursued him, and eventually trapped him into a skiing trip.

On the drive north, Sally pestered him with questions: about his childhood, about the orphanage, about his mother. This confused and angered Bradley. "Why are you doing this to me?" he asked.

"Don't you see?" she replied. "Dan, I love you."

"What do you mean, you love me?" said Bradley. That weekend, he watched her make love to him. Passive and frightened once again, he made the experience palatable by fantasizing about Tom the sailor. After he dropped Sally off at her home back in Atlanta, Bradley drove through the downtown area, looking for a man. "I was so confused that I wanted to reassure myself that I was a homosexual," he says. "But I didn't know where to look."

Within a few days, he began a homosexual sex life for the first time, based in a fast-food restaurant in Atlanta called the Varsity. He found men at the Varsity and brought them home for one-night stands, giving them a phony name and phone number, never the same man twice.

Meanwhile, he and Sally became "an item" in the heterosexual world. "It definitely helped my reputation at Legal Services," says Bradley. Three or four times that year he made heterosexual love, and the act always precipitated an immediate emotional crisis. Finally, when there was widespread talk of marriage, guilt pushed Bradley to seek a way out. He broke off the affair by concocting a desperate story about being all balled up inside over growing up in the orphanage, and promising Sally that he would see a psychiatrist.

Alone one Friday night in his Atlanta apartment,

* A pseudonym.

reading Eisenhower's memoirs, Bradley toyed with the idea of visiting one of the gay bars he had been reading about in Atlanta's underground newspaper, the *Great Speckled Bird*. He thought of horror stories, fought them off with suitable cover stories, and finally wandered into the Cove at nine o'clock. "It was empty," he says. "I didn't realize that those places don't get going until nearly midnight." A kindly bartender explained the customs of night life and wrote out for him, on a napkin, the names of other local gay bars. A week later, sitting at a gay bar, Bradley found himself staring at one of his Sigma Nu fraternity brothers from Mercer. The two of them played cat and mouse with each other before the fraternity brother took the initiative, volunteering that he knew all the gay bars from Key West to Provincetown. In parlance, he was "coming out" to Bradley.

The fraternity brother introduced Bradley to a group of about ten closeted professionals who saw one another every weekend. One of them would cook dinner for the rest, and they would go out to one or more "cruising bars" at the "witching hour," looking for sex. Bradley joined them occasionally. The gatherings offered a lot of gossip and some chance of friendship. They also gave Bradley his first inkling that the closet could be a social place; for him it had always been solitary. But he was frightened that so many people knew his real name. He disliked their habit of asking new people to join the group. He refused to invite them to *his* apartment for dinner. And much of what he came to know about them was depressing. His fraternity brother, a chronic alcoholic, began calling him at home late at night, begging for help. Another member of the group overdosed on PCP pills and suffered a complete breakdown. To Bradley, these were some of the many signs that homosexuals were badly damaged people, a fraternity of despair. Gradually, he withdrew from the group and resumed the solitary life of the dedicated workaholic.

III.

The Wedding Ring

BUT BRADLEY couldn't sustain this pose. After a frightening episode when he found himself leaving a note with his real name and phone number on the car of a handsome blond student who lived across the street, Bradley resolved, with the help of yet another psychiatrist, to design a secure closet life for himself. The solution, he concluded, was to adopt an elaborate double identity. Knowing that he could not suppress his homosexual impulses entirely, he resolved to channel them into anonymous sex. To attain security he would give up any hope of emotional attachment, which he was convinced he didn't need.

Bradley resolved to shape an imaginary heterosexual life in Washington that he could talk about in Atlanta, and vice versa. He wanted to regularize and systematize the imaginary love letters, dates, and dilemmas, to minimize the risk of being discovered in a contradiction. So as not to neglect the small touches, he took out a subscription to *Playboy* magazine and displayed the copies prominently on his coffee table for the benefit of his visitors.

As for sex, he made a heartening discovery. He found the baths. Having read about the gay baths, he finally worked up the courage to visit one in Miami after delivering a speech to a local bar association. He joined under the name Doug Bailey. Then he walked behind the forbidding walls and saw hundreds of gay men wearing towels. It took Bradley about five minutes to discern that the whole place was expressly designed for promiscuous, anonymous sex, which was exactly what he had in mind. He felt secure behind the great walls. "I must have had sex with ten different guys that first night," he says. "I was like a kid in a candy store. Nobody talked about what anybody did for a living."

The Club Bath chain alone owned outlets in thirty-seven American cities. Bradley visited most of them. They were listed in his *Gay Guide* (which comes in a plain gray cover marked ADDRESS BOOK, suitable for the closet), along with the gay bars and nightclubs. To facilitate his secret gay exploits, Bradley instructed his secretary to tell all those who invited him to conferences that he *must* stay in a hotel and not with a host family. He told everyone that he liked to work in his room and go to bed early. Citing these unbreakable habits, he could excuse himself to his hotel room and then slip off to the baths.

Growing bolder with time, he bought a gold wedding band at a pawnshop and carried it with him wherever he went. He put it on during out-of-town meetings whenever he was sure that no one there knew his marital status. To Bradley, the ring was a magic time-saver. It kept strangers from trying to set him up with dates. People made fewer social demands on a married man traveling alone.

During a bar-association conference in New York, Bradley told his colleagues that he had to leave early to see relatives on Long Island, and went off to see the musical *Hair*. In the dark he fell under the spell of a particular member of the cast. After some anguish, he managed to get a note to this actor, and soon they arranged a rendezvous in Washington—the first time Bradley dared indulge his gayness in the heart of his professional world. Eddie was also the first man Bradley went to bed with more than once. "And we talked for days," he says. "He completed my gay education." Bradley learned that the closet would always be a fearful adventure, with more shadowy corners than he could imagine. He learned the rudiments of the lingo and the standard personality types. He learned that the macho, short-haired "clone" look was coming into fashion, and he mastered the difference between "nellies," "twinkies," and "chickens." He asked a hundred questions about the "Hankie Code," which was printed in the front of his *Gay Guide*. A man entering a "cruiser bar" with a handkerchief on his left hip signaled a desire to be the active one, the doer. Those with one on the right hip wanted to be passive. Colors indicated the favorite sport. A dark blue hankie on the left wanted to "give" anal sex—on the right to "receive" it. There were fourteen colors in the code, reaching down to Dante and beyond. Maroon on the right wanted to receive an enema. Yellow on the left wanted to urinate in someone's face.

Comforted to find out that only a small percentage of homosexuals take part in such practices, Bradley sought to understand the far reaches of his new sociology. By now he was no longer the naïve Georgia preacher.

For every new low of closet life, there was a high. Primarily, for Bradley, it was the thrill of living in two separate worlds that came together but did not touch, saw each other but did not understand. He could live separately as Judd with pickups, Doug in the baths, and Dan in the halls of Congress. In camp circles, he was called Elizabeth. When Eddie left forever after a three-day spree, Bradley invented a new character in his life named Edie. He told people at Legal Services that he had fallen for her. He told them about letters from Edie, about phone calls and secret trysts—all based on the afterglow of the chorus boy from *Hair*. "I became a master of deception," says Bradley. "And it brought me vicarious joy every day to pull it off. That's one of the joys of the closet. There's no denying it."

In recent years, gay scholars have laid claim of kinship to an astonishing number of big names in the history of art and ideas. Their list is quite impressive, even when it is stripped of the weaker and more tentative assertions (such as Shakespeare): Plato, Walt Whitman, Somerset Maugham, Noel Coward, Leonardo da Vinci, Cole Porter, Aristotle, King James I (sponsor of the King James version of the Bible), W. H. Auden, Tchaikovsky, Francis Bacon, George Santayana, Herman Melville, John Maynard Keynes, Michelangelo, E. M. Forster, and Horatio Alger, Jr., to name a few. Gay scholars usually lament the failure of nearly all the masters to come out and write explicitly about homosexual themes. The argument assumes that homosexuality is an engine of creativity and that the closet is a brake. Neither assumption is necessarily true. Maugham or Melville out of the closet might have written duller, not better, books. The closet itself may be a prime source of the internal friction that produced the works claimed for the gay hall of fame. After all, coming out is now associated with improved mental health, contentment, self-acceptance, and a host of states inimical to the unruly artistic temperament.

AFTER HIS landslide reelection in 1972, President Nixon moved swiftly to dismantle the poverty program, including Legal Services. The great political battle of Bradley's life was engaged. Nixon's director of the Office of Economic Opportunity was a flinty Kentucky Republican named Alvin Arnett, who surprised the poverty-law network by being open-minded. Arnett was so impressed by an impassioned three-hour speech Bradley gave in defense of legal aid for the poor that he tried to appoint Bradley head of the national Legal Services program. But the White House vetoed the idea. Bradley proposed a bureaucratic maneuver: Arnett should bypass the White House by appointing *himself* head of Legal Services and making Bradley his special assistant, to run the program in everything but title. Arnett agreed. Thus Bradley arrived for his first full-time stint in Washington with both his sexual life and his political mission in the closet.

Before leaving Atlanta, Bradley invited his old girlfriend Sally to dinner at an elegant French restaurant. She was getting married. Bradley felt guilty about having manipulated her during their bizarre affair and thought that she, of all people, would be happy to hear that he was homosexual. It would explain why he had hurt her.

At dinner he dropped teasing hints about a big secret. Sally pounced on them as usual, wanting to know instantly. Then Bradley backpedaled, unable to say the words. He promised the secret after dessert, then after coffee. Finally, he stopped stirring the coffee and said bluntly, "Sally, I'm a homosexual."

She looked stricken. Bradley knew instantly that his plan had gone awry. When she insisted that it was impossible, he could only reply that he ought to know better than she.

"What about those times we made love?" she asked.

Bradley sighed. "Well, that's not easy to talk about. But if you must know, I got through them by fantasizing that you were another man."

She swallowed and began to cry, softly and then hysterically. Before Bradley could say anything else, she ran through the restaurant into the ladies' room.

Bradley absorbed stares from the surrounding tables. Fifteen minutes later, he asked the manager to send someone to check on Sally, who returned looking spent and resigned. "Dan, it's sad that you're a homosexual," she said. "Does it mean you'll never get married and have children?"

Bradley was too busy and too frightened to lead a homosexual life in the capital. Whenever he became sexually desperate, he would arrange a quick business trip to Philadelphia and sneak off to the Spartan Baths. In Washington, he lived only politics. He thought he liked it that way.

Since Nixon was determined to abolish the OEO, Bradley and his cohorts determined to save Legal

Services by installing them in an independent corporation. Nixon vetoed one bill, and another fell by the wayside, but a third attempt passed Congress, and Nixon, weakened by Watergate, signed it. Bradley was triumphant.

One day, without warning, he started crying in his office at OEO headquarters. It came so suddenly that Bradley had to make up a story of family tragedy for his secretary. Then, when he could not stop, he locked the door and waited for the fit to pass. After an hour, he was panicky. Still crying, he placed a call to a closeted psychiatrist he had met during his brief social period in Atlanta. He begged for help, saying over and over that he was "incapacitated" for no reason, just when everything was going well.

The Atlanta psychiatrist advised Bradley that his [the psychiatrist's] old college lover was now a professor in the psychiatry department at a medical school in the Baltimore-Washington area. That same afternoon, still crying, Bradley drove to the psychiatrist's private office. The doctor talked openly of his being gay, but he was deeply closeted himself, with photographs of his wife and children on his desk. Bradley introduced himself and said, "I *think* I'm a homosexual." He emphasized his doubts. Years later, Bradley still marvels at the power of retrenchment. "After all I'd been through, I tried to act like it was something completely new," he says. He and the doctor plunged back into the fundamental questions.

IV.

What Makes the Blood Rise

IN HIS *Problemata*, Aristotle (lover of his student Hermias) explained that some men are constructed physically so that some or all of their semen "settles" in their "fundament" instead of their testicles. In these cases, he declared, there cannot be enough "force" to expel the residue of semen, which then cools and congeals. Aristotle concluded that these fundament-oriented men naturally desired to submit to sexual intercourse, adding that if the semen "collected" in both places in the proper mixture, a man might be required to seek two pleasures.

Plato took a different approach in his *Symposium*, arguing that man had descended from an ideal type of being with four legs and four arms. When the gods divided this being into two human types, Plato suggested, some of the resulting males and females retained yearnings for the lost half of themselves. The human psyche, having been originally both male and female, would always have a fluidity at its core that could become manifest as homosexuality.

Plato and Aristotle established the two broad schools of theory that have been in contention ever since: the "physical" school and the ethereal, "environmental" one. The former holds that homosexuality is a predetermined aspect of a person's physical inheritance—like baldness or flat feet or eye color, except that it is invisible. In modern terms, a physicalist would argue that homosexuality is a mysterious part of the genetic package. An environmentalist, on the other hand, believes that the condition is not fixed, that it can be affected by factors ranging from mass culture to individual will. This notion introduces the dreaded or welcome element of choice; homosexuality is a taste to be acquired or rejected. Sigmund Freud, patron of the modern environmentalists, asserted that all human beings have pansexual urges when they are young, that with maturity these urges are resolved into healthy heterosexual channels, and that homosexuality is an "arrested development" caused by parent-child maladjustment. He was vague on the last point, leaving his followers to quarrel inconclusively over whether the culprit was a weak father, an overbearing mother, or something else. The essential environmental thesis is that the cause, and the cure, lie somewhere within the potential reach of psychoanalysis, though they would not be easy to find.

Each of the two major schools lives in part off the failure of the other. Otherwise, the physicalists argue that only a physical, rigidly determined homosexuality could have survived the unspeakable tortures of history. Through a thousand years of ghastly executions, homosexuals refused to renounce their practices—with a tenacity that rivaled the more highly publicized religious martyrs. Even during the decadent years of the Roman Empire, the law condemned homosexuals to execution by fire "in the sight of the people." In 1327, English noblemen executed the homosexual King Edward II by ramming a hot iron into his bowels. During the religious wars after the Reformation, sexual deviance was perhaps the commonest expression of heresy, and religious tribunals sent homosexuals to the stake.

In more recent times, homosexuals have been consigned to mental institutions, where doctors have tried to cure them with no-nonsense applications such as castration, lobotomy, and electric shock treatment. None of these has worked. Remarkably, many homosexuals have *volunteered* for these procedures in the desperate hope of escaping their torment. In 1894, Guy Olmstead had himself castrated in Chicago after all other treatments had failed, but the miserable Olmstead soon told his doctor that men still caused him to "have erections, commit masturbation, and have the same passion as before." From 1941 to 1943, Dr. Samuel Liebman subjected a black transvestite homosexual to enough shock treatment to electrify a small town, with many regrettable side effects but no effect at all on his sexual preference. More recently, Dr. J. Srnec and Dr. K. Freund reported to the scientific community the disheartening results of their experimental aversion therapy. "Psychic driving" and assorted miracle drugs have failed, along with countless home remedies and psychoanalytic tricks.

If sexuality were fungible, say the physicalists, homosexuality would have been expunged long ago at the stake or in the laboratory. This leads to the notion that homosexuals cannot reform "any more than a leopard can change its spots," which in turn supports the gay-rights position that homosexuals should be treated like any other physically determined minority group.

The environmentalists are more comfortable in theory than in the laboratory. They say homosexuality is *behavior*, not a pigment or a shape of the skull, and that it is difficult to change and explain only because it comes from the deepest chambers of the human psyche, where sex and survival wrestle with the awareness of death. Admittedly, they say, cures are rare, but at least they are not nonsensical, as is the idea of changing an African into an Oriental. They point to examples of voluntary homosexuality, citing feminists who claim to have "adopted" lesbianism for political reasons. On the mass scale, they say that fluctuations in the incidence of homosexuality throughout history are incompatible with physicalist theory.

But sexuality is a way to be, not a way to think. No person works through these essentially emotional questions on a plane of weightless rationality, and it is all too easy to be an environmentalist in theory and a physicalist in practice. Fear and anxiety tend to produce physicalists, dividing humanity into sexual camps. The shifting, polymorphous sexuality that one might expect from environmental theory does not exist. People become one thing or another, with most homosexuals wanting to believe they had no choice of becoming otherwise and most heterosexuals wanting to believe they have no chance. Fear brings the elements of confusion together on the wispy issue of bisexuality, which is a threat to both sides. Homosexuals laugh at bisexuality as a pretense or as a mode of transportation—today's bisexual is tomorrow's homosexual. Heterosexuals tend to look at bisexuality as the trapdoor on a scaffold of sex. Both see bisexuals as arid, deathly utopians, utterly liberated and therefore inhuman.

The unbearable, wonderful urgency of sex divides the camps. Homosexuals fear heterosexuals because they have always performed the lobotomies and made the rules—and also because they carry all the advantages of cultural transmission, such as children, a clear meaning for the word "generation," and membership in the most resilient and universal institution in human history (however battered the family has become). Looking in the other direction, heterosexuals are daunted by the thought of gay people living without these very amulets—casting them off, breaking taboos, and then somehow going on with life more or less like everyone else. Gays are reminders of each life as a discrete, vanishing particle, separate from the glue of custom.

On the issue of homosexuality, ignorance and dogmatism stick closely together, as they often do, but there are also odd combinations of hatred, deception, righteousness, debasement, and joy. As a species, human beings usually refuse to be humbled by the most prosaic aspects of our condition. We come in different colors, and we copulate in different ways, with different things at heart. These simple matters of affect raise passions that regularly confound the pretensions of civil society.

As a theoretical question, the nature and cause of homosexuality continues to mock the pretenders to knowledge. They make bold assertions in the high ether of abstraction, and they hold firm opinions on the more humdrum issues of taste, such as what it is about each gender that makes the blood rise—the smile, the thigh, or the giggle of passion. Only rarely do they see or care how difficult it is to escape character in order to gain the perspective to define it. Homosexuals, driven by need for an answer, often come to the conclusion Bradley reached with the counsel of five learned psychiatrists. "I believe I was a homosexual from the moment I was born," he says. "But I don't know what that means."

V.

The Recognition Game

IN 1974, as President Ford was preparing to name the board members for the new Legal Services Corporation, Bradley decided to retreat to his old job in Atlanta, where there was less risk of being fired by the Republicans. Before leaving, he told his secret to a married woman friend named Susan, whose air of wise maternity had always elicited his trust. During the long, convoluted buildup to his speech, Bradley projected such a piercing melancholy that she began crying in anticipation of the worst. When Bradley finally got the words out, she cried, "I thought you had leukemia or something. I don't care if you're gay. My *father's* gay!"

In Atlanta, Bradley found that poverty law had lost the spark of a ministry for him. He told his fifth psychiatrist that he was basically a frustrated politician. But he knew running for office would mean going even deeper into the closet. Coldly analyzing his past, he decided that he had already made too many mistakes. He would be exposed. Careful as he had been, he had gone to too many bars in Atlanta.

Fate intervened again when his Washington bosses drafted him to become the new Legal Services regional director in San Francisco, gay capital of the United States. Bradley pretended the transfer would be onerous, but secretly he was celebrating the move as a stroke of luck. He was headed for the briar patch, where he could "deal with" his homosexuality at last. Perhaps he could drift out of the closet there and even find a long-term lover.

None of this was to be. In San Francisco, Bradley lived in the famous Castro area, surrounded by 35,000 homosexual neighbors. The entire support structure of his life was gay—his bank tellers, grocers, pharmacists, landlords, and street venders. But he kept his distance, behaving like a closeted heterosexual. Now he lived in *two* closets, one at the office and one at home. He confined his social life to the anonymity of the baths. He shunned the bars and never attended parties.

When Jimmy Carter's presidential campaign came along in 1976, Bradley made use of his old Georgia connections to sign on. After Carter's victory over Gerald Ford, Bradley closed his affairs in San Francisco and moved to Miami to contemplate his future. He believed that homosexuality had capped his career in politics, but he could not bring himself to forswear politics and come out of the closet. His objection to homosexuality was no longer exclusively moral. He was between worlds. He thought of rejecting politics for legal practice, freeing himself for whatever private life felt comfortable.

SHORTLY AFTER the Carter inauguration, Bradley was approached about becoming the Florida commissioner of racing and pari-mutuel wagering. Gov. Reubin Askew was looking for someone above reproach, and Bradley, who didn't know a bookie from a bookmark, was perfect. No one could suspect him of ties to gamblers or the Mafia.

Bradley visited Hialeah Race Track and was captivated by the manicured grounds, the pink flamingoes inside the track, the splashes of color, and the rhythmic theater of horses, money, and people. Governor Askew soon talked him into taking the job, provided, of course, that Bradley passed the exhaustive state security investigation. The mere thought of it threw Bradley into a panic. Everything changed overnight. He ceased contemplating the possibility of drifting into a gay lifestyle and began feverishly erasing all traces of it from his past. Since leaving the government payroll he had allowed himself to spend some time in gay bars. When state investigators asked for snapshots of him, Bradley became obsessed with fear that they would show his photograph to the bartenders, or, even worse, to the attendants at the Club Bath, which Bradley had been frequenting now for five years.

Bradley nearly went to pieces when one of his Coconut Grove neighbors stopped by to tell him that the state investigators had asked her a number of questions, mostly about his sex life. They had asked specifically if he was a "queer." Bradley suffered a thousand visions of exposure and ruin before the woman volunteered that she thought it outrageous that the state was delving into a man's private life, and she didn't mind admitting that she had lied to them, saying that Bradley was seeing a lot of her own daughter. This was not true, of course, and the woman told Bradley that it could not be true since the daughter was a lesbian. This announcement made Bradley's jaw drop and his mind spin. He found himself thanking her profusely, and she eventually became a trusted friend.

The news of the sexual emphasis put Bradley's cover-up into high gear. He enlisted the help of two lawyers in Miami, a married couple with whom he had shared his secret. He coached them with plausible stories of heterosexual romance. They could say they'd heard him talk a lot about Sally, Bradley's old girlfriend, and about Barbara, Terry Lenzner's former assistant (now a lawyer). Bradley had shared his secret with Barbara a year earlier, only to hear her say she had already figured it out for herself (which had disturbed him). Bradley also threw in the name of his neighbor's lesbian daughter. He and his two accomplices agreed on the dates and places of incidents they would cite, complete with details of lovers' quarrels, public necking, and a pregnancy scare or two. Bradley backstopped the whole plan with calls to Susan and Sally, and then held his breath. Some weeks later, Florida's chief investigator summoned Bradley to a hurried meeting at Miami Airport and told him, "Dan, either you are a man who is completely clean and above suspicion, or you are the biggest fraud I've ever investigated."

As commissioner, Bradley was the Jehovah figure of the Florida gambling industry, scowling from the front pages when angry and smiling on the society pages when he pronounced his blessing on a new season. And as a public figure in the state, he attended at least two or three major social functions a week, which presented an escort problem. The same friends who had covered for him in the security investigation came through with a mixture of unwitting dates and willing "beards." Sometimes he would go alone. As a result of this socializing, a *Miami Herald* reporter called one day to announce that Bradley would be featured in a series on Miami's most eligible bachelors.

Bradley had to submit to the established treatment: posed photographs, a guided tour of his "bachelor home," and a two-hour interview at which a bubbly blonde reporter wanted to know everything. She quizzed Bradley on his ideal woman, his marriage and family plans, his romantic history, his favorite singles bars, his advice for young lovers, his turn-ons and his turn-offs. "That was the most difficult interview I ever had," Bradley recalls, laughing painfully. "I had to make up the whole thing."

When the story appeared in the *Herald*, Bradley's gay friends in Miami teased him mercilessly. Attendants at the Club Bath or drinking buddies from the gay bars would quote from his remarks and howl with laughter. Bradley decided to lie low for a while, which his demanding schedule made easy. This had been an asexual period for him anyway, even by his standards. He had been sneaking into the Club Bath one night every few weeks and into a gay bar perhaps once a month.

The danger and the contradictions intensified the thrill of his double life as Commissioner Bradley, the upright official who tried to ferret out, expose, and eliminate the secret underworld of gambling, and as "Doug Bailey," who would sneak off to join a different underworld in restaurants and gay bars, some of which, he heard, were controlled by the same organized-crime figures he chased in the day.

Matters became even more complicated when Anita Bryant's antihomosexual crusade sprang up in Miami and swept the nation. Bradley's boss, Governor Askew, announced his support of Bryant's movement at a press conference just after a meeting with Bradley. So the racing commissioner found himself standing in a room full of reporters and television cameras when, in response to a question, Askew said he would never tolerate any homosexuals in his administration. "I was amused, mostly," says Bradley. "And I was proud of pulling it off."

VI.

Bachelor Lawyers of Washington

WHEN ASKEW left office early in 1979, Bradley temporarily agreed to return to Washington as consultant to the Legal Services Corporation, pending appointment of a new president in June. He checked into a hotel in the capital, where he had not lived for nearly five years, and resolved not to be a hermit. He was out of politics forever, he told himself. He would soon take an extended vacation to Europe and "find himself." Meanwhile, he would enjoy himself in Washington for the first time.

He went to a different gay bar nearly every night —Equus, Rascals, the Eagle, and many others. At first he was surprised to see so many people he knew from his political past. There were lawyers, lobbyists, bureaucrats, and aides from Capitol Hill. After playing the recognition game, Bradley would gossip with them about the closet. Not surprisingly, he found that there were many different levels of paranoia. Some of the Capitol Hill aides would speak rather openly about their bosses, their jobs, and even their lovers. Others would say only that they worked "on the Hill." They all spoke of people they knew who were more snugly in the closet—of people who avoided gay bars altogether and confined their gay lives to parties, mostly in Georgetown. More secretively, some officials seemed to have relatively stable lovers and hardly ever ventured out at all. Others might or might not have been spotted at various "cruising areas" in the capital. Finally, there was a "mystery group" of congressmen, military men, and others whose sexual nature was debated even among the homosexual cognoscenti.

Some of Bradley's contemporaries introduced him to some younger, Adonis types among Capitol Hill aides. These being his chosen sexual partners, he pursued brief affairs with a few of them and became talking friends with several others. He attended a few all-gay dinners and parties, including one in Virginia that turned out to be an orgy. (Bradley wound up in bed with a lawyer from the Department of Justice.) He heard about gay art classes and softball teams, about the lively debates at the Gertrude Stein Club (Democratic) and the Walt Whitman Club (Republican), and he was invited to join a rather campy organization called Bachelor Lawyers of Washington (BLOW). He concluded that closeted life in the capital might not be as grim as he had always assumed.

This became a factor in Bradley' plans when the consensus candidate of the various Legal Services cabals, F.A.O. Schwartz, Jr., decided at the last moment that he would not accept the job as president. This caused a crisis. Pressure mounted for Bradley to offer himself as the emergency choice. He equivocated. Although he had sworn to himself never to take a step back deeper into the closet, his brief sojourn in Washington had changed his view of the situation. He wanted the job. "I finally decided that I was not going to come out of the closet, but at the same time I was not going to be uptight about it all the time," he recalls.

He moved into a spacious Washington office and spent the first few months lobbying a $321 million appropriation bill through Congress. At night, he went to BLOW meetings and to all-gay cocktail parties in Georgetown. The parties became a new dimension in his life. He learned that many closeted officials were in the habit of sleeping in the early evening so they could party and "cruise" late at night. He learned the informal etiquette by which gay politicians communicated their level of secretiveness. One rule, for example, was never to introduce anyone more specifically than they introduced themselves. Bradley never introduced himself as president of Legal Services, and he came to expect others to follow his cue.

Gossip among friends was another matter. Everyone was fair game then, and "who's who in the closet" was a leading subject of conversation. Bradley was skeptical of some of the names he heard bandied about in Congress, even when he heard them from staff members. But when some of those congressmen themselves showed up at the cocktail parties to gossip about their colleagues, he began to change his mind. Only two or three congressmen dared to show themselves at the parties, but Bradley came to know a score of others—first by gossip, then by one or two coded remarks at a private meeting, and finally when he pleaded with some closeted members of Congress not to vote against gay-rights legislation.

His official duties required him to attend more straight parties than gay ones. Bradley impressed his old friend Barbara into duty as his regular date. She went, and all was well until election year, 1980. Then he slipped back into the familiar depression. When a hysterical crying fit came over him one afternoon, he finally called his fourth psychiatrist, the closeted ex-lover of number five. Bradley arranged to begin emergency treatments once a day at 4:45 P.M., which caused security problems. By a long-standing rule, his secretary was required to know his whereabouts at all times. So Bradley had to make up stories every day that would make him temporarily unavailable. He was meeting the plumber in the basement, far away from the phone. Or he was picking up his car from a repair shop whose name he couldn't remember. Some days he would simply flout the rules and declare that he was disappearing. Years earlier, he might have encouraged the speculation that he was trysting with a secret female lover, but now he refused that much of a concession to the closet.

BRADLEY had long since accepted the idea that homosexuality was powerful enough to twist a person into any shape and to make him lie to himself and anyone else, as necessary. "There's no end to it," he says. Still, he was surprised at first to hear gossip that some of the most visible leaders of the anti-homosexual Moral Majority and New Right were themselves closeted gays. He knew better than to place hard bets against the drumbeat of the gay grapevine, but he still associated homosexuals with civil libertarians. His friends among the closeted congressmen were liberal Democrats like himself.

For at least a year before their arrests he had been hearing about Rep. Jon Hinson and Rep. Robert Bauman at the gay parties. Hinson, a conservative Mississippi Republican, was said to cruise the roughneck bars, and Bauman was said to have been picking up "chickens" (young male hustlers) for many years outside a gay bar called the Chesapeake House. The tawdry aspects of the sex did not bother Bradley, since he took them for granted as a consequence of life in the closet. Congressmen, he assumed, might avoid even the baths for fear of being recognized.

What bothered Bradley was the politics, particularly Bauman's. A married Roman Catholic with four children, Bauman was a founder and former national chairman of Young Americans for Freedom. He was also co-founder and national chairman of the American Conservative Union. In the House, he was widely considered the most intelligent, promising leader of the New Right—a crusader against busing, abortion, deficit spending, communism, and homosexuality. Bradley had heard the rumors about J. Edgar Hoover and others who were said to have expressed their self-hatred on a grand scale in politics, but he could not quite understand how anyone could strive for leadership of a movement that sought to persecute his own kind. Yet both Hinson and Bauman were arrested in 1980 for precisely the kinds of homosexual solicitations that the gay grapevine had ascribed to them.

The Reagan administration took power in 1981 on a pledge to abolish the Legal Services Corporation. Bradley sent up the emergency battle flags once again and tried to rally support in Congress. Ironically, to Bradley's utter mortification, the first test came on an amendment proposed by Rep. Larry McDonald of Georgia to bar Legal Services lawyers from cases involving discrimination against homosexuals. Numerous liberal congressmen told Bradley that they would have to vote with McDonald against their principles. They spoke of political suicide and asked his understanding. Bradley kept nodding, but he knew that more than a dozen of these liberals were themselves closeted homosexuals. He second-guessed their motives, and then his own. It seemed impossible for closeted people to separate political interests from personal ones. The McDonald Amendment passed the House in June 1981 but failed in the Senate.

Bradley raged against the hypocrisy that he saw in his own second thoughts and in the defections of the gay congressmen. They were working against themselves. Ominously, the threat to Legal Services and to gay rights in general seemed to be growing, and Bradley thought that some of the very congressmen leading McDonald's movement were themselves closeted homosexuals. This he could not fathom, except to believe that it all came from the insidious workings of the closet. Having finally isolated the closet as the archenemy in his private life, Bradley now faced it in politics as well.

VII.

The Homosexual Wars

HOMOSEXUALITY has long been associated with the political Left. After Sen. Joseph McCarthy made sensational news with his long lists of alleged "communists" in the government, few people noticed that most of the government employees actually sacked in the witch-hunt were classified as "perverts." At the height of the McCarthy era, the word "subversive" was commonly used as a synonym for "pervert," "deviate," and "communist" alike. "I don't say every homosexual is a subversive, and I don't say every subversive is a homosexual," conceded Sen. Kenneth Wherry of Nebraska in 1950. "But a man of low morality is a menace in the government, whatever he is, and they are all tied up together."

This attitude survived the Cold War. When Walter Jenkins, President Johnson's closest aide, was arrested for homosexual acts in 1964, commentators expressed the utmost shock that the malady had afflicted someone from the mainstream of American politics. It was a novel development, but at least Jenkins was a Democrat in a liberal administration.

In the 1970s, Judge G. Harrold Carswell, who had been President Nixon's Supreme Court nominee, was arrested in a public rest room for homosexual acts, and so was Gen. Edwin Walker, the flamboyant John Bircher who had "commanded" the white students during the 1962 Ole Miss riots. They were dismissed as kooks who had been unable to make it in the "real world" of Washington politics.

Then, in 1978 and 1979, stories broke about the arrests of two certified Washingtonians—Reps. Fred Richmond and Joseph P. Wyatt. In 1980, an underground Washington newspaper alleged that Rep. William Moorhead had been having an extramarital affair with a male/female "hermaphrodite" named Terri Hall, who had taken grievances against the congressman to lawyers and the press. Moorhead did not seek reelection in 1980, and has become a political consultant. These three were mainstream politicians—but at least they were Democrats. Finally, with the arrests of Hinson and Bauman, political homosexuality seemed to have spread across the entire political spectrum.

If this trend has dismayed the previously immune Republican stalwarts, it has brought surprisingly little joy to homosexual activists, many of whom had grown fond of their leftish political conceptions. They thought of their enemy as the system, represented by conservative, capitalist Republicans. Now they found themselves with a conundrum: if gay liberation is the antithesis of capitalist values, why is it that the burgeoning homosexual subculture of the last decade has manifested itself largely in crass, commercial hedonism—in an explosion of discos, hotels, nightclubs, and gay bars, all designed for maximum luxury and the ten-minute sexual affair? In Washington and other large cities, the most active, visible members of the homosexual community tend to be affluent white professionals, whose sexual identity is their only claim to oppressed status. Highly privileged otherwise, they agitate for entrepreneurial freedom and a stable currency, like good Republicans.

As sexual solidarity diminishes and political antagonism grows, homosexuals tend to behave more like traditional grasping politicians, who will use any weapon at their command. The most dangerous weapon available to both sides is the closet. As a political issue, the closet raises explosive psychological forces of hatred and self-hatred.

Closeted homosexuals have been lining up on both sides of an impending war. Right-wing activists, including many closeted homosexuals, have sought to drive homosexuals from public life. Before the 1980 elections, the National Conservative Political Action Committee (NCPAC) and allied groups targeted House and Senate liberals for defeat partly because of their tolerance of homosexuality. The Reagan administration supported the McDonald Amendment to prohibit the representation of homosexuals by the Legal Services Corporation. In September 1981, the Rev. Jerry Falwell held a press conference on the steps of the Capitol, urging Congress to veto a revision of the District of Columbia legal code that would have legalized all forms of sexual activity between consenting adults. Falwell sent out a nationwide funding appeal, headlined: SODOMY AND BESTIALITY WILL BE LEGAL IN OUR NATION'S CAPITAL UNLESS YOU ACT NOW! Congress vetoed the revision in October (the only time it has ever overridden the District's home-rule powers on a matter unrelated to the prerogatives of the federal government), and Falwell's campaign received such enthusiastic support that he sent out more appeals for money. "If this gay conspiracy succeeds," he wrote, "it will be just one more step downward for America, towards moral decadence."

In February 1982, Falwell promised his followers that he would turn over a list of the "gay conspirators" to Congress. (Ironically, the "page scandal" broke not long thereafter, indicating once again that many of the gay conspirators may be *in* Congress.) Meanwhile, editors from the *Spotlight*, journal of the far-Right Liberty Lobby, began publishing a scandal sheet called *Deep Backgrounder*, naming more than a dozen allegedly homosexual members of Congress in the first issue. And on the spy front, word leaked out about HOMEX (Homosexual Extortion), the FBI's twenty-year operation to identify prominent homosexuals in Washington, ostensibly to prevent their being compromised by the Russians. Columnists quoted unnamed investigators to the effect that the Russian KGB had been actively recruiting homosexuals in the capital.

THUS the pressure builds on the Right, and if President Reagan continues to be "Carterized" into vacillating impotence on the economy and the Russians, the chance of a scapegoating crusade increases. No one is more aware of this possibility than homosexual activists themselves, and they have been engaged in a lively debate over how to respond.

Handicapped, as always, by the fact that every one of their influential officials in Washington is closeted, they have tended to the traditional posture, which means lying low, hoping that the attack will not be severe, and trusting in the power of the civil libertarians and their own hidden numbers. There is, however, a minority school of thought that disparages this posture as similar to that of some European Jews before the Holocaust. The militants want to fight fire with fire by exposing the closeted homosexual leaders of the Republican Party and the New Right. They propose to deprive the homosexual question of its political slant by giving unfriendly politicians a shove toward the closet door. This tactic of enforced honesty is called "outage."

Perry Deane Young will strike the first major blow for "outage" this November, when his new book *God's Bullies* will be published, naming NCPAC president Terry Dolan as a closeted homosexual. Young, an openly gay Washington writer who is the co-author of Dave Kopay's best-selling book about homosexuality in professional football, believes that the paramount issue is hypocrisy. Dolan, he says, forfeited his right to privacy by advocating political measures inimical to the rights of his fellow closeted homosexuals.

Young says that Terry Dolan is a more important figure than Robert Bauman, his former colleague on the staff of the Young Americans for Freedom. As the man in control of the wealthiest political-action committee on the far Right, Dolan meets regularly with members of Reagan's staff and has breakfast once a week with Jerry Falwell. But at night, says Young, he goes to gay bars, including a popular "leather bar" called the Eagle. In his book, Young describes one of Dolan's evenings that began in the Eagle and ended in bed with a man named Richard Anderson, from whom Young has a supporting affidavit.

Young says that the closeted subculture in Washington is so large that its members have adopted the traditional habits of the capital, in which political enemies often roast each other on the job and then fraternize that evening. As a result, antihomosexual homosexuals like Robert Bauman and (allegedly) Terry Dolan are frequently encountered by their political opponents, who are sometimes friends or lovers. "I know of at least ten other prominent leaders of the Republican Right who have either had sex with friends of mine or gone to gay parties with them," Young writes. Dan Bradley has had similar experiences. So has Larry Bush, a gay reporter for the *Advocate*. And so have their friends.

Other gay activists are collecting affidavits, too. If there were a war of outage, they say, its victims would include members of the elected Republican leadership in Congress, some of the leaders who pushed the McDonald Amendment, and also some of the principal supporters of the Hyde Amendment, which prohibits federally funded abortions. The Reagan administration would not be spared, they say, as the president has associated with closeted homosexuals before and since the scandal that cost him a couple of aides when he was governor of California. The target list includes at least one member of his White House staff and several of his earliest political supporters, now lobbyists and political consultants in Washington. One of the latter group is a master of style at parties and is known casually in the closet as "Reagan's Capote."

As for recent political history, the outage searchlight seems to be hovering over Sen. Joseph McCarthy and the famous men who helped him find subversives. Gay activists and historians are collecting rumors and affidavits on those leaders, hoping to be able to prove soon that some of them flew broomsticks to the witch-hunt. If true, the news would add a new dimension of travesty to that era.

Like the Jewish member of the Nazi Party, the homosexual in antihomosexual organizations surfaces from time to time, and the world pays little interest. In July of this year, a veteran reporter of the Liberty Lobby's *Spotlight* told a gay newspaper in Washington that he had been fired because of his homosexuality.

Joel Passinault says he violated one of the cardinal rules of the closet by allowing himself to take phone calls at the office from his lover, who was (and is) dying of cancer at Bethesda Naval Hospital. "He was frightened," says Passinault. "So I talked to him. I couldn't not talk to him under those circumstances. And somebody at the *Spotlight* overheard me say 'I love you' to him several times, and that was that. They fired me."

Anyone unfamiliar with the hidden recesses of the closet may find it astonishing that Passinault wants to go back to the *Spotlight*. He winces when he says that his best friend at the *Spotlight* wrote the most violent antihomosexual diatribes, but he takes solace from the memory of a "common ground" between them. "We shared a belief about the direction the country should be taking," he says. "We both want more spending for national defense and less for wasteful social programs."

THE CENTRAL issue of closet politics is self-denial or self-hatred. It lies beneath the charges of hypocrisy and the differences between liberals and conservatives. Perry Deane Young and the gay activists contemplating acts of outage against right-wing activists would be the first to condemn the identical acts when committed against someone else. They hate the closet passionately, but they respect almost anyone's right to choose the time and place of exit. The exception—the only sin that could induce them to violate the protective code among homosexuals—comes from Robert Bauman and people like him, whom the activists describe as "classic, self-hating, schizophrenic, closeted gays." Bauman and his ilk do more than threaten political warfare against homosexuals. By absorbing, intensifying, and projecting antihomosexual values from positions of leadership, they give the most vivid conceivable demonstrations of self-hatred as a motivation for staying in the closet. The demonstrations threaten *all* homosexuals, among most of whom it is an article of faith that the closet is a prison justified only by prudent, reasoned fear of oppression by the straight world. Almost everyone in the closet wants to believe that it is legitimate fear that keeps him there, not self-loathing. As the outside world grows more tolerant, many have found it more difficult to tolerate Bauman-like reminders of the power of self-loathing to produce psychological contortions.

The heterosexual world remains generally oblivious to the possibility that the pro- and antihomosexual forces, both led by homosexuals, may start a war by lobbing napalm at each other. Indeed, the established order has taken little notice of stirrings about and among gays. The official position of establishment Washington is that homosexuality per se is not objectionable in public life, but that the closet is bad because it introduces a susceptibility to blackmail. This is the rationale behind the FBI's HOMEX operation, which is further predicated on the assumption that the best way to protect against possible espionage in this area is, first, to identify *all* homosexuals in public life, especially in Washington. Conveniently, the strategy justifies the existence of numerous FBI specialists, but it is probably not the most economical way of proceeding. The scarcity of blackmail-related homosexual-espionage cases and the FBI's failure to invite troubled homosexuals to make disclosures with immunity both suggest that the bureau has a surpassing negative interest in homosexuality itself.

The CIA operates under a stated public position similar to the FBI's. Recently, an agency technician challenged the sincerity of the policy by filing a lawsuit, claiming that he took the security-risk rationale at face value and decided to confess his homosexuality to his CIA boss—thereby removing leverage against him as a blackmail target—but that the CIA fired him anyway. The technician charges that the security-risk rationale is a fraud behind which the agency hides its dislike of homosexuals.

Most major organs of the American media take the official position, declaring editorially that sexual preference should not be held against a citizen in public life. Still, no television or radio network, major newspaper, or national magazine has an openly homosexual reporter among its employees—with a single exception, the *San Francisco Chronicle*, which has one. The homosexuals who already work for major media organs have given evidence by their unanimous behavior that they believe they would suffer if they declared themselves. They are all deeply closeted. "My reporter friends at the *Washington Post* always shy away from me after lunch when we get near the *Post* building," says Larry Bush. "They are more uptight than any closeted people I deal with, except possibly military officers in uniform."

Most newspapers are skittish about gay stories. Columnist Dave Anderson of *The New York Times* says that in his long career the *Times* editors killed only one sports column, which was about Dave Kopay and homosexuality in professional football. Roger Wilkins, formerly of the *Times* editorial page, has said that his bosses stopped only three of his editorials, two of which were about gay issues.

By all evidence, the newspapers and other media organs would simply prefer to avoid the issue. Perhaps this has something to do with congenital machismo among journalists and writers, who frequently betray the worry that they are mere typists or observers of those who make real decisions, perform real work, and really deserve their Miller Time. More likely, the avoidance comes from the fact that heterosexuals live in their own closet, hiding from homosexuals while homosexuals hide from them. It hasn't occurred to them to inquire. Or they don't want to inquire because they know it will be a big mess. Or perhaps they sense that questions about the nature and causes of homosexuality will lead inevitably to the same questions about heterosexuality, which is unnerving.

Whatever the reason, avoidance is less becoming to journalists than to other professional groups. Its practical effect has been to ignore one of the most explosive social changes of the past decade. If the "war of outage" comes, and readers suddenly look up to find a homosexual on every street corner and a prominent official coming out of every closet, journalists will more than likely join in a panic they could have helped avoid.

VIII.

Out of the Closet

DAN BRADLEY often discussed the politics of the closet with his gay friends in Congress. They agreed that it would serve the public interest for them to declare themselves. To do so would fulfill their obligations of honesty to the voters and to themselves, and possibly would prepare the way for less fear in politics. Two liberal Democrats told Bradley they planned to "come out" if they survived the 1980 elections, but after winning they returned to the usual talk of "political suicide" and decided to postpone the announcement once again. Bradley's conclusion was that no one fights his way out of the closet for reasons of political idealism.

One Sunday afternoon, in May 1981, he ate a

sandwich in a bookstore near Dupont Circle and began walking home to watch "60 Minutes." It was then that he saw, sitting on the fender of a car, the young blond man of his dreams. "I heard trumpets blaring and angels singing," he recalls. He backtracked past the car and then turned around again, groping for a plan. Finally, he struck up a conversation with Richard,* who turned out to be the son of a Secret Service agent on the White House detail. "I fell in love for the first time," says Bradley. "That was the beginning of my downfall."

Richard was the first time Bradley had ever felt any emotion in his sex life. "There were emotions I didn't even know I had," he says. Within a few weeks, Richard was spending most of his nights at Bradley's house, and Bradley was rushing home early from the office in the hope of greeting him. Soon he was making plans to leave government service and make a life with his new lover. When his psychiatrist suggested caution, observing that Richard was a construction worker with a high school education twenty years Bradley's junior, Bradley scoffed at the difficulties. "I didn't give a damn if I had to go out and drive a taxi," he says.

As a couple, they learned to accommodate two closets instead of one. They made it a rule never to venture into Virginia, as Richard knew too many people there, and they coached each other on how to behave in a crisis. Once, in Georgetown, Richard gave the signal between clenched teeth, saying, "Dan! Keep walking," and Bradley tried to look normal as he circled the block, giving Richard enough time to talk with a girlfriend. Another time in Georgetown there was no time to separate, and Bradley used the backup plan, introducing Richard to a White House aide as a man who was hired to build a patio in Bradley's backyard. Richard tried to look like a sullen employee. Still another time, standing in line with Richard for a movie, Bradley saw Sen. Alan Cranston and his wife walk up behind them. Bradley abandoned Richard in the line without a word or sign of explanation. After chatting amiably with the Cranstons about President Reagan's threat to abolish the Legal Services Corporation, Bradley went back to the end of the line and then stealthily located Richard's seat in the theater, keeping an eye on the Cranstons to make sure they did not notice where he was sitting.

These denials took a greater toll on Bradley than any of his previous misadventures in the closet. "I wanted to tell everybody that Richard was the man I loved," he says. "I was proud of him, but the closet made me treat him like a leper. That hurt, and it hurt when he did the same thing to me."

One night a woman called Bradley at home and identified herself as Richard's mother. "How well do you know my son, Mr. Bradley?" she asked, and Bradley mumbled an answer, suppressing terror. He had visions that Secret Service agents would kick in his door. "Finally, she asked me if he was a good worker on the patio," says Bradley, "and I realized that she had bought his whole cover story."

* A pseudonym.

WHILE adjusting to the new trials of life with a closeted lover, Bradley had to fulfill his duties as president of the Legal Services Corporation and also keep up the appearance of a heterosexual cover life. His friend Barbara was his most frequent date, as she had been for years, but the role was especially wearing to her because a number of friends were mounting separate, escalating campaigns directed at her and Bradley, urging each to marry the other.

One night Bradley and Barbara went to dinner with an influential Washington lawyer and his wife. The lawyer, who, like many Washingtonians, was as obtuse in personal matters as he was shrewd in political ones, decided to resolve the marriage matter by confrontation. "Barbara, I might as well tell you right in front of Dan, since you both know what's going on," he said. "I think you ought to ask him to marry *you*, and be done with it. We all know that he loves you, and he won't say no if you ask, but he's so shy that nothing will ever happen if we keep waiting for him to ask you."

This speech finally broke Barbara's loyalty. "Goddamn it!" she shouted, jumping to her feet. "Dan's never going to marry *any* woman, because he's gay! Can't you see that?"

After an unbearable silence, the lawyer's wife said, "Excuse me, I don't feel well." She walked unsteadily to the kitchen.

Barbara collapsed back into her seat, as the well-meaning lawyer stared blankly at his plate. Finally he looked up, took a breath, and said, "Well, Dan, what are you planning to do when you leave Legal Services?"

At less poignant moments, Bradley's future career was no conversational dodge. His days as president of the corporation had been numbered since Ronald Reagan's victory in the 1980 election. Inexplicably, Jimmy Carter had failed to appoint the six board members allotted to him, and the terms of the five others expired in July 1981—meaning that President Reagan could appoint all eleven board members, who would have fired Bradley summarily. But Reagan didn't appoint anyone. Like Nixon before him, he didn't bother to seize control of Legal Services because he intended to abolish it. Legal Services was the only one of the forty programs in the famous "Black Book" that was targeted for extinction rather than a budget cut.

Tentatively, Bradley planned to move to Miami, come out of the closet, and lead an openly gay life. But he came to doubt that he was ready to take Richard with him. "There were bad signs," he says. "After a few months, it began to dawn on me that he liked to watch all these terrible television programs. And whenever we talked about going to the movies, he always wanted to see Clint Eastwood. Things like that. I began to realize that we had nothing in common except love, and we couldn't stay in bed and be in love twenty-four hours a day."

One afternoon, Richard appeared in Bradley's office, wanting to borrow his car. He seemed uncomprehending and unapologetic when Bradley explained the trouble this visit was causing him. Not long after, Bradley told him that he would be moving to Florida alone. A long period of guilt and recrimination ensued, during which Bradley tried to explain that he still loved Richard even though he did not want to live with him forever.

Both the good and bad aspects of the love affair convinced Bradley that he would come out of the closet sooner or later. "I was determined that I would never again panic when my lover dropped by the office," he says. "And I wouldn't walk down the street with him like a fugitive criminal, always on the lookout for people who might recognize me."

By December 1981, Bradley and the poverty-law supporters in Congress had beaten back President Reagan's attempt to kill the corporation. They celebrated the victory again, even though they knew that the administration would soon oust all the incumbents. Bradley, ever conscious of legal detail, resolved to save the existing program for yet another year if he could. He did so by spending $260 million in two weeks, before the new board could take power and stop him. Bradley stayed up late many nights signing checks and cover letters, personally dropping packets into the mail for programs all over the country. When he mailed the last checks on December 15, there was not a dime left in the next year's budget. He was in Miami on New Year's Eve when the news flashed that Reagan had appointed eleven new board members and that the board had posted legal notices on Bradley's home and office doors, ordering him not to sign another check or letter. But it was too late, as Bradley would soon inform them.

Personally, he lapsed into another deep depression. Several lucrative job offers were pending, including one as president of Hialeah Race Track, but Bradley realized that every one of them required him to stay in the closet. His noble intentions dissolved into dreams. His professional desires demanded that he stay in the closet, but his insides demanded that he come out.

Bradley knew that the closet had limitless powers of deception. Numerous friends claimed to be out, only to have embarrassing circumstances make them admit that they wanted to keep the news from certain old friends, or relatives, or from strangers, or from newspapers and the general public. Bradley decided that he would have to force himself out, so he began announcing his intentions to friends who already knew he was gay. One of them, fatefully, was his old girlfriend Sally. "Richard caused my downfall," Bradley says, laughing, "but Sally was there to help it along."

This time she did so by passing the news along to her friend Phil Gailey, a reporter for *The New York Times*. Gailey, of course, wanted to write a story, and Bradley found himself trapped by his own bravado. He refused Gailey and pretended to scold Sally. However, he decided to write personal letters to twenty-five friends—fellow poverty-lawyers, old teachers from Mercer, clergymen from the Baptist Church. He cried all day while writing them. Then he submitted to Gailey's interview, as a clean break, and then he went to Washington's main post office to mail the letters. He walked indecisively back and forth, but he could not bring himself to drop them through the slot. It was too irrevocable.

A chagrined Phil Gailey called a few days later to say that the story was ready but that his *Times* editors refused to use the word "gay" in headlines or the body of the text—only in direct quotation. Did Bradley mind being called a homosexual?

This struck Bradley as funny. "Phil, I *am* a homosexual," he said. "I don't care what the *Times* wants to call it."

Bradley mailed the letters, and the *Times* story ran on March 31, 1981, his last day as president of Legal Services.

SINCE THEN, Bradley has become a national celebrity among gay people, traveling the country for the Gay Rights National Lobby. All the leading Democratic presidential contenders, including his old boss Reubin Askew, have asked him to talk with them about gay issues. In Miami, he addressed a large crowd on Gay Pride Day, which he calls "our Fourth of July." But what he remembers best are the countless nervous people who have come up to him after his speeches, from Oregon to Tennessee. They have talked to him about their children, their jobs, their friends who have committed suicide. Always it is the closet. Now, whenever Bradley looks over an audience, he is burdened by the thought of all the cover stories that make that audience possible—of those who tell the lies and those who believe them, or pretend to.

Romantically, he wishes he could start over at college age—the age of all his gay lovers—when he first knew he was homosexual. Now that a life's weight of denial is suddenly lifted, he has a sense of being unbalanced almost as badly as when he was carrying the weight. He hopes to adjust and to catch up, but he does not even know what is possible in gay relationships. Homosexuality, it seems, sets an exquisite table but is usually no picnic.

"But at least I don't have to lie anymore," he says. "Nobody who hasn't come out of the closet can ever know what a blessing that is." ■

OBSTACLES TO EQUALITY: GOVERNMENT RESPONSES TO THE GAY RIGHTS MOVEMENT IN THE UNITED STATES

A. S. COHAN

University of Lancaster

Abstract: The Gay Rights movement in the United States, like other social movements, may achieve its goal of full equality before the law through actions by the legislatures or courts. Generally, action by the latter opens the door to concessions by the former. But the Gay Rights movement has not progressed as its adherents have wished for four reasons: (1) the unpopularity of homosexuals; (2) the disjointed nature of American government(s); (3) the absence of cohesiveness of the movement itself, possibly as a result of a lack of economic deprivation among homosexuals; and (4) most significant, the unwillingness of the Supreme Court to accord to homosexuals the same rights it has extended to other minority groups, thereby giving a lead to legislatures as they did in the area of civil rights for Blacks.

GOVERNMENTS deal with a myriad of problems, all of which involve the allocation of societal resources in whatever form those resources may take.[1] Most problems, such as social welfare provisions and defence arrangements, require vast expenditures of money, and the expenditures, through money raising methods and where the money goes, affect entire populations of such societies. Because of the salience of those problems, they have tended to be the ones on which political scientists with a special interest in public policy have focused. Thus, public policy analysts have often been concerned with budgets because 'if one looks at politics as a process by which the government mobilizes resources to meet pressing problems, then the budget is a focus of these efforts'.[2] Further, taking all of its facets, the budget is an ideal operational definition of 'whatever governments choose to do or not to do'.[3] Budgets are the most easily manipulable data in policy analysis which actually tell us something important about problems affecting virtually all members of a society.

Some problems, however, involve the allocation of societal resources other than money. Often, these problems to not pertain to whole, or even majorities of, societies. Instead, groups, often very small, may require government intervention for assistance in some way. But because these problems usually do

[1] My view of the allocation of such resources is most strongly influenced by Harold Lasswell. See, especially, *Politics: Who Gets What, When, How* (Cleveland, Meridian Books, 1958), first published 1936.

[2] Aaron Wildavsky, *The Politics of the Budgetary Process*, 2nd edn (Boston, Little Brown, 1974), p. 4.

[3] Thomas R. Dye, *Understanding Public Policy*, 2nd edn (Englewood Cliffs, N.J., Prentice Hall, 1975), p. 3.

Political Studies, Vol. XXX, No. 1 (59 76)

not affect majorities, or even significant minorities, governments respond slowly, if at all, in meeting such problems.[4] In turn, political scientists have given relatively little attention to them. Problems typical of this category relate to questions of civil liberties. While civil liberties questions may entail economic factors, such as the generally lower standard of living among certain minority groups, many do not.

Civil liberties problems arise because members of a group, almost inevitably a minority,[5] collectively believe that the formal and/or informal rules of their society discriminate against them. But the very existence of such rules suggests that for some reason those comprising the majority disapprove of something about that group. Majority disapproval permits decision makers to avoid alleviating whatever grievance members of the minority group may feel. In this paper, by focusing upon the activities of the Gay Rights movement in the United States, the difficulties encountered by such minority groups in bringing about social change will be explored. In this section, two propositions concerning the balance between legislatures and courts in dealing with civil liberties questions will be suggested. Then the activities of the Gay Rights movement will be considered in the context of the American system with a discussion of the differences between agitation for gay rights and for other causes such as equal civil rights for women and Blacks. This will be followed by an analysis of the obstacles to progress for the Gay Rights movement in achieving its goals with special emphasis upon the lack of any major progress in the courts.

Although this is a case study,[6] many of the problems which confront American homosexuals are common to all societies in which citizens take pride in democratic traditions. Indeed, it is not especially easy being a homosexual in any Western democracy. The impulse toward civil liberties that characterizes such societies is often thwarted by public prejudices which affect those who differ from the majority. While fewer states maintain the level of legal discrimination against homosexuals that they once did, some enforce laws

[4] The concept of the significant minority is not an easy one with which to deal as it is fraught with problems of tautology. Generally, a significant minority may be seen as one which has the ability to affect the workings of a government, even, perhaps, to help being it down. By this definition, coal miners in the United Kingdom would be a significant minority while university teachers are almost certainly not. Blacks may be a significant minority, or they may not be, depending upon the strength they are able to mobilize in certain areas. Anomic group activity as in Bristol, for example, may have scant impact upon government policy thus suggesting insignificance. But government recognition of significance may often come too late. The transition from insignificance to significance is very shadowy.

[5] Women are the exception, although only a minority of women are interested in the women's movement in whatever country one wishes to study.

[6] While there is no great need to justify the case study, this approach had fallen on hard times until recently. Often, works which were really case studies were placed in other categories by their authors. This was usually done in order to justify 'theoretical relevance', a notion which many people still take seriously without considering the theoretical relevance of case studies, even those which make no mention of similar literature. Two works which do extol the virtues of case studies and which are worth reading are Arend Lijphart, 'Comparative Politics and Comparative Method', *American Political Science Review*, 65 (1971), 682–93, and Jorgen Rasmussen, '"Once You've Made a Revolution, Everything's the Same": Comparative Politics', in G. J. Graham, Jr., and G. W. Carey (eds), *The Post-Behavioural Era: Perspectives on Political Science* (New York, David Mackay, 1972), pp. 71–87. See, especially, p. 85.

which are directed largely, if not exclusively, against homosexuals. Even where homosexuals are granted consensual rights, those rights are generally not as extensive as rights enjoyed by heterosexuals. Ages of consent often differ for heterosexuals and homosexuals, and admitted homosexuals may be excluded from government positions. If leaders of the state and/or professional associations believe an individual's sexual preference detracts from his or her relationship with a client, or affects job performance, then the life chances of the homosexual may be limited by exclusion from those professions either through formal or informal means. Such professions may include medicine, law, teaching, and, in most societies, the military.

No Western democracy has been as inhospitable to homosexuals in terms of its laws as the United States during the past half century. While other countries have abolished, or at least substantially modified, the laws which once placed homosexuals at great risk, even, possibly, the loss of one's life,[7] the legal restrictions directed against homosexuals in the United States are still extensive and, of course, intimidating.

In all Western countries with relatively democratic institutions, homophile organizations have sought to alter laws which affect their affiliates. Perhaps because of the degree of legal discrimination directed against them, politically active homosexuals in the United States have become the most militantly outspoken in their denunciation of a society they perceive oppresses them. The activists have come together in what may loosely be called a Gay Rights movement. The most widely supported aim of participants is the removal of laws which discriminate against homosexuals.

It is the underlying assumption of this essay that, while the American ethos of individualism and personal liberty against the whims of the state encourages the growth of groups devoted to the enhancement of civil liberties, the disjointed and cumbersome nature of the American policy process enables decision makers to avoid dealing with such questions. When unpopular groups find that the legislative mechanism offers scant relief, only the courts remain where laws which are perceived as being restrictive and discriminatory may be challenged. But the court procedure, too, is difficult in terms of the expenditure of both time and resources, and those who require the assistance of the courts are more often than not least equipped to avail themselves of its services.

The practice of avoiding dealing with questions concerning minorities in society is not unique to the United States. Such questions are seldom high on the policy agenda of any country. Besides overriding government concern with the management of the economy, defence, and social welfare problems, another consideration must be taken into account by decision makers. However apathetic or predictable in terms of traditional voting patterns an electorate may be, civil liberties issues are potentially damaging to the electoral prospects of a political party or to the unity of the different political parties involved in the policy process. Thus, taking the United Kingdom as an example, highly contentious issues tinged with a civil liberties element are often left to the Private Members' Bill mechanism which allows MPs to debate and

[7] This latter point ought not to be underestimated. Among the less publicized occurrences since the collapse of the Shah's regime in Iran has been the execution of homosexuals.

pass legislation which government and opposition leadership may wish to avoid adopting as an element of a party programme.[8]

In the United States, governments are generally unlikely to act on questions concerned with civil liberties unless either of two conditions is met. The first condition is that the courts order those governments to do so explicitly, or create situations in which change may occur because the state interest is removed. Thus, a court rules that state practices are unlawful as in the maintenance of segregation in the schools. In *Brown* v. *Board of Education* (347 U.S. 483, 1954), officials in states were segregation existed were instructed to desegregate their schools. Alternatively, a court orders the state to desist enforcing private forms of discrimination as in *Shelley* v. *Kraemer* (334 U.S. 1, 1948). In that case, the Supreme Court found that, while a restrictive covenant was legal, it could not be enforced by the state because it was not a contract.

The second condition is that the public is seen to be overwhelmingly in favour of legislative action in the particular problem area. Following President Kennedy's assassination and the civil rights march in Selma, Alabama, President Johnson was able to bring about the passage of the Civil Rights Act of 1964 and the Voting Rights Act of 1965. Both Acts were far-reaching in terms of their impact, but it is doubtful if they would have enjoyed the easy passage through Congress had the combination of circumstances, as well as the belief that there was widespread support for the legislation, not occurred. Generally, however, success in the courts by minority groups is the first step in any expansion of civil liberties.

THE GAY RIGHTS MOVEMENT

It may be argued that describing agitation for gay rights as a movement is to accept some preliminary conditions about organization and self-conscious purpose as given. But such is not the case in this paper. Instead, the term, movement, will be used uncritically to consider the various activities that have been occurring if only because those involved in the work for full civil liberties for homosexuals tend to describe the agitation as such. It should be noted, however, that the concept of the social movement suggests certain factors which may not be present.[9]

Because they all grew out of the general restlessness that characterized American society in the aftermath of the Second World War, it is tempting to link the Gay Rights movement to the Black, Hispanic-American and, more lately, the Women's Movements. During the 1950s, the Supreme Court opened the doors through which Blacks first went only to be followed by other groups as well. So, although the radicalism that was to characterize the 1960s had not yet appeared, the foundations for social upheaval had already been laid by

[8] Perhaps because of the lack of emphasis placed on civil liberties legislation generally, and the limited amount of time allocated to Private Members' bills, there are relatively few works on the subject. See, for example, Michael Ryles, 'Private Members' Bills', *Political Quarterly*, 37 (1966), 385–93.

[9] Much depends upon the definition one uses. For an introduction to social movements literature, see Paul Wilkinson, *Social Movement* (London, Macmillan, 1971); Hans Toch, *The Social Psychology of Social Movements* (London, Methuen, 1966); and Rudolf Heberle, *Social Movements: An Introduction to Political Sociology* (New York, Appleton-Century-Crofts, 1951).

what had happened earlier and was, at least in part, initiated by a branch of the central government.

All minority movements owe much to the Black leaders who chose to challenge laws which permitted discrimination against Blacks for no reasons other than race. What was especially significant about most of the movements was the close link between political and economic discrimination. Blacks were, and remain, poorer than the majority Whites. This may also be said about the Hispanic-Americans and groups such as American Indians. The same condition may also be said to have affected women generally and minority women in particular. Although women have made tremendous strides over the past decade, as a group they have not yet attained the economic status of men, and it will, no doubt, be a long time before they do. Thus, residues of discrimination and the coincident economic deprivation affect all of these groups despite the extension of laws protecting them.

It is this close linkage between political and economic deprivation which distinguishes such movements from the Gay Rights movement. As a group, homosexuals cannot be said to have suffered the economic deprivation common to other minority groups for it is only with public openness that a homosexual is at risk. Thus, the motivation for organization into protest groups or a social movement, has probably been less developed than for Blacks.[10] Post-war organizations devoted to the rights of homosexuals did, however, appear in a few of the major liberal cities, most notably New York and San Francisco. Washington, DC, the national capital, also drew politically committed homosexuals. Most of these early activists were in a financial position to contribute their time, efforts and skills and could, therefore, risk the social and legal sanctions that might be applied. But unlike Blacks, Hispanic-Americans, and, of course, women, most of whom are readily identifiable as that with which they are labelled, homosexuals are generally unrecognizable as homosexuals. Most may live relatively anonymous lives, placing themselves at risk only when they choose to declare that they are homosexuals.

The early movement, especially, had no particular attraction for the vast majority of homosexuals. The laws were very restrictive even though unevenly enforced. While police harassment was and remains commonplace, gay bars managed to survive and thrive, and large cities provided some refuge from what could be a repressive and isolated life. Above all, self-declaration carried with it severe sanctions. Social and familial ostracism were common enough as was the possibility of the loss of one's job. If one were in a position to live a double life, it was probably better to do so rather than be involved in risk-taking in which everything could be lost for the sake of a principle that attracted little public attention and even less public sympathy.

Still, events in the 1960s began to disrupt such attitudes. After the Selma March, and subsequent police reaction, the Civil Rights Act of 1964 and Voting Rights Act of 1965 were passed. The Vietnam War and wasteful affluence among some groups in American society while many were poor gave rise to both the anti-war movement and 'drop-out generation' as well as to

[10] Here, I am especially influenced by Rudolf Heberle who saw social movements largely in terms of being class based. See Heberle, *Social Movements: An Introduction to Political Sociology*.

more open attitudes toward sex and sexuality. Pornography became readily available and less expensive, people actually talked about abortion, and new forms of contraception provided women with the opportunity of a freer attitude toward sex, which must certainly have had a great impact upon the directions of the women's movement.

So in June, 1969, when police raided a bar in the most pronounced gay ghetto in New York, it was not altogether surprising that many who were present reacted angrily. Homosexuals were simply the latest in the list of minority and/or socially oppressed groups to rebel against harassment by the state. The so-called Stonewall Riots in June, 1969, became the starting point for the Gay Rights movement; for the first time the collective anger felt by members of a group, who had suffered their oppression in silence but usually with profound humiliation, was demonstrated.[11]

Still, it is difficult to accept the view of one commentator who has suggested that 'by the end of the 1960s, it was apparent that the homophile movement had grown stronger. More local organizations were formed throughout the nation. Then regional and national organizations emerged to coordinate local efforts, while in San Francisco, gay people were beginning to learn how to use political power.'[12] Although, socially, gays had become more visible, this statement is clearly an exaggeration of what had happened. Even now, national co-ordination does not exist. San Francisco may be cited as a locale where political activism among homosexuals is common, but in that respect San Francisco is an uncommon city. What is more, most homosexuals are still 'in the closet', wherever they happen to live.

What has occurred is that legislatures in twenty states have rescinded at least parts of the laws that have discriminated against homosexuals. More than fifty cities and municipalities have adopted gay rights ordinances. Since Stonewall, hundreds of groups have been formed throughout the country. On college and university campuses, gay rights and/or gay social groups flourish. There must be no doubt that this follows on from the heady days of the late 1960s, but strong, more centrally orientated organizations have thus far eluded gay rights activists.

Reflecting the generally disjointed nature of both American society and its governmental structures, it is thought that more than two thousand gay rights groups are in existence.[13] Of this vast number, only two organizations, the National Gay Task Force (NGTF), and the Gay Rights National Lobby (GRNL), exist which are concerned primarily with fighting for the rights of

[11] The literature on Gay Rights and the development of the movement is idiosyncratic. A fairly useful work is Dennis Altman, *Homosexual: Liberation and Oppression* (New York, Avon Books, 1973). I disagree with many of Altman's conclusions—indeed, with some of his premises as well—but it is possibly the one restrained, non-personal account of a particularly vital period for Gay Rights activists.

[12] Sal Licata, 'A History of the Gay Rights Movement in America', *The Advocate*, no. 246, p. 8.

[13] This figure is, of course, subject to debate. It is an estimate derived from interviews with NGTF leaders in 1978. Another estimate, by the American Civil Liberties Union, puts the figure at about eight hundred. See E. Carrington Boggan, *et al.*, *The Rights of Gay People: The Basic ACLU Guide to a Gay Person's Rights* (New York, Discus Books, 1975). My own view is that the NGTF estimate is more likely. If one takes into account all of the colleges and universities in the United States that would possibly have gay groups of either a social or political nature, the figure is easily reached. Of course, many of these groups will be small and relatively inactive.

homosexuals at a national level. But their respective methods of operation differ markedly from each other as well as the resources they have at their disposal. The NGTF is a large, New York-based organization which acts as the major group when speaking for homosexuals. The GRNL is a small, Washington-based lobbying group which has attempted to influence Senators and Representatives particularly in amending the Civil Rights Act of 1964 to bring homosexuals under the protection of that Act.

The most significant lobbying activities of Gay Rights groups take place at the state and local, rather than at the national levels partly because the efforts that are being made to amend the Civil Rights Act are unlikely to bear fruit in the foreseeable future. Indeed, the failure to make dramatic strides at the federal level has not impeded—and, indeed, may have influenced—the work of local organizations. Such groups have lobbied various state, city, and municipal governments to repeal laws or ordinances which discriminate against homosexuals or to adopt laws or ordinances which protect homosexuals.

The efforts at local reform have proceeded in a piecemeal fashion with some successes and some failures. Since 1971, more than fifty municipalities have adopted ordinances ostensibly protecting the rights of homosexuals. The ordinances have ranged from reasonably strong guarantees of protection in areas such as housing and public employment to weak statements of respect for human rights with no enforcement procedures. Often such statements coexist with laws that still discriminate against homosexuals.[14] A major problem with such ordinances is that they have occasionally provoked anti-homosexual groups to work toward repeal, often through the method of the referendum, a pattern of public decision making which is widespread throughout the United States. When such local referendums have been held, Gay Rights Ordinances were generally defeated.

Leaders of different Gay Rights groups such as the NGTF, and the more broadly-based civil liberties groups, especially the American Civil Liberties Union, are antipathetic toward the activity leading to local ordinances because of what popular voting in referendums implies. According to the view that they hold, civil rights are not privileges that the state, as the representative of the majority, may choose to allow the people of that state to have. On the contrary, the constitutional guarantees are specifically designed to protect the individual from the potential tyranny of the state although it must be obvious that throughout American history such protection has not always been available. But, in theory at least, rights inhere in the individual, and it is the state's function to protect rather than allow or disallow those rights.

Aside from contempt for the notion that rights may be extended or removed by popular vote, recourse to the referendum is feared by advocates of civil liberties for two other reasons. First, the majority is more likely than not to be intolerant of minority rights given that the exercise of those rights may be

[14] Washington, DC, for example, has a strongly worded human rights ordinance which ostensibly recognizes the privacy of its residents. This ordinance coexists with laws against sexual activities common among homosexuals. While laws in the latter category are not really enforced any more, that they remain on the statute books does suggest some danger to homosexuals should less sympathetic public figures attain office.

offensive to the majority. And second, financial resources of the different civil liberties groups are almost never as strong as those which the anti-civil liberties forces are able to marshal. Consequently, in defending rights against the vagaries of the popular vote, civil liberties groups are forced into defensive postures whereas they see their real and most effective function in terms of legal challenges, in the courts, of laws they perceive to be unjust. Rights, they believe, are too vulnerable to be trusted to the electoral market place.

OBSTACLES TO THE GAY RIGHTS MOVEMENT

Unlike most organized minority groups, homosexuals have been unsuccessful in achieving a redefinition of their legal position through the legislative process in the United States. Government at the national level, and governments at the state and local levels, have usually been unwilling to meet the demands that various Gay Rights groups have placed before them. Many reasons may be cited for governments avoiding dealing with the Gay Rights issue, but, generally, four obstacles have impeded the Gay Rights movement. They are (1) the general hostility, real or perceived, of the public towards homosexuals, (2) the shape of the movement itself, (3) the structure of United States government(s), and (4) perhaps most significant to any group(s) organized to promote civil liberties in the United States, the failure of litigation in the courts to provide at least a framework within which the various legislative bodies would be forced to act.

Public hostility toward homosexuals is well known. Polls have demonstrated a general antagonism toward the notion that all laws which restrict the liberties of homosexuals ought to be repealed.[15] This hostility is magnified when questions are raised concerning whether homosexuals should be permitted to teach in schools, particularly in the primary schools. Probably as a result of this known hostility, as well as the possibility that the individual politician may actually share the public attitude, political figures, generally, have been unwilling to take up the cause of Gay Rights. Of course, leading politicians in cities such as New York, Washington, and San Francisco have been outspoken on the issue, but they have large and vocal gay communities to which they may be electorally accountable.

Politicians at the national level have been loath to take up full civil liberties for homosexuals. During President Carter's outspoken campaign for human rights, for example, he did not extend this concern to the rights of homosexuals. Further, no presidential, or would-be presidential, candidate has ever demonstrated any willingness to support the amendment to the Civil Rights Act which would end legal discrimination against homosexuals in much the same way that Act did for Blacks.

[15] A comprehensive Gallup Survey in 1977 (July) indicated that even though a majority (56 per cent) favoured equal rights in job opportunities for homosexuals, this majority turned into a minority when the jobs were teaching or the clergy. Only such employment as sales-persons or, interestingly, the military had majorities in favour of no discrimination. With regard to the question of whether homosexual relations between consenting adults should be legal, the numbers for and against were the same (43 per cent), thus suggesting a fair degree of hostility. Perhaps more pronounced is the question of adoption of children. Those against homosexuals adopting children constituted 77 per cent. Those for the proposition were only 14 per cent of the total (with 9 per cent don't knows).

This lack of sponsorship is most significant because by the time the Black civil rights movement began scoring its major successes with President and Congress in the 1960s, that movement enjoyed a wide base of support within the Federal Government as well as wide support from White Americans. From the end of the Second World War until the Civil Rights Act of 1964 finally was passed, a large proportion, perhaps a majority, of the members of Congress were favourably disposed to the premise of equal rights for Blacks although they were thwarted by the southern minority's use of procedural rules in the Senate. But this majority support has never been forthcoming when the matter of equal rights for homosexuals is raised.

The shape of the movement itself is the second obstacle to its success in bringing about an alteration of the laws as they now exist. Part of the reason for this is the structure of American political institutions, which will be discussed below. Perhaps the key factor other than the disjointed American political system is the fear many homosexuals feel about possible discovery and the accommodation most have made with their environments.

The Gay Rights movement has traditionally involved only a minority of homosexuals. Although, as suggested earlier, the number of organizations is quite large, few of these groups are composed of many participants. Except in more liberal cities, any homosexual affiliating with an organization in an open manner is potentially at risk. No civil rights act prevents a business or government authority from dismissing that homosexual although the courts are beginning to limit the reasons for dismissal when the particular individual shows any willingness to take the matter through the courts.

The various political organizations within the movement must compete with the variety of social attractions that also exist, something that cannot be said for other movements. Not all homosexuals who enjoy what the gay scene has to offer, including many who are open about their homosexuality, are particularly interested in politics. After all, homosexuals share only two basic characteristics. The first is a common sexual orientation in that they prefer partners of their own sex. Second, they suffer a number of social disadvantages because the vast majority of non-homosexuals disapprove of that first characteristic. Other than these factors, the many features that bind members of minority ethnic groups together are missing in the homosexual 'community'. Unlike the poor, homosexuals are located along whatever economic and social scale one wishes to construct. So the factors that bring homosexuals together are frequently insufficient to forge the bonds which are required to build determined social movements.

This is not to underestimate how vital the characteristics held in common are. But despite them, the vast majority of people who are gay, be it for reasons of fear of retribution, of contempt for what 'straight' society has come to represent, or of apathy, have not yet seen fit to declare openly that they are gay. Within the United States, the gay sub-cultures have managed to provide enough of a diversion for most homosexuals to discourage political activity. It is easy to fade in and out of the majority society, and this is what most homosexuals do.

From the perspective of the way which the movement has organized, it tends to reflect the dispersal of governmental authority in the United States. Social movements, pressure groups, and all varieties of groups that seek to bring about change in society, grow in accordance with the organization of political institutions in that society. In the American system, the decentralized nature of the government—indeed, of the society—has frequently led to large numbers of organizations springing up which all foster the same cause. These groups may operate relatively independently, and, occasionally, in direct competition with each other. They may concentrate on change at the national level or at the state and local levels. With the separation of powers, they may approach legislatures, courts, executives, or a combination of the three. During the early part of the civil rights era, the National Association for the Advancement of Coloured People was quite prepared to assist those who would pursue legal claims through the courts while the Southern Christian Leadership Conference organized campaigns of civil disobedience in order to demonstrate both numbers and determination to legislators and to the public as well as to other Blacks who had not become involved in the agitation. In the later years of the movement, the SCLC was viewed as a conservative organization when it was compared with the newer groups devoted to the more evocative cause of Black Power. But each of the main Black civil rights organizations was able to gain the support of large numbers of people probably because of the widescale economic deprivation that existed. Without the numbers, the challenges to discriminatory state and Federal laws would have been virtually impossible.

Yet all of these obstacles would be surmountable in terms of the extent of legal protection afforded to homosexuals if the major obstacle were to be overcome. If the Supreme Court placed the rights of homosexuals under the same cover that others have received, other problems would be less significant. The classic American method of avoiding civil liberties questions until pressure is overwhelming is simply to leave certain problems to the courts. In much the same way as in Britain where, as was suggested, controversial problems concerning minorities could be left to the mechanism of the Private Members' Bill, so in the United States, legislatures ignore certain types of problems as long as the possibility exists that the courts will eventually draw the fire that might otherwise be directed toward them.

But the courts, especially the Supreme Court, have demonstrated over the years that they are just as able to avoid confronting certain problems as elected politicians. The courts do this through a variety of ways ranging from the grounds upon which they base their decisions to refusing to hear particular cases, thus allowing decisions of lower courts that tend to uphold existing law to stand.

Against this background, however, Americans have long prided themselves on rights they had ostensibly possessed against state activity. Over time such rights have expanded as wider interpretation of the Constitution, especially through the courts, has brought more people under the protection of its clauses. The evolution of the meaning of the Constitution is central to any expansion of rights, and the significance of the flexibility of that document was expressed in 1910 by Justice McKenna who wrote:

> Time works changes, brings into existence new conditions and purposes. Therefore a principle to be vital must be capable of wider application than the mischief which gave it birth. This is particularly true of constitutions. They are not ephemeral enactments, designed to meet passing occasions. [*Weems* v. *U.S.*, 217 U.S. 349, 373]

Change has been most pronounced in recent years over the issue of the right of privacy. Increasingly, the question of what an individual may do before that action conflicts with a legitimate state interest is one with which the courts have been forced to deal. In a relatively early case in which privacy was of paramount concern, Justice Brandeis argued that

> The makers of our Constitution undertook to secure conditions favourable to the pursuit of happiness. They recognized the significance of man's spiritual nature, of his feelings and of his intellect. They knew that only part of the pain, pleasure and satisfactions of life are to be found in material things. They sought to protect Americans in their beliefs, their thoughts, their emotions and their sensations. *They conferred, as against the Government, the right to be let alone*—the most comprehensive of rights and the most valued by civilized men. [*Olmstead* v. *U.S.*, 277 U.S. 438, 478–9 emphasis mine.]

But Brandeis's view was contained in a dissenting opinion. The majority still held to a very narrow interpretation of the extent of the right of privacy.

Generally, all cases that deal with the right of the individual to be a homosexual without danger to his or her life and life chances or to engage in 'homosexual activities'—sexual participation of any kind with a person or persons of the same sex—have some connection with the idea of a right of privacy. The difficulty arises because

> no one can confidently draw up a list of American rights in outline form to be carried around by all citizens (and some aliens) because an accurate understanding of the scope and impact of American rights requires a keen appreciation of the definitions which courts and public officials have given to certain key phrases in the Constitution.[16]

The phrase, right of privacy, appears nowhere in the Constitution, so if such a right may be said to exist, it must spring from less explicit sources.

The most significant case in raising the right of privacy issue as it may relate to homosexuals came in 1965 when the Supreme Court ruled that a state could not interfere with the private lives of married couples if they chose to use contraceptives. The decision was based upon rights enumerated in the First, Third, Fourth, Fifth, and Ninth Amendments to the Constitution (*Griswold* v. *Connecticut*, 381 U.S. 779). A concurring opinion, written by Justice Goldberg, concentrated on the possible significance of the Ninth Amendment as it may pertain to a right of privacy. The Ninth Amendment states that 'The enumeration in the Constitution, of certain rights, shall not be construed to deny or disparage others retained by the people', which suggests 'a belief of the Constitution's authors that fundamental rights exist that are not expressly enumerated in the first eight amendments and an intent that the list of rights included there not to be deemed exhaustive.' (*Griswold* v. *Connecticut*, p. 492). The suggestion of a much more extensive range of rights was tempered by Goldberg's reliance upon a dissent in *Poe* v. *Ullman* (367 U.S. 497, 1960) in which Justice Harlan argued 'The right of privacy most manifestly is not an absolute. Thus, I would not suggest that adultery, homosexuality, fornication, and incest are immune from criminal inquiry, however privately practiced. So much has been explicitly recognized in acknowledging the State's rightful concern for its people's moral welfare' (*Poe* v. *Ullman*, 552–553). So the first

[16] See J. A. Sigler, *American Rights Policies* (Homewood, Illinois, Dorsey Press, 1975), p. 11.

step to extend the idea of the right of privacy through the Ninth Amendment was only tentative with homosexuality probably excluded.

But *Griswold*, and the possibilities it raised, became clearer eight years later when the question of abortion was decided by the Supreme Court. While other questions, such as the standing of the case, were raised, the central issue in the abortion decision was the right of privacy. The lower court decision extending the right of a woman to obtain an abortion without state interference was founded upon the Ninth Amendment, but the Supreme Court decision was more broadly based. In striking down the stringent laws of forty-nine states Justice Blackmun argued

> This right of privacy, whether founded in the Fourteenth Amendment's concept of reasonable liberty and restrictions upon state action, as we here think it is, or as the District Court determined in the Ninth Amendment's reservation of rights to the people, is broad enough to encompass a woman's decision whether or not to terminate her pregnancy. (*Roe* v. *Wade*, 410 U.S. 113, p. 153, 1973. See also *Doe* v. *Bolton*, 410 U.S. 179).

Privacy, however, 'is not unqualified and must be considered against important state interests in regulation' (*Roe* v. *Wade*, p. 157). This view is of great significance because guidelines determining the weight to be attached to rights inhering in the individual when compared with legitimate state interests do not exist.

The movement by the courts into the area of the right of privacy was not exactly without reservation. Yet those interested in civil liberties perceived that the Supreme Court could not for long avoid the inevitable decision regarding general relations among members of the same sex if it were to be consistent with its earlier rulings concerning private activities. One commentator, for example, argued in 1975, 'the developing right of privacy offers a traditional constitutional argument that requires no major doctrinal change in order to protect homosexuality. In extending the right of privacy to all forms of heterosexual conduct, the courts have gone so far that exclusion of homosexuality cannot be justified.'[17]

The opportunity the Supreme Court had to alter the restrictions on individual freedom through reliance on the right of privacy came in 1977 when an appeal was made from Virginia (*Doe* v. *Commonwealths' Attorney for City of Richmond*, 403 *F. Supp.* 1199, 1975). In that case, the District Court found that the state statute which, loosely stated, forbade crimes against nature was constitutional. Using the section of *Griswold* which excluded homosexuality from coverage by that decision the Senior Judge stated that

> No judgement is made upon the wisdom of policy of the statute. It is simply that we cannot say that the statute offends the Bill of Rights or any other of the Amendments and the wisdom on policy is a matter for the state's resolve [*Doe* v. *Commonwealth*, 1200] ... We believe that the statute, so long in Virginia, has a rational basis of State interest demonstrably legitimate and mirrored in the cited decisional law of the Supreme Court [*Doe* v. *Commonwealth*, 1203].[18]

[17] 72, *Michigan Law Review*, 1613 (1975), p. 1637.

[18] The case upon which the decision was largely based was a ruling which dealt with a Florida Statute (*Wainwright, Corrections Director, et al.* v. *Stone et al.* 414 U.S. 21, 1973). The *Doe* case was not unanimous at the District level. In a dissent it was argued that 'To say, as the majority

The Supreme Court chose not to hear the case on appeal and, by so doing it implied that the right of privacy, under certain circumstances, must take second place when weighed against what might be termed the legitimate state interest in areas of morality. In this instance, one can only assume that the avoidance by the Supreme Court of dealing with potentially highly controversial matter is based, at least in part, upon a perception by the Supreme Court that a decision striking down the laws of most states for so unpopular a cause would be impolitic. But it is difficult to separate the private acts of mature people of the same sex from the category that contains the right of privacy with regard to questions such as abortion or the use of contraception.

If the Supreme Court and law courts have avoided decisions about the right of privacy, they have done so in other areas as well. Another category of cases deals with the general question of discrimination against an individual simply because he or she is a homosexual. Once again, it could be reasonably assumed that just as it may be said that discrimination against different classes of people on the basis of race or sex in fields such as employment (job security) or housing violates clauses in the Constitution, so it is the case with homosexuals, but this is not so. Even when finding for homosexuals, the courts have avoided the Constitutional questions of the rights a homosexual may possess against such discrimination, and the courts have also found that discrimination may be practised against homosexuals partly because of a lack of precision concerning the nature of homosexuality. By this, the issue of whether homosexuality constitutes some type of sickness may be raised.

At the federal level, discrimination against homosexuals occurs largely within the bureaucracy, usually in either one of two ways. The first is through bureaucratic rule-making which may happen when laws enacted by Congress, frequently years earlier, are vague or purposely permit the bureaucracy to have great latitude in law making; and the second is job security, a question that has arisen both in the civilian and military sides of employment. The lack of any recent action by the Supreme Court has not helped to clarify the situation of homosexuals with regard to these particular problems. The Supreme Court has left the matter to the lower courts which have in turn hesitated in taking any radical steps.

The clearest use of authority in the area of bureaucratic rule making with regard to homosexuals is the question of immigration and naturalization. The law which affects homosexuals is the Immigration and Nationality Act of 1954. Section 212 states:

> Except as otherwise provided in this Act, the following classes of aliens shall be ineligible to receive visas and shall be excluded from admission into the United States . . .
> (4) Aliens afflicted with psychopathic personality
> (9) Aliens who have been convicted of a crime involving moral turpitude (other than a purely political offence).

does, that the right of privacy, which every citizen has, is limited to matters of marital, home or family life is unwarranted under the law.' (*Doe* v. *Commonwealth*, p. 1203.) The dissent concluded 'That the sole basis of the prescription of homosexuality was what the majority refers to as the promotion of morality and decency. As salutary a legislative goal as this may be, I can find no authority for intrusion by the state into the private dwelling of a citizen.' (*Doe* v. *Commonwealth*, p. 1205.)

According to the definition of the law, homosexuals fall under the category of Clause 4. Cases arising under the Act which have come before the Supreme Court have had various interpretations, some favourable to the homosexual involved (*Rosenberg, District Director, Immigration and Nationalization Service* v. *Fleuti*, 347 U.S. 449, 1963), others unfavourable (*Boutilier* v. *Immigration and Nationalization Service*, 387 U.S. 118, 1967). But the Court has yet to decide a case on constitutional grounds, i.e., whether the particular part of the act which suggests that homosexuals are afflicted with a psychopathic personality is valid. Because of this lack of direction, lower courts have varied in their interpretation, but the general rule that seems to have emerged is that if the alien is considered to be of good 'moral character' (*In Re Labady*, 326 F. Supp. 924, 1971) and/or has not lied about his/her homosexuality on the application for a visa (*Kovacs* v. *United States*, 476, *F. 2d.* 843, 1973), the person can be admitted to the United States and considered for citizenship. But the state of the law is so indefinite that homosexuals who had never been convicted of some offence related to being a homosexual would be foolish to admit to homosexuality. While nothing might happen to disadvantage the individual, no guarantee could be given that this would, in fact, be the case. Indeed, in 1980, a German homosexual in Virginia was denied citizenship in the United States after fourteen years residence simply because he was a homosexual.

Once one leaves the problem of bureaucratic rule making, three themes appear to have emerged from the different cases that have come before the courts in the general area of employment in the civil service and armed forces. First, private homosexual acts probably do not constitute grounds for dismissal from the civil service. The US Court of Appeals in DC ruled that:

> We are not prepared to say that the Commission [Civil Service Commission] could not reasonably find appellant's homosexual advance to be 'immoral', 'indecent', or 'notoriously disgraceful' under dominant conventional terms. But the notion that it could be an appropriate function of the federal bureaucracy to enforce the majority's conventional codes of conduct in the private lives of its employees is at war with elementary concepts of liberty, privacy, and diversity. [*Norton* v. *Macy*, 417 *F. 2d.* 1161, 1969].

Related to this is the issue and the question of security clearance for homosexuals, especially given the possibility of blackmail. The view that seems to be current suggests:

> The applicant's own public revelation avoids the usual blackmail threat, of disclosure of homosexuality ordinarily relied upon as a reason for such denial. That does not necessarily end the enquiry, but it suffices to establish that if the agency seeks to justify further enquiry into the details of what would ordinarily be considered the private sexual life of the applicant, as a matter required by the public interest, it must identify with particularity the relevance of such further enquiry with respect of applicable data. [*Gayer* v. *Schlesinger*, 490 *F. 2d.* 740, 1973, Leventhal concurring, 755].

But the general view holds that the Commission, or any body granting security clearance, has the right to make reasonable enquiries into a person's homosexuality which may be relevant to that clearance. Each case must be treated on its merits and no constitutional rights protect the individual from the enquiries (*Wentworth* v. *Schlesinger*, as part of *Gayer*, 490 *F. 2d.* 740, esp. 744).

A second theme is that people who openly 'flaunt' their homosexuality may not be protected by an appeal to First Amendment rights. In a case involving a Gay Rights activist who had been dismissed by the Equal Employment Opportunities Commission (the Director of which had been informed that the new employee was a homosexual before that individual was hired) the Circuit Court of Appeals ruled 'that notorious conduct and open flaunting and careless display of unorthodox sexual conduct in public might be relevant to the efficiency of the service' (*Singer* v. *United States Civil Service Commission*, 530 *F. 2d.* 247, 1976, p. 255). Further, where First Amendment rights are weighed against possible damage to the efficiency of the service, those rights are outweighed by the good of the majority. So appeal to First Amendment rights of free speech over perceived state interest seems not to hold, although once again, in the absence of any definite rule, each case may go through the courts. The question of what constitutes 'flaunting', however, is a vexing one. Does the decision imply that any political activity outside of work time might affect 'the efficiency of the service'?

A third theme relates directly to military service. As the situation now exists, known homosexuals cannot serve in the armed forces although the proportion of homosexuals in the military probably reflects the number in the country. As a result of the *Doe* case, a recent decision held 'that there is no constitutional right to engage in homosexual activity'; therefore, the decision by the Air Force to discharge honourably a career officer had to be upheld (*Matlovich* v. *Secretary of Air Force*, 13 *FEP Cases*, 267 and 269). The judge in this case, however, was clearly troubled by the limits he believed were placed upon him by the absence of leadership by the Supreme Court. He argued that he had no authority, given the current state of the law, to order the Air Force to grant reinstatement of the discharged officer. But, he concluded:

> While the Court has reached its conclusions, as a judge must do, on the law, I hope it will be recognized that after months of intense study of this problem, matters within and without the record the Court, individually, for what it is worth, has reached the conclusion that it is desirable for the military to re-examine the homosexual problem, to approach it in perhaps a more sensitive and precise way. [*Matlovich* v. *Secretary of Air Force*, 13 *FEP Cases*, 269, p. 272].

At the state and local level the issues before the courts remain basically the same: job security and laws which protect the civil rights of homosexuals. In certain respects, the laws at this level are more significant than federal practices because they deal with the more sensitive areas such as avowed or, as is usually the case, closet homosexuals, holding positions as school teachers, as well as the rights of landlords to evict homosexual tenants, not because the homosexual has been noisy or destructive, but because the landlord in question finds homosexuals offensive. The level of hostility directed openly to the homosexual in teaching is especially well known and was seized upon during the Dade County referendum on the extension of Gay Rights with, it is assumed, particular effect.

This antagonism to homosexual teachers may be extracted from the various court decisions. In a California case, the court seemed to have been saying that an individual's private life was beyond the reach of individual authorities by arguing that 'the power of the state to regulate professions and conditions of government employment must not arbitrarily impair the right of the individual to live his private life, apart from his job, as he deems fit' (*Morrison* v. *State Board of Education*, 461 *P. 2d.* 375, 1969, p. 394). But, the court did not go so far as to uphold the absolute right of homosexuals to hold teaching positions. Instead, the court stated

> we do not, of course, hold that homosexuals must be permitted to teach in the public schools of California. As we have explained, the relevant statutes, as well as the applicable principles of constitutional law, require only that the board properly find, pursuant to the precepts set forth in this opinion, that an individual is not fit to teach. (*Morrison* v. *State Board of Education*, 461 *P. 2d.* 375, 1969, p. 394).

As it turns out, while widely cited in books dealing with the rights of homosexuals, this rule does not seem to be the guiding principle. In a number of recent cases, for example, as the Gay Rights campaign has developed and homosexuals have attained greater visibility, more homosexual teachers have lost their jobs. Such dismissals have been implicitly and practically upheld by the Supreme Court which refused to hear appeals in the cases (*Gaylord* v. *Tacoma School District*, 435 U.S. 879, 1977, *Gish* v. *Board of Education*, 434 U.S. 879, 1977; see also, *Burton* v. *Cascade School District No. 5*, 512 *F. 2d.* 850, 1975).

But some slight shift in policy may be detected in two cases. The first involved the removal of a school teacher from a position in a Maryland school district (*Acanfora* v. *Board of Education of Montgomery County*, 491 *F. 2d.* 498, 1974). What is confusing about this case is that the Court of Appeals did not uphold the right of that Board of Education to remove the individual from his teaching post because of his homosexuality; instead, it did so on the ground that his application form could be construed as being incomplete. He had failed to inform the employers that he had been an active member of a homophile organization while at university. Indeed, the Court stated that public statements regarding his homosexuality were not grounds for dismissal. But given the reaction by the Board of Education when it learned that Acanfora was a homosexual it is clear that he would not have been employed by Montgomery County had he revealed his homosexuality on his job application.

On the higher education level, it seems that homosexuality *per se* may not be used as a reason for non-renewal of contract provided that there is no evidence that such sexual orientation impairs the individual's abilities to teach. Further, the university cannot infringe upon that individual's First Amendment rights of free speech if the interests of that institution are not really affected by the exercise of those individual rights (see *Aumiller* v. *University of Delaware*, 434 *F. Supp.* 1273, 1977). The problem with this case, of course, is that while it appears to uphold the individual's First Amendment rights, it extends the constitutional rules with regard to homosexuals no further than they are now. So, it may be concluded that 'there can be little doubt that many judges and others are still strongly influenced by fear of "contagion". Any evidence or suggestion that students may be influenced by a teacher's sexual preferences may be regarded by such judges as enough to sustain a dismissal.'[19] Unless a teacher has been arrested for public indecency, or something carrying greater

[19] Boggan *et al.*, *The Rights of Gay People*, p. 29.

penalties, a revelation about homosexuality will not make that job any more secure.

. The cases discussed in this essay are by no means exhaustive. Dozens of cases have been before the various courts ranging from the right of privacy to the activities of gay student groups on university campuses. Through all of the cases, the overriding theme is one of uncertainty. Without some lead from the Supreme Court, the lower courts have tended to act on the side of caution. The Supreme Court has avoided any clarifying decision either by refusing to hear the case, thus upholding the decision of the lower court without comment, or by finding against the homosexual litigant. Where crimes against nature such as sodomy or buggery exist, they are still binding in law although enforcement varies radically from location to location. But overall the Supreme Court has continued to avoid dealing with the constitutionality of such laws and, therefore, has failed to provide the protection activist homosexuals have required before challenging other disadvantages in legal and social terms when compared with other groups. Until the most stringent legal impediments are removed by the courts, homosexuals are unlikely to commit themselves to activities which may be directed to the alleviation of other social disadvantages. It is no accident that the Black civil rights movement expanded after the 1954 *Brown* decision.

CONCLUSION

In the Introduction, two conditions were suggested, either of which would be necessary before controversial matters, especially those with a civil liberties component, would be resolved in the United States. The first was that the courts at the different levels, but usually the Supreme Court, rule that certain laws clash with constitutionally protected rights. The second is that legislatures act to alter laws which are restrictive to particular groups. Of course, the two are not mutually exclusive. More often than not action in the courts is the spur to legislative action, but legislative action without some impetus from the courts in civil liberties areas is generally unlikely because such problems affect minorities usually possessing fewer political resources than other groups in society who are demanding the attention of decision makers.

Theoretically, the courts are seen to be immune from public pressure. Judges reach decisions based upon the application of precedent and rules of equity, and they ostensibly disregard the popularity or unpopularity of the litigant seeking redress of the particular grievance. Realistically, however, the courts do reflect public opinion and popular attitudes to a varying extent. During some periods, the Supreme Court has been more liberal than in others. In addition, members of the judiciary may have the same prejudices and biases that other members of the elite, even those less insulated than the judges from the electorate, may have. Further, the courts traditionally have not been trail-blazing. Indeed, civil liberties groups may have become too expectant of support by the judges as a result of the Warren Court's judicial activism. While the Burger Court has probably not been as conservative as some would suggest, given its qualified support of access to abortion, bussing, and the very difficult problem of affirmative action, it is not as adventurous as the Warren

Court was.[20] Still, were consistency to be a general attribute of the Supreme Court—and it is not—one might have expected the Court to be somewhat more open to the arguments of those homosexuals who have pursued cases through the courts, at least in the area of the individual's right of privacy.

The existence of multiple centres of power in the United States has never made life easy for groups who have made claims against the national rules. Successful groups, such as Blacks, have been able to gain the attention of national decision makers largely through their ability to mobilize large numbers of people to fight for what is generally accepted to be a just cause by the majority. But the Gay Rights movement has been less a movement than a loose aggregate of groups seeking, with greater or lesser fervour, vaguely similar goals. These groups, however, represent a relatively small proportion of homosexuals in the United States for the majority have been unwilling to commit themselves to the quest for full and equal civil rights. Further, the justness of the cause is not widely accepted by non-homosexuals perhaps because of continued perceptions by many of homosexuality as mental illness or depravity.

Thus, governments are able to avoid dealing with such minority claims if the cause is unpopular and the group ill-organized even if those claims are consistent with decisions which have been reached in related situations. For homosexuals in the United States, especially those activists who have, often with considerable personal risk, pursued goals both through the courts and legislatures with only occasionally favourable results, the changes in other areas must be both exhilarating and frustrating. They are exhilarating because such expansion of rights demonstrates the possibilities for the future. They are frustrating because that same expansion shows that bestowing rights still rests with authorities, who are more often than not more concerned with the possibly adverse reaction of the majority than they are with the justness of the claim by the minority.

[20] There is ample evidence that the Supreme Court and the lower courts have never been especially keen to rush into rights disputes. See, for example, Richard Funston, *A Vital National Seminar: The Supreme Court in American Life* (Palo Alto, Calif., May Field, 1978); and Stephen L. Wasby, *The Supreme Court in the Federal Judicial System* (New York, Holt, Rinehart and Winston, 1978).

Blanche Wiesen Cook

Female Support Networks and Political Activism: Lillian Wald, Crystal Eastman, Emma Goldman

photo: Visiting Nurse Service, New York

The "Family" about 1900. Standing, left to right: Jane Hitchcock, Sue Foote, Jeanne Travis. Second row (seated): Mary Magoun Brown, Lavinia Dock, Lillian D. Wald, Ysabela Waters, Henrietta Van Cleft. In front: "Little Sammy" Brofsky and "Florrie" Long.

In Vera Brittain's *Testament of Friendship,* the biography of her beloved friend Winifred Holtby, the British activist and author wrote that

From the days of Homer the friendships of men have enjoyed glory and acclamation, but the friendships of women, in spite of Ruth and Naomi, have usually been not merely unsung, but mocked, belittled and falsely interpreted. . . .[1]

Part of the problem is general in scope and involves a distorted vision of the historian's craft that is no longer operable. Historians of my generation were trained to believe that the proper study of our past should be limited to the activities of great men – the wars of kings, the hero's quest for power. We were taught that the personal was separate from the political and that emotions were irrelevant to history.

Recent history and the movements of the sixties, the decade of our professional maturing, have revealed the absurdity of that tradition. It has beome clear that in history, no less than in life, our personal choices and the nature of our human relationships were and remain inseparable from our political, our public efforts. Once the personal impact of such confined historical perspective emerged, the need for revision became clear.

In my own work, 10 years of work on the historical peace movement – studies that included such significant women as Lillian Wald, Jane Addams, Crystal Eastman, and Emma Goldman – I had focused entirely on women's political contributions. I wrote about their programs for social justice and their opposition to international war. Nothing else. Whenever I came across a love letter by Lillian Wald, for example, I would note "love letter," and move on.

This paper is the result of a long overdue recognition that the personal is the political: that networks of love and support are crucial to our ability as women to work in a hostile world where we are not in fact expected to survive. And it comes out of a recognition that frequently the networks of love and support that enable politically and professionally active women to function independently and intensively consist largely of other women.

Lillian Wald, Crystal Eastman, Emma Goldman

Beyond their commitment to economic and social change and their opposition to America's entrance into World War I, Lillian Wald, Crystal Eastman, Emma Goldman, and Jane Addams had very little in common. They are of different generations, represent contrary political solutions, and in their private lives reflect a broad range of choice. Yet all four women expanded the narrow contours of women's role and all four left a legacy of struggle against poverty and discrimination.

Jane Addams and Lillian Wald were progressive social reformers.* The most famous of the settlement-house crusaders, Wald created the Henry Street Settlement and Visiting Nurse Service in New York while Addams founded Hull House in Chicago.

Crystal Eastman, a generation younger than Addams and Wald, was an attorney and journalist who investigated labor conditions and work accidents. In 1907 she authored New York State's first workman's compensation law, which became the model for most such laws in the United States. One of the three founders of Alice Paul's Congressional Union for suffrage, Eastman was a socialist and radical feminist who believed in "free love."

More outspoken and less respectful of authority than Addams and Wald, Eastman nevertheless worked closely with them in the peace movement. Wald was president of the American Union Against Militarism, the parent organization of the American Civil Liberties Union, and Eastman was its executive secretary. Addams was president of the Women's Peace Party (renamed the Women's International League for Peace and Freedom), and Eastman, also one of its founders, was president of the New York branch. Their differences of temperament and tactics tell us much about the nature of the women's movement during the rapidly changing era of WWI.[2]

Emma Goldman was outside their company, but always in the vanguard of their activity. Addams, Wald, and Eastman worked to improve immigrant and labor conditions. Goldman, an anarchist immigrant worker, sought to recreate society. They worked within the law to modify it. Goldman worked without the law to replace it with anarchist principles of voluntary communism.

Goldman frequently visited the Nurses' Settlement on Henry Street and liked Lillian Wald and her co-workers, particularly Lavinia Dock, well enough. She thought them "women of ideals, capable of fine, generous deeds." But she disapproved of their work and feared that their activities created "snobbery among the very people they were trying to help." Although Jane Addams was influenced by anarchist writings, Goldman regarded her even more critically. She thought Addams an elitist snob.[3]

* Because of the complexity of Lillian Wald's life and the fact that the only significant biography is dated 1938, I will focus on Wald rather than Jane Addams – about whom many people have written and are now writing.

Emma Goldman's work with Crystal Eastman on behalf of birth control, the legalization of prostitution, and free speech in wartime was also dissatisfying. They agreed on more issues: but when Eastman and her circle were on the same picket line or in the same park distributing birth-control literature with Goldman and her allies, only Goldman's group would be arrested. That was the nature of class in America.

Wald, Eastman, and Addams worked to keep America out of war through the American Union Against Militarism (AUAM). They dined at the White House with Wilson and his advisors. They hired professional lobbyists to influence Congress. Goldman worked through the Antimilitarist League and spoke throughout the United States on the capitalist nature of war and the cruelties of the class system. When she was arrested, the Civil Liberties Bureau of the AUAM defended her; but the members of the AUAM were not themselves arrested. Goldman's wartime activities resulted in her deportation. Wald and Addams received commendations from the government because, in addition to their antiwar work, they allowed their settlement houses to be used as conscription centers.[4]

As different as their political visions and choice of strategies were, Addams and Wald, Eastman and Goldman were dedicated to a future society that guaranteed economic security and the full development of individual potential for women and men on the basis of absolute equality. Reformists, socialist, anarchist, all four women made contributions toward progressive change that are today being dismantled. The playgrounds, parks, and school lunch facilities they built are falling apart all over America because of lack of funding and a callous disregard for the needs of our country's children. The free-speech and human-rights issues they heralded are today facing a reawakened backlash that features the needs of "national security" and a fundamentalist Christianity that seems more appropriate to the 17th century.

The historical denial of lesbianism

The vigor and strength of these four women, born daughters in a society that reared daughters to be dependent and servile, cannot be explained without an understanding of their support networks and the nature of their private lives. Their lifestyles varied as dramatically as did their public activities from the prescribed norm of "wife-mother in obedient service to husband-father" that their culture and their era valued above all.

Of the four women, only Emma Goldman relied predominantly on men for emotional sustenance and political support. Although she was close to many anarchist and radical women, there were few with whom she had intimate and lasting relations. The kind of communal and noncompetitive intimacy of the settlement houses or the younger feminist movement Crystal Eastman was associated with was never a feature of Goldman's life.

Yet throughout her life, Goldman wrote, she "longed for a friend of my own sex, a kindred spirit with whom I could share the innermost thoughts and feelings I could not express to men....Instead of friendship from women I had met with much antagonism, petty envy and jealousy because men liked me." There were exceptions, and Goldman listed them in her autobiography. But basically, she concluded, "there was no personal, intimate point of contact."[5]

Like Goldman, Crystal Eastman was also surrounded by men who shared her work, her vision, and her commitment to social change. Unlike Goldman, she had a feminist support group as well. Her allies consisted of her husband (particularly her second husband, Walter Fuller), her brother Max, and the women who were her friends, many of them from childhood and Vassar until her early death in 1928. Eastman's comrades were the "new women" of Greenwich Village. Radical feminists and socialists, they considered men splendid lovers and friends, but they believed that women needed the more egalitarian support of other women. For Crystal Eastman and her associates this was not only an emotional choice, it was a political necessity.

Jane Addams and Lillian Wald were involved almost exclusively with women who remained throughout their lives a nurturing source of love and support. Henry Street and Hull House were staffed by their closest friend, who, night and day, made possible their unrelenting schedules.

In the past, historians tended to ignore the crucial role played by the networks of love and support that have been the very sources of strength that enabled political women to function. Women's friendships were obscured and trivialized. Whether heterosexual or

Homophobia has . . . erased a variety of role models whose existence would tend to obliterate crude and dehumanizing stereotypes.

homosexual, the private lives of political women were declared beyond the acceptable boundaries of historical inquiry. As a result, much of our history and the facts that define our heritage have been removed from our consciousness. Homophobia, a bigotry that declares woman-loving women an evil before God or a mental disease or both, has served to erase the very aspects of our history that would have enabled us to deal healthfully with what has been for most lesbians an isolating and cruel experience. Homophobia has also erased a variety of role-models whose existence would tend to obliterate crude and dehumanizing stereotypes.

The very existence of networks of women such as the creative community that flourished in France between 1880 and 1940 and beyond was unknown to us. Only recently have we begun to recover the work and correspondence of such independent women as Margaret Anderson (founder of the *Little Review*), poet and essayist Natalie Barney, artist Romaine Brooks, poet Renée Vivien, and novelist Djuna Barnes. Except for the recent and severely flawed biography of Romaine Brooks and the more recent and also flawed biography of Natalie Barney, no serious study of that generation of self-styled Amazons, the expatriate lesbians of America, has yet been attempted.[6]

This denial has persisted over time. The figures that serve as the frontispiece for Dolores Klaich's book *Woman + Woman* symbolize the problem. We see a sculpture, dated *c.* 200 B.C., of two women in a tender and erotic embrace. It has been called by the curators of the British Museum, "Women Gossiping."

Similarly, companionate women who have lived together all their adult lives have been branded "lonely spinsters." When their letters might reveal their love, their papers have often been rendered unavailable.* Interpreting Freud through a Victorian prism and thinking it enlightened, male historians have concluded that the settlement-house reformers were asexual women who sublimated their passionate energies into their work. Since they were not recognizably "dykes" on the order of Radclyffe Hall or Gertrude Stein, and they always functioned too successfully to be called "sick," the historical evidence was juggled to deny the meaning of their lifestyles altogether.

So, for example, William O'Neill can refer to the 40-year relationship between Mary Rozet Smith and Jane Addams as that of "spouse-surrogates" and then conclude: "Finally, one suspects, the very qualities that led [Addams] to reject the family claim prevented her from experiencing the human

* See Dolores Klaich, *Woman+Woman: Attitudes Toward Lesbianism* (Morrow, 1974). The recently successful pressure to open the Mary E. Woolley Papers at Mt. Holyoke is a case in point. The famous college president lived with the chairwoman of the English Department, Jeannette Marks, for many years. They were lovers. When that fact was discovered their papers were closed.

At a Mt. Holyoke alumni meeting called to discuss this issue, the comments ranged from queries as to why the papers were not simply burned to wonder as to what the fuss was about. When it was suggested that tales of lesbianism on campus might decrease enrollment, an older woman who knew Woolley and Marks reassured her young younger sisters: "That's ridiculous! They worried about that when they agreed to end compulsory chapel." See also Carroll Smith-Rosenberg, "The Female World of Love and Ritual: Relations Between Women in 19th Century America," *Signs* (Autumn 1975), pp. 1-29.

reality that she celebrated in her writings and defied convention to encounter. She gave her time, money, and talents entirely to the interests of the poor. . . . In a sense she rejected the personal claims upon her, . . . and remained largely untouched by the passionate currents that swirled around her. The crowning irony of Jane Addams' life, therefore, was that she compromised her intellect for the sake of human experiences which her nature prevented her from having. Life, as she meant the term, forever eluded her."[7]

Allen Davis observes a different phenomenon. "It would be easy to misunderstand," Davis writes, the friendship and affection between Jane Addams and her early companion Ellen Gates Starr. Quoting Gordon Haight, Davis concludes: " 'The Victorian conception of love between those of the same sex cannot be fairly understood by an age steeped in Freud – where they say only beautiful friendship, the modern reader suspects perversion.' "[8]

It is important to understand the language here. We are being told that, since Jane Addams was a conventional lady with pearls, her intense "romantic attachments" to other women could not possibly be suspected of "perversion." As a result, the perfectly ordinary nature of women's differing sexual preferences has been denied expression. Without information and history, we have become ignorant of the range of our choices. Repression and conformity have been fostered and an entire generation of activist and passionate women branded by historians, on no evidence whatsoever, as "asexual."

Our prejudices are such that it has been considered less critical – kinder, even – to label a woman "asexual" rather than "lesbian." Allen Reznick, for example, assures us that life did not elude Lillian Wald. His 1973 dissertation is the only study that deals with Wald's personal life, and Reznick is eager to inform us – which he does in the title of his forward – that she was made "Not of Glazed China, But of Flesh and Blood." But Reznick is entirely unprepared to deal with the implications of women's relationships. In his view, the fact that Wald answered so many admiring letters and made no "documented effort at denial or discouragement" hints that she accepted female affection, even solicited it." Then, he concludes, she was undoubtedly too busy for social relations anyway.[9]

In their analyses, Davis and O'Neill distinguished between Victorian attitudes and our post-Freudian "enlightenment." Yet the denial of lesbianism is literally Victorian. The Queen herself was appalled by the inclusion of a paragraph on lesbianism in the 1885 Criminal Law that sought to penalize private homosexual acts by two years' imprisonment. She "expressed complete ignorance of female inversion or perversion and refused to sign the Bill, unless all reference to such practices was omitted."[10]

More sensitive than most male historians, Allen Davis notes that although the romantic words and the love letters "can be easily misinterpreted," what is important is "that many unmarried women drew warmth and strength from their supportive relationships with other women." But he concludes that "whether or not these women were actually lesbians is essentially irrelevant." [11]

If we lived in a society where individual choice and the diversity of our human rhythms were honored, the actuality of lesbianism would in fact be irrelevant. But we live in a society where children are taken away from lesbian mothers, where teachers are fired for bedroom activities, where in June 1976 the Supreme Court endorsed the imprisonment of consenting adults for homosexual relations, and where as I sit typing this paper – in June 1977 – the radio announces that Dade County, Florida, by a vote of 2:1, has supported Anita Bryant's hate campaign against homosexuals.

Such legal and social manifestations of bigotry and repression have been reenforced and are validated by the historical rejection and denial of diversity in general and of independent and alternative lifestyles among women in particular. It is the very conventionality of women like Jane Addams and Lillian Wald that is significant. Not until our society fully accepts as moral and ordinary the wide range of personal choice will differences be "essentially irrelevant."

As I think about Anita Bryant's campaign to "Save Our Children" from homosexuality, my thoughts turn to Lillian Wald, who insisted that every NYC public school should have a trained nurse in residence and who established free lunch programs for the city's school children. My thoughts then turn to Jane Addams, who, in an essay called, "Women, War and Babies," wrote:

As women we are the custodians of the life of the ages and we will not longer consent to its reckless destruction. We are particularly charged with the future of childhood, the care of the helpless and the unfortunate, and we will not

longer endure without protest that added burden of maimed and invalid men and poverty-stricken women and orphans which war places on us.
We have builded by the patient drudgery of the past the basic foundations of the home and of peaceful industry; we will not longer endure that hoary evil which in an hour destroys or tolerate that denial of the sovereignty of reason and justice by which war and all that makes for war today render impotent the idealism of the race. [12]

And in the wake of the first mid-20th-century American vote to discriminate against an entire group of people,* my thoughts turn again to Lillian Wald and Jane Addams, who campaigned for the creation of the United States Children's Bureau. That bureau set up programs throughout the United States to care for battered wives and battered children; it crusaded against child labor and for humane child care. [14] Yet Anita Bryant would demand that we save our children from Jane Addams if Anita Bryant knew that Jane Addams slept in the same house, in the same room, in the same bed with Mary Rozet Smith for 40 years. (And when they travelled, Addams even wired ahead to order a large double bed for their hotel room.)

*The campaign, featuring "KILL A QUEER FOR CHRIST" bumper stickers – and couched in fundamentalist rhetoric urging TV America to understand that "God hates homosexuality" and that "the Bible says homosexuals should be put to death and their blood shed over their heads" – was supported by millions of dollars of free press coverage with pictures in all the glossy magazines. It was supported by a *Newsweek* editorial insisting that "The homosexual subculture based on brief, barren assignations is, in part, a dark mirror of the sex-obsessed majority culture."[13] It was even supported by an ambivalent New York *Times* editorial (24 May 1977) that reluctantly agreed homosexuals might be teachers, despite "feelings of repugnance and hostility. . . especially among parents concerned about their children's development."

The assumption that gay people do not love and do not work persists. The fact that hard-working and deeply loving lesbians and homosexual men lead a great variety of the most ordinary lives is hidden because they themselves have been hidden.

Because difference arouses fear and condemnation, there are serious methodological problems involved in writing about women who, for political and economic reasons, kept their private lives as secret as possible. The advent of the homosexual "closet" at the end of the 19th century was not accidental. Oscar Wilde had, after all, been released from prison on 19 May 1897. In addition to the criminal stigma now attached to homosexuality, a sudden explosion of "scientific" publications on "sexual disorders" and "perversions" appeared at the turn of the century. Nancy Sahli, historian and archivist, reports that in the first series of 16 volumes of the *Index Catalogue of the Library of the Surgeon General's Office, U.S. Army,* covering the years 1740 to 1895, only one article ("A Case of Man-Impersonation") dealt specifically with lesbians. In the second series, published between 1896 and 1916, there were over 90 books and 566 articles listed that related to women's "perversions," "inversions," and "disorders." [15]

Secrecy is not a surprising response to this psychoanalytic assault. How then, male historians continually ask, do you know these women were lesbians? Even if we were to assume that Adams and Smith never in 40 years in the same bed touched each other, we can still argue that they were lesbians because they chose each other. Women who love women, who choose women to nurture and support and to create a living environment in which to work creatively and independently, are lesbians.

It may seem elementary to state here that lesbians cannot be defined simply as women who practice certain physical rites together. Unfortunately, the heterosexist image – and sometimes even the feminist image – of the lesbian is defined by sexual behavior alone, and sexual in the most limited sense. It therefore seems important to reiterate that physical love between women is one expression of a whole range of emotions and responses to each other that involves all the mysteries of our human nature. Woman-related women feel attraction, yearning, and excitement with women. Nobody and no theory has yet explained why for some women, despite all cultural conditioning and societal penalties, both intellectual and emotional excitement are aroused in response to women.

Lillian Wald

Besides, there *is* evidence of these women's lesbianism. Although Lillian Wald's two volumes of memoirs are about as personal as her entry in *Who's Who Among American Women,* her letters underscore the absurdity of a taxi conversation that Mabel Hyde Kittredge reported to Wald after a meeting at Henry Street:

1st man: *Those women are really lonely.*
Second man: *Why under the sun are they lonely?*
1st man: *Any woman is lonely without a man.*

Unlike Jane Addams, Lillian Wald seems not to have had one particular "great friend," and the chronology of the women in her life, with their comings and goings, is impossible to follow. There are gaps and surprises throughout over 150 boxes of correspondence. But all of Lillian Wald's companions appear to have been friends for life.

Wald's basic support group consisted of the long-term residents of Henry Street, Ysabella Waters, Anne Goodrich, Florence Kelley, Helene MacDowell, and Lavinia L. Dock. They worked together on all projects, lived and vacationed together for over 50 years, and, often in company with the women of Hull House, travelled together to Europe, Japan, Mexico, and the West Indies.

But the letters are insufficient to tell us the specifics of her life. There are turmoils that we will probably never know anything about – upheavals that result, for example, in a 10-year hiatus in Wald's correspondence with Lavinia Dock. This hiatus, combined with the fact that in November 1915, after 20 years, "Docky" moved out of the Henry Street Settlement and, in an icy and formal note of March 1916, even resigned from the Henry Street Corporation, remains unexplained. There is also the puzzling fact that Dock, the ardent suffragist, feminist and socialist, a pioneer of American nursing education and organization, appears to be R. L. Duffus' major source of information – beyond Wald herself – for his 1938 biography, *Lillian Wald: Neighbor and Crusader.* The first letter to appear in the collection after Dock's 1916 resignation is dated 1925 and implies that the two women have not had a long-term falling out at all:

> *why-dear-I was imagining you radiating around the town telling about Mexico and here you are in the hospital just like any commonplace person – oh dear oh dear! . . . Dearest I would scrape up some money if you need – you have often done the same for me . . . . and I am not telling anyone that you are ill and in the hospital for I know how you would dislike being thought just a mere mortal . . . .*[16]

It is clear from another letter that Dock went to New York to be with Wald during her first operation. She wrote Wald's nurse that she was so relieved the tumor turned out to be benign that "for the first time my knees wobbled as I went down the steps to go to the train . . . ." The next week Dock wrote to Wald: "Dearest – I'm not sure whether to give you letters yet so I havent written before and just send this line to tell you that you do your illnesses and recoveries in the same dazzling form and with the same vivacity and originality as all your other deeds! With Love/Ever yours/Docky"

Why then did Dock leave? Was there a personal reason? A new lover? An old anger? Or was it connected with the political differences that emerged between them in 1915 when Wald became more absorbed by antimilitarist activities and Dock, also a pacifist, joined the radical suffragist movement of Alice Paul's Congressional Union? All the evidence indicates that the only significant differences between these women at this time were political. Their lives were dedicated to work each regarded as just and right. When they disagreed so intensively that they could no longer support and nurture each other's activities, they temporarily parted.

In 1914 Dock joined the Advisory Council of the Congressional Union. But she was the only member of the Henry Street community to do so. She wrote to Alice Paul that "you know I love everything you do," but "the people I live with here all have so many undertakings that they are involved up to the neck." Specifically, Lillian Wald "cannot ally herself exclusively to any suffrage group because she has close friends in all – for instance your invitation . . . was balanced by women in the National Association asking her not to [join] – this is confidential. She decided to remain independent of all and my own judgment for her is that it is best for her to do so – she has first and foremost her own immense responsibilities. . . ."

During the war, while Wald was meeting with President Wilson and being as conciliatory as possible on behalf of the peace movement, Dock and the militant suffragists were infuriating official Washington, getting themselves arrested, and generally aggravating the very people Wald was attempting to persuade – and for a different purpose.

Dock considered Paul's Congressional Union "fresh-young-glorious." She wrote to Paul in June 1915: "Pay no attention to criticism. Go right ahead with your splendid daring and resourcefulness of youth." Dock reacted furiously to criticism that the Congressional Union's confrontational tactics not only harmed the suffrage movement but threatened the peace movement. And Lillian Wald was one of the leading critics of such tactics. On this issue they disagreed utterly. Dock was adamant: "And what is this terrible burden of responsibility and anxiety now resting on the American Men's President? Is it arising from anything women have done or are going to do? Not at all. . . . I can't see it – surely there could be no more appropriate moment for women to press forward with their demand for a voice – women – who are at this moment going on errands of peace, – and who are being called a national menace for doing so – followed wherever he goes, by the demand which, so long as it remains unanswered shows a painful insincerity in those rounded and sonorous paragraphs on American ideals and American freedom that he utters so eloquently. . . ."[17]

Five months after this exchange, Lavina Dock moved permanently out of her Henry Street home of 20 years. I have not yet found one correspondence between her and Wald that deals with the event. And all Wald says about Dock in *Windows on Henry Street* is that "Everyone admired her, none feared her, though she was sometimes very fierce in her denunciations. Reputed a man-hater, we knew her as a lover of mankind."

Wald's other support network

There were two other categories of women close to Wald and the settlement. The first consisted of affluent women such as Irene and Alice Lewisohn and Rita Morgenthau. Younger than Wald, they admired her and regarded her as a maternal figure. She in turn nurtured their spirits, supported their ambitions, and provided them with sustaining and secure friendship. They, together with Wald's "friend of friends" Jacob Schiff, contributed tirelessly and abundantly to Henry Street. The Lewisohns founded the Neighborhood Play House and supported the famous music and dance education projects that continue to this day. They were also coworkers in the Woman's Peace Party and the American Union Against Militarism. On occasion they travelled with Wald. And they wrote numerous letters of affection and devotion to their dear "Lady Light." Alice Lewisohn frequently signed her letters "Your Baby Alice." One letter from Irene, conveying love and gratitude after a trip the Lewisohn sisters took with Ysabella Waters and Wald, is replicated in the collection by scores of others:

Why attempt to tell a clairvoyant all that is in one's mind? You know even better than I what those months of companionship with you and Sister Waters have meant. For way and beyond even the joys of our wanderings I have some memories that are holier by far than temples or graves or blossoms. A fireside romance and a moonlight night are among the treasures carefully guarded. . . . As an offering for such inspirations, I am making a special vow to be and to do. . . . /Much of my heart to you/

Wald's closest friend among the younger nonresidents appears to have been Rita Wallach Morgenthau, who generally signed her letters with love from "Your Daughter," "Your Foolish Daughter," or "Your Spoiled Child." However much Wald may have spoiled her "adoptive daughters," the very fact of her nurturing presence helped establish the nature of their life's work; and their work focused on social change and the education, dance, and theatre programs they created.

In 1906 Rita wrote to Wald that "everything that has stood for beauty has been inspired by you, and the thankfulness I feel for my share of you, and the dear settlement can never be whispered . . . ." During Wald's final, protracted illness in the 1930's, Rita wrote following Wald's operation:

You always have been and always will be my "Leading Lady" and I have a feeling of deep gratitude and humility that there will spark in me that fire kindled by your flame . . .[18]

All of Wald's friends and correspondents wrote of how she inspired them, fired their imaginations, and directed their lives to greater heights of consciousness and activity. Lavinia Dock referred to this quality in a letter to Duffus for his biography of Wald: "She believed absolutely in human nature and as a result the best of it was shown to her. People just naturally turned their best natures to her scrutiny and developed what she perceived in them, when it had been dormant and unseen in them before. I remember often being greatly impressed by this inner vision that she had. . . ."[19]

The last group of women involved with Wald and the settlement differed basically from the other two. Although they also served as residents or volunteered their time to Henry Street, they were "society women" perhaps more interested in Wald than in social change. Such long-term residents as Dock, Waters, and MacDowell, and Wald's younger friends, Morgenthau and the Lewisohns, supported Wald emotionally and politically and shared collectively in all her interests. The society women, however, attempted to possess or monopolize Wald, lamented that her activities kept her from them, and were finally rebuffed in what must have been thoroughly specific terms. Generally they fell into that trap that Margaret Anderson defined so well: "In real love you want the other person's good. In romantic love you want the other person."[20]

Lillian Wald had structured her life to avoid becoming anybody's possession. While she did get involved in emotional enthusiasms, as soon as the woman involved sought to redirect her priorities Wald's enthusiasm evaporated.

The clearest representatives of the society group were Mabel Hyde Kittredge and Helen Arthur. Both women were rich "uptowners" who spent many years "downtown." Both were highly educated, hardworking, and demanding. Both devoted their time to good works, in large part because their friendship with Wald encouraged them to think politically, and not because social change was their life's commitment. But they were loyal. Kittredge, for example, evidently left Henry Street because Wald encouraged her to do so. Yet she continued to be involved in settlement activities, helped organize the free lunch program in public schools in 1908, and founded the Association of Practical Housekeeping Centers that operated as a subsidiary organization for many years.

To understand Lillian Wald fully, it is necessary to deal with her relationship with Mabel Hyde Kittredge. Kittredge's demands seem on occasion outrageous, and her biases are transparent. Yet it is clear that for a time Wald was not only smitten by this lady, but relied upon her for comfort and trusted her deeply.

A Park Avenue socialite who frequently played bridge whist all night after she had played in a golf tournament all day, Kittredge was the daughter of Reverend Abbott E. Kittredge of the prominent Madison Avenue Church. After she had lived at Henry Street for several years, she wrote to Wald on 28 April 1904 that she understood Wald's objections to what appears to have been a moment of flagrant ethnic bigotry: "I believe that I will never again say 'my people and *your* people.' It may be that even though I have no prejudice I have used words and expressions that have done something to keep the lines drawn between the two peoples. . . ."

Whatever her views, it appears that when Wald was troubled she turned for a time to Kittredge. In a long letter of tender assurance and sensible advice to Wald concerning a bereaved friend, Kittredge wrote:

. . . I seemed to hold you in my arms and whisper all this. . . . If you want me to stay all night tomorrow night just say so when you see me. . . . Please dont feel that I keep before me the signs of sorrow that you trusted me enough to let me see – of the things of Thursday evening that are consciously with me are first the fact that in a slight degree I can share with you the pain that you suffer. Then I can hear you say 'I love you' – and again and again I can see in your eyes the strength, and the power and the truth that I love – but the confidence in yourself not there. All this I have before me – never a thought of weakness because you dared to be human. Why dear I knew that you were human before Thursday night – I think though that our love never seemed quite so real a thing before then. Good night.

But after 1904 most of Kittredge's letters became competitive – Kittredge *vs.* humanity in their claims on Wald's attentions. Wald evidently reserved one night in the week for Kittredge and then occasionally cancelled their date, infuriating her friend:

Just because you have reformed on Tuesday night – I havent got to give you entirely to humanity. I am human too and tonight I'd keep you up until – well later than Miss McDowell would approve of – if I had you. . . .

On a similar evening Kittredge wrote that she had just done two very sensible things, not telephoned to say good night and torn up a whiny letter:

But what business has a great grown woman like myself to sit up in her nightclothes and write nothings. . . . I am getting altogether too close to you Lady Wald – or is it . . . all those doors that you have pushed open for me? Half open-dear-just half open. And then I come up here and grow hungry for more knowledge. . . . And I feel that my strength ends and love you so. . . . I can feel your arms around me as you say I really must go.

When Wald cancelled a visit to Kittredge at Monmouth Beach, she wrote: "And so the verdict has gone forth – I cant have you. . . . But even you must want the ocean at times instead of Henry Street. . . ."

Wald did want the ocean at times. More than that, she sought the relaxation and comfort of Kittredge's friendship. During a business trip that was evidently particularly hectic, Wald wrote to Kittredge from Chattanooga that she looked forward to long, quiet, cosy evenings on the back porch. Kittredge replied that Wald's letter "was a real life-giving thing." But she no longer believed that Wald would actually make such free time possible and wrote: "When Lady Lillian is that cosy time to be? Miss McDowell says not after midnight and your humanity world would not let me have you before. 'Long evenings on the back porch' - it sounds fine – and improbable. . . ."

Eventually Kittredge's jealousy extended from humanity in general to the other residents of Henry Street in particular:

If you think that I wasnt damned mad today it is simply that I have inherited so much self-control and sweetness from my minister parent that the fact was hidden. . . .

There are times when to know that Miss Clark is standing behind one curtain, Miss MacDowell behind another and to feel an endless lot of people forever pressing the door or presenting unsigned papers makes me lack that perfect sympathy with "work for others" as exemplified by a settlement. No wonder I am called "one of your crushes" . . . . It is kiss and run or run without kissing – there really isnt time for anything else. . . .

After what appears to have been for Kittredge a particularly difficult

photo: Visiting Nurse Service, New York

Lillian Wald (*circa* 1903).

Christmas season, she gave up entirely the competition for Wald's affections:

These may be "Merry" days but they starve one to death as far as any satisfaction in calm, every day loving and talking goes. . . . I would very much like to meet you on a desert island or a farm where the people cease from coming and the weary are at rest – will the day ever come? Or is that white ring, those long, lazy drives, the quiet and the yellow trees only a lost dream? And yet you love me – the plant on my table tells me so. The new coffee tray tells me so. . . and a look that I see in your eyes makes me sure. . . .

Refusing to participate, evidently for the first time, in Henry Street's Christmas festivities, Kittredge wrote that she was

. . . not loveless nor lonely. I am free and strong and alive and awfully happy – But someway as I think back over this year, I believe that I needed you – it may be as much as the others – . . . . I know that it would be a loss out of my life if my thoughts of you, my love for you and my confidence in you were taken away – I don't believe they ever could be less than they are tonight. . . . [21]

Judging from the letters, whatever gap the loss of Mabel Hyde Kittredge's friendship may have opened Wald seems to have filled by that summer. Wald vacationed through August and September 1906 with another society woman, Helen Arthur, an attorney and director of the research department of the Woman's Municipal League. Helen Arthur seems to have been more spontaneous and less complaining than Kittredge; and she had a sense of humor: ". . . I have a report to write yet tonight and read to a bunch of elegantly attired ladies who do not care a darn so long as they get home for luncheon. What a farce this old world is – remember Oliver Herford's dedication 'to the world at large,' ending up with 'why is the world at large?' "

Arthur was also more dependent on Wald, and in this relationship Wald's maternal aspects were more evident. She coaxed Arthur out of repeated depressions, encouraged her law practice, managed her finances, and kept her bankbook so that she would not overspend. This last made Arthur pout, especially during one Christmas season when she wrote to Wald that she tried to buy "exactly 28 presents for $10 worth of currency without visiting the 5 and 10 cent store which is, I regret to say, not on the Consumer's League list! If you were at 265 Henry Street – I should hold you up for my bankbook – What's vacation money compared to Christmas toys – Surely it is more blessed to give than to receive interest on deposits! Couldnt you be an old dear and let me rob it for a month? Please, mommy."

When Wald travelled, Arthur wrote long newsy letters about her law cases and activities; but they all concluded or began with a note of despair that her good mother had left her sad or naughty "son" all alone: "Such a strange feeling – no one to telephone me no 'Hello-de-e-ar' to listen for – Rainy horrid day outside and a lonesome atmosphere within. . . ." At another time she wrote: "I am as near blue tonight as green can ever get and if I just had my nicest mommy to snuggle up to and talk it out straight for her son, I'd feel less like a disbarred judge. . . . Couldnt you write me a note and tell me – something?"

Eventually, Wald's busy schedule resulted in disappointments, cancelled dates, loneliness for Arthur, and what must have been for Wald familiar letters of discontent:

Dearest, nothing could have relieved the gloom of this day except the presence of the one person her secretary notified me not to expect. . . . Now that I am being severely left alone – I have much time to spend in my own room – the walls of which formerly saw . . . me only from 2 until 7 a.m. . . . I've put you – the dear old you in your silver frame on my desk and close to me when I write and I shoved my decanter and cigarette case to the other side – If I had you, the real you instead of one-ten-thousandth part of you I might shove the unworthy things way off – Summertime has spoiled the judge who longs to get back to your comfortable lap and the delights of kicking her pajammaed legs in peace and comfort instead of being solicitously hustled from your room at 10 o'clock. . . .

In another letter, Arthur, like so many others, expressed her desire to live up to Wald's expectations of her: "If only I could pull out of my easy ways – the pleasant vices which hinder me so. . . ." But her physical longing for Wald was equally powerful. The two combined to explain Wald's magnetism: "If only August and September, 1906 were all the year round for me, but their memories stay by and perhaps some day you'll be proud of your small judge. . . . I think so often of the hundreds who remember you with affection and of the tens who openly adore you and I appreciate a little what it all means and I'm grateful to think that your arms have been close around me and that you did once upon a time, kiss me goodnight and even good morning, and I am your lonesome little/Judge."

Arthur, more than many others, was genuinely mindful of Wald's time and her emotional needs. On 30 January 1907, she wrote that "Little by little there is being brought in upon me, the presumption of my love for you – the selfishness of its demands, the triviality of its complaints – and more slowly still, is coming the realization of what it ought to bring to you and what I mean it shall. . . ."[22]

Whatever special friend came or went in Lillian Wald's life, the women of Henry Street, the residents who called themselves her "steadies," were the mainstay of her support. The women in Wald's communal family served each other as well as society. There was nothing self-sacrificing about that community: It was a positive choice. For Wald it was the essential key to her life – and the only aspect of her personal life about which she wrote clearly. On the 40th anniversary of the settlement, Wald wrote: "I came with very little program of what could or should be done. I was perhaps conscious only of a passionate desire to have people, who had been separated and who for various causes were not likely to come together, know each other that they might sympathize and understand the problems and difficulties of each other. I made no sacrifices. My friend Mary Brewster [the first coworker at Henry Street] and I were engrossed in the edifice which was taking form and in which my friends and I might dwell together."[23]

Wald and her friends lived together for over 50 years. At the end, during long years of pain and poor health, she was surrounded by love and support. After her first operation, Mabel Hyde Kittredge wrote to Wald that "at least you must feel that this is a world full of friends and love and sympathy. I hope all the bread you ever cast upon any waters has come back fresh and lovely and so much as to be a surprise. . . ." On the morning of her death, Lillian Wald turned to her nurse and said, "I'm a very happy woman. . . because I've had so many people to love, and so many to love me."[24]

The letters in the Wald collections document only a fragment of her life, and they raise as many questions as they answer. Because we can never know the intimate details of people's lives if they are censored, withheld, or destroyed, we are confined to the details we have. But the details we have make it abundantly clear that Lillian Wald lived in a homosocial world that was also erotic. Her primary emotional needs and desires were fulfilled by women. She was woman-supported, woman-allied. Once that has been established, it becomes entirely unnecessary to pursue evidence of a specific variety of genital contact. Beyond a certain point, we get into fairly small-minded questions of technique. Since society's presumption of heterosexuality stops short of any inquiry as to what the husband and wife do atop their conjugal bed, it is only to indulge our prejudices that we demand "evidence" of lesbianism from conventional or famous women. Insistence on genital evidence of proof for a lesbian identity derives from a male model that has very little to do with the love, support, and sensuality that exist between women.

Emma Goldman wrote vividly about the difficulties faced by people who attempt to express themselves in harmony with their own nature. In a 1906 essay, "The Child and Its Enemies," she wrote that society employs all its forces to mould out of all our human differences a thing of dehumanized, patterned regularity: "Every institution. . . , the family, the state, our moral codes, sees in every strong, beautiful uncompromising personality a deadly enemy." Every effort is made, from earliest infancy, "to cramp human emotion and originality of thought" in order to create "a patient work slave, professional automaton, taxpaying citizen, or righteous moralist." To that end, all the child's questions "are met with narrow, conventional, ridiculous replies mostly based on falsehoods." Thus uniformity and order, rather than "eternal change, thousandfold variation, continual innovation," have become the hallmarks of our culture.

The full implications of our brutally deforming institutions were clear to Goldman: "Since every effort in our educational life seems to be directed toward making of the child a being foreign to itself, it must of necessity produce individuals foreign to one another. . . ."25

Urged to deny the secrets within our natures and to reject the differences of others, we are taught to be fearful of ourselves and contemptuous of others. Separated from ourselves and isolated from each other, we are encouraged to huddle together for comfort under the socially acceptable banners of racism, sexism, classism, and homophobia. While people are called "human resources" in advanced industrial societies, we are discouraged from seeing the ways in which we are all connected. We are thus rendered powerless and immobilized by our prejudices. This is not an accident.

Emma Goldman

Ardent feminists and fiercely independent, Emma Goldman and Crystal Eastman depended on men for the comradeship and pleasure Lillian Wald and Jane Addams sought from women. Far more specific about their sexual orientation, Eastman and Goldman wrote about their private lives and their commitment to free love. They made it clear that they refused to be trapped by conventional or legal arrangements such as marriage.

Both were, in the larger sense, maternal women. Crystal Eastman considered the status of the unmarried mother and decided to get married largely for the sake of the two children she would have. Emma Goldman nurtured all her friends and associates. According to Kate Richards O'Hare, Emma Goldman while in prison was, above all, "the tender cosmic mother."

Contrary to popular notions of "free love" as promiscuous and amoral, Goldman's long-term relations with the men she loved – Sasha Berkman, Ed Brady, Ben Reitman, Max Baginsky, and Hippolyte Havel – were nurturing and tender on her part and devoted and supportive on theirs. They worked for her and cared for her. Ed Brady enabled her to go to Europe to study. Ben Reitman, her manager, served as her "advance man"; he raised money for *Mother Earth* and arranged her speaking tours. These men did not possess her, control her, dominate her, or expect from her more than she would give freely because she loved them as a free woman.

Free love, for Emma Goldman and Crystal Eastman, meant simply love given freely to the lover of one's choice. Both rejected the notion that love was a limited commodity. They believed that it was an undefinable sentiment that expanded in proportion to the number of people who evoked it. Possession and jealousy were anathema to them. They rejected the notion that women were love objects to be married into the service and control of men.

Despite the clarity of their writings, their views were frequently misunderstood. The refusal of Eastman and Goldman to separate the personal from the political, their contempt for sham and hypocrisy, and their unfaltering openness about the most intimate subjects horrified their contemporaries. Among the social reformers with whom Crystal Eastman worked, she acquired a reputation as a reckless revolutionary. Her attitudes on free love and her frank affirmation of women's right to physical sexuality appeared hedonistic and horrible. A frequent contributor to feminist journals, her attitudes and behavior – notably her "affairs," divorce, and remarriage – were perceived as scandalous. After years of leadership in the peace movement, as founder and president of the Woman's Peace Party of New York and as executive director of the American Union Against Militarism, she was blocked from attending the second meeting at the Hague in 1919 by a committee chaired by Jane Addams, specifically because of Eastman's radical socialism and her espousal of free love.26

The reaction of the older social-reform women such as Jane Addams to Crystal Eastman's lifestyle is not explained by the simple fact that the sword of bigotry is many-edged. The failure of Jane Addams and most social-reform women to analyze traditional assumptions about marriage and sexuality is another byproduct of the societal pressure that kept alternative lifestyles of any kind in the closet for so many years. The settlement-house women were supplicants to the rich on behalf of the poor. Steadfast about their priorities, they frequently made political decisions which were not in harmony with their lives and which locked them into a conservative public position regarding such issues as sexuality.

Crystal Eastman's vision

Emma Goldman was adamant in her opposition to marriage, which she considered an economic arrangement. Since a wife's body is "capital to be exploited and manipulated, she came to look on success as the size of her husband's income." For Goldman marriage was the very antithesis of love. Why, she asked, should two people who love each other get married? Marriage is an arbitrary, mercenary, legal tie; while it does not bind, it fetters. Only love is free. Love for Emma was "the strongest and deepest element in all life; . . . love, the freest, the most powerful moulder of human destiny; how can such an all-compelling force be synonymous with that poor State-and-Church begotten weed, marriage?"[27]

Although Crystal Eastman shared Goldman's views on marriage, she married twice. But she was not limited or stifled in these marriages and arranged them to suit both her work and her emotional needs. According to one of her closest friends, Jeannette Lowe, Crystal Eastman was free – "You would not believe how free she was."[28] Vigorous and bold, Crystal Eastman discarded her first marriage with alacrity and then sought to revolutionize the institution. In her own life she extended the contours of marriage beyond recognition. During the first years of her second marriage, she and her husband, her brother Max, and several of their friends lived communally.

After the war she, her two children, and her husband, Walter Fuller, lived in England "under two roofs" as ordinary lovers. "He keeps a change of clothes and all the essentials for night and morning comfort at my house, as might a favorite and frequent guest." They phoned each other daily and often met for the theatre or dinner or at a friend's house. After the evening's entertainment they decided, "like married lovers," whether to part on the street or go home together. "Marriage under two roofs makes room for moods." As for the children, "without a scowling father around for breakfast, the entire day began cheerfully. . . ."

Crystal Eastman was, above all, a feminist. She considered the true feminist the most radical member of society. The true feminist, Eastman wrote, begins with the knowledge "that the vast majority of women as well as men are without property, and are of necessity bread and butter slaves under a system which allows the very sources of life to be privately owned by a few, and she counts herself a loyal soldier in the working-class army that is marching to overthrow that system." But she had no illusions about where men in that army placed women. "If we should graduate into communism tomorrow. . . man's attitude to his wife would not be changed." For Eastman, the creation of a communistic society based on sex equality was the task of the organized feminist movement.[29]

Unlike Emma Goldman, who lived almost exclusively among men, Crystal Eastman always had a feminist support group of considerable importance to her life. She was supported by women with whom she had deep and lasting relations: many of the ardent suffragists of the Congressional Union, her friends from Vassar who worked with her in the Woman's Peace Party of New York and who were part of her communal family in Greenwich Village. On several occasions she lived with one or more of these friends, and her experiences enabled her to write in "Now We Can Begin":

Two business women can "make a home" together without either one being over-burdened or over-bored. It is because they both know how and both feel responsible. But it is a rare man who can marry one of them and continue the home-making partnership. Yet if there are no children, there is nothing essentially different in the combination. Two self-supporting adults decide to make a home together: if both are women it is a pleasant partnership, more fun than work; if one is a man, it is almost never a partnership – the woman simply adds running the home to her regular outside job. Unless she is very strong, it is too much for her, she gets tired and bitter over it, and finally perhaps gives up her outside work and condemns herself to the tiresome half-job of housekeeping for two.

Crystal Eastman evidently solved that problem for herself by spending her summers in the south of France with Jeannette Lowe and their children, leaving her husband under his separate roof and in his separate country.

Throughout the postwar years Eastman had planned to write a book about women. But in 1928, one year after returning to New York to look for new work, she died of a kidney ailment. She was 47 years old, and her death came as a shock to her friends. Claude McKay wrote: "Crystal Eastman was a great-hearted woman whose life was big with primitive and exceptional gestures. She never wrote that Book of Woman which was imprinted on her mind. She was poor, and fettered with a family. She had a grand idea for a group of us to go off to write in some quiet corner of the world, where living was cheap and easy. But it couldn't be realized. And so life was cheated of one contribution about women that no other woman could write."[30]

Emma Goldman and women

Emma Goldman's lack of a feminist support group did not affect her adversely until the postwar years. Before and during the war she was surrounded by her anarchist comrades and Ben Reitman. But even then her friends found Reitman distasteful and tended to admonish Goldman for her choice of lovers. Sasha Berkman in particular hated Reitman because he was not dedicated to the revolution, anarchism, or even social change. Margaret Anderson thought that the "fantastic" Dr. Reitman was not "so bad if you could hastily drop all your ideas as to how human beings should look and act. . . ." But Emma loved him and wrote that he "gave without measure or restraint. His best years, his tremendous zest for work, he had devoted to me. It is not unusual for a woman to do as much for the man she loves. Thousands of my sex had sacrificed their own talents and ambitions for the sake of the man. But few men had done so for women. Ben was one of the few; he had dedicated himself completely to my interests."

During her last years in America, Goldman spent a good deal of time with Margaret Anderson and the women associated with *The Little Review.* In *My Thirty Years War,* Anderson described the days Emma Goldman spent in Chicago, with her and Harriet Dean, and in California, where she lived with Jane Heap. She presents a unique portrait of a gentle Emma Goldman, who was "gay, communicative, tender" and who sang Russian folk songs "in a low and husky voice" on the beach at night.

Goldman's reaction to *The Little Review* was intense: "I felt like a desert wanderer who unexpectedly discovers a stream of fresh water. At last a magazine to sound a note of rebellion in creative endeavor!" Although she was disappointed in the magazine's lack of clarity on social issues, she delighted in the fact that it was "free from the mawkish sentimentality of most American publications. Its main appeal to me lay in its strong and fearless critique of conventional standards, something I had been looking for in the United States for 25 years."

And Goldman's feelings about her generous new friends, "who were rarely away from my side for very long," were cordial:

Harriet Dean was as much a novel type to me as Margaret, yet the two were entirely unlike. Harriet was athletic, masculine-looking, . . . Margaret, on the contrary, was feminine in the extreme. Constantly bubbling over with enthusiasm. . . . Underneath her apparent lightness was depth and strength of character to pursue whatever aim in life she might choose. . . . I regretted their lack of social consciousness, but as rebels for their own liberation Margaret Anderson and Harriet Dean strengthened my faith in the possibilities of my adopted country.[31]

In this case it was Emma who had been adopted. She, for herself, had emotional support only from Reitman, with whom she was to break over his vacillation concerning the war, and Berkman, who was involved with others. That lack was keenly felt during the latter years of her life in exile.

But before the war Goldman idealized heterosexual relations. In many of her writings she scorned the bourgeois American feminists whose "narrow puritanical vision banished man as a disturber and doubtful character out of their emotional life. . . ." In a March 1906 essay, "The Tragedy of Woman's Emancipation," she argued that the "greatest shortcoming" of the feminist movement was "its narrow respectabilities which produce an emptiness in woman's soul that will not let her drink from the fountain of life." In September 1915 she published a similar editorial in *Mother Earth* by one "R.A.P.," who argued that "American feminists are the exponents of a new slavery," which denied sexual activity, encouraged inhibition, and crusaded against the "sexual victimization of virtuous females by some low, vulgar male." R.A.P. judged the bourgeois feminist movement classist and hypocritical and of "no interest except as an amusing and typical instance of feminine intellectual homosexuality."[32]

This is not to imply that Emma Goldman was homophobic in any intellectual or traditional sense. On the contrary, she was the only woman in America who defended homosexuality in general and the conviction of Oscar Wilde in particular. Although she was absolute about a person's right to sexual choice, she felt a profound ambivalence about lesbianism as a lifestyle. She believed that "the body, in all its splendid sexuality, had to be reclaimed from the repressive hands of the prudes and the philistines." When she was criticized by her comrades for dealing with such "unnatural themes as homosexuality," thereby increasing the difficulties of the already misunderstood anarchist movement, she persisted. "I minded the censors of my own ranks as little as I did those in the enemy's camp." Censorship from her comrades had, she wrote, "the same effect on me as police persecution; it made me... more determined to plead for every victim, be it of social wrong or of moral prejudice."33

There is even some evidence that Goldman may have experimented with a woman herself. The 1912 letters of an anarchist worker, Almeda Sperry, to Goldman are very one-sided. They consist in part of affirmations of passionate love by Sperry and apparent rebuffs by Goldman. These do not deter Sperry, who evidently luxuriated for a time in a state of unrequited yearning: "God how I dream of you! You say that you would like to have me near you always if you were a man, or if you felt as I do. I would not if I could. . . ." In response to Goldman's queries about Sperry's feelings toward men, she replies: "If you mean have I ever loved a man I will frankly say that I never *saw* a man. No, I have never deeply loved any man." Sperry was, however, married, and several letters refer to her affection for her husband.

Then, in the summer of 1912, the letters take a different turn. Sperry thanks Goldman for addressing her with terms of endearment, and she evades Goldman's suggestion that they spend a week in the country together by noting that "I am with you in spirit, at any rate." But she tells Goldman to know, just before she sleeps, that "I kiss your body with biting kisses – I inhale the sweet pungent odor of you and you plead with me for relief." A month later Sperry refers to the week they spent together after all in the country:

Dearest. I have been flitting about from one thing to another... to quell my terrible longing for you . . . I am . . . seized with a fire that races over my body in recurrent waves. My last thoughts at night are of you . . . and that hellish alarm clock is losing some of its terrors for me for my first waking thoughts are of you.

Dear, that day you were so kind to me and afterwards took me in your arms, your beautiful throat, that I kissed with a reverent tenderness. . . .

Do you know, sweet cherry-blossom, that my week with you has filled me with such an energy, such an eagerness to become worthy of your friendship, that I feel that I must either use my intensity towards living up to my best self or ending it all quickly in one last, grand debauch. . . .

How I wish I [were] with you on the farm! You are so sweet in the mornings – your eyes are like violets and you seem to forget, for a time, the sorrows of the world. And your bosom – ah, your sweet bosom, unconfined. 34

There is nothing simple about Goldman's attitude toward lesbianism. She never refers to Almeda Sperry, and it is impossible to know the significance of this correspondence in her life. Her absolute commitment to personal liberty and her total respect for individual choice prompted Magnus Hirschfeld, a leading homosexual rights advocate in Germany and the founder of the Scientific Humanitarian Committee, organized in 1897, to write that Goldman was the "only human being of importance in America to carry the issue of homosexual love to the broadest layers of the public." 35

But in a long article in the 1923 Yearbook of Hirschfeld's committee, Goldman criticizes an earlier article on Louise Michel in puzzling terms. Goldman reaffirms her political commitment to free sexual choice and affirms her disinterest in "protecting" Louise Michel from the charge of lesbianism. "Louise Michel's service to humanity and her great work of social liberation are such that they can be neither enlarged nor reduced, whatever her sexual habits were." Then follows a long tirade against minorities who claim for themselves all the earth's significant people, and a longer analysis of why it would be "nonsensical" to assume that Louise Michel was a lesbian. In an ultimately vague and paradoxical paragraph, Goldman concludes: "In short, Louise Michel was a complete woman, free of all the prejudices and traditions which for centuries held women in chains and degraded them to household slaves and objects of sexual lust. The new woman celebrated her resurrection in the figure of Louise, the woman capable of heroic deeds but one who remains a woman in her passion and in her love." 36

It appears that, in Goldman's mind, to be a lesbian was an absolute right, and nothing nasty about it. But it was also to be rendered somehow less a woman.

Emma Goldman in exile

In the long years of Emma Goldman's exile, years made lonelier by her political isolation, she wrote a series of letters that explored the difficulties and the pain of being a free and independent woman without a support group that provided emotional nurturance as well as a shared vision of the work to be done. After two years of disappointment in Soviet Russia, Goldman travelled back and forth between England, France, and Germany, seeking to rebuild her shattered life and attempting to convince her friends on the left that her critical analysis of the Soviet experiment was correct. In these letters she revealed the toll on her spirit taken by her personal loneliness and her political isolation. Also revealed is the brutal double standard to which even advanced women in progressive anarchist circles are subjected if their friendships are limited to men. On 28 May 1925 she wrote to Berkman:

I agree with you that both men and women need some person who really cares. The woman needs it more and finds it impossible to meet anyone when she has reached a certain age. That is her tragedy. . . . I think in the case of one who gave out so much in her life, it is doubly tragic not to have anyone, to really be quite alone. . . . I am consumed by longing for love and affection for some human being of my own. . . .

It is significant that the above passage ends a letter otherwise devoted to Goldman's visit with Edward Carpenter, one of the first British crusaders for homosexual rights, and his younger lover, Goe, who had been his companion for 35 years. Carpenter at the time was 82, and, Goldman noted, Goe had his own younger lover, the cook. But, she observed, Goe "takes good care of Ed. . . and Ed treats Goe every bit as a man treats his younger wife. It really was funny."

At this time Goldman was torn apart by her own truncated love affair with Arthur Swenson, a much younger man. There is something tragic in her dismissal of Carpenter's relationship as "screamingly comic . . . really dear, life is a circus if only one has enough sense of humor, which I do not. . . ." But the derision was possibly mixed with envy as she noted, "Well, as long as EC has a pleasant and comfortable (old) age, what is the difference?"[37]

As Goldman looked back over her life while in exile, even the good times seemed bitter. In a heartbreaking letter to Sasha she deals with the sexist double standard of her closest comrades:

Where did you ever get the idea that I suspected you of being jealous of Ben in any sexual sense. . . . What I did suspect – more than that what I knew – was that you are a prig who constantly worries about what the comrades will say and how it will affect the movement when you yourself lived your life to suit yourself, I mean as far as women are concerned. It was painful to me, at the time, as it has been on many other occasions, to see you fly the movement in the face a hundred times and then condemn me for doing the same. . . . Do I mean to deny Ben's faults? Of course not, my dear. . . . I knew Ben inside and out two weeks after we went on tour; I not only knew but loathed his sensational ways, his bombast, his braggadocio, and his promiscuity, which lacked the least sense of selection. But above all that there was something large, primitive, unpremeditated, and simple about Ben which had terrific charm. Had you and the other friends concerned in my salvation recognized this . . . instead of writing to the university to find out about his medical degree (which the boy never could forget). . . . Ben would not have become a renegade. . . . The trouble with you was . . . as with all our comrades, you are a puritan at heart. . . .

I have been too long in the movement not to know how narrow and moral it is, how unforgiving and lacking in understanding toward everyone different from them. . . . You will repeat your objections to Ben were because . . . "he did not belong in our ranks." All right, but what were your objections to Arthur Swenson? He never was in our ranks. Why did you treat him like a dog after he came to Berlin? Why did you fail to understand the terrific turmoil the boy created in my being? . . . Of course it is nonsense to say that the attitude of men and women in their love to younger people is the same. . . . It is nothing of the kind. . . . Hundreds of men marry women much younger than themselves; they have circles of friends; they are accepted by the world. Everybody objects, resents, in fact dislikes a woman who lives with a younger man; they think her a god-damned fool; no doubt she is that, but it is not the business or concern of friends to make her look and feel like a fool. . . .

In another letter Emma tried to console Sasha after the sudden departure of his former lover Fitzie. Secretary of the Provincetown Players, Eleanor Fitzgerald had been Sasha's companion until his arrest during World War I. In 1928 she arrived in St. Tropez to be with Djuna Barnes and to visit Berkman. Although the events are unclear, Goldman's letters of explanation for Fitzie's behavior over several years formulate her own reflections on the struggle of women to be liberated: "Here we have been worrying about who should meet Fitzie, then that crazy Djuna kidnaps her. Damned fool. . . . Really, the Lesbians are a crazy lot. Their antagonism to the male is almost a disease with them. I simply cant bear such narrowness. . . ."

By implication, Goldman denied that Fitzie's affair with Barnes might have been a positive choice. To understand Fitzie, Goldman wrote, it was necessary to understand that all her relations with men had been disastrous. Her tragedy "is the tragedy of all emancipated women, myself included. We are still rooted in the old soil, though our visions are of the future and our desire is to be free and independent . . . . It is a longing for fulfillment which very few modern women find because most men too are rooted in the old tradition. They too want the woman as wife and mother in the old sense, and the new medium has not yet been devised, I mean the way of being wife, mother, friend and yet retain one's complete freedom. Will it ever? . . ."[38]

Emma Goldman doubted it. Ultimately she even doubted that women could enjoy real satisfaction even physically with men. After a lifetime of celebrating woman's absolute right to full sexual pleasure, there is something intensively poignant about a letter to Dr. Samuel D. Schmulhausen in which she implied that all through the years the pleasure she received from the men she loved had been inadequate. Schmulhausen had written *Woman's Coming of Age*, and on 26 January 1935 Goldman wrote that ever since her "intellectual awakening" she had had the same thought. Namely,

that the sex act of the man lasts from the moment of its dominant motivation to its climax. After that the brute has done of his share. The brute can go to sleep. Not so the woman. The climax of the embrace, far from leaving her relaxed or stupefied as it does the man, raises all her sensibilities to the highest pitch. All her yearning for love, affection, tenderness becomes more vibrant and carries her to ecstatic heights. At that moment she needs the understanding of and communion with her mate perhaps more than the physical. But the brute is asleep and she remains in her own world far removed from him. I know this from my personal experience and experiences of scores of women who have talked freely with me. I am certain that the cause for the conflict between the sexes which continues to exist regardless of woman's emancipation is due to the differences in quality of the sex embrace. Perhaps it will always be that way. Certainly I find very few men who have the same need, or who know how to minister that of the woman's. Naturally, I felt elated to read your analysis . . . which actually expresses what I have felt and voiced for well nigh 45 years. . . . [39]

Despite anger, isolation, and disappointment, Emma Goldman remained active and enthusiastic to the end of her life. After her despondent years in London, several friends presented her with a cottage on St. Tropez: "Georgette LeBlanc, Margaret Anderson, Peggy Guggenheim, Lawrence Vail and many others came for an hour or a day to discuss serious matters or in jolly company." Life in St. Tropez, Goldman wrote, restored her health and her "fighting spirit." It was there that she decided to write her memoirs, tour Canada, and cable friends in the United States for loans to continue her important work, now focused mainly in Spain.[40] But she never found the one great friend who could understand her empty places, and she never acknowledged the value of feminist alliances for active women whose very activity, depths of passion, and committed independence alienated them from the men with whom they worked and struggled.

Even today the myth persists that women unattached to men are lonely, bitter, and without community . . .

Lillian Wald, Jane Addams, Crystal Eastman, and Emma Goldman all had visions of social change and economic justice that, 60 years later, we have yet to see fulfilled. They lived as they did at a time when, as Vera Brittain noted, women were programmed to monopolize their husbands, dominate their sons, possess their daughters, and make fetishes of their kitchens and shrines of their homes. These four women present a range of choices and affinities that were charged with courage, experiment, fulfillment, and intensity. In viewing women of the past it has been a common practice to assume that feminists, spinsters, woman-related women, and most women engaged in social reform were asexual, self-denying, and puritanical, sublimating their sexual passions in their work. Even today the myth persists that women unattached to men are lonely, bitter, and without community; that women who are political activists working with men can function effectively without a support network of women. In the lives of Wald, Addams, and Eastman, we see clearly the energy and strength they received from feminist networks. Crystal Eastman's feminism drew upon and allowed her to appreciate the woman-identification of her lesbian friends. On the other hand, despite Emma Goldman's intellectual and political identification with the oppressed, including women and homosexuals, she never did understand or identify with the feminist movement, and she never did find a friend of her own sex, "a kindred spirit with whom she could share her innermost thoughts and feelings."

For Jane Addams and Lillian Wald, service to humanity and leadership in public life were constantly refueled by their female support communities and by personal relationships with women who gave them passionate loyalty and love. The power of communities of independent women, and of the love between individual women, expressed not only sensually but in a range of ways, is part of the history that has been taken from us by heterosexist culture. To recognize this history is to recognize our own personal forces of energy and courage and the power to change.

Acknowledgments

This paper would not have been possible without the encouragement of several members of my own support group. I want to thank in particular Clare Coss, Audre Lorde, Adrienne Rich, and Joan Kelly-Gadol, who read and commented and every day helped to make it all possible. I also want to thank Bernice Goodman, who helps to make it more possible.

Many friends commented generously and helpfully on this paper before and after I first presented it to the Berkshire Conference on the History of Women on 9 June 1976. I am particularly grateful to Alice Kessler Harris, Claudia Koonz, Bert Hanson, and Carroll Smith-Rosenberg. In addition to their thoughts, Richard Drinnon and Jonathan Katz shared with me some of their unpublished documents.

Endnotes

1. See Vera Brittain, *Testament of Friendship: The Story of Winifred Holtby* (London: Macmillan, 1947), p. 2: "Within the framework of this biography I have tried to tell . . . the story of a friendship which continued unbroken and unspoilt for sixteen incomparable years. . . ."

2. See Blanche Wiesen Cook, "Democracy in Wartime: Antimilitarism in England and the United States, 1914-1918," *American Studies* (Spring 1972), reprinted in Charles Chatfield, ed., *Peace Movements in America* (Shocken Books, 1973), pp. 39-57; Cook, "Woodrow Wilson and the Antimilitarists, 1914-1918" (unpublished Ph.D. dissertation, The Johns Hopkins University, 1970); and Cook, ed., *Toward the Great Change: Crystal and Max Eastman on Feminism, Antimilitarism and Revolution* (Garland Publishing, 1976).

3. Emma Goldman, *Living My Life*, Vol. I (Dover Reprint, 1970), pp. 160, 375, *passim*.

4. Blanche Wiesen Cook, "The Woman's Peace Party: Collaboration and Non-Cooperation," *Peace and Change* (Fall 1972), pp. 36 ff.

5. Goldman, *op. cit.*, pp. 157-160.

6. See Margaret Anderson, *My Thirty Years' War*, *The Fiery Fountains*, and *The Strange Necessity;* Natalie Clifford Barney, *The One Who Is Legion* (London, 1930) and *Souvenirs Indiscrets* (Paris, 1960); Meryl Secrest, *Between Me and Life: A Biography of Romaine Brooks* (Doubleday, 1974); Jean Chalon, *Portrait d'une Seductrice* (Editions Stock, 1976); George Wickes, *The Amazon of Letters: The Life and Loves of Natalie Barney* (Putnam, 1976); and Gayle Rubin, introduction to Renée Vivien, *A Woman Appeared to Me* (The Naiad Press, 1976), a 1904 novel translated by Jeannette Foster. See also Jeannette Foster, *Sex Variant Women in Literature* (Diana Press, 1975 [1956]; Bertha Harris, "Lesbian Society in Paris in the 1920's," in Phyllis Birkby *et al.*, eds., *Amazon Expedition* (Times Change Press, 1973); and Dame Ethel Smythe, *Impressions That Remained,* 3 vols. (Longman's Green, 1920).

7. William O'Neill, *Everyone Was Brave: Feminism in America* (Quadrangle, 1969), p. 120.

8. Allen Davis, *American Heroine: The Life and Legend of Jane Addams* (Oxford University Press, 1973), p. 46.

9. Allen Reznick, "Lillian Wald: The Years at Henry Street" (unpublished Ph.D. dissertation, University of Wisconsin, 1973), pp. 153, 158, and foreword.

10. Vera Brittain, *Radclyffe Hall: A Case of Obscenity?* (London: A Femina Book, 1968), p. 21.

11. Davis, *op. cit.*, p. 91.

12. Jane Addams, "Women, War and Babies" (31 July 1915), reprinted in Allen Davis, ed., *Jane Addams on Peace, War and International Understanding, 1895-1932* (Garland Publishing, 1976).

13. George Will, "How Far Out of the Closet?" *Newsweek*, 3 May 1977, p. 92.

14. For information about the U.S. Children's Bureau, see Nancy P. Weiss, "The Children's Bureau: A Case Study of Women's Voluntary Networks," an unpublished paper presented at the Berkshire Conference on the History of Women, 10 June 1976, Bryn Mawr.

15. See Nancy Sahli's unpublished paper, "Changing Patterns of Sexuality and Female Interaction in 19th Century America," presented at the Berkshire Conference, 11 June 1976, pp. 12-13.

16. Lillian Wald's correspondence is divided between the New York Public Library and Columbia University. See Dock to Wald, 27 April 1925; 10 May 1925; 10 March 1916, Columbia University.

17. Lavinia Dock's correspondence with the Congressional Union is in the Woman's Party Papers, Library of Congress. See especially Dock to Paul, 8 September 1914, tray 1, box 6; 28 June 1915, New York, tray 1, box 6; Dock to C.U., 22 May 1915, tray 1, box 5.

18. Irene Lewisohn to Dear Lady Light, n.d., Wald Papers, Columbia. This probably refers to a round-the-world trip that lasted six months (1910). See R.L. Duffus, *Lillian Wald* (Macmillan, 1938), pp. 123 ff; Rita Morgenthau to Wald, 1 January 1905, box 14; 10 June 1906; n.d., 1930's, Wald Papers, Columbia.

19. Dock to Duffus, 28 May 1936, in Duffus, *op. cit.*, pp. 346-347.

20. Margaret Anderson, *The Fiery Fountains* (Horizon Press, 1969 [1951], p. 84.

21. Mabel Hyde Kittredge to Wald, 28 April 1904; all Kittredge letters, Wald Papers, Columbia.

22. Helen Arthur's correspondence with Wald is generally undated between 1906 and 1908. *Ibid.*

23. Wald quoted in Duffus, *op. cit.*, p. 55.

24. Kittredge to Wald, 11 May 1925, Wald Papers, Columbia; George W. Alger, Oral History, Columbia, pp. 251-252; Reznick, *op. cit.*, p. ii.

25. Emma Goldman, "The Child and Its Enemies," *Mother Earth* (April 1906), pp. 107-109.

26. A long correspondence to block Eastman's participation at the Hague may be found in the Balch and Addams Papers at the Swarthmore College Peace Collection; see especially Lucia Ames Mead to Emily Green Balch, Balch Papers. See also Nan Bauer Maglin, "Early Feminist Fiction: The Dilemma of Personal Life," *Prospects* (1976), pp. 167 ff., for an overview of the reformists' unwillingness to deal with changing social and sexual mores.

27. See Richard Drinnon, *Rebel in Paradise: A Biography of Emma Goldman* (University of Chicago Press, 1961), pp. 149-151; and Goldman, "Marriage and Love," in Alix Shulman, ed., *Red Emma Speaks* (Vintage, 1972), pp. 158 ff. See also Shulman, *To the Barricades: The Anarchist Life of Emma Goldman* (Crowell, 1971).

28. Jeannette Lowe to author, 27 March 1973.

29. Crystal Eastman, "Marriage Under Two Roofs" (1923); "Feminists Must Fight" (1924); and "Now We Can Begin" (1920) — all reprinted in Blanche Wiesen Cook, *Toward the Great Change.*

30. Claude McKay, *A Long Way From Home* (Harcourt, 1970 [1935]), pp. 154-155.

31. Margaret Anderson, *My Thirty Years' War*, pp. 54-55; Goldman, *Living My Life*, Vol. II, pp. 530-533.

32. Goldman, "The Tragedy of Woman's Emancipation," *Mother Earth* (No. 3, 1906), pp. 9-18 (reprinted in *Red Emma Speaks)*; R.A.P., "Feminism in America," *Mother Earth* (February 1915), pp. 392-394.

33. Goldman, *Living My Life*, Vol. I, p. 555.

34. See Sperry to Goldman in Jonathan Katz, *Gay American History* (Crowell, 1976), pp. 523-530.

35. John Lauritsen and David Thorstad, *The Early Homosexual Rights Movement, 1864-1935* (Times Change Press, 1974), pp. 36-37.

36. Katz, *op. cit.*, pp. 376-380.

37. Richard and Anna Maria Drinnon, eds., *Nowhere At Home: Letters From Exile of Emma Goldman and Alexander Berkman* (Schocken Books, 1975), pp. 126-128.

38. *Ibid.*, pp. 132-133, p. 86.

39. Goldman to Dr. Samuel Schmulhausen, 26 January 1935, Goldman Papers, Labadie Collection, University of Michigan.

40. Goldman, *Living My Life*, Vol. II, pp. 985-986; see also Goldman to Margaret Anderson, ed., *The Little Review Anthology* (Horizon Press, 1953), p. 363.

MILITARY POLICY TOWARD HOMOSEXUALS: SCIENTIFIC, HISTORICAL, AND LEGAL PERSPECTIVES

by Major Jeffrey S. Davis*

I. INTRODUCTION

Department of Defense Directive 1332.14 states that homosexuality is incompatible with military service.[1] Accordingly, current policy prohibits homosexuals from entering military service.[2] If a homosexual manages to enter the service in spite of this prohibition, the service will separate that individual as soon as possible.[3] To facilitate this process, current policy allows separation based on homosexual tendencies alone, without requiring proof of any homosexual acts.[4] Many military homosexuals, however, have resisted their separations from the military by strenuously defending their positions at administrative elimination hearings and by vigorously litigating their causes.

These cases often involve a soldier, sailor, or airman who, but for being a homosexual, is outstanding in every respect.[5] Using the testimony of supervisors and co-workers, these service members try to demonstrate the inapplicability of each of the policy reasons the military uses to justify their exclusion.[6] The current policy, however, contains no exceptions.[7] Commanders have no discretion to retain homosexuals and are themselves derelict if they do not initiate separation action.[8] Should commanders have this discretion? Can the retention policy be altered without altering the accession policy?

---

*Judge Advocate General's Corps. Currently assigned as the Officer-in-Charge, Butzbach Branch, Office of the Staff Judge Advocate, 3d Armored Division. Previously assigned as Chief of Legal Assistance, Trial Counsel, and Chief of Military Justice, Fort Sill, 1986-1989; Funded Legal Education Program, 1982-1985; Medical Service Corps Officer, 1977-1982. B.S., Texas A&M University, 1977; J.D., University of Texas Law School, 1985; and LL.M., The Judge Advocate General's School, 1990. This article is based upon a thesis submitted in partial satisfaction of the requirements of the 38th Judge Advocate Officer Graduate Course.

[1]Dep't of Defense Directive 1332.14, Enlisted Administrative Separations (Jan. 28, 1982) [hereinafter DOD Dir. 1332.14].

[2]*See, e.g.*, Army Reg. 601-210, Regular Army and Army Reserve Enlistment Program, para. 4-4 (1 Dec. 1988).

[3]DOD Dir. 1332.14.

[4]*Id.*

[5]*See, e.g.*, Watkins v. United States Army, 875 F.2d 699, 702-04 (9th Cir. 1989) (en banc); Matlovich v. Secretary of the Air Force, 591 F.2d 852, 854 n.4, 856 (D.C. Cir. 1978).

[6]*See, e.g.*, cases cited *supra* note 5.

[7]DOD Dir. 1332.14. There is a limited exception. Enclosure 3, Standards and Procedures, para. H.3.g.(2) authorizes retention of a member for a limited period of time in the interests of national security as authorized by the Secretary concerned.

[8]Uniform Code of Military Justice art. 92, 10 U.S.C. § 892 (1982) [hereinafter UCMJ].

Separating people from the military solely because of their sexual orientation or status may lead to a successful legal challenge under the fundamental rights prong of equal protection.[9] Although the Supreme Court recently declined to hear *Ben-Shalom v. Marsh*, a case raising a challenge under the suspect/quasi-suspect class prong of equal protection, the Court never has squarely addressed either prong of equal protection in a homosexuality case.[10]

The policy also may lead to problems if the Selective Service System is ever reactivated. The draft could be avoided by anyone claiming to be a homosexual. Should the military modify this policy, which is based on sexual orientation?

Sodomy, whether heterosexual or homosexual, is against the law for members of the armed services.[11] The Supreme Court has determined that sodomy statutes are constitutional.[12] Nevertheless, is sodomy the real problem, or is the problem sexual activity in general? Should the Uniform Code of Military Justice continue to prohibit sodomy?

Some people do not realize they have homosexual tendencies until after they have enlisted or have been commissioned.[13] Should they be treated differently than people who lie about their sexual orientation to enter military service?

This article contends that current policy on accession of homosexuals should be altered so that homosexuality becomes a waivable disqualification. As to separation, Service Secretaries and commanders should have the discretion to retain homosexuals who meet certain criteria. Finally, the military should not separate personnel based solely on statements of sexual orientation, but should require evidence of prejudice to good order and discipline.

---

[9]*See infra* text accompanying notes 232-38.

[10]*See* Ben-Shalom v. Marsh, 881 F.2d 454 (7th Cir. 1989), *cert. denied*, 110 S. Ct. 1296 (1990) [hereinafter Ben-Shalom III]. Ben-Shalom II involved procedural issues not relevant to this article. Ben-Shalom v. Secretary of the Army, 826 F.2d 722 (7th Cir. 1987) [hereinafter Ben-Shalom II]. Ben-Shalom I was a 1980 case in which the Eastern District of Wisconsin determined that the homosexual regulation violated the first amendment. Ben-Shalom v. Secretary of the Army, 489 F. Supp. 964 (E.D. Wis. 1980) [hereinafter Ben-Shalom I].

[11]UCMJ art. 125.

[12]Bowers v. Hardwick, 478 U.S. 186 (1986), *reh'g denied*, 478 U.S. 1039 (1986).

[13]Harry, *Homosexual Men and Women Who Have Served Their Country*, 10 J. Homosexuality 117, 121 (1984).

A multidisciplinary approach is used to reach these conclusions. Part II relies on science to explain why homosexuals exist, in what numbers, and the relationship of homosexuality to concerns other than sexual orientation. Part III is a history of the treatment of homosexuals in the Armed Forces, with emphasis on treatment in the United States Army. National and international trends also are addressed. Part IV is an analysis of the legal arguments that have been made for and against allowing homosexuals to serve in the Armed Forces. Emphasis is placed on equal protection analysis, as the fundamental rights prong of that analysis seems to be the homosexuals' best remaining argument. Part V is a critical appraisal of current policy, with suggestions for improvement.

II. SCIENTIFIC PERSPECTIVES

A. HOMOSEXUALITY DEFINED AND THEORIES ON CAUSATION

The military has its own definitions for "homosexual," "bisexual," and "homosexual act." A homosexual is defined as "a person, regardless of sex, who engages in, desires to engage in, or intends to engage in homosexual acts." A bisexual is defined as "a person who engages in, desires to engage in, or intends to engage in homosexual and heterosexual acts." A homosexual act is defined as "bodily contact, actively undertaken or passively permitted, between members of the same sex for the purpose of satisfying sexual desires."[14]

Homosexuality is a topic that often leads to heated discussion of divergent views. Science lends objectivity to the discussion. A great deal of scientific research has been conducted on the possible causes and effects of homosexuality.

1. The Kinsey Model

In 1948, Dr. Alfred C. Kinsey and two research associates at Indiana University published a nine-year case history study on human sexual behavior.[15] Their sample, intended to represent a cross section of the population of the United States, consisted of about 5300 white males from across the country.[16]

---

[14]DOD Dir. 1332.14.

[15]A. Kinsey, W. Pomeroy, and C. Martin, Sexual Behavior in the Human Male (1948) [hereinafter A. Kinsey].

[16]*Id.* at 3-9.

Kinsey did not adopt the common practice of labeling people as heterosexuals, homosexuals, or bisexuals. He developed a seven-point continuum based on psychologic reactions (specific arousal by same or opposite sex stimuli) and overt heterosexual and homosexual experience. The scale ranges from exclusively heterosexual (rate 0) to exclusively homosexual (rate 6). The middle (rate 3) is equally heterosexual and homosexual. Individuals can be assigned a different position on the scale for each age period of their lives.[17]

Kinsey used the term homosexual in connection with human behavior to mean sexual relations, either overt or psychic, between persons of the same sex.[18] He did not attempt to demonstrate what caused homosexuality. He believed that questions generated from data that he had gathered should be addressed by those scientists attempting to discover biologic, psychologic, social, or hereditary bases of homosexuality.[19]

2. Causation

Causation is of interest because it relates to the notion of fault, which relates to conscious choices. "Many homosexuals claim that their sexual orientation is the result of biological forces over which they have no control or choice."[20]

Sexual orientation refers to a consistent preference or ambivalence in regard to the gender of a sexual partner. Heterosexuals consistently prefer the opposite sex, homosexuals consistently prefer the same sex, and bisexuals have varying degrees of ambivalence.[21] The question is: What factor or combination of factors causes or leads to sexual preference?

Throughout the twentieth century, scientists have attempted to discover what causes sexual orientation. Most have taken heterosexuality as the norm and tried to explain why a minority of people deviate from it.[22] Some scientists have focused on personal ex-

---

[17]*Id.* at 636-47. The other rates are: 1) predominantly heterosexual, only incidentally homosexual; 2) predominantly heterosexual, but more than incidentally homosexual; 3) predominantly homosexual, but more than incidentally heterosexual; and 4) predominantly homosexual, but incidentally heterosexual.

[18]*Id.* at 612.

[19]*Id.* at 660-66.

[20]W. Masters, V. Johnson, and R. Kolodny, Masters and Johnson on Sex and Human Loving 349 (1986).

[21]Ellis & Ames, *Neurohormonal Functioning and Sexual Orientation: A Theory of Homosexuality-Heterosexuality,* 101 Psychological Bull. 233 (1987).

[22]*Id.*

perience and environment, while others have considered genetic and physiological explanations.[23]

Researchers recently have proposed a theory of how the entire spectrum of human sexual orientation is determined.[24] The theory is that hormonal and neurological variables operating during gestation are the main determinants of sexual orientation. Activation of the sexual orientation does not occur until puberty and may not stabilize until early adulthood. Personal experience and environment may be involved in sexual orientation, but it would be very unusual for such variables to overcome a strong predisposition to either heterosexuality or homosexuality.

a. Normal Development

From conception, females have two of the same sex chromosomes (XX), while males have two different sex chromosomes (XY). A fetus naturally will develop into a female unless certain events occur. Soon after conception of a male, genes in the Y chromosome trigger the production of biochemicals, such as testosterone, that cause male sex organs to appear. Other cells (called sertoli cells) also form and prevent the formation of structures that would otherwise become the uterus and fallopian tubes of a female.[25]

For fetuses being masculinized, testosterone creates hormone receptor sites within cells. During puberty, testosterone is produced in large quantities and bonds to the receptor sites formed during gestation.[26]

Separate areas of the brain control masculine and feminine behavior, and the masculine areas normally develop at the expense of the feminine areas. For example, the preoptic anterior nucleus of the hypothalamus generally is over twice as large in men as it is in women. This area appears to regulate the masculine sexual orientation tendency to mount in response to various feminine cues. Neurological organization for this area occurs during the third and fourth months of gestation.[27]

The norm is for males and females to develop a heterosexual orientation after a complex series of biochemical reactions that occur dur-

[23] *Id.*
[24] *Id.*
[25] *Id.* at 236-37.
[26] *Id.* at 237-38.
[27] *Id.* at 239.

ing gestation. A bisexual or homosexual orientation may result if these reactions are modified because of genetic variations, biochemicals produced in response to stressful situations, drugs taken by the pregnant mother, or other variables.[28]

b. Deviations From the Norm

Scientists have modified the above-described variables in laboratory experiments. Male rats with testes removed and female rats that have received testosterone injections, both prior to completion of neuro-organization, have been induced to display homosexual behavior. Similar work has been done with rhesus monkeys.[29]

Drugs called antiandrogens block the effects of testosterone and other sex hormones. Administration of antiandrogens to a pregnant rat often will result in homosexual behavior among the offspring after they reach puberty. Barbiturates, marijuana, and other drugs also can partially divert or block masculinization of the nervous system during neuro-organization.[30] Alcohol has been found to have both demasculinizing and defeminizing effects on the brains of both sexes of rats.[31]

Severe stress to a mother during neuro-organization of a fetus can lead to bisexual and homosexual male offspring. Stress causes depressed testosterone production in many species of mammals. The stress hormones such as adrenalin appear to inhibit production of testosterone. The hormones from the mother then pass through the placenta and affect the fetus.[32]

The only behavioral variable found to induce homosexual activity is total sexual segregation. Rhesus monkeys in this situation have displayed homosexual behavior. When later integrated with members of the opposite sex, however, most monkeys have displayed heterosexual behavior.[33]

Though scientists cannot conduct sexual orientation experiments on humans, evidence exists that many of the methods used to in-

---

[28] *Id.* at 243-48.
[29] *Id.* at 240-41.
[30] *Id.* at 241. Other drugs include chlorimipramine, diazepam, diethylstilbesterol (DES), pargyline, and reserpine.
[31] *Id.* at 242.
[32] *Id.*
[33] *Id.* at 243.

duce homosexual behavior in lab animals would have similar effects on humans.[34]

Four types of genetic mutations have been identified as probably causing homosexual or bisexual traits in humans. They all seem to involve chromosomes other than the sex chromosomes. Only one of the four types affects genetic females (XX).[35] These are not situations in which a person simply has a different sexual orientation. Depending on the type of mutation, a genetic male may have the physical appearance of a female, or a genetic female may have male genitalia.

A drug used to lessen the risk of miscarriage, the synthetic estrogen diethylstilbesterol (DES), has been linked to lesbian daughters of mothers who took the drug during pregnancy. One study found lesbianism to be more common among women whose mothers had taken DES than among women whose mothers had not.[36]

Stress on the mother also has been linked to homosexuals and bisexuals. A study of males born in Germany between 1934 and 1953 indicated an unusually high proportion of homosexuals were born during and immediately after World War II (from 1941 to 1946).[37] Another study involved asking mothers to recall any stressful episodes they experienced during pregnancy, such as deaths of close relatives, divorces, separations, traumatic financial or sexual experiences, or feelings of severe anxiety. The mothers who could recall such episodes included nearly two-thirds of the mothers of male homosexuals, one-third of the mothers of bisexuals, and less than ten percent of the mothers of heterosexuals.[38]

Several hypotheses follow from the prenatal neurohormone theory, and many have been tested. For example, homosexuality primarily should be a male phenomenon.[39] This is because mammals are fundamentally female and become male only when all the genetic and biochemical reactions associated with the addition of the Y chromosome work in the normal manner. Natural selection also would tend to favor fewer deviations in females, because only females can gestate

---

[34] *Id.*

[35] *Id.* at 244-47. The four types are alphareductase deficiency, androgen insensitivity syndrome, faulty testosterone synthesis, and congenital adrenal hyperplasia syndrome (which affects females).

[36] *Id.* at 247.

[37] *Id.*

[38] *Id.*

[39] *Id.* at 249.

offspring. Evidence from humans worldwide and from all other mammals studied supports the idea that homosexuality is more common among males than among females.[40]

Another hypothesis is that homosexuality should be an inherited trait, because there are likely to be many genetic factors that increase the chance of a deviation from the biochemical norm. "Support for this deduction can be found in studies reporting considerably higher concordance rates for homosexuality among identical twins than among fraternal twins. . .[S]everal studies have found that close relatives of homosexuals have higher incidences of homosexuality than the general population."[41] One study, for example, found "that nearly one-quarter of all brothers of male homosexuals also were homosexuals, a much higher rate than the 3-7% typically reported among human males generally."[42]

The prenatal hormone theory also "implies that efforts to change sexual orientation should be essentially confined to modifying where, when, and how sexual orientation is expressed; the orientation itself should not change."[43] This is because

> sexual orientation appears to be largely determined by hypothalamic-limbic system brain functioning, and most conditioning procedures, and certainly all counseling methods, gear their corrective efforts at neocortical functioning ("rational thought"). Although the neocortex's ability to learn ways to override and circumvent lower brain functioning should never be underestimated, basically a homosexual's neocortex would have to learn how to prevent hypothalamic-limbic areas of the brain from functioning as they were organized to function.[44]

The vast majority of homosexuals never seek treatment.[45] Of those who have, there have been some reports of successfully changing homosexuals into heterosexuals, but the criteria for success often have been "either vague or considerably less than exclusive heterosexual behavior."[46] The best predictor of whether a homosexu-

---

[40]*Id.*
[41]*Id.* at 250.
[42]*Id.*
[43]*Id.* at 251.
[44]*Id.*
[45]Sultan, Elsner & Smith, *Ego-Dystonic Homosexuality and Treatment Alternatives*, in Male and Female Homosexuality: Psychological Approaches 192 (L. Diamant, ed. 1987).
[46]Ellis and Ames, *supra* note 21, at 251.

al will respond to treatment is the amount of heterosexual experience the individual had prior to treatment.[47] Those who seek treatment are thus more likely to be bisexuals than homosexuals. At any rate, the reports on treatment of homosexuality seem consistent with the hypothesis that efforts to change sexual orientation should be minimally effective.[48]

The prenatal neurohormone theory, if correct, would indicate that those homosexuals who attribute their sexual orientation to biological forces beyond their control are right. Many social scientists, however, do not share this view. For example, many behavioral scientists favor experiential explanations for sexual orientation,[49] and some psychoanalysts maintain that homosexuality is a neurosis that can be cured.[50] Still, the prevailing view among psychologists is that "the diversity among sexual orientations is likely to be understood from a combination of sociological, cultural, and biological factors."[51] The prenatal hormone theory combines these factors and makes sense.

B. THE INCIDENCE OF HOMOSEXUALITY

1. Homosexuals in Society

The sexual histories of the 5300 subjects in the Kinsey study revealed a surprising incidence of homosexual experience in the general population.[52] For the purpose of reporting incidence, Kinsey defined a homosexual experience as physical contact to the point of orgasm with another male.[53] Kinsey's data indicated that:

> [A]t least 37% of the male population has some homosexual experience between the beginning of adolescence and old age. . . . Some of these persons have but a single experience, and some of them have much more or even a lifetime of experience; but all of them have at least some experience to the point of orgasm.[54]

---

[47]*Id.*

[48]*Id.*

[49]*Id.*

[50]Fine, *Psychoanalytic Theory*, in Male and Female Homosexuality: Psychological Approaches 86-87 (L. Diamant, ed. 1987).

[51]Gladue, *Psychobiological Contributions*, in Male and Female Homosexuality: Psychological Approaches 130 (L. Diamant, ed. 1987).

[52]A. Kinsey, *supra* note 15, at 625.

[53]*Id.* at 623.

[54]*Id.*

Kinsey made generalizations from his data with his seven-point heterosexual/homosexual scale.[55] The generalizations all pertained to white males after the onset of adolescence up to age fifty-five, and included the following: sixty-three percent never have an overt homosexual experience to the point of orgasm; approximately thirteen percent react erotically to other males without having overt homosexual contacts; twenty-five percent have more than incidental homosexual experience or reactions (rates 2-6) for at least three years; eighteen percent have at least as much homosexual as heterosexual in their histories (rates 3-6) for at least three years; thirteen percent have more of the homosexual than the heterosexual (rates 4-6) for at least three years, ten percent are more or less exclusively homosexual (rates 5 or 6) for at least three years, eight percent are exclusively homosexual (rate 6) for at least three years, and four percent are exclusively homosexual throughout their lives.[56]

> Since only 50 per cent of the population is exclusively heterosexual throughout its adult life, and since only 4 per cent of the population is exclusively homosexual throughout its life, it appears that nearly half (46%) of the population engages in both heterosexual and homosexual activities, or reacts to persons of both sexes, in the course of their adult lives.[57]

Kinsey was looking at American white males in the 1940's. Worldwide, as of the 1980's, the incidence of exclusively homosexual males was estimated at three to five percent, regardless of varying degrees of social tolerance, intolerance, or repression.[58]

The incidence of "feminized males" or "queens," who are often caricatured, is estimated at about ten percent of the male homosexual population.[59] Evidence also exists that homosexuality is more common among males than among females, both in humans worldwide and in all other mammals that have been studied.[60] Kinsey found that only two or three percent of women were mostly or exclusively homosexual on a lifelong basis.[61]

---

[55] *See supra* text accompanying notes 15-19.
[56] A. Kinsey, *supra* note 15, at 650-51.
[57] *Id.* at 656.
[58] T. Sarbin & K. Karols, Nonconforming Sexual Orientations and Military Suitability 8-9 (1988) (draft study of the Defense Personnel Security Research and Education Center).
[59] *Id.* at 26.
[60] Ellis & Ames, *supra* note 21, at 249.
[61] W. Masters, V. Johnson & R. Kolodny, *supra* note 20, at 345.

2. Homosexuals in the Military

If the incidence of homosexuals in the military is the same as the incidence in the general population, about three to five percent of the military is exclusively homosexual. Data that impact upon incidence include separations for homosexuality and studies of known homosexuals who report military service in their histories.

There were few discharges for homosexuality during World War II.[62] Data for separations because of homosexuality in the post-war 1940's through the 1950's can only be estimated because of the nature of military recordkeeping during those periods.[63] The Army, for example, did not record the number of enlisted personnel separated for homosexuality until mid-1960.[64] Nevertheless, data reviewed by Williams and Weinberg (1971) suggest that about 2000 persons per year, or one out of every 1500 servicemen (.066%), were separated from the Armed Forces for homosexuality between the late forties and mid-fifties.[65]

Even in the 1960's, the services did not have uniform data collection on homosexual separations. The Army separated 6139 enlisted soldiers for homosexuality during a seven and one-half year period from 1960-1967 (averaging 818 per year).[66] From 1957 to 1965, the Army allowed an average of thirty officers per year to resign in lieu of administrative elimination action for homosexuality.[67] From 1950 to 1965, the Navy separated a total of 17,392 enlisted men for homosexuality for an average of 1087 per year.[68] No statistics are available for naval officers during this period.[69]

When similar data for the Marine Corps and Air Force are considered, the average estimate of personnel separated from all Armed Forces for homosexuality from the mid-fifties through the sixties is between 2000 and 3000 per year.[70] The Navy accounted for the highest percentage of separations, and in 1961 the Navy stated that

---

[62]W. Menninger, Psychiatry in a Troubled World: Yesterday's War and Today's Challenge 225 (1948) (of 20,620 soldiers diagnosed as constitutional psychopaths by the Army in 1943, 1625 were of the homosexual type).

[63]C. Williams & M. Weinberg, Homosexuals and the Military 45-46 (1971).

[64]*Id.* at 47.

[65]*Id.* at 46-47.

[66]*Id.* at 47-48.

[67]*Id.* at 48.

[68]*Id.* at 49.

[69]*Id.*

[70]*Id.* at 53.

homosexuality and other sexual abnormalities accounted for approximately forty percent of all its Undesirable Discharges.[71]

More recent and complete data of administrative separations for homosexuality for all services are available for fiscal years 1985 to 1987.[72] The reported categories include enlisted and officer personnel by gender.

The Army had 1197 separations, which included 829 enlisted males (.05%, or 5 in 10,000), 354 enlisted women (.17%), 11 male officers (.004%), and 3 female officers (.007%). The Navy had 2241, which included 1825 enlisted males (.13%), 382 enlisted females (.27%), 30 male officers (.02%), and 4 female officers (.02%). Two of the Navy personnel were separated judicially rather than administratively. The Marine Corps had 309 separations, which included 213 enlisted males (.04%), 90 enlisted females (.33%), 6 male officers (.01%), and no female officers. The Air Force had 912, which included 644 enlisted males (.043%), 220 enlisted females (.1%), 41 male officers (.01%), and 7 female officers (.02%).

The data from fiscal years 1985 to 1987 show that all of the services except the Navy were separating about 4 or 5 enlisted men per 10,000 for homosexuality, while the Navy was separating 13 enlisted men per 10,000. Naval officers of both sexes also have higher separation rates than are found in the other services. The Marine Corps has the highest rate of separations for enlisted women at 33 per 10,000, followed by the Navy at 27 per 10,000.

The important finding is the relatively small number of separations for homosexuality in all services (from 1:10,000 to 33:10,000) in relation to the incidence of exclusive homosexual orientation in the general population (from 300:10,000 to 500:10,000).[73] This raises the question of how many homosexuals serve in the military without ever being identified.

One study from the World War II era addresses this question.[74] It traced 183 men known to be homosexual prior to entering the military. Of these, 51 were rejected at induction, and 14 were ad-

[71]*Military Justice: Hearings Before the Subcomm. on Constitutional Rights of the Senate Comm. on the Judiciary*, 89th Cong., 2d Sess. 1006 (1966), *quoted in* Williams and Weinberg, *supra* note 63, at 50.

[72]T. Sarbin & K. Karols, *supra* note 58, at 21, app. B.

[73]*Id.* at 22.

[74]W. Menninger, *supra* note 62, at 227, *quoted in* C. Williams & M. Weinberg, *supra* note 63, at 60 (interim report by C. Fry and E. Rostow reported by W. Menninger).

mitted but later discharged. The remaining 118 served from 1 to 5 years, and 68 of them served as officers. Two studies with results similar to the World War II study were reported in 1967.[75] In one, 550 white homosexual males who had served in the military indicated that 80% experienced no difficulties. The other study included 214 male homosexuals who had served, with 77% receiving honorable discharges. In 1971, Williams and Weinberg reported that 76% of the 136 homosexuals in their study received honorable discharges.[76]

Dr. Joseph Harry, in a study of 1456 men and women interviewed in 1969 and 1970, found that homosexual and heterosexual men seemed equally likely to have served in the military, while lesbians were more likely than heterosexual women to have served.[77] Sexual orientation was determined using the Kinsey heterosexual-homosexual rating scale, with homosexuals being defined at those scoring four or higher.[78] No findings explained why higher numbers of lesbians entered the service.[79]

Harry reported that one-third of the homosexual males who did not serve in the military avoided service by declaring their homosexuality. This figure represented fourteen percent of all homosexuals (those who did not serve and those who did serve), and raised the question of why more homosexuals did not declare their homosexuality.[80] One explanation was that many did not know they were homosexuals at the time they volunteered or were drafted.

Harry found that the median age of fully realizing one's homosexuality and becoming socially and sexually active was approximately nineteen or twenty, and that most men realize their homosexuality by their mid-twenties.[81] Kinsey earlier had found homosexual behavior patterns in males to be "largely established" by age sixteen, with only a small portion of men materially modifying their sexual behavior patterns upon entering military service.[82] Harry found:

> Those who defined themselves as homosexual at later ages were more likely to have had military service. Similarly, those who became socially active homosexuals after the age of 22 were

[75]C. Williams & M. Weinberg, *supra* note 63, at 60.
[76]*Id.*
[77]Harry, *supra* note 13, at 119.
[78]*Id.*; *see supra* note 17 and accompanying text.
[79]Harry, *supra* note 13, at 119.
[80]*Id.* at 121.
[81]*Id.* at 121, 124.
[82]A. Kinsey, *supra* note 15, at 416.

> a good deal more likely to have served in the military. Those who came to an early realization of their homosexuality, and those who came out earlier, are more likely to have declared their homosexuality to the military.[83]

Some support for Harry's findings comes from a study of homosexuals living in the Chicago area conducted by the Institute for Sex Research in 1967. Of those with prior military service, twenty-seven of eighty, or thirty-four percent, reported that they did not consider themselves homosexual before induction.[84]

From this data it appears that the incidence of homosexual men in the general population may approximate the incidence of homosexual men in the military, and the incidence of homosexual women may be greater in the military than in the general population. It appears that seventy-five percent or more of the homosexuals who serve in the military are never identified, and a significant percentage may not realize they have a homosexual orientation until after entering the military.

Homosexuals are identified by the military in three main ways: discovery through another person (sometimes related to jealousy, a lovers' argument, or blackmail); voluntary admissions (usually for the purpose of getting out of the military); and the homosexual's own indiscretion.[85] Variables related to detection include frequency of homosexual behavior prior to entering the military, sexual behavior in the military, and status of partner (military or nonmilitary).[86]

The following conclusions result from the Williams and Weinberg study: Those engaging in more frequent homosexual activity prior to entering the military are more likely to be identified, as are those who do the same while in the military. Homosexuals who have a military as opposed to a nonmilitary sex partner also are more likely to be detected. Even more interesting, however, is that those who engage in more frequent sex prior to entering the military and use nonmilitary partners are the least likely to be identified. Those who engage in sex more frequently upon entering the military are more likely to come to the attention of the military voluntarily, whereas those who engage in sex less frequently upon entry are more likely to be discovered through their own indiscretion.[87]

---

[83]Harry, *supra* note 13, at 122.
[84]C. Williams & M. Weinberg, *supra* note 63, at 92.
[85]*Id.* at 88-91.
[86]*Id.* at 91-99.
[87]*Id.*

Still, it appears that the great majority of homosexuals who serve in the military are never detected at all.

C. NONSEXUAL DIFFERENCES BETWEEN HOMOSEXUALS AND HETEROSEXUALS

"The vast majority of homosexual men and women never consult with a mental health professional of any sort."[88] In 1973 the American Psychiatric Association voted to stop classifying homosexuality as a mental disorder.[89] Nevertheless, some homosexuals still seek the assistance of psychiatrists because they do not want to be homosexual.[90] Homosexuality unwanted by a patient is called ego dystonic homosexuality.[91] These patients range from those wishing to increase their heterosexual responsiveness to those with low self-esteem who want to adjust to a homosexual orientation.[92] Either way, the psychological baggage carried by ego dystonic homosexuals sets them apart from heterosexuals and most homosexuals.

The important question is whether the majority of homosexuals have more emotional and psychological problems than heterosexuals. The bottom line is that they do not.

> For the last fifteen years, many research studies have evaluated the performance of homosexuals and heterosexuals on a variety of psychological tests. A recent review of data from dozens of these studies concluded that there are no psychological tests that can distinguish between homosexuals and heterosexuals and there is no evidence of higher rates of emotional instability or psychiatric illness among homosexuals than among heterosexuals.[93]

The two problem areas in which homosexuals are over-represented are alcohol abuse[94] and the acquired immune deficiency syndrome (AIDS).[95] In a 1980 report of problems surfaced by homosexuals during contacts with family physicians, alcoholism was found to be slight-

---

[88]Sultan, Elsner & Smith, *supra* note 45, at 192.
[89]L. Diamant, Male and Female Homosexuality: Psychological Approaches 13 (1987).
[90]*Id.*
[91]*Id.*
[92]Sultan, Elsner & Smith, *supra* note 45, at 195.
[93]W. Masters, V. Johnson & R. Kolodny, *supra* note 20, at 354.
[94]Diamant & Simono, *The Relationship of Homosexuality to Mental Disorders*, in Male and Female Homosexuality: Psychological Approaches 174-78 (L. Diamant, ed. 1987).
[95]W. Masters, V. Johnson & R. Kolodny, *supra* note 20, at 543.

69

ly more prevalent in the homosexual population.[96] A study of the lifetime drinking histories of homosexual and heterosexual women interviewed in the late 1960's suggested significantly more problem drinking in the lesbian sample.[97]

A 1978 study of four urban areas in the Midwest reported that about one-third of male homosexuals surveyed were alcoholics.[98] More recently, in a study comparing the preservice adjustment of homosexual and heterosexual military accessions tested in 1983, homosexuals who had been discovered and discharged did as well or better than heterosexuals in most tested areas, except in preservice drug and alcohol use.[99]

The acquired immune deficiency syndrome (AIDS) is a fatal disease with no known cure. The virus that causes the disease, the human immunodeficiency virus (HIV), is transmitted by body fluids such as blood and semen. By February 1990, sixty percent of the 119,590 known cases of AIDS in the United States were homosexual or bisexual men, twenty-one percent were female and heterosexual male intravenous drug users, seven percent were homosexual or bisexual men who were also intravenous drug users, and five percent were attributed to heterosexual contacts.[100]

Anyone can get AIDS. Homosexual and bisexual men are particularly susceptible because often they have multiple sex partners, thereby increasing the risk of contact with an infected person, and because anal sodomy lends itself to transmission of the disease. The military has an active program to screen personnel and potential accessions for HIV.[101] This screening program probably keeps some homosexuals out of the military. Ironically, it also makes the military one of the safest places to engage in sodomy—at least medically speaking.

III. HISTORICAL PERSPECTIVES

Don't talk to me about naval tradition. It's nothing but rum, sodomy, and the lash.

—Winston Churchill

---

[96]Diamant & Simono, *supra* note 94, at 175.

[97]*Id.* at 176.

[98]*Id.* at 177.

[99]M. McDaniel, Preservice Adjustment of Homosexual and Heterosexual Military Accessions: Implications for Security Clearance Suitability (1989) (draft study PERS-TR-89-004 of the Defense Personnel Security Research and Education Center).

[100]Centers for Disease Control, HIV/AIDS Surveillance Report, February 1990, at 8.

[101]*See, e.g.*, Army Reg. 600-110, Identification, Surveillance, and Administration of Personnel Infected with Human Immunodeficiency Virus (HIV), para. 1-14 (11 Mar. 1988).

A. HISTORICAL ANTECEDENTS

Homosexuality and bisexuality are nothing new. Forms of each were accepted widely in ancient Greece.[102] The poet Sappho lived circa 600 B.C. on the Isle of Lesbos, from which the term lesbian is derived.[103]

Plato lived from about 427-347 B.C.[104] His *Symposium* praised the virtues of male homosexuality and suggested that pairs of homosexual lovers would make the best soldiers.[105] One Greek bisexual known to have done well was Alexander the Great, who lived from 356-323 B.C. and conquered an empire that stretched from present-day Yugoslavia to the Himalayas.[106]

Jewish homosexuals presumably were not doing so well. The Old Testament has some of the earliest writings on the subject, such as Leviticus 20:13: "If a man also lie with mankind, as he lieth with a woman, both of them have committed an abomination: they shall surely be put to death; their blood shall be upon them."[107] Most historians have written that Christianity embraced the persecution and condemnation of homosexuals from its beginnings as well, but there is also evidence that Catholic Europe more or less tolerated homosexuality until the Middle Ages.[108]

> The primary ammunition for the Church's position against homosexuality came from the writings of Saints Augustine and Thomas Aquinas, who both suggested that any sexual acts that could not lead to conception were unnatural and therefor sinful. Using this line of reasoning, the Church became a potent force in the regulation (and punishment) of sexual behavior. While some homosexuals were mildly rebuked and given prayer as penitence, others were tortured or burned at the stake.[109]

In England, the ecclesiastical law against buggery (anal intercourse) became established as the criminal law of the state in 1563.[110] What had been one of the sins against nature became one of the "crimes

---

[102]W. Masters, V. Johnson & R. Kolodny, *supra* note 20, at 346.
[103]L. Diamant, *supra* note 89, at 4.
[104]T. Cowan, Gay Men & Women Who Enriched the World 17 (1988).
[105]W. Masters, V. Johnson & R. Kolodny, *supra* note 20, at 346.
[106]T. Cowan, *supra* note 104, at 11-16.
[107]L. Diamant, *supra* note 89, at 5. Other Biblical references to homosexual conduct include Genesis 9, Genesis 19, and Romans 1:26, 27.
[108]W. Masters, V. Johnson & R. Kolodny, *supra* note 20, at 346.
[109]*Id.* at 347.
[110]Sarbin & Karols, *supra* note 58, at 14.

against nature.'' This terminology still is used to describe sodomy in many jurisdictions.[111]

Ecclesiastical law served as the basis for punishing homosexual behavior in Europe until the nineteenth century, when the Napoleonic Code led to a liberalization of attitudes.[112] The nineteenth century also saw homosexuality take on the status of a sickness to be treated by the medical community.[113]

The history of anti-sodomy laws in America was stated succinctly in *Bowers v. Hardwick*, the Supreme Court case holding anti-sodomy statutes constitutional:

> Sodomy was a criminal offense at common law and was forbidden by the laws of the original thirteen States when they ratified the Bill of Rights. In 1868, when the Fourteenth Amendment was ratified, all but 5 of the 37 States in the Union had criminal sodomy laws. In fact, until 1961, all 50 states outlawed sodomy, and today, 24 states and the District of Columbia continue to provide criminal penalties for sodomy performed in private and between consenting adults.[114]

B. MILITARY LAW

Military law, as applied to homosexuals and homosexual acts, can be divided into statutes used to prosecute and regulations used to exclude or remove homosexuals from the service. Both have evolved over the years.

1. Sodomy Statutes

The Articles of War of 1916 became effective March 1, 1917, and were the first complete revision of military law since the Articles of War of 1806.[115] The ninety-third article of this revision, which addressed ''miscellaneous crimes and offenses,'' proscribed assault with intent to commit any felony, including assault with intent to commit sodomy.[116] This was the first mention of sodomy in military law. It did not proscribe sodomy—only assault with intent to commit

---

[111]*Id.*
[112]L. Diamant, *supra* note 89, at 6.
[113]*Id.* at 15.
[114]*Bowers*, 478 U.S. at 192-94.
[115]W. Aycock & S. Wurfel, Military Law Under the Uniform Code of Military Justice 14 (1955).
[116]Manual for Courts-Martial, United States, 1917, para. 443 [hereinafter MCM, 1917].

sodomy. The Manual for Courts-Martial, 1917, provided the following guidance:

> Sodomy consists in sexual connection with any brute animal, or in sexual connection, per anum, by a man with any man or woman. (Wharton, vol. 2, p. 538.) Penetration of the mouth of the person does not constitute this offense. Both parties are liable as principals if each is adult and consents; but if either be a boy of tender age the adult alone is liable, and although the boy consent the act is still by force. Penetration alone is sufficient. An assault with intent to commit this offense consists of an assault on a human being with intent to penetrate his or her person per anum.[117]

This rather narrowly drafted statute, proscribing only assault with the intent to commit anal sodomy, did not last long. Following World War I, Congress enacted new Articles of War in 1920.[118] For the first time, sodomy was included as a separate offense among the "miscellaneous crimes and offenses."[119] The definition was expanded to include oral sodomy; it read, "Penetration of the mouth of the person also constitutes this offense."[120] Curiously, though, assault with intent to commit sodomy was still limited to assault "with intent to penetrate his or her person per anum."[121] This remained the law through World War II. The sodomy statute did not change again until 1951, with the adoption of article 125 of the Uniform Code of Military Justice.[122] Article 125 states: "Any person subject to this chapter who engages in unnatural carnal copulation with another person of the same or opposite sex or with an animal is guilty of sodomy. Penetration, however slight, is sufficient to complete the offense."[123] The Manual for Courts-Martial, 1951, provided the following discussion:

> It is unnatural carnal copulation for a person to take into his or her mouth or anus the sexual organ of another person or of an animal; or to place his or her sexual organ in the mouth or anus of another person or of an animal; or to have carnal copulation in any opening of the body, except the sexual parts, with another person; or to have carnal copulation in any opening of the body of an animal.[124]

---

[117] *Id.*
[118] Act of June 4, 1920, ch. II, 41 Stat. 787.
[119] Manual for Courts-Martial, United States, 1921, para. 443 [hereinafter MCM, 1921].
[120] *Id.*
[121] *Id.*
[122] UCMJ art. 125 (1951).
[123] *Id.*
[124] MCM, 1951, para. 204.

Assault with intent to commit sodomy became part of article 134, UCMJ, and was not limited to any particular variety of sodomy.[125] These laws have remained substantially unchanged except for altering the maximum punishments for certain forms of the offenses.[126]

The courts-martial cases tend to have aggravating factors such as assaultive conduct, coercion, involvement of a minor, or abuse of rank. Though a court-martial offense since 1920, consensual sodomy without aggravating factors, when detected, historically has led to administrative separation.[127]

2. Regulations

Regulations pertaining to homosexuality or homosexual acts are generally of three interrelated varieties: accession, reenlistment, and separation. The rules for officers are the same as the rules for enlisted personnel, although they are found in different regulations. The different services have substantially similar regulations, because they are all derived from the same Department of Defense directives.[128]

Both the Army and the Navy announced at the beginning of World War II that they intended to exclude all persons with homosexual histories.[129] The social climate being as it was, however, "few men with any common sense would admit their homosexual experience to draft boards or to psychiatrists at induction centers or in the services."[130]

From 1922 to 1945, Army enlisted personnel suspected or charged with homosexual attempts or acts faced the prospect of a "Section VIII" discharge.[131] The general heading for Section VIII was "inaptness or undesirable habits or traits of character." Specific traits, such as homosexual behavior, were not listed. Most soldiers discharged

---

[125]UCMJ art. 134.

[126]For example, the Manual for Courts-Martial, 1984, increased the maximum punishment for forcible sodomy to dishonorable discharge, forfeiture of all pay and allowances, and confinement for 20 years.

[127]*See generally* C. Williams & M. Weinberg, *supra* note 63, at 33, 38-53 (explaining that few homosexuals receive punitive discharges from courts-martial; most are separated administratively).

[128]DOD Dir. 1332.14; Dep't of Defense Directive 1332.30, Separation of Regular Commissioned Officers for Cause (Feb. 12, 1986).

[129]A. Kinsey, *supra* note 15, at 621.

[130]*Id.* at 622.

[131]Army Reg. 615-360, Enlisted Men, Discharge; Release From Active Duty, para. 51-56 (26 Nov. 1942); para. 51-56 (4 Apr. 1935); para. 49-54 (14 Sep. 1927); para. 49-54 (6 Dec. 1922).

under Section VIII received an honorable discharge. In cases of psychopathic behavior, chronic alcoholism, or sexual perversion including homosexuality, the discharge was without honor.[132]

In 1945 War Department policy concerning homosexuals was either to court-martial them or to hospitalize those deemed to be "reclaimable." Hospitalization was to be followed by return to duty, separation, or court-martial. Mere confession of homosexual tendencies to a psychiatrist was not sufficient cause for discharge. Hospitalization was required, to be followed by return to duty or separation.[133]

The postwar homosexual policy reached its most liberal point on March 23, 1946, with the publication of War Department Circular No. 85.

> This order made it clear that enlisted personnel who were to be discharged because of homosexual tendencies, yet had not committed any sexual offense while in the service, could be discharged honorably. For officers in this category, it was further provided that they be permitted to resign under honorable conditions.[134]

The pendulum began to swing the other way in 1948. The provision for honorable discharge was deleted. Homosexuals were to be tried by court-martial or separated as unfit with an undesirable discharge. The category of those "unfit" at this time included criminals, pathological liars, homosexuals, drug addicts, individuals committing misconduct, and sexual perverts. In those cases in which there had been a long period of good service, however, a homosexual could be separated as "unsuitable" (with a general discharge) rather than as unfit.[135]

In 1949 the newly created Department of Defense issued a directive outlining a harsher policy on homosexuality for all branches of the service.[136] The 1950 Army Regulation implementing this policy divided homosexuals into three classes.

---

[132]Honorable discharges were characterized as "white" and discharges without honor were characterized as "blue." L. West & A. Glass, Sexual Behavior and the Military Law 252 (R. Slovenko, ed. 1965); *see also* Note, *Homosexuals in the Military*, 37 Fordham L. Rev. 465 (1969).

[133]Army Reg. 615-368, Enlisted Men, Discharge, Undesirable Habits or Traits of Character, para. 2.b. (7 Mar. 1945) (C1, 10 Apr. 1945) [hereinafter AR 615-368].

[134]C. Williams & M. Weinberg, *supra* note 63, at 27. This policy later was published in AR 615-368, para. 3 (14 May 1947).

[135]AR 615-368, para. 2 (27 Oct. 1948).

[136]C. Williams & M. Weinberg, *supra* note 63, at 27.

Class I homosexuals were those whose homosexual offenses involved assault or coercion as characterized by force, fraud, intimidation, or the seduction of a minor (regardless of the minor's cooperation). A general court-martial was mandatory for this category. Class II homosexuals were those who either engaged in or attempted to engage in homosexual acts. Preferral of court-martial charges was mandatory, but a resignation in lieu of court-martial could be accepted from officers, or a statement accepting a dishonorable discharge could be accepted from enlisted soldiers. Class III homosexuals were personnel who exhibited, professed, or admitted homosexual tendencies, but who had not committed any provable acts or offenses. Class III also included personnel who committed homosexual acts outside military jurisdiction. Class III homosexuals could receive either an honorable or a general discharge.[137]

In 1955 a Class III homosexual could get an honorable discharge if he or she had admitted to homosexual tendencies at induction but was inducted anyway, or if there was "heroic service" indicated in the soldier's record. Provisions were made to retain personnel who became involved in homosexual acts but were not "true, confirmed, or habitual" homosexuals.[138] By 1958 an honorable discharge was mandatory for Class III homosexuals. Convening authorities also could approve an honorable or general discharge for Class II homosexuals if it would be in the best interests of the service and if the individual concerned disclosed his or her homosexual tendencies upon entering the service, had performed outstanding or heroic service, or had performed service over an extended period.[139]

In 1966 the Army required a psychiatric examination prior to separation for homosexuality.[140] In 1970 the homosexuality regulation was superseded and was integrated into regulations that covered all types of unfitness and unsuitability discharges.[141] Unsuitability could be demonstrated by evidence of homosexual "tendencies, desires, or interests" (language later found to be unconstitutional).[142]

---

[137]Army Regulation 600-443, Personnel, Separation of Homosexuals, para. 3 (12 Jan. 1950) [hereinafter AR 600-443].

[138]Army Regulation 635-89, Personnel Separations, Homosexuals, para. 3 (21 Jan. 1955) [hereinafter AR 635-89].

[139]AR 635-89, para. 3 (8 Sep. 1955).

[140]AR 635-89, para. 5 (15 Jul. 1966).

[141]Army Reg. 635-212, Personnel Separations, Discharge, Unfitness and Unsuitability, para. 6 (15 Jul. 1966) (C8, 21 Jan. 1970); Army Reg. 635-100, Personnel Separations, Officer Personnel, para. 5-5 (19 Feb. 1969)(C4, 21 Jan. 1970) [hereinafter AR 635-100].

[142]*Ben-Shalom*, 489 F. Supp. 964.

In 1972 the unfitness and unsuitability provisions for enlisted personnel became chapters 14 and 13 of Army Regulation 635-200 (AR 635-200), the regulation pertaining to all types of enlisted personnel separations.[143]

This regulatory scheme was significant because separation boards convened pursuant to AR 635-200 generally had the authority to recommend retention of soldiers being processed for elimination, and commanders could disapprove a board's recommendation to separate. This provided two loopholes for some homosexuals, even though the Army policy was that homosexuality is incompatible with military service. A similar situation developed with officer separations, because the officer elimination regulation implied that separation was discretionary.[144] Indeed, prior to February 1977, the Army's litigation posture was that there was discretion to retain homosexuals.[145]

Meanwhile, the Air Force and the Navy were suffering some setbacks with their homosexuality regulations. The Navy regulation on homosexuality, dated July 31, 1972, did not provide any terms of exception to the general policy of separating homosexuals.[146] In litigation in 1974, however, the Navy argued that the regulation did not require mandatory discharge of homosexuals.[147]

The application of the Navy regulation became an issue in *Berg v. Claytor*, a case involving a homosexual officer.[148] The separation board deciding Ensign Berg's case was instructed that it had discretion to recommend retention. The court reviewing the case on appeal could not find in the record any indication of "the actual considerations which went into the Navy's ultimate decision not to retain Berg."[149] The court remanded the case to the Secretary of the Navy for a fuller articulation of the Navy policy on retention of homosexuals. Subsequent case history does not indicate whether such matters ever were presented.

In *Matlovich v. Secretary of the Air Force*,[150] a companion case to *Berg v. Claytor*, application of the Air Force regulation on discharge

[143]Army Reg. 635-200, Personnel Separations, Enlisted Personnel, paras. 13, 14 (15 Jul. 1966) (C39, 23 Nov. 1972) [hereinafter AR 635-200].
[144]AR 635-100, para. 5.
[145]DAJA-AL 1978/4168, 2 Jan. 1979.
[146]SECNAV INSTR. 1900.9A (31 Jul. 1972).
[147]Champagne v. Schlesinger, 506 F.2d 979, 983-84, (7th Cir. 1974).
[148]Berg v. Claytor, 591 F.2d 849 (D.C. Cir. 1978).
[149]*Id.* at 851.
[150]Matlovich v. Secretary of the Air Force, 591 F.2d 852 (D.C. Cir. 1978).

77

of homosexuals was at issue.[151] Technical Sergeant Matlovich, after twelve years of service, applied in 1975 for an exception to the policy of discharging homosexuals. The Air Force regulation expressly provided for exceptions when "the most unusual circumstances exist and provided the airman's ability to perform military service has not been compromised," and added that "an exception is not warranted simply because the airman has extensive service."[152]

Matlovich's request was denied, and discharge proceedings were initiated. During judicial review following his discharge, the Air Force stipulated that other homosexuals had been retained in the past.[153] Despite Matlovich's outstanding record, the Air Force said his case lacked the "unusual circumstances" that existed in some other cases. The Air Force did not articulate what constituted "unusual circumstances." The court remanded the case for the Air Force to clarify its policy on retention of homosexuals.[154] Subsequent case history does not indicate whether such matters ever were presented.

In *Ben-Shalom v. Secretary of Army* (*Ben-Shalom I*),[155] the Army in 1980 was told that the language it had been using since 1970 to define unsuitability because of homosexual "tendencies, desires, and interests" was unconstitutional. The court held that the language violated the first amendment and the constitutional right to privacy.[156] The Army had been using this language in several different regulations concerning active duty and reserve officer and enlisted accessions, reenlistments, and separations.[157] The definition was changed after *Ben-Shalom I* so that discharge for homosexual tendencies included those "admitted homosexuals, but as to whom there is no evidence that they engaged in homosexual acts either before or during military service. A homosexual is an individual, regardless of sex, who desires bodily contact . . . ."[158]

In 1981 the Army revised the enlisted separations regulation, AR 635-200, to create a separate chapter for separations due to homosexuality.[159] The policy made it clear that all personnel fitting the defini-

---

[151]*Id.* at 855. The regulation was Air Force Manual 39-12, para. 2-103 (C4, 21 Oct. 1970).
[152]*Id.*
[153]*Id.* at 854.
[154]*Id.*
[155]*Ben-Shalom*, 489 F. Supp. 964.
[156]*Id.* at 972-77.
[157]DAJA-AL 1980-2213 (7 Jul. 1980) (enclosing proposed changes to AR 135-178, AR 635-100, AR 635-200, AR 140-111, and AR 601- 210).
[158]AR 635-200, para. 13 (21 Nov. 1977) (IO2, 28 Nov. 1980).
[159]AR 635-200, para. 15 (21 Nov. 1977) (C4, 10 Mar. 1981).

tion of a homosexual were to be separated, with no exceptions. In the area of homosexual acts, an exception could be made if a soldier met five criteria that essentially meant the soldier was not really a homosexual.[160] The Department of Defense issued a directive in 1982 that made this total exclusion policy uniform throughout all the services.[161] There have been no major changes to regulations that address homosexuality since 1982.

C. NATIONAL AND INTERNATIONAL TRENDS

During the 1950's, the American Law Institute recommended that states adopt a Model Penal Code that decriminalized all non-violent consensual sexual activity between adults in private, but retained a prohibition on public solicitation to engage in deviate sexual activity.[162] As of 1987, twenty-four states either had adopted the Model Penal Code or had otherwise removed criminal penalties for consensual sodomy.[163] Attempts to get other states to repeal sodomy statutes have not been successful since the June 1986 *Bowers v. Hardwick* decision.[164]

Internationally, the status of laws concerning homosexual behavior as of 1988 was:

> In 5 countries (and in some parts of the USA, Canada, and Australia) the law protects gays and lesbians against discrimination. In 64 countries homosexual behavior is not illegal (although different ages of consent for homo- and heterosexual behavior may exist), but there is no protection against discrimination on the basis of sexual orientation. In 55 countries homosexual behavior is illegal (in most cases between men,

---

[160]A soldier will be separated. . .unless there are approved further findings that (1) Such conduct is a departure from the soldier's usual and customary behavior; and (2) Such conduct is unlikely to recur because it is shown, for example, that the act occurred because of immaturity, intoxication, coercion, or a desire to avoid military service; and (3) Such conduct was not accomplished by use of force, coercion, or intimidation by the soldier during a period of military service; and (4) Under the particular circumstances of the case, the soldier's continued presence in the Army is consistent with the interest of the Army in proper discipline, good order, and morale; and (5) The soldier does not desire to engage in or intend to engage in homosexual acts.

[161]DOD Dir. 1332.14.

[162]*See* American Law Institute, Model Penal Code § 213.2 (Proposed Official Draft 1962), *noted in* Leonard, *The Legal Position of Lesbians and Gay Men in the United States*, in Second ILGA Pink Book 104 (1988).

[163]Leonard, *supra* note 162, at 104.

[164]*Id.* at 105.

> but that doesn't mean that the situation of lesbians is any better), and in 58 countries no information is yet available. Legally speaking, the situation is . . . worst in Africa and rather better in Europe.[165]

A number of countries have tackled the issue of whether homosexuals should be allowed in the military. Many countries do not allow homosexuals to serve, in spite of the fact that they consider homosexual acts between consenting adults to be legal. These countries include Canada, Peru, Venezuela, New Zealand, Italy, Great Britain, and Northern Ireland.[166]

Some countries proscribe homosexual acts without addressing homosexual status. Brazil does not outlaw homosexual acts outside the military, but criminalizes "indecent acts, homosexual or not" between soldiers.[167] In Spain, homosexual acts have not been illegal since 1978, but sexual acts between soldiers on duty inside barracks are illegal.[168]

At least five countries in addition to Brazil and Spain allow homosexuals in the military. In Israel, homosexuality has not been a reason for dismissal from the Armed Forces since 1988, but homosexuals are not allowed to have security-related jobs.[169] It has been legal for homosexuals to serve in the Armed Forces of Denmark since 1979.[170] Homosexuals were permitted to serve in the Armed Forces of the Federal Republic of Germany, but they were not considered to be suitable for senior positions.[171] In the Netherlands, the Dutch have allowed homosexuals to serve since 1974.[172] Sweden has allowed homosexuals in the Armed Forces since 1979.[173]

---

[165]Tielman and de Jonge, *Country-by-Country Survey*, in Second ILGA Pink Book 186 (1988).
[166]*Id.* at 188-242.
[167]*Id.* at 199.
[168]*Id.* at 240.
[169]*Id.* at 213.
[170]*Id.* at 228.
[171]*Id.* at 230.
[172]*Id.* at 237.
[173]*Id.* at 240.

IV. LEGAL PERSPECTIVES

It is revolting to have no better reason for a rule of law than that it was laid down in the time of Henry IV. It is still more revolting if the grounds upon which it was laid down have vanished long since, and the rule simply persists from blind imitation of the past.[174]

—O.W. Holmes

For a number of years, most of the litigation in this area involved former military personnel who had been discharged for homosexuality suing to get their records amended because they were not really homosexuals.[175] These attacks proceeded mostly on procedural grounds, and many involved claims that the military did not follow its own regulations.[176] In the 1970's the focus changed, and more of the litigation was from homosexuals who admitted their homosexuality, but were attacking military policy and regulations on constitutional grounds.[177] Some of the cases were decided on the constitutional issues. Others never got that far. This section reviews some of the legal theories advocated for and against these efforts.

A. SODOMY STATUTES

The statutory proscription of sodomy provides the moral bedrock on which the military builds its policy against homosexuals. The military statute, article 125, UCMJ, proscribes both homosexual and heterosexual sodomy. In *Hatheway v. Secretary of the Army*[178] Lieutenant Hatheway claimed that selective prosecution of homosexual sodomy under article 125 violated equal protection and that article 125 was unconstitutional as to private heterosexual acts. He also claimed that article 125 violated the first amendment prohibition respecting establishment of religion and that article 125 unconstitutionally violated his right to personal autonomy.

---

[174]Holmes, *The Path of the Law*, 10 Harv. L. Rev. 457, 469 (1897), *quoted in Bowers*, 478 U.S. at 199.

[175]*See* Rivera, *Our Straight-Laced Judges: The Legal Position of Homosexuals in the United States*, 30 Hastings L.J. 799, 841 (1979).

[176]*Id.*

[177]*Id.*

[178]Hatheway v. Secretary of the Army, 641 F.2d 1376 (9th Cir. 1981), *cert. denied*, 454 U.S. 864 (1981).

Hatheway lost. The Ninth Circuit Court of Appeals held that the convening authority selectively could prosecute those cases most likely to undermine military order and discipline, that Hatheway lacked standing as to private heterosexual acts, that article 125 has a legitimate secular purpose and effect, and that Hatheway's personal autonomy argument carried less weight than the government interests, especially because Hatheway's acts with a subordinate enlisted soldier had been viewed in a barracks by other enlisted soldiers.

The Supreme Court squarely addressed the constitutionality of a state's sodomy statute in 1986 in *Bowers v. Hardwick*. Framing the issue as "whether the Federal Constitution confers a fundamental right upon homosexuals to engage in sodomy and hence invalidates the laws of the many States that still make such conduct illegal and have done so for a very long time," the Court held that it did not.[179] Hardwick had challenged the Georgia sodomy statute, which prohibited all sodomy—both homosexual and heterosexual[180]—and which had been the law in Georgia since 1816.[181]

The Eleventh Circuit had held "that the Georgia statute violated Hardwick's fundamental rights because his homosexual activity is a private and intimate association that is beyond the reach of state regulation by reason of the Ninth Amendment and the Due Process Clause of the Fourteenth Amendment."[182]

Had the Supreme Court agreed to recognize a fundamental right to engage in sodomy, any law affecting the exercise of that right would have to be supported by a compelling government interest.[183] In deciding against Hardwick, the Court stated that there should be great resistance to expanding the substantive reach of the due process clause, particularly if it required redefining the category of fundamental rights.[184] Although Hardwick did not defend at the Supreme Court on the basis of the ninth amendment, the equal protection clause, or the eighth amendment, a four-justice dissent observed that those theories should have been considered anyway.[185]

---

[179] *Bowers*, 478 U.S. at 190, 196.

[180] *Id.* at 188 n.1.

[181] *Id.* at 197.

[182] *Id.* at 189. The Eleventh Circuit had relied on decisions in Roe v. Wade, 410 U.S. 113 (1973) (abortion case); Eisenstadt v. Baird, 405 U.S. 438 (1972) (contraception case); Stanley v. Georgia, 394 U.S. 557 (1969) (obscene material in privacy of home); and Griswold v. Connecticut, 381 U.S. 479 (1965) (contraception case).

[183] *See* cases cited *infra* note 200 and accompanying text.

[184] *Bowers*, 478 U.S. at 195.

[185] *Id.* at 197 n.8, 201-03.

B. LITIGATION ISSUES CONCERNING HOMOSEXUALITY REGULATIONS

1. Judicial Review of Military Discharge Determinations

Some litigation has involved homosexuals trying to get back into the military, and some has involved those trying legally to prevent their separation. In the latter category, personnel have sought declaratory and injunctive relief to preclude their discharge. Two such cases were *Berg v. Claytor*[186] and *Matlovich v. Secretary of the Air Force*.[187] Berg and Matlovich each raised the issue of whether private consensual homosexual activity between adults is protected constitutionally, but that issue was never resolved.

Judicial review of discretionary military administrative determinations generally is limited to ensuring that the action complained of is supported by substantial evidence and that it is not arbitrary, capricious, or unlawful.[188] The military enjoys a long history of judicial deference to military affairs.[189] One area in which the military is scrutinized closely is the application of its own regulations. The government lost both *Berg* and *Matlovich* because neither the Navy nor the Air Force could explain what criteria were used to determine whether to retain homosexual personnel. The court took the position that it could not provide review of either case until the services provided standards on which to base the review.[190]

Matlovich and *Berg* are the exceptions. The government ultimately has prevailed in most requests by homosexuals to preclude discharge.[191] *Rich v. Secretary of the Army*[192] illustrates the dilemma homosexuals sometimes face. In *Rich* an Army medical specialist challenged his involuntary discharge for fraudulent enlistment. The Army had determined that Rich falsely represented that he was not a homosexual on his reenlistment documents.

[186] 591 F.2d 849 (D.C. Cir. 1978).

[187] *Matlovich*, 591 F.2d 852; *see supra* text accompanying notes 150-58.

[188] *See, e.g.*, Miller v. Lehman, 801 F.2d 492, 496 (D.C. Cir. 1986) (decision of Board of Correction of Naval Records to deny relief); Smith v. Marsh, 787 F.2d 510, 512 (10th Cir. 1986) (decision of Army Board for Correction of Military Records to deny relief).

[189] *See, e.g.*, Goldman v. Weinberger, 475 U.S. 503 (1986); Brown v. Glines, 444 U.S. 348 (1980); Orloff v. Willoughby, 345 U.S. 83 (1953).

[190] Berg v. Claytor, 591 F.2d at 851, 857; *see also* Martinez v. Brown, 449 F. Supp. 207, 211 (N.D.Cal. 1978) (district court seeking articulation of factors used by Navy to retain homosexuals).

[191] *See, e.g.*, Beller v. Middendorf, 632 F.2d 788, 792, 798-99 (9th Cir. 1980), *cert. denied*, 452 U.S. 905 (1980) (plaintiff Beller), 454 U.S. 855 (1981) (plaintiff Miller) (three cases consolidated).

[192] Rich v. Secretary of the Army, 735 F.2d 1220 (10th Cir. 1984).

After noting that "the composition and qualifications of the armed forces is a matter for Congress and the military," the court held that "concealing or failing to disclose homosexuality in the enlistment process is material, and one doing so may be discharged for fraudulent enlistment."[193] Even though Rich claimed that he was not sure of his homosexuality until after he reenlisted, the court found enough evidence from a number of Rich's admissions to conclude that the Army's conclusions were not arbitrary, capricious, or unsupported by substantial evidence.

2. Fighting a War of Attrition: Exhaustion of Administrative Remedies as a Government Defense

Sometimes the constitutional issues never are reached because the homosexual plaintiff fails to exhaust administrative remedies, which usually means review by one of the various boards for correction of military or naval records.[194] Although that process can take from months to years,[195] it is favored because it gives the administrative agency an opportunity to correct the problem, possibly eliminating the need for judicial action, and because it develops a factual record upon which a court later can rely. An incidental benefit to the government is that during this process plaintiffs sometimes fail to pursue their claims and never are heard from again.

Courts will not require exhaustion of administrative remedies if the plaintiff can demonstrate that exhaustion would be a futile exercise. Elimination of the exhaustion requirement sometimes is seen in the homosexual cases, such as when a known homosexual faces an absolute prohibition against reenlisting.[196]

3. Constitutional Issues

a. Due Process

Homosexual litigants have raised a number of issues in their attempts to remain in the military. Two issues of historical interest are

---

[193]*Id.* at 1224 n.1, 1225.

[194]*E.g.*, Lauritzen v. Lehman, 736 F.2d 550 (9th Cir. 1984) (district court ordered plaintiff to seek review of discharge order from Board of Correction of Naval records, which granted plaintiff's request for relief); Von Hoffburg v. Alexander, 615 F.2d 633 (5th Cir. 1980) (female enlistee discharged after marrying a transsexual); Champagne v. Schlesinger, 506 F.2d 979 (7th Cir. 1974) (two Navy enlisted women appealing discharge for homosexuality); Krugler v. United States Army, 594 F. Supp. 565 (N.D. Ill. 1984) (dismissed for failure to exhaust).

[195]*E.g.*, *Von Hoffburg*, 615 F.2d at 642 n.17 (expressing concern that plaintiff's case had been pending before the ABCMR for two years).

[196]*E.g.*, *Beller*, 632 F.2d at 801.

fifth amendment procedural and substantive due process. Both of these issues were raised in *Beller v. Middendorf*,[197] a consolidation of three Navy cases.

The procedural due process issue requires inquiry into whether military discharge procedures deprive homosexuals of property or liberty interests without due process.[198] The property interest is the expectation of continued employment. In *Beller* all three plaintiffs had committed homosexual acts, which provided cause for dismissal under the Navy regulations. Once cause for dismissal existed, there could be no expectation of continued employment. "Therefore, unless the Navy as a substantive matter may not discharge all homosexuals, or unless it must consider factors in addition to homosexuality in its decision . . . we see no basis for inferring any expectation of continued service sufficient to constitute a constitutional property interest."[199]

Deprivation of a liberty interest could occur if military charges of homosexuality were false, made public, and followed by discharge. These actions might damage standing and associations within the community. They also might impose a stigma or disability affecting employment opportunities.[200] The *Beller* court found that liberty interests were protected by the military practice of conducting predischarge hearings at which respondents could present evidence to support their arguments that they should be retained.[201]

Substantive due process requires that laws be at least rationally related to some legitimate government interest. If the law in question impacts on what the Supreme Court has described as fundamental rights—such as procreation, choice of a marriage partner, or family planning—the law is given heightened scrutiny.[202] In these cases, the law must further a compelling state interest and provide the least restrictive way to meet that interest. Prior to *Bowers v. Hardwick*, homosexuals often argued that private, consensual, adult homosexual activity should be protected as an aspect of the fundamental right of privacy.

---

[197] *Id.*

[198] *Id.* at 805 (citing Board of Regents v. Roth, 408 U.S. 564 (1972)).

[199] *Id.*

[200] *Id.* at 806 (citing *Roth*, 408 U.S. at 573).

[201] *Id.*

[202] *See, e.g.*, Griswold v. Connecticut, 381 U.S. 479 (1965) (contraceptive statute infringed on fundamental right of privacy); Loving v. Virginia, 388 U.S. 1 (1967) (miscegenation statute infringed on fundamental right to marry); Roe v. Wade, 410 U.S. 113 (1973) (concerning abortion statute); Eisenstadt v. Baird, 405 U.S. 438 (1972) (statute prohibiting distribution of contraceptives to unmarried persons infringed on fundamental right of privacy).

The *Beller* court avoided the issue of whether consensual private homosexual conduct was a fundamental right, and instead focused on whether the military regulation violated due process. In doing so, the court abandoned the rational basis and compelling state interest tests used in equal protection analysis. It chose instead a "case-by-case balancing of the nature of the individual interest allegedly infringed, the importance of the government interests furthered, the degree of infringement, and the sensitivity of the government entity responsible for the regulation to more carefully tailored alternative means of achieving its goals."[203]

In this balance, the court was more impressed with the weight of the Navy arguments. The Navy provided several reasons for its policy.

> The Navy "perceive[s] that homosexuality adversely impacts on the effective and efficient performance of the mission . . . in several particulars." The Navy is concerned about tensions between known homosexuals and other members who "despise/detest homosexuality"; undue influence in various contexts caused by an emotional relationship between two members; doubts concerning a homosexual officer's ability to command the respect and trust of the personnel he or she commands; and possible adverse impact on recruiting. These concerns are especially serious, says the Navy, where enlisted personnel must on occasion be in confined situations for long periods.[204]

The court concluded that the regulation was a reasonable effort to accommodate the needs of the government with the interests of the individual.[205] The court also noted that "[t]he due process clause does not require the Government to show with particularity that the reasons for the general policy of discharging homosexuals from the Navy exist in a particular case before discharge is permitted," and that discharge of the plaintiffs "would be rational, under minimal scrutiny, not because their particular cases present the dangers which justify Navy policy, but instead because the general policy of discharging all homosexuals is rational."[206]

---

[203] *Beller*, 632 F.2d at 807.
[204] *Id.* at 811.
[205] *Id.* at 812.
[206] *Id.* at 808 n.20.

b. The First Amendment

The government has not won all of the homosexuality cases. In *Ben-Shalom v. Secretary of the Army*, a case involving a homosexual Army reservist, Army regulations promulgated in the 1970's were held to be unconstitutional insofar as they allowed discharge for homosexual tendencies, desire, or interest.[207] The issue had been framed as "whether petitioner can be discharged from the Army (even if the discharge is 'honorable') simply because she is a homosexual, although there is no showing that her sexual preferences interfered with her abilities as a soldier or adversely affected other members of the Service."[208]

All prior military homosexual litigation had involved homosexual acts. Miriam Ben-Shalom admitted she was a homosexual, but the Army had no proof that she had engaged in homosexual acts or had made homosexual advances. After being discharged as unsuitable because of her homosexuality, Ben-Shalom brought a mandamus action to compel her reinstatement.

The problematic word in the regulation was "interest." The court found the regulation to be overbroad because it substantially impinged upon the first amendment rights of every soldier to free association, expression, and speech.[209]

> The Army's interests in protecting the national defense, maintaining discipline and upholding the law of obedience under the "peculiar" conditions of military life, are time-honored and given great respect by all courts, including this one. They are, however, substantially outweighed by the "chill" imposed on the First Amendment liberties of its soldiers by this regulation. The court can see no detrimental effect on any legitimate military interest caused by a soldier who merely "evidences" a "tendency, desire, or interest" in most anything, including homosexuality.[210]

The court found violations of the constitutionally protected right of personal privacy at two different levels. On one level, the regulation chilled the right of soldiers to associate freely with known or

[207] *Ben-Shalom*, 489 F. Supp. 964; *see supra* text accompanying notes 155-58.
[208] *Ben-Shalom*, 489 F. Supp. at 969.
[209] *Id.* at 973-74.
[210] *Id.* at 974.

87

suspected homosexuals (the court having found the right of association in the penumbral zone of privacy created by the first amendment).[211] On a different level, the regulation was defective insofar as personnel could be discharged for having a homosexual personality.

> Certainly, the "peculiar" nature of military life and the need for discipline gives the Army substantial leeway in exercising control over the sexual conduct of its soldiers, at least while on duty and at the barracks. This court, however, will not defer to the Army's attempt to control a soldier's sexual preferences, absent a showing of actual deviant conduct and absent proof of a nexus between the sexual preference and the soldier's military capabilities.[212]

The writ of mandamus was issued, the Army did not appeal, and the Army changed its regulations.[213] Soon after, the Department of Defense directed all the services to implement new regulations.[214] The issue of the homosexual personality, however, keeps coming back.

Consider Reverend (former Captain) Dusty Pruitt.[215] The Army had no evidence that she had committed any homosexual acts, but learned of her homosexual status after the Los Angeles Times article, *Pastor Resolves Gay, God Conflict*, described her as a lesbian.[216] Captain Pruitt admitted to her commander that she was a homosexual, and she was discharged. She claimed that the regulation under which she was discharged from the Army reserve violated the first amendment because it called for punishment solely on the basis of her assertion of homosexual status.[217]

The court did not question the constitutionality of the Army policy. Nor did it find the regulation to be overly broad. It noted that the Army "understandably would be apprehensive of the prospect that desire would ripen into attempt or actual performance."[218]

---

[211]*Id.* at 975-76 (citing *Griswold*, 381 U.S. at 484-85).
[212]*Id.* at 976.
[213]*See supra* text accompanying notes 155-58.
[214]*Id.*
[215]Pruitt v. Weinberger, 659 F. Supp. 625 (C.D. Cal. 1987), *appeal filed*, No. 83-2035 (9th Cir. 1989).
[216]*Id.* at 627.
[217]*Id.*
[218]*Id.*

Miriam Ben-Shalom raised the issue again in 1988 after the Army refused to reenlist her into the Army reserve under its new policy.[219] She argued "that the new regulation had the effect of chilling her freedom of expression as she would no longer be able to make statements regarding her sexual orientation, statements that she would otherwise be free to make."[220] The district court agreed, but the Seventh Circuit Court of Appeals did not.

> Ben-Shalom is free under the regulation to say anything she pleases *about* homosexuality and about the Army's policy toward homosexuality. She is free to advocate that the Army change its stance; she is free to know and talk to homosexuals if she wishes. What Ben-Shalom cannot do, and remain in the Army, is to declare herself to *be* a homosexual.[221]

Exclusion based on being a homosexual, as opposed to talking about homosexuality or committing homosexual acts, raises the issue of equal protection.

c. Equal Protection

The equal protection clause requires that all persons similarly situated be treated alike.[222] The Supreme Court has found an implied equal protection component in the fifth amendment due process clause,[223] and the Court has treated federal equal protection claims under the fifth amendment the same as state equal protection claims under the fourteenth amendment.[224]

1. Levels of Scrutiny Under Equal Protection Analysis

The highest level of equal protection scrutiny is strict scrutiny. At this level, legislation (and, by extension, regulations) burdening a class unequally will be sustained only if tailored to serve a compelling governmental interest. Two categories of legislation are subject to strict scrutiny: statutes that classify by race, alienage, or national origin (often called suspect classes); and statutes that impinge on personal rights protected by the Constitution.[225]

---

[219]*Ben-Shalom*, 881 F.2d 454.
[220]*Id.* at 457.
[221]*Id.* at 462.
[222]Plyler v. Doe, 457 U.S. 202, 216 (1982).
[223]*See* Bolling v. Sharpe, 347 U.S. 497, 499 (1954).
[224]*See, e.g.*, Weinberger v. Wiesenfeld, 420 U.S. 636, 638 n.2 (1975).
[225]*Id.*

89

The Supreme Court also has recognized a middle area of somewhat heightened scrutiny when legislation burdening a class unequally fails unless it is substantially related to a sufficiently important governmental interest. Classifications based on gender and illegitimacy (often called quasi-suspect classes) are given such review.[226] The Court has not extended suspect or quasi-suspect class status beyond the categories mentioned.[227]

If legislation does not qualify for strict or heightened scrutiny, it must pass the rational basis test.

> The general rule is that legislation is presumed valid and will be sustained if the classification drawn by the statute is rationally related to a legitimate interest. When social or economic legislation is at issue, the Equal Protection Clause allows the States wide latitude, and the Constitution presumes that even improvident decisions will eventually be rectified by the democratic processes.[228]

Under this deferential standard of scrutiny, it does not matter if an individual member of the burdened class is an exception.[229] Therefore, if regulations pertaining to homosexual service members need only meet the rational basis test, the fact that a homosexual service member might be outstanding in every respect is irrelevant. The inquiry is directed at the regulation, not the service member.

2. The Two Prongs of Equal Protection

As Justice Brennan once wrote, "discrimination against homosexuals or bisexuals based solely on their sexual preference raises significant constitutional questions under both prongs of our settled equal protection analysis."[230] The prongs, which require different analysis, are whether the regulation burdening a class unequally does so by 1) impinging on a fundamental right protected by the Constitution, or 2) affecting a class entitled to heightened scrutiny or suspect class status.[231]

---

[226]*Id.* at 440-41.

[227]The suspect class cases include: Graham v. Richardson, 403 U.S. 365, 372 (1971) (alienage); Loving v. Virginia, 388 U.S. 1, 11 (1967) (race); and Korematsu v. United States, 323 U.S. 214, 216 (1944) (national origin). The quasi-suspect class cases include: Mississippi University for Women v. Hogan, 458 U.S. 718, 723-24 (1982) (gender); Lalli v. Lalli, 439 U.S. 259, 265 (1978) (illegitimacy).

[228]City of Cleburne v. Cleburne Living Center, 473 U.S. 432, 440 (1984).

[229]Massachusetts Bd. of Retirement v. Murgia, 427 U.S. 307, 310-11 (1976).

[230]Rowland v. Mad River Local School Dist., 470 U.S. 1009, 1014 (1985) (Brennan, J., dissenting from denial of cert.).

[231]*See, e.g.*, Plyler v. Doe, 457 U.S. 202, 216-17 (1982).

a. Fundamental Rights

The "fundamental rights" prong of equal protection easily is confused with substantive due process fundamental rights analysis, but it involves a different inquiry. *Bowers v. Hardwick* illustrates this.[232] The Supreme Court held that there is no fundamental right to engage in sodomy. Applying substantive due process analysis, the Court refused to invalidate a longstanding law that presumably reflected the will of the Georgia citizenry. It is tempting to leap to the conclusion that because homosexuals traditionally have been defined by their acts (engaging in sodomy), and because those acts are not protected, then there cannot be a fundamental right to be a homosexual.

The equal protection focus should not be on whether a homosexual has the fundamental right to engage in sodomy; it should be on whether a homosexual has the fundamental right to be a homosexual. Clearly, since *Bowers v. Hardwick*, there is no constitutional right to engage in homosexual sodomy. Still, a person can have a homosexual orientation without engaging in proscribed homosexual acts, just as a person can have a heterosexual orientation without engaging in proscribed heterosexual acts.

The question of whether a person has a fundamental right to have the sexual orientation that he or she develops through forces beyond personal control is far different from the question of whether there is a right to commit sodomy. Laws and regulations can and do change. While anyone can refrain from doing an act proscribed by law or regulation, however, no one can refrain from being who he or she is.

Bowers v. Hardwick did not foreclose either branch of the equal protection analysis as to homosexual orientation.[233] It was a due process case, and the Court explicitly did not decide it on the basis of the equal protection clause.[234] The only reference to equal protection analysis was in a footnote of the dissent. Justice Blackmun, after referring to the possible equal protection issue of discriminatory enforcement of gender-neutral sodomy statutes, said "a claim under the Equal Protection Clause may well be available without having to reach the more controversial question whether homosexuals are a suspect class."[235]

[232] *Bowers*, 478 U.S. 186.

[233] *Contra* Padula v. Webster, 822 F.2d 97 (D.C. Cir. 1987) (holding that homosexuality could not be a suspect classification because conduct that defines the class is not constitutionally protected).

[234] 478 U.S. at 196 n.8.

[235] *Id.* at 202 n.2.

Under the fundamental rights prong of equal protection, regulations that burden a particular class by impinging on a fundamental right must meet strict scrutiny. To the extent that homosexuality regulations impinge upon the right to be homosexual, as opposed to the commission of an illegal act, these regulations should be required to meet a compelling state interest. Future litigation should focus on this prong.[236]

But, given the Court's disinclination to take a more expansive view of its authority to discover new fundamental rights imbedded in the due process clause, it seems unlikely that the Court will be inclined to discover new fundamental rights based on equal protection.[237] That is unfortunate for homosexuals because, regardless of the Constitution, their homosexual orientation is a fundamental aspect of their lives. The remaining inquiry, raised by *Watkins v. United States Army*, is whether the other prong of equal protection analysis applies.[238]

b. Suspect/Quasi-Suspect Class

The Supreme Court has identified a number of factors for deciding whether a statute burdens a suspect or quasi-suspect class. These include the following: whether the class in question has suffered a history of purposeful discrimination;[239] whether it is defined by a trait that frequently bears no relation to ability to perform or contribute to society;[240] whether the class has been saddled with unique disabilities because of prejudice or inaccurate stereotypes;[241] whether the trait defining the class is immutable;[242] and whether the class has the political power necessary to obtain redress from the political branches of government.[243]

---

[236]*But see* Rich v. Secretary of the Army, 735 F.2d 1220, 1229 (10th Cir. 1984) (homosexuality classification not suspect, but valid even under heightened scrutiny in light of Army's demonstration of a compelling government interest).

[237]*See* 478 U.S. at 194.

[238]Watkins v. United States Army, 875 F.2d 699 (9th Cir. 1989) (en banc).

[239]*See, e.g.*, *Cleburne*, 473 U.S. at 441; *Murgia*, 427 U.S. at 307; San Antonio School Dist. v. Rodriguez, 411 U.S. 1, 28 (1973).

[240]Mathews v. Lucas, 427 U.S. 495, 505 (1976) (illegitimacy); Frontiero v. Richardson, 411 U.S. 677, 686 (1973) (gender).

[241]*See Cleburne*, 473 U.S. at 440-41.

[242]*See Plyler*, 457 U.S. at 216 n.14, 219 n.19, 220, 223; *Frontiero*, 411 U.S. at 685-87. *But see Cleburne*, 473 U.S. at 440-41 (defining characteristics of suspect classes without mentioning immutability); *Murgia*, 427 U.S. at 313 (same); *Rodriguez*, 411 U.S. at 28 (same).

[243]*See, e.g.*, *Cleburne*, 473 U.S. at 441; *Plyler*, 457 U.S. at 216 n.14; *Rodriguez*, 411 U.S. at 28.

Judge Norris, concurring in *Watkins*, found all of these factors applicable to homosexuals. Nevertheless, there is room for disagreement with some of his conclusions.[244] There is no doubt that homosexuals have suffered a history of purposeful discrimination. In *Watkins*, the Army conceded this point.[245] Likewise, the trait of homosexual orientation does not correlate with ability to perform or contribute to society. Not only is history replete with accounts of homosexuals who have contributed a great deal to society,[246] but aside from sexual orientation, researchers cannot distinguish between homosexuals and heterosexuals.[247]

The question of whether homosexuals have been saddled with unique disabilities because of prejudice or inaccurate stereotypes is more difficult. Asking the question begs the issue. The criminalization of some of the behavior that identifies a homosexual as such is a unique disability, but it is also constitutional. In the military context, the unique disability is not being allowed to serve, which also has been upheld as constitutional. The law often is based on notions of morality that may be prejudicial and based on inaccurate stereotypes. Judge Norris suggests that the "irrelevance of sexual orientation to the quality of a person's contribution to society also suggests that classifications based on sexual orientation reflect prejudice and inaccurate stereotypes."[248]

Homosexual orientation is immutable. While it is not a visible manifestation like skin color or gender, as Justice Blackmun wrote in *Bowers v. Hardwick*, "neither is it simply a matter of deliberate personal election. Homosexual orientation may well form part of the very fiber of an individual's personality."[249] If homosexual orientation is mutable, it is only so with great difficulty, and the likelihood of it truly being changed is very low.[250]

The final factor is whether the class has the political power necessary to obtain redress from the political branches of government. About half the states have repealed their sodomy laws, and as of 1990 there were two openly homosexual members of Con-

---

[244] *Watkins*, 875 F.2d at 724-28.

[245] *Id.* at 724.

[246] *See, e.g.*, T. Cowan, *supra* note 104.

[247] *See supra* text accompanying note 93.

[248] 875 F.2d at 725.

[249] *Bowers*, 478 U.S. at 202 n.2. *Contra* Woodward v. United States, 871 F.2d 1068, 1076 (Fed. Cir. 1989) (homosexuality not immutable because primarily behavioral in nature).

[250] *See supra* text accompanying notes 43-44.

gress.[251] California and Wisconsin have passed statutes prohibiting discrimination against homosexuals.[252] The Civil Service Reform Act of 1978 has been interpreted to mean that homosexuality by itself is not a disqualification for federal employment.[253] The most significant display of homosexual political power has been in the cities:

> In many major cities with significant gay populations, political organization of the gay community has advanced far enough to secure the enactment of local ordinances prohibiting such [anti-gay] discrimination. Since the early 1970s, more than fifty cities or other political subdivisions (counties or districts) have passed such ordinances, including most of the major centers of gay life in America, such as Boston, New York, Los Angeles, San Francisco, Atlanta, the District of Columbia (Washington, D.C.) and Philadelphia.[254]

Judge Norris noted that the relevant political level for seeking protection from military discrimination is the national level, "where homosexuals have been wholly unsuccessful in getting legislation passed that protects them from discrimination."[255] He stated that "homosexuals as a group cannot protect their right to be free from invidious discrimination by appealing to the political branches."[256] There is much evidence to the contrary, however, and it is unlikely that the Supreme Court would hold that homosexuals are such a politically powerless group.

Homosexuals should not get suspect class status under this prong of equal protection analysis because they are not politically powerless. Because they have suffered purposeful discrimination and are defined by an immutable trait unrelated to their contributions to society, homosexuals may yet achieve quasi-suspect status. Without this status, regulations impinging upon homosexuals need only be rationally related to a legitimate government interest.

3. Equal Protection Applied to Homosexuality Regulations

The fifth amendment equal protection issue, as framed in *Ben-Shalom III*, is "whether homosexuals, defined by the status of hav-

---

[251]A. Leonard, *supra* note 162, at 103-04.
[252]*Watkins*, 875 F.2d at 727 n.30.
[253]A. Leonard, *supra* note 162, at 102.
[254]*Id.* at 106.
[255]*Watkins*, 875 F.2d at 727 n.30.
[256]*Id.* at 727.

ing a particular sexual orientation and absent any allegations of sexual misconduct, constitute a suspect or quasi-suspect class."[257] The same issue was raised in *Watkins*.[258]

The appellate courts in both *Watkins* and *Ben-Shalom III* declined to extend suspect or quasi-suspect class status to homosexuals. These cases were not argued on the basis of the fundamental rights prong of equal protection. In *Watkins* a panel of the Ninth Circuit found that homosexuals were a suspect class and that the Army failed to provide a compelling reason for its homosexuality regulations.[259] The Ninth Circuit, en banc, then decided the case in favor of Watkins on an estoppel theory, and withdrew the earlier *Watkins* opinion.[260] The equal protection issues were addressed only in the en banc concurring opinion of Judge Norris, joined by Judge Canby.

The *Ben-Shalom III* court reasoned that if "homosexual conduct may constitutionally be criminalized, then homosexuals do not constitute a suspect or quasi-suspect class entitled to greater than rational basis scrutiny for equal protection purposes."[261] The court applied rational basis scrutiny and found that the Army met that standard without difficulty.[262]

The Supreme Court declined to hear *Ben-Shalom III* without comment. A denial of certiorari does not carry the weight of an affirmance, nor does it mean that the Supreme Court agreed with the decision of the Court of Appeals.[263] Nevertheless, it does signal that the Court is not likely to hear similar cases any time soon unless a split develops among the circuits.

Judge Norris, concurring in *Watkins*, evaluated the equal protection claim with a three-stage inquiry.[264] First, do the regulations actually discriminate based on sexual orientation? Second, which level of judicial scrutiny applies? Third, do the regulations survive the applicable level of scrutiny?

a. Do Regulations Discriminate Based on Homosexual Orientation?

Equal protection requires that people be treated equally. If a

---

[257] *Ben-Shalom*, 881 F.2d at 463.
[258] *Watkins*, 875 F.2d at 699.
[259] Watkins v. United States Army, 847 F.2d 1329 (9th Cir. 1988).
[260] *Watkins*, 875 F.2d at 711.
[261] *Ben-Shalom*, 881 F.2d at 464.
[262] *Id.*
[263] 36 C.J.S. *Federal Courts* § 204 (1960).
[264] *Watkins*, 875 F.2d at 712.

regulation affects everyone equally, there should be no equal protection problem. Everyone in the military is capable of committing homosexual acts, and there is little disagreement that the military lawfully can proscribe these acts by its personnel. Everyone in the military does not have a homosexual orientation, however, and there is much disagreement over regulating what a person is, as opposed to what a person does. To the extent that a regulation affects or burdens only one class of the population—those with the homosexual orientation—the threshold inquiry is met.

Military homosexuality regulations since 1982 uniformly have emphasized the unsuitability for military purposes of people with homosexual orientations.[265] In contrast, the military has exceptions allowing accession and retention of people who have committed homosexual acts, but they only apply to people who do not have a homosexual orientation. There are no exceptions for people with homosexual orientations.

Judge Wood, writing for the *Ben-Shalom III* court, resolved the issue by finding that homosexuals are likely to commit prohibited homosexual acts. He found that the regulation classified upon reasonable inferences of probable conduct in the past and in the future. "The Army need not shut its eyes to the practical realities of this situation, nor be compelled to engage in the sleuthing of soldiers' personal relationships for evidence of homosexual conduct in order to enforce its ban on homosexual acts, a ban not challenged here."[266]

Whether the military decides to go sleuthing after the class most likely to commit the proscribed acts, the inquiry still is whether the regulations affect or burden everyone equally. The answer is that they do not. At least as far as this threshold question is concerned, Judge Norris provided the correct analysis in his concurring opinion in *Watkins.*[267]

> On their face, these regulations discriminate against homosexuals on the basis of their sexual orientation. Under the regulations any homosexual act or statement of homosexuality gives rise to a presumption of homosexual orientation, and anyone who fails to rebut that presumption is conclusively barred from Army service. In other words, the regulations target homosex-

[265]*See* sources cited *supra* notes 14, 158-61.
[266]*Ben-Shalom*, 881 F.2d at 464.
[267]*Watkins*, 875 F.2d at 712-16.

ual orientation itself. The homosexual acts and statements are merely relevant, and rebuttable, indicators of that orientation.[268]

b. Which Level of Judicial Scrutiny Applies?

The question of whether a regulation affecting homosexuals as a class should be given strict scrutiny, heightened scrutiny, or rational basis scrutiny depends on whether the regulation is more like one affecting the following: 1) race, alienage, or national origin; 2) gender or legitimacy; or 3) a legitimate government interest.

Almost all courts that have considered this issue have applied rational basis scrutiny. Those not applying rational basis scrutiny have been overruled.[269] Judge Norris, concurring in *Watkins*, supported strict scrutiny,[270] but he believed homosexuals are a politically powerless group. Homosexual regulations may one day be judged with heightened scrutiny because homosexuals have several of the characteristics of a suspect class.[271]

c. Do the Regulations Survive the Applicable Level of Scrutiny?

If the strict scrutiny standard applied, the homosexuality regulations would have to be tailored to meet a compelling government interest. Even under a standard of review deferential to the military, it is unlikely that the current regulations could withstand this scrutiny. The government has won only one compelling state interest case—the World War II era national origin case of *Korematsu v. United States*.[272] A review of homosexuality regulations is not likely to succeed under the equal protection suspect class theory, but it could with a fundamental rights theory.

If heightened scrutiny applied, the regulation would have to be substantially related to a sufficiently important government interest. The government interest is articulated in Department of Defense Directive 1332.14:

> Homosexuality is incompatible with military service. The presence in the military environment of persons who engage in homosexual conduct or who, by their statements, demon-

[268] *Id.* at 714.
[269] *See, e.g.*, *Ben-Shalom*, 881 F.2d at 454; *Watkins*, 875 F.2d at 699.
[270] *Watkins*, 875 F.2d at 724-28.
[271] *See supra* text accompanying notes 240-57.
[272] Korematsu v. United States, 323 U.S. 214 (1944).

strate a propensity to engage in homosexual conduct, seriously impairs the accomplishment of the military mission. The presence of such members adversely affects the ability of the Military Services to maintain discipline, good order, and morale; to foster mutual trust and confidence among service members; to ensure the integrity of the system of rank and command; to facilitate assignment and worldwide deployment of service members who frequently must live and work under close conditions affording minimal privacy; to recruit and retain members of the Military Services; to maintain the public acceptability of military service; and to prevent breaches of security.[273]

The military mission is an important government interest. The question is whether the military policy of excluding all homosexuals is substantially related to accomplishment of the mission. This inquiry first requires an examination of whether the presence of homosexuals prevents or hinders the military from accomplishing the mission. During this examination, the military gets deferential treatment. In military affairs, a court should not substitute its views for the "considered professional judgment" of the military.[274]

Because there always have been and probably always will be homosexuals in the military, it cannot tenably be argued that homosexuals prevent the military from accomplishing its mission. Nevertheless, any disruption to military affairs arguably hinders the military mission. Given the deference normally accorded the military, an assault on the regulations under heightened scrutiny probably would be resolved in the military's favor.

The remaining question is similar to the one raised by Justice Brennan in *Rowland*:

> Finally, even if adverse state action based on homosexual *conduct* were held valid under application of traditional equal protection principles, such approval would not answer the question, posed here, whether the mere nondisruptive *expression* of homosexual preference can pass muster even under a minimum rationality standard as the basis for discharge from public employment.[275]

---

[273]DOD Dir. 1332.14.

[274]Goldman v. Weinberger, 475 U.S. 503, 508 (1986); Rostker v. Goldberg, 453 U.S. 57, 65-66 (1981); Orloff v. Willoughby, 345 U.S. 83, 93, 94 (1953).

[275]Rowland v. Mad River Local School Dist., 470 U.S. 1009, 1016 (1985) (Brennan, J., dissenting from denial of cert.).

Is there such thing as "nondisruptive expression of homosexual preference" in the military setting? The minimum rationality standard requires only that the classification drawn by the government regulation rationally further some legitimate, articulated governmental purpose.[276]

The first question is whether the purpose of military homosexuality policy constitutes a legitimate governmental purpose. The stated purpose is preventing the impairment of the military mission. It would be difficult to attack such a broad statement of purpose. The government clearly has an interest in the accomplishment of the military mission.

The second question is whether the regulation rationally furthers the stated purpose. To the extent that homosexual activity is regulated, it does. In the military environment, any sexual activity tends to be disruptive. To the extent that homosexual orientation is regulated, it does not. A person's sexual orientation has nothing to do with the military mission. With the issues commingled, the regulation has so far passed minimum scrutiny.[277]

The fact that military homosexuality regulations have survived legal attacks does not mean that they cannot or should not be improved. It means only that the courts are not going to make it happen. It is up to the military to come up with the best policy without court intervention.

V. POLICY PERSPECTIVES

In January 1982 the Department of Defense issued new guidelines stating that homosexual offenses did not actually have to be committed to separate military personnel from the service; intent was what mattered.[278]

A. BASIS FOR CURRENT POLICY

"Homosexuality is incompatible with military service. The presence in the military environment of persons who engage in homosexual conduct or who, by their statements, demonstrate a propensity to engage in homosexual conduct, seriously impairs the accomplishment

[276]McGinnis v. Royster, 410 U.S. 268, 270 (1973).
[277]*E.g.*, *Ben-Shalom*, 881 F.2d at 464; *Woodward*, 871 F.2d at 1076; Dronenburg v. Zech, 741 F.2d 1388, 1398 (D.C. Cir. 1984).
[278]DOD Dir. 1332.14.

of the military mission."[279] These opening sentences of the policy refer to both conduct and speech that seriously impair the mission.

A person, whether homosexual or heterosexual, engaging in sexual conduct in a military environment, may well distract or detract from the mission. There are also situations in which the statements of a person with homosexual tendencies could create a problem for the mission, such as if a homosexual soldier were to solicit another soldier to engage in homosexual acts. Presumably, this is what the drafters of the policy had in mind. What is not clear is how missions are impaired by statements not involving solicitation, but which still demonstrate a propensity to engage in homosexual conduct.

"The presence of such members adversely affects the ability of the Military Services to maintain discipline, good order, and morale . . . ."[280] There is little argument as to personnel who commit homosexual acts in barracks, aircraft, on board ship, or on duty. Similar problems would be expected with personnel who commit heterosexual acts in such places or situations. Even with homosexual acts, though, it becomes difficult to see how these discipline problems occur when the acts are off government property with nonmilitary personnel. These cases often involve an act of sodomy, which, if discovered, can be prosecuted or dealt with administratively. The real effect on discipline is negligible. Outside those with an official need to know, few military personnel even will be aware of these acts until the military initiates adverse action.

It also is difficult to see how the presence of personnel who admit to a homosexual orientation adversely affects the maintenance of good order. About seventy-five percent of the homosexual personnel never are discovered at all, so they are not causing these problems.[281] Of course, neither are they talking about the fact of their homosexual orientation. If they had the freedom to discuss it openly, it is doubtful that they would choose to do so in a hostile environment. If such a person does cause a problem with order, morale, or discipline, and it can be articulated and proven, then he or she should be separated. Conversely, if a real problem cannot be articulated or proven, there should be no separation.

"The presence of such members adversely affects the ability of the Military Services to. . . foster mutual trust and confidence among

[279] *Id.*
[280] *Id.*
[281] *See supra* text accompanying notes 73-85.

servicemembers. . . ."[282] Here the military position is that the great majority of service members "despise/detest homosexuality."[283] Even if that is so, it does not necessarily follow that the great majority despise homosexuals. Personnel who work hard and make an effort to get along foster mutual trust and confidence. Those who do not tend to be despised and detested and are bid good riddance if they can be separated for any reason.

There also have been times when the "great majority" was not too keen on the idea of allowing minorities and women in the military. "The peculiar nature of Army life has always required the melding together of disparate personalities. For much of our history, the military's fear of racial tension kept black soldiers segregated from whites. Fear of sexual tensions, until very recently, kept the participation of female soldiers to a minimum."[284]

The military should not allow the fear of prejudice to drive its personnel policy. Even if the basic homosexuality policy does not change, the supporting rationale should be purged of arguments based on prejudice.

"The presence of such members adversely affects the ability of the Military Services to. . .ensure the integrity of the system of rank and command. . ."[285] The fear is that openly homosexual supervisors could not command respect.[286] This problem, however, is solved best by leadership training and by rating supervisors on their leadership abilities. Cases such as those of Technical Sergeant Leonard Matlovich and Staff Sergeant Perry Watkins—homosexual personnel who received outstanding ratings in all aspects of performance—demonstrate that even openly homosexual supervisors can do well in the military.[287] Perhaps the ability to command respect is more a function of leadership than sexual orientation. "The presence of such members adversely affects the ability of the Military Services to. . .facilitate assignment and worldwide deployment of service members who frequently must live and work under close conditions affording minimal privacy. . . ."[288] Even in a sexually integrated military, men and women do not share showers and close living

---

[282]DOD Dir. 1332.14.
[283]*See, e.g.*, *Watkins*, 875 F.2d at 728; *Beller*, 632 F.2d at 811 n.22.
[284]*Ben-Shalom*, 489 F. Supp. at 976.
[285]DOD Dir. 1332.14.
[286]*See, e.g.*, *Watkins*, 875 F.2d at 729; *Beller*, 632 F.2d at 811 n.22.
[287]*Matlovich*, 591 F.2d at 854; *Watkins*, 875 F.2d at 704.
[288]DOD Dir. 1332.14.

quarters because of basic privacy considerations. These privacy considerations are just as applicable to heterosexuals and homosexuals of the same gender. Nevertheless, that appears to be a unit level management problem, not an "assignment and worldwide deployment problem."

"The presence of such members adversely affects the ability of the Military Services to. . . recruit and retain members of the Military Services. . . ."[289] As the American military historically has excluded homosexuals, it is difficult to understand what leads to this conclusion other than conjecture. It is just as easy to surmise that a more limited policy to exclude or punish personnel who commit homosexual acts in barracks or on ship would be sufficient to meet these concerns.

"The presence of such members adversely affects the ability of the Military Services to. . . maintain the public acceptability of military service. . . ."[290] There always will be some people for whom military service will not be acceptable under any policies or circumstances. Assuming the fears are legitimate, they arguably could be assuaged with a focus on acts rather than orientation.

"The presence of such members adversely affects the ability of the Military Services to. . . prevent breaches of security."[291] A breach of security could occur if a homosexual or bisexual with access to classified information was blackmailed with the threat of disclosure to his family or superiors. Judge Norris addressed this issue in *Watkins.*

> It is evident, however, that homosexuality poses a special risk of blackmail only if a homosexual is secretive about his or her sexual orientation. The Army's regulations do nothing to lessen this problem. Quite the opposite, the regulations ban homosexuals only after they have declared their homosexuality or have engaged in known homosexual acts. The Army's concern about security risks among gays could be addressed in a more sensible and less restrictive manner by adopting a regulation banning only those gays who had lied about or failed to admit their sexual orientation. In that way the Army would *encourage*, rather than discourage, declarations of homosexuality, thereby reducing the number of closet homosexuals who might indeed pose a security risk.[292]

---

[289] *Id.*
[290] *Id.*
[291] *Id.*
[292] *Watkins*, 875 F.2d at 731.

Or, as stated by Representative Gerry Studds in 1989: "The question is not whether gay men and women will serve. The only question is will they be compelled by Defense Department policy to hide."[293]

B. PROBLEMS WITH CURRENT POLICY

Is the current policy in need of adjustment? Yes. The military views a person who admits to a homosexual orientation as a crime waiting to happen who should be expelled immediately.

A policy that deprives people of opportunity because of what they are, as opposed to what they do, is contrary to American ideals. The letter of the law may not be violated, but the spirit is. In equating admissions of homosexual orientation with illegal homosexual conduct, military policy turns the presumption of innocence on its head.

Does the policy work? It is taken as a given that people with a homosexual orientation simply are incompatible with military service. Yet, the incidence of homosexual men is about the same in the military as it is in the general population, and the incidence of homosexual women is greater in the military than in the general population.[294] While seventy-five percent never are detected, a portion of the twenty-five percent who are detected simply turn themselves in when they decide they want to get out.[295] The system is not broken; it never worked to begin with.

People who know they have a homosexual orientation and who want to serve in the military are faced with a dilemma: disclose and be excluded, or lie and hide. The policy excludes those who are truthful, while accepting those who choose to lie. Personnel who do not discover their orientation until after they are on active duty face a similar dilemma. If they are troubled by their discovery, they cannot seek help without being separated. The people needing help the most, therefore, are discouraged from seeking it, but they still will be operating our multi-million dollar weapon systems while they try to sort out their sexuality.

None of this is to say that personnel who are disruptive should be admitted or retained on active duty. Some homosexual personnel are and will be disruptive, just as some heterosexual personnel are and

---

[293]*Rethinking DOD Policy on Gays*, The Washington Post, Nov. 6, 1989, at A 11, col. 1.
[294]*See supra* text accompanying notes 73-85.
[295]*See supra* text accompanying notes 88-96.

will be disruptive. Policy should be crafted to allow the exclusion of disruptive personnel, but it should be crafted so it does not create as many problems as it solves.

C. PROPOSALS FOR MODIFICATION

1. Statutory

The military sodomy statute, article 125, UCMJ, is overbroad.[296] The real problem for the military is not the service member who engages in sexual activity on his or her own time, away from the military installation or vessel. The problem is the service member who disrupts the military mission through an inappropriate choice of the place or partner for the sexual activity. Sexual intercourse, whether of the homosexual or heterosexual variety, should be prohibited on duty, in the barracks, on board ships or aircraft, or in situations that would create the appearance or prospect of favoritism within a chain of command.

2. Regulatory

a. Accessions

Homosexuality currently is a nonwaivable disqualification for service in the military.[297] It should be a waivable disqualification. To qualify for a waiver, an applicant should be required to sign a statement that explains the sodomy statute and the fact that violations may lead to either an adverse administrative separation or a court-martial. Personnel with a homosexual orientation would know the rules, and those who gain entry after disclosing their orientation would be less likely to become security risks. A waiver provision also would help in the event that the Selective Service System has to be used for national mobilization.

b. Separations

The current separation policy includes a list of questionable conclusions about how the presence of homosexuals adversely affects the military.[298] The policy is not all bad, it just says too much. The military has a legitimate interest in keeping disruptive activity to

[296]UCMJ art. 125.

[297]*See, e.g.*, Army Reg. 601-210, Regular Army and Army Reserve Enlistment Program, para. 4-4 (1 Dec. 1988).

[298]DOD Dir. 1332.14.

a minimum. The basis for separation should be homosexual activity, not homosexual orientation. Sexual activity on duty, in barracks, on ship or aircraft, or between members of the same chain of command can be disruptive, whether it is homosexual or heterosexual.

The administrative proscription of homosexual acts also is justified to the extent that these acts are illegal when they involve sodomy.[299] Even if Congress repeals the military sodomy statute—which does not appear likely anytime soon—sodomy still will be illegal for military personnel in about half of the fifty states via the Assimilated Crimes Act.[300] The basis for the policy should say this, and should refrain from using a laundry list that easily is assailed as reminiscent of old arguments used to exclude minorities from the military.[301]

The bases for separation of homosexuals may include preservice, prior service, or current service conduct or statements.[302] This goes too far only in the situation of personnel who acknowledge a homosexual orientation, but for whom there is no evidence of any proscribed homosexual activity. Personnel who lie by failing to disclose prior homosexual acts or a known homosexual orientation should face separation for fraudulent entry. Personnel who commit homosexual acts that are prejudicial to good order and discipline should face separation for that conduct. Nevertheless, personnel who admit their homosexual orientation and for whom there is no evidence of homosexual activity should not be separated without proof of real prejudice to good order and discipline.

Commanders and Service Secretaries should have the discretion to retain homosexuals. Commanders are in the best position to judge whether a person has value to the military. This discretion existed once before, but it was taken away when the current policy was promulgated in 1982.[303] For example, Staff Sergeant Perry Watkins was retained in 1975 (as a Specialist Five) after a board of officers unanimously recommended "that SP5 Perry J. Watkins be retained in the military service because there is no evidence suggesting that his behavior has had either a degrading effect upon unit performance, morale or discipline, or upon his own job performance."[304]

---

[299]UCMJ art. 125.
[300]18 U.S.C. § 13 (1982).
[301]*E.g.*, *Watkins*, 875 F.2d at 729.
[302]DOD Dir. 1332.14.
[303]*See supra* text accompanying notes 139-45.
[304]*Watkins*, 875 F.2d at 702.

If the discretion to retain homosexuals is returned to commanders and Service Secretaries, homosexual personnel should be retained only if they meet standards consistent with military interests. Retention should be authorized for anyone with a homosexual orientation who has not engaged in homosexual acts that are prejudicial to good order and discipline. Retention should be authorized for personnel who commit homosexual acts, as long as they do not occur on duty, in the barracks, on board ship or aircraft, in a situation that would create the appearance or prospect of favoritism within a chain of command, or in a situation that otherwise causes actual prejudice to good order and discipline.

VI. CONCLUSION

A policy must be legally sound, but it also should reflect an understanding of historical and scientific facts. There are going to be personnel with homosexual orientations in the military regardless of the policy. Some will come in knowing that they are homosexual, and some will not discover their sexual orientation until after they are on active duty. The policy should reflect that reality.

People who identify themselves as heterosexuals, bisexuals, and homosexuals exist on all points of the continuum of human sexual behavior. While the majority is exclusively heterosexual, a significant segment is exclusively homosexual, and even more could be considered bisexual during different periods of adult life.

There seem to be a number of causes for the continuum of sexual orientation, almost all of which occur prior to birth. People do not choose their place on the continuum of sexual preference, but they can choose whether, when, and how they are going to act. It is logical to assume that most are going to act in accordance with their preference.

One of the acts associated with the homosexual and bisexual preference is sodomy, which is illegal in the military. Other homosexual acts, while not illegal, provide a basis for administrative separation from the military.

Other than sexual preference, there are no discernible differences between those who are exclusively heterosexual and everyone else. In terms of behavior, a small percentage of homosexual men will exhibit effeminate characteristics. There is some evidence that homosexuals as a class may be more prone to alcoholism than the general population, but that could be because more of them may have reason to drink. People who engage in anal sodomy also are at greater risk of acquiring AIDS than any other group.

As homosexuals have become politically organized, many states and countries have become more tolerant and have repealed many anti-sodomy laws. Some countries, such as Great Britain and Canada, have legalized homosexual acts between consenting adults, but still prohibit homosexuals from serving in the military. A number of countries, such as Israel and Spain, now allow homosexuals to serve in the military.

American homosexual military personnel have advanced a number of legal arguments to stay in the military. They have won a few battles, but for the most part, they have lost the war. Since *Bowers v. Hardwick* was decided in 1986—establishing conclusively that there is no fundamental right to engage in sodomy—homosexuals have had an uphill battle on all fronts.

The equal protection theory is the best remaining argument for homosexuals attempting to remain in the military. Though the suspect class prong of equal protection appears to be a lost cause because the Supreme Court declined to issue a writ of certiorari in *Ben-Shalom v. Marsh*, the fundamental rights prong still may prove to be successful. To succeed, a homosexual litigant will have to prevail on the issue of whether there is a fundamental right to be a homosexual. Even the Supreme Court would have a difficult time trying to decree homosexuals out of existence.

If the right case gets before the Court under the fundamental rights prong of equal protection, homosexuality legislation and regulations could be subject to strict scrutiny, even without a fundamental right to engage in sodomy. If that happens with the current regulations, the military almost certainly will lose the challenge. In the meantime, the rational basis test is the appropriate level of scrutiny, and the current regulations pass such scrutiny. The fact that the current policy is constitutional, however, does not mean that it works, that it is wise, or that the military cannot improve upon it.

The policy should advance and protect true military interests. It should not be crafted so that entry is denied those who are truthful, while granted for those who are untruthful. It should not discourage those in need of help from seeking it. The current policy is easy to administer, but it is ineffective at keeping homosexuals out of the military. It creates a number of problems that could be avoided by a few modifications. If homosexuals are going to be in the military regardless of all efforts to keep them out—a point reinforced by history—the military should adjust to that reality.

Current policy on accession of homosexuals should be altered so that homosexuality becomes a waivable disqualification. Service Secretaries and commanders should have the discretion to retain homosexuals who meet certain criteria. Finally, the military should not separate personnel based on statements of sexual orientation alone, but should require evidence of prejudice to good order and discipline.

MAKING AND UNMAKING MINORITIES: THE TENSIONS BETWEEN GAY POLITICS AND HISTORY

JOHN D'EMILIO*

Since 1969, when the Stonewall Riots in Greenwich Village gave birth to the current phase of gay and lesbian political struggles in the United States, the gay and lesbian movement has evolved from one emphasizing gay liberation to one emphasizing gay rights.[1] Within that shift in terminology lies a major alteration in social analysis, political strategy, and ultimate goals. In its gay liberation phase, the lesbian and gay movement employed a language of political radicalism. It saw itself as one piece of a much larger political impulse that strove for a complete reorganization of institutions, values, and the structure of power in American life. Gay liberation sought to achieve its aims by organizing masses of gay men and lesbians whose political activity would occur largely outside courts and legislatures. These activists viewed accepted categories of homosexuality and heterosexuality as oppressive social constructs. The movement perceived human sexuality as diffuse and polymorphous in nature, and potentially destructive of rigid social hierarchies.[2]

Over the last fifteen years, the movement has become exceedingly diverse. Today, gay and lesbian organizations include a host of constituencies—men and women, black, hispanic, Asian and white, young and old, entrepreneurs, middle-class professionals, and unionized workers. Homosexuals have formed political clubs, churches, synagogues, health centers, and theater companies. Although no unified vision or political strategy animates these constituencies, we can say that as Stonewall has receded into the past, the movement as a whole has become less politically and socially radical. Its portrayal by the media, the statements of many movement leaders, and the program of action of individuals and organizations convey an image of the gay movement as one in quest of equal rights. That evolution, from gay liberation to gay rights, places the political and social struggles of lesbians and gay men in a familiar, well-established equal rights framework, deeply rooted in American history.[3]

---

* Assistant Professor of History, University of North Carolina at Greensboro. B.A., Columbia University, 1970; Ph.D., Columbia University, 1982. Author of SEXUAL POLITICS, SEXUAL COMMUNITIES: THE MAKING OF A HOMOSEXUAL MINORITY IN THE UNITED STATES, 1940-1970 (1983).

1. The complex reasons for that transformation are beyond the scope of this paper.

2. *See* D. TEAL, THE GAY MILITANTS(1971); OUT OF THE CLOSETS: VOICES OF GAY LIBERATION (K. Jay and A. Young eds. 1972); D. ALTMAN, HOMOSEXUAL: OPPRESSION AND LIBERATION (1972); and T. MAROTTA, THE POLITICS OF HOMOSEXUALITY (1981).

3. This tradition is manifested in American equal protection jurisprudence. For a description of this tradition, see L. TRIBE, AMERICAN CONSTITUTIONAL LAW 991-1136 (1978).

This history has provided gay men and lesbians with several models of struggles employed by minorities in search of equality. Blacks, women, ethnic groups, and religious minorities seek this equality through social movements, legislative agendas, and litigation. Recommending an analogous course of action for gay men and lesbians may be tempting.

Although I would not dispute the value of either judicial or legislative protections that guarantee due process, equal protection, and equal access, I would suggest that the "traditional" minority group model raises certain problems when applied to gay men and lesbians.[4] These difficulties emerge most clearly if one approaches the question from an historical perspective. Over the last decade, historians have done pioneering research that goes far beyond the uncovering of gay heroes. Historians have advanced toward a reconceptualization of the nature of human sexuality, and are creating theories with implications for both lawyers and social activists. My goal, therefore, is to interpret the work of gay and lesbian historians for an audience that may be unfamiliar with it.[5]

I shall begin with my own book, which is a history of the gay and lesbian movement in its formative stages — the two decades between the founding of the Mattachine Society in Los Angeles in 1950, and the Stonewall riot in 1969.[6] The book's subtitle, "The Making of a Homosexual Minority in the United States," goes to the heart of this new conceptualization. During this period, a gay and lesbian minority emerged as a definable social group with a self-conscious sense of itself as different from the majority. This minority did not always exist; it lacks a historical presence in American society.[7]

Central to this argument is a view of human sexuality as exceedingly malleable. Sex is more than a configuration of bodies in space; it takes its definition from the values and structures of particular cultures, and from the consciousness of individuals within a society. Sexuality consists of acts with meanings. Although the acts may have a universal existence, the meanings may vary considerably. And it is through meaning, through an understanding of behavior which culture provides, that patterns of behavior take on social significance.[8]

---

4. When a minority group pursues equal rights by identifying itself as a minority, it may, to some extent, defeat its objectives. To accept an identity as a fixed minority may reinforce the very oppression that we seek to dispel. For a description of equal rights models, see L. TRIBE, *supra* note 3.

5. *See* J. KATZ, GAY AMERICAN HISTORY(1976), and GAY/LESBIAN ALMANAC (1983); J. WEEKS, COMING OUT: HOMOSEXUAL POLITICS IN BRITAIN FROM THE NINETEENTH CENTURY TO THE PRESENT (1977); and J. STEAKLEY, THE HOMOSEXUAL EMANCIPATION MOVEMENT IN GERMANY (1975).

6. J. D'EMILIO, SEXUAL POLITICS, SEXUAL COMMUNITIES: THE MAKING OF A HOMOSEXUAL MINORITY IN THE UNITED STATES, 1940-1970(1983).

7. *Id.*

8. *See* J. WEEKS, COMING OUT (1977); THE MAKING OF THE MODERN HOMOSEXUAL (K. Plummer ed. 1981); J. H. GAGNON & W. SIMON, SEXUAL CONDUCT: THE SOCIAL SOURCES OF HUMAN SEXUALITY (1973); and Padgug, *Sexual Matters: On Conceptualizing Sexuality in History*, 20 RADICAL HIST. REV. 3 (Spring/Summer 1979).

This view of human sexuality as socially constructed has led many historians, on the basis of the evidence uncovered thus far, to conclude that sexual identity — in particular, a social world divided into homosexuals and heterosexuals — is a fairly recent historical invention. To phrase it more baldly, the reason a gay political movement did not exist before the post-World War II era was not because gay men and lesbians were slower to recognize injustice than were blacks or women, nor because the oppression was so severe that protest was too dangerous. Rather, the explanation lies in the fact that until the modern era, a gay and lesbian "minority" did not exist.[9] Many contemporary Americans take for granted that sexual orientation is a fixed category that indicates an essential difference in human beings. Yet, in the mid-18th century, or even mid-19th century, American society did not label people as heterosexuals or homosexuals.

Jonathan Katz's book, *Gay/Lesbian Almanac*, illustrates this conceptual distinction.[10] Katz divides his book into two parts: "The Age of Sodomitical Sin, 1607-1740," and "The Invention of the Homosexual, 1880-1950."[11] By examining in detail two eras separated by more than a century, Katz highlights the sharply distinctive sexual characteristics of each. In the former period, sodomy and sodomitical behavior were punished and excoriated as sin and crime.[12] Clerics and magistrates were preoccupied with certain proscribed behaviors, with discrete sexual acts. Sodomy was but one of many sexual activities prosecuted under the law. Others were adultery, fornication, rape, buggery, and public lewdness.[13] Sodomy was not an offense unto itself, a category that demarcated one type of individual from another. Instead, it represented a capacity for sin inherent in everyone.[14]

Katz describes a profoundly different social reality during the years 1880-1950. In medical writing, in literature, and in the testimony of men and women themselves, one finds an effort to redefine the meaning and the experience of homosexual behavior into a distinctive identity.[15] Sex becomes the distinguishing characteristic that describes the essential nature of some men and women. No longer simply an act, homosexual behavior instead serves as a marker of identity.[16] That identity encompasses personality, emotional state, sexual desire, and even, according to some, physical characteristics.[17] The homosexual can exist apart from any sexual activity: if one feels that one is a homosexual, that is sufficient. Colonial Americans would have found such assertions incomprehensible. To them, a sodomite was someone who had

---

9. *Supra* note 8.

10. J. KATZ, GAY/LESBIAN ALMANAC (1983).

11. *Id.*

12. *Id.* at 23-65.

13. *Id.* at 66-133.

14. *See generally* D'EMILIO, *supra* note 6; WEEKS, *supra* note 5; *see also* KATZ, *supra* note 10.

15. KATZ, *supra* note 10, at 137-74.

16. *Id.*

17. *Id.* at 175-653.

committed the sin of sodomy.[18]

The distinction between homosexual acts and homosexual identity represents more than playing with words. The concepts describe two profoundly different forms of homosexual expression, rooted in different social contexts. The process of creating a sexual identity involves a complex dialectic between external labeling and self-definition. In the century since the 1880s, the medical profession, courts, legislatures, government agencies, the mass media, educational institutions, and religious bodies have articulated a system that both describes and controls the social category they helped to create. In tandem with this categorization process, men and women have elaborated complex, diverse ways of living based upon their sexual desires. They have adopted distinctive styles of dress, have evolved an argot of their own, and have carved out social spaces — private friendship networks, public cruising areas, bars, bathhouses, clubs, and most recently, political organizations — that have allowed this sexual identity to take shape. Along the way, communities of mutual interest and experience have evolved. This reinforcing process of social labeling and individual self-definition has created a homosexual minority in the last half century.[19]

Although there seems to be a fair consensus among gay and lesbian historians that a homosexual minority has come into being in the modern era,[20] fewer of these historians agree about precisely why this phenomenon occurred. One hypothesis is that the emergence of American industrial capitalism in the late 1800s provided an opportunity for individual autonomy that was a precondition for the development of a gay identity.[21]

Throughout the United States diverse gay and lesbian identities and communities developed. These communities emerged among female faculty of women's colleges, among the single working women and prostitutes of boardinghouse districts in large cities, among entertainers in Harlem, and along the fringes of bohemian communities in places such as New York City's Greenwich Village. As time went on, they interacted with one another and were all subject to the external forces of social control in ways that may not have homogenized them, but that did nonetheless create commonalities among them: blacks and whites crossed paths in the clubs and cabarets of Harlem; college-educated social workers and prison administrators encountered prostitutes and other working-class lesbians in the courts and in penal

18. *Supra* note 14.

19. *See* D'Emilio, *Capitalism and Gay Identity* at 100-13 in POWERS OF DESIRE: THE POLITICS OF SEXUALITY (A. Snitow, C. Stansell, and S. Thompson, eds. 1983).

20. *Supra* note 14.

21. *See, e.g.*, LILLIAN FADERMAN, SURPASSING THE LOVE OF MEN (1981); E. GARBER, *T'Ain't Nobody's Bizness: Homosexuality in 1920's Harlem*, in BLACK MEN/WHITE MEN: A GAY ANTHOLOGY 7-16 (Michael J. Smith, ed., 1983); and Chauncey, *Christian Brotherhood or Sexual Perversion: Homosexual Identities and the Construction of Sexual Boundaries in the World War One Era*, 19 J. SOC. HIST. 189 (Winter 1985).

institutions. Distinctive subcultures were forming, but the lines between them were sometimes blurred.

Before moving on to suggest some of the implications that this historical analysis has for contemporary legal and political strategies, let me add one more word about history. What many historians are saying about sexuality departs from common folk belief in another significant way. Popular wisdom might summarize the history of sex as follows: first, there were moralistic Puritans, then repressed Victorians, followed by liberated moderns. Individuals, the story goes, have become sexually freer since the 1920s.

In contrast, historical writers have argued that this repression/freedom model misses the essential nature of the last two centuries of change in Western attitudes toward sex. Sexual activity has gradually, though not completely, been detached from a reproductive, gender-based matrix, and has been reconstituted as an entity in itself. Sexuality has been elevated in importance; it has become, for heterosexual and homosexual alike, a marker of personal identity. Our happiness and our sense of self-worth often revolve around our sexuality, and the emotional relationships that attach to it. Perhaps this elevated importance of sexuality is a sign of freedom. But, it has also amplified the possibilities for public intervention in personal life and for new methods of social control.[22]

From this perspective, it is perhaps easier to understand why public conflicts over sexuality have become so significant in the last century. From the seventeenth through the mid-nineteenth century, one searches in vain for a politics of sexuality in America. As long as social and economic conditions kept sexual expression deeply embedded in a procreative family-centered context, neither motive nor opportunity existed for social battles to rage around sexual issues. Since the Civil War, however, sex has generated political controversy of growing intensity and scope. Issues such as obscenity, birth control, prostitution, homosexuality, and abortion have proven capable of mobilizing vast numbers of Americans.[23] In this century, sexual issues have situated themselves nearer to the center of political concerns. At times, the leading edge of sexual politics seems to represent "freedom," while at other times the forces of "repression" appear to have the upper hand. Yet, both sides are united in the magnified importance that they attach to sexuality. If we have more sexual freedom than the Victorians had, that freedom is at best double-edged.

Are there ways in which this historical interpretation can clarify political

22. *See* M. Foucault, The History of Sexuality (R. Hurley trans. 1978); J. Weeks, Sex, Politics, and Society: The Regulation of Sexuality Since 1800 (1981).

23. *See, e.g.*, L. Gordon, Woman's Body, Woman's Right: A Social History of Birth Control in America (1977); J. Mohr, Abortion in America: The Origins and Evolution of National Policy, 1800-1900 (1978); J. Walkowitz, Prostitution and Victorian Society: Women, Class, and the State (1980); M. Thomas Connelly, The Response to Prostitution in the Progressive Era (1980); and K. Luker, Abortion and the Politics of Motherhood(1984).

strategies and tactics, especially in relation to the law? My comments about the present will not be as neat as my historical analysis. But let me at least describe some of the tensions and problems that arise when we place history alongside contemporary politics.

Take, for instance, the possibility of moving the courts to rule that gay men and lesbians deserve judicial intervention to guarantee equal protection under the law, *i.e.*, that we are a minority subject to discrimination. To achieve this, one would at least have to demonstrate convincingly a history of discrimination. This task is feasible if we restrict ourselves to the last generation. Unquestionably, gay men and lesbians have been subject since the 1940s to pervasive, systematic discrimination in many spheres of public life.[24] The military moved from simply court-martialing and discharging personnel who engaged in proscribed sexual behavior to excluding a whole class of men and women, regardless of their sexual activities, on the basis of their sexual inclinations — in other words, on the basis of their sexual identities.[25] The federal government banned the employment of gay men and lesbians, and many state governments and private employers followed suit.[26] Urban police forces arbitrarily conducted mass arrests at gay bars; probably tens of thousands of men and women were arrested every year.[27]

For the pre-World War II generations, however, there is little courtroom-ready evidence of discrimination. Homosexuality was a far less visible phenomenon. Society did not so clearly categorize on the basis of sexual orientation. The laws and public policies of a later time had not yet taken shape. Unlike blacks, against whom discriminatory laws stretch back to the seventeenth century, the "gay minority" has captured legislative attention only recently. A minority must exist before it can be oppressed, but a socially-defined, self-conscious homosexual minority simply does not exist very far back in the nation's past. In addition, some discriminatory practices, such as the ban on civil service employment, have already been abolished. Given this historical record and the recent Supreme Court decision in *Bowers v. Hardwick*,[28] what is the likelihood federal courts will consider gay men and lesbians in need of protection?

As another example, consider a key item of a gay rights agenda — the modification of municipal, state, and federal civil rights statutes to include sexual preference. Clearly it is desirable to prohibit discrimination in housing, employment, and other areas of life. Yet central to the oppression of lesbians and gay men, and to society's ability to shape and enforce it, are the homosexual and heterosexual categories themselves. The identity and the oppression are bound together. Is it not deeply ironic and troubling that a strategy which

---

24. *See* D'EMILIO, *supra* note 6, at ch.3.
25. *Id.*
26. *Id.*
27. *Id.*
28. 106 S. Ct. 2841 (1986) (Georgia's criminalization of consensual sodomy held constitutional).

relies on civil rights laws is a strategy which strengthens the categories that allow a system of oppression to continue? Is it possible that other approaches — litigation based on the freedoms of speech and assembly or legislative proposals that blur gender-based distinctions — might be both more successful and be more consistent with the history we have uncovered?

Whatever the legislative goals we choose to pursue, however, I am certain of two things. First, the issue that gay men and lesbians are facing is not simply one of a minority struggling for civil rights or equality. The issue is sex and its place in society and individual lives. The call for minority rights is simply one way of framing part of this larger issue — an issue that taps into the deepest layers of human and social irrationality. Secondly, whatever our short-term goals, we need to frame arguments for them consistent with the core of historians' discovery that sex is a malleable social construct. In this way we will achieve an educative goal beyond our immediate aim.

Let me illustrate this second point with a personal experience. About three years ago, I found myself in a debate concerning gay rights. On one side were a congressman and a retired Navy admiral; a representative of a prominent national gay rights organization and I were on the other side. The congressman made statements to the effect that homosexuals are willful, perverse sinners violating biblical law. In response, my partner declared that all the best medical evidence demonstrated conclusively that there was no choice involved, and that sexual identity is determined long before puberty.

Now, there was nothing new or startling about that statement. It is an argument made frequently in courts and legislatures, and articulated by many of our most committed activists and allies. But I heard it more clearly during this debate than I ever had before. It is a sincerely held viewpoint that squares well with the gut-level feelings of most of us. It also seems to promise political benefits; surely you will not punish us for something we cannot help.

This statement, however, ignores several valid arguments. Magnus Hirschfeld and other German activists used a variant of this argument earlier in the century when they claimed that homosexuality was not a willful perversion, but a congenital condition.[29] The argument did not deter Nazi persecution. Secondly, at a psychological level, there is something dreadfully wrong about basing a political movement on individual and collective helplessness. Do we really expect to bid for real power from a position of "I can't help it"? And thirdly, what if the argument is simply not true?

A fatal weakness attends any gay political movement which defines itself as a fixed minority in quest of equal protection based on its minority status.[30] To do so implies acceptance of a sexual paradigm that itself shapes and strengthens the oppression we are battling. To argue that our identity, our sexuality, is in effect an accident of birth or of early conditioning is to embrace a sexual ideology that negates the choices we have made. So long as we accept

29. *See generally* J. STEAKLEY, *supra* note 5.

30. *See supra* note 3.

these pre-set terms we have lost much of our freedom of choice. Fifteen years ago we supposed the terms of gay oppression to be that gay was bad, sick, and criminal. So the movement proclaimed that gay is good. Now it is clear that the terms of that proclamation are the acceptance of the mutually exclusive categories of heterosexuality and homosexuality.

All of us have made sexual choices throughout our lives. This phenomenon exists for heterosexuals and homosexuals alike. Because the hegemonic models of sexuality offer only two possible self-definitions, we have retrospectively interpreted our activities as the unambiguous manifestation of our one true being. Francis Matthiessen, as a young gay man in the 1920s, illustrates this process in a comment he made after reading Havelock Ellis: "How clearly," he said, "I can now see every act and friendship of my boyhood interpreted from my proper sexual temperament."[31] Many of us have likewise experienced a moment when we said, "This is who I am" — and in the process homogenized and flattened the complexity of our lives.

A century ago, certain American men and women were making radical personal choices, pursuing untrodden paths of sexual desire. The paths they marked became the outlines both of new sexual definitions, and of new oppressions. In many ways, we are still traveling those same paths. It is time to carve out new personal and political paths, to lay claim to the possibility of choice, to embark on new journeys of sexual definition. In doing so, we will challenge not merely the particular inequalities which a minority faces, but also the meaning, the structure, and the place of sexuality in our society for everyone. A multifaceted movement which takes on that task, in its own community and in society, will provide lawyers and lobbyists with a social and political context that can radically reshape our legal and legislative strategies.

31. RAT AND THE DEVIL: JOURNAL LETTERS OF F.O. MATTHIESSEN AND RUSSEL CHENEY 47 (L. Hyde, ed. 1978).

Gay Politics, Ethnic Identity: The Limits of Social Constructionism

Steven Epstein

"I seem to be surrounded at all times in all ways by who I am. . . . It goes with me wherever I go . . . and my life is gay and where I go I take my gay life with me. I don't consciously sit and think while I'm eating soup that I'm eating this 'gayly,' but, you know, it surrounds me."

* * *

"To me, being gay is like having a tan. When you are in a gay relationship, you're gay. When you're not in a gay relationship, you're not gay."

* * *

"As I sit at a concert or engage volubly in a conversation in the office or at home, or as I look up from my newspaper and glance at the people occupying the seats of the bus, my mind will suddenly jump from the words, the thoughts, or the music around me, and with horrible impact I will hear, pounding within myself, the fateful words: *I am different.* I am different from these people, and I must always be different from them. I do not belong to them, nor they to me."

* * *

This paper could not have been written without the encouragement, advice, and criticisms offered by a good number of people (many of whom, it should be said, do not agree with aspects of my argument). I would particularly like to thank Jeffrey Escoffier for a series of inspiring conversations on these topics. I also owe a debt to the following people for their comments on an earlier version of this essay: Tomás Almaguer, Jeanne Bergman, Alan Bérubé, Ellyn Kestnbaum, David Kirp, Lisa Orlando, Gayle Rubin, Arlene Stein, Indi Talwani, Jackie Urla, Carole Vance, Chris Waters, Jeff Weintraub, and the members of the Bay Area SR *collective.* —S. E.

> "There's nothing in me that is not in everybody else, and nothing in everybody else that is not in me. We're trapped in language, of course. But homosexual is not a noun. A least not in my book."

WHAT DOES IT MEAN to be gay? Do lesbians and gay men constitute a "deviant subculture"? A "sexual minority"? A privileged "revolutionary subject"? Is homosexuality a "preference" (like a taste for chocolate ice cream)? Or perhaps an "orientation" (a fixed position relative to the points of a compass)? Or maybe it's a "lifestyle," like being a "yuppie" or a surfer? Is being gay something that has some importance? Or is it a relatively inconsequential difference?

The gay men and women quoted above are undoubtedly not a representative sample, but the range of contradictory opinions certainly testifies to the difficulties involved in answering these questions.[1] And the types of disagreements observed in these quotes are present not only between individuals, but also within them. Most people who identify as gay or practice homosexuality adopt some variety of relatively inconsistent positions regarding their identity over the course of time, often depending on the needs of the moment. These contradictions are paralleled by the attitudes of homophobic opponents of the gay movement, which are typically even less consistent; for example, one frequently hears the belief that homosexuality is an "illness" combined with a simultaneous concern that youngsters can be "seduced" into it. The whole issue, it seems, is a terminological and conceptual minefield. Yet given the startling newness of the idea of there being such a thing as a "gay identity"—neither that term, nor "lesbian identity," nor "homosexual identity" appeared in writing by or about gays and lesbians before the mid-1970s—the confusion is hardly surprising.[2]

This article does not address the question of what "causes" homosexuality, or what "causes" heterosexuality. Instead, what I seek to explore is how lesbians and gay men, on a day-to-day basis, interpret their sexual desires and practices so as to situate themselves in the world; how these self-understandings relate to social theories about homosexuals; and how both the theories and the self-understandings can shape—or block—different varieties of political activism by gays.* I take as given that power inheres in

*This analysis does not systematically explore the self-understandings or politics of people who identify as bisexuals, though the category of "bi-

the ability to name, and that what we call ourselves has implications for political practice. An additional assumption is that lesbians and gay men in our society consciously seek, in a wide variety of ways, to *legitimate* their forms of sexual expression, by developing explanations, strategies, and defenses. These legitimations are articulated both on an individual level ("This is who I am, and this is why I am that way") and on a collective level ("This is what we are, and here is what we should do"). Legitimation strategies play a mediating function between self-understandings and political programs, and between groups and their individual members.

EXISTING THEORIES of sexuality fail to address these concerns adequately. For some time now, sexual theory has been preoccupied with a debate between "essentialism" and "constructionism"—a debate which, despite its importance in reorienting our thinking about sexuality, may well have outlived its usefulness. "Essentialists" treat sexuality as a biological force and consider sexual identities to be cognitive realizations of genuine, underlying differences; "constructionists," on the other hand, stress that sexuality, and sexual identities, are social constructions, and belong to the world of culture and meaning, not biology. In the first case, there is considered to be some "essence" within homosexuals that makes them homosexual—some gay "core" of their being, or their psyche, or their genetic make-up. In the second case, "homosexual," "gay," and "lesbian" are just labels, created by cultures and applied to the self.

Both essentialist and constructionist views are ingrained in the folk understandings of homosexuality in our society—often in a highly contradictory fashion. In a recent letter to Ann Landers, "Worried in Montana" expresses concern that her fourteen-year-old son may be "seduced" into homosexuality (folk constructionism) by the boy's friend, who she has "no question" is gay, because of his "feminine mannerisms" (folk essentialism). Ann reassures

sexual" itself is important to the discussion. For an analysis of bisexuality that touches on many of the issues explored here, see Lisa Orlando's article cited in reference 99.

At times, I will discuss gay men separately from lesbians; at other points, the analysis will refer to both at the same time. While this may be confusing from an analytic standpoint, it seems unavoidable if one wants to avoid simplistic assumptions of parallelism between the experiences of gay men and women.

the mother that the only way her son would turn out to be gay is if "the seeds of homosexuality were already present" (folk essentialism). At the same time, she questions the mother's certainty about the sexual orientation of the friend, claiming that it is "presumptuous" to label a fourteen-year-old as "gay" (folk constructionism).[3] But if such inconsistent views can at times exist side by side, it is equally true that at other times they clash violently. Homosexuals who are advised to "change" and become straight, for example, might have more than a passing investment in the claim that they've "always been that way"—that their gayness is a fundamental part of who they "really are."

This debate is not restricted to the field of sexuality; it parallels similar ones that have taken place in many other domains, including gender, race, and class. For example, while some feminists have proposed that qualities such as nurturance constitute a feminine "essence," others have insisted that any differences between men and women, beyond the strictly biological, are the products of culture and history: men and women have no essential "nature."[4] But while the issues may be generalizable, they have a special salience for contemporary gay politics, because of a peculiar historical irony. With regard to sexuality, the constructionist critique of essentialism has become the received wisdom in left academic circles. And yet, curiously, the historical ascendancy of the new constructionist orthodoxy has paralleled a growing inclination within the gay movement in the United States to understand itself and project an image of itself in ever more "essentialist" terms.

As many observers have noted, gays in the 1970s increasingly came to conceptualize themselves as a legitimate minority group, having a certain quasi-"ethnic" status, and deserving the same protections against discrimination that are claimed by other groups in our society.[5] To be gay, then, became something like being Italian, or black, or Jewish. The "politics of identity" have crystallized around a notion of "gayness" as a real, and not arbitrary, difference. So while constructionist theorists have been preaching the gospel that the hetero/homosexual distinction is a social fiction, gays and lesbians, in everyday life and in political action, have been busy hardening the categories. Theory, it seems, has not been informing practice. Perhaps the practitioners are misguided; or perhaps there is something about the strict constructionist perspective which neither adequately describes the experiences of gays and lesbians nor speaks to their need to understand and legitimate their places in the world.*

To address these questions, my analysis will proceed as follows. First, I will recapitulate the constructionist-essentialist debate and discuss why neither side proves altogether useful in understanding or guiding contemporary gay politics. Then, I will argue that other theoretical perspectives on identity and ethnicity can provide valuable help in understanding recent political trends and in defending some version of an "ethnic/minority group model." In the process, I will return to the theoretical debate, examine some more subtle expressions of it, and show that the "ethnic" model is congruent with a modified constructionist position. Finally, I will explore the implications of this analysis for the future directions of gay politics.

The Debate

AT HEART, the theoretical debate is located on the all-too-familiar terrain of nature vs. nurture. As against the essentialist position that sexuality is a biological force seeking expression in ways that are preordained, constructionists treat sexuality as a blank slate, capable of bearing whatever meanings are generated by the society in question. In addition, the debaters line up on opposite sides of an old epistemological argument concerning categorization.[7] Essentialists are "realists" in their insistence that social categories (e.g., "homosexual," "heterosexual," "bisexual") reflect an underlying reality of difference; constructionists are "nominalists" in their contrary assertion that such categories are arbitrary, human-imposed divisions of the continuum of experience—categories create social types, rather than revealing them.

"Essentialism"is often equated with "traditional" views on sexuality in general, but can be linked specifically to the work of nineteenth-century "sexologists," such as Havelock Ellis and Krafft-Ebing; to certain aspects of Freud's work; and to deterministic theories such as sociobiology.[8] Essentialist views stress the "natu-

*I do not mean to suggest that constructionism is the *only* theoretical perspective on homosexuality proposed by left academics. Clearly, feminist theory has played a significant role in informing debates on sexual politics. However, feminism has often been guilty of "gender reductionism" by treating questions of sexual identity as epiphenoma of gender debates. To the extent that there is a coherent theoretical perspective on homosexuality *as* homosexuality, it is constructionism.[6]

ral" dimensions of sex; and essentialist conceptions of homosexuality seek to account for such persons on the basis of some core of difference, whether that difference be hormonal, or medical, or a consequence of early child-rearing, or "just the way we are."

The constructionist critique of sexual essentialism has played an important role in debunking this traditional view. Much like essentialism, though, constructionism should not be thought of as a specific school, but rather as a broader tendency of thinking that has found representations in a number of disciplines. At the risk of oversimplifying, it can be said that recent historical and sociological work on gays and lesbians in Western societies[9] traces its roots to two schools of sociology: *symbolic interactionists,* particularly the pathbreaking work of John Gagnon and William Simon on "sexual conduct" (1973); and *labeling theorists,* especially Mary McIntosh's analysis of the "homosexual role" (1968) and Kenneth Plummer on "sexual stigma" (1975).[10] To a lesser degree, analyses of sexual constructionism in Western societies have also been influenced by the cross-cultural work of constructionist anthropology; these studies of "sex/gender systems" trace a somewhat different history from the mid-century cultural anthropology of Boas, Benedict, and Mead.[11] Finally, in the 1980s, the work of Michel Foucault has become a new rallying point for sexual constructionism, and has served as the impetus for further investigations.[12] I will briefly discuss some of these sources of constructionism, in order to describe the main contours of the perspective as it has evolved.

In keeping with the central thrust of symbolic interactionism, constructionists propose that sexuality be investigated on the level of subjective meaning. Sexual acts have no inherent meaning, and in fact, no act is inherently sexual. Rather, in the course of interactions and over the course of time, individuals and societies spin webs of significance around the realm designated as "sexual." People *learn* to be sexual, Gagnon and Simon stress, in the same way they learn everything else: "Without much reflection, they pick up directions from their social environment."[13] As actors attribute subjective meanings to their interactions with others, they begin to develop "sexual scripts" which guide them in their future sexual interactions. Unlike "drives," which are understood as fixed essences destined to seek a particular expression, "scripts" are highly variable and fluid, subject to constant revision and editing.[14]

CENTRAL TO THE constructionist critique of essentialist "drive theory" is a repudiation of the popular imagery of sex. In this view we tend to see sex as

> an overpowering, instinctual force, whose characteristics are built into the biology of the human animal, which shapes human institutions and whose will will out, either in the form of direct sexual expression, or if blocked, in the form of perversion or neuroses.[15]

In this view, which preceded but was popularized by Freud, "society" must restrain "sexuality," and social order depends on the proper channeling of sexual energy. In the left-wing version of the same ideology, "sex radicals" such as Wilhelm Reich and Herbert Marcuse have treated sexual repression as the cornerstone of social repression, hailing sex as the liberator from bondage.[16] More generally, in the popularizations of this imagery, the sex drive is treated as some sort of magical energy; hence the idea that athletes shouldn't have sex before the big game, or that masturbation constitutes a waste of one's potency. In all these views the sex drive is credited "with enormous—almost mystical—power."[17]

While symbolic interactionists debunked the notion of a "natural" sexuality, it was labeling theory that first provided the means to challenge essentialist views of "the homosexual" as a natural, transhistorical category. This challenge, which lies at the very crux of the constructionist argument about homosexuality, can be expressed in the following claim: although every known society has examples of homosexual *behavior,* only recently has there arisen a conception of "the homosexual" as a distinct type of *person.* In Mary McIntosh's important essay on the modern "homosexual role," her immediate target was the medical conception of the homosexual person. McIntosh argued vehemently against the prevailing medical logic:

> Many scientists and ordinary people assume that there are two kinds of people in the world: homosexuals and heterosexuals. Some of them recognize that homosexual feelings and behaviour are not confined to the persons they would like to call "homosexuals" and that some of these persons do not actually engage in homosexual behaviour. This should pose a crucial problem, but they evade the crux by retaining their assumption and puzzling over the question of how to tell whether someone is "really" homosexual or not. Lay people too will discuss whether a certain person is "queer" in much the same way as they might question whether a certain pain indicated cancer. And in much the same

> way they will often turn to scientists or to medical men for a surer diagnosis.[18]

In place of this essentialism, McIntosh argues that "the homosexual" has come to occupy a distinct "social role" in modern societies. Since homosexual *practices* are widespread but socially threatening, a special, stigmatized category of *individuals* is created so as to keep the rest of society pure. By this means, a "clear-cut, publicized and recognizable threshold between permissible and impermissible behaviour" is constructed; anyone who begins to approach that threshold is immediately threatened with being labeled a full-fledged deviant: one of "them."[19] A homosexual identity, then, is created not so much through homosexual activity per se (what labeling theorists would call "primary deviance"), but through the reactions of the deviant individual to being so described, and through the internalization of the imposed categorization ("secondary deviance").

THESE SOCIOLOGICAL THEORIES were employed by historians who, in empirical studies, have traced the genesis of the modern homosexual.[20] More recently, the work of Foucault has helped us to theorize a historical dimension to the constructionist arguments. According to Foucault, sexuality in the modern Western world has been the site of an explosion of discourses of power and knowledge; sexual meanings, sexual doctrines, and sexual beings have been generated incessantly by a culture that has come to be obsessed with the significance of the sexual, has elevated it to unprecedented dimensions, and has sought in it "the truth of our being."[21]

Foucault has tried to use this perspective to account for the origin of "the homosexual." In Foucault's view, the transformation from sexual behavior to sexual personhood is attributable to three factors: the increasing importance attached to sexuality in general; a more widespread transformation in structures of social control, from control that operates through sanctions against specific acts to control based on highly individualized discipline; and the growing power of professionals, and especially doctors, to define social problems and enforce social norms. In an oft-cited passage, Foucault argues:

> As defined by the ancient civil or canonical codes, sodomy was a category of forbidden acts; their perpetrator was nothing more

> than the juridical subject of them. The nineteenth-century homosexual became a personage, a past, a case history, and a childhood, in addition to being a type of life, a life form, and a morphology.... Homosexuality appeared as one of the forms of sexuality when it was transposed form the practice of sodomy onto a kind of interior androgyny, a hermaphrodism of the soul. The sodomite had been a temporary aberration; the homosexual was now a species.[22]

As summarized in this brief sketch, constructionism posed a serious challenge to the prevailing essentialist orthodoxy concerning homosexuality. Where essentialism took for granted that all societies consist of people who are either heterosexuals or homosexuals (with perhaps some bisexuals), constructionists demonstrated that the notion of "the homosexual" is a sociohistorical product, not universally applicable, and worthy of explanation in its own right. And where essentialism would treat the self-attribution of a "homosexual identity" as unproblematic—as simply the conscious recognition of a true, underlying "orientation"—constructionism focused attention on identity as a complex developmental outcome, the consequence of an interactive process of social labeling and self-identification. Finally, by refusing to privilege any particular expression of sexuality as "natural," constructionism shifted the whole framework of debate on the question of homosexuality: instead of asking, why is there homosexuality? the constructionists took variation for granted and asked, why is there homophobia?[23]

Unfortunately, while constituting a significant advance in our understanding of sexuality and homosexuality, constructionism also posed some inherent difficulties. However, before attempting a critique of constructionism, it is important to situate the debate within a social and political context. Rather than juxtaposing ideas in the abstract, we need to examine the politics of gay communities during the postwar period and the connection between those politics and the evolving theoretical stances.

The Political Context

As Foucault notes, the labeling practices of the nineteenth-century doctors who invented the term "homosexual" created the possibility for a "reverse affirmation," by which the stigmatized could gradually begin to organize around their label and assert the legitimacy of that identity.[24] Foucault, however, neglects the material bases for these practices. As Jeffrey Weeks and John D'Emilio have argued, the medical categorization itself presupposes certain social conditions, including changes in family structure that were linked to the Industrial Revolution, and urbanization, which provided the social space for a homosexual subculture to develop.[25] By mid-century, such subcultures were firmly established in most major cities in the United States.

Homosexual politics of the 1950s and early 1960s preached liberal tolerance and stressed the goal of integration into the larger society.[26] The birth of the gay liberation movement marked a radical break with these accommodationist politics. When American gay liberation burst out of quiescence with the Stonewall riot in Greenwich Village in 1969, the politics that were espoused represented a mixture of new-left ideology and left Freudian arguments that anticipated constructionism.[27] Activists with groups such as the Gay Liberation Front portrayed homosexuals as revolutionary subjects who were uniquely situated to advance the cause of sexual liberation for society as a whole. However, the notion of "the homosexual" as a distinct type of person was specifically repudiated, in favor of a left Freudian view of human sexuality as "polymorphously perverse." In utopian fashion, activists prophesied the disappearance of both "the homosexual" and "the heterosexual" through the abolition of constraining categories:

> The reason so few of us are bisexual is because society made such a big stink about homosexuality that we got forced into seeing ourselves as either straight or nonstraight. . . . We'll be gay until everyone has forgotten that it's an issue. Then we'll begin to be complete people.[28]

Or in the words of a lesbian activist:

> I will tell you what we want, we radical homosexuals: not for you to tolerate us, to accept us, but to understand us. And this you can do only by becoming one of us. We want to reach the homosexuals entombed in you, to liberate our brothers and sisters, locked in the prisons of your skulls. . . . We will never go straight until you go gay. As long as you divide yourselves, we will be divided from you—separated by a mirror trick of your mind.[29]

Perhaps the most sophisticated expression of this ideology is Dennis Altman's, whose *Homosexual: Oppression and Liberation*

(1971) remains the classic statement of early post-Stonewall gay male politics. In the final chapter, entitled "The End of the Homosexual?," Altman looks forward to not only the abolition of sexual categorization but also the elimination of "masculinity" and "femininity," along with the creation of a "new human" for whom such distinctions would simply be irrelevant.[30]

While such arguments are not exactly "constructionist"—Gagnon and Simon, after all, would criticize the lingering essentialism of left Freudians such as Marcuse—they resonated fairly closely with the gay and lesbian constructionist history that began to be written soon afterward; this history, in fact, was inspired by the events of the early gay liberation movement, and many of the historians had been active in it from the start. What the liberationist position shared with the constructionist arguments was an insistence that sexual typologies are social, rather than natural facts; that these categories are highly fluid; and that they need to be transcended. Both shared a sense of the openness of historical possibilities that was inspired by the political climate of the day.

NEEDLESS TO SAY, the radical liberationist politics did not achieve its goals. However, the greater irony is that, to the extent that the activists did succeed in advancing the situation of gays and lesbians, they undermined the logical supports for their own arguments. That is, simply by advancing the cause of gay liberation, the liberationists helped to further the notion, among both gays and straights, that gays constitute a distinct social group with their own political and social interests. This is a familiar dilemma, and one that is by no means peculiar to the gay movement: How do you protest a socially imposed categorization, except by organizing around the category? Just as blacks cannot fight the arbitrariness of racial classification without organizing *as blacks,* so gays could not advocate the overthrow of the sexual order without making their gayness the very basis of their claims.

The 1970s witnessed a phenomenal growth in the institutionalization of a gay identity, as "deviant subcultures" gave way to "gay communities." And contrary to the "proto-constructionist" perspective that had been espoused by the early liberationists, the next generation of gay activists embraced a conception of gay identity that was significantly essentialist. To some extent, these essentialist notions had been around from the start; and in the political climate of the late 1970s, one can imagine why they would have more appeal than the utopian vision of the early liberationism, with its focus on historical openness. What this meant, however, is that a disjuncture developed between theory and practice: in place of the rough congruence between early gay liberation politics and evolving constructionist theory, we now find a growing tension between an evolving essentialist politics and a constructionist theory that is firmly in place.

Each variant of essentialism is based on some sort of legitimation strategy. In some cases, activists have legitimated their claims with reference to the trans-historical unity of homosexuals or their trans-cultural functional role. Perhaps most prominently, Adrienne Rich has proposed the existence of a "lesbian continuum" which links the resisters of heterosexist patriarchy across cultures and throughout history.[31]* In a somewhat analogous vein, a male activist claimed: "We look forward to regaining our ancient historical role as medicine people, healers, prophets, shamans, and sorcerers."[32] Others have sought legitimations of a more "scientific" sort, making reference to a biological or genetic basis for homosexuality. Most typically, and far more usefully, gays and lesbians have adopted what Altman has in recent writings characterized as an "ethnic" identification.[33]

THIS "ETHNIC" self-characterization by gays and lesbians has a clear political utility, for it has permitted a form of group organizing that is particularly suited to the American experience, with its history of civil-rights struggles and ethnic-based, interest-group competition. In fact, an irony that Altman points out is that, by appealing to civil rights, gays as a group have been able to claim a legitimacy that homosexuals as individuals are often denied:

> One of the paradoxes of the present situation is that even where the old laws defining homosexual behavior as a major crime remain, there is a growing de facto recognition of a gay minority, deserving of full civil and political rights *as* a minority. Thus for years the mayor of New York could proclaim an official Gay Pride Week while the very people being honored remained criminals under state law.[34]

*Other forms of lesbian essentialism are actually gender essentialism, stressing the superiority of the intrinsic qualities of women. For a striking example, see Karla Jay, "No Man's Land," in Jay and Allen Young, eds., *Lavender Culture* (New York: Jove, 1978), pp. 48–68.

Gay people's sense of themselves as belonging to a "minority group" was not altogether new; this view had been stated publicly at least as early as 1951, when Donald Webster Cory discussed the "invisible minority" in *The Homosexual in America.*[35] However, this self-conception could not really take root at a time when the institutional and cultural content of the gay subculture was so relatively impoverished. By the late 1970s, however, the "ethnic" self-understanding truly seemed to correspond to the reality of the burgeoning gay male communities, which had become, at least in New York and San Francisco, wholly contained cities-within-cities (or "ghettoes," as they were not infrequently called). Inhabitants of these "urban villages" need never leave them to satisfy their desires, whether those desires be sexual, recreational, cultural, or commercial. There were gay churches, gay banks, gay theaters, gay hiking clubs, gay bookstores, and gay yellow pages listing hundreds of gay-owned businesses. While lesbian communities were neither as visible nor as territorially based, they, too, provided a variety of cultural supports and institutions, fostering a sense of minority-group identity that was furthered by separatist tendencies. Little wonder, then, that lesbians and gay men began to be seen as, and to think of themselves as, almost a distinct type of being, on an ontological par with "Irish-Americans" or "Japanese-Americans."* Gone were the dreams of liberating society by releasing "the homosexual in everyone." Instead, homosexuals concentrated their energies on social advancement *as homosexuals.*

It should be noted that the "ethnic" self-understanding is a much looser form of essentialism than, say, a strict genetic or hormonal theory of homosexuality. Based on an analogy that is not necessarily intended literally, this form of group identification is peculiarly vague about where the essential "core" of gayness resides. Nonetheless, the notion does tend toward a reification of the category "homosexual," implying that lesbians and gay men

*Granted, the majority of self-identified gays and lesbians did not live in these communities, but many of them did make their pilgrimages to the "Gay Mecca" or were exposed to it through the mass media. And beyond that, to use a different religious metaphor, San Francisco came to symbolize for gays around the United States what Israel represents for Jews around the world: a focal point for cultural identity, that functions even for those who are not firmly integrated into the culture.

It should be clear, of course, that there is no *single* gay or lesbian "culture," but rather a variety of them that are loosely integrated.

are in some fundamental sense different from heterosexuals. Such viewpoints can be quite dangerous: they can lend support to eugenicist arguments and are also disturbingly compatible with the contemporary understanding of AIDS as a "gay disease."

Moreover, there are a number of questions that can be raised, from a progressive standpoint, about the political manifestations of "ethnicity." It would be unfortunate to reduce the politics of gay liberation to nothing more than the self-interested actions of an interest group, in competition with other such groups for various resources; such a model would imply that gays have no interests in common with other oppressed groups, and would almost entirely abandon any notion of a broader role for the gay movement in radical politics. In addition, such a move would further separate gay men from gay women, by questioning whether even they have sufficient common interests to overcome their senses of difference. Finally, as many critics have noted, the politics of gay "ethnicity" have tended to foster the hegemonic role in community-building played by white males within the gay movement,[36] and have been articulated to an uncomfortable extent through capitalist enterprise and the commodification of sexual desire.[37]

Given the problems posed by "ethnic" essentialism, one might think that the role of gay and lesbian theorists should be to continue promoting a constructionist critique. In a certain sense, I think this is true; but it is a project that needs some rethinking. Is constructionism to be defended unproblematically? If so, the defenders must grapple with the problem that their theoretical perspective is "out of sync" with the self-understandings of many gay people. From the standpoint of the defenders of constructionism, lesbians and gay men must be seen as victims of "false consciousness," unaware of the constructedness of their identities. Moreover, we might predict that constructionists would experience considerable difficulties in leading the gay masses to a state of "true consciousness," given that constructionism poses a real and direct threat to the ethnic legitimation: people who base their claims to social rights on the basis of a group identity will not appreciate being told that that identity is just a social construct; and people who see their sexual desires as fixed—as "just the way we are"—are unlikely to adopt a viewpoint that presents "sexual scripting" as a fluid, changeable process open to intentional redefinition. Altman has recognized this dilemma:

> Few arguments have caused as much controversy among gay audiences as the assertion of a universal bisexual potential. I was once interrupted during the taping of a gay radio program in Los Angeles by a producer very concerned by this position, which he said justified Anita Bryant's claim that all homosexuals could be "cured." He was only partially mollified by my pointing out that the reverse was equally true.[38]

While it is important to challenge essentialism, particularly in its most insidious forms, we need not do so by reverting to a dogmatic constructionism. A strict constructionist position of the kind outlined above not only poses a threat to contemporary legitimations of lesbians and gay men: it is also theoretically unsound and analytically incomplete. Having situated the essentialist-constructionist debate within contemporary politics, I would now like to return to the examination of constructionism and spell out its shortcomings.

Constructionist Pitfalls

For all its radical potential, constructionism has trapped itself in the basic dualisms of classic liberalism. Liberal discourse goes back and forth between two extreme views of the relation between the individual and society: either it asserts that individuals are free to create themselves, rise above their environments, and take control over their lives; or it sees individuals as simply the product of their environment (or their genes, or what have you), molded like clay into various shapes.[39] Similarly, constructionism vacillates between a certain type of libertarian individualism (the left Freudian variant is the best example here)[40] in which sexual categories may be appropriated, transcended, and deconstructed at will; and just the opposite conception of the individual's sexual identity as created for him or her by the social and historical context (a strand of thinking best represented by Foucault). In either case, the "individual" is pitted against "Society"; and what is missing is any dynamic sense of how society comes to dwell within individuals or how individuality comes to be socially constituted.

Put more simply, constructionism is unable to theorize the issue of determination. This is true both on the societal level and on the level of individual lives. As Jeffrey Weeks has acknowledged, though constructionism would predict an infinite variety of sexual identities, sexual acts, and sexual scripts, practical experience indicates that only the tiniest fraction of these possibilities are realized.[41] Stephen Murray points out that if we take the constructionist assumption that gender identity, gender roles, sexual identity, sex roles, and object choice can all vary independently of each other, and if we assume that each feature might take on one of three possible values (e.g., "masculine," "feminine," and neither/both), then there are 243 potential permutations of sexual beings. Needless to say, even if we combed through the entire history of human civilization, we would not find anywhere near that many variations.[42] Each society seems to have a limited range of potential storylines for its sexual scripts—and constructionists have surprisingly little to say about how that limiting process takes place. Moreover, strict constructionism implies a lack of determination in the sexual histories of *individuals* as well: their scripts are assumed to be in a constant state of revision. While this is no doubt true to a point, it would seem to belie most people's experiences of a relatively fixed sexual identity. It may be that we're all acting out scripts—but most of us seem to be typecast.

It is precisely this perceived non-voluntary component of identity that cannot be accounted for within a strict constructionist perspective. Constructionism has no theory of the intrapsychic; it is unable to specify the ways in which desire comes to be structured over the course of people's lives. While it asserts that people are social products, it has no way of explaining how it is that social meanings come to resonate with the core of who people are.* Falling into the dualistic traps of liberal theory, constructionism then lends itself to further misunderstanding on the part of those who encounter the theory. A "folk constructionism" comes to be disseminated: the view that sexual identities are willful self-creations. And in reaction against this folk constructionism, which denies the experience of a non-voluntary component to identity, lesbians and gays operating within the liberal discourse slide to the

*In a more recent revision that deserves attention, Gagnon and Simon speak of three levels of scripting: "cultural scenarios," "interpersonal scripts," and "intrapsychic scripts." While this is a drastic improvement over the original definition of scripts, it still does not go far enough. The intrapsychic is conceptualized primarily as the realm in which the self "rehearses" for interpersonal experience; there is no real dynamic theory of intrapsychic processes in relation to actions in the external world. Also, a conception of unconscious mental processes, as opposed to conscious ones, is missing from their version of intrapsychic scripts. See Simon and Gagnon (ref. 55), pp. 53-60.

opposite extreme: they assert that there is something "real" about their identity, and then try to locate that felt reality in their genes, or their earliest experiences, or their mystical nature. In this way, constructionism becomes its own worst enemy, driving its potential converts into the enemy camp.

A final point can be made about the theoretical inadequacies of constructionism as well as essentialism. If such theories are to be politically useful, then they should provide some means of evaluating concrete political strategies. In fact, the debate can at times appear quite beside the point, for there are many gay political strategies which cannot be cleanly conceptualized as either "essentialist" or "constructionist." For example, consider the situation of "political lesbians" living in separatist communities of women. Such women have consolidated an (essentialist) conception of group difference to a significant extent—but the emphasis on identity as a conscious political choice would seem to place them squarely within the constructionist camp. Alternately, we might examine the politics of the pre-Stonewall homophile movement in the United States in the 1950s and '60s. The leaders of this integrationist movement stressed in no uncertain terms that homosexuality was not a consequential difference, and that homosexuals were really just the same as straights and wanted to be treated as such. But this more-or-less constructionist viewpoint was mixed with an equally rigid essentialist insistence that homosexuals could not help being the way they were, and should therefore not be asked or forced to "change."[43]

IT SEEMS THAT when we scrutinize the essentialist-constructionist debate closely, it immediately unravels into two underlying dualisms: "sameness" vs. "difference," and "choice" vs. "constraint." Constructionism insists that homosexuals and heterosexuals are basically the same, and not fundamentally distinct types of beings; and it emphasizes the possibilities for the self-conscious creation of sexual identities ("choice"). Essentialism, conversely, stresses the politics of difference and presumes the existence of constraint on one's sexual identity: sexual desires are not a "preference" but a fixed "orientation."

However, when we separate out the two dimensions, we find that there are four logical possibilities (chart 1), rather than the two presumed by the constructionist-essentialist debate. First, there is

CHART 1: POLITICAL EMBODIMENTS OF A DECONSTRUCTED DEBATE

	CHOICE	CONSTRAINT
SAMENESS	Post-Stonewall (transformative) gay liberation Civil libertarianism	Integrationism (e.g., 1950s–60s homophile movements)
DIFFERENCE	Political lesbians Cultural radicalism	Civil rights Minority/ethnicity Cultural radicalism

CHART 2: CORRESPONDING LEGITIMATION STRATEGIES AND DELEGITIMATING THREATS

		CHOICE	CONSTRAINT
SAMENESS	*Strategies*	Free expression Social liberation	Liberal tolerance
	Threats	Sin; criminality	Curable illness
DIFFERENCE	*Strategies*	Oppositional culture	Civil rights Cultural pluralism
	Threats	Deviant group	Degenerate group Incurable illness

sameness-choice, which is exemplified by the early 1970s gay liberationist perspective, as well as by certain civil-libertarian arguments. Gay liberationists of the early seventies, for example, thought that all people were bisexual and hence fundamentally similar; and they stressed the role of volition in identity-formation. Next, there is *sameness-constraint,* the position of the pre-Stonewall homophile movements. Then, there is *difference-constraint,* best exemplified by the ethnic/civil rights model. Actors within such a model possess a strong sense of group difference and a notion of sexual identity as a fixed orientation. Finally, there is *difference-choice,* which would characterize "political lesbians" as well as certain expressions of cultural radicalism within the gay male community.* Each box, then, has its political embodiments, and each box also implies specific legitimating strategies which would need to confront specific ideological challenges (chart 2). The problem, though, is that the politics of only two of the boxes (sameness-choice and difference-constraint) are explicable within the context of the constructionist-essentialist debate. That is, sameness-choice can be seen as pure constructionist, while difference-constraint is pure essentialist. The other two boxes would seem to indiscriminately criss-cross the bounds of the argument—and yet they are no less logically defensible or worthy of theoretical attention. It follows that to explore systematically the essentialist-constructionist debate, we really need to delve more deeply into these two oppositions—choice vs. constraint, and sameness vs. difference—and see if they are really so opposing.

In order to build up a stronger constructionist position, my strategy will be as follows. First, I will examine more closely the idea of a gay "ethnic identity," exploring, from the standpoint of theories of identity and of ethnicity, the historical conjuncture in which this idea appeared. I will argue that the debates on identity and ethnicity have been bogged down by certain polar oppositions that parallel the essentialism-constructionism divide. By staking out an alternative position in these debates, I will further argue that it is reasonable, with certain qualifications, to accept the "ethnic" model—both as a relatively accurate characterization of contemporary gay identity formation, and as a politically defensible starting point from which the gay movement can evolve in a pro-

*It should be clear that groups or individuals can be "located" within these boxes only in a highly ideal-typical fashion. In the real world, at some point or another, most of us are all over the map.

gressive direction. In the course of this analysis, I will return to the oppositions that undergird the essentialism-constructionism debate—choice vs. constraint, and sameness vs. difference—and once again seek some way of transcending the dualisms, in a way that helps sexual theory to resonate more closely with the politics of gay "ethnic" identity.

Identity

THE CONCEPT OF "homosexual identity," as mentioned earlier, is a surprisingly new one; though the term is now ubiquitous, it first appeared in the relevant literature little more than a decade ago.[44] Perhaps it is not so surprising, then, that the term has been used in a consistently haphazard fashion. In her survey of the literature on homosexual identity, Vivienne Cass has found that

> in these articles it is possible to infer diverse meanings such as (1) defining oneself as gay, (2) a sense of self as gay, (3) image of self as homosexual, (4) the way a homosexual person *is*, and (5) consistent behavior in relation to homosexual-related activity.[45]

General definitions of identity are equally problematic. In an interesting "semantic history" of the term, Philip Gleason notes that it, too, is a new concept, having entered the general social-science literature only in the 1950s. Popularized initially by psychoanalyst Erik Erikson, "identity" then wound its way through various sociological "feeder streams," including role theory, reference-group theory, and symbolic interactionism. By the mid-1960s, the term "was used so widely and so loosely that to determine its provenance in every context would be impossible."[46]

Nevertheless, Gleason observes that most definitions tend to fall toward one or the other pole of an opposition between two conceptions of identity, one a psychological reductionism, the other a sociological reductionism. The first conception of identity—which might be called "intrapsychic"—treats identity as a relatively fixed and stable characteristic of a person, which, from a developmental standpoint, more or less unwinds from within. In a word, this sense of identity is essentialist: it is the type of "identity" that we mean when we speak of identity as describing who someone *really is*. Quite distinct is the sense of "identity" which I will call "acquired" (although the term "constructionist" would not be inappropriate). In this sense, identity is the internalization or conscious adoption of socially imposed or socially constructed labels or roles. According to the "acquired" definition, identity is not so deeply entrenched in the psyche of the individual, and can vary considerably over the course of one's life. This is the type of "identity" that we have in mind when we say that someone "identifies as" a such-and-such.[47]

It should be clear that not all psychologists adopt a simplistic intrapsychic definition, nor do all sociologists see identity as purely acquired. Erikson, for example, was quite specific on the point that identity emerged through an interactive developmental process between self and others.[48] Conversely, the symbolic interactionists Berger and Luckmann argue that "identity is a phenomenon that emerges from the dialectic between individual and society."[49] Nonetheless, these two polar senses have each become prevalent, and it is not uncommon to encounter fairly pure expression of either type.*

Mediating between the poles of intrapsychic and acquired identity is Habermas's useful discussion of identity:

> [Ego] identity is produced through *socialization,* that is, through the fact that the growing child first of all integrates itself into a specific social system by appropriating symbolic generalities; it is later secured and developed through *individuation,* that is, precisely through a growing independence in relation to social systems.[50]

Ego identity, then, is a *socialized sense of individuality,* an internal organization of self-perceptions concerning one's relationship to social categories, that also incorporates views of the self perceived to be held by others. At its core, identity is constituted relationally, through involvement with—and incorporation of—significant others and integration into communities. The relationship of ego

*Lee Rainwater, for example, has used a definition of identity as something completely acquired, treating identities as things that people "try on," like hats: "Individuals are led to announce a particular identity when they feel it is congruent with their needs, and the society influences these needs by its willingness to validate such announcements by a congruent placement.... Each individual tries on identities that emerge from the cultural material available to him and tests them by making appropriate announcements." See Lee Rainwater, *Behind Ghetto Walls: Black Families in a Federal Slum* (Chicago: Aldine, 1970), p. 375; quoted in Laud Humphreys, "Exodus and Identity: The Emerging Gay Culture," in Martin P. Levine, ed., *Gay Men: The Sociology of Male Homosexuality* (New York: Harper & Row, 1979), p. 144.

identity to subsidiary identities (such as occupational, class, racial, gender, or sexual identities) is an interactive one, in which all subsidiary identities are integrated into a relatively coherent and unique life history.[51]

Where then do these subsidiary identities come from, and in what circumstances can they be appropriated and incorporated? As Berger and Luckmann maintain, it is important to recognize that such identities are, at the same time, both human self-creations and constraining structures. To paraphrase Marx, people make their own identities, but they do not make them just as they please. Identities are phenomena that permit people to become acting "subjects" who define who they are in the world, but at the same time identities "subject" those people to the controlling power of external categorization.[52]

In this regard, it is vital to note that identity has increasingly come to be seen as something quite important. In modern, fluid, "mass" society, the relationship of the individual to the social whole is rendered problematic; as part of a continual "quest for identity," we go through "identity crises"; we seek to "find ourselves." It is not surprising that group identities—occupational, racial, ethnic, sexual—become increasingly attractive, since they provide an intermediate link between the individual and the mass.[53] As we accept more and more identities, it does indeed begin to seem that they are all somewhat arbitrary, tried on like hats and discarded for next year's style. And yet the fundamental irony of this apparent freedom to define ourselves is that in a world where identity has been transformed into a problem—where identity "crises" must be resolved, and where we all search for our identities—external cues and definitions become increasingly authoritative. The more we feel impelled to discover our "true" identity, the more we are likely to grasp at the reassurance provided by the adoption of available identity types.

THE PRESSURE to define oneself *sexually* is particularly keenly felt. This is true in part because labels such as "homosexual" are powerfully charged, carrying with them the risk of strong social disapproval. But beyond that, a Foucaultian argument can be made about the increasing importance of sex, in general, to the constitution of identity. As Dennis Altman notes,

> sex remains one of the few areas of life where we feel able to be more than passive spectators. It is a feature of modern society that we increasingly define achievement in terms of immediate gratification, and the move to burden sexuality with greater expectations is closely related to the stress on ideas of "self-fulfillment" and "personal actualization."[54]

In a similar vein, Jeffrey Weeks observes:

> As divorce rates rise, fertility declines, and the distinction between married and unmarried tends to blur, "the couple" rather than marriage emerges as the one seeming constant of western life. But sex becomes even more central to its success. . . . Sex has become the cement that binds people together.[55]

Gay, lesbian, and bisexual identities must be understood as arising out of this historical conjuncture.[56] Their emergence reflects a world in which group identity has assumed paramount importance, and where sexuality has become a central dimension of identity formation in general. In addition, as already suggested, these identities constitute "reverse affirmations" of social labels, adoptive contestations of imposed stigma categories. As labeling theory indicates, deviant identities are particularly likely to assume totalizing dimensions: *all* behavior of persons so categorized becomes interpreted by others through the prism of the perceived difference: "One will be identified as a deviant first, before other identifications are made."[57] And as Erving Goffman points out, the need for the stigmatized to "manage" their stigma in social situations—to tell or not to tell, to confront or to excuse—causes the stigma-identity to assume substantial proportions within the overall ego identity—to become, in some cases, an all-consuming preoccupation.[58] Attempts to assert the legitimacy of one's position and claim that one's stigma is not grounds for social exclusion tend to have the ironic effect, also noted by Goffman, of furthering the process by which the particular identity consumes the overall ego.[59]

FINALLY, the emergence of various types of sexual identity as important components of ego identity presumes the existence of individuals who are in some loose sense qualified to fill the categories—people who are capable of interpreting their erotic and emotional desires and actions as corresponding to their understanding of the meaning of these social terms.[60] This is the point at which both labeling theory and symbolic interactionism falter, for they have nothing to say about how such people come to exist. The rigid temporal sequence laid down by labeling theory is particularly inadequate. In that model, the individual commits an act of "primary" deviance (in this case, a homosexual act), is in consequence met with a stigmatizing label ("You're a queer"), and by internalizing this label becomes fixed in a "secondary" deviant identity ("I'm a homosexual").[61]* But in the real world, the developmental sequences vary tremendously. Interview data suggest, in fact, the relationship among the processes of engaging in homosexual activity, being labeled a homosexual, and having suspicions that one is a homosexual can come in various orders; typical patterns seem to include "engaged, suspicious, labeled," "engaged, labeled," "suspicious, engaged, labeled," and "suspicious, labeled, engaged." As Plummer has pointed out in his review of several studies, some gay men and lesbians report a fixity and clarity of sexual preferences dating to early childhood; others experience several shifts in sexual identity and the structure of desire over the course of their lives.[62] Research into the lives of homosexuals increasingly suggests that there is no "homosexuality," but rather "homosexualities."[63]

A theory of sexual identity formation, therefore, must be able to identify a wide range of potential developmental strategies by which individuals, in relation with significant others, compare (or fail to compare) their experiences and feelings against their comprehension (or lack of comprehension) of existing sexual and gender typologies.[64] As a result of these processes, individuals arrive (or fail to arrive) at consistent or variable interpretations of their sexual identity.† This is a complex and never-ending activity, involving both conscious and unconscious dimensions. Consciously, people perform what Barbara Ponse has called "identity work": they actively seek to organize into a coherent whole their thoughts, motivations, and experiences with others—to create a consistent

* A notable exception to this presumption of a standard sequence of deviant identity-formation is Goffman's discussion of the "moral career" of the stigmatized individual, which can unfold in several distinctive fashions, depending upon the relative timing of (1) developing a stigma and (2) learning that the world considers this to *be* a "stigma." Goffman (ref. 58), pp. 32–34.

† To complicate the above discussion even further, it should probably be added that, to the extent that sexual identity and gender identity are ideologically linked, the individual's perception of his or her relationship to the gender categories (e.g., gender "conformity" or "nonconformity") can influence the developmental understanding of sexual identity.

biography which legitimates their places in the world.[65] Critical phases, such as the "coming out" process, may represent cognitive strategies for handling breaks and discontinuities in these biographies. To the extent that such processes remain unconscious, people are often subject to constraints that they but dimly perceive; their needs, desires, actions, cognitions and self-concepts may all be out of sync with one another, and a consistent biography may not be achieved.

THIS DISCUSSION sheds new light on the polarity between "choice" and "constraint," which was observed to be one dimension underlying the essentialist-constructionist debate. If the question is, Are sexual identities the outcome of choice or constraint?, then the whole thrust of the preceding argument is to suggest that the only possible answer is "neither and both." Choice and constraint constitute a false opposition; and the way to transcend this dualism, I think, is with some form of psychoanalytic theory. Such a perspective can account for the ways that sexual and emotional desires can be structured, developmentally, into relatively well-defined directions. In particular, the "object relations" school of psychoanalysis, with its focus on relational experience, and with its theory of the ego as possessing a "relational core," might be usefully applied to an analysis of sexual identity.[66] Object relations theory describes, in a vivid way, how from a child's earliest moments onward a sense of self is constituted through "introjections" of significant others. The child's needs and desires, which can only be satisfied externally, come to be mediated and shaped through these encounters; while aspects of these desires may remain highly fluid and subject to what constructionists want to call scripting, other dimensions may be sharply structured and come to comprise fundamental parts of the ego core.* Without

*It may even be useful to reintroduce a concept of "drives"—stripped of its essentialist Freudian baggage. Rather than treat drives as pre-social and biological, Chodorow (following Edith Jacobson) suggests that "the infant is born with undifferentiated drive potentials, which are transformed and used in the process of development, in the interest of internal and external relationships, to become aggressive and libidinal drives." Chodorow, "Beyond Drive Theory" (ref. 40), p. 308. From this perspective, it might be possible to conceptualize a developmental organization of drives that results in a homosexual "object choice." However, it could be argued that the term "drive" has been so contaminated by Freud's biologism, ahistoricism, prescriptive claims about "normality," and assumptions that drives serve to "channel" sexuality in order to stabilize the moral and social order, that it would be best to avoid the term altogether.

displacing the symbolic interactionist focus on conscious, adult experience, psychoanalysis also permits us to conceptualize the unconscious and to appreciate the formative element of early childhood experiences. From such a perspective, identity becomes more than just a serial enactment of roles; it takes on a socially constituted reality.

In light of this discussion, the organization of the gay community around the "politics of identity" would seem to have strong social roots. Once we abandon both the strict essentialist notion of identity as forever fixed within the psyche, as well as the strict constructionist conception of identity as an arbitrary acquisition, we can recognize that a gay or lesbian identity might have a clear resonance for individuals without necessarily binding them to any specific definition of what that identity "means." An intermediate position between the poles of intrapsychic and acquired identity allows us to recognize that these sexual identities are *both inescapable and transformable,* and are capable of giving rise to a variety of political expressions. The question that must now be asked is why the contemporary gay identity in the United States has particularly assumed an "ethnic" dimension, and what this implies for gay politics.

Ethnicity

HOW CAN WE SPEAK seriously of gays and lesbians as an "ethnic" group—or even a minority group? After all, there would seem to be some rather fundamental differences between gays and the other groups that we normally associate with these terms. In the first place, ethnic or racial identifications are normally conferred at birth and transmitted through the family. In place of this "primary socialization" into a racial or ethnic identity, the entrance into a gay community constitutes a "secondary socialization," occurring later in life.

A process of secondary socialization is typically seen as less formative than primary socialization, because "it must deal with an already formed self and an already internalized world. It cannot construct subjective reality *ex nihilo*."[67] In particular, it is unclear what sort of coherent cultural content can be transmitted through a secondary socialization into a gay community, and whether this cultural distinctiveness corresponds with the kinds of cultural differences that we normally consider to be ethnic. Ethnic culture is presumed to be handed down through the generations; gay "culture" lacks both the historical roots and the standard transmission devices. This problem is compounded by the fact that individuals being socialized into a gay community will already possess a variety of cross-cutting identities—ethnic, racial, class, gender, religious, occupational, and so on—which may claim much greater allegiance and inhibit the secondary socialization process.[68]

The treatment of these objections rests ultimately on the particular definition of "ethnicity" that is adopted. And once again, an investigation into the existing definitional possibilities reveals a debate between two polar opposite conceptions. Lining up on one side are the "primordialists," who treat ethnicity as an inescapable given, an absolute ascription. And in opposition to this traditional view has arisen the "optionalist" (a.k.a. "circumstantialist") critique, which in its most vulgar manifestations argues that "ethnicity may be shed, resurrected, or adopted as the situation warrants."[69] It should be clear that a "primordialist" conception of ethnicity implies an "intrapsychic" notion of ethnic identity; while conversely, an understanding of ethnicity in the "optionalist" sense is quite compatible with a definition of ethnic identity as "acquired."[70]

Once again, we need to transcend a false dualism: on the one hand, it seems ridiculous to claim that we can shed or adopt ethnicities as we please. Clearly, there are major constraints on this process. But on the other hand, it is quite true that racial and ethnic categories are historical products that are subject to extensive redefinition over time. Omi and Winant give an interesting example of the definitional crisis surrounding the influx of Mexicans and Chinese into the United States in the mid-nineteenth century. Confused over what sort of racial/legal status to accord these groups, courts eventually ruled that Mexicans were "white" but that Chinese were "Indian."[71] Even in the lives of individuals, racial designations can change. In South Africa, where race, of course, is of paramount importance, there is a special government agency responsible for adjudicating claims about one's racial classification; and each year many people officially "upgrade" their racial identity.[72]

Donald Horowitz strikes a good intermediate note between primordialism and optionalism:

> Ascription is, of course, the key characteristic that distinguishes ethnicity from voluntary affiliation. *Ethnic identity is generally acquired at birth. But this is a matter of degree.* In the first place, in greater or lesser measure, there are possibilities for changing individual identity. Linguistic or religious conversion will suffice in some cases, but in others the changes may require a generation or more to accomplish by means of intermarriage and procreation. In the second place, collective action, in the sense of conscious modification of group behavior and identification, may effect shifts of boundaries.... It is, therefore, a putative ascription, rather than an absolute one, that we are dealing with.... Ethnicity thus differs from voluntary affiliation, not because the two are dichotomous, but because they occupy *different positions on a continuum.*[73]

This definition brings us a step closer to feeling comfortable with the idea that the ethnic analogy is a reasonable one for gays and lesbians. If ethnicity does not necessarily begin at birth, and if ethnicity involves some combination of external ascription and chosen affiliation, then a gay identity as described above seems not wholly unlike an ethnic identity. But we can better understand the adoption of the ethnic model by gays and lesbians if we spell out the particular ways in which ethnicity has come to be understood in the contemporary United States.

IN THE 1970S, social scientists announced that the United States was in the throes of an "ethnic revival"—a "resurgence" of ethnicity.[74] Though heavily influenced by the cultural and political assertiveness of racial minorities in the late 1960s, the revival was essentially a phenomenon of white European ethnic groups, manifesting a rediscovered pride in their heritage.* It was quickly observed that, despite the implications of a turn toward the past, there was something quite new about this form of ethnicity. As Frank Parkin notes,

> the nature of collective action mounted by ethnic groups has undergone a significant change in recent times. Originally dedicated to fighting rearguard actions of cultural preservation, they

*This occurrence posed a bit of a puzzle to social scientists, many of whom had previously adopted the assumptions of the "melting pot" theory, or who, following the predictions of classical social theorists such as Karl Marx and Max Weber, had assumed that "irrational," "communal" ties such as ethnicity would be progressively swept away by the advance of capitalism and the inexorable processes of rationalization.[75]

> have now adopted more combative forms of activity expressly designed to alter the distribution of rewards in their members' favour.[76]

The "new ethnicity" differs from traditional ethnicity in a variety of respects. First, as Daniel Bell points out, the new ethnicity combines an affective tie with the pursuit of explicitly sociopolitical goals in "interest group" form: ethnic groups become "instrumental" and not just "expressive."[77] Second, the new ethnicity places ethnic-group activity firmly on the terrain of the state.[78] Third, and as a corollary to the preceding arguments, the new ethnicity is "forward-looking," seeking to expand the group's social position, while the old ethnicity was "backward-looking," aimed at "preserv[ing] the past against the encroachments of centralization and 'modernization.'"[79] Fourth, as a reaction against "mass society," the new ethnicity is not so much a new form of aggregation as a "disaggregation" or "de-assimilation" from the mass.[80] Fifth, lacking the type of structural power possessed by subordinate social classes (i.e., the ability to disrupt production), the new ethnic groups are increasingly inclined to press their demands by appealing to, and manipulating, hegemonic ideologies (such as "equal rights").[81] And finally, neo-ethnic politics frequently take on a localist character, organized around a specific geographic space or community, leading to a distinctively ethnic involvement in urban political affairs.[82] While to some extent a general feature of contemporary Western politics, the "new ethnicity" manifested itself most prominently in the United States, where the political possibilities for organizing around ethnicity were the greatest (and, conversely, class-based organizing had proven relatively ineffective).[83]

Of course, it would be a mistake to exaggerate the changes that have occurred and ignore either the continuities between the "old" and the "new" ethnicity, or the extent to which both varieties have always been present. Nonetheless, it seems that a somewhat new understanding of what ethnicity is all about emerged in the United States in the 1970s—that is to say, at the very same time that gay and lesbian identity was taking on an ethnic cast.* And indeed, on the basis of the preceding discussion, this notion of gay ethnic

*Other countries that have gay political movements have failed to develop gay "ethnicity." French activist Guy Hocquenghem, for example, has commented that France does not have a "gay community." Mark Blasius, "Interview with Guy Hocquenghem," *Christopher Street,* April 1980, p. 36. This identity seems increasingly comprehensible and plausible. Like the archetypal "new ethnicity," gay ethnicity is a "future-oriented" identity linking an affective bond with an instrumental goal of influencing state policy and securing social rewards on behalf of the group. Like the other ethnic groups, gay ethnicity functions typically through appeals to the professed beliefs of the dominant culture, emphasizing traditional American values such as equality, fairness, and freedom from persecution. And finally, in neo-ethnic fashion, gay identity (in this case, gay *male* identity in particular) operates by using the control of a specific geographic space to influence urban political decision-making.[84]

The final question that must be addressed, to understand and assess the gay community's adoption of an ethnic self-understanding, has to do with the issue of culture and tradition. No matter how much ethnicity may now be articulated in the sociopolitical realm, most conceptions of ethnicity would certainly still include some sense of a unique ethnic culture heritage; indeed, one manifestation of the new ethnicity that was frequently alluded to in the 1970s was the resurgence of pride in one's ethnic cuisine, ethnic costume, and so on. And no matter how much ethnic groups may now be "forward looking," many of the legitimations for group allegiance are focused on the past and argue for the preservation of traditional forms. Can the lesbian and gay communities claim to be ethnic, given these considerations?

THE ANSWER IS that the analogy holds. On the one hand, gay communities have developed a variety of cultural forms which, despite the considerable internal variation, serve to unify those communities.[85] And on the other hand, the cultural potency of at least the European ethnic groups would seem to be much less than it's often cracked up to be. In an interesting twist on the "new ethnicity" argument, Stephen Steinberg has characterized the recent "ethnic fever" as sort of a Freudian reaction-formation: an assertion that ethnicity is still culturally and psychologically meaningful, voiced with such rigid insistence as to imply that even the proponents themselves are not convinced. He quotes Irving Howe to this effect:

---

would tend to support the argument that the United States has structural spaces for "ethnic" organizing that other countries lack.

> These ethnic groups now turn back—and as they nervously insist, "with pride"—to look for fragments of a racial or national or religious identity that moves them to the extent that it is no longer available. Perhaps, also, *because* it is no longer available.[86]

Because ethnicity no longer provides the institutional supports capable of integrating individuals into the community and providing them with a sense of belonging, individuals futilely attempt to re-create that sense of belonging by grasping at a *psychological* affiliation. In the process, they fail to observe that the ground has fallen away beneath their feet:

> Indeed, it is precisely because the real and objective basis for ethnic culture is rapidly disappearing that identity has been elevated to a "symbolic" plane and a premium is placed on the subjective dimensions of ethnicity. People desperately wish to "feel" ethnic precisely because they have all but lost the prerequisites for "being" ethnic.[87]

Steinberg's analysis would lead one to characterize the gay community's adoption of an ethnic identity as profoundly ironic. It would seem to be precisely the fact that ethnic culture has been *evacuated of content* that has permitted the transposition of the category of "ethnicity" onto a group that, in the traditional sense of the term, clearly would not qualify for the designation. Thus it is true that lesbians and gay men don't really fit the original definition of what an ethnic group is: but then, neither really, do contemporary Jews, or Italian-Americans, or anyone else. In this way, the decline of the old ethnicity permits and encourages new groups to adopt the mantle and revive the phenomenon. Indeed, to the extent that the gay community has succeeded in creating new institutional supports that link individuals into the community and provide their lives with a sense of meaning, gays may now be more "ethnic" than the original ethnic groups.* And in any event, as the term progressively loses its original significations and acquires a more future-oriented, sociopolitical connotation, there is a diminishing tendency to assume that an ethnic group needs to provide those original functions anyway.

Now that we have explored the historical conjuncture in which the idea of a "gay ethnicity" made its appearance, we can see that

*This process is limited, of course, by the extensive variation within and among gay communities and the fact that integration of individuals into those "communities" is often extremely partial.

the term is more than a simple catch-phrase, as it appears in Altman's analysis. Rather, it is at the very least a compelling analogy, and perhaps even the most accurate designation we can come up with.*

THIS DISCUSSION of the particular sense in which "gay identity" has come to resemble an "ethnic" identity also sheds light on the "sameness-difference" dichotomy that underlies the essentialism-constructionism debate. Just as "choice" and "constraint" proved to be a false polarity with regard to gay *identity,* so are "sameness" and "difference" an unhelpful analytical distinction with regard to gay *ethnicity:* it makes little sense to quarrel over whether homosexuals and heterosexuals are fundamentally the same or fundamentally different. First, we need to rethink what we mean by the terms, and escape a sense of "sameness" as meaning a coercive uniformity, or "difference" as the clash of opposites. As Chodorow argues in the analogous case of gender difference, a rigid assertion of differentness reflects a defensive need to separate: it stems from anxieties about one's sense of self that are manifested in a refusal to recognize the other as also a "self"—as an active subject. It is possible to be differentiated, she argues, "without turning the cognitive fact into an emotional, moral, or political one."[88]

In this regard, it may be useful to talk about the relationship between gay "ethnic" communities and the larger society in terms of varying combinations of "sameness-in-difference," or "difference-in-sameness." This is true in several senses. First, the adoption of a neo-ethnic form of social closure combined with a civil-rights political strategy implies that gays are asserting their difference partly as a way of gaining entry into the system. By consolidating as a group, they are essentially following the rules of the modern American pluralist myth, which portrays a harmonious competition among distinct social groups. Neither "sameness" nor "difference" would seem to capture the peculiar ambiguity of this political expression.

---

*Purists who wish to preserve a more conventional sense of the term "ethnicity" that would be applicable outside of the contemporary American context might instead prefer to call the gay community a "status group" of a "communal" character, organized around sexual expression.

While Parkin does not discuss sexual minorities, it would not be hard to incorporate them into his neo-Weberian argument on "communal" forms of usurpationary social closure. See Parkin (ref. 75), p. 67, and Almaguer (ref. 23).

Second, as many commentators have noted, the more coherent an ethnic group in the United State becomes, the greater its cultural influence upon the larger society. That is, at the times when Jews, or blacks, have been most "separatist," the diffusion of those cultures has also been the greatest. In the areas of sexual practices and urban lifestyles, lesbians and gays have indeed had an influence on the general culture in opening up possibilities for new forms of sexual and aesthetic expressions.[89]

This leads to another point, which is that the "lifestyles" of homosexuals and heterosexuals (at least among the white middle class) would seem in some ways to be moving closer together, even as the identity categories congeal. Once again, neither "sameness" nor "difference" seems to adequately characterize the phenomenon. As D'Emilio indicates, the conventional nuclear family is less and less the norm; the variety of living arrangements has multiplied; and sexuality has been increasingly divorced from a procreative intent: "As the life cycle of heterosexuals exhibits greater variety and less predictability, they have come to face many of the choices and experiences that gay men and women confront."[90] And conversely, D'Emilio argues that homosexuals are moving closer to heterosexuals:

> The gay liberation movement allowed many lesbians and homosexuals to break out of the ideological prison that confined them to a sexual self-definition. It also began the transformation of a sexual subculture into an urban community. The group life of gay men and women came to encompass not only erotic interaction but also political, religious, and cultural activity. Homosexuality and lesbianism have become less of a sexual category and more of a human identity.[91]

D'Emilio would seem to be exaggerating somewhat the convergence that has taken place; moreover, his endorsement of a "desexualized" lesbian and gay identity is certainly controversial.*

---

*Much of the early panic surrounding AIDS within the gay male community would seem to cast doubts on the viability of a "desexualized" notion of gay identity. The view was frequently expressed that if gay men couldn't have sex with each other, they would lose their identity altogether and the community would fall apart. Clearly, sex is unlikely ever to become an incidental part of a gay male identity.

Conversely, the general public seems unprepared to grant gays a "desexualized" gay identity, even if gays want that. Here again, AIDS is a good example: much of the "moral panic" surrounding AIDS can be interpreted as an attempt to "re-sexualize" gay (male) identity, by asserting that "the

Nonetheless, to the extent that there is some truth in the argument, it would seem that gays are becoming "the same" as straights to the extent that they are "different."

A final point in this regard relates to the potency of sexual classification itself. Jeffrey Weeks points out that the consolidation of typologies of sexual "persons" can have the paradoxical effect of challenging the whole system of categorization. Initially, labels such as "homosexual" were applied by doctors and sex researchers to describe deviations from a presumed norm. But once the people so labeled, in a "reverse" affirmation, began to assert the legitimacy of their sexual identity—and once that legitimacy began to be more widely recognized—then the whole classificatory schema began to lose its cultural force:

> For the elaborate taxonomies and distinctions existed in the end only to explain the variations in relationship to an assumed norm. Once the norm itself was challenged, then the category of the perverse became redundant, and with them the whole elaborate edifice of "sexuality"—the belief that the erotic is a unified domain, governed by its own laws, organised around a norm and its variations—began to crumble.[92]

Weeks's argument is misleading because it presumes that categorization can be abolished—that the elimination of one set of norms somehow precludes the installation of others. In fact, as Weeks himself has noted elsewhere, not only is categorization a never-ending process, but gays and lesbians have increasingly become the new categorizers, subdividing and stratifying their communities into a variety of new types.[93] But clearly Weeks has a point. By consolidating their sense of difference *and* asserting their legitimacy, lesbians and gays may be helping to usher in a world where they no longer seem so different. But neither an essentialist claim of basic difference, nor a constructionist insistence on fundamental similitude, alone seems adequate to capture this ambiguous process.

---

homosexual" (as a person) is inherently diseased, due to the diseased nature of his sexuality.

Similarly, for lesbians, the issue of a "desexualized" identity has been controversial. While some lesbian-feminists have proposed "desexualized" definitions of "lesbian" that would be more inclusive of feminists in general, others have protested against these "'women-loving-women' definitions, which too often hide the genital homophobia of an otherwise purified and cleansed reconstruction of the term." Jacquelyn N. Zita (ref. 93), p. 173.

Conclusion

In making sense of the notion of "gay 'ethnic' identity," I have deliberately steered clear of both the strict essentialist and the strict constructionist understandings of ethnicity as well as identity. The constitution of a gay identity is not something that simply unwinds from within, nor is it just an amalgam of roles that proceed according to scripts; only an intermediate, and dialectical, definition makes sense in this case. Similarly, if "ethnicity" is to serve even as an analogy for comprehending gay and lesbian group identity, then ethnicity must be understood as something that is neither an absolutely inescapable ascription nor something chosen and discarded at will; as something neither there from birth, nor something one joins like a club; as something that makes one neither fundamentally different from others, nor fundamentally the same. It is in the dialectics between choice and constraint, and between the individual, the group, and the larger society, that "identities," "ethnic identities," and "gay and lesbian identities" emerge.

Neither strict constructionism nor strict essentialism are capable of explaining what it means to be gay. The fact that contemporary gay self-understandings and political expressions are inexplicable within the bounds of these theoretical perspectives therefore should come as no surprise. No sexual theory can inform sexual practice without transcending the limitations imposed by aligning oneself on either fringe of a bootless philosophical argument between "nature" and "society." This whole discussion so far has really been a series of variations on that theme, since all the oppositions that have been described can be located at one or the other pole of what is basically the same debate:

essentialist	constructionist
realist	nominalist
constraint	choice
difference	sameness
intrapsychic	acquired
primordialist	optionalist
nature	society
internal	external
real	fictive

The fact that, in seeking to transcend these oppositions, I have ended up quoting the arguments of many constructionists, is not incidental. Constructionists have become increasingly aware of the complexities of these debates, and have continued to provide the most insightful analyses of the changing character of the gay community and gay identity. But what constructionists have failed to acknowledge are the ways in which their own observations are increasingly at odds with the basic premises of the theoretical perspective. Plummer, in an interesting article aimed at a "synthetic" position, has gone so far as to embrace the possibility of the existence of fixed sexual "orientations"—while carefully skirting the question of how such a concept accords with his general theoretical stance.[94] Altman, one of the most subtle chroniclers of the gay ethnic experience, can never seem to quite escape his own suspicion that ethnicity rests on an illusion that is also a trap. Weeks, who is perhaps the most sensitive to the theoretical limitations of strict constructionism, and who provides the most insightful discussions of both the limitations and the possibilities inherent in gay identities, is also capable of lapsing into the most utopian constructionist arguments about the abolition of sexual categories. The hold of strict constructionism remains tenacious; and its expositors seem unwilling to clarify their relationship to the doctrine.[95]

CLARIFICATION would require a number of modifications to strict constructionism, yet would in no way amount to an endorsement of essentialism. First, there is a need to understand the issue of determination: out of the range of potential forms of sexual expression, how are limitations created on that expression, both socially and within the individual psyche? On the individual level, this implies the systematic introduction of psychoanalytic conceptions of needs and desires and of the development of the self in relation to others. On the social level, it implies a more comprehensive understanding of power, and of the dialectical relationship between identities as self-expressions and identities as ascriptive impositions. Anthropological analyses of "sex/gender systems" in kinship-based societies have something to offer here. As Harriet Whitehead has pointed out, "To say that gender definitions and concepts pertaining to sex and gender are culturally variable is not necessarily to say that they can vary infinitely or along any old axis." Analyses such as hers have attempted to connect cultural meanings about gender and sexuality with specific social-structural relations, so as to show how culture can structure the possibilities for personhood in distinctive ways.[96]

An example of how such an analysis might proceed for Western societies is offered by Michael Omi and Howard Winant's analysis of a different domain, "racial formation."

> Racial formation . . . should be understood as a *process:* (1) through which an unstable and contradictory set of social practices and beliefs are articulated in an ideology based fundamentally on race; (2) through which the particular ideology thus generated is enforced by a system of racial subjection having both institutional and individual means of reproduction at its disposal; and (3) through which new instabilities and contradictions emerge at a subsequent historical point and challenge the pre-existing system once more.[77]

Substitute "sexuality" for "race" in the above quote, and its relevance to the present discussion would be apparent. It is important to note, however, that Omi and Winant also intend "subjection" to be understood in the dual sense discussed earlier: both the creation of political *subjects,* and their simultaneous *subjection* to structural and ideological controls. For as Omi and Winant point out in their evaluation of the black movement:

> Probably the greatest triumph of the movement was not its legislative accomplishments or even the extent of its mass mobilization. The social movement for racial equality had its greatest success in its ability to create new racial "subjects," in its ability to *redefine the meaning of racial identity,* and consequently, of race *itself,* in American society.[98]

Similarly, the creation of a positive identity, and the simultaneous redefinition of legitimate sexual and affectional possibilities, is the overriding accomplishment of the lesbian and gay movements to date.

BEYOND THE ISSUE of determination, a second requirement for the reinvigoration of constructionism is a better understanding of the "collectivization of subjectivity." We must be able to speak of sexually based group identities without assuming *either* that the group has some mystical or biological unity, *or* that the "group" doesn't exist and that its "members" are indulging in a dangerous mystification. "Ethnicity" is a metaphor; but the relationships that it entails can come to be internalized as a fundamental part of the self. To the extent that this is consciously recognized—to the extent that "ethnicity" can be seen as both strategy and reality—

then the dangers of it being misunderstood in a rigidly essentialist sense become greatly reduced. Furthermore, this sense of what it means to be part of a distinctive community can rescue us from investing "difference" with moral implications. Rather than reifying difference into a defensive separatism or dissolving it into a false vision of homogeneity, we need to acquire an appreciation for difference as harmless, perhaps synergistic.[99]

A modified constructionist perspective of this sort would address the deficiencies of constructionism that were noted earlier in this paper. Not only would it permit a fuller description of the complex experiences of being homosexual, but it might also permit lesbians and gay men to feel that constructionism described the world and themselves as they experience it, rather than inducing them to flee from constructionism and into the arms of essentialism.

A modified constructionism could also allow theory to play a more helpful role in the analysis of the contemporary political expressions of gays and lesbians. In fact, the preceding analysis of the complexities and ironies of gay identity and ethnicity raises several important political dilemmas. The first of these has to do with the political manifestations of ethnicity. As I indicated, the gay movement's (and in this case, particularly the gay male movement's) subscription to the tenets of pluralism—its attempt to simply get its "piece of the pie" by appealing to hegemonic ideologies—raises questions about its potential (or desire) to mount a serious challenge to the structural roots of inequality—whether that be sexual inequality or any other kind. However, we might be better off avoiding facile distinctions between "reformist" and "revolutionary" strategies. As Omi and Winant note, civil-rights movements have an inherently radical dimension:

> By asserting that society denied minorities their rights *as groups,* they challenged the overall legitimacy of a hegemonic social order whose political logic and cultural coherence was based fundamentally in ideologies of competitive individualism.[100]

Moreover, rights movements that are organized around the politics of identity tend, by their nature, to imbue political actors with the capacity to make radical demands that they may not even intend. When the leader of the New York Gay Men's Chorus proclaims: "We show the straight community that we're just as normal as they are,"[101] this would seem on the face of it to be a rather conservative proposition, reminiscent of the accommodationist politics of the 1950s homophile movements. And yet in fact the comparison is inappropriate. When the members of homophile organizations stressed their "normality," they meant: We're the same as you, so please stop excluding us. But the sense of the above quote is quite different; it is saying: We're different from you, and that doesn't make us any less human. In this sense, it would seem that the modern adherents of identity politics are engaged, willy-nilly, in a process of changing the very bounds of the normal.

GAY "ETHNIC" POLITICS, therefore, certainly have capacities for moving in a more radical direction. Part of what would be required, however, is a recognition that the freedom from discrimination of homosexual *persons* is an insufficient goal, if homosexuality as a *practice* retains its inferior status. The disjuncture that Altman has noted between "homosexuality" and "the homosexual"—whereby the former remains stigmatized while the latter increasingly is awarded civil rights and civil liberties—presents an opportunity, in the short run, and a hurdle to be leaped, in the long run. Overcoming this obstacle would entail the adoption of political methods beyond those appropriate for electoral and established institutional politics.

But part of what may determine the political direction in which gays move is the particular model of minority-group organizing and political consciousness that is employed. Despite the adoption of a goal of civil rights, gay collective identity is at present closer in form to that of the white ethnic groups than to those of racial minorities. Movement away from a political consciousness based on white "ethnicity" and toward a "sexual minority" self-understanding might increase the gay movement's capacity to pose a more fundamental challenge to the socio-sexual order.

This, however, raises other dilemmas, regarding both the internal composition of the gay movement and its leadership, and the relationship of the gay movement to other social movements. The adoption of a "white ethnic" model, in other words, is not unexpected in a movement dominated by white, middle-class males. An adequate discussion of these issues is beyond the scope of this essay; however, it seems clear enough that the gay movement will never be able to forge effective alliances with other social movements unless it can address the inequalities that plague its internal organization. In this light it is worth noting a peculiar paradox of identity politics: while affirming a distinctive group identity that legitimately differs from the larger society, this form of political expression simultaneously imposes a "totalizing" sameness *within* the group: it says, this is who we "really are."[102] A greater appreciation for internal diversity—on racial, gender, class, and even sexual dimensions—is a prerequisite if the gay movement is to move beyond "ethnic" insularity and join with other progressive causes.[103] The obvious first step in that direction would be improved understandings between lesbians and gay men—and a better articulation of feminist theory with theoretical perspectives on sexuality.

FINALLY, in considering the political dilemmas confronting lesbians and gays, it is vital to discuss the most serious crisis that the movement has yet faced, namely, AIDS. The "moral panic" surrounding AIDS demonstrates some of the inherent fragility of identity politics. By hardening a notion of group difference, identity politics present a highly visible target. Those social groups who see their understandings of the world as called into question by changing conceptions of sexuality, gender, and morality more broadly defined, have found in the consolidated notion of "gayness" a potent and available symbol upon which they can easily discharge their anxieties—and vent their wrath. And if there is perceived to be such a thing as a "homosexual person," then it is only a small step to the conclusion that there is such a thing as a "homosexual disease," itself the peculiar consequence of the "homosexual lifestyle."[104]

Thus the ideological and practical consequences of a complete solidification of identity into a reified notion of "the gay person" would seem to be quite grave. But to reiterate, this is not an argument for the maintenance of a strict-constructionist pose; for both the "politics of constructionism" and the "politics of essentialism" present legitimating possibilities as well as dangers of delegitimation. The task of melding theory with practice will involve creatively capitalizing on the most effective legitimations of the moment, while still remaining true both to theoretical insights and to the contemporary self-understandings of the women and men who populate the movement.

REFERENCES

1 The four quotes, in order, are: (1) an unnamed lesbian, interviewed by Barbara Ponse in *Identities in the Lesbian World: The Social Construction of Self* (Westport, Conn.: Greenwood Press, 1978), p. 178; (2) a different lesbian interview subject, quoted in Ponse, p. 189; (3) Donald Webster Cory [pseud.], *The Homosexual in America* (New York: Castle Books, 1951), p. 9; (4) James Baldwin, interviewed by Richard Goldstein, "Go the Way Your Blood Beats: An Interview with James Baldwin," *Village Voice,* 26 June 1984, p. 14.

2 Vivienne C. Cass, "Homosexual Identity: A Concept in Need of Definition," *Journal of Homosexuality,* vol. 9, nos. 2/3 (Winter 1983/Spring 1984), p. 105.

3 *Oakland Tribune,* 6 March 1987, p. F-7.

4 See Nancy Chodorow, "Feminism and Difference: Gender, Relation, and Difference in Psychoanalytic Perspective," *Socialist Review,* no. 46 (July-August 1979), pp. 51-69. For an analogous discussion in the domain of race, see Michael Omi and Howard Winant, *Racial Formation in the United States: From the 1960s to the 1980s* (New York: Routledge & Kegan Paul, 1986), p. 68 and passim. For class, see Ernesto Laclau and Chantal Mouffe, *Hegemony and Socialist Strategy: Towards a Radical Democratic Theory of Politics* (London: Verso, 1985); or Pierre Bourdieu, "The Social Space and the Genesis of Groups," *Theory and Society,* vol. 14, no. 6 (November 1985), pp. 723-744. Similar arguments have also taken place with regard to mental illness, alcoholism, and drug addiction.

5 See, in particular, Dennis Altman, *The Homosexualization of America* (Boston: Beacon Press, 1982).

6 For a discussion of the contributions and limitations of feminist theory (and, somewhat analogously, Marxism) to the study of sex, see Gayle Rubin, "Thinking Sex: Notes for a Radical Theory of the Politics of Sexuality," in Carole Vance, ed., *Pleasure and Danger: Exploring Female Sexuality* (Boston: Routledge & Kegan Paul, 1984), pp. 300-309.

7 This argument about "nominalism" and "realism" is taken from John Boswell, "Revolutions, Universals and Sexual Categories," *Salmagundi,* nos. 58-59 (Fall 1982-Winter 1983), pp. 89-113. See also Ian Hacking, "Making Up People," in Thomas C. Heller, Morton Sosna, and David Weilbery, eds., *Reconstructing Individualism: Autonomy, Individuality, and the Self in Western Thought* (Stanford, Calif.: Stanford University Press, 1986), pp. 222-236.

8 Gay and lesbian exponents of essentialist positions include John Boswell, *Christianity, Social Tolerance, and Homosexuality: Gay People in Western Europe from the Beginning of the Christian Era to the Fourteenth Century* (Chicago: University of Chicago Press, 1980); and Adrienne Rich, "Compulsory Heterosexuality and Lesbian Existence," in Ann Snitow, et al., eds., *Powers of Desire: The Politics of Sexuality* (New York: Monthly Review Press, 1983), pp. 177-206.

9 Prime examples of this recent scholarship would be Jeffrey Weeks, *Coming Out: Homosexual Politics in Britain, from the Nineteenth Century to the Present* (London: Quartet Books, 1977): and John D'Emilio, *Sexual Politics, Sexual Communities: The Making of a Homosexual Minority in the United States, 1940-1970* (Chicago: University of Chicago Press, 1983); and the essays in Kenneth Plummer, ed., *The Making of the Modern Homosexual* (London: Hutchinson, 1981). Many

other examples could be added. In the bibliography to *Coming Out,* Weeks identifies the main influences on his thinking as Plummer, McIntosh, and Gagnon and Simon (p., 239); in later essays, he has testified to the importance of Foucault. D'Emilio (p. 4n) cites the same cast of characters, with a few additions, such as Jonathan Katz and Estelle Freedman.

10 John M. Gagnon and William Simon, *Sexual Conduct* (Chicago: Aldine, 1973); Mary McIntosh, "The Homosexual Role," *Social Problems,* vol. 17, no. 2 (Fall 1986), pp. 262-270; Ken Plummer, *Sexual Stigma* (London: Routledge & Kegan Paul, 1975).

11 The phrase "sex/gender system" is from Gayle Rubin, "The Traffic in Women: Notes on the 'Political Economy' of Sex," in Rayna Reiter, ed., *Toward an Anthropology of Women* (New York: Monthly Review, 1975), pp. 157-210. Good examples of anthropological studies in this vein include the essays in Sherry B. Ortner and Harriet Whitehead, eds., *Sexual Meanings: The Cultural Construction of Gender and Sexuality* (Cambridge: Cambridge University Press, 1981). Anthropological constructionism escapes some, but not all of the problems I identify in the sociological and historical forms, for reasons I return to in the conclusion.

12 Michel Foucault, *The History of Sexuality,* volume 1 (New York: Vintage, 1980).

13 John Gagnon, *Human Sexualities* (Chicago: Scott, Foresman & Co., 1977), p. 2; quoted in Kenneth Plummer, "Symbolic Interactionism and Sexual Conduct," in Mike Brake, ed., *Human Sexual Relations* (New York: Pantheon, 1982), p. 226.

14 Gagnon and Simon, *Sexual Conduct,* p. 19.

15 Jeffrey Weeks, "The Development of Sexual Theory and Sexual Politics," in Brake, ed., *Human Sexual Relations,* p. 294.

16 Wilhelm Reich, *The Sexual Revolution* (New York: Farrar, Straus & Giroux, 1969); Herbert Marcuse, *Eros and Civilization* (Boston: Beacon Press, 1966).

17 Weeks, "Development of Sexual Theory," p. 295.

18 McIntosh, "Homosexual Role," p. 182.

19 Ibid., pp. 183-184.

20 The first and most influential of these was Weeks's study of Britain, *Coming Out.*

21 Foucault, *History of Sexuality.*

22 Ibid., p. 43.

23 Tomás Almaguer, "Conceptualizing Sexual Stratification: Notes toward a Sociology of Sexuality" (unpublished essay, 1986), p. 8.

24 Foucault, *History of Sexuality,* p. 101.

25 Weeks, *Coming Out,* p. 2 and parts I-III; John D'Emilio, *Sexual Politics,* pp. 9-22; also John D'Emilio, "Capitalism and Gay Identity," in Snitow et al., eds., *Powers of Desire,* pp. 100-113.

26 Jeffrey Escoffier, "Sexual Revolution and the Politics of Gay Identity," *Socialist Review,* nos. 82-83 (July-October 1985), pp. 119-153; D'Emilio, *Sexual Politics,* chapters 5-7.

27 The most influential of the left Freudians was Herbert Marcuse, *Eros and Civilization.*

28 Carl Wittman, "Refugees from Amerika: A Gay Manifesto," in Joseph A. McCaffrey, *The Homosexual Dialectic* (Englewood Cliffs, N.J.: Prentice-Hall, 1972), p. 159.

29 Quoted in Ponse, *Identities,* p. 95.

30 Dennis Altman, *Homosexual: Oppression and Liberation* (New York: Avon, 1971). Altman's radical Freudian views can be seen in the frequent references to Marcuse.
31 Rich, "Compulsory Heterosexuality."
32 Quoted in Altman, *Homosexualization of America,* p. 161.
33 This is one of the prime arguments made by Altman in *Homosexualization of America,* written a decade after his earlier "liberationist" book.
34 Altman, *Homosexualization of America,* p. 9.
35 Cory, *The Homosexual in America.* It is interesting to note that while the term "minority" is indexed frequently, "identity" does not appear.
36 Almaguer, "Conceptualizing Sexual Stratification," p. 25; Frances Fitzgerald, *Cities on a Hill: A Journey through Contemporary American Cultures* (New York: Simon & Schuster, 1986), p. 58.
37 Jeffrey Weeks, *Sexuality and Its Discontents: Meanings, Myths & Modern Sexualities* (London: Routledge & Kegan Paul, 1985), pp. 21-25; Altman, *Homosexualization of America,* chapter 3.
38 Altman, *Homosexualization of America,* p. 45.
39 On the dualisms of liberal thought, see Roberto M. Unger, *Knowledge and Politics* (New York: Free Press, 1975), esp. chapter 5. I want to thank Steve McMahon for pointing out this argument to me.
40 For a discussion of the underlying asocial individualism in Marcuse, see Nancy Chodorow, "Beyond Drive Theory: Object Relations and the Limits of Radical Individualism," *Theory and Society,* vol. 14, no. 3 (May 1985), pp. 271-319.
41 Jeffrey Weeks, "Discourse, Desire, and Sexual Deviance: Some Problems in a History of Homosexuality," in Ken Plummer, ed., *The Making of the Modern Homosexual* (London: Hutchinson, 1981), pp. 94-95.
42 Stephen O. Murray, *Social Theory, Homosexual Realities* (New York: Gay Academic Union, 1984), pp. 19-20.
43 On the politics of the homophile movement, see D'Emilio, *Sexual Politics,* chapters 5-7; and Escoffier, "Sexual Revolution."
44 Cass, "Homosexual Identity," p. 107-108. A comparison of the indexes of Altman's *Homosexual: Oppression and Liberation* (1971) and *The Homosexualization of America* (1982) is instructive. In the earlier book, the term "identity" does not appear in any form in the index. In the more recent book, "Identity, homosexual" has eleven direct page references, and six subheadings with further page references.
45 Cass, "Homosexual Identity," p. 108
46 Philip Gleason, "Identifying Identity: A Semantic History," *Journal of American History,* vol. 69, no. 4 (March 1983), pp. 910-931. The quote is from p. 918.
47 Ibid., pp. 918-919.
48 Ibid.
49 Peter L. Berger and Thomas Luckmann, *The Social Construction of Reality* (New York: Anchor Books, 1967), p. 174.
50 Jürgen Habermas, "Moral Development and Ego Identity," in *Communication and the Evolution of Society* (Boston: Beacon Press, 1979), p. 74.
51 Ibid., pp. 90-91; Cass, "Homosexual Identity," p. 110; Unger, *Knowledge and Politics,* p. 195; Chodorow, "Feminism and Difference," p. 60.
52 Louis Althusser, "Ideology and Ideological State Apparatuses," in *Lenin and Philosophy* (New York: Monthly Review, 1971), p. 182.
53 Kenneth Plummer, "Homosexual Categories: Some Research Problems

in the Labelling Perspective of Homosexuality," in Plummer, ed., *Making of the Modern Homosexual," pp.* 60-61.

54 Altman, *Homosexualization of America,* p. 82.

55 Weeks, *Sexuality and Its Discontents,* p. 28. See also Simon and Gagnon's recent discussion of how "the erotic" historically has come to be separated out as a distinct realm of human experience: William Simon and John H. Gagnon, "Sexual Scripts," *Society,* vol. 22, no. 1 (November-December 1984), pp. 53-60.

56 In a somewhat different, though clearly related sense, the notion of "straight" identity emerges out of the same historical conjuncture. The idea of a "heterosexual" person is also quite new, and has been created in some sense by its opposite. Cf. Omi and Winant's discussion of the changing conceptions of "white" identity through redefinitions of "black" identity: Michael Omi and Howard Winant, "By the Rivers of Babylon: Race in the United States (Part 2)," *Socialist Review,* no. 72 (November-December 1983), p. 45.

57 Howard Becker, *Outsiders: Studies in the Sociology of Deviance* (New York: Free Press, 1963), pp. 33-34.

58 Erving Goffman, *Stigma: Notes on the Management of Spoiled Identity* (Englewood Cliffs, N.J.: Prentice-Hall, 1963), pp. 14, 88.

59 Ibid., p. 114.

60 Cass, "Homosexual Identity," pp. 110, 114.

61 See, for example, Becker, *Outsiders.*

62 Plummer, "Homosexual Categories," pp. 66-72. See also the critique of the "stages" in labeling theory, as applied to homosexual identity development, in Murray, *Social Theory," p.* 17.

63 Alan P. Bell and Martin S. Weinberg, *Homosexualities: A Study of Diversity among Men and Women* (New York: Touchstone, 1978).

64 I would like to thank Ellyn Kestnbaum for substantially helping me to clarify and rethink the discussion that follows.

65 Ponse, *Identities.* This much underrated book may be the best symbolic interactionist study of identity and legitimacy; the discussion of methods of biographical reconstruction, drawing on Berger and Luckmann, is particularly excellent. Still, the notion of identity never really sneaks beneath the level of "roles"; Ponse has no conception of the intrapsychic, or of unconscious processes. Also, she focuses almost exclusively on adult life, to the exclusion of childhood.

66 See Nancy Chodorow, *The Reproduction of Mothering: Psychoanalysis and the Sociology of Gender* (Berkeley: University of California Press, 1978); also Chodorow, "Feminism and Difference," pp. 54-60. For differences between the object-relations school and the appropriation of Freud by Marcuse that has influenced gay liberation so far, See Chodorow, "Beyond Drive Theory."

67 Berger and Luckmann, *Social Construction of Reality,* p. 140; Escoffier, "Sexual Revolution," p. 127.

68 Almaguer, "Conceptualizing Sexual Stratification," p. 27.

69 Peter K. Eisenger, "Ethnicity as a Strategic Option: An Emerging View," *Public Administration Review,* vol. 38 (January-February 1978), p. 90. The terms "primordialist" and "circumstantialist" are used by Nathan Glazer and Daniel P. Moynihan in their introduction to *Ethnicity: Theory and Experience* (Cambridge: Harvard University Press, 1975), pp. 19-20. "Optionalist" is used in place of "circumstantialist" by Eisinger and by Gleason.

70 This point is made by Gleason, "Identifying Identity," pp. 919-920.

71 Michael Omi and Howard Winant, "By the Rivers of Babylon: Race in the United States (Part 1)," *Socialist Review*, no. 71 (September-October, 1983), p. 52.
72 Ibid., p. 47.
73 Donald L. Horowitz, "Ethnic Identity," in Glazer and Moynihan, eds., *Ethnicity*, pp. 113-114; emphasis added.
74 Glazer and Moynihan, *Ethnicity*.
75 See Stephen Steinberg, *The Ethnic Myth: Race, Ethnicity, and Class in America* (Boston: Beacon Press, 1981), pp. 3-4; also Frank Parkin, *Marxism and Class Theory: A Bourgeois Critique* (New York: Columbia University Press, 1979), pp. 32.
76 Parkin, *Marxism and Class Theory*, pp. 33-34.
77 Daniel Bell, "Ethnicity and Social Change," in Glazer and Moynihan, *Ethnicity*, pp. 169-170.
78 Glazer and Moynihan, *Ethnicity*, pp. 9-10; Parkin, *Marxism and Class Theory*, p. 95.
79 Eisenger, "Ethnicity as a Strategic Option," p. 90. The quote is from Altman, *Homosexualization of America*, p. 223.
80 Glazer and Moynihan discuss ethnic "disaggregation," *Ethnicity*, p. 9. Murray makes a parallel argument about gay "de-assimilation," *Social Theory*, p. 38.
81 Parkin, *Marxism and Class Theory*, pp. 85-86.
82 Ira Katznelson, *City Trenches: Urban Politics and the Patterning of Class in the United States* (New York: Pantheon, 1981).
83 Ibid.
84 On this last point, see Manuel Castells, *The City and the Grassroots* (Berkeley: University of California Press, 1983), chapter 14.
85 Michael Bronski, *Culture Clash: The Making of Gay Sensibility* (Boston: South End Press, 1984).
86 Irving Howe, "The Limits of Ethnicity," *New Republic*, 25 June 1977, p. 18; quoted in Steinberg, *Ethnic Myth*, p. 73.
87 Steinberg, *Ethnic Myth*, p. 63.
88 Chodorow, "Feminism and Difference," p. 57.
89 Altman, *Homosexualization of America*, pp. 223-224.
90 D'Emilio, *Sexual Politics*, p. 248.
91 Ibid.
92 Weeks, *Sexuality and Its Discontents*, p. 244.
93 Weeks, "Development of Sexual Theory," pp. 305-307. See also Plummer, "Homosexual Categories," pp. 55-57; and Jacquelyn N. Zita, "Historical Amnesia and the Lesbian Continuum," part of "On 'Compulsory Heterosexuality and Lesbian Existence': Defining the Issues," *Signs*, vol. 7 (Autumn 1981), p. 173.
94 Plummer, "Homosexual Categories," pp. 71-72.
95 And on the other side of the divide are scholars such as John Boswell, who rightly claim the need to develop some sort of middle ground, but continue to conceive of "gay history" in fundamentally essentialist terms. See Boswell, "Revolutions."
96 Harriet Whitehead, "The Bow and the Burden Strap: A New Look at Institutionalized Homosexuality in Native North America," in Ortner and Whitehead, eds., *Sexual Meanings*, pp. 80-115 (quote from p. 110). The idea that culture structures the possibilities of personhood is developed more generally in Clifford Geertz, *The Interpretation of Cultures* (New York: Basic Books, 1973), chapter 2. See the analogous argument by Hacking, *Making Up People*.

97 Omi and Winant, "By the Rivers of Babylon (Part 1)," p. 50. See also their *Racial Formation.*
98 Omi and Winant, "By the Rivers of Babylon (Part 2)," p. 35; emphasis in the original.
99 This implies a greater degree of acceptance among the gay community of those who stand at the "boundary," namely, bisexuals. See Lisa Orlando, "Bisexuality: Loving Whom We Choose," *Gay Community News,* 25 February 1984, p. 6.
100 Omi and Winant, "By the Rivers of Babylon (Part 2)," p. 53.
101 Altman, *Homosexualization of America,* p. viii.
102 Escoffier, "Sexual Revolution," pp. 148–149; Weeks, *Sexuality and Its Discontents,* p. 187.
103 On sexual intolerance *within* the gay community, see Rubin, "Thinking Sex."
104 See Steven Epstein, "Moral Contagion and the Medicalizing of Gay Identity: AIDS in Historical Perspective," *Research in Law, Deviance, and Social Control,* vol. 9 (forthcoming, 1987).

Sexual Revolution and the Politics of Gay Identity

Jeffrey Escoffier

The dispersion and reconstitution of the *self*. That's the whole story.
—*Baudelaire*

THE LESBIAN AND GAY movements have achieved a recognized presence in American life. There are open communities of lesbians and gay men in many cities. Community organizations and businesses cater specifically to the needs of the homosexual population. Until recently there was a lesbian and gay caucus in the Democratic Party, and there are lesbian and gay political clubs in most major cities. Openly gay men and lesbians have been elected to city councils, state legislatures, and the United States Congress. These remarkable developments have occurred because the lesbian and gay movements have stressed a politics of identity closely modeled on the politics of ethnic and racial minorities.

The homosexual politics of identity successfully married interest-group politics to a radical reinterpretation of the social definitions of gender and sexuality. The original sense of identity was based on people's shared sexual preferences and on similar encounters with homophobia. The fundamental ambivalence of homosexuals originating in their being raised to be heterosexuals made the discursive process of identity formation central to gay and lesbian politics. The "ethnic model" of homosexual identity emerged when

This essay would never have been written without the constant encouragement of four people: Dick Bunce, Mark Leger, Ilene Philipson, and Gayle Rubin. In addition to them, I would also like to thank Dennis Altman, Jeanne Bergman, Allan Berubè, George Chauncey, William Simon, Howard Winant, and the Bay Area Socialist Review *collective for their extensive comments and suggestions. I owe a special debt to the students of my course on homosexuality and social change at the University of California, Berkeley, during the summer and fall of 1983, whose critical, passionate, and intelligent arguments contributed to the development of many of the ideas presented in this essay.* —J. E.

lesbians and gay men had accumulated enough political and economic resources to contend with other interest groups.

Recently lesbian and gay male communities may have entered a new period in relation to the homosexual identity developed over the past decade. Both lesbians and gay men have created a network of institutions that reaches outside their shared sexual preferences; these have adopted norms of conduct that guide their members, and they have a small degree of power in American society. Within this context other forms of sexual expression (e.g., bisexuality, S/M, or butch/femme role-playing) have provoked intense and highly politicized debates. Most recently the AIDS crisis in the gay male community has aroused a full-scale re-evaluation of sexual behavior and its relationship to gay identity.

These recent developments have put into question the belief in a fixed homosexual identity that has permanent sexual and political significance.[1] Questioning this belief poses problems of great theoretical and political urgency. Should the lesbian and gay movements abandon the politics of identity? Why are sexual identities political? What historical conditions underlie the emergence of the gay and lesbian movements? Before we can address the political and strategic question of whether or not we must abandon a politics of identity we must address the theoretical and historical issues of why and how sexual identities are politicized.

Transformations of the Sex/Gender System

SINCE WORLD WAR II various groups dissatisfied with the social relations of sex and gender have become political subjects and mobilized to reorganize the social relations and norms regulating gender and sexuality. It is not possible to understand this history without reference to the ensemble of discourses, practices, and institutions that structure and regulate the social relations of gender as well as the varieties of sexual behavior. This ensemble of discourses, practices, and institutions—called the sex/gender system by Gayle Rubin—codes biological capacities into the symbolic and social patterns that constitute our lives as gendered and sexual human beings.[2] The sex/gender system embodies *forms of domination* with their concentrations of power (such as the male-headed nuclear family, urban sexual spaces as "back regions," or segmented labor markets); *normative regulations* (such as the sexual double standard, the heterosexual assumption, or the male breadwinner ethic); and *symbolic codes* (such as the ideology of romantic love, the Christian conception of marriage, the idea of sexual reproduction as an evolutionary responsibility, or the belief in the sexual innocence of children).[3] Sexual identities are the results of struggles among concrete historical actors (for example, between prostitutes and the state) and shaped by the social relations of the sex/gender system. As forms of subjectivity and agency, sexual identities are in the process of formation at any particular moment. They are not uniquely determined by the economic, political, normative, or symbolic aspects of the sex/gender system. Precisely because the formation of sexual identities is the result of social struggles, the outcomes and meanings of this process are reconstituted at each moment of history. Transformations in the sex/gender system are the result of struggles among historical actors with gender and sexual identities. The historical struggles of politicized sexual identities thereby modify the conditions under which they are formed. The sex/gender system is not an isolated system of institutions and practices; it interacts with the economy and the state as well as with other social ensembles such as those devoted to racial formation, class structure, or generations.[4]

THE MASSIVE MOBILIZATION of civilians and armed services during World War II transformed the American sex/gender system beginning in 1940. This transformation is an immense and contradictory process (very much like the "industrial revolution" as a process of long-term historical change) that should not be understood as a coherent or "progressive" process but as one in which antagonistic movements and ideologies contend for their own visions of possible sexual and gender arrangements. This dynamic process of historical change—with its moments of rupture and periods of stability—is what I mean by "sexual revolution."

I will chart the postwar sexual revolution through three politically and analytically distinct "moments" (which are *not* meant to be chronological moments). The first moment was the discovery of a gap between sexual norms and sexual behavior. This discovery was made by Alfred Kinsey and his colleagues. On the basis of this discovery Kinsey formulated a critique of sexual norms. The second moment emerged during the highly contradictory period of postwar prosperity brought on by Keynesian economic policies. This period showed marked reactionary tendencies toward gender roles (the attempt to keep women in the home), sexuality (violent repression of homosexuals), and an extreme pronatalism (the baby boom). The consumption ethos of the period, however, tended to undermine the repressive measures toward women and sexual minorities. In this period a number of intellectuals developed critiques of sexual repression, i.e., of the power to enforce the norms of gender and sexuality. The works of these intellectuals helped give the sexual revolution political subjects. The third moment appeared with the political emergence of the gay liberation movement in the wake of the women's movement. The women's movement emerged from both the decline of the paternalistic family and women's reaction to sexism in the student movement and the new left. The gay movement followed closely on the emergence of the women's movement. Building on a gay urban subculture that had existed since World War II, gay people were able to forge a collective sexual culture and thus, to some extent, reinterpret the symbolic significance of sexuality and gender.

Before we can examine these developments in the post–World War II period, however, it is necessary to abandon the Reichian model of sexual revolution so effectively criticized by Michel Foucault in his critique of the "repression hypothesis."[5] The transformation of the sex/gender system not only involves the elimination of repressive strictures on sexual behavior but also entails a constant reconstitution of new forms of gender and sexuality. Moreover these transformations affect economic and political relations, attitudes, and laws and, in turn, the symbolic and imaginative meanings of gender and sexuality.

Historical and anthropological research has shown that homosexual *persons* (i.e., people who occupy a social position or role as homosexuals) do not exist in many societies while homosexual behavior is found in virtually every society.[6] Therefore we must make a distinction between homosexual *behavior* and homosexual *identity*. This distinction refers to the difference between homosexual activity per se (whether casual or regular) and the social definition of oneself as a homosexual person both emotionally and sexually. Such a distinction is consciously rooted in historical and cross-cultural comparisons between homosexuality in advanced industrial societies and homosexuality in other cultures or time periods. For instance, in ancient Greece, homosexual relationships between older men and younger men were commonly accepted. The relationships were viewed as pedagogic. Within the context of an erotic relation the older man passed on to the younger man military, intellectual, and political skills. But the older men were also often married and the fathers of children. Neither sexual relation excluded the other. Thus although the societies of ancient Greece recognized homosexual activity for men as a valid form of sexuality, the men involved in these relationships rarely defined themselves as primarily "homosexual."[7]

Another institutionalized form of homosexuality took place in many American Indian societies. In these societies girls and boys could refuse initiation into their adult gender roles and instead adopt the social role of the other gender. For example, men who dressed and performed the adult female role were known as "berdache"—originally the French term for these Indians. The *berdache* often married Indian men. Yet the partners in these marriages did not define themselves, nor were they recognized by their societies, as homosexuals, although their marital sex life consisted of homosexual sexual relations.

The theoretical distinction between behavior and identity has been important in histories of homosexuality, and in a number of histories of the gay and lesbian emancipation movements.[8]

Kinsey and the Liberal Imagination

THE MOBILIZATION for World War II profoundly rocked the social relations of gender and sexuality in the United States. Young men and women left the haven of their families and lived for four years among other young people far from parental guidance.

Recognition of sexual revolution dawned slowly after the war. The publication of Alfred Kinsey's two pathbreaking volumes on human sexuality in 1948 (*Sexual Behavior in the Human Male*) and 1953 (*Sexual Behavior in the Human Female*) probably exerted greater influence on modern conceptions of sexuality than any work since Freud's. Kinsey's work represented the detailed mapping of a submerged continent known only from the archipelagos of exposed mountaintops. Moral outrage and a great deal of professional hypocrisy greeted the report, but few Americans remained immune to a new awareness of the gap between public attitudes toward sexual behavior and daily sexual activities.

In his critical review of the first volume, the conservative cultural critic Lionel Trilling saw the Kinsey report as a symptomatic failure of the liberal imagination. "The *Report* has the intention of habituating its readers to sexuality in all its manifestations: it wants to establish as it were, a democratic pluralism of sexuality. . . . That this generosity of mind is much to be admired goes without saying. . . . [But] it goes with a nearly conscious aversion from making intellectual distinctions, almost as if out of the belief that an intellectual distinction must inevitably lead to a social discrimination or exclusion."[9]

While many of Kinsey's analyses and assumptions can be criticized, both volumes offer sophisticated and often subtle discussions of many aspects of sexual life. Nevertheless, many intellectuals and readers expressed moral objections to Kinsey's project for its empirical, materialistic, and ostensibly value-free investigation into the subject of human sexuality. Although he never saw it as a moral position, Kinsey's fundamental ethical tenet throughout his work was tolerance; in both volumes he stressed "sympathetic acceptance of people as they are" and repeatedly noted the limits of a person's ability to modify his or her sexual behavior.[10] Kinsey was so struck by the extraordinary extent of individual variation in sexual behavior that he argued that any attempt to establish uniform standards of sexual behavior was both impracticable and unjust. Kinsey supplemented this theme of individual variation by stressing what Paul Robinson has called "our common deviance."[11] He believed that his discovery of the widespread deviation from accepted sexual standards showed that attempts to regulate sexual behavior were doomed to failure and "the only proper sexual policy was no policy at all."[12] As texts Kinsey's studies united a positivistic-empirical investigation of sexual behavior and a moral attitude of tolerance. This harmonization was achieved partly by virtue of Kinsey's radical materialism which led him to measure sexual experience in quantitative terms as orgasms and by tabulating the number of orgasms. This resulted in the demotion of heterosexual intercourse to only one of six possible forms of "sexual outlet" that also included masturbation, nocturnal emission, heterosexual petting, homosexual relations, and intercourse with animals. Kinsey's tolerance was a statistical concept. From this perspective the sole distinction between heterosexuals and homosexuals is that the former are sexually attracted to people of the other gender while the latter are attracted to those of the same gender. Wherever Kinsey discusses the religious and moral attitudes that regulate sexual behavior, the behavior is valorized and the norms are characterized as naïve, mystifying, and ideological.

One of the major shortcomings of Kinsey's volumes is the absence of any historical perspective. While the actual collection of Kinsey's statistical material was stretched out over a decade (1938–1947), the analysis in the published volumes collapses any possible diachronic dimension into cross-sections. The historical dimension survives only in the analysis of sexual behavior by age, but even then age as a stage of life cycle is given analytical priority over cohort differences. Kinsey's blindness toward history obscured the political horizon within which the Kinsey volumes were published. While the Kinsey reports were published at the beginning of a second wave of modern "sexual revolution" (a first wave took place in the late nineteenth century and early twentieth century—1890–1919), Kinsey's data reflected the sexual behavior of the generations that came to adulthood between 1920 and 1940, a period which evidenced little sexual change.

Kinsey's data did show traces of the earlier wave of "sexual revolution," but these data were not published in either of the two reports.[13] An earlier survey of sexual behavior had already revealed that the proportion of women born between 1890 and 1899 (and therefore reaching maturity between 1910 and 1920) who had premarital intercourse had increased by 100 per cent over those born before 1890.[14] While the Kinsey reports did not capture the postwar sexual revolution (partly because they studied the interwar generations and partly because they assumed that sexuality as physiological activity did not have a history), they did come to symbolize it in the popular consciousness and in the history of ideas. For American liberals, the Kinsey reports unified heterogeneous intellectual and political elements. They offered an interpretation of sexual acts that was empirically grounded, embedded in a critique of accepted sexual norms and politically held together by an ethics of tolerance. The Kinsey reports served as the basis of the liberal theory of sexual liberation (all orgasms were equally valid!)

Kinsey's findings on homosexuality were among the most controversial and widely publicized. His volume on male sexuality concluded that 37 per cent of the male population of the United States had had at least one homosexual experience to orgasm between adolescence and old age. The data also seemed to suggest that many adults were neither permanently nor exclusively homosexual or heterosexual but evidenced a fluid continuum of sexual behavior. Kinsey measured this fluidity along the "Kinsey scale" of hetero- to homosexual behavior and fantasy which ranged from 0 (exclusively heterosexual) through 6 (exclusively homosexual). While Kinsey's findings clearly encouraged him to reject homosexuality as a pathological syndrome, the range and fluidity of many Americans' sexual behavior also led him to reject the idea of a sexual identity; he believed that there were no homosexual persons, only homosexual acts.

Kinsey's emphasis on acts and the number of orgasms ideologically closed off his analysis from its political and historical meaning. If his synchronic analysis of sexual outlets obscured the emergence of "sexual revolution," his ontology of acts obscured the emergence of political subjects—such as youth, women, and homosexuals—who would make the postwar sexual revolution. While the Kinseyan paradigm had an enormous emancipatory impact on American society (another major contribution was its recognition of female sexuality), its positivistic methodology and even its "liberal" presupposition of tolerance had the effect of suppressing the significance of gay cultural developments in the early fifties.

HOMOSEXUALS THEMSELVES were divided over the significance of the emerging sense of "group consciousness." The Mattachine Society, founded in Los Angeles in 1951, marked the beginning of an unbroken history of homosexual emancipation movements in the United States.[15] Many of the founders of the Mattachine Society had extensive political experience before they turned their energies to organizing among homosexuals. Most of the founders' earlier political experience had been in the Communist Party or on the left. The parallels between the experience of Communist Party members and homosexuals in the late forties and early fifties led the early leaders of the Mattachine to model their new organization on the Communist Party, emphasizing secrecy, centralized leadership, and a hierarchy of "cells." Marxist analysis also helped the early leaders of Mattachine develop a political analysis of homosexual oppression that emphasized its "socially determined pattern." From their early group discussions, these Mattachine members concluded that homosexuals were an oppressed cultural minority. They believed the rigid definitions of gender behavior led men and women to accept unquestioningly social roles which equated "male, masculine, man *only* with husband and Father . . . and which [equated] female, feminine, women *only* with wife and Mother." Thus for these early homosexual emancipationists, homosexual women and men were victimized by a "language and culture that did not admit the existence of a Homosexual Minority." For those activists homosexuals constituted "a social minority imprisoned within a dominant culture" and largely they were "a minority unaware."

Although this analysis seemed consistent with the experience of many gay women and men at the time as well as with subsequent history, other homosexuals in the Mattachine Society argued that the cultural and social characteristics of gay life were the results of ostracism and oppression itself. And against the "cultural minority" thesis these critics often adopted the Kinseyan argument that homosexuals and heterosexuals differed only in their sexual preferences.

Each line of argument conceptualized the homosexual self differently and each implied alternative political strategies. The cultural-minority thesis argued that homosexuals had developed differently because they had been excluded from dominant heterosexual culture. The "secondary socialization" of homosexuals into a distinct subculture helped them to develop appropriate new values, relationships, and cultural forms because homosexual life "did not fit the patterns of heterosexual love, marriage, children, etc. upon which the dominant culture rests."[16] While the proponents of the cultural-minority thesis recognized that homosexuals also internalized the dominant culture's view of themselves as aberrant and were often forced by social stigma to lead lives of secrecy, hypocrisy, and emotional stress, they emphasized the need for a critique of this internalized self-oppression and the development of "an ethical homosexual culture."

The alternative "assimilationist" position sought to open the way to acceptance of homosexuals by emphasizing the similarities between homosexuals and heterosexuals. Because the "secondary socialization" of homosexuals resulted from a life given over to hiding, isolation, and internalized self-hatred, homosexuals should adopt a "pattern of behavior that is acceptable to society in general and compatible with [the] recognized institutions . . . of home, church and state," rather than creating an "ethical homosexual culture," which would only accentuate the perceived differences between homosexuals and heterosexuals and provoke continued hostility. The "cultural minority" analysis was hotly debated in the early years of the Mattachine Society but after many battles, marked also by anti-communism, the assimilationist thesis prevailed and served as the ideological basis for the homosexual rights movement during the fifties and sixties.

THUS THROUGHOUT the fifties and sixties the Kinseyan paradigm permeated the political discourses of sexual emancipation. We find its marks on homosexual politics,[17] on popular conceptions of female sexuality, on the sociological analysis of the premarital sexual activities of young men and women,[18] and on the "philosophy" of *Playboy* magazine.[19] The Kinsey paradigm validated sexual activity (lots of orgasms) and criticized the normative regulation of sexual behavior. But the Kinseyan approach offered no theory of sexual coding (i.e., the symbolic and cultural significance of sexual acts). Not only did it therefore ignore the mundane importance of "romantic love" but it also played down the social construction of sexuality and the role of subcultures and secondary socialization in an individual's sexual development. In a corresponding fashion the assimilation position of the Mattachine Society suffered from blindness to the possible significance of sexual culture. This made it not only difficult to conceive of homosexuals as political subjects but also impossible to imagine the gay subculture as a community that had resources to mobilize and could organize politically.

The Kinsey reports' lack of a historical perspective on sexuality also made it difficult to interpret the radical transformation of the sex/gender system that in the wake of World War II began to modify the everyday significance of family life, gender roles, and sexual behavior. Both the cultural-minority thesis and the assimilation argument also suffered from their lack of historical perspective. While the cultural minority thesis could easily have accommodated an account of the historical development of a homosexual minority, it did not find the ideological space to do so. The assimilationist perspective implied a history of sexual oppression (since no difference "really" existed between homosexuals and heterosexuals, history alone could explain the peculiar reasons and means heterosexuals had for repressing homosexuality), but such a history was not articulated. Both kinds of history would have been useful but neither developed during the late fifties and early sixties.

Both the liberal imagination and the homophile movement (as the homosexual emancipation movement of that time called itself in order to play down the "sexual") conceptualized sexual emancipation as a critique of ideological and unrealistic sexual norms in favor of people's actual sexual behavior. Neither perspective emphasized the family as a form of dominance nor criticized sexual repression for its impact on the culture and institutions of American society. A critique of sexual repression in American society eventually emerged from a left analysis of the economic role of sexual repression.

The Sexual Contradictions of Keynesianism

ALL THROUGH THE WAR YEARS most economists, politicians, and the general public had no doubt that the most important postwar economic and political problem was that of providing full employment. Many people feared a return to the grim economic realities of the thirties. Among policy-makers other postwar economic and social policies were subordinated to the goal of full employment.[20] In addition the labor movement also pushed hard for full-employment legislation.

Even if the weakened version of the Employment Act that eventually passed in 1946 only established the principle of the federal government maintaining "maximum employment, production and purchasing power," additional legislation bolstered the rather vague guidelines of the act, creating unemployment compensation, minimum-wage legislation, and old-age and survivor insurance. If the 1946 Employment Act provided the Keynesian rationale in the postwar period, the military budget supplied the bulk of federal spending that sustained high levels of aggregate demand throughout the fifties and sixties.[21]

Through a series of important pieces of labor legislation (the Wagner Act of 1935, the Social Security Act of 1935 and the postwar Taft-Hartley and McCarran acts), the Employment Act became the centerpiece of postwar capital-labor relations.[22] In conjunction with the restrictive immigration legislation of the 1920s and the decline of the United States birth rate through the 1920s and 1930s, the Employment Act helped to alter the historical relations between labor demand and labor supply. Consequently the high level of aggregate demand and the tight labor markets of the

1940s and 1950s provided the economic resources that helped spur on the postwar baby boom.[23]

Through these long-term modifications in labor relations and macroeconomic policy, the Keynesian-welfare state exercised a considerable impact on the relations of autonomy and dependence (of men, women, and children) within the family. Other aspects of the immediate postwar economic situation also helped to destabilize relations within the family. The effect of reconversion (toward a peacetime economy) on the labor market led to a temporary drop in the labor-force participation of women. By January 1946, four million fewer women were in the labor force than at the 1944 wartime employment peak, while at the same time total civilian employment increased from 52.8 million to 57.8 million as soldiers were released from the armed services and civilian workers (mostly women) were laid off from wartime jobs.[24]

Throughout the immediate postwar period there was a concerted effort to re-establish "traditional values." The male-headed family had not only been disrupted by the war but the "male breadwinner role" had already been severely undermined by the depression.[25] The social upheavals, the unprecedented migration and breakup of families, and the entry of women into the industrial labor force during the war years were counteracted in the postwar period with a barrage of publicity. For instance, many sociologists argued that if women continued to work, children would be neglected and the home would be endangered. They argued for restoring the paternalistic family.[26] The postwar ideological campaigns that portrayed women's place in the home, and postwar federal economic policies as well as private industry's personnel policies, were all intended to revitalize the male-headed nuclear family and re-establish the pre-depression relations of autonomy and dependence in the family.

During the depression the high level of male unemployment and the economic difficulties experienced by most households had begun to alter the relations of autonomy and dependence within the family. Many married women and children entered the labor market in order to compensate for the decline of the male breadwinner's earnings.[27] Children took on adult responsibilities at an early age. Girls were drawn into the domestic management of the household, while boys were forced to take on breadwinning responsibilities. Following on this the war experience offered unprecedented personal autonomy and economic independence to the generation reared in the thirties. Because of this many men and women found it difficult to return to more traditional gender roles when the war ended. Many married women re-entered the labor force soon after the demobilization was complete. By 1952 some 10.4 million wives held jobs—two million more than at the height of World War II. Substantial numbers of these women were the middle-aged wives who first found it respectable to be employed outside the home during the war.

A SIGNIFICANT DEVELOPMENT in heterosexual behavior during the postwar period was the baby boom. It temporarily reversed the steady decline in marital fertility rates that had been going on since 1800. The baby boom resulted from a higher proportion of women who were born in the 1920s and 1930s marrying, marrying at earlier ages, and having children more quickly.[28] The extended postwar prosperity may have had a lot to do with encouraging marriage and childbearing by its implicit promise of an economic future that differed considerably from the childhood experience of most people during the thirties.[29] This period also saw unprecedented attention paid to sexual pleasure in marriage, while the National Fertility Studies of 1965 and 1970 revealed a great deal of unwanted fertility in the 1950s.[30] The postwar ideological and attitudinal shifts towards home, family, and children also were affected by the process of suburbanization, which established new communities on the fringes of large cities from which husbands made a long commute in to work while community life centered on the activities of children and mothers.

These demographic trends merge with certain political developments that surfaced in the period immediately after the war (1945–1955). For example, the pronatalism and the attempted restoration of the "patriarchal" family also coincided with the postwar "moral panic" about the "homosexual menace" and the "sexual offender." Throughout the period, many states and cities launched campaigns to control sexual psychopaths and "deviants." The McCarthy witchhunts focused on homosexuals in government employment as "security risks" and morally-politically suspect.[31]

The Keynesian prosperity of the 1950s and 1960s created a double bind for the postwar family. The baby boom household—with the exploding cost of raising children and its members' rising consumer expectations—eventually rendered the family wage (based on the earnings of the male breadwinner) insufficient to attain the new postwar standard of living without a supplemental income. While a wife's earnings were usually below even her own subsistence level, nevertheless they were high enough to affect the family's standard of living.[32] This Keynesian double bind is what Daniel Bell has called the "cultural contradictions of capitalism"—the tension between work, accumulation, and production as ends in themselves and work as a means to consumption and hedonistic gratification.[33]

As married women increasingly entered the labor force, gender roles within the family were under pressure to change.[34] Thus women's labor-force participation has continued to undermine the male-dominated family in the postwar sex/gender system. This type of family's normative regulations—"the breadwinner ethic" and "woman's place is in the home"—have had less and less relevance to most people's behavior. Wage and job discrimination against women and single men as well as the segmented labor market do perpetuate some of the economic imbalances in power and resources. But the steady increase in individuals living outside family households has fueled a host of cultural revolts and urban subcultures since the late fifties.

Throughout this period (1950–1964) there were frequent skirmishes against the norms of gender and sex by men. Even with the economic support of Keynesian full-employment policies, many men resisted the strenuous burden of the primary breadwinner, as Barbara Ehrenreich has recently shown in her book *The Hearts of Men*. Failure to sustain the breadwinner role implied immaturity and was considered symptomatic of latent homosexuality or mother-fixation.[35] These minor revolts ranged from "the Gray Flannel dissidents" and the Beat generation to the readers of *Playboy* magazine. The male rebellions of the fifties took place within the context of the attempted revival of male-dominated sex/gender arrangements. Men's resentments were often directed against the women and children for whom a man had to commit himself to a boring and unsatisfactory job, while female resentments were often displaced onto their fellow prisoners in the home, their children.[36]

Moreover, as the fifties wore on, postwar affluence did not allay these frustrations and anxieties. Many workers were dissatisfied with the meaninglessness of their work and their feelings of powerlessness to affect the course of production. Family responsibilities also bore heavily on many male workers, while increasingly many wives went to work in order to maintain the family standard of living. Increasingly the problems of labor and the discontents of workers received public attention.[37]

BY 1960 THREE BOOKS had been published which became extremely influential in the sixties: Herbert Marcuse's *Eros and Civilization* (1955), Norman O. Brown's *Life Against Death* (1959), and Paul Goodman's *Growing Up Absurd* (1960). While substantial differences exist among these authors, all three articulated a critique of what Marcuse called the "performance principle" in the name of erotic and sensual gratification. All three examined the consequences of the social repression of "instinctual" erotic needs. Although each work explored different aspects, they all questioned the organization of work (particularly Goodman and Marcuse) and the role of family in the repression of sexual desire. In recognition of American society's display of economic abundance, Marcuse claimed that there was "surplus repression," i.e., repression above the minimum necessary for society to function. Marcuse and Goodman also identified possible sources of political and historical change; in other words, they named political subjects.

Marcuse saw the "perversions" as the champions of the pleasure principle; they upheld sexuality as an end in itself. He claimed that "they thus place themselves outside the domination of the performance principle and challenge its very foundation."[38] He gave "narcissism" and "homosexuality" as examples of revolutionary sexualities which resisted the restriction of eros to procreative sexuality. Both Marcuse and Brown championed "polymorphous perversity," a sexuality not narrowly focused on any specific object or activity.

Paul Goodman's argument rested on a more orthodox Reichian foundation. In an essay published right after the war he had argued that "the repression of infantile and adolescent sexuality is the direct cause of submissiveness of the people to present political rule of whatever kind."[39] Thus in *Growing Up Absurd* he identified youth as the political subject who must rebel against meaningless work and sensual repression.

In some form or another, all three writers managed to capture the tangled web of sexuality and economics that marked the fifties.

All assumed the possibility of economic abundance as a necessary condition for eliminating any "surplus repression." All criticized the repressive expectations of work life and family life, the tight linking of procreation and work and the denial of pleasure in work and sexuality.

In identifying the homosexual as a champion of pleasure and eros, Marcuse named one of the moral bogeymen of the fifties as a figure of liberation. But both Brown and Marcuse resisted identification of sex with Kinsey's notion of outlets—that is orgasm. They both criticized the "tyranny of the orgasm" as a form of repressed sexuality. Instead they argued for the primeval innocence of polymorphous perversity. And Goodman argued that youth was the group most likely to break the stranglehold of repression. And indeed it was this postwar generation who really made the sexual revolution in all its aspects.

While the radical critique of sexual repression may have encouraged politically conscious youth to effectively challenge the norms of sexual and gender behavior, the affluence and the consumption ethic of "permissive" Keynesianism probably had a larger impact by undermining the disciplinary effect of the breadwinner ethic on the cohesiveness of the paternalistic family. But the radical critique did offer a more effective basis for sexual politics than the Kinsey critique, which restricted itself merely to a critique of sexual norms. Neither a critique of norms nor a critique of repression, however, could help change the symbolic significance of sex. For that we need to turn to a third "moment"—the creation of a collective sexual culture.

The Sex/Gender Code

WHILE THE KINSEY REPORTS helped homosexuals recognize that a large number of Americans had had homosexual experiences, recognizing the gap between sexual norms and behavior did not provide an adequate ideological basis for mobilizing the homosexual population. The quantitative empiricism of the Kinsey perspective excluded a vigorous conception of the homosexual identity. The behavioral continuum of the Kinsey scale created uncertainty about the validity of a collective subjectivity that primarily seemed to be a response to social stigma. The contemporary sense of "homosexual identity" did not first appear in the period after 1945; it had been in process of elaboration at least since the end of the nineteenth century. In the United States the theoretical problem of homosexual persons was first posed as a problem in medical discourse.[40]

Nineteenth-century physicians were puzzled by a broad range of deviant gender behavior, such as expressions of lust by women, dressing in clothes of the other gender (i.e., some women chose to dress as men in order to work and travel), women who could "whistle admirably," men who "never smoked and never married [and were] entirely adverse to outdoor games," and women who drank, smoked, and were very independent in their ways.[41] The term "sexual inversion" was applied to a whole spectrum of gender-role reversals only one of which was the sexual desire for someone of the same gender. Inverts were men and women who did not conform to accepted norms of gender behavior. But the theory of sexual inversion was not able to explain the traditionally "feminine" partners of female inverts or the "masculine" partners of male inverts. Thus, increasingly physicians began to distinguish homosexual desire (or sexual perversion in nineteenth-century terms) from gender-role nonconformity (or inversion).

Once homosexual desire became analytically distinct from gender behavior physicians attempted to explain homosexuality by arguing that homosexuals were in fact hermaphrodites—incorporating the biological traits of both genders. While medical research in this period often claimed to find evidence of hermaphroditism (i.e., lesbians with large clitorises or male homosexuals with feminine bodily characteristics), concepts of somatic hermaphroditism gave way to psychic hermaphroditism in which a person had the anatomical characteristics of his or her own gender but the "soul" of the other gender.

The need to clarify these issues was important to homosexual intellectuals of the nineteenth century. Karl Ulrichs, a German writer who first envisioned a homosexual emancipation movement in the 1860s, represented the male homosexual as a "woman's spirit in a man's body."[42] In the early twentieth century, political homosexuals Magnus Hirschfield and Edward Carpenter proposed a version of this, characterizing homosexuals as an "intermediate sex," which incorporates psychological qualities of both males and females.[43]

In all these theories homosexuality is explained in relation to the biological or behavioral definitions of gender. This remained the case up until the late 1960s. The psychoanalytic tradition and especially the work of Irving Bieber continued to rely on the assumption that there is a necessary relationship between the development of masculinity and femininity and heterosexuality or homosexuality.[44]

UNDERLYING ALL THESE attempts to formulate theories of homosexuality whether by physicians or homosexuals themselves is a deeply held "code" that has historically shaped our interpretation of the sex/gender system. In a pathbreaking formulation, Barbara Ponse has called this master code "the principle of consistency."[45] The principle of consistency ideologically links social roles of the sex/gender system into what Gagnon and Simon have called "the gender identity-sexual identity-family formation-reproduction pattern."

The principle of consistency ideologically links *genetic assignment* (i.e., whether a person has XX or XY chromosomes) to *anatomy* (there are in fact syndromes where this link does not hold) to a *gender identity* which is usually based on the gender assignment at birth.[46] *Gender identity* is the privately held awareness of oneself as male or female. The principle of consistency then projects the *gender role* as a function of gender identity. Gender role is learned behavior, and while usually related to one's genetic assignment and gender identity, is not necessarily determined by them, i.e., in reality to be born female does not guarantee femininity; women are not biologically nurturant. For the next step in the principle of consistency's coding of the sex/gender system, gender roles imply *sexual object choice*. The principle of consistency assumes that one's gender role determines the gender of those one finds sexually attractive. The principle of consistency ideologically ties all these elements together and portrays them as "natural."

The principle of consistency as a master code for interpreting the sex/gender system expains why any reversal or "inversion" of one element suggests that the other elements must be consistently inverted as well. A woman who wears men's clothes (or indeed chooses to pass as a man) must be a man either biologically or psychologically ("a man's spirit in a female body") and also a lesbian.

In recent years, the emergence of lesbian and gay identities has led to modifications in some versions of the principle of consistency. Ponse herself includes *sexual identity* (whether a person is homosexual, heterosexual, or bisexual) as an element, and this can be further elaborated by adding sexual role which allows for active/passive, top/bottom, butch/ femme.[47] But these amendments already imply a weaker interpretation of the principle in which the rigid categorization of sex/gender behavior into male/female/heterosexual no longer holds with the force of earlier interpretations.

If the principle of consistency ideologically holds together the ensemble of practices, discourses, and institutions of the sex/gender system, then the emergence of the homosexual as a subject and particularly as a political subject can only take place on the basis of reinterpreting the *meaning* of sexuality and gender. Otherwise, as long as homosexuals remain within the discourses of "consistency," most aspects of homosexual life will be interpreted and treated as *anomalous* and *unnatural*.

Cultural Politics in the City of Night

How powerful is the principle of consistency as an interpretative scheme in our culture? Everyday social interactions are shaped by the principle in the form of the *heterosexual assumption*. This is the common presumption made by most people that everyone is heterosexual. While the assumption has been weakened in certain cities with large homosexual populations and in certain occupational or cultural milieus, most social interactions are still governed by it. In the years before the rebirth of the gay movement in 1969, the heterosexual assumption was reinforced by the social stigma attached to homosexuality. Together the heterosexual assumption and the stigma against homosexuality forced most lesbians and gay men to keep their homosexual feelings or activities secret. The force of stigma and the heterosexual assumption established the *political horizon* for all homosexual acts—they were physical and symbolic acts at the same time.

In the period after the end of World War II, most homosexuals were in the closet. Most of them sought to "pass" as heterosexual in public settings such as the workplace or even within their families. Nevertheless, a vigorous underground subculture emerged in cities like New York, Chicago, San Francisco, Los Angeles, and Philadelphia. The urban homosexual subculture was created by the routine activities of women and men in search of sexual partners. Unlike ethnic or racial subcultures, the homosexual subculture was not transmitted and shared by families. Most women and men with homosexual desires had been raised in heterosexual families that reared them with the expectation that they would adopt heterosexual roles in adult life. Thus homosexuals often adopted and shared those heterosexual expectations and social values for many years of their lives. But outside of lucky accidents (which are often important in crystallizing one's sexual desires), most homosexual women or men had to go outside their social circles to seek out partners who shared their sexual desires. How was this possible when there were no public or explicit avowals of homosexuality? When there were no publicly acknowledged social spaces where lesbians or gay men could meet each other? When the heterosexual assumption or the stigma on homosexuality enforced silence, invisibility, and hostility?

Special tactics devised by lesbians and gay men were necessary in order to identify sexual partners. The tactics originated in the need to coordinate sexual activities without much *explicit* discussion. In a study of oppositional social practices in everyday life, Michel de Certeau has emphasized that "tactics" are ways of using imposed cultural systems to achieve one's own desires. They introduce alternative or heterogeneous meanings into the dominant cultural system. Tactics are an art of the weak; they make use of cracks in the system. Like wit, tactics require the seizing of opportunities, or timing.[48]

Communication with a desired partner (but of unknown sexual preference) requires great "tact" and must use the language of innuendo, well-placed pauses, carefully worded jokes, or ambiguous expression. For example, in John Rechy's novel *City of Night,* the narrator is propositioned on his first night in New York City at a YMCA by another resident:

> "They dont call this Y the French Embassy for nothing," the merchant marine laughs. He has sized me up slyly: broke and green in the big city—and he said: "You wouldnt believe if youd been at Mary's last night—thats a place in the Village and everything goes." He watches me evenly for some reaction, determining, Im sure, how far he can go how quickly. "So I spot this cute kid there—" Hes still studying me carefully, and when I dont say anything, he continues with more assurance: "So I spot him and I want him—yeah sure Im queer—whatya expect?" he challenges. He pauses

> longer this time, watching me still calculatingly. He goes on: "And the kid's looking for maybe a pad to flop in and breakfast—hes not queer himself. I dont like em queer: If I did Id go with a woman—why fuck around with substitutes?... So this kid goes with me—Im feeling Good, just off the ship flush—I lay 50 bucks on him."[49]

Rechy's account captures the ambiguities: "a place in the Village and everything goes"; the well-placed pauses and innuendos like "So I spot this cute kid...." He doesn't say anything about the kid's gender, somehow it's understood but not yet explicit until after the pause he continues, "So I spot *him* and I *want* him" and then after a momentary pause "Yeah, sure Im queer, whatya expect."

THE TACTICAL USES of language were central to the lesbian and gay experience of the forties, fifties, and sixties. But sexual coordination problems often required "tactical" elaborations on a larger scale. Sacha Lewis quotes from one such account:

> When I was in high school I didn't even know the word *lesbian*, much less how to be one. I just knew I wanted to be with women. I wanted to go steady, date and have a woman to share intimate sexual feelings with. So I looked very carefully at how the boys in school got girls to date, go steady, neck and the rest. What I saw was that boys had short hair. What I saw was that boys wore shirts and pants. And what I saw at the time was that the most desirable boys were into leather jackets and chains and these huge silver rings that were kind of like brass knuckles—a real '40's thing. "Okay," I said, "that must be how you get girls." So that's what I did.... I must have looked pretty funny, but it [was a] very serious thing with me at the time because it worked. There were other girls who were gay and I guess I was so obvious that they had an easy time following me."[50]

This woman's solution to the problem of satisfying her homosexual desires was to reinterpret the principle of consistency. She wanted to attract women, so she modeled herself on males. Thus she created a code that communicated a desire to establish sexual relations with women by adopting male role behavior. By adopting that tactic she became "obvious," thus attracting other women with homosexual preferences who chose to maintain their female role behavior. The woman in this anecdote became a "butch." Others chose to relate to a butch lesbian in the traditional female role; these women were called "femme." Butch/femme roles were common (though certainly not universal) in the lesbian culture of the 1950s.

Because butch/femme roles appeared to be imitations of heterosexual roles, they were later denigrated in the early days of lesbian feminism. But butch/femme roles *reinterpreted* male/female roles and because both roles were adopted by women, they were *in fact* different. Butch/femme dynamics became what John Gagnon and William Simon have called a "sexual script."[51] Butch and femme lesbians elaborated a mutually shared interpretative scheme that orchestrated their desires with a person of the preferred gender and integrated their biological capacities for arousal, climax, and resolution into sexually significant events. Joan Nestle saw her butch/femme relationships as "complex erotic statements." Butch women were "tabooed women who were willing to identify their passion for other women by wearing clothes that symbolized the taking of responsibility. Part of this responsibility was sexual expertise. In the 1950s this courage to feel comfortable with arousing another woman became a political act."[52]

Butch and femme lesbian roles involved neither a repudiation of gender role nor an exaltation of it. For example, while the lesbian butch may have adopted masculine behavior for its "initiatory" or "managerial" qualities, her primary preoccupation in sex was to please the femme rather than macho behavior of pleasing oneself first. Both roles allowed women to play with and to extend the range of possible behavior within a firm personal sense of female gender identity.[53]

There was similar playfulness among gay men on the gender "inversion" theme, in gay slang called "camping it up." Camping involved men adopting feminine mannerisms and playing on the male homosexual's "incongruous" behavior as a man having sex with another man. Camp was built on the assumption that gender behavior is a *role,* something that can be adopted, changed, or dropped. It was a style of humor that allowed homosexuals to laugh at their situation rather than despair over it.[54] Camp as an aesthetic philosophy received public recognition in Susan Sontag's famous essay "Notes on Camp," published in *Partisan Review* in 1964. Sontag acknowledged its roots in the homosexual community—"The peculiar relation between Camp taste and homosexuality has to be explained. While it's not true that Camp taste *is* homosexual taste, there is no doubt a peculiar affinity and overlap.

But homosexuals, by and large, constitute the vanguard—and most articulate audience—of Camp."[55] But she ignored that camp grew out of the gay culture's process of recoding the sexual significance of the dominant definitions of gender and of the principle of consistency. Thus although the camp sensibility, like butch/femme, cannot be attributed to all gay men and lesbians, it offered a counter-hegemonic challenge to the sex/gender system.[56] Both butch/femme role-playing and the camp sensibility were reinterpretations of the relationship of sexual preference and sexual behavior to gender. Thus, homosexuals drove a wedge between gender and sexuality by their wit and role-playing. The everyday sexual practices, the butch/femme role-playing, and the camp sensibility significantly modified the symbolic meaning of the dominant culture's notions of gender/sex for lesbians and gay men. Camp was the ideology of the homosexual subculture in the 1950s which promulgated the view of gender roles *as* performances with a sense of bitter irony.

IN A PREDOMINANTLY hostile world, one way that homosexuals limited their vulnerability was to keep their social and sexual transactions as invisible as possible. Many homosexuals joined highly closeted social circles in the hope of meeting other homosexuals in a relatively safe social setting. The homosexual stigma kept homosexual social spaces in "back regions" hidden from public view,[57] but therefore vulnerable to illegal intrusions like criminal activity (many cities had and have Mafia-controlled bars) and police brutality and corruption (gay sexual activity often "hides" in red-light districts). Nevertheless, homosexuals (more often male, because public space has been traditionally dominated by men) established physical and social spaces within urban areas—bars, hotel lobbies, Y's, bathhouses, street corners, men's rooms, and gyms. They appropriated space from its uses by the dominant culture (gay bars often evolved from bohemian or artists' bars) by introducing heterogeneous practices (e.g., certain men's rooms become sites of sexual activities).[58] Throughout the 1950s and early 1960s urban police departments all over the United States attempted to close gay bars and other homosexual meetingplaces.[60] While these drives severely disrupted the lives of homosexuals, they provoked political responses over and over again.

These developments in gay life since the end of World War II—the increasingly elaborate cultural expressions, the proliferation of gay spaces, and the numerous, if minor, political mobilizations—created a sense of social identity. Almost all gay life required *role-playing;* that is, playing a straight man or woman to many people, which gay cultural expressions such as camp generalized into a fundamental challenge to the notions of gender, sexual preference, and sexual identity as *natural.*

The Search for a Gay Identity

IN THE UNITED STATES, the debate between the homosexual assimilationist perspective and the cultural-minority thesis resurfaced in the mid-sixties.[61] An important contribution to this debate both here and in Britain was made in 1968 by Mary McIntosh, a lesbian sociologist long active on the British left. She wrote her seminal article "The Homosexual Role" as a direct response to the narrowly civil-libertarian approach of the homophile movement in England.[62] Her article helped to revive the debate that had taken place during the 1950s in the Mattachine Society between the assimilation approach and the cultural-minority thesis.[63] McIntosh argued that the homosexual role did not simply describe a "sexual behavior pattern" but a whole pattern of feelings, expectations, and strategies that emerged in response to the stigmatized labeling of homosexuals as pathological outcasts. McIntosh's analysis of the distinction between sexual behavior and role or "identity" (as later theorists have called it) was amplified by her historical account of the development of the homosexual role in England.

Only one year later, hustlers, drag queens, and gay-bar patrons fought against police when they raided the Stonewall Inn in New York City. Several days of demonstrations followed. Established homosexual leaders from the Mattachine Society of New York and the lesbian organization Daughters of Bilitis responded cautiously. Mattachine leaders still held that "demonstrations which define the homosexual as a unique minority defeat the very cause for which the homosexual strives—*to be an integral part of society.*" A new group, modeled on new-left organizations, was founded—the Gay Liberation Front. Many of its members had been participants in the anti-war movement and the counterculture. But GLF leaders broke with the "old line" homosexuals.

The explosion of gay liberation (as the wave of homosexual emancipation that emerged after the 1969 Stonewall riots is called) was produced by a clash of two cultures and two generations—the homosexual subculture of the fifties and sixties and the new-left-counterculture of 1960s youth. Ideologically, the camp of the fifties and early sixties had served as a strategy of containment; it balanced its scorn for the principle of consistency with a bitter consciousness of oppression in a framework that offered no vision of historical change (like the Kinseyan paradigm). The gay liberationists, who rarely had much appreciation for traditional gay life, proposed a radical cultural revolution. Instead of protecting the right to privacy, gay-liberation radicals insisted on "coming out"—the public disclosure of one's homosexuality—which then became the centerpiece of gay political strategy. For the gay movement *coming out* was what Gramsci called a "catharsis" which occurs when a "structure ceases to be an external force which causes man, assimilates him to itself and makes him passive and is transformed into a means of freedom, an instrument to create a new ethno-political form and a source of new initiatives."[64] Coming "out of the closet" (originally a phrase of gay slang) was to do the very thing most feared in the gay culture of the fifties and early sixties.

THE MOST SOPHISTICATED theoretical elaboration of the new gay politics was made by Dennis Altman in his book *Homosexual: Oppression and Liberation,* published in 1971.[65] The process of "coming out" is at the center of his analysis. A frequently difficult and painful process, it is both a personal and a political one. The process could involve years of coming to terms with the specific cultural or religious beliefs that stigmatize homosexual behavior. The gay liberation movement gave a political meaning to this by extending the psychological-personal process into public life by encouraging lesbians and gay men to publicly acknowledge their homosexuality. Coming out thus became praxis. Altman interpreted this extended process of coming out as a search for identity, an already existing identity, not one to be self-consciously or politically constructed.[66]

Altman linked his analysis of the gay search for identity to the views of Herbert Marcuse and Norman O. Brown that sexual liberation involved "a resurrection of our original impulse to take enjoyment from the total body" and that with liberation homosexuality and heterosexuality would cease to be viewed as separate sexualities.[67]

Like Marcuse and Brown, Altman analyzed the repression of polymorphous perversity by the removal of the erotic from all areas of life and the denial of our inherent bisexuality by the polarization of gender roles. He went on to argue, "How far sexual freedom can be conceived without coming to grips with the basic features of our society is a key ideological concern of both the women's and gay movements. Yet there is a sense in which we should be suspicious of attempts to deny the centrality of sexuality in any discussion of liberation."[68]

In his synthesis Altman attempted to bridge the "old line" gay culture of the fifties and sixties and the countercultural gay movement of the late sixties and early seventies.[69] The gay identity of the fifties and sixties would be politicized through coming out. But Altman situated both the "old" gay culture and the "new" gay identity within the framework of the utopian sexual theory of Herbert Marcuse and Norman O. Brown. In his concluding chapter, "The End of the Homosexual?" Altman saw gay liberation as "part of a much wider movement that is challenging the basic cultural norms of our advanced industrial, capitalist, and bureaucratic individual consciousness and new identities and life styles. He concluded that "one hopes that the answer lies in the creation of a new human for whom such distinctions no longer are necessary for the establishment of identity. The creation of this new human demands the acceptance of new definitions of man- and womanhood such as are being urged by gay and women's liberation."[70]

While many gay activists shared Altman's utopian sexual hopes, their political activities crystallized a strategy of encouraging and supporting the decision to come out. The focus on coming out created an altogether new type of gay politics. The public announcement of one's homosexuality became a signal act of self-acceptance, and as vast numbers of homosexuals felt encouraged to emerge from their closets the movement grew until it achieved a political impact that the homophile movement never attained.

Coming out achieved two important effects. First was the creation of a network of formal institutions serving a range of previously unsatisfied needs—religious, educational, political, recreational, professional; the publication of newspapers and periodicals, social service institutions (e.g., counseling services) and mutual-aid societies. Second, the mobilization of those who came out and the availability of community institutions helped to create a well-defined public identity for homosexuals.

Visibility was the precondition for the establishment of lesbian and gay communities that resembled the urban neighborhoods of the immigrant groups in the late nineteenth and early twentieth centuries. Visible homosexuals created gay residential neighborhoods, political groups that influenced elections, and gay-owned or -serving businesses that thrived. Many homosexuals left their communities, their families, and jobs and careers that conflicted with their being openly gay, and migrated to those cities with visible lesbian and gay communities.

In the mid-seventies among gay intellectuals, particularly those who had been active in the anti-war movement and the new left, there was a movement to explore the "gay experience" in a way modeled on black intellectuals' recovery of black culture and history in order to reclaim the historical and cultural experience of homosexuals. In addition, gay historians soon discovered the sources of homosexual emancipation on the political left. Many lesbians and gay men had only a vague awareness that a homophile movement had existed before the 1969 Stonewall riots, and most were completely surprised to discover that homosexual emancipation movements had antedated World War II.

Probably the most important book to explore the American gay experience was *Gay American History* by Jonathan Katz. Published in 1975, this documentary history of homosexuality in the United States included material from 1528 through to the mid-seventies. Katz's definition of homosexuals was framed by the cathartic experience of the gay movement in the early seventies. In his introduction, Katz wrote that "we were a people perceived out of time and out of place—socially unsituated, without a history. . . . That time is over. The people of the shadows have seen the light; Gay People are coming out—and moving on—to organized action against an oppressive society."[71]

But Katz's pioneering work also unintentionally undermined the definition of homosexual identity that the movement had assumed. The section on "Native Americans/Gay Americans" showed homosexual behavior embedded in societies that had institutionalized social relations for men and women who wished to trade gender roles. While homosexuality followed from trading gender roles, the sexual partner who had not traded gender roles was not stigmatized or labeled. Katz also categorized some passionate male-male or female-female relations as homosexual which may not have had any homoerotic component at all—for instance a passionate correspondence between Alexander Hamilton and John Laurens. The long history of coding homosexual feelings as "friendship" makes Katz's decision to include such material plausible but not necessarily always valid. Katz's research also unearthed an important new category of deviants—women who chose to pass as men in order to work for good wages or to travel. No doubt some of these were lesbians but certainly many were not. In his *Gay American History,* Katz had intended to offer the history of homosexuals, but instead rediscovered the history of gender nonconformity and of homosexual *behavior.* Katz was torn between a history of homosexuals as a distinct and fixed minority and the radical historicism that "all homosexuality is situational."

Finally a history of the homosexual *identity* was articulated by a group of activists and historians associated with a British journal called *Gay Left* (1975–1980).[72] Among this group, Jeffrey Weeks explored the implications of Mary McIntosh's 1968 essay on the "homosexual role" in a series of essays and in his history of homosexual politics in Britain, *Coming Out.*[73] The *Gay Left* approach combined symbolic interactionism with Marxist analysis. Jeffrey Weeks, Kenneth Plummer, and other gay left historians identified the specific social and economic conditions that permitted the growth of a homosexual subculture and its psychological-political outgrowth—the modern lesbian and gay-male identity. They saw sexual identity as the result of a historical process, not a natural process. John D'Emilio, in a theoretical essay, "Capitalism and Gay Identity," and in his history of the pre-Stonewall gay movement, *Sexual Politics, Sexual Communities,* has also contributed to this tradition of analysis.[74]

This search for a theory of gay identity originated among gay left intellectuals. Starting out from an "ethnic model" of history which assumed an already existing identity or social group, they discovered that homosexuals were historically constructed subjects. Both for these leftists, as well as for many other lesbian and gay activists, the theory of a lesbian or gay identity is believed to be a description of reality *and* a normative basis for politics.

The lesbian and gay movements certify—politically and socially—

the existence of the homosexual identity. The lesbian and gay contribution to the transformation of the sex/gender system was to split sexual object preference from gender, and by challenging the heterosexual assumption, legitimate the social construction of sexual identity. These developments seriously weakened the grip of the principle of consistency.

Identity and Transgression: A Conclusion

LESBIAN AND GAY IDENTITIES emerged from the political mobilization of a subculture which has started to recode the sexual significance of gender and sexual preference. Today the existence of large visible communities of lesbians and gay men has helped to institutionalize homosexual identities. The extension of the principle of consistency to include "sexual identity" is an uneasy form of incorporation of homosexuality into the principle of consistency. But its incorporation has seriously weakened the symbolic significance of the "natural" relationship between gender identity, family formation, and reproduction that the principle of consistency signifies.

The cumulative modifications in the American postwar sex/gender system—the increased independence of adolescent youth from parental control, the growing equality of women, and the political emergence of homosexuals—have threatened the beliefs and privileges of many Americans who, for religious or other reasons, are committed to traditional family patterns. The new right as a political movement has mobilized the resentments generated by the postwar transformation of the sex/gender system. The political mobilization of women and homosexuals during the seventies has threatened the economic and social status of the lower middle class and white Christian working class. Thus the new right is the most recent political subject to emerge from the turmoil of the sexual revolution.[75] But the new right is attempting to restore the principle of consistency as a natural law. Conservative critics of gay rights have argued that "the case for homosexuality is a vulgarization of a philosophical anarchism which denies the existence of nature," which also denies the "overwhelmingly obvious fact that human bodies are better designed for heterosexual intercourse than homosexual."[76] But the principle of consistency as symbolic order or master code works only as long as it is taken for granted. The political mobilization of the new right can only succeed in defending a particular sex/gender subculture. It cannot restore the heterosexual and paternalistic family form to its position of dominance.

The sex/gender arrangements that held in American society in 1940 have been radically modified—by the mobilization of World War II; by the contradictory postwar demands for family discipline and mass consumption; and by the series of grassroots political mobilizations by youth, women, and the new right. Each of these mobilizations has, like the gay movement, created a particular form of political subjectivity. And each form of political identity is vulnerable to recodings due to shifts in age, social context, and political developments. In the early stages of creating a collective subjectivity, politically mobilized homosexuals (or women, for example) adopted norms and codes of conduct that served as "recipes for an appropriate attitude regarding the self."[77] These norms, often articulated in opposition to homophobia, provided a platform for politics and social criticism. But they also addressed the personal distress and thematized the experience of humiliation that homosexuals had suffered. Thus the personal became the political. While the initial political mobilization drew on these feelings of oppression, the political distance that the lesbian and gay communities had been able to go was fueled by the process by which an individual lesbian or gay man modified her or his behavior and feelings according to these "recipes for being." The mobilization of homosexuals as collective subjects emphasized our *shared* experiences of oppression. It therefore was a militant affirmation of all that is the same among us.*

But every form of political subjectivity is only a relay that gets us from one point to another. The affirmation of the shared experience within any group soon encounters limits and differences. Everyone's identity exists at the nexus of a web of opposing, contradictory, or merely different group affiliations and personal

* The breakdown of the sex/gender system organized along the principle of consistency into a plurality of autonomous practices and identities around age, gender, sexuality, and form of family suggests the rise of a new sex/gender code which could be called the *combinatorial principle*—in which the social relations of gender and sex will be more fluid. Thus distinct sexualities would emerge based on permutations of the "elements" (not necessarily immutable elements) of the sex/gender system—for example butch heterosexual women and femme heterosexual men. The combinatorial principle of the sex/gender system would offer an ideological framework for these permutations of diverse components of sexualities and genders.

commitments. In gay politics not only has the affirmation of shared experience resulted in the consolidation of homosexual differentness, but in the lesbian and gay-male communities' drive for affirmation differences have emerged among the members of both communities that cannot be eradicated. Political action eventually provokes internal conflict or splits political movements along the most significant social fault lines of a historical period—such as class, religion, race, or generation. But not even an individual's identity is ever completely harmonious or unified with itself. This is the transgressive experience through which we discover the limits of our membership, our real heterogeneity. Thus the politics of identity must also be a politics of difference. The politics of identity is a totalizing drive that attempts to universalize its norms and conduct; the politics of difference affirms limited, partial being.[78] Thus the emergence of intense and controversial differences about sexuality within the lesbian and gay-male communities. New forms of sexual politics are emerging throughout American society.

REFERENCES

1 For a theoretical discussion of the political ontology of identities see Ernesto Laclau and Chantal Mouffe, *Hegemony and Socialist Strategy: Towards a Radical Democratic Politics* (London: Verso Books, 1985), pp. 114–122.

2 Gayle Rubin, "The Traffic in Women: Notes on the Political Economy of Sex," in Rayna R. Reiter, ed., *Toward an Anthropology of Women* (New York: Monthly Review Press, 1975), pp. 159, 199-200. Recently Rubin has modified her earlier formulation to distinguish between the gender and sexual components of the sex/gender system and to outline a model of "sexual transformation," in Gayle Rubin, "Thinking Sex; Notes for a Radical Theory of the Politics of Sexuality," in Carole S. Vance, ed., *Pleasure and Danger: Exploring Female Sexuality* (Boston: Routledge & Kegan Paul, 1984) on sexual transformation, pp. 284–287; and on modifications of her conceptualization of the sex/gender system, pp. 307-309. George Chauncey has also used the sex/gender system as an analytical framework in his history of the medical theories of gender deviance and homosexuality. In George Chauncey, Jr., "From Sexual Inversion to Homosexuality: Medicine and the Changing Conceptualization of Female Deviance," *Salmagundi*, no. 58-99 (Fall 1982-Winter 1983), pp. 114-146. Chantal Mouffe has argued that the sex/gender paradigm is more useful than concepts of "patriarchy" or the "social relations of reproduction" for understanding the different practices, discourses, and institutions by which women's subordination is constructed. See Chantal Mouffe, "The Sex/Gender System and the Discursive Construction of Women's Subordination" in I. Bessenyei, et al., *Rethinking Ideology: A Marxist Debate* (New York: International General/IMMRC, 1983), pp. 139-143.

3 Anthony Giddens' analysis specifies these three dimensions (domination, normative regulation, and coding) as aspects of social reproduction. See

his *Central Problems in Social Theory: Action, Structure, and Contradiction in Social Analysis* (Berkeley: University of California Press, 1979), esp. pp. 96–115 and 225–233 for his discussion of the analysis I draw on here.

4 For an account of racial formation see Michael Omi and Howard Winant, "By the Rivers of Babylon: Race in the United States," *Socialist Review*, nos. 71 and 72 (September-October, November-December 1983). For an analysis of class formation in the same spirit, see Adam Przeworski, "Proletariat into a Class: The Process of Class Formation from Karl Kautsky's *The Class Struggle* to Recent Controversies," *Politics and Society*, vol. 7, no. 4 (1977). Authors who have mapped some of the interactions of the sex/gender system with other sectors of society include Jeffrey Weeks, *Sex, Politics, and Society: The Regulation of Sexuality since 1800* (London: Longman, 1981), pp. 12–16; and the pioneering work of John H. Gagnon and William Simon, *Sexual Conduct: The Social Sources of Human Sexuality* (Chicago: Aldine, 1973), pp. 287–307.

5 Michel Foucault, *The History of Sexuality*, vol. 1: *An Introduction* (New York: Pantheon Books, 1978), pp. 15–50.

6 Clellon S. Ford and Frank A. Beach, *Patterns of Sexual Behavior* (New York: Harper & Row, 1951).

7 K. J. Dover, *Greek Homosexuality* (New York: Vintage Books, 1980), pp. 39–57.

8 Jeffrey Weeks, *Coming Out: Homosexual Politics in Britain, from the Nineteenth Century to the Present* (London: Quartet Books, 1977); John D'Emilio, *Sexual Politics, Sexual Communities: The Making of a Homosexual Minority in the United States, 1940–1970* (Chicago: University of Chicago Press, 1983); Kenneth Plummer, ed., *The Making of the Modern Homosexual* (London: Hutchinson, 1981).

9 Lionel Trilling, "The Kinsey Report," in *The Liberal Imagination* (New York: Anchor Books, 1953), p. 234.

10 Alfred C. Kinsey, Wardell B. Pomeroy, and Clyde E. Martin, *Sexual Behavior in the Human Male* (Philadelphia: Saunders, 1948), and Alfred C. Kinsey, et al., *Sexual Behavior in the Human Female* (Philadelphia: Saunders, 1953), p. 10.

11 Paul Robinson, *The Modernization of Sex* (New York: Harper & Row, 1976), p. 51.

12 Ibid.

13 From Ira L. Reiss, "Standards of Sexual Behavior," in Albert Ellis and Albert Abarbanel, eds., *The Encyclopedia of Sexual Behavior* (New York, 1961), calculated from unpublished data from the Institute for Sex Research quoted in Daniel Scott Smith, "The Dating of the American Sexual Revolution: Evidence and Interpretation," in Michael Gordon, ed., *The American Family in Social-Historical Perspective*, 2nd ed. (New York: St. Martin's Press, 1978); Linda Gordon, *Woman's Body, Woman's Right: Birth Control in America* (New York: Penguin, 1977), p. 193.

14 Lewis M. Terman, *Psychological Factors in Marital Happiness* (New York: McGraw-Hill, 1938), quoted in Gordon, *Woman's Body*, p. 193.

15 D'Emilio, *Sexual Politics*, pp. 57–91.

16 The quotations from and material about the Mattachine Society are from ibid., pp. 65, 77–91.

17 Donald G. Cory, *The Homosexual in America* (New York: Greenberg, 1951).

18 Ira L. Reiss, *Premarital Sexual Standards in America* (New York: Free Press, 1960); Robert R. Bell, *Premarital Sex in a Changing Society* (Englewood Cliffs, N.J.: Prentice-Hall, 1966).

19 Barbara Ehrenreich, *The Hearts of Men* (New York: Doubleday/Anchor, 1984), pp. 42–51.
20 H. W. Arndt, *The Rise and Fall of Economic Growth* (Chicago: University of Chicago Press, 1984), p. 27.
21 Robert A. Gordon, *Economic Instability and Growth: The American Record* (New York: Harper & Row, 1974), pp. 105–107; Harry N. Scheiber, Harold G. Vatter, and Harold Underwood Faulkner, *American Economic History* (New York: Harper & Row, 1976), pp. 422–427.
22 Samuel Bowles and Herbert Gintis, "The Crisis of Liberal Democratic Capitalism: The Case of the United States," *Politics and Society*, vol. 11, no. 1 (1982), pp. 65–66.
23 Richard A. Easterlin, "What Will 1984 Be Like? Socioeconomic Implications of Recent Twists in Age Structure," *Demography*, vol. 15, no. 4 (November 1978). See also Richard A. Easterlin, "American Population since 1940," in Martin Feldstein, ed., *The American Economy in Transition* (Chicago: University of Chicago Press, 1980).
24 See Ruth Milkman, "Organizing the Sexual Division of Labor: Historical Perspectives on Women's Work and the American Labor Movement," *Socialist Review*, no. 49 (vol. 10, no. 1; January–February 1980), pp. 128–141; and Ruth Milkman, "Women's Work and the Economic Crisis: Some Lessons from the Great Depression," in Nancy F. Cott and Elizabeth H. Pleck, eds., *A Heritage of Her Own* (New York: Simon & Schuster, 1979), p. 532.
25 See Winifred D. Wandersee, *Women's Work and Family Values, 1920–1940* (Cambridge, Mass.: Harvard University Press, 1981), esp. pp. 27–54, 103–117.
26 William H. Chafe, "Looking Backward in Order to Look Forward," in Juanita Kreps, ed., *Women and the American Economy* (Englewood Cliffs, N.J.: Prentice-Hall, 1976), p. 17.
27 See Wandersee, *Women's Work*, pp. 111–117.
28 John Modell, Frank Furstenberg, and Douglas Strong, "The Timing of Marriage in the Transition to Adulthood, 1860–1975," *American Journal of Sociology*, vol. 84 Supplement (1978), and Andrew Cherlin, *Marriage, Divorce, Remarriage* (Cambridge, Mass.: Harvard University Press, 1981), pp. 8–12, 19–21.
29 Easterlin, "American Population."
30 Norman Ryder, "Recent Trends and Group Differences in Fertility," in Charles F. Westoff, ed., *Toward the End of Growth: Population in America* (Englewood Cliffs, N.J.: Prentice-Hall, 1973), p. 61; see also Judith Blake, "Coercive Pronatalism and American Population Policy," prepared for the Commission on Population Growth and the American Future, 1972.
31 Rubin, "Thinking Sex," pp. 269–270; see also Allan Berubè, "Behind the Spectre of San Francisco," *Body Politic*, April 1980; Allen Berubè, "Marching to a Different Drummer," in Ann Snitow, et al., eds., *Powers of Desire: The Politics of Sexuality* (New York: Monthly Review Press, 1983); D'Emilio, *Sexual Politics*; John D'Emilio, "Gay Politics, Gay Community: San Francisco's Experience," *Socialist Review*, no. 55 (vol. 11, no. 1; January–February 1981).
32 Eileen Applebaum, "Women in the Stagflation Economy," in Sidney Weintraub and Marvin Goodstein, eds., *Reaganomics in the Stagflation Economy* (Philadelphia: University of Pennsylvania Press, 1983), p. 38. For more recent data see George Masnick and Mary Jo Bane, *The Nation's Families: 1960–1990* (Boston: Auburn House, 1980).

33 Daniel Bell, *The Cultural Contradictions of Capitalism* (New York: Basic Books, 1976), pp. 33–84.
34 See Mark Poster, *Critical Theory of the Family* (New York: Seabury Press, 1978), pp. 166–205; and Masnick and Bane, *Nation's Families*, pp. 95–116.
35 Ehrenreich, *Hearts of Men*, pp. 14–28.
36 Ilene Philipson, "Heterosexual Antagonisms and the Politics of Mothering," *Socialist Review*, no. 66 (vol. 12, no. 6; November-December 1982).
37 For example, Daniel Bell's "*Work and Its Discontents*" (1956), reprinted in *The End of Ideology* (Glencoe, Ill.: Free Press, 1960); and Ely Chinoy, *Automobile Workers and the American Dream* (New York: Random House, 1955).
38 Herbert Marcuse, *Eros and Civilization* (Boston: Beacon Press, 1955).
39 Quoted in Richard King, *The Party of Eros: Radical Social Thought and the Realm of Freedom* (Chapel Hill: University of North Carolina Press, 1972), p. 84.
40 Chauncey, "Sexual Inversion," pp. 114–146.
41 Ibid., p. 120.
42 See James D. Steakley, *The Homosexual Emancipation Movement in Germany* (New York: Arno Press, 1975).
43 Edward Carpenter, *The Intermediate Sex* (London, 1908), reprinted in Edward Carpenter, *Selected Writings*, vol. 1 (London: Gay Men's Press, 1984).
44 For a critical discussion of this assumption see John H. Gagnon and William Simon, *Sexual Conduct: The Social Sources of Human Sexuality* (Chicago: Aldine, 1973), pp. 132–136.
45 Barbara Ponse, *Identities in the Lesbian World: The Social Construction of Self* (Westport, Conn.: Greenwood Press, 1978), pp. 24–30; see also Gagnon and Simon, *Sexual Conduct*, pp. 99–109.
46 John Money and Anke Ehrhardt, *Man and Woman Boy and Girl: The Differentiation and Dimorphism of Gender Identity from Conception to Maturity* (Baltimore: Johns Hopkins University Press, 1972); see also Nancy Chodorow, *The Reproduction of Mothering* (Berkeley: University of California Press, 1978), for an analysis of the social construction of gender identity.
47 See Esther Newton and Shirley Walton, "The Misunderstanding: Towards a More Precise Sexual Vocabulary," in Vance, ed., *Pleasure and Danger*.
48 Michel de Certeau, *The Practice of Everyday Life* (Berkeley: University of California Press, 1984), pp. 29–42.
49 John Rechy, *City of Night* (New York: Grove Press, 1963), p. 22.
50 Quoted in Sacha G. Lewis, *Sunday's Women: Lesbian Life Today* (Boston: Beacon Press, 1979), p. 30.
51 William Simon and John H. Gagnon, "Sexual Scripts," *Transaction/Society*, November-December 1984.
52 Joan Nestle, "Butch/Femme Relationships: Sexual Courage in the 1950's," *Heresies*, no. 12 (1981), p. 21–24.
53 See Amber Hollibaugh and Cherrie Moraga, "What We're Rollin Around in Bed With: Sexual Silences in Feminism," *Heresies*, no. 12 (1981), pp. 58–62.
54 For the best account of camp and its importance in gay male culture of the fifties and early sixties, see Esther Newton, *Mother Camp: Female Impersonators in America* (Englewood Cliffs, N.J.: Prentice-Hall, 1972). For a somewhat priggish critique of camp from a gay liberationist perspective see Jeffrey Escoffier, "Breaking Camp," *Gay Alternative*, no. 4 (1973), pp. 6–8.
55 Reprinted in Susan Sontag, *A Susan Sontag Reader* (New York: Vintage Books, 1983), p. 117.

56 For an excellent analysis of subcultures as counter-hegemonic cultural responses see Dick Hebdige, *Subculture: The Meaning of Style* (New York: Methuen, 1979), esp. pp. 73–99.
57 Erving Goffman, *The Presentation of Self in Everyday Life* (New York: Doubleday Anchor Book, 1959), pp. 106–140.
58 Laud Humphries, *Tearoom Trade: Impersonal Sex in Public Places* (Chicago: Aldine, 1970).
59 See Michel de Certeau's discussion of "tactics" vs. spatial "strategies" in *The Practice of Everyday Life*, esp. pp. 34–39.
60 See Berubè, "Behind the Spectre"; and also Allan Berubè, "The History of Gay Bathhouses," *Coming Up!*, December 1984, p. 18; Ellen Klages, "When the Bar Was the Only Place in Town," in *1984 International Lesbian/Gay Freedom Day Parade Celebration* (San Francisco, 1984), pp. 39–41.
61 Toby Marotta, *The Politics of Homosexuality* (Boston: Houghton Mifflin, 1981); see esp. pp. 48–68.
62 Mary McIntosh, "The Homosexual Role," *Social Problems*, vol. 16, no. 2 (Fall 1968).
63 See the interview with Mary McIntosh, "Postscript: 'The Homosexual Role' Revisited," in Plummer, ed., *Making of the Modern Homosexual*, pp. 44–49.
64 Antonio Gramsci, "Problems of Philosophy and History," *Selections from the Prison Notebooks* (New York; International Publishers, 1971), pp. 366–367.
65 Dennis Altman, *Homosexual: Oppression and Liberation* (New York: Avon Books, 1973). Altman has recently published another important evaluation of the lesbian and gay movements, *The Homosexualization of America* (Boston: Beacon Press, 1983).
66 Altman, *Homosexual*, pp. 13–41.
67 Ibid., p. 98.
68 Ibid., p. 94.
69 Ibid., pp. 108–151.
70 Ibid., pp. 234, 237.
71 Jonathan Katz, *Gay American History: Lesbians and Gay Men in the U.S.A.* (reprinted, New York: Avon Books, 1978), p. 1.
72 Gay Left Collective, *Homosexuality: Power and Politics* (London: Allison & Busby, 1980).
73 Jeffrey Weeks, *Coming Out: Homosexual Politics in Britain* (London: Quartet Books, 1977).
74 John D'Emilio, "Capitalism and Gay Identity," in Ann Snitow, et al., eds., *Powers of Desire*.
75 Alan Crawford, *Thunder on the Right: The "New Right" and the Politics of Resentment* (New York: Pantheon Books, 1980), pp. 144–164.
76 Robert Reilly, "Homosexual Rights and the Foundations of Human Rights," *Family Policy Insights*, vol. 1, no. 3 (10 December 1981), pp. 539–540.
77 Erving Goffman, *Stigma: Notes on the Management of Spoiled Identity* (Englewood Cliffs, N.J.: Prentice-Hall, 1963), p. 111.
78 Michel Foucault, "A Preface to Transgression," in *Language, Counter-Memory, Practice* (Ithaca, N.Y.: Cornell University Press, 1977), pp. 34–36.

THE ETIOLOGY OF INTOLERANCE OF HOMOSEXUAL POLITICS[1]

James L. GIBSON, *University of Houston*

Kent L. TEDIN, *University of Houston*

A model of the origins of political intolerance of homosexual rights is presented and analyzed. Political intolerance is shown to be a function of two basic attributes of individuals: level of education and degree of psychological dogmatism. Not only do education and dogmatism contribute to intolerance directly, but there are important indirect effects through such variables as perceptions of threat from homosexuals, support for the norms of democracy, and support for the agenda of the New Right. The article concludes by tracing some of the implications of the findings for the political repression of homosexuals.

Over the course of the last several years, the politics of homosexuality has become an increasingly salient component of the U.S. political scene. Gays have asserted themselves politically throughout the country; they have been the objects of public referenda in several cities; and opposition to homosexuality is an important component of the New Right social agenda. The emergence of the disease AIDS has also generated widespread attention to homosexual life-styles.

It is clear that the American people do not approve of homosexuals or homosexuality. When asked in a national survey in 1985 whether homosexual relationships are wrong, nearly three-quarters of the American people asserted that they believe them to be "always wrong" (Davis and Smith, 1986: 237). Only 13 percent of the respondents in the 1984 National Election Survey rated homosexuals positively on the feeling thermometer. For most Americans, gays may well be among the groups they like the least.

Throughout American political history, antipathy toward unpopular political minorities has frequently generated political intolerance and repression. As "out-groups" become threatening and salient, propensities

[1]This is a revised version of a paper delivered at the 1986 annual meeting of the Midwest Political Science Association, Chicago, Illinois. This research was supported by funds from the Limited-Grant-in-Aid Committee at the University of Houston, to whom we are indebted. We also appreciate the comments of Glendon Schubert on an earlier version of this article. Some data from the General Social Survey are used in this article.

toward intolerance become manifest and focused. To the extent that intolerance becomes focused on a particular group, political repression is the likely result (see Sullivan, Piereson, and Marcus, 1982). One might predict, therefore, that the unpopularity of gays will generate political repression. Thus, it is important to consider the degree to which ordinary Americans favor "putting up with" homosexuals.

In this article, we test a model of the origins of political intolerance of homosexuals. The analysis is based on a survey of registered voters in Houston, Texas. The survey was conducted shortly after a heated—and quite salient—referendum on whether the city government should be prohibited from discriminating against gays in its hiring practices. The model tested has been found to be useful for understanding political intolerance in the abstract (Sullivan, Piereson, and Marcus, 1982; Sullivan et al., 1981; Shamir and Sullivan, 1983; Sullivan et al., 1985; Gibson, 1987a). We consider whether it has similar utility for explaining intolerance of homosexual rights within a concrete civil liberties dispute.

The Politics of Homosexuality in Houston

Homosexuals have become a salient and active force in Houston city politics. They have organized politically through the Gay Political Caucus (GPC). The GPC openly supports and endorses candidates for public office. Gays have considerable political influence in Houston: the gay community is commonly given some degree of credit for the electoral success of Houston's mayor, as well as for several members of the city council.

On 19 January 1985 Houstonians voted on a referendum aimed at repealing an ordinance that forbade discrimination against homosexuals in city employment (see Gibson and Tedin, 1986). Voters turned out in record numbers and resoundingly voted to repeal the ordinance. Encouraged by the overwhelming rejection of gay employment rights, a former Houston mayor challenged the incumbent in the next mayoral election. The challenger ran on a latent platform of opposition to gay rights. Midway through the campaign the challenger succeeded in bringing the issue of homosexuality to the foreground. When asked off the air at a local television station what the challenger would do about the AIDS problem, he responded, "Shoot the queers!" Unfortunately for him, his microphone was in fact turned on, and the comment was broadcast. The challenger himself believes that the comment was fatal to his campaign, and many observers suggest that the gaffe may have served to delegitimize anti-gay sentiments. The incumbent won reelection easily.

The purpose of this article is to consider how the citizens of Houston feel about "putting up with" this unpopular political minority. That is, our purpose is to assess the degree of intolerance of homosexual rights, as well as to try to account for that intolerance.

TABLE 1

Willingness among Houston's Registered Voters to Repress Homosexuals

	Percent Supporting Political Repression against Homosexual Political Organizations[a]		
	Support	Unsure	Oppose
Require gay organizations to register with the government	19	21	61
Prohibit gay organizations from holding demonstrations	19	12	70
Outlaw gay organizations	16	11	73
Tap gays' telephones	4	8	88
Prohibit gays from running for public office	19	10	71
Prohibit gays from teaching in public schools	37	16	47

Percent supporting no repression against gays: 31%

Percent supporting no repression except against gays teaching in public schools: 44%

[a]611 ≤ N ≤ 616.

Support for Political Repression of Homosexuals

Like Americans in general, Houstonians do not like homosexuals (see below for the details of the Houston survey). Over two-thirds of those with an opinion believe that homosexual relationships are always wrong. While nearly one-third of the sample claims to have no opinion on whether they "like" homosexuals, among those with opinions, one-half dislike them a great deal. Approximately 17 percent view homosexuals as a great threat to Houston, while 41 percent perceive them as some threat. Only 42 percent see gays as no threat at all. Perceptions of the homosexual threat are roughly the same as perceptions of threats from Communists and from the Ku Klux Klan. Indeed, it is difficult to imagine a political minority that is more disliked in Houston than gays.

Table 1 reports that only a minority of registered voters in Houston are willing to support any particular form of political repression against gays.[2] Even on the sensitive question of whether gays should be allowed to teach in the public schools, only slightly more than one-third would forbid homosexuals to be teachers. Though these data seem to reveal a great deal of tolerance, less than one-third of the respondents oppose *all* of the forms

[2]Gibson and Bingham (1985) have earlier defined political tolerance as "opposition to state actions that limit opportunities for citizens, individually or in groups, to compete for political power" (p. 106). We adopt that definition in this research.

of repression against homosexuals. Even discounting the question of gays teaching in schools, less than a majority would allow gays all of the political rights enjoyed by members of mainstream political organizations.

Given this degree of intolerance of homosexual rights, it is important to attempt to determine its origins. Existing research is quite helpful in that regard.

Origins of Political Intolerance

Sullivan, Piereson, and Marcus (1982) have reported the most thorough analysis to date of the sources of political intolerance (see also Shamir and Sullivan, 1983; Sullivan et al., 1981; Sullivan et al., 1985; and Gibson, 1987a). They began their inquiry by classifying possible determinants as *political* (ideology, perceptions of threats, support for the general norms of democracy, political information, and political involvement), *psychological* (self-esteem, authoritarianism, dogmatism, trust, and value actualization), and *social* (education, social status, age, and religion). The relevance of each of these classes of factors for understanding intolerance of homosexuals will be considered in turn.

Political Origins of Intolerance. One of the strongest predictors of intolerance is support for the general norms of democracy. Those who value democratic rights and processes in the abstract are more likely to be willing to put up with unpopular political minorities. Important norms of democracy include the values of freedom of speech, freedom of assembly, the right to public employment, and freedom of publication.[3] We hypothesize that greater support for the norms of democracy is associated with greater political tolerance of homosexuals.

Political activism has long been considered a major source of tolerance. Beginning with Stouffer's (1955) work in the mid-1950s, a succession of projects has demonstrated greater tolerance among elites, local influentials, opinion leaders, and activists than among the ordinary mass public (see also Prothro and Grigg, 1960; McClosky, 1964; McClosky and Brill, 1983; and Gibson and Bingham, 1985). Partially due to practice at politics, activists learn the necessity and utility of accommodation, bargaining, compromise, and therefore tolerance. Elites are also drawn from the more tolerant segments of the general population (Nunn, Crockett, and Williams, 1978). Intolerance is also less socially acceptable among political leaders and activists (Jackman, 1972), in part because the formal norms of the political system are supportive of toleration of political minori-

[3]Though tolerance is itself one of the norms of democracy, we conceptualize intolerance more concretely as support for political repression against homosexuals. This is not unlike the distinction first made by Prothro and Grigg (1960) between abstract and concrete forms of political tolerance.

ties. In addition, those assuming positions of influence in U.S. politics may be resocialized to these more tolerant norms (Key, 1961).[4] Consequently, we hypothesize that greater political activism is associated with greater willingness to tolerate homosexual rights.

Political liberalism is also commonly associated with tolerance. This position has been most cogently argued by McClosky and Brill (1983). They asserted:

> Over the past two centuries, conservatives have repeatedly shown their fear of political and social instability. With rare exceptions, the conservatives have been the party of tradition, stability, duty, respect for authority, and the primacy of "law and order" over all competing values.
>
> Liberals, although sharing some of these values to a degree, differ from conservatives in their willingness to risk a measure of social instability for the sake of promoting certain changes and reforms. . . . To bring about institutional change and economic reforms, liberals are inclined to go further than conservatives in permitting or even encouraging dissent, protest, and the dissemination of unorthodox opinions—activities that obviously presuppose extensive opportunities for freedom of speech, press, and assembly, as well as other forms of freedom of expression. (McClosky and Brill, 1983:275)

On the other hand, Sullivan, Piereson, and Marcus (1982) indicated that the traditional correlation of liberalism and tolerance is in part an artifact of the use of left-wing target groups in the measures used to indicate political tolerance. Because their own results revealed that conservatives are less supportive of the general norms of democracy, if not less politically tolerant, we hypothesize that liberals are more tolerant of the rights of homosexuals.

In addition to political ideology measured in terms of liberalism–conservatism, we are interested in conservatives who endorse the political agenda of the New Right. This agenda includes the issues of creationism, abortion, the Equal Rights Amendment, prayer in the public schools, and political involvement on the part of religious leaders. The literature on the far right indicates that beyond political convictions, there are certain psychological predispositions among members of the far right that may contribute to intolerance. Among those predispositions are dogmatism, scapegoatism, ethnocentrism, authoritarianism, prejudice, and a conspiratorial outlook (Rother, 1969; Lipset and Raab, 1981; Tedin, 1978). These characteristics often result in heightened feelings of threat from out-groups, and an exaggeration of inconsistencies in one's own thinking (Reynolds, 1973:196–212). Even nonextremist New Right supporters

[4] The research of Sullivan et al. (1985) suggests that this might not be true of other countries. While the relationship is positive in the United States, it is negative in New Zealand, and there is no relationship at all in Israel. They argue that there is nothing inherent in political activism that produces political tolerance. Rather activism is related to the learning of system values, values that differ in different political systems. (Sullivan et al., 1985:186–95).

may be expected to be intolerant to the extent that they are unusually threatened by political disagreements and to the extent that tolerance requires some degree of permissiveness.

Conflicts over the ERA, abortion, and gay rights are especially important because they extend beyond the specific content of the issue. They symbolize broad life-style outlooks. The ERA, abortion, and gay rights are direct challenges to the conventional American lifestyle. On the part of those involved, the stakes and the intensity of conflict are often surprisingly high from the viewpoint of outsiders. As Conover (1983) asserted, "Membership in the New Right represents a way of combating more than just specific issues like abortion and the E.R.A.; it is a way of fighting the deeper life style changes that those issues appear to symbolize. With the stakes so high, then, it is no wonder that the battle has been so intense" (p. 646). Homosexuality is one of the most fundamental threats imaginable to the life-style of the New Right. We hypothesize, therefore, that greater support for New Right issues is associated with greater intolerance of homosexual rights.

One of the most enduring hypotheses in tolerance research is that intolerance is a function of the degree of threat posed by the political minority (e.g., Stouffer, 1955; Nunn, Crockett, and Williams, 1978; Sullivan, Piereson, and Marcus, 1982; Gibson and Bingham, 1985). More specifically, even those who are favorably predisposed toward tolerance may be dissuaded from adopting a tolerant position within a specific context due to the high degree of threat posed by the group. We hypothesize that those who are especially threatened by homosexuals are more likely to favor political repression against them.

Psychological Sources of Intolerance. A host of personality attributes are typically associated with political intolerance. For instance, self-esteem is commonly found to predict intolerance (e.g., Sniderman, 1975). Those low in self-esteem tend to be more intolerant in part because they do not interact with others enough to learn the dominant social norms of the society, which are in the main tolerant (see also McClosky and Brill, 1983). They are also less tolerant because they are more likely to perceive threats from others. Similarly, dogmatism—or "closed-mindedness"—has also been found to predict intolerance. Because they tend to perceive the world in dichotomous "us versus them" and "good versus evil" terms, those who are dogmatic tend to perceive greater threat from political minorities and tend to evaluate the cost of compromise as very high. Sullivan, Piereson, and Marcus (1982:212) have generalized several personality attributes to the concept "psychological insecurity" (more dogmatism, lower on the needs hierarchy, and lower in self-esteem) and have found it to be a useful predictor of intolerance. We focus here exclusively on the personality attribute dogmatism and hypothesize that those who are more dogmatic are more intolerant of homosexuals.

Social Determinants of Intolerance. Finally, a variety of social attributes have been found to be related to tolerance. Most commonly investigated is level of education, although social class, age, and especially religiosity have received some attention as well. Education has been shown in the past to be a major predictor of tolerance (e.g., Stouffer, 1955; Nunn, Crockett, and Williams, 1978), largely because education leads to an exposure to social and cultural diversity, which in turn enhances tolerance. Sullivan, Piereson, and Marcus (1982) have argued, on the other hand, that education is related to tolerance at least in part due to the use of left-wing targets of intolerance in the typical measures. Nonetheless, they still found at least a weak relationship between education and tolerance. Income, age, religiosity, and race have also received some attention, although none has as powerful an effect as education. Consistent with existing literature, we hypothesize that high levels of education and income, youth, and low levels of religiosity contribute to the tolerance of homosexual rights.

We expect that most social attribute variables affect political tolerance through other variables that are more proximate causes. For example, Stouffer (1955) argued that tolerance is learned through exposure to cultural diversity, and it is education that is the linchpin to this exposure (see also Williams, Nunn, and St. Peter, 1976). Since exposure to diversity affects tolerance mainly by reducing threat, perception of threat is the more proximate cause. Thus, we treat social attribute variables largely as exogenous factors.

The model to be tested posits that tolerance of gay rights is a direct function of attitudes toward democratic norms, as well as perceptions of threats from gays. Further, democratic attitudes and threat perceptions are hypothesized to be a function of levels of political activism, ideology, personality attributes, and social background characteristics. Thus, a fairly comprehensive analysis of the attitudes of the relevant population can be considered.

The Sample

Following the 19 January 1985 gay rights referendum, 619 registered voters were interviewed in Houston by telephone. The sample was selected by dividing the city into seven strata—five white, one black, and one predominantly Hispanic. Within these strata, 30 precincts were selected using probability methods. At the precinct level, respondents were chosen using a skip interval with a random entry point.

TABLE 2

Intolerance of Homosexuals in Houston and the United States

	Percent Tolerant[a]		
	General Social Survey		Houston
	1985	1982	1985
Homosexuals speaking in the community	67	64	65
Homosexuals teaching in a university	58	55	62
Homosexual books in the public library	56	56	54
Average index of intolerance of homosexuals	1.4	1.4	1.4
Percent completely tolerant of homosexuals	46	44	43

[a]The numbers of cases for the GSS are approximately 1,500. For the Houston survey, the number of cases is approximately 618.

Due to our analytical needs, two independent samples were chosen—one of voters and one of nonvoters. The information on who voted was taken from the poll lists. Turnout in the referendum was 31 percent. However, we oversampled voters in order to include an adequate number for analysis. We interviewed 372 voters and 247 nonvoters, resulting in a 60/40 split favoring the former in the overall sample. For this analysis, the sample was weighted to be representative of the Houston registered electorate.

We are, of course, somewhat concerned about comparing a sample taken from Houston, Texas, with the national data upon which much of the tolerance literature is based. No national data exist on the willingness to repress homosexuals (a measure we developed) so we cannot make direct comparisons. It is possible, however, to address the question indirectly. Table 2 presents a comparison between the Houston sample and the 1982 and 1985 General Social Surveys (national probability samples) on tolerance for homosexual civil liberties. The results of the three surveys are remarkably similar. Based on the data in Table 2 we also created an intolerance index and computed bivariate correlations between that index and a variety of variables common to both the Houston survey and the GSS (data not shown).[5] Again, the predictors were remarkably similar

[5]The results of this analysis are available from the authors.

for both studies. Given these results, we are confident that it is appropriate to make limited inferences from our local survey to the larger population.[6]

The Etiology of Intolerance of Homosexual Rights

Table 3 reports the bivariate correlations between willingness to support the political repression of homosexuals (the dependent variable, see Table 1 for the items that comprise the scale) and a variety of social, political, and personality attributes of the respondents. Several aspects of this table are noteworthy. First, the best predictor of intolerance toward gays is support for the norms of democracy.[7] Those who value free speech, free assembly, the right to teach and to publish are least likely to support the political repression of homosexuals in Houston. The second strongest correlation is between a scale measuring perceptions of threat[8] and support for repression. Using the simple measure of threat, the mean repression score for those "greatly" threatened by homosexuals is 1.5; for those perceiving "some" threat, the mean is 1.7; for those perceiving no threat, it is 1.9 (overall standard deviation = 0.3; minimum = 1.0; maxi-

[6] Some important caveats about this conclusion must be noted. First, the Houston sample was drawn from registered voters, not simple residents. To the extent that the regular correlates of tolerance (e.g., education, interest) are associated with registration to vote, one would expect the Houston sample to be *more* tolerant than the national sample. Similarly, because residents of cities tend to be more tolerant than those living in the country, we would expect the Houston sample to exhibit more tolerance. On the other hand, as residents of a southern city, the Houston respondents should be more intolerant than a national sample. On balance, the various differences in the two samples seem to cancel themselves out, resulting in very similar frequencies for the tolerance measures.

[7] We employ the traditional measures of these norms first used by Stouffer (1955) and later by Nunn, Crockett, and Williams (1978) and the GSS (e.g., Davis, 1975). These items ask whether certain unpopular groups should have the right to engage in various political activities. The rights we focus on in this research are four: the right to freedom of speech; the right to freedom of assembly; the right to free communication of ideas; and the right to be treated equally by the government regardless of one's political beliefs. In order to neutralize the Sullivan, Piereson, and Marcus (1979, 1982) critique of these items, we used both a left-wing (Communists) and a right-wing (Ku Klux Klan) stimulus for all respondents. Furthermore, we ascertained through an independent measure that virtually none of the sample likes (even a little) Communists or Klansmen. Because these measures specify little of the context of the activity (e.g., what is to be said or where specifically it will be said), we consider them to be indicators of political tolerance in the abstract (cf. Prothro and Grigg, 1960). It should be noted, however, that this measure of support for democratic norms is derived from items that are quite similar in content and level of abstraction to the items comprising the dependent variable.

[8] Respondents were directly asked how threatened they feel by homosexuals. Instead of relying on only a single indicator, however, we also asked them about a variety of specific homophobic beliefs. These include beliefs about (1) whether homosexual teachers encourage children to become homosexual; (2) whether homosexuals generally encourage others to become homosexual; (3) the degree of threat posed by AIDS; and (4) whether private homosexual behavior is one's "own business." When factor analyzed, these items formed a single strong dimension. Factor scores were computed as the indicator of the concept. The results of the factor analysis are available from the authors.

TABLE 3

Correlates of Support for Political Repression of Homosexuals

	Bivariate Correlation with Support for Political Repression[a]
Support for norms of democracy (scale)	−.58
Freedom of speech	−.51
Freedom of assembly	−.48
Freedom to teach	−.43
Freedom to publish	−.48
Perceptions of threats from gays and homosexuality (scale)	.57
Threat of gays	.53
Fear of AIDS	.35
Gays encourage others	.42
Gay teachers encourage students	.40
Right to private behavior	−.15
Political involvement	
Political interest	−.14
Political participation	−.24
Frequency of voting	−.09
Conservatism–liberalism	
Social conservatism	.21
Political conservatism	.09
Democratic party identification	.10
Support for New Right positions (scale)	.30
Opposition to abortion	.23
Opposition to Equal Rights Amendment	.10
Support for prayer in schools	.22
Support for creationism in schools	−.16
Support for religious influence in politics	−.18
Personality	
Dogmatism	.34
Social attributes	
Baptist identification	.17
Religious fundamentalism (belief in the Devil)	.25
Secular detachment (frequency of church attendance)	.17
Age	−.15
Education	−.41
Income	−.29
Gender	.09
Years lived in Texas	.27
Minority group membership	.07
Black race	.13

[a] $471 \leq N \leq 619$.

mum = 2.0). Strong bivariate relationships are observed for the individual variables indicating fear of AIDS and the various homophobic beliefs. These findings are consonant with existing research on political tolerance: those who feel threatened by a political minority are quite unwilling to extend full civil liberties to it.

Most of the traditional findings in tolerance research are also supported by this analysis. Political activists tend to be somewhat more tolerant, though the relationship is not strong.[9] Intolerance of homosexuals is related to conservatism, though it is mainly to social conservatism—as reflected in self-identifications and support for New Right positions—rather than to traditional political conservatism.[10] There is a moderate relationship between the personality attribute dogmatism[11] and intolerance of gay rights, a finding that is also well established. Some tendency toward intolerance among those who are religious is observed. Those who believe that the devil exists—a better measure of religiosity—are also somewhat more intolerant of homosexuals (cf. Nunn, Crockett, and Williams, 1978). Education has a strong impact on tolerance, and intolerance is found to be somewhat greater among longtime residents of Texas and those with lower incomes. Blacks are slightly more intolerant of homosexuals than are whites. Generally, a wide variety of factors seem to contribute to the intolerance of homosexual rights.

It is difficult to sort out the independent effects of the various predictors of intolerance toward homosexuals without multivariate analysis. Table 4 reports the path coefficients from an analysis of a fully specified model of the origins of political intolerance. A simplified path analysis of the general model is shown in Figure 1. The model reported eliminates all variables that do not make at least a modest contribution to the explanation of the variance in the dependent variable.[12] Several of the exogenous variables have been discarded using this criterion.

Variation in support for political repression against homosexuals is quite well explained in this model: nearly one-half of the variance can be accounted for by just two variables—perceptions of threats from homo-

[9]The respondents were asked to report how interested they are in politics, how frequently they vote, and whether they have engaged in a variety of political activities (e.g., trying to convince others to vote). The activities were summed to form an index.

[10]The New Right scale is composed of questions concerning abortion, the proper role of religious leaders in politics, creationism in the public schools, prayer in the public schools, and the Equal Rights Amendment. The items were factor analyzed; a single factor emerged, from which factor scores were computed. Details on the analysis are available from the authors.

[11]We use the same dogmatism items as Sullivan, Piereson, and Marcus (1982). These items originated with Rokeach (1960).

[12]We have required that the semipart coefficient for each variable exceed .025 in order to be included in the simplified model. This results in eliminating some variables that exhibit statistically significant path coefficients, but that do not produce any meaningful increment in R^2.

sexuals and support for the norms of democracy. Those who are threatened by gays are considerably more willing to support political repression against them. Similarly, those who are generally supportive of the democratic norms including free speech and assembly are less inclined to support repression of homosexuals. These findings closely parallel those of Sullivan, Piereson, and Marcus (1982) and are also similar to earlier findings on the strong influence of perceptions of threat on political tolerance.

The variance in the democratic norms and threat variables is also reasonably well explained. Those who support the norms of democracy tend to be higher in education, less dogmatic, and less fearful of homosexuals. The direct effect of level of education on support for the norms of democracy—though it is not great—is inconsistent with the earlier findings of Sullivan, Piereson, and Marcus. They observed that the influence of education is largely through political conservatism and psychological security (Sullivan, Piereson, and Marcus, 1982:225, Figure 8-6). Our analysis shows that, in addition to its direct effect, education also influences dogmatism, which in turn influences support for the norms of democracy. Education also has other indirect effects on support for democratic norms. Those high in education tend not to support the New Right political

TABLE 4

Analysis of a Fully Specified Model of Political Tolerance

	Support for Repression		Norms of Democracy		Perceived Threat	
	r	*β*	*r*	*β*	*r*	*β*
Norms of democracy	−.58	−.35	—	—	—	—
Perceived threat	.57	.37	−.50	−.28	—	—
Political involvement	−.24	−.01	.35	.15	−.16	−.03
Support for New Right positions	.30	−.01	−.34	−.11	.42	.29
Religious fundamentalism (belief in the Devil)	.25	.03	−.25	.03	.31	.08
Dogmatism	.34	−.00	−.46	−.17	.37	.20
Education	−.41	−.14	.44	.10	−.32	−.12
Social status (income)	−.29	−.03	.38	.15	−.17	.02
Age	.15	−.06	−.31	−.16	.21	.10
Secular detachment (frequency of church attendance)	.17	−.04	−.25	−.02	.27	.03
R^2	.47		.46		.29	

NOTE: $407 \leq N \leq 619$.

FIGURE 1

A Simplified Path Analysis of Support among Houston's Registered Voters for Political Repression of Homosexuals

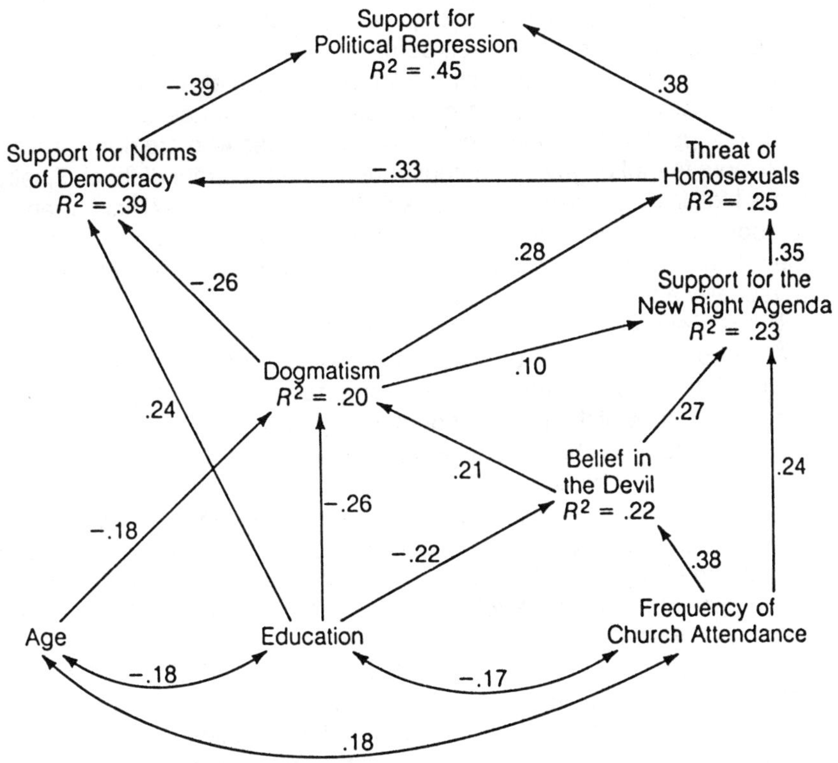

NOTE: All relationships with a semipart coefficient greater than or equal to .025 are shown. All coefficients shown are statistically significant beyond .05.

agenda, a variable that is in turn related to perceptions of threats from homosexuals, and ultimately to support for democratic norms. Thus, the direct and indirect effects of education on support for the norms of democracy (and ultimately, on tolerance for gay rights), while not large in magnitude, are pervasive.[13]

Though perceptions of threat had a substantial impact on intolerance in the Sullivan, Piereson, and Marcus analysis, they were unable to explain

[13]The causally interpretable indirect effect of education on support for democratic norms is .18.

why some feel threatened and others do not. In our analysis, which is focused on a single group, not a multitude of groups,[14] one-fourth of the variance in perceptions of threat from homosexuals can be attributed to support for the New Right political agenda and to dogmatism. New Right supporters are threatened by homosexuals, as are individuals high in dogmatism. This latter relationship is one that is often the subject of speculation, but has rarely been demonstrated in previous work.

This research also reveals strong indirect effects of dogmatism on political intolerance. Dogmatism contributes to intolerance of gays by reducing support for the norms of democracy. Those who are dogmatic are also more fearful of gays, and consequently less tolerant of them. Finally, those high in dogmatism are more likely to support the New Right agenda, support that is associated with fear of homosexuals and intolerance of them.[15] This is impressive evidence indeed of the linkage between this personality attribute and political intolerance.[16]

Virtually every variable in the model is affected to at least some degree by level of education. Those high in education are less certain that the devil exists, are less likely to support the agenda of the New Right, are more supportive of the norms of democracy, and are less dogmatic. That levels of education have such a pervasive impact is at once both surprising and not surprising. The finding is not surprising in the context of the long-standing research literature showing the more educated to be more tolerant (e.g., Stouffer, 1955; Nunn, Crockett, and Williams, 1978; Hyman and Wright, 1979; Corbett, 1980; McClosky and Brill, 1983; Hall, Rodeghier, and Useem, 1986). On the other hand, Sullivan, Piereson, and Marcus (1982) have challenged these findings, arguing that the education-tolerance relationship is in part an artifact of the use of left-wing targets of intolerance in earlier research. Since gays might be considered a left-wing group, the argument requires further investigation.

Sullivan, Piereson, and Marcus found that education is only weakly related to political tolerance. They account for findings to the contrary by asserting: (1) most studies use left-wing targets of intolerance; (2) this creates a spurious correlation between ideology and tolerance; (3) there is a positive relationship between levels of education and political liber-

[14] It should be noted that the Sullivan, Piereson, and Marcus measure of perceptions of threat was based on their content-controlled measure, and consequently is derived from perceptions of a wide variety of groups. Perception of threat in this research is specifically limited to homosexuals.

[15] The causally interpretable indirect effect of dogmatism on support for political repression is .26.

[16] It should be noted that while Sullivan, Piereson, and Marcus (1982:218, Figure 8-4) labeled their personality construct "Psychological Security," in fact the largest single epistemic correlation is with dogmatism (.81). This is followed by self-esteem (.67), faith in people (.50), and value-actualization (.43). Thus, there is greater similarity between our findings and theirs than might be apparent from the labels attached to the concepts.

alism; and therefore (4) the relationship of education and tolerance is (at least in part) spurious.

It is true that gays are perceived by Houstonians as being on the political left. Fully 79 percent of those able to locate gays on a liberal–conservative scale named them as liberal or very liberal. However, 41 percent of the respondents could not locate gays, presumably because gays are too heterogeneous to be placed on the scale as a group, or because the respondents did not possess sufficient information to form a judgment. Of more direct relevance to the Sullivan, Piereson, and Marcus argument, self-identified liberals in Houston are *not* more tolerant of homosexuals than conservatives.[17] Moreover, there is little relationship between level of education and liberalism. Within ideological groups, level of education is still strongly related to political tolerance; and within categories of education, liberalism–conservatism bears little relationship to political tolerance. Thus, we conclude that the pervasive effect of education on political tolerance is *not* an artifact of our focus on gays as the objects of intolerance.

On the other hand, we certainly recognize that some aspects of these findings are colored by the particular nature of the dispute. Homosexuals are more threatening to those with low education and to New Right conservatives. We suspect, however, that *nearly all unpopular minorities* are more threatening to those with low education and those who support the New Right social agenda. Would our results differ were the objects of intolerance atheists, Communists, Klansmen, or Nazis? Though we do not know, we suspect not. The intolerance of this segment of the population is more generalized and could be mobilized to support the repression of any group, left or right, that threatened its basic values.

The effect of education is a little surprising for a quite different reason. One might expect that as levels of education increase in society, the variation in education declines, and hence its impact on tolerance would lessen (cf. Davis, 1975). Moreover, with greater social diversity and geographic mobility, people may be able to acquire exposure to social and cultural diversity without having to rely on formal educational experiences. While this may be true of the country as a whole, these relationships may differ in the South. The South still has a disproportionate number of poorly educated residents. Having low education in the South is especially significant for political intolerance because the region has traditionally been more parochial than the rest of the country. Compensatory experiences are not as readily available to southerners with low education. This leads to the prediction that southerners with low education are among the least tolerant groups in the United States—a finding that is

[17]Liberalism–conservatism is measured through self-identification on a five-point scale.

typically reported—but also that the effect of education on tolerance would be greatest in the South. They may be what we are observing here.

It should also be noted that political tolerance may also be connected to education through a more directly cognitive process. Tolerance of unpopular political groups requires an understanding of the reasons for tolerance. The natural reaction toward something threatening or that one opposes is to suppress it. Tolerance requires what Stouffer called a "sober second thought," that is, reflection about the political and social costs and benefits of tolerance. Unless the arguments—which are intellectually demanding—are accessible to citizens, tolerance is an unlikely response. Tolerance, as McClosky and Brill (1983) strongly argued, requires significant intellectual skills.

To simplify our findings, we conclude that political tolerance of homosexual rights ultimately flows from two distinguishable sources. The first is experiential, having to do with exposure to diversity, and its best measure is education. Tolerance of disliked groups also requires psychological security and flexibility. Those who are psychologically inflexible are more easily threatened by political differences. The common response to threat is an intolerant one.

Finally, we note that this research has demonstrated that the models typically used to predict intolerance in hypothetical questions ("should a Communist be allowed to make a speech") are also useful for predicting intolerance within a more realistic conflict over the civil liberties of an unpopular political minority. This implies that the difference between the hypothetical and the concrete may not be as substantial as is sometimes thought.

Implications

Only a minority of registered voters in Houston are willing to allow homosexuals the same rights to compete fully and openly for political power as other groups. That homosexuals are not currently the victims of widespread political repression in Houston speaks to the caution with which all tolerance research must be approached. Though a majority of the mass public in Houston may be intolerant of homosexuals, the incumbent political leaders are not. A significant number of local elites support political rights for homosexuals. It is perhaps the ability of these elites to block demands from the majority for political repression that keeps the repression from materializing.

At the same time, however, mass preferences are not unimportant. The gay rights referendum was resoundingly defeated in a highly salient referendum. Perhaps the fear of mass involvement in politics significantly affects the manner in which politics is played out in Houston. That is, while the mass public may not generate demands for political repression of unpopular political minorities, it does set the constraints within which political leaders must work. If so, then the political intolerance of the majority may be important even if it does not directly determine public policy. Thus, in the end, whether citizens are willing to tolerate unpopular political minorities has a significant impact on political freedom and democracy.

We cannot be certain that these findings are generalizable to the nation as a whole. To the extent that they are generalizable, they suggest that there is a substantial possibility of increasingly political repression of homosexuals in the United States. The increasing threat from AIDS (as it becomes more widespread) and the increasing conservatism of the country can only serve to exacerbate intolerance. On the other hand, increases in levels of education, as well as the increased availability of alternative means of acquiring exposure to diversity (e.g., the greater participation of women in the work force) may neutralize this to some degree.[18] Thus, the final conclusion of this article is that it is important to continue to monitor intolerance of homosexual rights in the United States in order to understand the causes and consequences of political intolerance. SSQ

REFERENCES

Conover, Pamela Johnston. 1983. "The Mobilization of the New Right: A Test of Various Explanations." *Western Political Quarterly* 36:632–49.

Corbett, Michael. 1980. "Education and Contextual Tolerance: Group-Relatedness and Consistency Reconsidered." *American Politics Quarterly* 8:345–59.

Davis, James A. 1975. "Communism, Conformity, Cohorts, and Categories: American Tolerance in 1954 and 1972–73." *American Journal of Sociology* 81:491–513.

Davis, James Allan, and Tom W. Smith. 1986. *General Social Surveys, 1972–1986*. Chicago: National Opinion Research Center.

Gibson, James L. 1987a. "Homosexuals and the Ku Klux Klan: A Contextual Analysis of Political Intolerance." *Western Political Quarterly* 40:427–48.

———. 1987b. "The Evolution of Intolerance in the United States." Paper delivered at the 1987 annual meeting of the American Political Science Association.

Gibson, James L., and Richard D. Bingham. 1985. *Civil Liberties and Nazis: The Skokie Free Speech Controversy*. New York: Praeger.

Gibson, James L., and Kent L. Tedin. 1986. "Political Tolerance and the Rights of Homosexuals: A Contextual Analysis." Paper delivered at the 1986 annual meeting of the Midwest Political Science Association.

Hall, Robert L., Mark Rodeghier, and Bert Useem. 1986. "Effects of Education on Attitude to Protest." *American Sociological Review* 51:564–73.

[18]Gibson (1987b) has reported that there has been little change in levels of intolerance in the United States throughout the period from 1972 to 1987.

Hyman, Herbert H., and Charles R. Wright. 1979. *Education's Lasting Influence on Values*. Chicago: University of Chicago Press.

Jackman, Robert. 1972. "Political Elites, Mass Publics, and Support for Democratic Principles." *Journal of Politics* 34:753–73.

Key, V. O., Jr. 1961. *Public Opinion and American Democracy*. New York: Knopf.

Lipset, Seymour Martin, and Earl Raab. 1981. "The Election and the Evangelicals." *Commentary* 71:25–31.

McClosky, Herbert. 1964. "Consensus and Ideology in American Politics." *American Political Science Review* 58:361–82.

McClosky, Herbert, and Alida Brill. 1983. *Dimensions of Tolerance: What Americans Believe about Civil Liberties*. New York: Russell Sage Foundation.

Nunn, Clyde Z., Harry J. Crockett, and J. Allen Williams, Jr. 1978. *Tolerance for Nonconformity*. San Francisco: Jossey-Bass.

Prothro, James W., and Charles M. Grigg. 1960. "Fundamental Principles of Democracy: Bases of Agreement and Disagreement." *Journal of Politics* 22:276–94.

Reynolds, H. T. 1973. *Politics and the Common Man*. Homewood, Ill.: Dorsey.

Rokeach, Milton. 1960. *The Open and Closed Mind*. New York: Basic Books.

Rother, Ira S. 1969. "Social and Psychological Determinants of Radical Rightism." In Robert A. Schoenberger, ed., *The American Right Wing*. New York: Holt, Rinehart & Winston, pp. 191–211.

Shamir, Michal, and John L. Sullivan. 1983. "The Political Context of Tolerance: Israel and the United States." *American Political Science Review* 77:911–28.

Sniderman, Paul M. 1975. *Personality and Democratic Politics*. Berkeley: University of California Press.

Stouffer, Samuel C. 1955. *Communism, Conformity, and Civil Liberties*. New York: Doubleday.

Sullivan, John L., George E. Marcus, Stanley Feldman, and James E. Piereson. 1981. "The Sources of Political Tolerance: A Multivariate Analysis." *American Political Science Review* 75:92–106.

Sullivan, John L., James E. Piereson, and George E. Marcus. 1979. "A Reconceptualization of Political Tolerance: Illusory Increases, 1950's–1970's." *American Political Science Review* 73:781–94.

———. 1982. *Political Tolerance and American Democracy*. Chicago: University of Chicago Press.

Sullivan, John L., Michal Shamir, Patrick Walsh, and Nigel S. Roberts. 1985. *Political Tolerance in Context: Support for Unpopular Political Minorities in Israel, New Zealand, and the United States*. Boulder, Colo.: Westview.

Tedin, Kent L. 1978. "Religious Preference and Pro-/Anti-ERA Activism on the Equal Rights Amendment." *Pacific Sociological Review* 21:21–37.

Williams, J. Allen, Jr., Clyde Z. Nunn, and Louis St. Peter. 1976. "Origins of Tolerance: Findings from a Replication of Stouffer's Communism, Conformity, and Civil Liberties." *Social Forces* 55:394–408.

POLITICS

Why Gay Leaders Don't Last

THE FIRST TEN YEARS AFTER STONEWALL

by David Jernigan

RICHARD C. WANDEL

1 2 3

Front row: Marty Robinson (1), Jim Owles (2), and Arthur Evans (3), original members of the Gay Activists Alliance, September 1970, New York

SOCIAL MOVEMENTS need leadership. Leaders offer role models, images of power and purpose. They also provide organizational acumen and direction, and for the press, a focal point for the articulation and publicizing of the concerns of the traditionally disfranchised. Betty Friedan, Gloria Steinem, Geraldine Ferraro and many others in the women's movement have served this function; Martin Luther King, Jr., Jesse Jackson and others have done so in the movement for black liberation. Although not always chosen democratically, they have nonetheless spearheaded impressive organizational efforts bringing political muscle and social change to disfranchised groups.

In this time of health crisis, more gay men and lesbians occupy positions of visible leadership than ever before. Yet there is still no gay or lesbian leader of national significance who leads gay and lesbian people. The gay movement has seen many leaders come and go. Some, like Harvey Milk, were killed off by forces outside the gay community; many more, though, apparently were forced out of visible

David Jernigan is a west coast writer, researcher, and activist who has conducted workshops on gay and lesbian leadership development in the United States and Europe.

RINK FOTO

José Sarria, left, 1984

leadership by "burnout," frustration, their own inability to maintain the allegiance of their followers, and a myriad of other reasons—stated and unstated.

Are there structural features peculiar to the gay movement that have made long-term, national leadership difficult? Do gay and lesbian people tend to attack or abandon our leaders more than others? Or is the lack of national leaders merely the result of the movement's relative youth? If there are any features of the gay movement that have rendered leadership particularly difficult, what does this tell us about the nature and state of the gay movement itself?

The homophile movement's dominant strategy lay not in developing gay and lesbian leaders, but rather in finding heterosexual experts to attest to the trustworthiness and respectability of homosexuals.

These are important questions which our movement must address. This essay offers at best a preliminary attempt to answer them, by looking at visible leadership in the gay movement in its first decade post-Stonewall. There are thousands of gay and lesbian people who played crucial roles in the movement in some form during this period. While their contributions should not go unrecognized, there is a good argument for emphasizing visible leadership. As a heavily stigmatized people, gay men and lesbians have had to use visibility as a major stratagem in taking on the negative images which gay oppression has painted of us. Positive image-building, and the development of visible, positive role models has been key.

Several themes about leadership can be drawn from our history as a movement:

1) The development of leaders as role models has been complicated by a changing and evolving understanding—both within and outside of the gay movement and community—of what it means to be gay or lesbian. This changing understanding is inseparable from the trajectory and gains of the gay liberation movement itself. As the movement made concrete gains, the possibilities for being publicly gay and publicly a gay leader broadened. Ironically, this progress in liberation led to changing and often conflicting "job descriptions" for the gay leader. Within the movement, disagreements over the definition of the gay identity have contributed to the failure of leaders to achieve broad national backing.

2) Within the gay movement, the internalization of gay and lesbian stereotypes by gay and lesbian people has impaired our ability to recognize and support leadership. Attacks on leaders have been endemic, and often have come in the same language as that of the external oppression. Leaders have faced charges of immaturity, of puerile fascination solely with things sexual, of being untrustworthy, of not being really committed to gay people, of not being "really gay," or conversely, of being "too gay."

3) Throughout the history of the movement, there has been a general ambivalence about leadership: Do we need it? Is it inherently oppressive? This, as well, has led to punishing those who take initiative.

4) Notoriety has been repeatedly confused with leadership. The importance of seizing media attention and turning stereotypes on their heads led to a series of so-called leaders who in fact were media creations with no organizational base and no strategy beyond their own self-presentation.

Early Models of Leadership

While the Stonewall riots in 1969 are generally considered the starting point of gay liberation, the leadership which emerged post-Stonewall actually fashioned itself in reaction to the "homophile" leadership of the fifties and sixties. In the homophile period, the relationship between the level of oppression which gay men and lesbians faced and the kinds of leadership that emerged is clear. Low profiles were the norm for homophile movement leaders. Despite the founding of a wide variety of homophile organizations in the fifties and sixties, by 1969 membership in gay organizations barely surpassed 5,000 men and women, with only a few hundred publicly identified as gay men or lesbians.[1] With so few members, there is a sense that every person who chose to become a part of the movement was a "leader," whether by actively founding an organization, editing a newsletter, or simply being among the first to join a professedly homophile group.

The homophile movement's dominant strategy lay not in developing gay and lesbian leaders, but rather in finding heterosexual experts—mental health practitioners, lawyers, educators and the like—to attest to the trustworthiness and respectability of homosexuals. Visible homosexual leadership first emerged in San Francisco in the early sixties, when drag entertainer José Sarria ran as an openly gay candidate for city supervisor in the wake of a campaign by police and Mayor Warren Christopher to "clean up" the city's "homosexual problem." Sarria, the first openly gay candidate in the nation, garnered only 6,000 votes, but his campaign inaugurated a tradition of openly gay electoral activism in San Francisco.

Sarria offered an early model of using the notoriety of open homosexuality to gain attention for gay rights. His candidacy provided an early focal point for organizing, as the self-sacrificial acts of other firsts—such as the first openly gay football player, army sergeant, public official—would do later.

Outside of San Francisco, the most visible leaders headed the Mattachine Society of Washington, D.C. (MSW), and the Mattachine Society of New York (MSNY). MSW founder Dr. Franklin Kameny, an astronomer fired by the Army when his homosexuality was discovered, lobbied the legislative and executive branches to end discrimination against homosexuals in federal employment. MSW's brand of direct action consisted of small groups of "appropriately groomed" gay men (in coats and ties) and lesbians (in skirts) picketing in front of the White House, or at Independence Hall in Philadelphia every Fourth of July. MSNY president Dick Leitsch also took on discrimination and legislative issues, but he carefully differentiated his own personal lobbying activities from the liberation activities occurring in other movements in the sixties:

> Power lies not in the number of members or the total of names on a list....It lies in how effective your organization is in achieving the goals of the homophile movement. This is not a plea for "gay power" or "lavender power." It is a plea for those charged with leadership positions in homophile organizations to make the voice of the homosexual heard in the community.[2]

PATSY LYNCH/COURTESY OF THE ADVOCATE

Frank Kameny, 1986

That Leitsch felt he had to make this differentiation is indicative of changes occurring outside the homophile movement which were expanding possibilities for visible gay and lesbian leaders. A new generation of leaders would reject the behind-the-scenes approach of the homophile activists in favor of the public and confrontive tactics used by the black and women's liberation movements.

Leading With Little to Lose

Rioting by New York City bar patrons who were responding to a routine police raid on the Stonewall Inn on June 27, 1969 brought the gay movement literally into the streets and into the mainstream of New Left protest. Whereas "gay" and "gay is good" had been used by homophile activists, in the hands of gay liberationists the term "gay" came to define a lifestyle, a personality, a commitment to a myriad of personal and social changes. "Homosexual," conversely, represented life without liberation, gay people without the gay consciousness or identity which came with liberation. For the first time, gay began to mean an identity that was self-determined, staking out a social territory by confronting dominant images of gay people.

Differing views of identity formed a strong line of demarcation between the gay and homophile movements. That "gay" was initially synonymous with confrontation is important to understanding the philosophy of the movement and the style of leadership which emerged in the first years after Stonewall. Simply to identify publicly as gay was a political act—a confrontation. The early gay liberation organizations capitalized on this as an almost exclusive organizing strategy. They encouraged and required gay visibility to confront societal stereotypes about gays. Gay pride parades epitomize this approach: mass visible confrontations of the dominant culture, establishing social space for open homosexuality. Leadership and organizational issues were secondary to the struggle to establish a beachhead of gay visibility.

The Gay Liberation Front (GLF) was the first major gay political organization founded post-Stonewall. Its chief targets were gatekeepers of social space: the police (a popular countercultural/New Left target anyway); the medical/psychiatric establishment; the media (one early effort focused on persuading the *Village Voice* to allow the word "gay" in news articles and personal advertisements); and the New York City Council, where activists lobbied for legislation protecting gays from discrimination in housing and employment.

GLF's New Left politics led to a commitment to rotating leadership, free-form discussion sessions, and ad hoc project groups and cells—rather than to the development of any sort of hierarchical structure. This lack of organization frustrated its own members' efforts to turn their organization's promise of a movement into reality. Such an atmosphere intentionally militated against the development of individual leadership. The odyssey of two gay male leaders of the period is instructive: Marty Robinson and Jim Owles had left MSNY for the more militant and confrontive atmosphere of GLF. They left GLF within a year of its founding because of its sexual politics and structural weaknesses. According to historian Toby Marotta,

> they had come to believe that since GLF's "structureless structure" permitted anyone to introduce any concern at any time, it ensured that no consensus could be protected from the unsettling arguments of newcomers and that nothing could be made binding on any who disagreed with decisions reached. In the end, Robinson, Owles, and others who set out to form a reformist alternative to GLF were motivated almost as much by their desire to have a group that was effectively organized as by their ideas of what its aims should be.[3]

Robinson, Owles and ten others set out to establish a gay liberation organization serving gay people. Like the homophile leaders (and unlike GLF), they wanted a single-issue focus—gay liberation—but using the confrontational politics and rhetoric that had informed GLF's efforts. They wanted to organize more explicitly on behalf of gay people in the present, as opposed to attaching a gay caboose onto the New Left railway. They eschewed any reference to revolution in the title they chose for the new organization: the Gay Activists Alliance (GAA).

It was in GAA's structure that the twelve founders most clearly strayed from prevailing models in the women's and gay movements, and more specifically, from the rotating monthly chairs and ad hoc committees of GLF. GAA's reformist constitution created titled leaders: a president; vice president; secretary; treasurer; and delegate-at-large (elected annually and paid small stipends). It also established standing committees which eventually grew to cover such areas as women's issues, publicity, the street, political action, legal issues, community relations, municipal and state government, and state and federal affairs. This structure enabled the members of GAA to work for the single goal of gay liberation on a variety of different fronts simultaneously and

Taking advantage of their ability to "pass" in largely heterosexual crowds, GAA members infiltrated everything.

RINK FOTO

Del Martin, center, 1984

with greater success than the more diffuse GLF.

Although it encouraged activism in many forms, GAA became best known for its tactic of simply making GAAers—and thereby gay people and gay concerns—visible. While GLF had been content to present gay issues as part of the revolutionary program of the New Left, GAA members went everywhere in pursuit of a hearing for gay people. GAA's signature was the "zap," a tactic somewhat akin to a gay kamikaze raid on "establishment" figures and strongholds. Taking advantage of their ability to "pass" in largely heterosexual crowds, GAA members infiltrated everything from political rallies to meetings of the Village Independent Democrats, to the offices of *Harper's* magazine and the studio audience of the "Dick Cavett Show."

The zaps succeeded at making gay individuals and gay issues more visible than ever before. They required participants to be more visible as gays than ever before, sometimes just in a crowd or a meeting, sometimes—as with Cavett—visible to a national audience. Mere participation in a zap could bring an individual high status within the movement. Individuals who chose to zap commanded respect from within the movement for their decision to be radically "out." In the social climate of 1969 and 1970, the decision to zap—or in any other way be fully and radically out—meant eschewing traditional career paths and throwing one's lot in with the movement.

The zaps were less successful, however, as a route to building a mass movement. Zapping encouraged notoriety rather than leadership. Those who participated had little to lose, and were self-selected. Only those with the means and leisure to put in long hours for next to no pay, but also to accept that for the foreseeable future most standard career routes would be closed to them, could afford to take leadership.

Zapping was also primarily a male activity. The growing visibility of the men, their sexism, and the growing self-consciousness of lesbians as a result of the women's movement led to early schisms along gender lines. While the men achieved notoriety and prominence, the legwork of building a movement—staffing committees and work groups, providing services and so on—seemed to come "naturally" to the lesbians, just as traditional forms of visible leadership came "naturally" to the men. Tension between the male and female wings fueled many of the early attacks on movement leaders. Lesbian activist Del Martin's letter of farewell to the men in 1970 exemplifies the ways in which movement activists echoed the language and stereotypes of gay oppression in their criticisms of each other:

> [I had hoped] that you were my brothers and that you would grow up, to recognize that freedom is not self-contained....I will not be your "nigger" any more. Nor was I ever your mother. Those were stultifying roles that you laid on me, and I shall no longer concern myself with your toilet training....As I bid you adieu, I leave each of you to your own device. Take care of it, stroke it gently, mouth it, fondle it. As the center of your consciousness, it's really all you have.[4]

Gay oppression defined gays as "immature"; it is no coincidence that a recurring criticism of gay leaders within the movement is for their alleged "immaturity."

Women left the united movement in large numbers in the early seventies. Their departure to form separate liberation groups, either around lesbian or more generally feminist issues, was part of the proliferation and fragmentation of organizations and activities which characterized the early seventies. Differing perceptions of gay experience and identity fed this fragmentation as well. Early movement writings were rife with "analyses" of who gay people are and what they are "really" like. Yet each such analysis implied a different strategy for organizing and leading. For instance, as Marotta writes, two of the co-founders of GAA began early on to move in very different directions:

> Owles gauged that most homosexuals thought they managed rather successfully and needed to be seduced into believing that they had anything to gain from becoming involved in politics. [Arthur] Evans, on the contrary, held that most homosexuals harbored repressed rage and that one had to prick gay facades to tap deep-seated anger and trigger political involvement.[5]

The deep disagreements over basic issues left the small group, which took leadership early on in New York, scarred by division and mutual attack. Jim Owles served two terms as president of New York's GAA. What was notable about his defeat in the 1971 GAA presidency race was not so much that fellow GAA founders Marty Robinson and Arthur Evans were also defeated, but that Owles is reported to have said that "he was running to stop Robinson from being elected, and Evans…said he was running to stop Owles."[6]

In 1972, GAA elected Dr. Bruce Voeller, a research biologist and former associate professor at Rockefeller University, to be its next president. While Voeller began his term as a well-credentialed radical activist, again issues of organization and leadership led to an exodus from a leading gay liberation organization. Voeller and several other GAA officers had grown increasingly dissatisfied with GAA's diffuse focus and politics, and with the limits on the executive's power to act without express consent of the membership. In a dispute over the latter issue at the group's regular business meeting on October 4 of that year, Voeller suddenly resigned. News and Media Relations Committee chair Ron Gold's resignation followed Voeller's. Vice-president Nathalie Rockhill had already resigned a month earlier for "personal reasons."

Together, the three then approached Dr.

DAVE WALTER / COURTESY OF THE ADVOCATE

Bruce Voeller

Harold Brown about a concept they already had been discussing. Brown had served as administrator of health services in the Lindsay administration from June 1966 to December 1967, and then as professor of public administration at New York University School of Medicine. On October 3, 1973 he announced his homosexuality and pledged his support for the gay rights movement in a major public address and a front page interview in the *New York Times* which appeared the same day. His announcement stunned the non-gay world and elated the gay press. The *Advocate* called Brown's coming out "perhaps the biggest single boost since a similar revelation by novelist Merle Miller nearly three years ago [also on the front page of the *New York Times*]."[7] Brown told the *Times* that his decision to come out had been prompted by the efforts of GAA to get a gay civil rights bill passed by the New York City Council. He later told the *Advocate*:

> Though I had helped [GAA members] behind the scenes, really I was like the other successful homosexuals I know [Brown subsequently claimed that between a quarter and a third of Lindsay's top advisers in the sixties had been homosexual]. I stayed hidden and let these gallant boys and girls work hours and days and even be beaten up in a fight that I really should have joined.[8]

While many of the public coming outs simply led to notoriety, Brown's act actually inspired organization. On October 15, 1973, the National Gay Task Force was born. Brown was the first chairman of the board; Voeller, Rockhill and Gold were among its first paid staff people, with Voeller as executive director. Brown's prestige and support enabled Voeller and company to put together the most credentialed openly gay group the movement or the non-gay world had ever seen. NGTF's founders planned an annual budget of $200,000, part of which would pay five full-time staff members.

NGTF was the most ambitious and tightly organized effort of the movement thus far. Modeled on the NAACP, it aimed to be a nationwide membership organization advocating for gay people. The planned relationship between membership and staff represented a major structural innovation over the GAA model. In NGTF, the members, who qualified as such by paying membership fees, would elect the board. The board then supervised the staff work. In practice, this set-up left a great deal of power and discretion in the hands of the executive director—Voeller—and the staff.

Voeller claimed that democracy within the new organization would eventually come through power of the purse—whether and how many gay people elected to join and pay annual membership fees. If joining was an indication of interest, however, most gay people wanted no part of NGTF. At the end of 1974, its staffers were working for $87.50 a week—less than they could have received on welfare or unemployment. NGTF received $65,858 in 1975, far below its projected $200,000 budget. At the end of 1976, NGTF had 2,500 members. In contrast, NAACP had 442,000, and NOW had 55,000.[9] Low wages and lack of support took their toll on the NGTF staff. By mid-1975, Voeller was the only original staffer remaining. At the New York gay pride parade in 1975, the crowd greeted mention of two entities with resounding hisses and boos: the Catholic Church, and Bruce Voeller.

NGTF's early failures can be written off, to some extent, to the growing pains of a new organization. But other factors militated against its success as well: GAA co-founder Arthur Evans' attacks on the structure of NGTF exemplify the ambivalence about leadership and the anti-authoritarian trend in the movement, as well as resentment at a perceived elitism and hegemonism:

> By the deliberate design of its founders, NGTF will be tightly controlled from the top down (much like a big-business corporation.) Those on the top will have "M.D." or "Ph.D." or "the well-known" attached to their names. The founders make no secret of one of their basic goals: to create a group where gay members of the professional class will be "comfortable."[10]

The *Advocate*'s New York correspondent at the time, George Whitmore, commented on the movement's ambivalence towards the Task Force and the leadership style it represented:

> Perhaps the Task Force brags too much about its accomplishments, but the fact is that it is accomplishing something. Others obviously disagree. Is it unpopular because it brags? Because it isn't radical enough? Because it's political? Your guess is as good as mine. I am positive that gay people don't want leaders. A simple recitation of the list of past leaders would illustrate that; most of them flaked out, burned out, or lost their credibility—fast.[11]

Had NGTF restricted its activities to the high-level lobbying and pressure campaigns for which it was probably best suited, it might have attained a higher level of popularity in the movement and community at large. But the organization's survival depended on a high profile and visible successes. Voeller's attempt to set up a nationwide emergency phone tree to be used for rapid community mobilization irritated the organizations it was designed to unite and sidestepped the basic issues of organizational democracy—what would be considered an emergency and who would decide. The need for visible victories led to a string of questionable press releases which undercut NGTF's credibility within the movement.

Voeller claimed that democracy within the new organization would eventually come through power of the purse. If joining was an indication of interest, however, most gay people wanted no part of NGTF.

Leadership of the Elect?

The aggressively public tactics of GLF and GAA drew attention to the events unfolding in New York. New York also seems to have been the center for early theoretical discussions about the nature of the movement. However, on the West Coast, and particularly in San Francisco, a corps of leaders was developing whose accomplishments and visibility would soon eclipse those of the New Yorkers. Since Sarria's 1962 supervisorial campaign, organizations such as the Society for Individual Rights (SIR) and the Tavern Guild nurtured a growing tradition of electoral work, and helped promote a community aware of itself as a legitimate political minority with a specific political agenda. The leaders who developed in San Francisco were expert at the very backroom lobbying activity which Evans and others in New York had decried.

By 1969, the concept of a gay voting bloc in San Francisco had already gained some credence. In late 1971 SIR co-founder Jim Foster came up with a new innovation—a gay Democratic club. According to Foster, "We organized the Alice B. Toklas Memorial Democratic Club for a single purpose:" to be eligible to attend the statewide convention of the California Democratic Council, an influential non-party coalition of grassroots Democratic Party activists, in early 1972. Alice, under Foster's leadership, drew on the expertise he and others had developed in the past eight years of mobilizing gay voters by taking campaigns to the heart of the gay community: the bars, baths, and businesses in the growing gay ghetto. On the strength of his work with Alice, Foster won a delegate seat at the Democratic National Convention in Miami where he and Madeline Davis, a lesbian delegate from upstate New York and a member of the Mattachine Society of the Niagara Frontier, argued on national television (albeit at six a.m.) for a gay rights plank in the party platform. In June 1972, Foster protégé Earl (Rick) Stokes garnered 44,469 votes in a losing bid for a seat on the San Francisco Community College Board. Although Stokes was unsuccessful, his showing was strong enough to dispel any doubts about the existence of a formidable gay voting bloc in San Francisco.

RINK FOTO

Rick Stokes, 1982

The differences between the New York and San Francisco experiences are instructive. One finds far less discussion and disagreement concerning identity issues in San Francisco during the late sixties and early seventies. The resulting higher level of unity facilitated the growth of a stronger political movement. Furthermore, the focus on electoral activism offered a route for mass participation in the gay movement that was considerably less risky than the radical coming out policy encouraged by GLF, GAA and their imitators. In the privacy of the voting booth, gay people could participate without publicly disclosing their gayness. The California electoral activists also could point to clear victories, including having a central role in the repeal of the state's anti-sodomy law in 1975.

But the electoral strategies also carried with them their own brand of leadership self-selection. Again, those who took visible leadership tended to be those who could afford to. In New York, the early leaders could afford it because they had nothing to lose, but in San Francisco it was because they had well-developed financial bases, either within the gay community or from independent wealth.

David B. Goodstein, who beginning in 1971 would provide much financial and managerial skill to the burgeoning lobbying and electoral work, was a former stockbroker and attorney who lost his job when he mentioned to his employer's wife that he was a homosexual. Goodstein subsequently used his professional skills as well as his considerable private fortune, first, to set up the Whitman-Radclyffe Foundation, originally a fundraising arm of the efforts to abolish California's anti-sodomy law and later a major social-service provider, and then to buy out the *Advocate* and convert it into a major nationwide magazine and a mouthpiece of the emerging gay "middle class." Goodstein founded Whitman-Radclyffe, and hired Foster to be its first executive director, with the "conviction that the gay movement had to find ways to build organizations controlled by stable, responsible persons who could enlist the support of Gays who are economically and professionally successful."[12]

Foster and Stokes, the two other most visible Alice leaders, did not come from wealthy backgrounds. Both, however, built their positions on the wealth of San Francisco's sizable gay ghetto—Foster by convincing bar and bathhouse owners to donate a portion of their profits and time to protecting their patrons through Foster-backed political organizations, Stokes by investing in one of the city's most popular bathhouses.

These men were frequently the first gay activists that non-gay politicians met. This, and their efforts to ingratiate themselves with those politicians, gave them increasing connections and clout as the gay movement grew. The result of this dual self-selection process was the creation of two strands in the gay movement, each working from different class positions and a very different view of how to effect change.

At times, they worked in tenuous coalition, as at the 1972 Democratic convention when 20 people sat-in outside while Foster and Davis watched the gay rights plank go down to defeat inside. But more often they were at odds. The radicals accused Foster and company of selling out street people and transvestites, and of using the movement to further their own careers. *The Advocate* generally sided with the "moderates." An early 1973 editorial referred to the radicals as immature "destroyers." Again, the language of accusation reflected social stereotypes of gay immaturity:

> But perhaps to some, helping gays isn't as important as the fun of pulling down the pillars, the joy of parliamentary maneuvering, the vicarious pleasure of plotting, then the final tantrum. Now *there's* the real fun—the climax of it all—more fun even than sex. Remember how mom and dad always caved in at the final tantrum? Wasn't that great? Isn't it still great, boys and girls? Wipe your nose, Johnny, your mental age is showing.[13]

Elaine Noble and Jim Foster, 1978

This kind of attack seems to have led many gay and lesbian people to eschew movement participation entirely, and to view those who participated in visible leadership positions with ridicule, at worst, and embarrassment, at best. In the midst of a particularly acrimonious struggle between the two camps over control of the Whitman-Radclyffe Foundation, Foster remarked,

> the fact of the matter is that when you look around, we are an infinitesimally small number of people compared to the gay community as a whole. If you doubt me, just go to the bars, the restaurants, the operas, the theatres....And the fact is, that somehow we have to convince these people who have money not to be hostile to us, not to look upon us as some kind of embarrassment—*which they do.*[14]

Conditions outside the gay movement also militated against broad participation. As long as the "job description" for a gay leader entailed loss of the freedom to pursue major non-gay careers, those who elected to offer their talents to the gay movement did so underground. An interesting underground partnership between openly-gay activists and high-ranking closeted gay city employees began mid-1974 in New York City. In a paper delivered to the American Political Science Association in June 1975, political scientist Kenneth Sherrill described the new organization as

> a gay political infrastructure that has ties to the government and the organizations of our state's political parties. A relatively recent and growing phenomenon, this infrastructure has been used for purposes ranging from getting gay people out of jail to getting gay people jobs to cutting bureaucratic red tape. In a sense, the functions of the political machine are being performed by gay politicians for gay people, yet the vast majority of politicians are unaware of this, and most gay people do not know where the functional equivalent of the clubhouse is.[15]

Until early 1974, all of the members of this infrastructure, dubbed the "New York Study Group," held executive-type positions in New York City or State government. They fell into one of two categories: either they held "sensitive establishment political jobs" and were "not known to have a gay sexual orientation by anyone other than members of the Study Group and possibly their immediate family and closest friends," or they had "establishment political jobs and have made their gay sexual preference known on the job and elsewhere—but not made it dramatically known."[16]

In 1974 Ethan Geto, Democratic party activist and special assistant to the Bronx borough president, proposed expanding the group. A member of the second category, Geto was then "living platonically" with GAA president and former student activist Morty Manford. Impressed by Manford, Geto convinced the Study Group to add a third category of members: officers of New York gay organizations. Eventually the Study Group included members of NGTF, GAA, Lesbian Feminist Liberation (an organization founded by disaffected lesbian GAA members), and the National Coalition of Gay Organizations (started by Manford in 1976 to coordinate demonstrations at the Democratic convention). None of the other members of these organizations knew of the Study Group's existence, or that their associates were members. All members pledged to maintain the confidentiality of those not "out" publicly.

David Goodstein, 1978

RICK GROSSE / COURTESY OF THE ADVOCATE

42

A sharp awareness of the price of visible gay leadership continued through the mid-seventies. When a closeted delegate to the 1976 Democratic National Convention was asked whether he would ever consider being an openly gay candidate, he replied, "Are you kidding? I want to get something done. If I were to come out that would have to become the main thrust of my politics...any other issue would get buried."[17] Even as the weight of oppression eased over the course of the decade, those willing to be openly gay resisted being stereotyped as "politically gay." An openly gay Carter press aide complained in 1976 that

> I only have so much time in my life to be politically gay. The movement has to understand that there are those of us who want to work the establishment side of the street....Sure it's fun to demonstrate when all it takes is one Sunday afternoon. But the way to change things is to work with campaign people on a one-to-one level. It takes more time, but it will produce far more change."[18]

Openly gay or lesbian political leadership, thus, remained heavily conditioned by the perceived limits (such as unemployment or pigeonholing) which gay oppression continued to place on those who chose it.

Notorious Or Not Gay Enough

Five gay or lesbian people achieved national prominence in the mid-seventies. None of them came from the ranks of the gay movement, and none of them lingered on the national stage past 1978. Two of these—Army sergeant Leonard Matlovich and football player David Kopay—gained notoriety rather than leadership status. Their notoriety helped push forward the ongoing debate with the dominant society over what gayness was or could be, and was derived in part from the fact that they were, as *Advocate* news editor Sascha Gregory-Lewis put it, people "heterosexual America can swallow."[19] By providing personal testimony that gay could be "normal," in terms of at least some aspects of the male sex role, they encouraged others who did not identify with the early seventies radical image of gay liberation to consider that the emerging gay identity might include them as well.

Three others gained fame through electoral successes. Allan Spear was elected to the Minnesota State Senate in 1972, where he still serves today. He came out publicly in 1974 shortly *after* being re-elected. Spear downplayed his homosexuality, commenting that "I don't want to be typecast as a gay legislator. I'm a legislator with concerns in a variety of areas, who also happens to be gay." Aside from stints on the boards of NGTF and Gay Rights National Legislation (GRNL), he eschewed national politics entirely, despite pressure from movement moderates to cut a wider swath.

Elaine Noble parlayed her Boston political connections into a successful bid for a seat in the Massachusetts House of Representatives in 1974, making no secret of her lesbianism. She elected not to run for a third term in 1978, citing a House redistricting plan that put her in competition with one of her closest political allies, Barney Frank. (Seven years later, having reached the U.S. House of Representatives, Frank would acknowledge his own homosexuality, but prior to this he was assumed to be, and supported the assumption that he was, heterosexual.)

Movement moderates besieged Noble with speaking engagement offers which carried the weight of imperatives. At the same time, both Noble and Spear came under heavy criticism from activists to their left in their home cities. The attacks on Noble and Spear generally came in the form of "not gay enough." In Minneapolis, former University of Minnesota student body president Jack Baker attacked Spear for not moving fast enough on gay rights and for not including the right to adopt children and civil rights protection for transvestites and transsexuals in his legislative efforts. In Boston, Noble's efforts at backroom lobbying, combined with her failure to get a gay rights bill through the House, brought her the dubious distinction of being the second most criticized public figure by Boston's collectively-run newspaper, *Gay Community News*.

MORGAN GWENWALD

Madeline Davis

A closeted delegate to the 1976 Democratic National Convention who was asked whether he would ever consider being an openly gay candidate replied, "Are you kidding? I want to get something done."

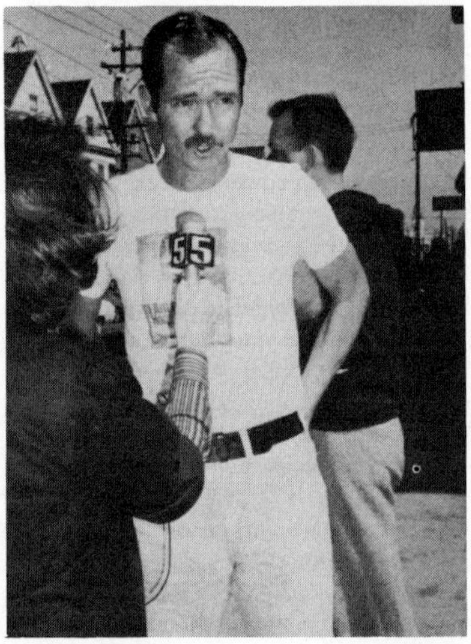

Leonard Matlovich, 1980

Noble's reflections on her experience are illustrative of the confusion in the "job description" of a gay leader which arose from the badly-divided movement. Noble felt she was in a

> no-win situation with gay people. If I tried to be the best politician I could be, some gay people gave me flak because I wasn't being gay enough or responding enough to the gay community....The gay community expected me to be on call 24 hours a day. It was like they felt they owned me....The irony of it is that these gay people didn't elect me. The majority of the gay people who are out in the gay community not only don't live in my district, they don't vote in my district....[Those gay people who were unhappy with me were] only a handful of individuals, but a handful's enough to make your life miserable....The only thing I can say is that a handful of people are far more comfortable being represented by somebody who is a straight male. It's sort of like blacks. There was a time in history when blacks, some blacks, felt they'd rather have a sympathetic liberal white speak for them. I think that's where we are....The level of self-hate right now among gay people is so damned high that if, when you start trying to work in a sane manner, you ask, "What are you doing constructively?" it has a self-hate backlash.... They can't swing at the straight world, so they swing at the person nearest them.[20]

The ambivalence about leadership, which Spear and Noble faced, grew in the mid-seventies with the rising influence, on young gay activists, of the women's movement's philosophies about collectivism and its own ambivalence about strong individual leadership. Even as they took leadership, these young activists avoided leadership roles. UCLA student Dave Johnson in 1974 singlehandedly convinced his university to fund a Gay Awareness Week and organized it himself. But he told the *Advocate* he feared a leadership role, because leading did not fit his definition of being gay. Johnson described his gayness as

> making a personal statement about myself...it involves not just talking about collectivism, not just talking about breaking down stereotyped roles, but actually doing it, in my own life. Men are bribed to be non-human, bribed with power. I was bribed, and the most radical thing I can say is I'm gay, which means I will not take your power; I will not take your domination. I'm going to be a human being; I'm going to love my way; I'm not going to play your roles.[21]

A significant segment of the gay and lesbian press—notably Boston's *Gay Community News*—was ready to attack any visible and reasonably forceful gay or lesbian leader for taking the bribe from the patriarchal society, and it gave little positive press to visible leaders of either sex. Distrust of any model of strong personal leadership was also a feature of most leftist gay organizations of the period. One of the founders of Bay Area Gay Liberation (BAGL), a mid-seventies group of gay leftists in San Francisco, spoke for many of his comrades when he told the *Advocate* that in his view, "it's probably healthier to have an extreme distrust than an extreme trust of leaders."[22]

Harvey Milk and the Flexible Identity

Although his untimely death in 1978 brought him greater national coverage than anything he did while living, Harvey Milk was nonetheless the most compelling and successful gay leader to emerge in the mid-seventies. Superficially he appeared to be a bundle of contradictions who alienated nearly every sector of the movement. He was a small businessman at odds with San Francisco's gay business association, the Golden Gate Business Association (GGBA), and a leftist who refused to work with the main gay left group in San Francisco, BAGL. These paradoxes were, in fact, part of Milk's success: not accepting a label as a certain type of gay leader, he proved able to work with a broad range of individuals and groups—gay and non-gay.

In August of 1973, the pony-tailed proprietor of Castro Camera took very practical issue with the Jim Foster/Alice club philosophy of backing sympathetic non-gay politicians instead of encouraging gays to run for office themselves. Harvey Milk decided to seek election to the San Francisco Board of Supervisors. In a column for the city's gay newspaper, the *Bay Area Reporter*, Milk wrote:

> Masturbation can be fun, but it does not take the place of the real thing. It is about time that the gay community stopped playing with itself and get [sic] down to the real thing. There are people who are satisfied with crumbs because that is all they think they can get when, in reality, if they demand the real thing, they will find that they indeed can get it.[23]

With five seats open, Milk placed tenth in the 1973 supervisorial elections, winning 17,002 votes. Out of step with the Alice club's strategy, Milk was denied its support. The two non-gay politicians backed by Foster and Alice placed seventh and eighth. Foster blamed Milk for his candidates' losses.

"Masturbation can be fun, but it does not take the place of the real thing. It is about time that the gay community stopped playing with itself and [got] down to the real thing."

Undaunted, Milk spent the next four years building a personal political base by running for office at every available opportunity. In 1975, he placed sixth in the supervisorial race. In 1976, he challenged Foster's choice, non-gay Art Agnos, for a state assembly seat and lost by 4000 votes. Milk's presence on the political scene split gay electoral efforts at the same time that his populism attracted to electoral work gay leftists who had previously shunned reformist politics. Within the gay community, he built a coalition based in his own neighborhood in the Castro, and included some of the gay constituencies that Foster et al. would have preferred to forget: transvestites (José Sarria was an early endorser), and recent gay immigrants to San Francisco (like Milk himself) with few financial resources but a strong interest in preserving and strengthening the safety of the ghetto.

But Milk's support stretched far beyond the gay community. Although he made no secret of his gayness, he seldom mentioned gay issues outside of the gay community, and his campaign literature did not indicate his homosexuality. For this, the *Advocate* dubbed him "the 'missing person' in gay lobbying efforts" and charged that he was "reluctant, outside the gay community, to speak to gay issues."[24] Milk debunked the concept of the "gay vote," claiming that

> there's a myth in San Francisco about the gay vote, a myth about the number of gays in San Francisco, a myth in San Francisco about the gay precinct. I live in a "gay precinct," and if 20% of the voters are gay here, that's high.[25]

Like Minnesota's Allan Spear, Milk refused to be merely a gay candidate. He combined fiscal conservatism and small-government populism with a strong pro-labor stance and a championing of the city's ethnic minorities. Gradually he garnered major endorsements from labor, Hispanic, and Chinese organizations.

Milk worked tirelessly in three elections without success, but each time building a slightly larger base of support. Foster and the Alice club continued to oppose him; in response to their attacks, Milk countered that

Milk used stereotypes of gays—both positive and negative—to attract attention to himself and his causes. He aggressively courted publicity, and used his gayness before and after his election as a media angle.

Foster and his entourage were part of machine politics, and that their end of the gay movement was dominated by "those who have the most money [who think it's enough] to show you can do it [be a successful gay person]. That's not what the gay movement is about."[26]

The success of a district elections initiative paved the way for Milk finally to win a seat on San Francisco's Board of Supervisors. In November of 1977, he beat Rick Stokes, the gay attorney who was the ex-president of the Council on Religion and the Homosexual, founding president of the Golden Gate Business Association, bathhouse investor, and Foster protégé. In his victory speech, Milk likened his gayness to Kennedy's Catholicism, saying, "If I do a good job, people won't care if I am green or have three heads."[27]

Milk thus established electoral credibility, but combined this with a growing notoriety. He used stereotypes of gays—both positive and negative—to attract attention to himself and his causes. He aggressively courted publicity and used his gayness before and after his election as a media angle. He was expert at coming up with quotable phrases like his standard opening line on the stump: "Hi, I'm Harvey Milk, and I'm here to recruit you." A former Broadway producer, Milk viewed politics as theater, and himself as a symbol. In his own way he carried forward the tactics of GAA in the early seventies, "zapping" the media with a constant stream of press releases, interviews and quotable speeches.

As a gay leader, Milk was unique in the mid-seventies: self-selected, but with electoral support; unafraid to be open, but with the political savvy not to let himself be limited by the confines of the gay movement or the gay ghetto. He drew on the traditions of the gay community and identity, employing camp humor and tapping into a communal sense of outrage at the injustice of oppression. But certainly one of the keys to his success was his ability to adjust his gay identity, when necessary, in order to work in coalition with and attract the support of other disfranchised groups.

In the crucial fight against the 1978 California Briggs Initiative [which would have prohibited employment of gay people in public shcools], Milk became a key statewide spokesperson. After his successful election effort, he turned his mobilizing know-how to recruiting even more volunteers to canvass against the Briggs Initiative. By June his San Francisco Gay Democratic Club had surpassed Alice in numbers, and ran major canvassing operations every weekend. Leftists in San Francisco formed the Bay Area Committee Against the Briggs Initiative (BACABI) and worked closely with the Milk machine. BACABI clones appeared in at least eight other California cities, using similar tactics and working in loose coalition. Wealthy gays joined with liberal non-gays to form Concerned Voters of California (CVC) to fight Briggs. CVC emphasized its compatibility with the grassroots effort, and devoted its resources to a statewide media campaign.

Milk challenged Briggs to one-on-one debates anywhere in the state. Whether the venue was conservative or liberal, he greeted Briggs with a prepared set of one-liners designed for their quotability. In response to Briggs' claim that the average homosexual had more than 500 sexual partners Milk remarked, "I wish." When Briggs argued that homosexual teachers would engender homosexuality in their students, Milk replied that if children really emulated their teachers, there would be many more nuns in the world.[28]

In the anti-Briggs campaign, the gay movement seemed at last really to have it all: money; unity; and a visible, capable, and credentialed spokesperson. Thousands of gay people took the risk of being publicly identified to assist in the campaign. The combination of unprecedented gay unity and visibility, and equally unprecedented bipartisan support from non-gays, left Briggs and his initiative completely isolated. By election day, he had garnered endorsements from only three organizations: the state Nazi Party, the KKK, and the Los Angeles Deputy Sheriffs Association. On election day, the ordinance went down to stunning defeat, losing by a two-thirds margin.

Elsewhere, gay rights ordinances were

repealed in Eugene and Wichita. But the movement's successes far outweighed these setbacks. Well-organized, amply-funded, and united campaigns run by professionals, defeated the backlash, not only in California, but in Seattle as well. In his *Advocate* column, Goodstein crowed that "we have entered a new phase of our community's development...1978 is marked by our community's being spearheaded by young, middle-aged and older gay men *and women* of substantial education, economic means and professional skills."[29]

The resources and discipline brought to bear in California and Seattle were impressive. In the wake of these major electoral challenges, the movement's national organizations also experienced a renaissance. NGTF swelled to a staff of fourteen and a budget of $350,000. At Milk's suggestion, grassroots activists across the country began to plan their first coordinated effort since the early seventies: a 1979 march on Washington, D.C.

Yet, for all the activity, the organizational growth and concrete progress made in 1978, by the end of that year only one major leader had emerged into national visibility: Harvey Milk. On November 27, 1978 former fellow Supervisor Dan White shot and killed Milk and pro-gay Mayor George Moscone. The aftermath of Milk's death and White's trial brought the first gay riots since Stonewall, but part of the tragedy of Harvey Milk's life and death is that there was no replacement ready to fill his shoes as an outrageous, aggressive, and visible movement spokesperson.

Lessons To Be Learned

Why was Harvey Milk the only gay leader of this period to even approach national prominence? What can be learned from his case, as well as from the negative examples of others, of relevance to the gay liberation movement today? The paucity of leadership in this period was certainly in part simply historical. The changing relative safety—or lack thereof—to identify as gay affected the development of leadership. The decisions of early leaders to go after visibility affected the risk/reward ratio of leadership. As they established a beachhead of visibility, and as more diverse kinds of gay and lesbian people came out, the job description of a visible gay leader began to change.

The early activists inadvertently caused their own obsolescence. By aping the rhetoric and forms of the civil rights and women's movements, they helped gay activism win legitimacy first in left-wing and then in liberal circles. Within four years, advocating for gay *rights* (not liberation) became a respectable form of political activity in the left wing of the Democratic Party. In the mid-seventies, NGTF and the gay democratic clubs began to present opportunities for activism as a part-time activity. This increased participation in the movement overall, but also transformed the job description of movement leader from a self-sacrificing "new human" living the revolution to the more traditional model of administrator,

Harvey Milk, Castro Street Fair, 1978

fundraiser and organizer of large groups of people towards specific goals. Leaders could either move with the changes, as did Owles in initiating New York electoral activism and Voeller in founding NGTF, or be left behind.

The definition of a "gay leader" reflected the evolution of the gay identity itself. Beyond the obvious commonality of engaging in homosexual behavior, no one knew for certain what gays had in common. In the face of oppression, the pre-Stonewall homosexuals had created a subculture with "back regions" of relative safety, and stigma symbols—words with double meanings, tonal inflections, clothing, or hair styles—to identify themselves to each other without risking discovery by the larger society.[30] When the post-Stonewall activists repudiated the homophile movement, they rejected these invented commonalities as well, replacing them with their own set which could serve more visibly to identify gays to each other and the rest of society. Those who disagreed with the new definition of being gay were dubbed "not really gay." They were "self-oppressed." That is, their definitions of their own gayness still retained vestiges of the oppressor-defined homosexuality of the pre-liberation era.

The development of leadership was further complicated by the fact that each conflicting view of "being gay" not only entailed its own gay agenda, but also its own image of the gay leader.

As the movement grew, definitions of gay identity proliferated. Homosexuality remained oppressor-defined, but the possibilities for what homosexual identification could mean mushroomed as gay men and lesbians with diverse public images achieved greater visibility. Initially, the meaning of "gay" within the movement was quite narrow: while GLFers assumed an inherent gay affinity with New Left ideals, GAA's founders assumed an inherent gay unity around issues of sexual liberties and gay civil rights. The *Advocate*, particularly during Goodstein's tenure, attempted to mold the gay identity into something approaching middle-class respectability: "You are employed and a useful, responsible citizen. You have an attractive body, nice clothes and an inviting home."[31]

Yet unity within that movement was always very tentative. Essentially, the movement had only two basic goals in common: eliminating the proscriptions against homosexual behavior and eradicating the stigma attached by the society to those who either appeared to engage, or admitted to engaging in such behavior. Not surprisingly, efforts aimed at achieving these narrow goals were the most successful undertakings of the movement. Efforts to build a "gay politics" beyond this least common denominator were largely unsuccessful. The factionalization of the movement may be attributed to the lack of an *a priori* common viewpoint provided by being gay. "Being gay" meant something very different to gay feminists, gay democrats, gay businesspeople, gay professionals, or gay leftists.

The development of leadership was further complicated by the fact that each conflicting view of "being gay" not only entailed its own gay agenda, but also its own image of the gay leader. Each faction felt and often expressed a need to project its vision of what gays are really like through exemplary figures (designated "leaders" by most, except for some of the left and feminist factions). If the leader promoted by one faction—NGTF's Voeller, for instance—exemplified the wrong qualities in the eyes of another faction, say the left-feminists running *Gay Community News*, the dissidents not only refused to follow him, but also considered it a necessity to repudiate him as a true member of the collectivity, as a "real gay." To succeed, a leader not only had to prove he or she could weather failure, criticism, and repudiation from fellow gays, but also had to be able to be gay visibly without embracing any unitary definition of gayness. Only Harvey Milk proved equal to the task.

Implications For 1988

Which of the four themes concerning the non-development of visible national leadership identified here remain relevant today? The growth and diversity of the gay movement and gay and lesbian communities has provided an answer of sorts to the first one. In proliferation, the gay identity has defined itself as diverse. The life or death threat posed by AIDS has markedly changed the risk/reward ratio of coming out. Rock Hudson exemplifies the degree to which post-diagnosis coming out loses much of its sting.

The notoriety which ten years ago went to Matlovich, the sergeant, today attaches to Matlovich, the person with AIDS. People with AIDS have taken important steps in leadership in recent years, but as long as cure and treatment remain distant hopes, this is a constituency which will be spokespersons on the basis of their condition rather than because they are able to provide long-term visible leadership.

To a certain extent, the AIDS crisis has required moving beyond our ambivalence about strong leadership, as it has made evident the need for visible and forceful advocates on the national and local scene. AIDS has also provided a place for the professional and organizational gay and lesbian leader, as it has required the development of permanent and effective service institutions within the gay community. In the training of service volunteers, we have the first organized leadership development in the gay movement outside of the gay churches.

We are still not unified around a gay liberation agenda, and are reluctant to claim as leaders or true fellow gay liberationists those who disagree with our agenda and our vision of the gay identity. The attacks continue to come in the language of internalized oppression. Throughout the AIDS crisis, those who have argued for safer sex have been targeted as "erotophobic" and "self-hating," the latest variants on "not really gay."

Milk's success came in creating a specific agenda for gay liberation in the context of a broader progressive agenda for all people. His refusal to be a "gay candidate" is instructive: his non-gay support helped him to weather the factionalism of the gay community. His solitary status in the seventies, and to a certain extent, in the movement's history since, speaks to our need to unify, to build coalitions, to laugh off attacks from without and within, and to offer support and assistance rather than criticism and rejection to those willing to lead nationally and visibly. ▼

Rink Foto has been photographing lesbian and gay life for 20 years, coast to coast.

Morgan Gwenwald is a photographer living in New York who has covered the lesbian and gay movement extensively.

Rich Wandel is a New York photographer who succeeded Jim Owles as president of GAA and photographed for the newspaper "Gay."

---

[1] John D'Emilio, *Sexual Politics, Sexual Communities: The Making of a Homosexual Minority in the United States, 1940-1970* (Chicago: University of Chicago Press, 1983), p. 219.

[2] Quoted in *ibid.*, p. 210.

[3] Toby Marotta, *The Politics of Homosexuality* (Boston: Houghton-Mifflin, 1981), p. 143.

[4] *The Advocate*, 10/28/70 - 11/10/70, pp. 21-22.

[5] Marotta, *op. cit.*, p. 208.

[6] *The Advocate* #79, 1/5/72, p. 16.

[7] *The Advocate* #125, 11/21/73, p. 2.

[8] *The Advocate* #125, 11/21/73, p. 2. See also Howard J. Brown, *Familiar Faces, Hidden Lives: The Story of Homosexual Men in America Today* (New York: Harcourt-Brace-Jovanovich, 1976).

[9] *The Advocate* #204, 12/1/76, p. 7.

[10] *The Advocate* #124, 11/7/73, p. 24.

[11] *The Advocate* #134, 3/27/74, p. 3.

[12] Interviewed by George Mendenhall in *The Advocate* #128, 1/2/74, p. 14 [11 months prior to Goodstein's purchase of *The Advocate*].

[13] *The Advocate* #106, 2/28/73, p. 36.

[14] Quoted in *The Advocate* #106, 2/28/73, p. 21. Emphasis in the original.

[15] Quoted in Lee H. Solomon, "The Closet Politics of New York's Study Group" in the *Advocate* #216, 6/1/77, p. 41.

[16] *Ibid.*, p 41.

[17] *The Advocate* #196, 8/11/76, p. 9.

[18] *Ibid.*, p. 9.

[19] Sascha Gregory-Lewis, "The Cannibalization of a Hero" in *The Advocate* #180, 12/31/75, p. 7.

[20] Interview by Sascha Gregory-Lewis in *The Advocate* #233, 1/25/78, p. 11.

[21] *The Advocate*, #143, 7/31/74, p. 14.

[22] *The Advocate*, #181, 1/14/76, p. 36.

[23] Quoted in Randy Shilts, *The Mayor of Castro Street: The Life and Times of Harvey Milk* (New York: St. Martin's Press, 1982), p. 75.

[24] *The Advocate* #191, 6/2/76, p. 4 of political supplement.

[25] Quoted in *The Advocate* #187, 4/7/76, p. 12.

[26] Quoted in *The Advocate* #187, 4/7/76, p. 12.

[27] Quoted in *The Advocate* #230, 12/14/77, p. 8.

[28] Shilts, *op. cit.*, pp. 230-231.

[29] *The Advocate* #259, 1/25/79, p. 5.

[30] See Erving Goffman, *Stigma: Notes on the Management of Identity* (Englewood Cliffs, N.J.: Prentice-Hall, 1963), pp. 81, 100 for a fuller discussion of back regions and stigma symbols.

[31] *The Advocate* #156, 1/29/75, p. 3.

Warren Johansson

Periods of the Movement

With the Stonewall Uprising on the early morning of June 28, 1969 the gay liberation movement in the United States began its massive upsurge. Twenty-one years have passed since that momentous event, commemorated by gay pride marches in a score of American cities. It was not, it should always be remembered, the absolute beginning of the movement: this had its start in Germany in January 1864, when Karl Heinrich Ulrichs published his first pamphlet under the title *Vindex*. Nor did it mark the commencement of organized activity for gay rights; this fell on May 14, 1897 when Magnus Hirschfeld and his collaborators formed the Wissenschaftlich-humanitäre Komitee (Scientific-Humanitarian Committee), a group that lasted until June 1933, when it was dissolved so that it would not be banned by the National Socialist regime.

Nor was the gay movement a total stranger to the American scene. At the end of 1950 Harry Hay and his circle in Los Angeles had formed the Mattachine Society, a daring assertion of the rights of a minority which until then had endured its oppression in passivity and silence. But in the climate created by McCarthyism and the conservative miasma of the Eisenhower years, the most that the few gay and lesbian organizations of the time could do was to survive and keep the tiny flame of resistance flickering. On the eve of Stonewall there were two score such groups in the entire country, with perhaps 150 activists. The anti-war movement, influenced by Stalinist and Maoist factions with their belief that homosexuality was nothing more than "bourgeois decadence", although it had convoked gigantic rallies and inspired strikes at such prestigious universities as Columbia and Harvard, largely scorned the appeals of the Student Homophile League for support.

The history of the movement that followed the Stonewall Uprising can best be divided into five phases, each with its own characteristic features and problems:

I. 1969-1973

The initial phase lasted from June 28, 1969 to the end of the Vietnam War on January 27, 1973. This was the heroic, the pioneering, the legendary era in which the movement drew strength and inspiration not just from the organized opposition to American intervention in the civil wars in Southeast Asia, but from the whole mood of cultural rebellion of a younger generation represented by the hippies and beatniks who angrily rejected the beliefs and values of the past.

The activists of that day had the task of seizing the initial beachheads that could serve as the points of departure for later advances. They struggled for bare recognition of the right to exist from an establishment that had long denied the homosexual minority - far more than any other - the rights that were now demanded by every ethnic group and religious denomination almost as a matter of course. Some of them had previous experience as organizers of the civil rights or anti-war movements where they opted to remain in the closet so as to maximize their effectiveness, and they put the skills they had acquired there to good use, but on the whole they knew exceedingly little of the ideology of the gay movement in the past. Many were totally unaware of the organizations that had lasted for decades in Germany, of the writings of their leaders and theoreticians, and of the issues that had divided these now historic groups. On the other hand, they were inspired by the ideology of 'liberation' that swept the Western world as part of the wave of sympathy with the struggles for national independence in the Third World. The identity of the anarcho-individualistic American left with these authoritarian Communist-led movements was largely a matter of illusion at best, of self-deception at worst, but the belief system was adaptable enough to the needs of the Gay Liberation Front to sustain its drive for recognition as part of the larger movement. The 'established' left such as Castro's regime in Cuba never accorded gay liberation any legitimacy.

For many would-be gay activists, the radicalism of the Gay Liberation Front was unpalatable, and by the winter of 1969-1970 the single-issue Gay Activists Alliance had come into being. On the other hand, the older groups that had survived from the 'homophile' phase of the movement, whose pleas for toleration had gone unheeded by an indifferent society, were now seen as hopelessly timid, closeted, and out of date, and so disintegrated and faded into the past.

II. 1973-1977

The second phase of the movement lasted from the end of the Vietnam War to Anita Bryant's victory in Dade County on June 7, 1977. With the radical mood of the country dissipated, gay liberation had to fight on alone for goals that could be accomplished only in decades, if not in a lifetime; but, while the Student Mobilization Committees and the like vanished forever, the movement survived as the enduring legacy of the 1968-1973 period - an era that contrasted strikingly with the normal conservatism and apolitical ambience of the American campus. Organized opposition to gay rights had not yet emerged, in part because until then all institutions of society had been homophobic in a multitude of ways: there was no need for a specific group. In some instances gay activists were able to win victories just because their opponents were totally unprepared for their claims and arguments.

Such groups as the National Gay Task Force and the Gay Academic Union formed with the conscious goal of increasing the presence and influence of homosexuals within the establishment - which they had no thought of overthrowing. Religious bodies such as Metropolitan Community Church, Dignity, Integrity, and the gay synagogues spread into the hinterland along with mainly social student organizations able to benefit from the more tolerant climate of the campus, even when surrounded by a hostile, fundamentalist Middle America. Local initiative spawned community groups, businesses with a specifically gay clientele, health centers, and clubs with shared interests apart from the gay identity of their members.

III. 1977-1981

The repeal by referendum of the gay rights law in Dade County, Florida was another milestone in movement history. It signaled the rise of an organized, religiously motivated and institutionally supported opposition to gay rights - but not the defeat of the larger movement, for which the challenge was also a stimulus for further initiatives. The political atmosphere of the Carter Administration, with its emphasis on human rights, conferred on the movement a legitimacy that made it possible to consolidate the gains of the preceding years. A gay press, national and local, now served to keep readers in the most distant corners of America informed and in contact and to shape a collective opinion on matters of common concern. The drive to repeal the survivals of medieval law that penalized homosexual expression scored successes in both legislatures and courts, so that by 1981 half of the 50 states ceased to make criminals out of otherwise law-abiding gay citizens. And in October 1979, the March on Washington demonstrated that from a handful of semi-clandestine organizations hiding in the bohemian quarters of the large cities, the gay movement had grown into a multitude of interlocking groups, caucuses, and organizations that reflected the innumerable facets of the America of which our community is a microcosm.

IV. 1981-1986

No one could have foreseen the phase that began with the report of the first cases of AIDS in March, 1981. The dark side of the sexual revolution - the spread of a mysterious, seemingly incurable disease among gay men - coincided with the conservative if not openly reactionary political climate ushered in by the Reagan Administration. On many fronts the movement was forced to defend itself against mounting attacks by fundamentalist religious groups such as the Moral Majority led by Jerry Falwell with a following of millions in the hinterland. But it persisted in its efforts to repeal the sodomy statues, and, more important, to assure civil rights that had been denied to gay people on the convenient pretext that they were suffering from a mental illness: privacy, recognition of one's "significant other", inheritance, child custody, freedom of speech for gay activists. In this campaign a signal victory was the ordinance adopted in New York City on March 20, 1986 after 15 years of struggle, in the final decade led by the Coalition for Lesbian and Gay Rights founded just after the fiasco in Dade County.

V. 1986-

Then on June 30, 1986 the movement entered its fifth phase: the Supreme Court of the United States by a 5-4 majority upheld the constitutionality of Georgia's sodomy law, refusing to extend to homosexual behavior the concept of privacy which it had first recognized in the criminal law in 1965 with reference to the use of contraceptives. This defeat was a blow to the legal campaign that had hoped to eliminate the sodomy laws at one stroke, but it also sparked the Second March on Washington in October, 1987, twice as large as the previous one.

This newest phase of movement history also saw a return to the kind of bold and heroic activism that had marked the first one. Even if AIDS was a single issue, such groups as ACT UP [AIDS Coalition To Unleash Power], founded in New York City on March 12, 1987, far outdid the Gay Liberation Front in their imaginative and resourceful tactics for building organizations, staging public protests, and winning the attention of the media.

Fund raising on a grand scale became a crucial need of the movement; the AIDS organizations of 1990 were spending more in a week than the annual budget of most gay liberation fronts in 1971. At the same time the AIDS Memorial Quilt, displayed in cities around the country, reminded all who viewed it of the toll which disease - and official indifference to the magnitude of the peril - had taken in the ranks of the gay community.

But another aspect of the post-1986 phase

was the arrival of a 'second generation' of movement activists, too young to remember the pre-Stonewall era, able to accept and affirm its gay identity proudly and even aggressively, but also faced with its own set of problems. Issues such as gay marriage, adoption, 'life partner' rights, and similar matters that the activists of 1969 could scarcely have envisioned now stood on the agenda of the movement. Gay people - for better or worse - were a fact of American life that no one could ignore. Even the tragedy of the AIDS epidemic, which brought so much sorrow to gay Americans and ended so many careers that might have lasted into the 30s of the next century, still reinforced the solidarity of the gay community in the face of suffering and death.

Overview

The American movement began in the 1950s on the West Coast, in Los Angeles and San Francisco. There the Mattachine Society and the Daughters of Bilitis were founded; there the first gay periodicals were issued. But since the mid-1960s there has been a division of labor, as it were, between the two coasts. The West Coast has continued to pioneer in the social and cultural domains, has given birth to the gay churches and synagogues, to the veterans' and athletic organizations, and similar groups united by a shared interest or identity apart from sexual orientation. The East Coast has spawned the political groups from the Gay Liberation Front (in July, 1969) to Queer Nation (in March 1990) and the academic ones, beginning with the Student Homophile League (at Columbia in April, 1967) and continuing with the Gay Academic Union (founded at John Jay College in November 1973) and now the Center for Lesbian and Gay Studies (CLAGS) at the City University of New York and the Columbia University Seminar on Homosexualities (CUSH). This complementarity reflects the differing roles of the two regions in American life in general.

So as it has happened, in only the first and third phases of its history did the gay rights movement coast with the tide of American politics. In the other three it held its own, consolidated its gains, and grew inwardly by its own strength. It has established the gay community as an interest group that is a stable and abiding part of the American nation and shares its common destiny, one that cuts across all other religious and ethnic divisions and still proudly asserts its own identity - and will not go away despite the rejection and hostility of its enemies. Whatever gay people have accomplished in all of the five periods has been their own doing - in many cases ignored and scorned by other 'outsider' groups, even other 'official' minorities, quite as much as by the majority. While the gay rights movement has had its leaders, its celebrities - and its martyrs, in most cases their peak of fame was brief. Far more than many others, it has been a movement of unknown soldiers - of men and women working tirelessly day after day and year after year to combat the ignorance, the prejudice, the hostility around them, trusting that their efforts would leave an enduring legacy to their spiritual if not physical descendants. So it is with confidence in the ultimate victory of their movement that gay Americans can look to the 1990s and to the tasks and challenges of the decade that lies ahead.

Warren Johansson is Associate Editor of the *Encyclopedia of Homosexuality* (1990) and lives in New York City. This paper first appeared in the *C·L·G·H Newsletter* of the American Historical Association, Vol. 4, No. 2, September, 1990.

Social theory, social movements and public policy:

recent accomplishments of the gay and lesbian movements in Minneapolis, Minnesota

by Lawrence Knopp

In recent years there has been a proliferation of ostensibly non class-based social movements throughout the world. In the west, movements organized around issues of gender, sexuality, the environment, and nuclear war have all but displaced more traditional and self consciously class-based ones. To be sure there are factions, sometimes strong, within each of these which stress the class origins of their particular concerns. But such analyses are rarely popularized, even within the movements.

This proliferation of seemingly non class-based movements poses both theoretical and practical problems for a political-economic analysis of contemporary capitalist society. Strict economistic approaches usually reduce to functionalism, and ignore the important substance of many of these movements' critiques of society. Thus the women's movement, for example, is all too often 'factored out' of analyses of urban restructuring (see Rose, 1984, 52). Similarly, Castells (1978, 152–66) regards the environmental movement in the US as simply an 'ideological mystification. What is needed here is the drawing of non-functionalist linkages between the class interests of human beings and their propensities to act politically on the basis of other affiliations.

Concomitant with this theoretical problem are the practical political dangers inherent in playing off traditional class-based movements against seemingly non-class-based ones. Class-based stratifications have developed within many movements which have resulted in the partial redefinition of their agendas by conservative interests (e.g. certain debates at the 1985 International Women's Conference and the growth of 'gay Republicanism' in the US).

The gay and lesbian movements are excellent examples of movements which warrant analysis from a non-functionalist political-economy perspective. Historically, they have been leaders in revealing the socially constructed nature of reality at the level of everyday experience. This is because they have combined powerful critiques of the prevailing social definitions of gender and sexuality in capitalist society. But the gay and lesbian movements themselves do not normally make linkages to the issue of class.[1]

The purpose of this paper is to examine the ways in which social definitions of

[1] This is more true of the US movement than of its European counterparts.

gender and sexuality were altered in a particular case through the struggles of gay and lesbian activists, and to make linkages between these struggles and a broader system of capitalist social relations. The class positions of various actors are identified, as are the class interests which their action served (these two are often not equivalent). The paper also explores the implications more generally of the challenge to contemporary capitalist social formations which the lesbian and gay movements represent.

I Social theory, social movements, and sexuality

Both liberal and much Marxist theory have failed to account adequately for the recent proliferation of seemingly non class-based social and political movements. To many Marxists, an America in which organized lesbians and gay men in some places rival organized labour for political clout (e.g. San Francisco) is highly problematical. A great many neo-Marxists have scrambled to account for these movements, but except for feminist and/or lesbian and gay scholars, they have tended to regard them as, at best epiphenomenal and, at worst, counter-revolutionary.[2]

In the liberal tradition, these movements could not have been anticipated at all, since it was expected that the sway of 'collective conscience' and small 'moral communities' over individuals would diminish as the division of labour in society increased, to be replaced by a primary allegiance to the social 'organism' (Saunders, 1981, 35–47; Murray, 1984, 11). Even liberal positivists like Kinsey *et al.* (1948; 1953) denied the ontological status of identities, focusing instead on (sexual) behaviours and thus denying the possibility of new political subjects emerging from their analyses. According to Kinsey, there were no sexual identities, only sexual acts. There could therefore be no social movements based on a shared sense of sexual identity. Neo-Weberian analyses, meanwhile, tend to ignore the substance of the critiques which these social movements represent. They focus instead on creating typologies, understanding personal motivations through *verstehen*, and establishing correlations between events. The result is often superficial and trivial analyses (see, for example, Wilson's (1973, 45–47) discussion of US campus activism in the 1960s).

These problems pose what may be the most important set of issues in social theory: What is the relationship between the motivations and consciousnesses of human subjects and the social structures which they (re)produce and transform through their actions? How are personal identities sufficiently meaningful to fuel these movements formed, even while the sway of other affiliations seems to be declining? In short, how can we account for social change, the face of which is

[2]There is a strong tradition among some Marxists which is openly hostile to movements for 'sexual liberation' (see Derbyshire, 1980, for a review of Marxist theory and practice regarding gay men and lesbians). Herbert Marcuses' *Eros and civilization* (1955) is an exception.

quite different from that for which our theories have prepared us?

Radical theory has tended to stress the importance of unperceived structures, in the context of capitalist societies imbued with 'voluntarist' ideology (e.g. Fainstein and Fainstein, 1983; Clark and Dear, 1984). But too often radical theory has failed to conceptualize important links between these real structures and the active human subjects whose social relations these structures *are*, in particular the capacities of these subjects to struggle against domination in a multiplicity of ways. Liberal and conservative theories (both positivists and hermeneutic),[3] meanwhile, have simplistically assumed the primacy of human agency (e.g. 'public choice' theory (Archer, 1981) and symbolic-interactionist studies of subcultures (e.g. Anderson, 1923)).

A considerable body of recently developed social theory recognizes these shortcomings (Giddens, 1979; 1981, Bhaskar, 1979). In political and economic geography, applications involve the development of new conceptualizations of 'explanation' which transcend the 'structure/agency' dichotomy (Sayer, 1982; Chouinard *et al.*, 1984; Thrift, 1983).[4] In feminist and lesbian/gay studies, similar developments are taking place. Here 'social constructionist' perspectives (Berger and Luckman, 1966) are gaining currency. Murray (1984, 56), for example, notes that the 'salience' of gender as an organizing principle varies from culture to culture. Escoffier (1985, 136) points out that even the link between genetic assignment and anatomy is not invariant. Similarly, concepts like 'sexual orientation', which categorize according to both the subjective perception of self and external labelling, have been shown to be highly culture-specific (Weeks, 1985; Murray, 1984; Carrier, 1980).

Lauria and Knopp (1985, 156–57) provide the rudiments of a political-economic accounting of the social construction of the modern 'gay identity'. They suggest that homosexual repression is tied to the repression of sexuality generally, and specifically to a form of gender relations in which women are dominated by men. Unrepressed homosexual relations are seen as a threat to the economically efficient (for capital) nuclear family, which, through its internal relations of gender and sexuality, sustains the ideological separation between the 'productive' and 'reproductive' spheres of daily life. The gay and lesbian movements are seen as reactions to this historically specific form of oppression.

More comprehensive efforts to approach the 'gay identity' (and social movements organized around it) from this perspective are found in the works of various feminist and lesbian/gay theorists (Snitow *et al.*, 1983; Ross and Rapp, 1983; Altman, 1982; D'Emilio, 1981; 1983a; 1983b; Escoffier, 1985; Weeks, 1981; 1981; 1985). Here, sexual identities (indeed, sexuality itself) are also seen as deriving from industrial capitalism's separation of 'productive' and 'reproductive'

[3] This is not meant to imply that hermeneutics are necessarily liberal or voluntarist; on the contrary, most are not.

[4] Thrift (1983) suggests that the 'structure/agency' dichotomy itself reflects the bifurcation at the level of appearances of everyday life into spheres of production and consumption under capitalism.

life. The argument is roughly as follows: As capitalism developed, and free-labour and exchange relations came to dominate production, the family became more narrowly defined in terms of the reproduction of labour-power. Many of the needs of labourers were now met within the family by unwaged (and hence 'unproductive' yet superexploited) domestic labour. An ideal of monogamous (and patriaarchal) heterosexuality underpinned the system ideologically. But at the same time, the autonomous 'personal' realm created by the intersection of waged-labour and industrialization made it possible (economically, if not ideologically) for waged-labourers to explore non family-centred avenues of fulfillment. Sexual (and other) subcultures thus emerged.[5] The labelling of people engaged in same-sex sexual relationships as 'homosexuals' by the medical profession in the late nineteenth century then provided the final link in the process of personal and group identity formation.

Escoffier (1985, 120–21) disaggregates the process of lesbian and gay identity formation even further. He views sexual identities as

> . . . the results of struggles among concrete historical actors (for example, between prostitutes and the state) and shaped by the social relations of . . . the ensemble of discourses, practices and institutions that structure and regulate the social relations of gender as well as the varieties of sexual behaviour (the 'sex/gender system').

In particular, he argues that the modern lesbian and gay identities emerged from the sexual revolution of the post-World War II era, which he links to the growth of the welfare state. As women entered the work force, and more people lived outside family households, 'cultural revolts' (e.g. the Beat Generation) and urban subcultures (including sexual subcultures), steadily grew. Fueled by these developments, and by the growth of the women's movement, the identity-based lesbian and gay political movements developed. But Escoffier also notes that these movements are currently attempting to cope with the realization that the 'identities' upon which they are based are not fixed:

> [By] reinterpret[ing] the symbolic significance of sexuality and gender . . . [by] split[ting] sexual object preference from gender, and by challenging the heterosexual assumption, [the movements have] legitimated the social construction of sexual identity (Escoffier, 1985, 147).

Escoffier argues that because of this, any movement based on identity will eventually have to stress a politics of at least limited *differentness* as well as of shared experience. Hence the emergence of separate lesbian and gay movements and of intense controversies within these communities regarding, for example, sexual ethics (e.g. debates about pornography, the practice of certain kinds of sexual 'play' (i.e. S/M), and how best to acknowledge and accommodate child sexuality) Escoffier, 1985, 147–49).

[5]This is not meant to suggest that 'heterosexism' is found only in capitalism or that sexual 'networks' have not existed in previous modes of production (see Boswell, 1980, for evidence to the contrary). I do mean to suggest, however, that the sexual identities and subcultures constructed in capitalism are *different* from those found elsewhere.

Lauria and Knopp (1985) contend that a modest redefinition of the social relations of gender and sexuality may be in the interest of certain factions of capital. 'Service-sector' jobs in the centre-city, for example, are quite easily filled by gay men (Gagnon and Simon, 1973; Harry and Devall, 1978), many of whom locate in centre-city areas because of the concentration of gay institutions there. Similarly, the development of 'rent gaps' in the urban land market (Smith, 1979) favours the development of consumer markets for 'gentrified' housing (and other 'higher and better' land uses) among lesbian and gay populations. This is due to a combination of the relatively high disposable incomes of middle-class lesbians and gay men (especially the latter) and these groups' frequent preferences for easy accessibility to lesbian and gay social and cultural institutions.

Still, the process of redefining the social relations of gender and sexuality, which the gay and lesbian movements have encouraged, has been an uneven one. Arguably, it is not very advanced. For every San Francisco or Amsterdam there are hundreds of Wichitas.[6] For every 'jet-set' there are thousands of traditional 'sets' that cling tenaciously to established norms. While the processes which Escoffier, Lauria and Knopp, and others identify are certainly occurring in the mass cultures of advanced capitalism, the actual struggles bringing about concrete changes have yet to be identified and analysed.[7] The present study is an attempt to identify, in the context of a specific case, the process whereby a concrete change *was* achieved though a conscious struggle to redefine the social relations of gender and sexuality at the level of everyday life and experience. This redefinition has important implications for the particular class-based social formation which is advanced capitalism.

II Gay and lesbian politics in Minneapolis in the seventies

The State of Minnesota has a liberal political culture. Except for a brief period during the 1930s, when its electoral politics were dominated by the left leaning Farm-Labor Party, the economic and social policies pursued by the state have been solidly Keynesian.

Postwar Keynesian liberalism has had contradictory social and cultural effects, however (Bell, 1976). On the one hand, the era's economic growth and rising material expectations have fostered the development of a libertarian individualist ethos, which translates into popular demands for equality of 'opportunity' and freedom from cultural 'constraints' of various kinds (e.g. traditional gender and sex roles). On the other hand, tight labour markets, the rising cost of living relative to the established family wage, and the attempted reconversion to a 'peacetime' (i.e. male-dominated) labour force, have created pressure for the reestablishment of

[6] Wichita, Kansas was one of several cities in the US where gay rights ordinances were repealed by popular referendum in 1977 and 1978.

[7] Exceptions may be New York (Teal, 1971; Marotta, 1981), San Francisco (D'Emilio, 1981; Castells and Murphy, 1982; Castells, 1983) and Weimar Germany (Steakley, 1975).

Table 1 The political development of Minneapolis's gay and lesbian communities

1969	
May 18 –	Fight Repression of Erotic Expression (FREE) founded at the University of Minnesota.
1970	
May 18 –	Jack Baker attempts to secure marriage license for himself and Michael McConnell.
Summer-fall –	State Board of Regents rescinds hiring of McConnell as university librarian; ACLU takes case, wins.
October –	National gay and lesbian conference at the University of Minnesota sponsored by FREE.
1971	
Spring –	Baker elected president of Minnesota Students' Association (MSA).
October –	Appeals court overturns lower court decision in McConnell case.
1972	
Fall –	100–200 gays participate in DFL (Democratic Party) precinct caucuses; gay rights, planks passed as State Convention; gay alternate elected to national Convention.
1973	
* * –	First attempt to pass statewide gay-rights bill is made.
* * –	FREE becomes Minnesota Gay Activists (MGA).
1974	
March 29 –	Minneapolis gay-rights ordinance passed.
May 11 –	Minnesota Committee for Gay Rights (MCGR) founded.
July 16 –	St Paul gay-rights ordinance passed.
December 9 –	State Senator Allan Spear acknowledges publicly that he is gay.
1975	
* * –	Baker brings suit against Big Brothers of Minneapolis.
* * –	MCGR compromises on language of statewide gay-rights bill; Baker faction protests.
June 13 –	City Council proclaims last day of June Gay Pride Day.
November –	Conservative ex-Mayor Stenvig defeats liberal DFL mayor.
1976	
October 9 –	City Council rescinds Gay Pride Day.
November –	Spear wins reelection over a Baker supporter.
1977	
May –	Statewide gay-rights bill nearly passes State Legislature.
June 23 –	Target City coalition founded.
Fall –	1300+ local gays and lesbians stage anti-Anita Bryant rally.
1978	
April 25 –	St Paul gay-rights ordinance is repealed.
November –	Rally held locally on evening of gay-rights victories in California and Seattle.
1979	
June-November –	8 murders of gay men in Minneapolis and St Paul.
June 28 –	First police raid on a local gay bathhouse.
July 27 –	State Supreme Court rules against Baker in Big Brothers case.

* * = Exact dates unavailable.

traditional (patriarchal) relations of gender and sexuality (among other sets of social relations). These contradictions were evidenced in Minneapolis during the 1970s by a profound ambivalence towards 'liberal' social agendas in elections. For the first four years of the decade (and two more later on), the city was presided over not by a DFL (Democratic Party) liberal, but by a conservative Independent mayor drawn from the ranks of the Police Department.

For the gay and lesbian movements the decade was a period of growth (Table 1). One of the first direct challenges to the prevailing social definitions of marriage, sexuality, and the family in Minneapolis was a well-publicized attempt to secure a marriage license by a leader of the city's first gay-oriented political organization, Jack Baker, and his male lover, in 1970. By appealing to the authority of the local state apparatus the two activists at once challenged and acknowledged the power of state sanction to legitimate the social construction of some kinds of social relations.

Others during the 1970s engaged in strictly pluralist, 'interest group'-orientated gay politics. Initial successes included the founding of a gay lobbying organization in 1971, the election of openly-gay delegates to the State DFL Convention in 1972, and the enactment of gay-rights ordinances in both Minneapolis and neighbouring St Paul in 1974.

But no sooner had these successes been achieved than pluralist tactics began to fail. In 1975, a liberal gay lobby agreed to compromise the language of a state-wide gay-rights bill. This was because of two widely publicized and very controversial lawsuits brought by Baker under the 'public services' provisions of the Twin Cities' gay-rights ordinances. Baker challenged the Big Brothers organization in Minneapolis, and an adoption agency in St Paul, for inquiring as to the sexual orientations of prospective Big Brothers and adoptive parents, and using this information to screen applicants. Here he was challenging the social definition of the relationship between sexuality and parenting. This precipitated a considerable amount of hostile reaction. Eventually he lost the Big Brothers case. But in so doing Baker demonstrated that the prevailing social definitions of sexuality and parenting, and the legal structure which supported them, were patently contradictory.

Reacting to the liberal gays' compromise, supporters of Baker conducted a high-visibility campaign to support the original version of the statewide gay-rights bill. This included a mock press conference in a Capitol building men's room and a parade of 'drag queens' (transvestites) testifying at committee hearings. The former was intended to expose the men's room as a place where many of the legislators voting 'no' on gay-rights were saying 'yes' to gay sex (i.e. actually having semi-anonymous gay sexual encounters) – an example of what Gofman (1959)and Giddens (1979, 207) call 'back regions', or locations in space and/or time where certain social contradictions are allowed to play themselves out.[8] The transvestites' actions, meanwhile, can be seen as an even more radical attack on traditional

[8]In this case, the contradiction was between many legislators' socially constructed 'personal' sexual proclivities and their internalization of a 'public' sexual morality which could not accommodate these proclivities.

notions of gender and sexual normalcy. These activists were symbolically reinterpreting the connections between gender, gender roles, and sexual preference (see Escoffier, 1985, 140–41). By demonstrating that men could affect feminine mannerisms and roles, including a sexual preference for other men, these actors validated the social construction of gender and sexuality.

Pluralist tactics, meanwhile, continued to fail through the end of the decade. In 1975, a conservative ex-mayor campaigned against gay-rights and was elected in an upset. In 1977, a statewide gay-rights bill, which appeared likely to pass the State Legislature, was defeated. Then, in 1978, a campaign to repeal gay-rights laws came to neighbouring St Paul and succeeded overwhelmingly. In 1979, trouble between the Police Department and the gay-male community began. Furthermore, there were eight murders of gay men in Minneapolis that year, so many that one issue of *Positively Gay*, a gay newspaper, featured the headline, 'Another month, another murder' (*Positively Gay*, 1979a).

These assaults mobilized the gay community. A 'radical' gay political organization, Target City, was formed.[9] It was composed of both leftist and non-leftist activists who were united by a conviction that high visibility, confrontational responses to oppression were necessary. Its members engaged in, among other things, a series of 'pie in the face' attacks on antigay public figures. Although Target City never achieved the 'official' clout of liberal gay organizations, its members' tactics were crucial to the outcome of the conflict between the Police Department and the gay male community which erupted in 1979.

III 1979–1985: the battle over 'indecent conduct'

Through most of the 1970s, the primary source of hostility towards gays and lesbians was not the Police Department but rather other local state apparatuses (e.g. the courts, the city administration, the State Legislature) and non-state actors. Friendly police walkthroughs of gay bars were in fact common, and reports of police brutality and harassment of gays were sporadic.

But on the morning of Gay Pride Day, 1979 (28 June), a series of events began which can only be characterized as open warfare between gays and certain members of the Minneapolis Police Department (MPD) (Table 2). At 4.00 am, the head of the MPD Vice Squad, along with the deputy mayor and a municipal bond salesman, forcibly entered a gay steambath and threw out the patrons. No arrests or citations were made. Affidavits signed by patrons claimed the intruders were drunk and abusive. A scandal ensued. At a meeting with the police chief, the head of the Vice Squad, and the deputy mayor (before it was learned that the latter was involved in

[9] Target City was so named because in 1978 antigay activist Anita Bryant had identified Minneapolis and St Paul as 'Target Cities' for her national gay-rights repeal campaign.

1979	
June 28 (Gay Pride Day) —	First bathhouse raid.
July 3 —	Gays meet with police chief, head of vice, and deputy mayor.
July —	Cover-up of June 28 incident charged by deputy police chief; deputy police chief demoted.
August 9 —	Police chief resigns; deputy mayor suspended.
Fall —	Large-scale arrests for 'indecent conduct' in adult bookstores begins; Tim Campbell runs for mayor, campaigns against police harassment.
December 1 —	Second bathhouse raid.
1980	
January 1 —	3 Popular gay bars raided for being open after hours on New Year's Eve.
January 10 —	Third bathhouse raid.
• • —	Meetings between gays, Mayor Fraser, city council members held; bathhouse raids stop.
November —	Target City runs slate of candidates for city offices; openly-lesbian Karen Clark elected to State House of Representatives.
1981–1982	
• • —	Meetings between gays and city officials held periodically.
• • —	Allegations of police brutality against gays escalates; civil suits cost city thousands of dollars.
November, 1981 —	Four openly-gay men run for sixth ward City Council seat.
1983	
November —	Openly-gay Brian Coyle elected to sixth ward City Council seat.
1984	
May 23 —	Coyle meets with police chief; 'got nowhere'.
May 24 —	Coyle, another council member, meets with Fraser, attorneys for arrestees; Fraser refuses to interfere with police practices.
Summer —	Allegations of police brutality, entrapment arrests escalate, spread to city parks and Park Police.
September 21 —	Coyle meets with Fraser; mayor claims directive was issued to cease entrapments.
November 7–8 —	Minneapolis Civil Rights Commission holds hearings on police bruality; 'seemed to favor' citizens review panel.
November 20 —	Intensive campaign by police against two bookstores downtown launched; 20+ visits a day; frequent arrests.
November 30 —	Gay aides to Coyle and Fraser stress 'equal enforcement' concerns to police chief and head of Vice Squad.
December —	Coyle pressures police chief publicly at appearance before gay business organization.
1985	
January 10 —	Municipal judge rules that bookstore cubicles are not public places.
February 15 —	Attorney for Tim Campbell arrested while attempting to serve summons on officers named in class-action suit.
February 19 —	Meeting between various gay and non-gay city officials; police chief tells *Star and Tribune* 'I caved in'.
February 21 —	Police chief orders Vice Squad to 'radically deemphasize' bookstore patrols; acknowledges effectiveness of gay lobbying.
Februry 22 —	Police chief denies gay lobbying influenced decision to change policy.
February 25 —	New policy formalized and 'accepted' by Fraser.
March 1 — May 20 —	Only four 'indecent conduct' arrests in Minneapolis

• • — = Exact dates unavailable.

the raid), members of the gay community were assured that the incident did not signal a change of policy towards gays in the Police Department or at City Hall (*Positively Gay*, 1979b).

But shortly thereafter, the attacks on gay men and gay establishments escalated. A pattern of large-scale arrests for 'indecent conduct' in adult bookstores began in the fall (Halfhill, 1984; *GLC Voice*, 1985a). Arrestees were almost always gay or bisexual men whose sexual proclivities were for the most part hidden from friends and family. Typically, the police would employ decoys and/or storm through the establishments, forcing open doors to viewing booths and roughing-up patrons. Numerous complaints were filed with the Police Internal Affairs Unit. Rarely, if ever, were these sustained.[10]

In December and January there were two more raids on bathhouses, resulting in over 200 arrests or citations, including nine for sodomy, which is a felony in Minnesota. Then three popular gay bars were raided for being open after hours on New Year's Eve, 1980.

Target City responded to eight murders, a hostile State Supreme Court ruling on the Big Brothers issue, and a sudden upsurge of antigay police harassment and violence by running a slate of third-party candidates for city offices and demanding meetings with the new mayor and members of the City Council. A list of demands was formulated which included abolition of the Vice Squad and reparations for victims of the bathhouse and bookstore raids. Although no policy concessions were made, the bathhouse raids did stop. The bookstore raids did not.

The city's daily newspapers, meanwhile, ran lurid stories about drugs and unusual sexual paraphernalia at one of the bathhouses (Halfhill, 1984). It was the conclusion of many in Target City, at the time, that the increased police harassment downtown, and the sensationalist press coverage of it, were part of an effort by the city to legitimate the redevelopment of a downtown street on which many gay businesses are located.

Over the next four and a half years there were between 3500 and 5000 arrests of gay and bisexual men for 'indecent conduct', most of them in adult bookstores (*GLC Voice*, 1984a; 1984c; 1985b; Halfhill, 1984; interviews). Allegations of police brutality against gays escalated, and meetings between representatives of the gay community and the city were held at least once a year (*GLC Voice*, 1985a).

Members of the local gay press took a very active role in these meetings and the conflict in general. Bruce Brockway and Tim Campbell (both of whom had ties to Target City) published *Positively Gay* and, later, *GLC Voice*, carefully documenting every arrest, beating, trial and election concerning the gay community. These journalist-activists always contrasted 'official' accounts of incidents involving the police with those of eyewitnesses, and exposed contradictory official accounts and missing or altered police reports, as well. They frequently helped coordinate meetings and public demonstrations. Their advocacy style of journalism made the

[10]Of 144 complaints filed from March 1 through August 31, 1984, none was sustained (*GLC Voice*, 1985c).

capricious and unequal enforcement of indecent conduct laws an indisputable fact in the gay community, and many of their findings were picked up by the mainstream press as well (e.g. Davies, 1985).

These gay activists also continually questioned prevailing sexual norms. *Positively Gay* pressed Mayor Fraser in a 1979 preelection interview to comment on the 'legitimacy' and 'morality' of gay sex (*Positively Gay,* 1979c). Fraser refused to discuss the issue in these terms. He did, however, evince mixed feelings about the Big Brothers case:

> . . . under these circumstances the question of sexual preference . . . is a different kind of issue than religion, color, race. (*Positively Gay*, 1979c, 8.)

In the case of morals code enforcement he drew the line at 'public sex'. This distinction between 'public' and 'private' sex had repeatedly been used by the police to justify their enforcement practices. It also raised important questions about where the line between 'public' and 'private' was to be drawn, and whether or not there was a public interest in holding gays to a different standard then straights in this regard.

Brockway, Campbell, and others relentlessly challenged the *purpose* of distinctions like 'public' versus 'private' sex, as well. In 1984, Campbell documented a correlation between police harassment of two adult bookstores, declining business at those stores, and an increased number of offers by property brokers to purchase the businesses (*GLC Voice*, 1984d). Campbell charged 'graft', asserting a connection between the city's December designation of an area adjacent to these bookstores as the site of a proposed convention centre, and a particularly intense campaign of police harassment at these locations in November. Furthermore, Campbell argued forecefully throughout the conflict that the place where most of the so-called 'public sex' was taking place (adult bookstore movie cubicles and certain portions of public parks late at night) constituted essentially *private* places, and moreover that they were the *only* private places available to some gay people, namely those who have not come to terms with their sexualities (*GLC Voice*, 1982b; 1984b; 1984c; 1985a; 1985d; 1985e). Thus like the Capitol building activists in 1975, he identified perfectly a set of 'back regions', the only difference being that this time their patrons were cast in a more sympathetic light. In both cases the 'back regions', and their patrons' confused 'identities', were presented unequivocally as *social* products. Campbell also argued that sexual activities had been going on in these places for years without apparent harm to anyone.[11]

'Radical' gay activists also stressed the *history* of morals codes and the 'gay experience' to present policies and practices. At one of the earlier meetings between

[11] Acquired Immune Deficiency Syndrome (AIDS) did not enter the public consciousness as an issue until relatively late in this conflict. Furthermore, the same gay press which struggled against harassment of bookstore patrons was at the same time painstakingly educating its readers about the disease and demanding that the city and the state devote more resources to coping with and preventing it.

gays, Fraser, and Police Chief Bouza, a non-traditional 'sensitivity training' was proposed for the police by gays. This included calls for a look at uneven patterns of law enforcement vis-a-vis morals codes, presentations of the history of the development of gay and other sexual subcultures, and an examination of the contradiction between the city's human rights ordinance and the state's sodomy laws (*GLC Voice*, 1982a). These proposals were clearly an attempt to raise consciousnesses and force an examination of the issues raised by Fraser's and Bouza's explanations.

Gays and lesbians in the DFL (and therefore in the city bureaucracy and on the staffs of DFL officeholders, including Fraser) also brought pressure on the mayor and the police chief to resolve the conflict. However, this was only after the problem became very large scale and these 'insiders' were either personally touched by it or pressured by their gay constituents because of it. An open lesbian, Karen Clark, was elected to the State Legislature from a central-Minneapolis district in 1980.[12] In 1983 a gay man, Brian Coyle, was elected to the City Council from the city's sixth ward, which includes most of the areas with heavy concentrations of gays. Neither of these two emphasized gay and lesbian politics, or this particular conflict, in their campaigns, however. Indeed, they generally opposed the high visibility tactics and specifically 'gay' agendas of Target City and people like Campbell and Baker.[13] Nevertheless, by 1984 Coyle (under pressure from gay constituents and Campbell's *GLC Voice*) was publicly pressuring Chief Bouza to change his enforcement policy.

The enforcement policy was finally changed in February, 1985. Chief Bouza's public reaction reveals both his bitterness at being forced into this position and his acknowledgement of the role played by gay activists in bringing it about:

> I caved in. I always cave in to every pressure group. Whatever they want. All they have to do is ask me (*GLC Voice*, 1985a, 3);

and

> I succumbed to the pressure . . . It's absolutely true, there's no doubt, I've never been involved with such a high-powered effort to influence policy involving gays (*Minneapolis Star and Tribune*, 1985a, 1A.)

The new policy calls for irregular Vice Squad entries into adult bookstores, usually only when uniformed officers report trouble (*Minneapolis Star and Tribune*, 1985c). Since its implementation, indecent conduct arrests have decreased significantly: only four were recorded between March 1 and May 20,1985 (*GLC Voice*, 1985b.) For the moment, arrests in city parks have declined as well.

The policy change does not mark an end to the battle over the redefinition of

[12] Clark, as a lesbian, did not have to interpret the bookstore arrests as a lesbian issue. Indeed, she could have allied herself with feminist antipornographers who opposed such establishments as a matter of principle. She did not.

[13] In subsequent races against other gays with ties to Target City, both Coyle and openly-gay State Senator Allan Spear have won handily.

the social relations of gender and sexuality in Minneapolis. Mayor Fraser still clings steadfastly to the importance of a police department being able to act independently, free of 'political' pressures. Thus he dislikes interfering in matters of police policy and continues to oppose a citizens' review board to handle complaints of police misconduct. And at the same time that he announced the 'radical deemphasis' of bookstore patrols, Chief Bouza told the *Minneapolis Star and Tribune*:

> I want to make it clear these places won't become privileged sanctuaries where the police won't ever intrude. We'll still patrol. And anything that spills into the public won't be tolerated if it's indecent conduct . . . I'm saying this: Keep it discreet and keep it very private. (*Minneapolis Star and Tribune*, 1985a, 6A.)

IV Discussion: identity politics and class

By the late 1970s liberal lesbians and gay men had finally secured more or less permanent access to most local state apparatuses in Minneapolis, through the DFL's lock on local electoral politics. Whereas previously their main opponents had been non-state actors and state apparatuses other than the police, the police were now the one state apparatus with which they (or, more specifically, gay men) were most in conflict. Liberal gays and their allies were unable to do anything about the massive assault waged by the police on gay men for over five years, just as they had failed to turn back other assaults earlier (e.g. the 1978 gay-rights repeal in St Paul). More 'tactically radical' gay activists struggled to expose the police campaign as contradictory and plainly homophobic. They effectively challenged official accounts of events *and* of motives, including arguing that the police campaign was linked to city and private developers' plans to redevelop a downtown street on which the majority of Minneapolis's gay establishments are located. But their success was also due, in part, to their enemies' overzealousness. Analysts of minority activism, from Suttles (1972) to Murray (1984) have acknowledged that hostile external assaults often galvanize oppressed groups so that they react.

These 'tactically radical' gays were not necessarily consciously anticapitalist. Tim Campbell, for example, describes himself as 'very comfortable in capitalism' (personal interview, 19 July, 1985). Conversely, Council member Coyle, while eschewing 'special interest' gay politics, comes from a background of tenants'-rights activism, and is generally sceptical of the public-private economic development 'partnerships' which have been the hallmark of liberal DFL urban policy in Minneapolis in recent years.[14] Similar contradictions can be found in the internal politics of Minneapolis's gay press. In April of 1982, a second gay newspaper, *Equal Time*, was founded. Although tactically much more 'conservative' than *GLC Voice*, it also claimed to be addressing needs of the usually more radical lesbian community, which *GLC Voice* was allegedly ignoring. *Equal Time's* downplaying of

[14] Very recently Coyle has strengthened his ties to the DFL establishment and Mayor Fraser, and muted his criticism of some forms of urban redevelopment and revitalization (e.g. gentrification – see Knopp, 1986).

explicitly sexual issues (its coverage of the bookstore issue was scarcely more extensive than that given it by the *Minneapolis Star and Tribune*) was regarded by at least one staffer as reflecting a desire to de-emphasize casual (and especially *commodified*) sex, which he felt the gay male subculture, and *GLC Voice*, promote irresponsibly (personal communication).

These contradictions are symptomatic of the heterogeneity inherent in any social movement organized around a socially constructed (and hence dynamic) identity which crosses class boundaries. But this is not to say that gay and lesbian actors are lacking in class interests, or that their actions' impacts are 'class-neutral'. Rather, there are divergences between the real class interests of some of these actors and those on behalf of which they may consciously (though incidentally) have been working. Confrontational yet avowedly accumulation-minded activists like Campbell, for instance, consistently challenged the limits of contemporary capitalism's relations of gender and sexuality during the course of the police-gay community conflict. In spite of their personal aspirations, such individuals paid a price for their activism. For example, the publication of an article on 'man-boy love' in the May, 1984 issue of *GLC Voice* (though not directly related to the police-gay community conflict) prompted several advertisers, both gay and non-gay, to withdraw their support for the paper permanently. Similarly, Jack Baker, though now an attorney, is not particularly influential, even within the gay community. On the other hand, gays like Brian Coyle, whose political backgrounds and personal histories are more traditionally 'progressive', have fared quite well, personally.

Thus the gay and lesbian activists who radically challenged contemporary capitalist social relations of gender and sexuality in Minneapolis were successful only in so far as they were able to expose members of the police department (and their actions) as deeply reactionary, or as acting in the interests of certain factions of local capital (i.e. developers). They helped bring about only a *partial* redefinition of gender and sexual relations in Minneapolis, the same redefinition which their liberal brethren had also been struggling to accomplish (with only limited success). This redefinition could only accommodate a very narrow and fixed form of homosexuality. It could not accommodate other, more radical redefinitions which recognize gender and sexuality as changing social constructions (e.g. transvestism, non-monogamy, and intergenerational sex). This is because such redefinition would undermine many of the foundations of contemporary capitalist social formations (e.g. gender divisions of labour, stable 'family' units, and the socialization of children into these). Liberal and middle-class gays, then, whose politics of a fixed gay identity had been losing ground to the political right through much of the 1970s, were, ironically, the primary beneficiaries of the actions of these more 'radical' gay activists.

V Conclusion

The gay and lesbian movements in Minneapolis have succeeded in altering the social relations of gender and sexuality which prevail there. Middle-class lesbians and gay men are now well integrated into the prevailing liberal political culture, and to a considerable extent into the popular culture as well. In contrast to the San Francisco experience (Castells, 1983, 138–70), this is the result of neither spatial concentration nor the development of gay community economic clout. Rather, it is the result of struggles between lesbian and gay activists (usually without a 'class analysis' of their own oppression) and various state actors representing traditional gender and sexual norms. Also in contrast to the San Francisco experience, this redefinition of social relations has been extremely modest.

The contradictions and tactical divisions within Minneapolis' gay and lesbian movements are a testament to the variety of 'gay identities' which exist there. The difference between the two tactical factions is that one recognizes this diversity as the product of an ongoing process of social construction while the other denies it. Neither camp, however, necessarily makes links between gender and sexual relations and the class structure of advanced capitalism. Yet both advance the interests of one or more factions of capital and/or labour. In the conflicts recounted here, liberal gay men and lesbians advanced the interests of what might be termed 'progressive capital' – those capitalist interests (e.g. the 'service sector' in the centre-city) which stand to benefit from a modest alteration in the social definitions of gender and sexuality – and those gay and lesbian people (disproportionately white, male and middle class) who can fit into these redefinitions. More 'radical' gay and lesbian activists, regardless of their conscious intentions, challenged contemporary capitalist social formations much more deeply, by challenging the present social relations of gender and sexuality almost completely. These social relations are critical links in the particular social formation which is advanced capitalism. Thus 'radical' lesbians and gay men undermined the interests of capital generally, and of many middle and upper-middle class lesbians and gay men, as well. The police, meanwhile, by attempting to enforce the'naturalness' (ideologically) of existing social definitions of gender and sexuality, advanced the interests of what might be called 'conservative capital' – those factions (e.g. manufacturing) which continue to benefit from strictly defined gender and sexual relations.

Gay men and lesbians have gained a certain amount of acceptance in Minneapolis. But, like other minorities, they face the dual obstacles of increasing internal heterogeneity and a tenacious system of social relations which cannot offer many of their members full 'citizenship'. The outcomes of similar battles elsewhere, and of struggles over other aspects of social relations (including other aspects of gender and sexual relations), will ultimately determine the extent to which all individuals are able consciously to participate in the social construction of their world.

Acknowledgements

I would like to thank Jim Blaut, Maggie Clover, Richard Kujawa, Mickey Lauria, David R. Reynolds. Joe Scarpaci, Fred Shelley, Fran Ufkes-Daniels, and an anonymous referee for comments of earlier drafts of this paper.

VI References

Altman, D. 1982: *The homosexualization of America*. Boston: Beacon Press.

Anderson, N. 1923: *The hobo*. Chicago: University of Chicago Press.

Archer, J.C. 1981: Public choice paradigms in political geography. In Burnett, A.D. and Taylor, P.J. editors, *Political studies from spatial perspectives*, New York: John Wiley and Sons Ltd.

Bell, D. 1976: *The cultural contradictions of capitalism*. New York: Basic Books.

Berger, P. and **Luckmann, T.** 1966: *The social construction of reality*. Baltimore: Penguin.

Bhaskar, R. 1979: *The possibility of naturalism*. Hassock, Sussex: Harvester Press.

Boswell, J. 1980: *Christianity, social tolerance, and homosexuality*. Chicago: University of Chicago Press.

Carrier, J.M. 1980: Homosexual behavior in cross-cultural perspective. In Marmor, J., editor, *Homosexual behavior: a modern reappraisal.*

Castells, M. 1978: *City, class, and power*. London: The Macmillan Press Ltd.
1983: *The city and the grassroots*. Berkeley: University of California Press.

Castell, M. and **Murphy, K.** 1982: Cultural identity and urban structure: the spatial organization of San Francisco's gay community. In Fainstein, N. and Fainstein, S., editors, *Urban policy under capitalism*, Beverly Hills: Sage.

Chouinard, V., Fincher, R. and **Webber, M.** 1984: Empirical research in scientific human geography. *Progress in Human Geography* 8, 347–80.

Clark, G.L. and **Dear, M.** 1984: *State apparatus: structures and language of legitimacy*. Boston: Allen and Unwin.

Davies, P. 1985: To protect and serve. *City Pages*, July 17.

D'Emilio, J. 1981: Gay politics, gay communities: the San Francisco experience. *Socialist review* 55,77–104.
1983a: *Sexual politics, sexual communities: the making of a homosexual minority in the United States, 1940–1970.* Chicago: University of Chicago Press.
1983b: Capitalism and gay identity. In Snitow, A., Stansell, C. and Thompon, S., editors, *Powers of desire: the politics of sexuality*, New York: Monthly Review Press.

Derbyshire, P. 1980: Sects and sexuality: trotskyism and the politics of homosexuality. In Gay Left Collective, editors, *Homosexuality: power and politics*, 104–15. London: Allison and Busby.

Escoffier, J. 1985: Sexual revolution and the politics of gay identity. *Socialist Review* 15, 119–53.

Fainstein, N. and **Fainstein, S.** 1984: Regime strategies, communal resistance, and economic forces. In Fainstein, N. and Fainstein, S., editors, *Restructuring the city: the political economy of urban redevelopment*, New York: Longman.

Gagnon, J. and **Simon, W.** 1973: *Sexual conduct*. Chicago: Aldine.

Giddens, A. 1979: *Central problems in social theory*. Berkeley: University of California Press.

GLC Voice 1982a: Bouza holding tight against inservice training on police-gay relations; Fraser thinking, stalling for time. Issue 7, February 1.

1982b: Judge Porter decision thought likely to slow down gay arrests. Issue 8, February 15.

1984a: Accounts of brutality against gays rivets panel. Issue 105, November 19.

1984b: Police decoys shift all efforts to gays and bisexuals. Issue 106, December 2.

1984c: Police decoy operations lead to third death. Issue 102, October 1.

1984d: Appearance of graft taints operations. Issue 107, December 17.

1985a: Fraser curbs sex sleuths. Issue 112, March 4.

1985b: Local courts hand down two friendly decisions and one unfriendly decision. Issue 117, May 20.

1985c: Minneapolis appointed board criticizes processing of complaints against police. Issue 108, January 7.

1985d: Vice practices reviewed. Issue 113, March 18.

1985e: Temporary restraining order: no more harassment and entrapment. Issue 113, March 18.

Goffman, E. 1959: *The presentation of self in everyday life*. Garden City, NY: Doubleday.

1963: *Stigma: notes on the management of spoiled identity*. Englewood Cliffs, NJ: Prentice-Hall.

Halfhill, R. 1984: *Oral history of the Minneapolis gay liberation movement, 1969–84*. Produced by the Gay Men's Political Discussion Group. Minneapolis.

Harry, J. and **DeVall, W.** 1978: *The social organization of gay males*. New York: Praeger.

Kinsey, A., Pomeroy, W. and **Martin C.**, 1948: *Sexual behaviour in the human male*. Philadelphia: Saunders.

1953: *Sexual behavior in the human female*. Philadelphia: Saunders.

Knopp, L. 1986: Gentrification and gay community development: a case study of Minneapolis, Minnesota. Paper presented to a special session on urban restructuring at the annual meetings of the Association of American Geographers, May, Minneapolis, MN.

Lauria, M. and **Knopp, L.** 1985: Toward an analysis of the role of gay communities in the urban renaissance. *Urban Geography* 6, 152–69.

Marcuse, Herbert 1955: *Eros and civilization*. Boston: Beacon Press.

Marotta, T. 1981: *The politics of homosexuality*. Boston: Houghton Miflin.

Minneapolis Star and Tribune 1985a: Bouza curtails bookstore patrols. February 22.

1985b: Bouza denies gay pressure on bookstores. February 23.

1985c: New policy will send vice squad into bookstores less frequently. February 26.

Murray, S. 1984: *Social theory, homosexual realities*. New York: Scholarship Committee of the Gay Academic Union.

Personal interview, Craig Anderson, August 1, 1985.

Personal interview, Tim Campbell, July 19, 1985.
Personal interview, Brian Coyle, July 15, 1985.
Personal interview, Bob Knight, July 24 and 29, 1985.
Personal interview, Jim St George, March 28, 1985.
Positively Gay 1979a: Another month, another murder. July.
1979b: A preposterous coverup of unlawful conduct. September.
1979c: special election pullout. September.
Rose, D. 1984: Rethinking gentrification: beyond the uneven development of marxist urban theory. *Environment and Planning D: Society and Space* 1, 47–74.
Ross, E. and **Rapp, R.** 1983: Sex and society: a research note from social history and anthropology. In Snitow, A., Stansell, C. and Thompson, S., editors, *Powers of desire: the politics of sexuality*. New York: Monthly Review Press.
Saunders, P. 1981: *Social theory and the urban question*. New York: Holmes and Meier Publishers, Inc.
Sayer, A. 1982: Explanation in economic geography. *Progress in Human Geography* 6, 68–88.
Smith, N. 1979: Toward a theory of gentrification: a back to the city movement by capital not people. *Journal of the American Planning Association* 45, 538–48.
Snitow, A., Stansell, C. and **Thompson, S.** 1983: Introduction to Powers of desire: the politics of sexuality. New York: Monthly Review Press.
Steakley, J. 1975: *The homosexual emancipation movement in Germany*. New York: Arno.
Suttles, G. 1972: *The social construction of communities*. Chicago: University of Chicago Press.
Teal, D. 1971: *The gay militants*. New York: Stein and Day.
Thrift, N. 1983: On the determination of social action in space and time. *Environment and Planning D: Society and Space* 1, 23–57.
Weeks, J. 1981: *Sex, politics and society: the regulation of sexuality since 1800*. London: Longman.
1985: *Sexuality and its discontents: meanings, myths and modern sexualities*. Oxford: Oxford Univeristy Press.
Wilson, J. 1973: *Introduction to social movements*. New York: Basic Books

La prolifération récente de mouvements sociaux apparemment non basés sur les classes pose des problèmes théoriques et pratiques pour l'analyse politico-économique d'une société capitaliste avancée. Il est nécessaire d'établir des liens non-fonctionnels entre les mobilisations basées sur la structure des classes et non basées sur elle. Les liens sociaux de genre et de sexualité sont des éléments importants de tout système de rapports de classes. Les mouvements de gais et de lesbiennes ont mis en question les rapports actuels du genre et de la sexualité. Ils méritent, de ce fait, une analyse politico-économique attentive (c.à.d. non-fonctionnelle). Cet article examine, dans cette perspective, ce qui a été récemment accompli à Minneapolis par les mouvements de gais et de lesbiennes. On s'attache tout particulièrement à étudier un conflit entre la communauté des homosexuals et la Police. Les acteurs, les événements examinés se situent dans un systéme assez lâche de rapports de classes, tel qu'on le rencontre á l'échelle locale. Les activistes, homosexuals et lesbiennes, ont fait appel à une stratégie de confrontation qui a exposé le caractère de genre et d'identité sexuelle élaboré par la société. L'une des conséquences non intentionnelles de cette stratégie est qu'elle sape un lien important dans le systéme élargi des rapports sociaux en société capitaliste.

Die Entstehung einer Fülle von scheinbar nicht auf Klassenunterschieden beruhenden Gesellschaftsbewegungen in jüngster Zeti wirft theoretische wie auch praktische Probleme bei einer politisch-wirtschaftlichen Betrachtung fortgeschrittener kapitalistischer Gesellschaften auf. Nicht-funktionalistische Verbindungen zwischen Klassenstruktur und nicht auf Klassenunterschieden beruhenden Initiativen werden erforderlich. Die gesellschaftlichen Beziehungen zwischen Geschlecht und Sexualität sind wichtige Elemente eines jeden Systems von Klassenbeziehungen. Die homosexuellen und lesbischen Bewegungen stellen eine Herausforderung der gegenwärtigen Beziehungen zwischen Geschlecht und Sexualität dar. Sie sollten deshalb sorgfältig (d.h.nicht-funktionalistisch) unter Berücksichtigung politisch-wirtschaftlicher Aspekte betrachtet werden. Diese Arbeit beschäftigt sich aus dieser Perspektive heraus mit den Errungenschaften homosexueller und lesbischer Bewegungen in Minneapolis. Besondere Aufmerksamkeit wird einem Konflikt zwischen der homosexuellen Gemeinschaft und der Polizei geschenkt. Die betrachteten Personen und Ereignisse sind innerhalb eines breiten Systems von Klassenbeziehungen anzusiedeln, wie sie auf lokaler Ebene zu beobachten sind. Vertreter homosexuelle und lesbischer Gruppen gingen auf Konfrontationskurs, der die gesellschaftlich bedingte Natur von geschlechtlicher und sexueller Identität bloßlegte. Eine unbeabsichtigte Folge dieser Strategie bestand in der Schwächung eines wichtigen Bindegliedes innerhalb des breiteren Systems der kapitalistischen Gesellschaftsbeziehungen.

La reciente proliferación de movimientos sociales aparentemente no clasistas plantea problemas teóricos y prácticos para un análisis político-económico de una sociedad capitalista avanzada. Es necesario establecer lazos no funcionales entre las movilizaciones basadas sobre la estructura de clases y las movilizaciones sin base clasista. Las relaciones sociales de género y sexualidad son componentes importantes de cualquier sistema de relaciones de clases. Los movimientos de hombres y mujeres homosexuales han puesto en tela de juicio las relaciones actuales de género y sexualidad. Por consiguiente, merecen un análisis político-económico profundo (es decir no funcional). Este documento examina los logros de los movimientos de hombres y mujeres homosexuales en Minneápolis desde dicha perspectiva. Se ha prestado especial atención a un conflicto entre la comunidad "gay" y la Policía. Los actores y acontecimientos considerados, están situados dentro de un sistema amplio de relaciones de clases, según se experimenta a escala local. Los activistas homosexuales emplearon una estrategia de confrontaciones que expuso el carácter de género e identidad sexual elaborado por la sociedad. Una consecuencia no prevista de esta estrategia fue el debilitamiento de un eslabón importante en el sistema más amplio de las relaciones sociales en una sociedad capitalista.

STUDENT HOMOPHILE LEAGUE: *FOUNDER'S RETROSPECT*

Robert A. Martin
("Stephen Donaldson")

The spring of 1982 saw the fifteenth anniversary of an historic moment in the history of the gay movement, an event which made the front page of *The New York Times* and reverberated around the world. In late April, 1967 (the 23rd or 27th, more likely the latter date, if memory serves me), Columbia University gave official recognition to the first known/public gay student group in North America, and quite possibly the world. This group, recognized then as the Student Homophile League, later changed its name to Gay People at Columbia-Barnard.

The historical memory of student groups, with their rapid turnover, is notoriously short, but there is a great deal of which to be proud. So that the history of that time, of the beginning of the gay student movement which now spans the globe, shall not be lost, I have undertaken to write this memoir. I must draw entirely on my own memory, for I have no access to the documents of the times. But I was there; I was the founder; and I am proud.

Background

Columbia has come a long, long way. I talked to Allen Ginsburg, the poet, one time in the late 'sixties. Allen told me that he was expelled from Columbia College in 1947 on suspicion of homosexuality, at a time when, according to him, he was still a virgin.

In the 1964-65 school year, the Board of Managers of Columbia's Ferris Booth Hall (FBH) created a furor by inviting a representative of the Mattachine Society of New York (MSNY) to speak as part of a series of FBH lectures. Prof. Gilbert Highet of the Classics Department cancelled his own lecture at FBH in protest against allowing a homosexual to speak on campus. In the same year, according to reports I heard two years later, one of the more athletic-oriented fraternities had a gay student playing piano at one of their parties. Getting drunk, they forced the pianist to perform sexually and then systematically broke his fingers. This was hushed up by the administration and the fraternity involved received a private slap on the writst.

In the summer of 1965, prior to my registration as a freshman in the College, I had a social worker from Traveler's Aid (I had run away from home) call the dean's office, not using my name, to find out whether Columbia would allow a homosexual student known to them to register. It took two weeks for the administration to make up its mind; I have no idea how far up the decision went, but there was clearly no precedent. When the decision came down, it was this: the student would be allowed to register, on condition that he undergo psychotherapy and not attempt to seduce other students.

With this understanding, I began my studies in the fall of 1965, as far as I could determine the first *officially cognized* homosexual student to be tolerated. I was and am actually bisexual, but orientational dualism was even stronger then that it is now, and anyone who related to the same gender was considered homosexual.

During my entire freshman year I did not discover any other gay students (or faculty, for that matter) at Columbia, which tells you a lot about the atmosphere at that time. I began in a four-man suite in Carman Hall, but in December of 1965 my suite-mates went to the dean's office and told the dean that they felt uncomfortable having a homosexual living with them. I was taken out of Carman and assigned a single, 322 Livingston Hall, where I resided for the rest of my undergraduate days. This incident left a deep impression on me.

Meanwhile, I had "come out" in the spring and summer of 1965 and joined MSNY at that time. Having run away from home due to my mother's hysteria over homosexuality, I accepted an ivitation from Julian Hodges, then president of MSNY (New York's major gay group at that time, founded in 1955), to stay at his apartment. So I began gay life with instruction from a movement activist. Spending August '65 with Hodges, I met Dr. Franklin E. Kameny at a meeting held in Hodges' Greenwich Village apartment.

Frank Kameny's significance to the gay movement is well recognized. He and I became friends; in the summer of 1966 I got a job as a House of Representatives intern (with Rep. Donald E. Lukens, R-Ohio) and lived with him in Washington. Frank, unemployed at the time, was an enormous influence on me, one of two people who most have shaped my thinking modes (the other being my "girlfriend" of that time, who is still close 16 years later). Frank gave me a complete education both in homosexuality and in the homophile movement, instructing me also in how to respond to attacks from psychiatry, religion, the law, etc., etc. He largely shaped my "gay ideology" and continued to influence me even after I split with him ideologically in '68-69. I, and indeed every gay person in America, owe him an enormous debt.

In the summer of 1966 Frank took me to Cherry Grove, Fire Island, at that time one of the few places in the USA where gay people could feel a sense of freedom. It was there that I ran into James Millham, a psychology major in the College.

Jim was living (during the school year) with his lover, a NYU student, in Furnald Hall, and he knew of five other gay Columbia students. The eight of us formed a "family" in the fall of 1966, and we had some pretty wild parties in that ground-floor Furnald Hall room. Jim was a senior.

Underground

Not long after school started, Jim and I were having coffee in the Lion's Den (then in FBH), and I was telling him about the homophile movement, as it was then called. Thinking of my freshman year experiences (and lack of them) stimulated me to suggest to him the need for a movement presence at Columbia. He agreed. Since I already knew that Columbia was not going to expel me for being gay, it did not seem like an unacceptable risk for me to take the lead in this. I gave little thought to the long-term implications for my own life. The "family" supported the idea with varying degrees of enthusiasm and "keep me out of it" and was finally won over with a promise of complete anonymity. Only Jim and I would be known to the Columbia authoritie .

Initially the idea was to form a chapter of MSNY, so that the group's first name was "Mattachine Society at Columbia." Dick Leitsch, however, had meanwhile become president of MSNY, and under the stimulus of his presidency it soon became clear to me that we would do better on our own, so the name "Student Homophile League" was chosen. I saw Columbia as the first chapter of a spreading confederation of student homophile groups.

In those days it was common for people in the homophile movement to use pseudonyms for protection. Thus, Jim Millham became Steele. Back in the summer I had used the name "Stephen Donaldson" in a piece I wrote for the Mattachine Society of Washington's publication, so Stephen Donaldson I was. (Sometime in 1968, I think, I ceased using the name and reverted to Bob Martin. I took it up again in 1977 for very different reasons and continue to write under that name as well as use it socially.)

Our first task was to find an ally and protector. This turned out to be John Dyson Cannon, Chaplain of the University, an Episcopal priest of great courage, unshakable devotion to his ideals, wisdom and a gentle understanding of the needs of gay students. To me, the Rev. Cannon cannot be praised too highly. Without him, we never would have gotten started. He put his own neck on the chopping block for us, and in no little measure because of his action, he was forced to leave Columbia in 1970; our last chaplain. After the SHL became public, he was deluged with hate mail, he and his wife were harassed with threatening phone calls, there was trouble from within the Episcopal Church. All of this he bore with cheerful grace. He was our formal sponsor, he brought us into Earl Hall, letting us use his own office as our mailing address, his phone as our phone, the rooms in Earl Hall for our meetings. He was our lighting rod.

In October I set up a meeting in Earl Hall to introduce the new organization—or more precisely, the idea of one—to the administration and the religious and psychological counselors. About fifty of the administrators dealing with student life and counselors were invited, and some twenty-five showed up in late October for a presentation which featured Frank Kameny, who came up from Washington for the occasion, as speaker. There was a fair amount of opposition expressed at that meeting, led by Associate Dean of the College, John Alexander and Unitarian-Universalist counselor, The Rev. Vilma Harrington (wife of the head of the New York Liberal Party). I consider this the birth day of the group.

Our next problem was getting university recognition. This proved to be very difficult. Proctor William Kahn, a jovial man, was head of the administration committee which passed on these things (for University-wide groups). I think he was personally on our side, but acting under orders from above. The University at that time required a membership list from each organization. We were only prepared to submit the names of officers: myself, Jim, and Barnard student Seana Alexander, a straight friend, who in those pre-feminist days was our secretary. Despite all our pleas, the University would not budge from its position, would make no concession to the needs of gay people for anonymity. One real concern of ours was government subpoena; the FBI and others were known to consider the fledgeling homophile movement to be subversive.

The struggle over this issue was protracted. I have little doubt that the issue served as a convenient cover for the University administration's real opposition to the group, which among other elements involved a fear of loss of alumni contributions, as I was later told.

So we functioned underground. In a way this period gave us valuable time to discuss issues, to formulate an ideology as it were, among ourselves, to educate ourselves and work on group cohesion.

Financial support came from Philadelphia's *Drum* magazine, which included a flyer asking for contributions with one of their soft-core porn issues, from the West Side Discussion Group, and from ONE's New York chapter. The MSNY and the lesbian Daughters of Bilitis (D.O.B.) were the only other gay groups in New York that time (indeed, the only ones on the East Coast north of Washington).

Breaking Out

In the spring of 1967, after most of an academic year underground, and with the Administration's Committee on Student Organizations (CSO) still refusing to budge, I had an inspiration. First I obtained an ironclad assurance from Kahn that if we submitted a membership list, there were no other barriers to recognition. Then I went around to the most prominent student leaders and asked them to become *pro forma* members. In this way, Dotson Rader, who went on to become a well-known writer, and John Ward, then chairman of the college's Citizenship Council, became charter members. The list was submitted, and the CSO capitulated; in late April we were recognized, and the Student Homophile League of Columbia University was history.

Obviously, this called for a press release. I wrote one up. A copy was given to the secretary to Dean of the College David B. Truman, then front-runner to succeed Grayson Kirk as President when Kirk stepped down. This release never reached Truman, and as a result he made some foolish remarks to the press after the story broke. I later learned that he was deliberately sabotaged to undercut his candidacy for the presidency.

The press release was sent out to all the city's media. Only WNEW, all-news radio, picked it up and used it, doing a phone interview with me. The student paper, *Spectator,* of course, did a big story. Being myself on the news staff of WKCR, I saw to it that the AM news also mentioned us. This was around April 27 or 28.

The world, however, ignored us for a week. Then somebody at the *New York*

Times saw the Spectator story, and decided it was news, never mind that they had ignored my press release. A front-page story began with the headline: COLUMBIA CHARTERS HOMOSEXUAL GROUP. The *Times* decides what is news. That afternoon (early May), the *World-Journal-Tribune* did a big, sensational story (the following issue was their last); all the papers, all the TV stations, radio stations suddenly were doing stories, the next couple days were frantic as media which had all ignored the press release suddenly wanted the information I had already given them. The story spread abroad: incoming mail told us of coverage in Paris' *Le Monde*, various London papers, and newspapers in Australia, Japan, and other distant points.

The University was deluged with outraged letters. Vice-President of the University Lawrence Chamberlain told me the University received more mail over the SHL than any issue he had seen in his 20-odd years at Columbia. (Chamberlain was an active ACLU member and one of our few sympathizers in the Administration.) A tide of letters also came pouring in to the Earl Hall office, and to the Chaplain as well. Some contained donations, which were most welcome.

The school year closed with an argument in the pages of *Spectator* with Dr. Phillips, head of the Columbia Counseling Service. Gay people were still sick in '67, not being cured by American Psychiatric Association fiat until years later. However, our subsequent relations with the Counseling Service were good ones, with some referrals in both directions.

Pioneering Days

The SHL was primarily interested in educating the campus, rights for gay people, and counseling. We were throughout the early years integrated with respect to orientations, gender and race. Membership ran around 15 to 30, from a wide variety of schools within the University, meetings were held about every two weeks. It was part of our understanding with the University that we would not embrace social functions—no dances. We did, however, have informal parties to which members were coincidentally invited. We were very active; I spent more time on the SHL than on my schoolwork (nevertheless finishing up with a B average in thos pre-grade-inflation years; having a Mensa-measured IQ of 175+ helped).

We had regular office hours in Earl Hall, and did a lot of counseling, mostly with students who were just "coming out" (a process triggered by exposure to us in many cases). One of our first programs was the series of dorm discussions, which were never less than interesting, and done in cooperation with the dorm counselors.

We issued a long series of statements, written by me, on homosexuality and the law, psychiatry, armed forces, etc., and circulated them widely. In our insistance on the goodness of gayness and the thoroughness of our application of this principle, we worked out the basic principles and approaches of what came later to be known as "gay liberation," but a couple years before Stonewall. These ideas filtered out into the rather conservative homophile movement and did much to pave the way for Stonewall. Any historian of the ideas of the gay movement who neglects the pioneering intellectual work of SHL has missed a key element of gay history. Nor was our pioneering limited to thought, as you will see.

> ***"In those days it was common for people in the homophile movement to use pseudonyms for protection"***

We had a number of "forums" at which we presented public speakers, heavily advertised, and usually heavily attended. Frank Kameny was the first such, a panel of prisoners from the Fortune Society, with David Rothenburg, was the second.

Only a few faculty members supported us in those days, Prof. of English Eric Bentley, one of Columbia's most famous scholars, being chief among them. We also had an alumni committee, which however never did a great deal; Foster Gunnison Jr. '49C, eventually headed it up (the late Lawrence May was the first alumni chair). Foster had been involved with the movement via his Hartford, CT Institute for Social Ethics and ONE, Inc. of New York. His archives contain virtually complete documentation on the SHL of this period.

In 1967, *Spectator* printed a two-page essay by me on the life of the gay student; I believe this is the first depiction of same in print, outside of fiction. It is worth looking up for a glimpse at what campus gay life was like 15 years ago.

Organizational

In the summer of 1967, I represented the SHL at the Washington meeting of what a year later was renamed the North American Conference of Homophile organizations (NACHO). Yes, in those years we actually had a national organization to which almost all the gay groups belonged. I myself became very active in NACHO, being at various times Treasurer, chair of the Credentials Committee, chair of the Youth Committee, and head of the radical caucus. NACHO's regional organization, ERCHO, elected me Secretary. The SHL was always a radicalizing force within these umbrella groupings.

I think it was in the fall of '67 that the New York University chapter was chartered, followed by the Cornell chapter in the spring of '68. Rita Mae Brown (*Rubyfruit Jungle*) was head of the NYU chapter, Jearld Moldenhauer, and then Robert Roth (now an NYC attorney) head of the Cornell branch, which incidentally was sponsored by the Rev. Phil Berrigan.

This expansion necessitated reorganization, under which I took the title of National Chairman and Nino Romano, a GS student (now living in the Village), became chairman of the Columbia chapter. Nino and I worked bery closely together, and I stayed very much involved with Columbia affairs even while devoting my time to SHL-national and the movement as a whole through NACHO/ERCHO. Nino was a good chairman. He was succeeded by Morty Manford, who joined us ("coming out" in the process) following the Fortune Society forum, but that changeover was after my time. Morty, of course, went on to become a major leader in the Gay Activists Alliance and movement.

In late 1968 John Baker established FREE at the University of Minnesota; this was the first non-SHL student gay group. John told me later that he was much influenced by the SHL literature I had sent him, and that he considered the SHL to be the true founder of "Gay Liberation."

It was in 1970, I think, that the SHL broke up as a national organization. Certainly the three chapters became autonomous in 1969, attaining separate representation (and votes) at ERCHO in that year. We still worked together in harmony, tho, whatever the formal arrangements, and the Columbia and NYU chapters or groups were often well-represented at each other's functions. Non-affiliated Student Homophile League groups were established for the Boston area schools and Rutgers; all, like Columbia, eventually changed their names.

One of our first public actions was going to the May 1967 March on Washington and distributing thousands of leaflets there calling the left to task on its anti-gay positions. In connection with this it should be noted that the SHL was never welcomed by the Columbia radical political groups, and the Progressive Labor Party (Maoist) group was overtly hostile. This attitude did not change until 1970 or so.

We also initiated our own campaign to rid Columbia of NROTC as long as the armed forces continued to discriminate against gays.This issue was taken up by the Columbia University Student Council in 1967-68, and resulted in a resolution from CUSC supporting our position. NROTC was dismantled not long afterwards.

Another activity of this time was integrating dances. We would go to dances, especially those held in the dorms and Ferris Booth Hall, and dance together. This caused a sensation the first time it happened, in Livingston Hall, but was eventually accepted. It was part of our consciousness-raising efforts as well as fun. At this time there was no gay lounge.

I am not sure when exactly we changed our policy and added social activities to our concerns, beginning the series of Earl Hall dances in the auditorium upstairs. I think it was 1969. This decision had far-reaching consequences, altering the focus of the group, changing its nature, and making it relatively wealthy.

1968

Nobody who was at Columbia in the spring of 1968 can ever forget that year.

In certain ways, the atmosphere in those days was a lot freer than it is now in respect to gay people. Experiments, including with sexual deviations, were encouraged by the psychedelic culture, love and a benevolent attitude towards people with different life-styles was part of the time. Pardon me if I wax nostalgic!

We liked to think that it was the SHL which started the Great Student Revolt, somewhat tongue-in-cheek. This came about in the following way:

Columbia's Medical School, P&S, scheduled a panel discussion on homosexuality, and advertised it at the Morningside Heights campus. Of the panelists, only the Kinsey Institute's Dr. Gebhard could be considered remotely favorable, all the others were psychiatrists known to be hostile. We decided to act by showing up and asking pointed questions. When P&S heard of this, they panicked and decided to limit admission to med students.

We then prepared a multi-page statement (with help from Kameny) on gays and psychiatry, and decided to undertake a picket and demonstration at the site, up at P&S. This we did. It was spectacularly successful. Medical students stopped to talk with us on the way in, read our statement, and handed us their tickets. We thus got in. As every member of the audience (the hall was jammed with several hundred) had a copy of that statement, the questioning was overwhelmingly on our side, and Gebhardt had a field day.

This event was, I believe, the first gay demonstration in New York City, one of the first in the nation. It was certainly the first to target the psychiatric establishment, and thus a step towards our cure-by-ballot in 1973. It predated Stonewall by over a year.

Flushed with our success, we returned that evening to find the Morningside campus in an uproar. It was April 23, and students had occupied Hamilton Hall and Low Library. The planned front-page story on our historic demonstration was lost in the epic events of that day.

We did seriously consider the SHL taking over a building, or part of one, to press our own demands; the major reson which stopped us, I think, was the fact that so many of our members were, by the 25th, already involved in the occupations by other groups. We did picket and issue a list of demands (very fashionable that spring).

And in May I ran for and was elected to the CUSC, one of six delegates from the College. Since everyone on campus knew who I was, I considered the election a triumph for non-discrimination.

In 1968-69, we were very heavily involved in the changes in Earl Hall, when the Student Governing Board was established and Chaplain Cannon handed over to it virtually all policy-making authority for the building.

Epilogue

I finished my studies in January 1970 (I had lost the fall '67 semester to illness) and left Columbia. Under Morty's leadership, the name was changed to Gay People at Columbia-Barnard and a new set of by-laws adopted, but the continuity of the group was maintained. Late in the spring of 1970 I dropped out of the gay movement, for a number of reasons, one of them the increased hostility from within the movement to my own bisexuality. I hope someday somebody does a study of why so many of the leaders of the movement have dropped or been forced out, but that is beyond the scope of this account.

I returned to Columbia as a graduate student in the fall of 1974, rejoined GPC, and was elected to represent it on the SGB. In December I became Chairperson of the SGB, a position I held until the spring of 1977, which was also my last semester at Columbia. During these three years I stayed with the GPC, which met in the Gay Lounge. I enjoyed my somewhat legendary status, but the socially-oriented group did not offer any outlets for my energy, so I gave my main attention to the SGB. Dances, parties and the dorm raps were the main activities; of political activism there was virtually none.

In the words of the Buddha, all things put together are subject to change; and so is GPC. But besides change there is continuity. I do not know what the GPC is like today, a whole generation of students having passed since I left Columbia. Let our struggles, our achievements, our history be not be forgotten as have those of so many minorities. □

Following his undergraduate studies, the author worked as a reporter for the Associated Press, served in the U.S. Navy for two years, then became a reporter covering the Pentagon, while founding the Committee of Friends on Bisexuality (1973--76). Arrested at a Quaker pray-in on the White House Lawn in 1973, he was gang-raped in a D.C. jail, and became the first victim of jail rape to speak out in public about it. He has been imprisoned since 1980 on a felony assault charge. The foregoing document was originally written in slightly different form as "An Open Letter to Gay People at Columbia."

33

A Punk's Song: View from the Inside

Donald Tucker

In jail; November, 1980

What you are about to read has been written specifically for this book in the conviction that the academics—researchers, armchair theorists, and others who have written on prison rape—have a good deal to learn from those who have lived in jails and prisons; that nice-sounding theories must yield to actual experiences; that our knowledge of prison rape and its context, prison sexuality, is pitifully small. I have attempted to criticize the academics—generally psychologists—wherever I feel they are vulnerable, for no one else is doing so, and their errors are many and in some cases fundamental. Some of my criticism will make more sense after reading the rest of this book, so I urge you to return to this article at that point.

Despite my criticisms, I do not wish to discourage the academics or cast doubt on the importance of their work, which I hope they continue, augmented by sociologists and sociobiologists. They are pioneers in a new field, most of which is yet unexplored, and I salute them for daring to break the ground. Mistakes are inevitable, for the culture of confinement is strange, forbidding, secretive, and resistant to standard research techniques. Take heart, and keep digging!

What I offer here is a hybrid account—my own experiences in the field, so to speak; the conclusions and theoretical observations derived from those experiences and from the accounts of scores of fellow prisoners, given to me with a candor seldom found when outlaws are questioned by "respectable" people; and—this has been the hardest—my own inner journey, the transformations in my own emotions, values, and perspectives which resulted from my experiences. It is this latter which separates me from the field anthropologist reporting on a strange and hitherto little-known culture, but I believe it is critical, for one must never lose sight of the fact that all those involved are human beings.

In this respect "A Punk's Song" is an authentic continuation of "The Account of the White House Seven." Some may conclude that, for this man, the darkness has overcome. I will not dispute that conclusion, for it has certainly ovecome much, including my Quakerism. And yet—despite all—I have never lost sight of the humanity of my fellow prisoners, and though I have become an outlaw myself, I have not lost the capacity for love. That light still shines in the darkness.

Gang Rape in D.C. Jail

Entering the multi-tiered Cell Block Two of the District of Columbia Jail on the afternoon of August 21, 1973, I was placed by myself in a two-man cell on the second tier, the next to the last one away from the guards' position at the entrance to the block, and locked in. Many prisoners were out in the block and a number of them stopped by my cell for a look at the new white boy. One of them was a fellow who called himself "Baseball" and looked to be about nineteen or twenty. We chatted briefly. He offered me what he said was LSD, but I declined. (Drugs—in this case LSD, but more often downers or homebrew alcohol—are not infrequently used to facilitate a prison rape.)

I was let out for supper and again around 7:30 p.m. for the indoor recreation period. I went down to the floor of the cell block which was crowded. The posted rules stated that during this period the cell doors would be locked—stay in or stay out—but this was not enforced. While walking around the floor, I was approached by one of the men who asked me what I was arrested for. Was I a pacifist? Receiving an affirmative answer, he told me that somebody wanted to talk to me and was waiting in his cell. I was eager to discuss the White House action and Quaker principles, so I followed him off the floor into the farthest cell on the first tier. In the old D.C. Jail guards could not see into the cells without entering the cell block, which they did not routinely do.

Entering the cell, I found several men already there; several more came right after me, so there was not much room. One of them was Baseball. Immediately I was ordered to take my pants off. "Like hell!" said I, but my avenue of retreat was completely blocked. (Having since learned that it is not uncommon administrative practice, I wonder now whether the D.C. Jail administrators were motivated by a desire to deflect some of the obvious tension and hostility building up in that cell block by literally throwing me to the Wolves—a jail term for rapists—to save themselves a riot.)

"Are you gonna cooperate or do we gotta get rough?"

"I may not be able to stop you, but I sure as hell ain't gonna help you!"

At this I was seized and my head was banged against the metal railing of the top bunk several times. Dazed, I was placed on the toilet bowl in the far corner of the small cell. Baseball stood in front of me with a hard cock. "If you bite anybody, or if you say one word about this to the Man," he warned, "you'll be dead, and there ain't no place in this motherfuckin' jail we can't get to you, so you better do what you're told." He pressed his dick against my lips, but I still wouldn't open my mouth, so he hit me in the head. I saw that resistance was useless and reluctantly opened my mouth which he quickly filled with his cock. At first I gagged a lot, and to the end continued to have trouble with large organs and guys who tried to get it down my throat. Fortunately, the men tended to come off very quickly; if anyone was taking too long, the guys in line behind him would make comments.

There are no words to describe the sensation of having a dick inside your own head. My emotional state was one of fear mixed with hope, for I figured that now they were getting what they wanted they wouldn't hurt me and soon it would all be over. In this way I was fucked in the mouth by five men in a row. (I later reckoned that three-fifths to two-thirds of my entire experience in D.C. was oral.)

Why the preference for head over ass? I suggest two factors: 1) head is far more intimate for the victim, being so much closer to the brain and the sense of identity (it is easier to withdraw mentally from your ass than your head) and it involves him so much more (somebody getting raped in the ass just lies there inert and takes it without really participating, but when you get raped in the mouth you have to do things to avoid suffocation and gagging, so you're much more involved and have to keep your mind on what is going on); it's more of a conquest; 2) although this second point did not apply so much in the D.C. experience, it is true that when a rapist is unhurried he can force his victim to provide maximum pleasure through use of his tongue—more of a demonstration of power and control than fucking an inert body.

I was then taken off the toilet bowl and my pants were removed (I still refused to cooperate by taking them off myself). They picked me up and placed me belly down on the lower bunk. A man climbed on top of me and tried to get his dick into my ass, but it wouldn't go, so he called for some "grease"—lubricant such as petroleum jelly, baby oil, or a hair preparation—and stuck it up my ass with his finger. He got back on and shoved himself into me. It hurt so much I cried out and somebody stuffed a towel in my mouth. Then another guy took his turn on top of me. At this point, the guy whose bunk I was in asked Baseball to move the show somewhere else, so they picked me up, checked to see if any guards were looking, and quickly dragged me to the cell next door.

I have lost any recollection of chronology from this point on until about 10:00 p.m. A pattern had developed in which I would be moved down one cell about every five guys. Baseball and a partner were collecting packs of cigarettes from the men. My fear increased greatly when they fucked my ass and even more so when I realized that there was no end in sight.

There was a wide variety of behavior among the men. A few were deliberately trying to hurt me, not by beatings, but by choking me or fucking me very hard from the start. One even told me, "Your ass belongs to the black man and don't you forget it!"

Others were relatively gentle. A surprising number of the men who fucked my ass were doing things like kissing the back of my neck, calling me by various girls' names, or whispering tenderly in my ear. These men as often as not stayed in me a while after climaxing and I came to welcome this as a relief from the interminable thrusting and hurt. I came to associate the feeling of a relaxed body covering me after his coming as a kind of protection from the next guy in line. That association has remained with me.

Two differences between prison rape and community rape are that the prison rapists apparently do not fantasize that their victims are sexually aroused and appreciative, and that there is little or no sexual dysfunction—impotence, premature ejaculation, inability to ejaculate, etc.—in prison rape, by my observation.

When I got fucked in the mouth the guys would keep my head in their hands and push me in and out. For a while they had me down on my knees doing this, but after I complained that my knees were giving out they put me back on the toilet.

Around ten o'clock they took me to the shower room, which was large and could not be seen by the guards outside the block. Here they had me get down on my hands and knees and took turns fucking me at both ends at the same time. I was in great pain by now. They were laughing a lot and joking about it, and when there was a break Baseball pissed all over me. Seeing this, a bunch of the guys—there were about fifteen or so in the shower room—did the same. As I was still on all fours, some of them came around to my head and told me to open my mouth and drink their piss. This startled me, but quickly I realized that it was not painful at least and afforded a kind of relief. Since I was soon wet with piss, nobody fucked me anymore. Then they turned the water on, cleaned me off, let me put my trousers back on, and led me back to a cell. They had switched people so that another man was in my cell and I took his place in a two-man cell. This was just before lock-in at 11:00 p.m., I think.

After lock-in and the count (I was told to cover myself completely so the guard wouldn't see a white face there), the guy on the top bunk came down and crawled on top of me. I begged him not to do it, telling him how painful it was. He said he would be real quick about it, because he didn't want me to hurt, and he was. After he finished he lay on top of me for a long time and I was very conscious of his body warmth. He had his arms around me and was licking my ears and stuff. He said he knew it was rough what I had gone through, but that it was only the first day that it would be like that.

At some point I completely surrendered my body to the rapists, and discovered that in some strange way, through all the pain and despite all the fear, it was utterly relaxing, but most of my feelings from that day have been wiped from my conscious memory.

The Second Day

The next day I returned to my own cell in the morning and stayed there, except for meals, outdoor yard, and a visit. Baseball insisted I eat with him, but there was no conversation. My main feeling was relief that it was over and done with. One guy stopped me on my way back to my cell and said he'd like to fuck me, but didn't approve of rape. I told him I wasn't about to volunteer and he turned away disappointed.

At indoor recreation that evening I was in my cell writing a letter when Baseball and his friends came in, and it all started over again, but this time in my own cell. Precisely because I had believed I was out of it, my emotional state now became pure panic, an animal consciousness in which my only thought was escape.

Baseball and his partner kept coming back to fuck my face, at least four times each, till they could no longer get a hard-on, but even then they made me take their soft dicks in my mouth to show their power, and called their friends to watch them piss in my mouth. My jaw was still aching so my reaction was that this was still better than getting fucked: it didn't hurt.

About 10:00 p.m. or so I was sitting on my bunk without pants when I saw my chance. My assailants had relaxed their vigilance enough so that the door was not blocked. One of their lookouts suddenly said, "Hey, the Man's watching!" At this I dove headfirst out the door, picked myself up and ran like hell down the catwalk to the end where I collapsed in tears and was pulled out by the guard. I had been fucked about sixty times in the two days of rape.

There were two guards down there and when I could talk again, they asked me how I had come to be there in Cell Block 2. I told them the story of Captain Cobb and the transfer, and one of them said to me, *"You were set up."* They sent me to the infirmary, where I spent a couple of hours shaking like a leaf without being given so much as an aspirin. Then I was taken to D.C. General Hospital in handcuffs and perfunctorily examined. So superficial was the examination that the staff did not even notice the tear in my rectum that would require surgery later at the D.C. Veterans' Administration Hospital. The staff regarded me with disdain and made it clear they'd prefer not to have anything to do with me at all; after all, I was a prisoner, wasn't I?

I spent the night in the infirmary and left the next afternoon, but not before another guard captain had given me a hostile grilling in which he was clearly trying to put the blame on *me*. "You sure you ain't homosexual?" he asked, as if a homosexual couldn't be raped. After the story broke in the press the Department of Corrections also suggested to reporters that I was probably homosexual and was just claiming to have been raped; when I heard about this I protested and the Corrections people backed off, saying it was only a suggestion and that they didn't stand behind it. I've wondered since then if any female rape victims have ever been told they couldn't be raped because they were heterosexual!

It should be clear from this account that there are wide differences among the participants in a gang rape; I think it is a mistake to lump them all together. Many would not initiate a rape, but would join in with a one-more-won't-make-any difference rationalization. Some of the D.C. group seem to have been told only that a white Punk could be had for cigarettes and not that it was a rape at all. A gang of "booty bandits," on the other hand, is just a collection of initiators.

Aftermath and Observations

Much of the subsequent reaction on my part and others is related in the preceding article from *Friends Journal;* I would like to relate some of the things that are missing there and conclude with observations based on the D.C. and later experiences.

One thing that bothered me was the frosty reaction I got when I telephoned the Rape Crisis Hot Line; the woman who answered just couldn't be bothered with a male caller. Later, at the D.C. City Council hearings, I came into contact with organizers of the Hot Line and found a more sympathetic response.

When I requested psychological counseling of some type at a meeting of a Quaker committee (see previous article), I was referred to a lay counseling program that was no help at all; what I really needed was heavy-duty psychotherapy. After enrolling in a local college, I met with their counseling service, but they also failed to recommend a program of treatment. It seems astonishing today, but nobody ever raised the question of whether the trauma of gang-rape was being adequately treated. The result was no treatment at all. *A great deal of my emotional reaction was immediately suppressed.*

I lost all interest in sex for months and the relationship I was in was severely damaged. Fortunately I met a girl who was understanding and who helped me regain sexual confidence in myself. It took about a year and a half before I was back to my usual level of sexual activity.

Having been the first victim of jail rape to speak out in public, I immediately became a "resource person" on the subject, appearing in television network news programs, talk shows, radio, magazine articles, a widely-read book, touring panels of former prisoners sponsored by the Fortune Society, etc. I met and received mail from numerous other victims of jail and prison rapes. I was also able to contact and communicate with admitted prison rapists. These contacts gave me a broader base of experiences from which to discuss sexuality in confinement.

In 1975, the suppressed emotions began to rise to the level of consciousness, primarily in the form of anger, aggression, and a vigorous reassertion of my own masculinity. I joined a "consciousness-raising" group of men and entered a program of individual Gestalt therapy (not being able to afford anything else) with a lay therapist, in 1976.

Punk to the Marine Corps

In late 1976, while travelling, I stopped over at a motel in a small town near a U.S. Marine Corps base. A parking lot that at 1:00 a.m. seemed deserted enough to take a piss in proved to be staked out by the local cops, who arrested me, searched my motel room, found the dread marijuana weed, and charged me with possession of same. I was delivered up to the county jail.

There I was placed in a small cell block, four rooms of four bunks each. The cells had no doors, only the block entrance was locked, facing a corridor. The block contained a dozen prisoners, four white marines and eight blacks, of whom six were marines. Identifying myself as a former enlisted navy man, I was greeted with a recitation of what the marines claimed was the well-known fact that all sailors suck dick, followed by a demand for a demonstration. (In the same spirit of fraternal rivalry, sailors usually claim that all marines take it up the ass.) Not wishing to repeat the battering I got in the D.C. Jail, I capitulated.

I was led into the end cell, where I was fucked in the mouth by nine and in the ass by two. The whites were at the end of the line and two of them fucked me at the same time. I considered myself lucky that the blocks were so small.

The next day the four white marines came up to me and said, "You're moving in with us!" and so I became the fifth occupant of the four-bunk cell. Each night one of the other four would take his turn sleeping on the floor across the entrance to the cell to keep any of the blacks from entering; I always slept in one of the lower bunks. My visits to the shower stall were made under marine escort, otherwise I never left their cell. They picked up my food tray and brought it to me, likewise with mail.

I had become the *Punk* of these four lads, who in jail lingo became my *Men:* nineteen, twenty, twenty-one and twenty-one years old, facing charges like armed robbery and assaulting a police officer; working class. Only one of them had ever made it with a guy before—the only one with previous jail experience. They provided me with protection and such things as stamps and snacks, in return wanting blowjobs (from three) and ass (in jail called "pussy") from one. To my surprise, they never put me down.

Dan the Man

One of the marines, Dan, a nineteen-year-old Californian with blue eyes and blond hair, related to me more than the others did. Dan discovered that he loved getting his dick sucked and demanded satisfaction whenever he had a hard-on, which was about three times a day. Dan also liked to read—usually Westerns—sitting on his bunk, with me stretched out on the bunk and my head in his lap, whereupon he would casually stroke my hair like one would a cat. In a word, he was not only friendly like the other three, but also affectionate. He explained that he treated his girlfriend the same way back home.

This experience was a critical turning point in my life. Instead of contempt I found not only warmth but real affection. I was guarded and protected night and day by four strong marines—greater physical security than I had ever known in life.

I was so grateful to these four lads that I decided to accept my role as their Punk and do my best to keep them happy. Instead of passive resistance, I figured out what would make them feel good, and did it. I felt protection in the hands that guided my head to its appointed rendezvous with that symbol of power, now seen as protective and benevolent. In retrospect, so powerful were these emotions that it is fair to say I fell in love, especially with Dan.

When I related my D.C. experiences to the boys, they picked up the idea of pissing on me and occasionally did so in the shower stall before I showered. I saw this as a mark of their *ownership* of me.

One of the marines was fairly small, and I warned him that he would be a likely target for rape when he went off to prison. He didn't think anybody would succeed, but later I got a letter from him saying that what I feared would happen to him did.

A Punk is a status symbol. My Men had the only Punk in the block, so they considered themselves top dogs, and that was to be our undoing. The blacks decided to fight them over me (Punks are not expected to fight at all), somebody spilled the beans to the jailor, and I got yanked out and put in the Hole, though I was not charged with anything. I was still in solitary when my bail was posted.

I was defended by the chief counsel of the state affiliate of the American Civil Liberties Union and, to everyone's astonishment, had the case thrown out when the Judge suppressed the pot charge due to unconstitutional police behavior.

Going Home: Adventures in the City Jail

The following spring, having become depressed enough to cut my wrist, I travelled to my home town and carefully arranged to have myself arrested for sale of LSD, so as to be lodged in the city jail. Here I hoped to find myself being wanted and needed, to find the warm security I had experienced with the marines in the county jail.

At first I was placed in an all-white dormitory housing about thirty-five guys and soon found myself taking on a dozen a night, more often than not in the form of a pair of buddies fucking head and tail at the same time. This ended when somebody told the guards I was being raped, and I was put in the Hole "for my own protection" despite vigorous protests on my part.

I think it is intolerable for people to be put in solitary against their will without being found guilty of violating regulations, "for protection." If somebody wants to go crazy in solitary, that's their business, but where I have seen this practice, which is widespread, no attempt was made to distinguish between the men in the Hole for punishment and those in the Hole for "protection": both are denied reading material, full meals, exercise, etc. Administrative convenience, of course. The same reasoning applies to "Queens' blocks" which usually are deprived of rights or privileges enjoyed by normal population blocks.

Coming out of solitary, I was put in a special section of four-man cells reserved for those needing protection and those taken out of population for starting fights. The fighters, of course, soon "took" the "protected" non-fighters.

At first I was put in a cell with blacks (supposedly $5 was paid to arrange this) and was again raped. When it happened I was paralyzed with terror, the emotions of DC Jail overwhelming me, but afterwards I fought my assailant. This brought me back to the Hole and thence into a white cell whose inhabitants greeted my arrival with "Why, it's Donny the Punk!" This became my jailhouse name.

The term "punk" is an interesting one. In modern usage, its root meaning is a young, usually small, outlaw. From this is derived punk rock, a rebellious rock & roll style, and the word is then extended to a subculture centered around that music: punk fashion, punk values, and so forth. In jail it is generally the youngest and smallest prisoners who get raped and "turned"—or "turned out"—a phrase suggesting an inversion of their sexual role, hence the jail application of the word "punk" to "one who gets fucked."

In jail the Punks are distinguished from the Queens—effeminate, semi-transvestite homosexuals to whom only feminine terms are applied: "she," "blouse," etc. In many institutions, queens are immediately segregated from the general population, thus increasing the pressure on the punks who remain. Punks generally retain some sense of masculinity and expect to resume relations with women when released. Punks are involuntarily recruited in the first place and adopt feminisms only when forced to. Nevertheless, in jail they are still substitutes for females and are expected to remain in the passive role sexually as well as perform such "wifely" tasks as housekeeping, laundry, and ironing for their men. Many men assign feminine pronouns to punks, but most do not.

At first there was no sexual activity in this cell, but soon the blacks in the other cells started taunting the guys, saying things like "them white boys don't know what to do with their dicks," suggesting they weren't man enough to fuck a Punk, and wondering if maybe they weren't getting fucked themselves. Before long the guys were demanding and getting head from me.

Under the impact of rape, battery, and robbery in this jail I came to abandon my Quaker belief in pacifism; my depression gradually changed to anger at the jail and the government in general. This was a turning point in my consciousness; I came to think of myself as an outlaw and began to adopt jailhouse attitudes. Eventually I accepted my identity as a punk and decided to make the best of it.

Eventually one of my cellmates, a twenty-one-year-old sailor and burglar named Terry, put a "public" claim on me and became my Man. We got to know each other well, and late at night Terry would tell me things about himself—his fears and anxieties for example—which he could not admit in front of the other men. In a good Man-Punk relationship the Man, feeling secure in his power over his Punk, is thereby enabled to relax with him and abandon the hard, competitive role he feels he has to play otherwise.

With his Punk, the Man can allow himself to be tender, to care about another person, to know parts of his humanity which would otherwise be considered "weakness"; his Punk is an extension of himself.

Terry always shared with me any marijuana he managed to get in, told cellmates he would not tolerate insults to me, etc. Following the violence I had just experienced, this relationship gave me a strong sense of security which expressed itself in an emotional attachment to him. I didn't even mind it when Terry occasionally pissed in my mouth as a way of graphically demonstrating that he was Boss and could make me do anything he wanted. To me, submission meant protection.

Patterns of Coercion

The emotional significance of this type of prison relationship to me cannot be understood except in the context of my experiences with rape; always I felt it to be my protection against rape, and this was a powerful motivation to become quite devoted to my Man. Nor is this unique to me, for most Punks fear rape with good reason and prefer a relationship with one Man or a small number of Men.

In the setting of jails and prisons, it is difficult to draw sharp distinctions between rape and other forms of sexuality; instead there is a broad spectrum in which a Punk's motivations range from fear of death (the classic rape with shiv at one's throat) to an attempt to escape emotional isolation—the closest I admit to a purely voluntary relationship. In between you have the victim of gang-rape who then takes up with one man in order to prevent more gang-rapes; the person intimidated into punkdom by a convincing threat of rape; the impoverished prisoner who becomes a Punk in order to maintain a nicotine addiction or secure other material needs from soap to dope; the victim of manipulative trustees who may control work schedules and assignments; the litigant who finds a high price for the services of the jailhouse lawyer; the weak prisoner who perhaps is not threatened with rape, but is being harassed in other ways and who accepts a man's offer of protection to escape that harassment. You just can't single out violent rape from the rest of prison sexuality without getting an incomplete and distorted picture as a result.

Looking at it from another angle, I doubt that the gays and bisexuals who get fucked on the Outside amount to as much as five per cent of the prison population, giving a natural ratio of some twenty guys who prefer to fuck to every one who prefers to get fucked. Since the actual Man-to-Punk ratio varies, but can get much closer than 20-to-1 (I am told that at Joliett prison in Illinois, a very long term facility, it approaches one to one!), the difference is made up of men who are coerced one way or another into the punk role. The vast majority of Punks are naturally heterosexual; it is stupid to call their status voluntary even when adapted to.

The most important social function of rape is the "turning" of men into Punks in order to meet the incessant demand for Punks to be paired off with individual Men. This practical function of rape, feeding the rest of the sexual system, has been overlooked by the psychologists—a major error induced by their preoccupation with psychological research and failure to place rape in the context of the whole sexual system; the sociologist and sociobiologist are needed here as well as the clinical psychologist.

While on the subject of sexual orientation, I would like to point out that most working-class guys, and thus most men coming into jail, look at this differently than do the middle-class academics who write books. While the middle class thinks the most important thing is the *gender* of one's sexual partner, *the working class is more concerned with the power relationship, which is linked to role and masculinity.* The guys are not as concerned about whom you are in bed with so much as who is in charge, that is, *who* is doing the fucking, the penetrating, *who* is the man, who is "normal." The one who is subordinate, who is getting fucked, being penetrated, is (if male) "queer"; the other is just using a "faggot" to get his rocks off. This identification of power with masculinity and normality (for men) is critical to any understanding of working-class sexuality. The terminology and conceptual framework of almost everything written about sex in working-class environments like jails and the armed forces is distorted by middle-class perspectives. Personally I find the working-class viewpoint to reflect better the psychological realities, and will use it henceforth.

The Sexual Power Structure

There is a wide variation between confinement institutions, ranging from the small, rural county jail in which sex is virtually absent, to the very long-term prison in which almost everyone is paired off, and rape is the main device to turn enough men into Punks to provide most of the surviving men with their own Punks. The comments that follow are necessarily based on a more average institution—the big-city jail or medium-term prison.

At the top of the prisoner power structure is the class of Men. In order to participate directly in the power structure, to be a decision-maker, a leader, a plotter, a hustler, you must be a *man.*

Most of the men in prison will take advantage of opportunities to fuck someone, with prisoners of middle age or older—a minority—most likely to abstain. Due to the usually unfavorable supply-demand situation, however, only a small minority of the fuckers have their own Punks. The remainder have these options: 1) prostitution—it is common for a man to enrich the family treasury by pimping for his Punk, virtually inevitable if he has no other good source of income; 2) borrowing the services of a Punk belonging to a buddy; 3) finding an independent Punk, which is rare; 4) joining in on a gang-rape; 5) turning out a new Punk, which more often than not means initiating a rape.

You may conclude from this, correctly, that there are a number of inmates especially in jails, who are not powerful enough to own their own Punk, too poor to pay for one, not blessed with a generous punk-owning buddy, not too old, and who did not check in their sex drive along with their civilian clothes when they got locked up. They are marginal men, socially and psychologically.

Masturbation is not the answer and those who, like Davis [Alan J. Davis, "Sexual Assault in the Philadelphia Prison system," reprinted elsewhere in this book], consider it an adequate sexual outlet have a lamentably simplistic understanding of sexuality. If masturbation were really satisfactory, there would be no interpersonal sex; this is particularly clear in the light of the Masters and Johnson findings on the superior physical intensity of masturbatory orgasm in comparison to interpersonal orgasm. It is clear by now that the human sexual drive is inextricably interpersonal. I am convinced that it includes a need for touch, intimacy, otherness, for the interruption of isolation, for warmth, for relationship. Professor Edward O. Wilson of Harvard has shown that human sexuality has evolved from a purely reproductive behavior to become primarily a bonding device.

The only option open to the marginal men is rape! I am aware that this is heresy to many academics who, from their comfortable offices, insist that rape is never motivated by sexual deprivation. I invite these theoreticians to spend a year as a prisoner in a maximum-security prison where they will learn the hard realities of life at first hand. They are flat out wrong!

Below the class of Men comes the class of Punks and Queens, though these may be known as "sweet boys," "squeeze," "bitches," "homos," or other terms in different localities. Theoretically the punk is totally powerless, having no more independence than a slave. In fact, there are ways for a Punk to influence his destiny: there are punk wiles just as there are feminine wiles.

A contented Punk is much more desirable than a sullen and reluctant one, so there is a definite incentive for the Men to back off from a confrontation with their Punks on an issue which they don't consider essential, though no Man will tolerate a rebellious Punk.

A discontented Punk can by judicious flirting cause other Men to challenge his own Man for ownership, either offering to buy the Punk (Punks are bought and sold like so many baseball players) or fighting for him. In some cases a Punk can put in for a transfer.

Punks tend to be involved in hypergamy—"marrying" upward in the power structure. A Punk is a status symbol and one can measure the pecking order on the basis of Punk location. (It should be noted that in comparison to ownership of a Punk, *rape confers little status,* a fact that I think is related to the last-option situation of marginal men described above.) The most desirable Punks end up with the cell block leaders, who also tend to be the ones with the most money one way or another.

A Man has a social obligation to share his wealth with his Punk, much as a rich man on the Outside is expected to keep his wife in furs and take her out to eat. As one Man put it: "You Punks have got it made; you don't have to fight, and you get all the dope and commissary from the men with the most money." The price you pay is the loss of automony and masculinity.

An ironclad rule is that, once fallen from the grace of manhood, no one can ever become a man again. Some escape this rule by changing institutions, but usually your reputation catches up with you. There is a relentless pressure on the men whose Man-status is marginal either to prove their manhood or be forced into Punkdom. This results in a lot of fights. A man who is perceived as weak or having a shaky claim to the prison concept of Manhood is likely to be challenged by another man who is without a Punk. The best way to preempt such challenges is to have your own Punk. Another way of reaffirming your "membership in the class of men" (Scacco) is to show it functionally—by acting as a fucker. This greatly increases the pressure on the marginal men to do so by joining in or initiating a rape.

The relationship between a Man and his Punk tends to reflect the Man's customary way of treating his woman on the Outside. A Man who beats his wife will more than likely beat his Punk. The converse is true, too: the man who treats his women well will usually respect his Punk. It is not uncommon for a Man to develop genuine concern and affection for his Punk, and passionate love affairs are common in prison. Some couples even go through imitation marriage ceremonies, complete with celebrants, guests, party, and presents. Imprisoned long enough, men can transfer any emotion they feel for women to their Punks. The one difference that stands out is that most men feel comfortable letting other men have access to their sexual partner, as long as the situation is under their control, so Punks are loaned as favors, exchanged for other services, or pimped out. The Man, however, makes the rules. In Terry's case, he not only allowed me to grow a moustache as an affirmation of my own maleness, but allowed me to acquire a Punk of my own.

The Turning of a Punk

Terry and I were alone in the cell when a nineteen-year-old boy who had never been in jail before was moved in. Feeling a need to assert my own masculinity in spite of my status as a Punk, I decided, with Terry's consent, to try to "turn" the boy myself. I didn't want to be violent about it, so I decided to try to take advantage of his emotional needs.

He was very lonely, insecure, frightened, and depressed: feelings I knew well. I approached him gently, without sexual vibes, offering friendship, protection, and advice. He took the bait, spilling out all his troubles and anxieties to me, coming out of his depression and becoming dependent on me.

The next day I told him I was horny and needed relief; it was time for him to do something for me, and that's the way jail was. He was shocked and protested that he wasn't "that way," but he was also afraid of being thrust into isolation or worse (Terry helped by acting in a generally tough manner; though nobody directly threatened rape, it wouldn't take much imagination for that possibility to suggest itself). As a result, his will to resist was paralyzed with indecision: just what I had hoped for.

I pried open his mouth and proceeded to fuck his face while tears trickled from his eyes, while Terry watched. As a cocksucker he was terrible, but the thrill of conquest was so strong that I soon had a powerful orgasm, and felt that my manhood was vindicated.

Then I pulled him into his bunk and lay on top of him. At first he was crying, but I soothed him, stroked his head, talked to him, did everything I could to calm him down, being as warm and affectionate and protective as I knew how. This was to get him used to the feel of my body covering his own in traditional Man-Punk fashion (each of us face down, my dick resting against his ass, my head next to his or kissing the back of his neck or ears). In this way he soon came to associate physical contact with warmth, affection, protection, etc., and came to accept his role as my Punk, much as I had once done myself.

I had some misgivings about all this, but I told myself that I was really being good to him and meeting his emotional needs, had not used real violence or threatened him, etc. For the most part, the exhilaration of demonstrating my masculinity, of conquest, of sexual release swept these reservations aside. Somewhere deep in my soul, I suppose, there lurks a jailhouse rapist....

Rape Is a Phony Issue

Prison rape is, undoubtedly, as the academics state, a vehicle for the expression of a power relationship, dominance, control. So, too, are what the writers are pleased to call "voluntary" sexual relationships in jail! In fact, the power/control element is never absent from the Man-Punk relationship, indeed, it defines that relationship: the Man controls the Punk. Period.

Another heresy: the academics are misleading us in linking the exercise of power and control with prison rape. It is not power and control that distinguishes prison *rape,* it is the violent means by which these are expressed. Nor is aggression confined to rape; the difference is one of degree.

Violence, then, is said to be the real issue. Yet violence—coercion by physical means—is another middle-class issue. The middle and upper classes control the various levers of power in our society: education, money, politics, law, religion, the media, culture, etc. The only lever even partially available to the poor in America is the physical one, and this is shared with the State, representing the controlling classes. The middle-class condemnation of violence does not even extend to the organized violence of police and prison guards! For all their professed devotion to non-violence and pacifism, I have yet to hear the Quakers call for the disarmament of the police force that protects their own class interests.

The poor are used to physical coercion as one of many types. So now am I. How can I condemn the prison rapist and not the judge who sends him there?

Coercion is no more than the exercise of contested power, a normal part of life. If violence is a phony issue, and for most of us it is, *what,* then, *are the real issues,* the ones that matter to us who are stuck with this world, who look out through these bars, and not the ones that intrigue armchair theorists?

One issue is *injury*—the unnecessary damaging of the victim, either sadistically or by overuse (as in my D.C. experience). Such injury is rarer than most people think: sadism is seldom encountered, prison rapes being power rapes, and I have never heard of another gang-rape coming anywhere near the number that hit me in D.C.; four is more typical, with seventeen the most I have heard of from others or read about.

Then there is *the institution of confinement* itself, and this is by far the most important issue, for all the coercion, the trauma, the demasculinization, the degradation are inherent in this abomination, with only differences of degree—important as these may be to us inside—between one human zoo and another. Part of that confinement is that which confines us to each other, barring us from sexual and emotional contact with those on the Outside.

There is, ultimately, no prison rape issue. There is only the prison issue.

Back on the Street

After several months, my case was dropped by the prosecution when my arresting officer committed suicide, and I was released once again. Unemployed, I used my time to explore the meanings of my new identity as a punk. I became heavily involved in the punk rock subculture, discovering in the aggressive defiance of the punk rockers an outlet for my own anger, and in their vulnerability, only partially obscured by their "tough boy" image, a reflection of my own feelings. Trying to look and act strong, I first took to wearing a marine combat knife, then acquired a gun.

Meanwhile I sought to fathom my changed feelings towards men, thinking I must be bisexual (my erotic feelings for women remaining apparently unchanged). Looking at the gay scene, I found that there the notion of prison sexuality was pornographic, with gay bars bearing names like The Cell Block, supposed replicas of cells built into them, and purported jailhouse scenes a mainstay of porno films, magazines, and books. These images, however, had little in common with reality; their creators didn't know what they were talking about.

Trying to understand the Man-Punk relationship, I even ventured into the sado-masochistic scene, only to discover a charade in which the actors had to resort to symbols like licking boots and calling someone "Master" in order to represent a dominance which had no reality to it; indeed, I discovered that it is the masochist who actually controls the game, giving subtle but definite signals to his partner to indicate the limits of the play. I could only shake my head and chuckle: what did these pretenders know about a sexual slavery from which there was no escaping?

Gay men failed to satisfy me; I just couldn't find in them the strength which to me spelled protection. I'd think, these guys wouldn't last two days in a big-city jail. Emotionally, they just weren't credible as Men.

I even tried to find straight men to relate to, but this proved to be not only dangerous but ultimately frustrating. With women available, who needs a Punk?

Power and Aggression

My sexuality was polarized on the question of power: I was comfortable as the boss—as when dominating women—or as the object of power, the dominated jail Punk, but I did not want to nor could I deal comfortably with the relationships in between where power flowed back and forth in a constant if usually friendly contest between two often opposing wills.

While there is no doubt that its prominence varies a great deal, the element of power is, I am convinced, impossible to extricate from male sexuality. This conclusion is no doubt bitter to the feminist idealogues, very few of whom seem to have taken the trouble to understand men. It is symbolized by the very word *potent,* from the Latin for power. At a deep, and even for many men subconscious level, fucking is an exercise of male power and dominion, if only in the mind or fantasy of the male. Not only is power erotic, as Kissinger reminds us, but eros is power-ful!

Academics have taken the power element and emphasized its role in prison rape (which I would amend to prison sex in general), and I am glad they have done so, since the public is generally not aware of its significance. In our understanding, however, the elements thus separated must be restored to their phenomenal unity. Neither in the head nor in the body does either the rapist or his victim separate the power from the sex; both constitute a unitary whole focused on the potent hard cock.

The academics have started with the sexual act and traced its roots back to aggression, which is laudable, but I think it may be even more important for them to look at it from the other end of the telescope. *How is aggression channeled into sexuality?* Why are the pecking-order contests so often given sexual form, and thus usually resolved without serious physical injury to the loser, rather than directed into maiming and killing? Sociobiologists in particular should look at this, for I suspect that the biopsychological mechanisms involved here are related to those that set limits on the violence of power contests within other related species, and may be found in the relationships between the reptilian, limbic, and neocortical portions of the brain. For my part, I am thankful that, in the context of prison life and its inevitable power struggles, rape is a ritual that does serve to limit the damage. If a Man is intent on taking out his hostility on me, I would rather suffer the sore asshole and bruised psyche than lose an eye or a life. It may be that this choice is characteristic of the Punk—a comment on my own metamorphosis—whereas the Man would rather be killed than fucked.

Racial Issues

I have noticed no particular effects of my jail experience on my racial attitudes. Since 1978 I've shared my home with my best friend, a black man; our friendship has no sexual element. In general I can confirm Scacco's primary thesis on interracial rape and extend it to the whole range of prison sexuality. There are, however, a number of things that need to be added to the picture he draws.

I have been told by prisoners and ex-cons alike that in a Southern state where I spent much of my life there are some cell blocks or other units, especially in juvenile institutions, where the whites outnumber the blacks, and in these places it is the black kids who are routinely raped by the whites, with the whites instituting a parody of slavery. It may be that this phenomenon is peculiar to the South; there just is not enough known about prison rape patterns to be sure.

A phenomenon I have clearly observed is a white minority banding together and "claiming" actual or potential white Punks in order to keep them out of black hands and prevent the loss of face that would entail. For a white boy, being a Punk to the blacks means in most cases a friendless isolation, shunned by other whites and looked down on by the blacks, immersed in a subculture he does not understand. Here the boy is given the choice of servicing the whites or being exiled into the black population; not much of a choice, and pretty coercive.

The observation has been made that whites tend to become more personally involved with the Punks; this goes hand-in-hand with a greater reluctance to get sexually involved at all. It would seem that the sexual threshold is higher for whites, but that once they cross it, they do so with more of themselves—a vast generalization, of course. The question that needs to be asked here is whether the same behavior applies as well to relations between black Men and black Punks. It may be that the differences cited are due to the difference between interracial and same-race relationships, there just is not enough information to be sure, and there is virtually none on white Men with black Punks. I have also observed and described instances of the cultural transmission of the more casual black attitudes towards fucking Punks to the white group, resulting in the lowering of the whites' sexual threshold. There is also, of course, a cultural transmission from experienced cons to first-timers of prison attitudes towards sexuality, but that is to be expected.

Darkness on the Edge of Town

At the beginning of 1980, circumstances arose which produced in me an overwhelming feeling of powerlessness, helplessness, of not being recognized as a human being but rather being treated in purely bureaucratic terms by a government agency to which I had turned in vain with an urgent need for help.

I felt that my masculinity was at stake, that I had to regain control of the situation or go under trying. As the Bruce Springsteen song goes, "Sometimes I feel so weak I just wanna explode. . . ." These feelngs are directly related to my D.C. experience, the subconscious emotions that are dredged up when I feel completely vulnerable. In this state I went out with a gun and violently confronted the government, though without injuring anyone. I knew I would be going back to jail for it, and this was probably a major factor as well in determining my action. It was in jail that I felt I knew the rules and could find security, a means of coping with my helplessness. The jail Punk in me was looking for a way home, even as the man in me was striking back, by force of arms assuming control of the situation, returning to the government some of the rape it had given me.

Having accomplished my objective, I surrendered to the police and was led away once more to the darkness on the edge of society, to the "darkness on the edge of town" that Springsteen sings about.

It is not just my case; no, I know from other victims of prison rape how the male seeks compensation for the trauma of the total loss of control by striking back and asserting control; as it was lost in violence so it is regained in violence. *It may be that the most serious cost of prison rape to society is that it takes non-violent offenders and turns them into people with a high potential for violence,* full of rage and eager to take vengeance on the society which they hold responsible for their utter humiliation and loss of manhood. If they do not turn their frustrated rage against themselves—I suspect that a majority of jail suicides are rape victims—they may turn it on the world outside, perhaps becoming rapists themselves in a desperate attempt to "regain their manhood."

In Harness Once More

And so, more than a half a year ago, I was locked up in my fourth jail, this time with years of prison ahead of me. While here, I have been raped once, assaulted once, and claimed by five different men. Soon I will be off to "the Big House," where an unknown fate awaits me. The advice I get from veterans of maximum-security prisons ranges all the way from "being pussy, you ain't got nothing to worry about," to a listing of the various reasons why Punks get killed. I am far better prepared than most Punks going to prison for the first time, yet anxiety gnaws away at my insides. I am afraid.

As this is written, I am happy in a good relationship with a man and I feel secure and at home. I am lucky with him; he is intelligent and likes to read, though he isn't formally educated; he's decent and good, and honest with me. He is a Man and will always be a Man in his relationship with me, but this does not mean he is incapable of tenderness or recognizing my need for affection.

When with him I am alone no more, the very strength in his arms which press my head against his body reassures me, give me security in an otherwise frightening jungleland. It is the power of such moments that stamps PUNK on my face in indelible ink.

I know that my experience seven years ago in the D.C. jail was the most terrifying event of my life. It was also the most intense sexual experience I have ever had. Memory suppresses the terror and retains the sexuality.

The once wild stallion has been broken and tamed, and now bears his rider easily. I look at the bridle and admire the quality of the leather, the workmanship of the chain, the finish of the saddle. I have been shaped and molded by my experiences and, like Martin Dysart in Peter Schaffer's great play, *Equus,* I look and observe,

> There is now, in my mouth, this sharp chain
> And it never comes out.

This Is Where It Counts

I will not leave you without some suggestions, recommendations, and observations.

To the academics, I recommend that you investigate the differences in incidence of rape and other sexual arrangements from one institution to another in an attempt to discover other factors at work to increase or decrease its frequency or savagery. Why are big-city jails and long-term prisons reputed to have the most rape as well as the highest levels of sexual involvement in general? I recommend also that you look into the age factor: why do men cease to be rapists when they reach their mid-thirties? Also, how does rape function as ritual?

What you call the problem of prison rape is not necessarily solvable, but this does not mean that nothing can be done. Look at the goal as one of reducing the damage and the frequency and intensity of coercion rather than abolishing it.

Beware of measures to de-sexualize *prison violence;* if successful, you may be left with only the violence.

Encourage experiments with *sexual visiting,* but beware of its problems. Conjugal visiting programs help the married, but increase the pressure on the men who cannot avail themselves of the program, and like all benefits in prison it quickly becomes a tool of administrators, its original purpose easily subordinated to carrot-dangling to maintain control of the prison population.

Do not segregate queens or known Punks from the rest of the prison population except at their request, for doing so merely leads to renewed pressure to "turn" someone to fill the vacancy.

Stop pretending that prison sexuality doesn't exist; remove the sanctions against the least coercive forms of sexual expression and in general adopt policies that recognize the facts of prison life and encourage less stressful sexual relationships at the expense of the most damaging ones!

Segregate cell blocks *by race* where racial tension is high.

Prisoners, especially in jails, need to be given meaningful activities to *keep them from getting bored.* Do not underestimate the importance of sheer boredom in motivating booty-bandits and other rapists. The evaluation of potential victims, the plotting, the execution of the rape, the observation of the victims' reactions: all these are diversions from an otherwise boring existence.

Perhaps the most useful small step would be to *prepare* honestly *the incoming first-timer* for what he is going to face. I wish I could design a booklet to be handed to each young man as he comes in, perhaps supplemented by an oral briefing. Tell the guys how to avoid rape, prepare them to fight back, and perhaps most importantly, prepare them as well as can be done for the possibility that they may be sexually penetrated, despite all, emphasizing that this does not mean the end of the world or of their heterosexuality, etc. Therapy in advance!

Prison administrators must cease using rape as a tool to control populations, break potential prison leaders, and recruit informers.

Not only prisons but jails must be provided with *effective psychologists and psychiatrists* trained to deal with the trauma of rape and other forms of sexual coercion, and these must advertise their availability and their independence from the administration, which must be real.

The only remedy that is guaranteed to work is not to send the young men to jail in the first place. Most prisoners in jail are there awaiting trial; their real offense is poverty, being unable to raise bail. Most sentenced prisoners are not enough of a threat to society to warrant the expenditure of $20,000 a year on their imprisonment.

Every legislator should know the facts about prison rape when he considers passing laws against non-violent offenses, particularly the "victimless crimes." Every policeman should consider this when deciding whether or not to use his discretion to arrest or not to arrest. Every judge should consider the likelihood of the convicted defendant being subjected to rape before he passes sentence.

My *advice to the first-timer* boils down to this: find allies quickly—men of your own race and ethnic group, or friends of friends. If you can, defend yourself; fight the first time you are tested—you may lose the fight and do time in the Hole, but you'll probably establish your membership in the class of Men. If you can't fight back but have income, find out who the leaders are and pay them for protection. Do not ever become an informer! And prepare yourself mentally for the possibility that, despite everything, you may not be able to prevent rape from happening to you.

Who Supports Rape?

Rape exists and will continue to exist in confinement institutions because it serves the interests of too many powerful elements of jail and prison societies, including the administration. Officials use it to divert prison aggression, destroy potential leaders, and intimidate prisoners into becoming informers (as before the New Mexico prison riot); the Men at the top of the prisoner power structure benefit sexually, psychologically, and financially from the Punks who are turned out by this process or the fear of it; and the rapists, initiators and followers themselves who come in for a share of the action.

The victims of rape, like most prisoners, leave confinement a good deal more "antisocial" than when they enter it. The practice of rape is but one mechanism in a system that takes non-violent people and efficiently processes them into men who rape, rob, assault, and kill. It seems to me that "society" must be self-destructive, an eager victim who maintains such institutions in order to punish itself for its own feelings of guilt over its exploitation of human beings. How otherwise could such institutions continue to exist?

I Walk with Delinquents with Passionate Love

I am the man, I suffer'd, I was there.
Agonies are one of my changes of garments.
I do not ask the wounded person how he feels, I myself become
the wounded person,
My hurts turn livid upon me as I lean on a cane and observe.
Embody all presences outlaw'd or suffering,
See myself in prison shaped like another man,
And feel the dull unintermitted pain.
For me the keepers of convicts shoulder their carbines
and keep watch,
It is I let out in the morning and barr'd at night.
Not a mutineer walks handcuff'd to jail but I am handcuff'd
to him and walk by his side,
Not a youngster is taken for larceny but I go up too, and
am tried and sentenced.

And whoever walks a furlong without sympathy walks to his
own funeral drest in his own shroud.

I seize the descending man and raise in him with resistless will,
O despairer, here is my neck,
By God, you shall not go down! hang your whole weight upon me.

Behold, I do not give lectures or a little charity,
When I give I give myself.

The male . . . is all qualities, he is action and power,
Scorn becomes him well, and appetite and defiance become him well,
The wildest largest passions, bliss that is utmost, sorrow

that is utmost become him well, pride is for him,
The full-spread pride of man is calming and excellent to the soul.

Give me the drench of my passions, give me life course and rank,
To-day I go consort with Nature's darlings, to-night too,
I am for those who believe in loose delights, I share the
midnight orgies of young men . . .
The echoes ring with our indecent calls, I pick out some low
person for my dearest friend,
He shall be lawless, rude, illiterate, he shall be one condemned
by others for deeds done,
I will play a part no longer, why should I exile myself from
my companions?
O you shunn'd persons, I at least do not shun you,
I come forthwith in your midst, I will be your poet,
I will be more to you than to any of the rest.

You felons on trial in courts,
You convicts in prison-cells, you sentenced assassins chain'd
and handcuff'd with iron,
Who am I too that I am not on trial or in prison?
I walk with delinquents with passionate love,
I feel I am one of them—I belong to those convicts . . . myself,
And henceforth I will not deny them—for how can I deny myself?

—Walt Whitman, speaking for me, from
Leaves of Grass

BEING DISCOVERED: A STUDY OF HOMOSEXUALS IN THE MILITARY

COLIN J. WILLIAMS and MARTIN S. WEINBERG
Indiana University

Current conceptions of deviance have placed less emphasis on the role played by the deviant himself in being assigned a deviant label. To examine the role of the deviant, a sample of male homosexuals who had received less than honorable discharges from the military for homosexual conduct (LHD group) were compared with a sample who had received honorable discharges (HD). It was found that, compared to the HD group, the LHD group was more likely (a) to have been engaging in homosexual sex more frequently before induction, (b) to have experienced more frequent homosexual sex while in the service, and (c) to have had predominately other servicemen as homosexual partners. Further examination of the data showed how these factors specified the manner in which members of the LHD group were discovered.

Current among sociological conceptions of deviance is an approach that concerns itself less with the attributes of the person or persons said to have violated a social rule than with the character of the reactions of other persons to these attributes and events. This approach, sometimes called the "labelling" approach to deviance, sees the deviant as a social product, the outcome of interaction sequences between labellers and labelled)cf. Becker, 1964a). The questions that are raised by this approach thus concern the behaviors that are labelled as deviant, what the processes are by which the labels are successfully applied or avoided, and what the consequences of such processes are for both labellers and labelled. However, despite the emphasis laid on deviance as a product of interaction, in practice most attention has been paid to the labeller's role in this process. Social control agencies have been especially focused on; most of the findings have documented the discrepancies between formal statements of procedures and actual operating procedures and the immense power of control agencies in the social production of deviants (cf. Scheff, 1964; Sudnow, 1965; Chambliss and Liell, 1966).

The emphasis on labelling, rather than the attributes of deviants, has been rich in its contribution to a better understanding of deviance as a social fact. However, a case can and has been made that the reaction to older conceptions of deviance has been an overreaction and that valuable truths in these earlier perspectives have been ignored. Bordua (1967) makes the following comment about labelling theory's conception of the deviant:

> . . .it assumes an essentially empty organism or at least one with little or no autonomous capacity to determine conduct. The process of developing deviance seems all societal response and no deviant stimulus.[1]

This is perhaps an overreaction to an overreaction. Becker, for example, does spell out a theory of why some people break rules and some do not in terms of what he calls "commitment," and for other labelling theorists, attributes of the deviant himself are not entirely irrelevant. The point is well taken, however; for example, in some of Goffman's writings (1961) on mental patients his use of the concept "career contingencies" appears to treat the mental patient as a pawn, subject to the vagaries of all kinds of situational exigencies.[2]

As a consequence of the above, labelling theory also has been viewed as taking the side of the "underdog"—that the deviant is seen as a victim of the somewhat arbitrary procedures of control agencies. He is more "sinned against than sinning," as it is a matter of chance, or racial or socioeconomic factors, rather than any behavior on his part, that decides whether he is cast as deviant (cf. Gouldner's criticism 1968).

This paper examines in one particular situation, what the effects of the *deviant's behavior* are on the application of the deviant label. Our focus is the contribution made by the deviant himself to his discovery; to what extent is he an active participant in the process?; are there any factors in his behavior which place him more or less "at risk" as regards the scanning operations of control agencies?

The particular situation in question concerns irregular discharge from the military for reasons of homosexual conduct. We shall examine the role played by the individual serviceman in having his sexual status called into question by military authorities. We are aware that the type and extent of surveillance and differential sanctioning activities on the part of these authorities are an important factor in this process.[3] For this study, however, this subject is bracketed; we propose that it is still possible to get some notion of the deviant's role in the labelling process.

It is important to note that the great majority of homosexuals in the armed forces do complete their service without incident and leave with an honorable discharge. Over 90 percent of all servicemen receive honorable discharges and many homosexuals are included in the majority. In a study done by the Institute for Sex Research in 1967, of some 458 male homosexuals, 214 had served in the military of whom 77 percent had received honorable discharges.

---

1 A similar point is raised by Gibbs and Lorber. In Gibbs's (1966) words: "Why do some persons commit a given act while others do not? . . .the new perspective does not generate an answer to this question." And Lorber (1967) says: "The theoretical bias of the labelling approach has helped form a more purely sociological analysis of deviance and social control. Neglect of the deviant, however, while possibly justified operationally, creates large gaps in the study of deviance."

2 For example (Goffman 1961:135), ". . .mental patients distinctively suffer not from mental illness, but from contingencies."

3 For an indication of some of the variability across time and the influence of other factors, cf. West and Glass (1965).

Earlier data reported by Simon and Gagnon (1967) indicate that only one-fifth of 550 homosexual males reported any difficulties in the military. Finally, in the present study, of 136 male homosexuals who had served in the military, 76 percent received honorable discharges.[4]

These should not be considered remarkable findings; to define them as such suggests a stereotyped view of the homosexual as a person having uncontrollable sex drives that demand constant and indiscriminate satisfaction (a view implicitly held by military authorities). Most homosexuals, not unlike most heterosexuals, pursue sex according to rules which reduce visibility and potential risk. The homosexual realizes the consequences of homosexual behavior in the military; as the consequences have similarities to discovery in civilian settings, he is likely to apply the same type of operative rules that he had learned before.

What of those who are discovered? It is our contention that such eventualities are mainly determined by transgressions from those rules, either to their not being learned in the first place or to situational conditions making them difficult to follow.

We considered the following to be possible contributing factors as to whether a homosexual comes to the attention of military authorities.

Homosexual Frequency prior to Induction into the Military

If a person is frequently engaging in homosexual behavior before he enters the military, then it is reasonable to expect that he is likely to perceive and evaluate the military situation in terms of the opportunities open to a homosexual to a greater degree than do those persons whose homosexual behavior is less frequent prior to their induction. For this reason we expected discovery to be positively related to frequency of homosexual sex before induction.

The Nature of Homosexual Conduct while in the Military

The way in which the homosexual manages his sex in the military was also expected to be related to discovery. We anticipated a positive relationship between discovery and (a) frequency of homosexual sex while in service and (b) the degree to which such sex is engaged in with other military personnel. Those homosexuals who frequently engage in sex while in the military place themselves more at risk than those who have little sex. Having other servicemen as partners also increases the risk of discovery. (For example, in prosecuting cases, military authorities endeavor to find out the names of all

[4] We are aware, of course, that a proportion of homosexuals do not serve at all because they either avoid induction or are rejected at induction. How large this proportion is we do not know for sure. Kinsey (1948) *et al.*, report some figures from the Second World War which state that less than one percent were turned down at induction centers or rejected by draft boards for being "homosexual."
The only other estimate we could find as to the proportion of those persons who avoid the draft comes from a reported statement by Col. Robert A. Bier, Chief Medical Officer for the National Selective Service System, who in a study of 1,500,000 men called for examination between 1960 and 1962, found that 382,000 (25.4 percent) were granted medical deferments. Psychiatric disorders including homosexuality accounted for 11 percent of the latter. What proportion homosexuality was of psychiatric disorders was not mentioned (*Time Magazine* 1968, p. 15). Estimates after this date must be read with caution as homosexuality apparently has been increasingly used as an excuse to avoid the draft by some of those opposed to the Vietnam War (cf. Anonymous, 1968).

partners of the accused who are also servicemen; this is often done by threats and promises to the accused, or through the inspection of personal effects—letters, diaries, and the like. Also, homosexuals who want to get out of the service and so admit their homosexuality often agree to provide the names of other homosexual servicemen. Cf. Williams and Weinberg 1970)

The manner in which a homosexual is discovered is also of interest. It is our contention, which we examine later, that manner of discovery is closely associated with the variables that determine discovery in the first place.

METHOD

The research design employed to answer the above questions was quite simple; it involved comparing male homosexuals who had been less than honorably discharged from the military with homosexuals who received honorable discharges.

Two sample sources were utilized: the Mattachine Society of New York and the Society for Individual Rights in San Francisco. Both are homophile organizations with large memberships. Using their mailing lists those persons who lived in the New York or San Francisco metropolitan areas were respectively selected out. The number of such persons totalled 1,372 (New York N = 872, San Francisco N = 500).

A short questionnaire was sent to each of these persons. This questionnaire was designed to assist in the selection of the sample. In addition to a number of demographic items it included the following three questions:

Whether the respondent had served in the military.

If so, what type of discharge he had received (honorable or less than honorable).

If less than honorable, whether this had anything to do with his homosexuality.

A set of questions was also asked to determine the stage of homosexual career at the time of induction into the military. Finally, permission for an interview was requested. If the respondent was willing to be interviewed he was asked to put his name, address, and telephone number on the questionnaire.

From the responses to this questionnaire it was possible to separate out those who received a less than honorable discharge due to homosexuality (hereinafter referred to as the LHD group) and a comparison group of homosexuals who had served in the military but who had received honorable discharges (the HD group). It was also possible to estimate the equivalence of both groups as to the stage of their homosexual careers at the time of their induction into the military.

The response to the questionnaire was as follows. Of 1,372 questionnaires sent out, 428 (31.2 percent) were returned completed. Of these 428, 292 (68.2 percent) were unable to be used due to the fact either that the person had not served in the military or that he did not give permission to be interviewed. The former reason was the more prevalent—of the 428 replies, 268 (62.6 percent) gave names and addresses.

There remained 136 questionnaires that were "usable" (31.8 percent of those returned, 10 percent of those sent out). Of these 136 respondents, 104 had received honorable discharges and 32 less than honorable discharges due to homosexuality. From the former group 32 respondents were randomly selected so that the final sample before interviewing involved two groups of 32 respondents. Unfortunately the LHD group was reduced by one person who at the last moment changed his mind about being interviewed. Regarding the demographic information obtained on the questionnaires, there were no significant differences between the HD and LHD groups.

Included in the personal interview were questions designed to tap the following: the stage of the respondent's homosexual career prior to induction into the military (as a check on the data gathered by the initial questionnaire); his homosexual behavior in the military (how often and with whom); and how his homosexuality was discovered (LHD group only). On both the initial questionnaire and in the interview a large number of other questions that had nothing to do with the military were also included. These were asked to gather data on other aspects of the homosexual's socio-psychological situation.[5] These other questions concealed the fact that military experiences were the main focus of interest and thereby limited some of the bias that could appear, for example, through the creation of a "sad tale." Thus questions on the military were the last questions to be asked.

Results

Manner of Discovery

The homosexuality of those respondents who were discovered came to the attention of military authorities in three main ways. Each is illustrated below.

The most common manner of discovery involved *discovery through another person*. Seventeen of the respondents were discovered in this way (54 percent of the LHD group). This mode of discovery is sometimes related to jealousy, a lover's tiff, or blackmail.

> (R 28 year old salesman. Served in the Navy for almost three years before receiving an Undesirable Discharge. Exclusively homosexual before service.)
> I was turned in by a civilian—he was a bartender. The ship came to Monterey and he fell in love with me. I couldn't stand him. . . . He said if I didn't become his lover he'd turn me in. I ignored him. He called ONI (Office of Naval Intelligence) and turned me in.

There were also cases where another serviceman was discovered and persuaded to reveal his previous sexual partners or whoever else he knew in the service to be homosexual. Through threats or promises or through a search of personal effects names are discovered.

> (R 45 year old policeman. Served in both the Army and the Navy for a period of about six years receiving an Undesirable Discharge from each service. R exclusively homosexual before entering service.)
> I was having an affair with a serviceman on a ship, who kept a diary. He was apprehended with another fellow and through this they got the diary and I was apprehended along with several other people.

This mode of discovery is often linked to many *voluntary admissions*—what we consider to be the second chief mode of discovery. To get out through voluntary admission the military requires proof of homosexuality. The best proof is to provide the name of a partner who is also a serviceman. Not only can he be interrogated at length by military authorities, but there

[5] These will be evaluated in terms of the effects of receiving a less than honorable discharge in our forthcoming book, *The Homosexual and the Military: A Study of Less than Honorable Discharge*, New York: Harper and Row, 1971.

is the further possibility that he will supply additional names. Six of the 17 cases who were discovered through another person were victims of servicemen who were onetime sexual partners and wished to get out of the service. An example of one such case is as follows:

> (R 31 year old male nurse. In the Navy seven years before receiving an Undesirable Discharge. No homosexual experience prior to service.)
> A drag queen asked if 'she' could stay in my apartment. I said yes, but don't hustle and don't bring tricks back. But she didn't listen to me. She brought two sailors back and we got into an orgy. They both wanted out of the service and used me as a reference. . . . I denied I was in the Navy but they went ahead and used my name.

Twenty-nine percent of the LHD group (nine cases) were voluntary admissions. The most frequent reason given for seeking discharge was disatisfaction with military life. Generally absent from such accounts were any pressures that the homosexual might undergo such as fear of exposure or the inability to control sexual tendencies. Such reasoning seems more an influence of stereotypical views of homosexuals, held especially by the military. Also of note is that few were unduly bothered by the potential stigma of a less than honorable discharge. Note the following case:

> (R 50 year old dress designer-manufacturer. Served in the Army for two and a half years before receiving an Undesirable Discharge. Exclusively homosexual before service.)
> I felt I was just wasting time. . . . I wanted out because I was bored to death . . . . I had the advantage of being able to get out as a homosexual. . . . If I had been doing something of value I would have stayed.

The final manner of discovery was through the *homosexual's own indiscretion*. There were five cases (16 percent of the LHD group) where discovery was due to imprudent action on the part of the respondent.

> (R 30 years old, hydraulic engineer. After serving two years in the Navy he was released with a General Discharge. No homosexual experience before service.)
> It's not a very good story. I was turning gay and one feels he's the only one in that category. It was coming to the surface and I didn't want to control it and had sex and was caught in the locker room.

It is obvious from these cases that the serviceman runs a risk in engaging in homosexual behavior. Not only may he be directly discovered but there is even more of a chance of indirect discovery due to being the "fall guy" in connection with another serviceman or through his name arising in connection with the other's case.

Having discussed the manner in which the homosexual serviceman is discovered, we turn to the factors associated with the probability of discovery and whether these factors are related to the particular manner of discovery.

Two sets of variables were conceptualized as related to discovery. These were: how "homosexual" in behavior the respondent was at the time of his induction and the nature of his homosexual behavior while in the military.

Prior Homosexual Frequency and Discharge Status

In an attempt to reconstruct the comparability of the HD and LHD groups when they entered the service the respondents were asked on the initial questionnaire how often they had been engaging in homosexual sex at the time of their induction. The results are shown in Table 1. The table shows that of those who before induction were having homosexual sex once a week or more, 69 percent received less than honorable discharges. Of those who were having homosexual sex less than once a week, 43 percent received less than honorable discharges. This 26 percent difference is significant at the .066 level (gamma = .50).[6]

Other data regarding the stage of the respondent's homosexual career at the time of induction support the conclusion that those who eventually received less than honorable discharges were more likely to be further advanced than were those who eventually received honorable discharges. The supportive data include the following: the gamma between nature of discharge and the exclusiveness of homosexuality (as measured by the Kinsey Scale) was .22; the gamma between nature of discharge and associating with other homosexuals was .34; and the gamma between nature of discharge and extent of social activity with other homosexuals was .34.

TABLE 1
DISCHARGE STATUS BY FREQUENCY OF HOMOSEXUAL SEX AT INDUCTION

	Frequency of Homosexual Sex at Induction	
Type of Discharge	High* (N = 16)	Low (N = 47)
LHD	69%	43%
HD	31	57
	100	100

$\gamma = .50$
$z = 1.509$, one-tailed $p = .066$

* Once a week or more.

Sexual Behavior in the Military and Discharge Status

Thus we concluded that there was a difference in sexual status between the LHD and HD groups at induction. We now consider whether there was a difference as regards homosexual behavior while in the military.

Frequency of sex. Table 2 shows that of those engaging in homosexual sex more frequently, 61 percent received less than honorable discharges. Of those engaging in homosexual sex less frequently, 38 percent received less than honorable discharges. This 23 percent difference is significant at the .052 level (gamma = .45).

Type of partner. With regard to sexual partners, respondents were asked whether they had sex predominantly with military personnel while they were in the forces. The results are shown in Table 3.

Of those who engaged in homosexual sex predominantly with other servicemen, 82 percent received less than honorable discharges. Of those who did not have predominantly military partners, 35 percent received less than

TABLE 2
DISCHARGE STATUS BY FREQUENCY OF HOMOSEXUAL SEX IN THE MILITARY

	Frequency of Homosexual Sex in Military	
Type of Discharge	High* (N = 31)	Low (N = 32)
LHD	61%	38%
HD	39	62
	100	100

$\gamma = .45$
$z = 1.624$, one-tailed $p = .052$

* Once a month or more. Since this was in response to an open-end interview question the nature of the replies precluded more precise categories than "at least once a month" or "less."

[6] Z is used as the test of significance in Tables 1-3. For a description of this procedure, see Freeman (1965:170-175).

TABLE 3
DISCHARGE STATUS BY USUAL TYPE OF SEX PARTNER

Type of Discharge	Usual Partner: Military (N = 22)	Usual Partner: Not Military (N = 26)
LHD	82%	35%
HD	18	65
	100	100

$\gamma = .79$
$z = 2.961$, one-tailed $p = .002$

The decreased total N is due to those cases who did not have homosexual sex while in service.

honorable discharges. This 47 percent difference is significant at the .002 level (gamma = .79).

In summary, we have seen thus far that not only are those who have more frequent homosexual sex before they enter the military less likely to receive honorable discharges, but that those who have more homosexual sex while in the military and who restrict this sex mostly to other servicemen are also less likely to receive honorable discharges.

There is thus a relationship between discharge status and the character of the respondent's homosexual career at induction as well as his sexual behavior in the military. The question now can be raised as to whether there is an interaction between these factors in increasing the probability of less than honorable discharge. To examine this, prior sex frequency was held constant, and discharge status was again run by in-service sexual frequency and type of sex partner. Goodman's (1964) test for analyzing interaction in contingency tables showed no significant interactions.

The data support our hypotheses regarding factors involved in the probability of discovery. The relationships, which appear quite straight forward, turned out, however, to be more complex when the *manner of discovery* was considered.

Prior Sexual Frequency and Manner of Discovery

Among those who received less than honorable discharges, what is the relationship between their homosexual frequency at induction and the manner of their discovery? Table 4 shows the following: that those who had higher frequencies at induction were more likely to come to the attention of military authorities by their own wish; those who were lower in frequency at induction were more likely to come to the attention of the authorities due to being caught through their own indiscretion. Sexual frequency at induction was not related to discovery through another person and the difference between the former categories has a p of only .628.

TABLE 4
MANNER OF DISCOVERY BY FREQUENCY OF HOMOSEXUAL SEX AT INDUCTION

Manner of Discovery	Frequency of Homosexual Sex at Induction: High (N = 11)	Frequency of Homosexual Sex at Induction: Low (N = 20)
Discovered through another person	55%	55%
Voluntarily admitted	36	25
Caught through indiscretion	9	20
	100	100

The difference between rows 2 and 3 provides a two-tailed Fisher Exact p = .628.

Sexual Behavior in the Military and Manner of Discovery

Sexual frequency in the military. Table 5 relates the frequency of in-service sexual behavior to manner of discovery. The table shows that those whose in-service activity was high were more likely to be discovered through another person. Those whose sexual behavior in the military was relatively infrequent were more likely to be caught through their own indiscretion or to voluntarily admit to their homosexuality (p = .019).

TABLE 5
MANNER OF DISCOVERY BY FREQUENCY OF HOMOSEXUAL SEX IN THE MILITARY

Manner of Discovery	Frequency of Homosexual Sex in Military: High (N = 19)	Low (N = 12)
Discovered through another person	73%	24%
Voluntarily admitted	21	42
Caught through indiscretion	5	33
	100	100

When frequencies are combined in rows 2 and 3 the difference between extent of homosexual activity and whether or not respondents were discovered through others provides a two-tailed Fisher Exact p = .019.

Usual type of sex partner while in the military. Table 6 relates the usual type of sex partner to manner of discovery. The table shows that those whose sexual partners were predominantly other servicemen were more likely to have been discovered through their own indiscretion, whereas those whose sexual partners were not predominantly other servicemen were more likely to have been discovered through another person (p = .062).

TABLE 6
MANNER OF DISCOVERY BY USUAL TYPE OF SEX PARTNER

Manner of Discovery	Usual Partner: Military (N = 18)	Not Military (N = 9)
Discovered through another person	56%	78%
Voluntarily admitted	22	22
Caught through indiscretion	22	0
	100	100

The difference between rows 1 and 3 provides a two-tailed Fisher Exact p = .062.

It is evident that of all variables considered, sexual frequency while in the military shows the strongest relationship to *manner of discovery.* If we look at sexual frequency in the military as specified by these other variables in its relationship to manner of discovery, we obtain findings which lead us to conclude that there are three main patterns that lead to the discovery of homosexuals by military authorities.

Two groups of LHD respondents had low frequency of sex while in the military. The first of these are those homosexuals caught through their own indiscretion. Their low frequency of sex while in the military is at variance with a frequency-probability model of risk, which would suggest that those discovered this way would be engaging most in the behavior. *All* such cases did, however, report that their frequency was greater than it had been prior to induction. As these respondents were *all* engaging in sex primarily with other military personnel, and were not high in sexual frequency *prior* to induction, it seems reasonable to say that their discovery was mainly due to inexperience in a deviant role; i.e., their indiscretion was not due to the extensity of their behavior but to ignorance of, or disregard for, the safest ways in which to engage in the behavior.

The second group of respondents who had low frequency of sex while in the military provide us with another pattern of discovery. These were those respondents who voluntarily admitted their homosexuality. Contrary to the above group, they tended to score high on sex frequency prior to induction,[7] and were more catholic in their choice of partners while in the military. From the interviews it was apparent that their disclosure was motivated by a desire to leave the service, the stigma of the discharge not being the major concern. Being further advanced in their homosexual career at induction seems to have made them less afraid to use their homosexuality to get out of the service.

The final pattern of discovery involves those respondents who differ from the above by having high frequencies of sex while in the military. This group was primarily discovered through another person. Nothing was specified by sexual frequency prior to induction and, as regards type of sex partner, they were represented somewhat less among those having sex primarily with other servicemen. This pattern of discovery was most common to our respondents and represents those who put themselves more at risk regarding involuntary discovery by military authorities.

[7] Also, all but one of the voluntary admissions had labelled themselves as homosexual before induction into the military.

CONCLUSION

The data reveal the deviant's role in his discovery. On the part of those who voluntarily admit their deviance, this influence is directly seen; in this case the homosexual uses a self label to gain a social label which can serve him. For those whose discovery is not voluntary, discovery involves placing one's self more at risk due to the frequency of the behavior and imprudent choice of sexual partners. With our respondents there were no cases of a "bum rap." All had engaged in a form of behavior proscribed by the organization in which they were involved.[8] With regard to our original hypotheses about the relationships between nature of discharge and frequency of homosexual sex within and prior to military service, it can be seen that the data become meaningful only after manner of discovery is taken into account.

In this study, official labelling was found to be related to the "quality and quantity" of the deviant's acts. As such, labelling theorists should perhaps make more precise the character of their "unconventional sentimentality."[9] Such a stance does not preclude a recognition of the deviant's role in his own plight; on the other hand, this need not imply the sociologist's endorsement of the policies or processes of control agencies.[10]

[8] This is not to say that "bum raps" do not occur. For a description of such cases cf. West and Glass (1965).

[9] This is Becker's (1964b:5) phrase, used to describe those who assume, ". . .that the underdog is always right and those in authority always wrong."

[10] Conversely, it should be mentioned that attributing a recognition of the role of control agencies in the labelling process by no means implies their moral condemnation.

References

Anonymous
1968 "How Faked Faggotry Can Lead to Your Honorable Discharge." *The Realist* 76(January): 11-14.

Becker, Howard S.
1964a Outsiders: Studies in the Sociology of Deviance. New York: The Free Press of Glencoe.
1964b The Other Side: Perspectives on Deviance. New York: The Free Press of Glencoe.

Bordua, David
1967 "Recent Trends: Deviant Behavior and Social Control." *Annals of the American Academy of Political and Social Science* 369(January): 149-163.

Chambliss, William J. and John T. Liell
1966 "The Legal Process in the Community Setting." *Crime and Delinquency* 12(October): 310-317.

Freeman, Linton C.
1965 *Elementary Applied Statistics: For Students in Behavioral Science.* New York: John Wiley.

Gibbs, Jack
1966 "Conceptions of Deviant Behavior: The Old and the New." *Pacific Sociological Review* 9(Spring): 9-14.

Goffman, Erving
1961 "The Moral Career of the Mental Patient." pp. 125-169 in Goffman (ed.), *Asylums: Essays on the Social Situation of Mental Patients and Other Inmates.* New York: Anchor Books.

Goodman, Leo
1964 "Simple Methods for Analyzing Three Factor Interaction in Contingency Tables." *Journal of the American Statistical Association* 59 (June): 319-352.

Gouldner, Alvin W.
1968 "The Sociologist as Partisan: Sociology and the Welfare State." *American Sociologist* 3(May): 103-116.

Kinsey, Alfred C., Wardell B. Pomeroy and Clyde Martin
1948 *Sexual Behavior in the Human Male.* Philadelphia: W. B. Saunders.

Lorber, Judith
1967 "Deviance as Performance: The Case of Illness." *Social Problems* 14(Winter): 302-310.

Scheff, Thomas J.
1964 "The Societal Reaction to Deviance: Ascriptive Elements in the Psychiatric Screening of Mental Patients in a Midwestern State." *Social Problems* 11(Spring): 401-413.

Simon, William and John H. Gagnon
1967 "Homosexuality: The Formulation of a Sociological Perspective." *Journal of Health and Social Behavior* 8(September): 177-185.

Sudnow, David
1965 "Normal Crimes: Sociological Features of the Penal Code in a Public Defender's Office." *Social Problems* 12(Winter): 255-276.

Time Magazine
1968 91(March 15): 15.

West, Louis Jolyon and Albert J. Glass
1965 "Sexual Behavior and the Military Law." Pp. 250-272 in Ralph Slovenko (ed.), *Sexual Behavior and the Law.* Springfield, Illinois: Charles C Thomas.

Williams, Colin J. and Martin S. Weinberg
1970 "The Military: Its Processing of Accused Homosexuals." *American Behavioral Scientist* 14(November/December): 203-217.

Carl Wittman

Refugees from Amerika: A Gay Manifesto

—Wittman's persuasive article has been referred to by some as the bible of the Gay Liberation Movement. The author carefully solidifies his argument that the homosexual is a viciously persecuted individual. In effect, this piece constitutes an elementary "bill of rights" for homosexuals—both male and female.

San Francisco is a refugee camp for homosexuals. We have fled here from every part of the nation, and like refugees elsewhere, we came not because it is so great here, but because it was so bad there. By the tens of thousands, we fled small towns where to be ourselves would endanger our jobs and any hope of a decent life; we have fled from blackmailing cops, from families who disowned or "tolerated" us; we have been drummed out of the armed services, thrown out of schools, fired from jobs, beaten by punks and policemen.

And we have formed a ghetto, out of self protection. It is a ghetto, rather than a free territory, because it is still theirs. Straight cops patrol us, straight legislators make our laws, straight employers keep us in line, straight money exploits us. And we have pretended everything is OK, because we haven't been able to see how to change it—we've been afraid.

From *San Francisco Free Press* (December 22–January 7, 1970).

In the past year, there has been an awakening of gay liberation ideas and energy. How it began we don't know: perhaps we were inspired by black people and their liberation movement; we learned how to stop pretending from the hip revolution. Amerika in all its ugliness has surfaced with the war and our national leaders. And we are revulsed by the quality of our ghetto life.

Where once there was frustration, alienation, and cynicism, there are new traits among liberated gays: we are full of love for each other and are showing it; we are full of anger at what has been done to us. And as we recall all the self-censorship and repression for so many years, a reservoir of tears pours out of our eyes. And we are euphoric, high, with the initial flourish of a movement.

We want to make ourselves clear; our first job is to liberate ourselves, and that means clearing our heads of the garbage that's been poured into them. This pamphlet is an attempt at raising a number of issues, and present some ideas to replace the old ones. It is primarily for ourselves—a starting point for discussion. If straight people of good will find it useful in understanding what gay liberation is about, so much the better.

It should also be clear that these ideas reflect the perspective of one person, and are determined not only by my homosexuality, but my being white, male, and middle class. It is my individual consciousness. Our group consciousness will evolve as we get ourselves together—we are only at the beginning.

I. ON ORIENTATION

1. WHAT HOMOSEXUALITY IS: Nature leaves undefined the object of sexual desire. The gender of that object has been imposed socially. Humans originally put a taboo on homosexuality because they needed every bit of energy to produce and raise children—survival of the species was a priority. With overpopulation and technological change, that taboo is absurd and continues only to exploit us and enslave us.

As kids, we refused to capitulate to demands that we smother our feeling toward each other. Somewhere we found the strength to resist being indoctrinated, and we should count that among our assets. We have to realize that our loving each other is a good thing, not an unfortunate thing, and that we have a lot to teach straights about sex, love, strength, and resistance.

Homosexuality is NOT a lot of things. It is not a makeshift in the absence of the opposite sex; it is not hatred or rejection of the opposite sex; it is not genetic; it is not the result of broken homes (except inasmuch as we could see the sham of American marriage). HOMOSEXUALITY IS THE CAPACITY TO LOVE SOMEONE OF THE SAME SEX.

2. BISEXUALITY: Bisexuality is good; it is the capacity to love people of either sex. The reason so few of us are bisexual is because society made such a big stink about homosexuality that we got forced into seeing ourselves as either straight or nonstraight. Also, many gays got turned off to the ways men are supposed to relate to women and vice-versa, which is pretty fucked up. Gays will begin to get turned onto women when 1) it's something that we do because we want to, and not because we should; 2) when women's liberation has changed the nature of heterosexual relationships.

We continue to call ourselves homosexual, rather than bisexual, even if we do make it with the opposite sex also, because saying "Oh, I'm Bi" is a cop out for a gay. We get told it's ok to sleep with guys as long as we sleep with women, too, and that's still putting homosexuality down. We'll be gay until everyone has forgotten that it's an issue. Then we'll begin to be complete people.

3. HETEROSEXUALITY: Exclusive heterosexuality is fucked up; it is a fear of people of the same sex, it is anti-homosexual, and it is fraught with frustrations. Heterosexual sex is fucked up, too; talk to women's liberation about what straight guys are like in bed. Sex is aggression for the male chauvinist; sex is obligation for the traditional woman. And among the young, the modern, the hip, it's only a subtle version of the same. For us to become heterosexual in the sense that our straight brothers and sisters are is not a cure, it is a disease to cop out.

II. ON WOMEN

1. LESBIANISM: It's been a male dominated society for too long, and that has warped both men and women. So gay women are going to see things differently from gay men; they are going to feel oppression as women, too. Their liberation is tied up with both gay liberation and women's liberation.

This paper speaks from the gay male point of view. Although some of the ideas in it may be equally relevant to gay women, it would be arrogant to presume this to be a manifesto for lesbians.

We look forward to the emergence of a lesbian liberation voice. The existence of a lesbian caucus within the New York Gay Liberation Front has been very helpful in challenging male chauvinism among gay guys and anti-gay feelings among women's lib.

2. MALE CHAUVINISM: All men are infected with male chauvinism—we were brought up that way. It means we assume that women play subordinate roles and are less human than ourselves. (At an early gay liberation meeting, one guy said, "Why don't we invite women's liberation, and they can bring sandwiches and coffee.") It is no wonder that so few gay women have become active in our groups.

Male chauvinism, however, is not central to us. We can junk it much more easily than straight men can. For we understand oppression. We have largely opted out of a system which oppresses women daily—our egos are not built on putting women down and having them build us up. Also, living in a mostly male world, we have become used to playing different roles and doing our own shit-work. And finally, we have a common enemy: the big male chauvinists are also the big anti-gays.

But we need to purge male chauvinist behavior and thought among us. Chick equals nigger equals queer. Think about it.

3. WOMEN'S LIBERATION: They are assuming their equality and dignity, and in doing so are challenging the same things we are: the insufferable roles, the exploitation of minorities by capitalism, the arrogance of straight white male middle class Amerika. They are our sisters in struggle.

Problems and differences will become clearer when we begin to work together. One major problem is our own male chauvinism. Another is the uptightness and hostility to homosexuality that many women have—that is the straight in them. A third problem is differing views on sex: sex for them has meant oppression, while it has been the symbol of our freedom. We must come to understand each other's style, jargon and humor.

We want to begin more intensive discussions with women's liberation. And in any case we must support their demands and understand their viewpoint.

III. ON ROLES

1. MIMICRY OF STRAIGHT SOCIETY: We are children of a straight society. We will think straight, and that is part of our oppression. One of the most fucked up of straight concepts is inequality. Straight (also white, English, male, capitalist) thinking sees things always in terms of order and comparison. A is before B, B is after A; 1st is higher than second is higher than 3rd; there is no room for equality. This idea gets extended to male/female, on top/on bottom, spouse/nonspouse, heterosexual/homosexual; boss/worker, rich/poor, white/black. Our social institutions cause and reflect this verbal heirarchy. This is Amerika.

We have lived in these institutions all our lives, so naturally we mimic the roles. For a long time we mimicked these roles to protect ourselves—a survival mechanism. Now we are becoming free enough to shed these roles which we've picked up from the institutions which have imprisoned us.

Stop mimicking straights, stop censoring ourselves.

2. MARRIAGE: Marriage is a prime example of a straight institution fraught with role playing. Traditional marriage is a rotten, oppressive institution. Those of us who have been in heterosexual marriages too often have blamed our gayness on the breakup of the marriages. No. They broke up because marriage is a contract which smothers both people, denies needs, and places impossible demands on both people. And we had the strength, again, to refuse to capitulate to the roles which were demanded of us.

Gay people must stop measuring their self respect by how well they mimic straight marriages. Gay marriages will have the same problems as straight ones, except in burlesque. For the usual legitimacy and pressures which keep straight marriages together are absent—kids, what will parents think, what will neighbors think.

To accept the idea that happiness comes through finding a nice spouse and settling down, showing the world that "We're just the same as you" is avoiding the real issues, and is an expression of self hatred.

3. ALTERNATIVES TO MARRIAGE: People want to get married for lots of good reasons, although marriage doesn't meet those

needs. We're all looking for security, a flow of love, a feeling of belonging and being needed.

These needs can be met through any number of social relationships and living situations. The things we want to get away from are: 1. exclusiveness, propertied attitudes toward each other, a mutual pact against the rest of the world; 2. promises about the future, which we have no right to make and which prevent us from, or make us feel guilty about, growing; 3. inflexible roles, roles which do not reflect us at the moment but are inherited through mimicry and inability to define equalitarian relationships.

We have to define for ourselves a new pluralistic, role-free social structure for ourselves. It must contain both the physical space and spiritual freedom for people to live alone, live together for a while, live together for a long time, either as couples or in larger numbers; and the ability to flow easily from one of these states to another as our needs change.

Liberation for gay people is to define for ourselves how and with whom we live, instead of measuring our relationships by straight values.

4. GAY "STEREOTYPE" ROLES. The straight's image of the gay community is defined largely by those of us who have violated straight roles. There is a tendency among "homophile" groups to deplore gays who play visible roles—the queens and the nellies. As liberated gays, we must take a clear stand: 1) gays who stand out have been the most courageous among us; they came out and withstood straight disapproval before the rest of us. They are our first martyrs; 2) if they have suffered from being open, it is straight society whom we blame for that suffering.

5. CLOSET QUEENS: This phrase is becoming the equivalent to "uncle Tom." To pretend to be straight sexually, or to pretend to be straight socially, is probably the most damaging pattern of behavior in the ghetto. It has many forms—the married guy who makes it on the side secretly; the guy who will go to bed once but who won't develop any gay relationships; the pretender at work or school or home who changes the gender of the friend he's talking about; the guy who'll suck cock in the bushes but who won't come home with you.

Closet queenery must end. If we are liberated, we are open with our sexuality. Come out. Come out. Come out.

BUT: in saying come out, we have to have our heads together about a few things: 1) closet queens are our brothers; they are to be defended against attacks by straight people. 2) Our fear of coming out is not totally paranoid: the stakes are high—loss of family ties, loss of job, loss of straight friends—these are all real risks. Each of us has to make the steps toward openness at our own speed and on our own impulses. Being open is the foundation of liberation, and it has to be built solidly. 3) Closet queen is a blanket term covering a multitude of patterns of defense, self-hatred, lack of strength, and habit. We are all closet queens in one way or another, and all of us had to come out—very few of us were "flagrant" at the age of seven! We must afford our brothers and sisters the same patience we afforded ourselves. And while their closetness is part of our oppression, it's more a part of their oppression; they alone can decide WHEN and HOW.

IV. ON OPPRESSION

It is important to catalog and understand the different facets of our oppression. There is no future in arguing about degrees of oppression. A lot of "movement" types come on with a line of shit about homosexuals not being oppressed as much as blacks or Vietnamese or workers or women. We don't happen to fit into their ideas of class (or caste). Bull—when people feel oppressed, they act on that feeling. And we feel oppressed. Talk about the priority of black liberation or ending imperialism over our "problem" is just antigay propaganda.

1. PHYSICAL ATTACKS: We are attacked, beaten, castrated and left dead over and over again. There are half a dozen known unsolved slayings in San Francisco parks in the last few years. Punks, often minority group members who look around for someone under them socially, feel encouraged to beat up on queers, and cops look the other way. If we recall, that used to be called lynching.

Cops in most cities have harassed our meeting places—bars, baths, parks. They set up entrapment squads. A Berkeley brother was murdered by a cop this spring when he tried to split after finding out that the trick who was making advances to him was a cop. Cities set up "pervert" registration, which if nothing else scares our brothers into the closet.

One of the most vicious slurs on us is to blame us for prison "gang rapes." These rapes are invariably done by people who consider themselves straight, and the objects of these rapes are us and other straights who can't defend themselves. The press campaign to link prison rapes with homosexuality is an attempt to make straights fear and despise us, so they can oppress us more. And it is typical of the fucked-up straight mind to think that homosexual sex means tying a guy down and fucking him. That's aggression, not sex—and if that's what sex is for a lot of straight people, that's their problem, not ours.

2. PSYCHOLOGICAL WARFARE: Right from the beginning we have been subjected to a barrage of straight propaganda. Since our parents don't know any homosexuals, we grow up thinking that we're all alone and different and perverted. Our school friends identify "queer" with any nonconformist or bad behavior. Our elementary school teachers tell us not to talk to strangers or accept rides in cars. The television, billboards and magazines pour forth an unreal idealization of male/female relationships, and make us wish we were different, we were "in." In family living classes we're taught how we're supposed to turn out. And all along, the best we hear, if anything, about homosexuality is that it's an unfortunate problem.

3. SELF OPPRESSION: As gay liberation grows, we will find our up tight brothers and sisters, particularly those who are making a buck off our ghetto, coming on strong to defend the status quo. This is self-oppression: "don't rock the boat"; "things in SF are ok"; "gay people just aren't together"; "I'm not oppressed." These lines are right out of the mouths of the straight establishment. A large part of our oppression would end if we would stop putting ourselves and our pride down.

4. INSTITUTIONAL: Discrimination against gays is blatant, if we open our eyes. Homosexual relationships are illegal, and even if these laws are not regularly enforced, they play the role of encouraging closet queenery. The vast bulk of the social work/psychiatric field looks upon homosexuality as a problem, and treats us as sick. Employers, particularly big business and (with some exceptions) government, let it be known that our skills are acceptable only as long as our sexuality is hidden.

The discrimination in the draft and armed services is a major pillar of the general attitude toward gays. If we are willing to label ourselves publicly not only as homosexual, but as sick, we can qualify for deferment; and if we're not "discreet" (read dishonest) we get drummed out of the service. Hell no, we won't go—of course—but we can't continue to stand back and let the army fuck us over this way, either.

V. ON SEX

1. WHAT SEX IS: Sex is both creative expression and communication: good when it is either, and better when it is both. Sex can also be aggression—and usually is when those involved do not see each other as equals; and it can also be perfunctory, when we are distracted or preoccupied. These uses of sex spoil what is good about it.

I like to think of good sex in terms of playing the violin—(on one level) with both people seeing the other's body as an object of producing beauty as long as they play it well; and on another level the players communicating through their mutual production and appreciation of a thing of beauty. As in good music, you get totally into it—and coming back out of that state of consciousness is like finishing a work of art, or coming back from an episode of an acid or mescaline trip. And to press the analogy further: the variety of music is infinite and varied, depending on the capabilities of the players, both as subjects and as objects. Solos, duets, quartets (symphonies, even, if you happen to dig Romantic music!) are possible. And the variations in gender, response, and bodies are like different instruments. And perhaps what we have called sexual "orientation" probably just means that we have learned to play certain kinds of music well, and have not yet turned on to other music.

2. OBJECTIFICATION: In this scheme of things, people are sexual objectives, but they are also subjects, and are human beings who appreciate themselves as object and subject. This use of human bodies as objects is legitimate (not harmful) only as long as it is reciprocal. If one person is always the object and the other the subject, it stifles the human being in both of them. Objectification must also be open and frank. By silence we often assume or let the other person assume that sex means commitments: if it does, ok, but if it doesn't, say so. (Of course, it's not all that simple: our capabilities for manipulation are unfathomed—all we can do is try.)

Gay liberation people must understand that women have been treated EXCLUSIVELY and DISHONESTLY as sexual objects. It is a major part of their liberation to play down sexual objectification and begin to develop other aspects of themselves which have been stifled so long. We respect this. We also understand that many liberated women will, for a while, be appalled or disgusted at the open and prominent place that we put sex in our lives—and while this is a natural response from their experience, they must learn what it means for us.

For us, sexual objectification is a focal point of our liberation. Sex is precisely that which we are not supposed to have with each other. And to learn how to be open and good with each other sexually is part of our liberation. And one major distinction is obvious: objectification of sex for us is something we choose to do among us, while for women it is imposed by their oppressors.

3. ON POSITIONS AND ROLES: Much of our sexuality has been perverted through mimicry of straights, and through warping from self-hatred. These sexual perversions are basically anti-gay:

"I like to make it with straight guys"
"I'm not gay, but I like to be 'done' "
"I like to fuck, but don't want to be fucked"
"I don't like to be touched above the neck"

This is role playing at its worst; we must transcend these roles—we strive for democratic, mutual, reciprocal sex. This doesn't mean that we are all mirror images of each other in bed, but that we break away from roles which enslave us. We already do better in bed than straights do, and we can do even better.

4. ON CHICKENS AND STUDS: Face it, nice bodies, and young bodies, are attributes, they're groovy. They are inspiration for art, for spiritual elevation, for good sex. The problem arises only in the inability to relate to people of the same age, or people who do not fit the plastic stereotypes of the good body. At that point, objectification eclipses people, and is an expression of self-hatred: "I don't like gay people, and I don't like my own sexuality, but if a stud (or chicken) will go to bed with me, I can pretend I'm not me."

A footnote on exploitation of children: kids can take care of themselves, and are sexual beings way earlier than we'd like to admit. Those of us who began cruising in our early teens know this, and we were doing cruising, not being debauched by our elders.

Scandals such as that in Boise, Idaho about homosexuals perverting the youth are dirty lies: the high school kids were exploiting gay people who were too scared to express the fullness of their homosexuality. And as for child molesting, the overwhelming amount is done by straight guys to little girls: it is not particularly a gay problem, and is a function of an antisex puritanism and its resulting frustrations.

5. PERVERSION: We've been called perverts enough to be automatically suspicious of this word. Still many of us shrink from the idea of certain kinds of sex: with animals, sado/masochism, "dirty" sex (involving piss and shit). Right off, even before we take the time to learn any more, there are some things to get straight: a) we shouldn't be apologetic to straights about gay people whose sex lives we don't understand or share; b) it's not particularly a gay issue, except that gays probably are less hung up about sexual experimentation; c) let's get some perspective—even if we were to get into the game of deciding what's good for someone else, the harm done to people in these "perversions" is undoubtedly less dangerous or unhealthy than is tobacco or alcohol. d) While they can be reflections of neurotic or self-hating patterns, they may also be enactments of spiritual or important things: e.g. sex with animals may be the beginning of interspecies communication: some dolphin-human breakthroughs have been made on the sexual level; e.g. one guy who says he digs eating shit during sex occasionally says it's not the taste or texture or role, but just a symbol that he's so far into the sex that those things no longer bother him; e.g. s/m, when consensual, can be described as highly developed artistic endeavor, a ballet the constraints of which are threshholds of pain and pleasure.

VI. ON OUR GHETTO

We are refugees from Amerika. So we came to the ghetto—and as other ghettos, it has its negative and positive aspects. Refugee camps are better than what preceded them, or people never would have come. But they are still enslaving, inasmuch as we are limited to being ourselves there and only there.

Ghettos breed self-hatred. We stagnate here, accepting the status quo. And the status quo is rotten. We are all warped by our oppression, and in the helplessness of the ghetto we blame ourselves rather than our oppressors.

Ghettos breed exploitation: Landlords realize they can charge exorbitant rents and get away with it, because there is a limited area which is safe to live in. The Mafia control of bars and baths in New York is only an extreme example of outside money controlling our institutions for their profit. In San Francisco, the Tavern Guild is in favor of maintaining the ghetto, because it is through the ghetto culture that they make a buck. We crowd their bars not because of their merit, but because of the absence of any other social institutions. And the Guild has refused to let us collect defense funds or pass out literature in their bars—need we ask why?

Police or con men who shake down the straight gays in return for not revealing them; the bookstores and movie makers who get away with outrageous prices because they are the only outlet for pornography; the heads of "modeling" agencies, and other pimps, who exploit both the hustlers and the customers—these are the parasites who flourish in the ghetto.

SAN FRANCISCO—GHETTO OR FREE TERRITORY: Our ghetto certainly is more beautiful, larger, and more diverse and freer than most ghettos, and certainly more than Amerika—that's why we're here. But it is not ours—capitalists make money off us, police patrol us, the government tolerates us as long as we shut up, and daily we work for and pay taxes to those who oppress us.

To be a free territory, we must govern ourselves, set up our own institutions, defend ourselves, and use our own energies to improve our lives. The emergence of gay liberation communes and our own paper is a good start. The talk about a gay liberation coffeeshop-dance hall, should be followed through. Rural retreats, political offices, food retail cooperatives, free school, unalienated gay bars and afterhours places—they must be developed if we are to have even the shadow of a free territory.

VII. ON COALITION

Right now the bulk of our work has to be among ourselves—selfeducating, fending off attacks, and building our free territory. Thus basically we have to have a gay/straight vision of the world, until the oppression of gays is ended.

But two problems exist with that as a total vision: 1) we can't change Amerika alone, we need coalition with other oppressed groups at some point; 2) many of us have "mixed" identities—we are gay, and also we are part of another group trying to free itself —women, blacks, other minority groups; we may also have taken on identities which are vital to us: dopers, ecologists, radicals.

Whom do we look to for coalition?

1. WOMEN'S LIBERATION: Without repeating earlier statements, 1) they are our closest ally—we have to try hard to get together with them; 2) a lesbian caucus is probably the easiest way to deal with gay guys' male chauvinism, and challenge the straightness of women's liberation; 3) we as males must be sensitive to their developing identities as women, and respect that; if we know what our liberation consists of, they certainly know what's best for them.

2. BLACK LIBERATION: This is tenuous right now, because of the uptightness and supermasculinity of many black males (which is understandable). Notwithstanding, we must support their movement and demands; we must show that we mean business; and we must figure out which our common enemies are: police, city hall, capitalism.

And they need us too: In New York, where blacks and whites are in a stalemate about community control of schools and police, a solid support from the very large gay population can make the difference between justice or continuing racism.

3. CHICANOS: Basically the same problem as with blacks: trying to overcome mutual animosity and fear, and finding ways to support their movement. The extra problem of superuptightness and machismo among Latin cultures, and the traditional pattern of Mexican "punks" beating on homosexuals, can be overcome: we're both oppressed, and by the same people at the top.

4. WHITE RADICALS AND IDEOLOGUES: We're not, as a group, Marxist or communist—we haven't figured out what kind of economic-political structure is good for us as gays. Nobody—capitalist or communist—has treated us as anything other than shit so far.

But we know we are radical, in the same sense that we know the system we're living under is the direct source of oppression, and it's not just a question of sharing the pie. The pie is rotten.

We can look forward to coalition and mutual inspiration with white radical groups if they are able to transcend their antigay and male chauvinist patterns. We must support radical and militant demands as they come up, e.g. Moratorium, People's Park; but only as a group; we can't compromise our gay identity.

Problems: because radicals are mostly doing somebody else's thing, they are likely to want to avoid issues which affect them directly, and may see us as jeopardizing their "work" with workers, blacks. Some years ago, a dignitary of SDS at the onset of a community organization project announced at an initial staff meeting that there would be no homosexuality (or dope) on the project. And recently in NYC, a movement group which had a coffeehouse get together after a political rally, told the gays to leave when they started dancing together.

Perhaps it would be useful to approach them by helping them free the homosexual within them.

5. HIP AND STREET PEOPLE: Perhaps the major dynamic of recent gay lib sentiment is the hip revolution within the gay community. Emphasis on love, drop out, be honest, stop dressing drably, hair, smoke dope. Those who are the least vulnerable to attack by the establishment are the freest to express themselves.

We can make a direct appeal to young people, who are increasingly not so up tight about homosexuality. One kid, after having his first sex with a man, said "I don't know what all the fuss is all about, it's not that different from making it with a girl!"

The hip/street culture has led people into a lot of other things: encounter/sensitivity, the quest for reality, liberating territory for the people, ecological consciousness, communes. These are real points of agreement.

6. HOMOPHILE GROUPS: 1) Reformist and pokey as they might sometimes be, they are our brothers. They will grow just as we have grown and will grow. Don't attack them, particularly in straight or mixed company. 2) Ignore their attacks on us. 3) Cooperate where cooperation is possible without essential compromise of our identity.

CONCLUSION: AN OUTLINE OF IMPERATIVES FOR GAY LIBERATION

1. Free ourselves: come out, everywhere; initiate self-defense and political activity; initiate community institutions; think

2. Turn other gay people on: talk all the time; understand, accept, forgive.

3. Free the homosexual in everyone: we'll be getting a lot of shit from threatened latents: be gentle and keep talking and acting free.

4. We've been playing an act for a long time: we're consummate actors. Now we can begin TO BE, and it'll be a good show!

Prisons

HOMOSEXUAL AND DRUG BEHAVIOR IN PRISON: A TEST OF THE FUNCTIONAL AND IMPORTATION MODELS OF THE INMATE SYSTEM*

RONALD L. AKERS
Florida State University

NORMAN S. HAYNER and WERNER GRUNINGER
University of Washington

Which of the two major models of the inmate system, the importation or the functional, better accounts for two forms of in-prison behavior of inmates, drug use and homosexual behavior, is tested in a sample of inmates from seven U.S. prisons. The prisons were classified into three types along a custody-treatment continuum. The reported levels of these two kinds of behavior in the different types of prisons are examined against their relationship to seven inmate background characteristics. The analysis reveals that the amount of drug and homosexual behavior among inmates is more a function of the type of prison which holds them than the social characteristics which they bring with them from the outside.

Our objective in this analysis is to present findings from a comparative study of prison organization in an attempt to account for differential levels of *homosexual* and *drug* behavior among prison inmates. There are, of course, many practical and theoretical issues in the study of drugs and homosexuality as forms of deviant behavior in society, whether they occur within or outside of correctional institutions. However, our attention to drug use and homosexual behavior here is part of the general concern with describing and explaining the inmate social system and culture which has been a major focus of sociological research and theory on correctional organizations at least since the pioneering work of Clemmer (1938) and others (see Hayner and Ash, 1939, 1940; Reimer, 1937; and Weinberg, 1942).

The inmate code, anti-staff hostility, inmate social roles, leadership structure, socialization (prisonization) into the system, and other aspects of the inmate system have been investigated. (See the various topics discussed in Cloward, et al., 1960; Cressey, 1961; Hazelrigg, 1969; Carter et al., 1972). The attempts to explain the existence and anti-conventional orientation of the inmate system revolve around two theoretical models. The first of these is a *functional* explanation, which views the inmate culture as a collective adaptation to the prison environment, more specifically the deprivations or "pains" and "degradation" of imprisonment, and also as serving control functions for the administration (Sykes, 1958; Sykes and Messinger, 1960; Cloward, 1960). The other is a diffusionist or *importation* model, which sees the nature of the inmate system as reflective primarily of

* The present analysis reports findings taken from a study of prisons in five countries—Mexico, Great Britain, West Germany, Spain, and the United States. Collection of the Mexican data was supported by NIMH Grant #MH 1340401, 1967. Analysis of data from all countries was supported by NIMH Grant #MH 1581301141, 1970-71 and NIMH Grant #MH 20032-01, 1971-72. This support is gratefully acknowledged. Appreciation is expressed to Charles Wellford for his helpful critical reading of the manuscript. We would also like to thank the prison administrators and the inmates in the prisons who so graciously cooperated in the study. It goes without saying that but for their participation there would be nothing to report.

the criminal roles played and values acquired by inmates on the outside and brought into the institution with them (Irwin and Cressey, 1962; Irwin, 1970), and, by extension, other pre-prison characteristics and experiences of the inmates.

Studies of prison homosexuality have fairly closely reflected the general interest in the whole inmate system; the emphasis has been on homosexual roles and relationships as integral to inmate social organization, and both the functional (Sykes, 1958; Kirkham, 1971) and importation (Ward and Kassebaum, 1965; Giallombardo, 1966; Gagnon and Simon, 1972) models have been invoked in the analysis of in-prison homosexual behavior. Drug use within prisons has not yet received the same attention. In the United States, correctional administrators, legislators, prosecutors, and others are becoming increasingly concerned about drugs in the prisons and make public statements about the extent of the problem. However, the phenomenon of significant amounts of drug taking by prisoners in the United States is recent enough that, to our knowledge, no systematic sociological research on it has yet been reported. Irwin (1970) does make reference to drug taking in the context of discussing the in-prison behavior of the "dope fiend" and the "head;" and since these are role types defined by pre-prison behavior, it is clear that he sees their drug use as simply an extension of behavior patterns established before imprisonment. However, drug use in prison can also be interpreted as one functional adaptation to the prison environment.

The contrast between the functional and importation models can be misleading, if it is taken to mean that the two are necessarily mutually exclusive, for prior experience and the prison situation may interact to produce the norms and behavior of the inmates. The existence of collective *solutions* in the form of an inmate culture and social structure may be explained by the need to solve common problems of adjusting to imprisonment, but the *content* of those solutions may be reflective of behavior patterns and values imported from the larger society (Thomas, 1970). While recognizing this interaction, we start with the hypothesis, consistent with the functional model, that the amount of drug and homosexual behavior among inmates is a function of the type of prison in which they are located. By *type of prison* we refer to the kind of total organizational atmosphere or milieu confronting the inmates provided by the style of architecture, administrative goals, orientation of the staff, visiting policies, rehabilitation programs, and other aspects of the prison organization. At one extreme, the type of prison climate facing the inmate is repressive, punitive, and degrading. At the other, this atmosphere is nonpunitive, open, and imbued with humanitarian concern for the welfare of the prisoners. A given prison can be typed by placement on the hypothetical continuum running between these two polar types of custodial and treatment institutions. We assume that the more custodial type of institution presents a more deprivational environment and greater problems of adjustment to inmates than does the more treatment-oriented institution.

Type of Prison Organization: The Custody-Treatment Continuum

The data presented here are from a larger study of prison organization and the inmate system in 25 prisons in five different countries—the United States, Mexico, Germany, Great Britain, and Spain. In selecting the prisons, the effort was made to include a variety of institutions, maximum security penitentiaries, reformatories, and modern treatment institutions to allow for both cross-national and within country comparisons. Although the actual classification procedure (described below) did not come until later, prisons were selected which, on the basis of initial information and observation, could be tentatively characterized as lying at various points on the custody-treatment continuum. This report presents analysis of data from the seven United States prisons only. One of these institutions is located on the West Coast, one in the Southeast, one in the Southwest, one in the West, two in the South, and one in the Northcentral section of the United States.

The custody-treatment continuum in prison organization and orientation and the conflict between custodial and treatment goals are widely discussed in the literature. However, the meaning of these terms have not been precisely delineated, and there are few guidelines to their empirical measurement in the literature.[1]

The procedure used in this study to classify institutions is as follows. Tape recorded interviews were held with the top administrators of the various prisons. These interviews were designed to elicit information about nine dimensions of the prison setting, operation, and administration which we thought to be especially relevant to defining a prison as relatively custodial or treatment: (1) architecture, (2) administrative goals and structure, (3) classification and diagnostic procedures, (4) work and employment of inmates, (5) education and training programs, (6) counselling and treatment programs, (7) security and custody practices, (8) ratios and qualifications of treatment and custodial personnel, and (9) policy on visiting and outside contact. Descriptive statements on each dimension were transcribed; and from these descriptions three judges, independently, but on the basis of previously agreed upon written specifications, rated each prison on each dimension on a seven-point scale. (Initial concordance was tau = .76; after discussion tau = .95.) The scores for the nine items for each prison were then summed and averaged for the three raters; this averaged sum represented the overall ranking on the custody-treatment continuum (mini-

[1] The words "custody" and "treatment" are in fact somewhat misleading because treatment in the sense of engaging in strategies which will change behavior is not strictly the polar opposite of custody. The difference seems to be one of degree of humane attention to the rights and dignity of the individual. But since these terms are recognized in the literature, we shall continue to use custody and treatment to denote the two ends of the continuum. However, "repressive-open," "inhumane-humane," and other pairs of terms would be suitable and perhaps more descriptive synonyms to indicate the differences we have in mind. The lack of agreed upon procedures for placing prisons on this continuum results partly from the fact that most studies of correctional organizations are case studies of single institutions, and thus there is no opportunity to array a number of institutions in these studies. In the few instances where more than one institution is included and the institutions are characterized as custody, treatment, or intermediate between the two, no detailed information is given on the basis for classification (see, Berk, 1966; Street, *et al.*, 1966). Moss (1968) does give sufficient detail on his measures of "social climate," but they are only indirectly applicable to the custody-treatment continuum.

mum possible score of 9 indicating the most severely custodial prison, and a maximum of 63 indicating the most treatment-oriented institution). For purposes of analysis, the possible range of scores was trichotomized as custody type (a score of 29 or less), intermediate type (scores from 30 to 44), and treatment type (score of 45 or more). The actual scores split into three fairly discontinuous groups, with the intermediate prison scoring closer to the custodial than to the treatment prisons, as follows:

Treatment—three prisons scoring 50, 52, and 57.
Intermediate—one prison with a score of 30.
Custodial—three prisons scoring 16, 18, and 21.

Measures of Levels of Homosexual and Drug Behavior

In addition to the interviews with prison administrators, questionnaires were administered to a sample of inmates from each institution.[2] The questionnaires were given under conditions designed to maximize confidentiality and elicit cooperation.[3] The inmates completed the questionnaires in groups of about 20 in a classroom or other room set aside specifically for the purpose. Only the investigator and his inmate assistants were present in the room during the time the questionnaire was being taken. No member of the prison staff was in the room. Few questionnaires were rejected as too incomplete to be used, and for the most part the per-item non-response rate is low. However, the non-response to a few questions, including the five of most interest in this paper, is fairly high.[4]

[2] The original intent was to draw a 10 percent interval sample of inmates from each prison. However, because of administrative restraint on access to files, in only three of the U.S. prisons was this strict sampling procedure followed. In the others, staff made the selection under specific instructions to use interval sampling from the files or (in two cases) inmates were selected, with the help of staff and inmates, to approximate the racial, age, offense, and security composition of the inmate population. The degree to which instructions were in fact followed or the extent to which the sampling plan was consciously or inadvertently modified by those actually selecting the respondents cannot be known with certainty. Nevertheless, we have assurances that lead us to conclude that administrators and inmates acted conscientiously within the limits set by particular situations. That some modification occurred, however, is attested to by the fact that we achieved an eight percent rather than the planned ten percent sample of the total number of inmates in all prisons.

[3] The assistance of a number of prisoners whom the staff felt were "respected" by other inmates was obtained (after private sessions in which the questionnaire and purpose of the research was explained and these prisoners answered the questionnaire themselves) in administering the questionnaire and assuring the inmates selected that there was no way in which their answers could be seen by prison staff or other inmates or individually identified by anyone.

[4] Our findings and conclusions must be read with this non-response rate in mind. There is a tendency for the respondents in the custodially oriented institutions to fail to respond more than the respondents in the treatment oriented institutions. But it is not clear in which direction this would produce systematic bias. If we assume that every failure to respond means that the respondent has knowledge of no one using drugs or engaging in homosexual behavior (and assign "no responses" to the "none" category), then the associations between type of institution and these two variables would be considerably weakened. If we assume, on the other hand, that failure to respond represents an effort to keep from "ratting" (however anonymously) on known users

The questionnaire covered several aspects of the inmate culture and social system, personal and criminal characteristics of the respondent, participation in prison programs, and other behavior and attitudes of the inmates, including questions on homosexual and drug behavior. Data on the amount of homosexual involvement were obtained from responses to the question, "How many inmates do you *know for sure* have participated in homosexual relations in this institution at least once in the past year?" The same question was asked separately for: drugs (no kind specified), marihuana, heroin, or drugs other than marihuana or heroin.[5] The inmate responded by writing in whatever number he was sure had been involved in homosexuality or drugs (including himself if applicable). For purposes of analysis, the responses were categorized as none, 1 to 5, and 6 or more. This procedure obviously does not allow for measuring or reliably estimating the absolute proportion of inmates participating in homosexual acts or using drugs. However, we believe that by emphasizing that we wanted to know the number about whose involvement the inmate had certain knowledge, thus avoiding reports based on vague feelings and uncertain or hearsay knowledge, we have a more valid measure of *relative* level of involvement in different institutions than we would if inmates or staff were asked to offer general estimates of percentages of the total population engaging in drug and homosexual behavior.[6]

Our measure may be affected by the total number of inmates in the given institution, however, for the larger the size of the inmate population, the greater the chance that more drug users and homosexual participants will be known to the respondent. Thus, size of the prison may be a contaminating intervening variable in the relationship between either of these two dependent

and homosexual participants and assign the "no responses" to the "1-5" or "6 or more" categories then the relationships reported would be considerably strengthened. We have, therefore, done neither and simply report the non-responses to allow the reader to make his own judgments about how they may or may not bias the results.

[5] We did not ask the inmate to report his own drug use or homosexual behavior. We felt that because admission to this kind of behavior would place the inmate in extreme jeopardy should his identity be discovered, he would be so threatened that, in spite of all efforts to assure confidentiality, we would have an extremely low response rate and largely invalid answers. This study still must contend, however, with the same difficulty of studies which use self-report as the behavioral measure; that is, we are dealing with *reported* behavior, not behavior which we have directly observed. The near impossibility of an outsider adequately observing the behavior in question, of course, leads to this reported approximation to the actual behavior. In the text we often call attention to this by referring to "reported" behavior, but even where the reference is simply to behavior, we do not lose sight of the fact that it is reported behavior.

[6] The percentage of inmates participating in homosexual relations has been estimated in other studies on the basis of official reports, estimates given by staff members, or estimates given by inmates (Clemmer, 1938; Ward and Kassebaum, 1965; Giallombordo, 1966, Kassebaum, Ward, and Wilner, 1971). This procedure involves problems of counting as equal the estimates of those who really have knowledge and those who have none, differential acquaintance with and ability in thinking in terms of percentages, and other biases. Thus, although the questionnaire administered in prisons in countries other than the United States contained an item asking the respondent to estimate the percentage of inmates engaged in homosexual behavior, we changed the items on the questionnaire administered in the U.S.

variables and any independent variable. This appears to be no problem in this instance, however, because there is only a small and non-significant relationship between prison size and the number of reported drug users (Gamma = .096) and a slightly *negative* association between prison size and reported homosexuality (Gamma = —.06).

Type of Prison and Differential Levels of Homosexual and Drug Behavior

Generally, it appears that the number of inmates taking part in homosexual behavior, which traditionally has been considered a major behavioral problem by prison authorities, has now been surpassed by the number of drug users. Of those responding in all seven prisons, 33.5 percent know more than five inmates who have been practicing homosexual acts in the institutions, whereas 43.6 percent are certain of more than five inmates who are drug users. In only one prison is the number of homosexual participants reported to be greater than the number of drug users. But these general figures conceal considerable variation among the prisons. For instance, in one place 80 percent of the respondents report at least six inmates engaging in homosexual behavior while only 12 percent report knowing this many in another institution. In one prison, no one admits knowing six or more heroin users (and only five percent know even one); but in another, 44 percent report this number of heroin takers.

The data make it clear, however, that these are not random variations. There is something about the prison which produces *both* homosexual and drug behavior. Without exception, those with high levels of reported drug use also experience high levels of homosexual behavior; and prisons with low levels of drug use also have low levels of reported homosexual behavior. The data support the hypothesis that these differences in both drug and homosexual behavior are accounted for by differences in the type of prison in which the inmates are incarcerated. Not only is the reported number of drug users and homosexual participants associated with the overall type of prison, but both are related to the ratings given the institutions on each of the nine separate dimensions, in the expected direction.

Table 1 shows that the more custodial the institution, the higher the level of reported homosexual behavior. More than half the inmate respondents in the treatment institutions report that they know no one for sure who has participated in homosexual relations. At the other extreme, more than half of the inmates in the custodial prisons report certain knowledge of six or more who have engaged in homosexual relations in the prison. Drug use of all kinds also increases from treatment to custodial prisons. The strongest association is that between type of prison and use of drugs other than marihuana or heroin (Table 2); these drugs are used more often in the custodial than in the intermediate prison, which in turn has more than the treatment institutions. However, as shown in Table 3, the relationships between prison type and overall drug use, marihuana use, and heroin use are slightly curvilinear; for the intermediate prison has more users of these drugs than do the custodial prisons. Thus, the consistent difference in drug use by inmates is in the low level of use in treatment institutions on the one hand, and the much higher level of use in intermediate and custodial prisons on the other hand.

TABLE 1
LEVEL OF HOMOSEXUAL BEHAVIOR IN DIFFERENT TYPES OF PRISONS IN THE UNITED STATES

(Percentage distribution of responses to "How many inmates do you *know for sure* have participated in homosexual relations in this institution at least once in the past year?")

Type of Prison	None	1-5	6 or more	N	No response N
Treatment (3 prisons)	52.2	32.3	15.4	201	12
Intermediate (1 prison)	39.9	25.5	35.3	102	27
Custodial (3 prisons)	31.3	12.7	56.0	150	55
All prisons	42.4	24.3	33.3	453	94

Gamma = .40, $P < .01$; $X^2 = 65.52$, df = 4, $p < .01$

The findings, then, do support the functional model. In all cases, the relationship between type of prison and reported level of homosexual behavior, marihuana use, heroin use, and other drugs is in the expected direction and statistically significant. Those institutions which present the inmate with a more punitive, repressive, and harsh environment have relatively more inmates using drugs and participating in homosexual liasons than those institutions which are more open, humane, and treatment-oriented.

INMATE CHARACTERISTICS AND LEVELS OF DRUG AND HOMOSEXUAL BEHAVIOR

Drug and homosexual behavior are not solely a function of prison life, of course. Indeed, while it can be assumed that there will be sexual behavior of some sort in any case, using drugs probably would not occur to the in-

TABLE 2
LEVELS OF USE OF DRUGS OTHER THAN MARIHUANA OR HEROIN, IN DIFFERENT TYPES OF PRISONS IN THE UNITED STATES

(Percentage distribution of responses to "How many inmates do you *know for sure* have used other drugs [other than marihuana or heroin] in this institution at least once in the past year?")

Type of Prison	None	1-5	6 or more	N	No Response N
Treatment (3 prisons)	61.5	23.1	15.4	169	44
Intermediate (1 prison)	34.4	17.8	47.8	90	39
Custodial (3 prisons)	30.2	16.3	53.5	129	76
All prisons	44.8	19.6	35.6	388	159

Gamma = .46, $P < .01$; $X^2 = 55.51$, df = 4, $p < .01$

TABLE 3
PERCENTAGES OF INMATES REPORTING HIGH LEVELS OF VARIOUS TYPES OF DRUG USE IN DIFFERENT TYPES OF PRISONS IN THE UNITED STATES

(Percentages reporting knowing for sure 6 *or more* inmates who have used)

Type of Prison	Drugs (any type)	Total N	Mari-huana	Total N	Heroin	Total N	Other Drugs	Total N
Treatment (3 prisons)	27.5	(200)	8.9	(179)	11.7	(180)	15.4	(169)
Intermediate (1 prison)	60.8	(97)	50.5	(95)	35.2	(88)	47.8	(90)
Custodial (3 prisons)	54.6	(141)	34.7	(121)	26.3	(118)	53.5	(129)
Gamma =	.35		.40		.25		.46	
P <	.01		.01		.05		.01	

mates as a way of adjusting to life inside if it were unknown in the larger society. The fact that there has been an increase in drug use within the walls during a period of time that has seen illicit drug taking become more widespread in American society as a whole indicates that inmate behavior reflects changes in the larger society. The fact that homosexuality seems more frequent in female than in male prisons (Ward and Kassebaum, 1965) indicates that in-prison adjustment may reflect differences in sex roles in the outside community. More specifically, some inmate types, such as the "queen," are homosexual prior to and after imprisonment (Sykes, 1958; Kirkham, 1971); and the kind of orientation to sex in prison populations may be an extension of the lower educational and social class from which most inmates come (Gagnon and Simon, 1972). There are inmates whose drug taking in the prison is just a continuation of habits developed prior to incarceration (Irwin, 1970). It may be, then, that the findings in this study are explained more readily by an importation hypothesis that the variations in drug use and homosexuality result from differential selection of inmates into the prisons; that the types of inmates who are more likely to use drugs or commit homosexual acts are more likely to be incarcerated in custodial and intermediate prisons than in treatment institutions.

We do not have direct measures of predisposition to drug use or homosexual behavior, but we do have measures of a number of background characteristics. Because we did not ask the respondent to report his own behavior, we are uninterested in the relationship between his characteristics and the number of drug users and participants in homosexual behavior known to him. (And our data show that they are, in fact, unrelated.) The meaningful relationship is that between the general distribution of characteristics among the inmate population and the level of reported homosexual and drug behavior. Therefore, we devised aggregate measures of seven inmate characteristics: criminal background, length of sentence currently being served, age, marital status, race, sentences being served for drug and sex offenses, and education.[7] Of these only the age distribution is strongly related to the level of homosexuality (Gamma = —.41). As presented in Table 4, the three prisons with a relatively young population have more reported homosexual behavior than the four prisons with older populations. Also, the proportion of inmates with prior criminal background and the mean length of sentence are related to reported homosexual behavior, but the relationships are not strong (Gammas = .18 and .15 respectively).

None of the seven inmate characteristic variables is related to all types of drug use in prisons. The mean length of sentence is significantly related to marihuana (Gamma = .49) and "other" drug use (Gamma = .35). The proportion of inmates with prior criminal histories is strongly related only to the level of heroin use (Gamma = .47), but is also slightly related to marihuana and other drug use. Surprisingly, reported marihuana use bears no relationship at all to the age distribution. Perhaps even more surprising, the percentage black in the inmate population is *negatively* related to the level of reported drug use of all types. (The association with heroin use is statistically significant at the .01 level, Gamma = —.29; but the other negative relationships are small and non-significant.) The age distribution is related to both the level of heroin use and "other" drug use, but in opposite directions. There are more heroin users in the institutions with older populations (Gamma = .40), while "other" drug use is more often reported in prisons with younger populations (Gamma = —.27).

These findings do not confirm the hypothesis that differences in levels of homosexuality and drug use among the prisons are the result of the differences in the backgrounds of the inmates. Of the seven inmate background characteristics, only the age structure has a significant impact on both homosexuality and drug use (with the exception of marihuana). In addition, homosexuality and at least one type of drug use are somewhat related to mean length of sentence and prior criminality.[8]

---

[7] With the exception of race, the measures are based on the distributions among the respondents. The distributions were categorized as follows for purposes of analysis:

(1) Criminal background. Proportion of inmates who were arrested at a young age, had a juvenile record, and are adult recidivists. Low = less than 50 percent, medium = 50-70 percent, high = more than 70 percent.
(2) Mean length of sentence for currently incarcerated inmates. Low = less than five years, medium = five to ten years, high = more than ten years.
(3) Age composition. Younger = 40 percent or more under age 25, older = less than 30 percent under 25.
(4) Marital status. Proportion of inmates not currently married (single, widowed, or divorced). High = 60 percent or more unmarried, low = less than 60 percent unmarried.
(5) Race. Percent black in each prison.

In both the case of (6) offense type (proportion serving time for drug offenses and proportion serving time for sex offenses) and (7) educational level, the distributions were so similar among the seven prisons that no meaningful classification could be made. The lack of variation in these two variables, of course, means that neither can explain the variation among prisons in drug use and homosexual behavior.

[8] Controlling for these two variables leaves the associations between prison type and levels of homosexual and drug behavior virtually unchanged.

TABLE 4
LEVELS OF HOMOSEXUAL BEHAVIOR IN PRISONS WITH YOUNGER INMATE POPULATIONS AND IN PRISONS WITH OLDER INMATE POPULATIONS

(Percentage distribution of responses to "How many inmates do you *know for sure* have participated in homosexual relations in this institution at least once in the past year?")

Age Composition	None	1-5	6 or more	N	No response N
Younger Inmates (3 prisons)	28.6	20.7	50.7	140	40
Older Inmates (4 prisons)	48.6	25.9	25.6	313	54
All prisons	42.4	24.3	33.3	453	94

Gamma $= -.41$, $p < .01$; $X^2 = 28.55$, df $= 2$, $p < .01$

TYPE OF PRISON, HOMOSEXUAL AND DRUG BEHAVIOR, AND AGE OF THE INMATE POPULATION

The failure to account for the consistently significant relationships of drugs and homosexuality to the type of prison by assignment of the inmates in this study with predisposing social or criminal characteristics to the different prisons is to be expected, since of the seven background variables only the age composition is significantly related to prison type; and it is related in the *opposite* direction from what would be expected (Gamma = —.21). Ordinarily, the more treatment-oriented institutions tend to receive younger offenders, and thus one would expect the age level to increase moving from treatment to custodial prisons, but this is not the case for the prisons in our sample. Rather, of the three treatment prisons, two have older populations, and of the three custodial prisons, two have younger populations.[9] However, since the age structure is also negatively related to the level of homosexual behavior as well as to the number of known users of heroin and "other" drugs, we should regard age as a probable intervening variable between prison type and these kinds of behavior. Therefore, we shall analyze the relationships between prison type and reported homosexual and drug behavior, controlling for age composition of the prison population.

The association between prison type and homosexual behavior remains after controlling for age composition. However, the relationship is weaker for institutions with older populations (Gamma = .29) and stronger for prisons with younger populations (Gamma = .56) than the uncontrolled relationship for all institutions (Gamma = .40). In other words, the type of prison in which inmates are incarcerated does make a difference in the amount of homosexuality for both younger and older populations, but it makes a bigger difference for prisons with *younger* populations. This is

[9] This is probably due to the fact that our treatment institutions and custodial prisons were not located in the same states. The two custodial prisons are located where there are no treatment alternatives in the state and hence receive even the young offenders. One of the treatment prisons is a special treatment facility for which age plays little part in commitment.

TABLE 5
PERCENTAGES OF INMATES REPORTING HIGH LEVELS OF HOMOSEXUAL BEHAVIOR IN DIFFERENT TYPES OF PRISONS IN THE UNITED STATES, BY RELATIVE AGE OF THE INMATE POPULATION

(Percentage of inmates reporting knowing *6 or more* inmates who have participated in homosexual relations)

Type of Prison	In Prisons With Younger Inmates	Total N	In Prisons With Older Inmates	Total N
Treatment	19.2 (1 prison)	(52)	14.1 (2 prisons)	(149)
Intermediate			35.3 (1 prison)	(102)
Custodial	69.3 (2 prisons)	(88)	37.1 (1 prison)	(62)

shown clearly in Table 5. This table also shows that the prison type is more important than the age structure. The differences in levels of homosexuality in younger and older inmate populations controlling for type of prison are much less than the differences in homosexual behavior in different types of prisons controlling for age composition.

The relationship between prison type and use of drugs other than marihuana or heroin remains essentially unchanged when the age structure is controlled.[10] But when the age composition is controlled, the association between prison type and heroin use stays the same for prisons with younger inmates (Gamma = .25) and increases for prisons with older inmates (Gamma = .40). This pattern for heroin is just the opposite of that for homosexual behavior. As Table 6 shows, the type of prison accounts for levels of heroin use for both younger and older populations, but accounts for more in prisons with *older* populations.

[10] The uncontrolled association is Gamma = .46; for prisons with younger populations it is .46; and for those with older populations it is .49.

CONCLUSION

One way to approach the question of which better accounts for the adoption of inmate culture and behavior patterns, the effects of the institutional stay or the imported characteristics and predispositions, is a *processual* one as in the studies of prisonization. That is, the length of time incarcerated and the phase of institutional career may be seen as measures of exposure to the prison environment (Wheeler, 1961). The effects of this "situational element" may be compared to the independent effects of some "actor characteristic" such as the inmate's social role or type (assuming that the inmate's role is reflective of his past criminal career) (Wellford, 1967; see also Garabedian, 1963).

We have taken a different more *structural* approach here by examining the impact of different types of prison environments and the distribution of inmate characteristics at a given time on the amount of homosexual and drug behavior in prison, rather than changes in behavior over time within the same prison. This approach to testing which of the two major models of the inmate

TABLE 6
PERCENTAGES OF INMATES REPORTING HIGH LEVELS OF HEROIN USE IN DIFFERENT TYPES OF PRISONS IN THE UNITED STATES, BY RELATIVE AGE OF THE INMATE POPULATION

(Percentage of inmates knowing *6 or more* heroin users)

Type of Prison	In Prisons With Younger Inmates	Total N	In Prisons With Older Inmates	Total N
Treatment	2.0 (1 prison)	(51)	15.5 (2 prisons)	(129)
Intermediate			35.3 (1 prison)	(88)
Custodial	14.3 (2 prisons)	(70)	43.8 (1 prison)	(48)

system, the functional-deprivational or importation models (or which combination of variables from the two theoretical perspectives), better explains various features of the inmate system has not progressed very far for at least two reasons. First, most studies of prison organization and the inmate system are case studies of single institutions, and there is no way to compare variations in organizational environment. Comparing findings from several separate case studies is hampered by the lack of comparable measures. Second, the type of prison to which inmates are sent is related to the criminal history, offense, age, and other social characteristics of the inmates. Thus, it is difficult to find two or more institutions which differ in prison type but are similar in social characteristics of the convicts (or two or more prisons which are similar in custody-treatment orientation but differ in the kind of inmates committed to them).

We were able to deal with both of these difficulties in this study. Not only are a number of prisons of varying types included from which comparable data were collected, but the prison types were sufficiently independent of the types of inmates in them to enable judgment of their relative importance in accounting for levels of drug and homosexual behavior. Such analysis suggests that the extent to which convicts are engaged in these two kinds of deviant behavior during the time of their incarceration is more a function of the type of prison which holds them than they are reflective of the social characteristics which they bring with them from the outside. Preliminary analysis of other findings in the study indicate that several other aspects of the inmate system, too, are more strongly related to prison type than to factors in inmates' social backgrounds.

REFERENCES

Berk, Bernard B.
1966 "Organizational goals and inmate organization." American Journal of Sociology 71(March): 522-534.

Carter, Robert M., Daniel Glaser, and Leslie T. Wilkins (eds.)
1972 Correctional Institutions. Philadelphia: J. B. Lippincott Co.

Clemmer, Donald
1938 The Prison Community. New York: Holt, Rinehart, and Winston.

Cloward, Richard

1960 "Social control in the prison." Pp. 20-48 in Richard Cloward et al., Theoretical Studies in Social Organization of the Prison. New York: Social Science Research Council.

Cloward, Richard, et al.
1960 Theoretical Studies in Social Organization of the Prison. New York: Social Science Research Council.

Cressey, Donald R. (ed.)
1961 The Prison: Studies in Institutional Organization and Change. New York: Holt, Rinehart, Winston.

Gagnon, John N., and William Simon
1972 "The social meaning of prison homosexuality." Pp. 221-232 in Robert M. Carter, Daniel Glaser, and Leslie T. Wilkins (eds.), Correctional Institutions. Philadelphia: J. B. Lippincott.

Garabedian, Peter G.
1963 "Social roles and processes of socialization in the prison community." Social Problems, 11(fall): 140-152.

Giallombordo, Rose
1966 Society of Women. New York: John Wiley and Sons.

Hayner, Norman, and Ellis Ash
1939 "The prisoner community as a social group." American Sociological Review 4(June): 362-369.
1940 "The prison as a community." American Sociological Review 5 (August): 577-583.

Hazelrigg, Lawrence (ed.)
1960 Prison Within Society. Garden City, New Jersey: Anchor Books.

Irwin, John, and Donald R. Cressey
1962 "Thieves, convicts, and the inmate culture." Social Problems 10 (fall): 142-155.

Irwin, John
1970 The Felon. Englewood Cliffs, New Jersey: Prentice-Hall.

Kassebaum, Gene G., David Ward, and Daniel Wilner
1970 Prison Treatment and Parole Survival. New York: Wiley.

Kirkham, George L.
1971 "Homosexuality in prison." Pp. 325-349 in James M. Henslin (ed.), Studies in the Sociology of Sex. New York: Appleton-Century-Crofts.

Moos, Rudolf H.
1968 "The assessment of the social climates of correctional institutions." Journal of Research in Crime and Delinquency 5(July): 174-188.

Reimer, Hans
1937 "Socialization in a prison community." Proceedings of the APA: 151-155.

Sykes, Gresham
1958 The Society of Captives. Princeton, New Jersey: Princeton University Press.

Sykes, Gresham, and Sheldon L. Messinger
1960 "The inmate social system." Pp. 5-20 in Richard Cloward et al. (eds.), Theoretical Studies in Social Organization of the Prison. New York: Social Science Research Council.

Street, David, Robert D. Vinter, and Charles Perrow
1966 Organization for Treatment. New York: Free Press.

Thomas, Charles W.
1970 "Toward a more inclusive model of the inmate contraculture." Criminology 8(November): 251-262.

Ward, David A., and Gene G. Kassenbaum
1965 Women's Prison: Sex and Social Structure. Chicago: Aldine.

Weinberg, S. Kirson
1942 "Aspects of prison's social structure." American Journal of Sociology, 47(March): 717-726.

Wheeler, Stanton
1961 "Socialization in correctional communities." American Sociological Review 26(October): 697-712.

Wellford, Charles
1967 "Factors associated with adoption of the inmate code: a study of normative socialization." Journal of Criminal Law, Criminology, and Police Science 58(2): 197-203.

‘Ladies’ behind bars

A liminal gender as cultural mirror

JOHN M. COGGESHALL

The author is assistant professor of anthropology at Clemson University, Clemson, South Carolina.

‘You here to see the show?’ the inmate leered. The focus of attention was the tall blond then receiving her food in the prison cafeteria. The workers filled her plate with polite deference, and as she walked between the tables her fine blond hair bounced over her shoulders. ‘Make you want to leave home?’ the guard next to me teased. His joke clarified the significance of the episode I had just witnessed. The object of attention was genetically a male, reconstructed as female according to the perception of gender within the cultural rule system of prison. Behind bars, certain males become redefined as ‘ladies’. I have not been able to discern any correlation between assigned gender and the type of crime for which an inmate was sentenced. The process by which this transformation occurs reveals not only clues about gender construction in prison culture, but also suggests perceptions of gender identity in American culture in general.

Prison culture involves one predominant theme: control. To establish identity, males profess a culturally-defined image to defend themselves from oppression by guards and other inmates. Men define themselves as males by juxtaposing maleness with femaleness, fabricating gender identity from the reflection. For inmates, the concept of female emerges from the concept of male. To borrow a well-known metaphor, the rib for Eve’s creation is taken from Adam’s side, and draws both its cultural significance and social status from the extraction. Woman is defined in contrast to man, and takes a lesser place at his side. In prison, males create females in their image, and by doing so, dominate and subjugate them.

The fieldwork upon which this study is based was conducted in two medium-security prisons in southern Illinois between 1984 and 1986. Within that time span I taught three university-level courses to about thirty adult inmates, constituting a range of racial group and criminal record diversity representative of the overall prison population. Their perceptions provided a portion of the field data, supplemented by my observations of and conversations with guards and staff. After having received some instruction on ethnographic data collection, a former student and then resident inmate, Gene Luetkemeyer, volunteered to collect additional information on ‘ladies’ behind bars. His nine detailed interviews of various categories of inmates, identified in the text by pseudonyms, significantly enhanced the scope and detail of the study.

Prison culture is extremely complex, and deserves much more detailed study by anthropologists (see for example the treatment by Goffman 1961, Davidson 1983, and Cardozo-Freeman 1984)[1]. Even my relatively brief ‘incarceration’ has suggested numerous leads for future research. Gender identity in prison could be explored in much greater detail, describing for example the abusive context whereby young males might become pawns by an administration concerned with pacifying gangs. Another productive line of inquiry might explore the overall cultural context of gender identity in prison culture, for themes of sexuality pervade prison, indicating its cultural significance for staff as well as inmates.

Gender perceptions of convicts

Here the research concentrates on the gender perceptions of convicts, i.e. the long-term residents (Davidson 1983). Convict attitudes toward homosexual behaviour vary considerably from one individual to the next. Not all participate, and not all do so with the same self-perception or with the same purposes. A subtle distinction is made by many inmates between individuals who engage entirely in submissive, recipient homosexual intercourse, and those who participate in mutual exchange of pleasure. Further distinctions also exist. Certain types or categories of homosexuals, some of which are discussed below, provide a ranking of these attitudes. Despite intra-cultural variation, widespread agreement prevails on cultural definitions of masculine and feminine gender identities.

Inmates have provided various estimates for the amount of homosexual activity in prison[2]. All agree that long-timers are more likely to engage in such practices, for they have less of a future to anticipate, more opportunities for sexual pleasure to utilize, and relatively lenient punishments for violations. For example, Paul and Sandy, homosexual lovers, and Frank, Paul’s straight friend, believe that about 65% of their prison population engages in homosexual activity, an estimate supported by Dr. B, an incarcerated medical doctor. While such numbers reveal the amount of control and coercion in prisoner culture, they also reveal the ‘need for love, affection, [and] intimate relationships’ denied by the system, another inmate observes. Some ties are based on affection, but these are relatively rare[3]. Homosexual behaviour fulfils numerous functions in the social and cultural system of prison. Thus most inmates see it as at worst a repugnant necessity and at best a tolerable alternative.

Despite varying views on prevalence, prisoners agree on the general gender constructs in prisoner culture. Males in prison adopt a ‘masculine role’, inmates assert. Robert describes ‘a big ... macho weight-lifting virile Tom Selleck type guy’ as typical of the stereotype. Weight lifters, in fact, seem to predominate in the category, for strength suggests masculinity. Real men vigorously protest sexual advances from other males by exhibiting a willingness to fight. Men are also seen as preoccupied with sexual gratification, and will obtain it at all costs.

Real men in prison are perceived as those who can keep, satisfy, and protect ‘women’. The dominant sex partner is termed a ‘daddy’, who watches out for and protects his ‘kid’ or ‘girl’. For some men, the acquisition of sex partners strongly resembles courting, where the pursuer flirts with and purchases commissary (snack foods, cosmetics, and similar items) for the object of his interest. Others acquire submissive sex partners by force. Ultimately, with either type, sexual partnerships are based on power and control, the complete domination of one person and one gender by another. In fact, domination defines the structure of the relationship which distinguishes the genders in prison.

However, in prison, since the culturally-defined females had been males at one time, this presents ‘real’ men with a gender identity problem: reconciling having sexual intercourse with males while maintaining a masculine self-concept. This adjustment is accomplished by means of a unique folk explanation of the origins of gender development and orientation. Basically, males in prison redefine selected males as females.

In direct contrast to these self-perceptions of males, men portray women in a painting of their own creation. Males see females as passive, subordinate, sexual objects. According to Robert, women are 'sweet and charming', 'fluid of movement', with 'seductive gestures'. Dr. B believes that he himself exhibits such effeminate qualities as 'mild manners' and a 'passive demeanour'. Women are also viewed as attractive, and they use that allure to their advantage by feigning helplessness; this allows women to maintain a 'certain power' over men, Paul feels. A woman might 'use her charms' to 'get what she wanted', while at the same time she might not 'put out' sexually, according to Dr. B. Women often tease to coerce men, and sometimes withhold what had apparently been promised, he adds.

Of course, nearly all female staff in prison culture do not meet these stereotypes. By inmate definition, then, they must not be women. Such 'non-women' do not challenge gender constructs but reinforce them further. Female guards and staff occupy positions of power and authority over inmates, decidedly atypical for women from a prisoner's perspective. Moreover, most of these women dress in ways to deliberately de-accentuate anatomical differences and to resemble their male counterparts uniformly. Because these women dress as 'non-women' and control men, they cannot be women and must therefore be homosexuals or 'dykes', as the convicts term them. To inmates, this can be the only explanation for women who do not act like women. Cultural reality persists as potentially disruptive anomalies disappear through redefinition.

Trapped between male and female roles

The process by which certain males become redefined as females in prison provides an example of Victor Turner's (1969) concept of liminality. Prisoner culture perceives certain males as being trapped in between male and female, thus necessitating the release of their true gender identities. The period of incarceration provides the 'time out of time' necessary for the transfiguration to occur. In fact, inmate terms for the metamorphosis reveal this gender ambiguity: males 'turn out' these non-males, transforming them into the cultural equivalent of females. The liminal gender is actually 'male as female', betwixt and between both. Such individuals figuratively 'turn out' to be females, reconstructed according to the prisoner cultural stereotypes of 'female'. They thus become their 'true' selves at last.

This duality creates additional complications in self-identity for such men. Goffman (1961) noted the struggle inmates have in reconciling the staff's perception of them from their own self-concept. Inmates readjusting a sexual orientation share a similar problem. Dr. B explains that individuals who make the transition from male to female must reconcile past heterosexual behaviour with their present homosexual identity. The homosexual in prison must convince herself that this new self-perception had been her true identity all along. Thus she now has adopted the normal role befitting her identity and gender adjustment.

Vindication for the transformation comes as those forced to become homosexuals remain as such. The acceptance by the homosexual of her new gender identity and associated behaviour justifies the conversion in the eyes of the rest of the prison population. If the 'male becoming female' had no natural proclivity or had not been submissive by nature and thus also female, she would never have agreed to have adopted a feminine identity. As Frank (an inmate) explains, those who surrender are weak, and females are weak. Therefore, those who surrender must be female by nature.

Folk conceptions of the origins of gender further support this perspective. Tommy (another inmate) notes that all humans are 'conceived as female, then either, as foetuses, develop genitalia or not'. Some individuals perpetuate, even unconsciously, this dualistic foetal identity into adulthood: they can be transformed or 'turned out'. Not resisting, or not resisting aggressively enough, merely validates this gender liminality. In a sense, it is only appropriate that those trapped betwixt and between be released, to unfetter their true natures. Even coercive gender conversion restores the natural order.

Prisoner culture divides homosexuals into several types, each defined on the basis of degree of sexual promiscuity, amount of self-conceptual pride, and severity of coercion used to turn them out. Generally, status declines as sexual promiscuity increases, self-concept decreases, and the types and intensity of coercion used in the conversion process increase.

The highest status category of homosexuals in prison is that of 'queens' or 'ladies', those who had come out both voluntarily and willingly. Prisoner cultural belief suggests that these individuals had been homosexual on the outside but may have lacked the freedom to have been themselves. Prison has provided them with a treasured opportunity to 'come out', and they have accepted the freedom gratefully. Such individuals maintain a high status by remaining in control of their own lives and of their own self-concept.

Other individuals volunteer to be females, transforming themselves in order to acquire material comforts or social prestige. Terms for this general category vary, depending on the amount of coercion or force needed to 'turn out' the female image. 'Kids', 'gumps', or 'punks' describe individuals who in effect have sold their male identities, surrendering their culturally-defined masculinity to be redefined as females.

Many other inmates, however, are forced to become homosexuals against their initial will. According to Wadley (another inmate):

> everyone is tested. The weak–of personality, personal power, willingness to fight, physical frailty, timidity–are especially susceptible.

'Respect is given to one who can control the life of another', he adds. Those unwilling or unable to control others are thus themselves controlled. According to the cultural rules of gender identity in prison, those who dominate, by natural right, are males, and those who submit, by natural temperament, are females.

A forced female role

Individuals forced to adopt a female role have the lowest status, and are termed 'girls', 'kids', 'gumps', or 'punks'. Kids are kept in servitude by others, as a sign of the owner's power and prestige. Gumps are generally owned or kept by a gang, which collects money by prostituting the sexual favours of the unfortunate inmate. A gump may at one time have volunteered to come out to her feminine identity, but due to lack of personal status or power she has been forced to become sexually promiscuous for money or her physical survival. A punk, most agree, initially hesitates, and is turned out by coercion.

However transformed, most homosexuals in prison

A slightly shorter version of this paper was presented at the 1987 American Anthropological Association meetings in Chicago, Il. A more detailed and more theoretical discussion, including discussants' comments, is planned.

1. In my other writings I have discussed various ways in which inmates successfully retaliate to maintain a sense of identity. Much more could be explored, but space constrains discussion.
2. There are obvious implications for study of the spread of the AIDS virus. From my research it seems that most inmates had not yet thought about acquiring AIDS, probably on account of a low self-concept paralleling that of intravenous drug users. Since homosexual behaviour in prison cannot be eliminated, education and protection should be

stressed.

3. I do not mean to suggest that homosexual relationships in society at large are similar. In this article, I do not deal with homosexuality outside of prison, nor with affectional homosexuality inside prison, which does exist.
4. Racial distinctions become exaggerated in prison. Some research indicates that prison administrations sometimes deliberately exacerbate racial antagonism to 'divide and conquer' gangs by rewarding leaders with homosexuals of the opposite 'race'.

take on a feminine persona and appearance, even assuming a feminine name and requesting feminine pronouns as referents. The external transformation from male to female often is remarkable. Despite the formal restrictions of a dress code in prison, clothing styles may be manipulated rather patently to proclaim gender identity. Hair is often styled or curled and worn long. Even cosmetics are possible: black felt-tip pens provide eye liner and shadow; kool-aid substitutes for blush; and baby powder disguises prominent cheekbones. The personal appearance of homosexuals enhances their identity by demarcating them as obviously different from men.

Homosexuals perform numerous functions depending upon their status and relative freedom. Generally, the higher the status the more control one has over one's activities and one's life. High status individuals such as Sandy select their own lovers. These couples live as husbands and wives, with the 'little woman' providing domestic services such as laundry, cell cleaning, grooming, and sex.

Those with less status perform much the same tasks, but less voluntarily and with less consideration from their daddies. Once an inmate has been forced to adopt a submissive lifestyle, the nightmare of domination becomes more intense. For example, gumps might be forced to pleasure a gang chief, or may be passed down to soldiers in the gang for enjoyment. A particularly attractive kid might be put 'on the stroll', forced to be a prostitute, for the financial benefit of the gang. Business may prove to be so lucrative that some homosexuals must seek protective custody (solitary confinement) to get some rest.

According to Dr. B, some homosexuals actually prefer to be dominated. The prevalent value system in prison suggests that those 'females' who resist sexual attacks vicariously enjoy being dominated physically and sexually by more powerful individuals.

Hated and abused, desired and adored, ladies in prison occupy an important niche: they are the women of that society, constructed as such by the male-based perception of gender identity. In prison, females are termed 'holes' and 'bitches', reflecting the contempt of what Dr. B believes to be characteristic of society's view of lower-class women in general. In prison, he adds, a homosexual 'is likely to receive much of the contempt [and] pent-up hostility that would otherwise be directed at women ...'. Herein lies the key to unlocking the deeper significance of gender construction in prisoner culture.

Gender construction in prison

Recall the general inmate perception of this liminal gender in prisoner culture. Homosexuals are owned and protected by daddies, who provide for their material and social comfort. In exchange, they provide sexual gratification. They often sell themselves and their bodies for material objects, promiscuously using their allure to manipulate men and to improve their social status. They feign helplessness in order to control their men. Ladies are emotional, helpless, and timid, while at the same time petulant, sassy, and demanding, nagging their men for attention. Best suited for certain tasks, homosexuals provide domestic and personal services for their daddies, serving their every whim.

Most fundamentally, homosexuals are sexual objects, to be used, abused, and discarded whenever necessary. Passive recipients of male power, they even enjoy being dominated and controlled. Males do them favours by releasing their 'true' female identities through rape. In prison, sexuality equals power. Males have power, females do not, and thus males dominate and exploit the 'weaker sex'.

Ultimately, in whose image and likeness are these 'males as females' created? Genetically female staff and administrators do not fit the stereotypical view, and thus provide no role models for ladies in prison. Males themselves draft the image of female in prison, forming her from their own perceptions. Males 'turned out' as females perform the cultural role allotted to them by males, a role of submission and passivity. In actuality, males produce, direct, cast, and write the script for the cultural performance of gender identity behind bars.

In prison, woman is made in contrast to the image and likeness of man. Men define women as 'not men', establishing their own self-identity from the juxtapositioning. Gender as a cultural construct is reflexive; each pole draws meaning from a negation of the other. As in Monteros (Brandes 1980:205, 207), folk concepts reinforce the differences, emphasizing maleness at the expense of femaleness and the powerful at the expense of the powerless. By means of sexual domination, women remain in a culturally-defined place of servitude and submission.

Prison culture as a distorting mirror

It is precisely this concept of gender identity that has proven most disquieting about the status of homosexuals in prison. Granted, prison culture fosters a terribly distorted view of American culture[4]. Nevertheless, one sees a shadowy reflection in the mirror of prisoner culture which remains hauntingly familiar. As ladies are viewed by males in prison culture, so are females perceived by many males in American culture. Gender roles and attitudes in prison do not contradict American male values, they merely exaggerate the domination and exploitation already present. In prison gender constructs, one sees not contrasts but caricatures of gender concepts 'on the street'. Thus, the liminal gender of ladies behind bars presents, in reality, a cultural mirror grotesquely reflecting the predominant sexism of American society in general, despite initiatives by women to redefine their position and change gender relationships.

Brandes, Stanley. 1980. *Metaphors of masculinity: sex and status in Andalusian folklore.* Publications of the American Folklore Society (n.s.) Vol.1. Philadelphia: U. of P.P.

Cardozo-Freeman, Inez. 1984. *The joint: language and culture in a maximum-security prison.* Springfield, Il: Thomas.

Davidson, R. Theodore. 1983. *Chicano prisoners: the key to San Quentin.* Prospect Heights, Il: Waveland P.

Goffman, Erving. 1961. *Asylums: essays on the social situation of mental patients and other inmates.* Garden City, NY: Anchor Books.

Turner, Victor. 1969. *The ritual process.* Chicago: Aldine.

Holmesburg Prison, Philadelphia, Pennsylvania

Sexual Assaults in the Philadelphia Prison System and Sheriff's Vans

ALAN J. DAVIS

In the summer of 1968, Joseph F. Mitchell, a slightly-built 19-year-old, was brought to trial before Alexander F. Barbieri, judge of the Court of Common Pleas No. 8 in Philadelphia County. Mitchell's lawyer, Joseph E. Alessandroni, told Judge Barbieri that his client, while being transported in a sheriff's van, had been repeatedly raped by a gang of criminals. A few weeks later, Alessandroni informed the judge that George DiAngelo, a slender 21-year-old whom Barbieri had committed to the Philadelphia Detention Center merely for pre-sentence evaluation, had been sexually assaulted within minutes of his admission.

Judge Barbieri thereupon appointed me, then Chief Assistant District Attorney of Philadelphia, to investigate these allegations. Police Commissioner Frank L. Rizzo started a parallel investigation; then these two investigations were merged.

In the Philadelphia prison system there are three facilities: the Detention Center, Holmesburg Prison, and the House of Correction. The period we chose to study was from June 1966 to July 31, 1968—a little over two years. Out of the 60,000 inmates who passed through the prison system in those 26 months, we interviewed 3,304—virtually all of them inmates during the period of our investigation. We also interviewed 561 out of the 570 custodial employees. We took 130 written statements from those who had given us important information, and gave polygraph ("lie-detector") examinations to 45 of them. We asked 26 employees to take polygraph tests: 25 refused, and the one employee who took the test "passed." We asked 48 inmates: seven refused, and of the 41 remaining, 10 failed the test and 31 passed. (We ignored the statements of those prisoners and employees who either would not take the test or who failed it.) In addition, we interviewed several people whom we believed had special information, and we reviewed all of the reports dealing with homosexuality issued by the prison system since June 1966. Finally, we made a number of detailed personal inspections of the prison facilities and of the sheriff's vans.

In brief, we found that sexual assaults in the Philadelphia prison system are epidemic. As Superintendent Hendrick and three of the wardens admitted, virtually every slightly-built young man committed by the courts is sexually approached within a day or two after his admission to prison. Many of these young men are repeatedly raped by gangs of inmates. Others, because of the threat of gang rape, seek protection by entering into a homosexual relationship with an individual tormentor. Only the tougher and more hardened young men, and those few so obviously frail that they are immediately locked up for their own protection, escape homosexual rape.

After a young man has been raped, he is marked as a sexual victim for the duration of his confinement. This mark follows him from institution to institution. Many of these young men return to their communities ashamed, and full of hatred.

This, then, is the sexual system that exists in the Philadelphia prisons. It is a system that imposes a punishment that is not, and could not be, included in the sentence of the court. Indeed, it is a system under which the least hardened criminals, and many men later found to be innocent, suffer the most.

A few typical examples of such sexual assaults may convey the enormity of the problem. In an early draft of our report, an attempt was made to couch this illustrative material in sociological, medical, and legal terminology less offensive than the raw, ugly language used by the witness and victims. This approach was abandoned. The incidents are raw and ugly. Any attempt to prettify them would be hypocrisy.

A witness describes the ordeal of *William McNichol*, 24 years old and mentally disturbed:

"That was June 11th, I was assigned to E Dorm. Right after the light went out I saw this colored male, Cheyenne—I think his last name is Boone. He went over and was talking to this kid and slapped him in the face with a belt. He was saying come on back with us and the kid kept saying I don't want to. After being slapped with the belt he walked back with Cheyenne and another colored fellow named Horse. They were walking him back into E Dorm. They were telling him to put his hand down and stop crying so the guard will not know what is going on. I looked up a couple of times. They had the kid on the floor. About 12 fellows took turns with him. This went on for about two hours.

"After this he came back to his bed and he was crying and he stated that 'They all took turns on me.' He laid there for about 20 minutes and Cheyenne came over to the kid's bed and pulled his pants down and got on top of him and raped him again. When he got done Horse did it again and then about four or five others got on him. While one of the guys was on him, raping him, Horse came over and said, 'Open your mouth and suck on this and don't bite it.' He then put his penis in his mouth and made him suck on it. The kid was hollering that he was gagging and Horse stated, 'you better not bite it or I will kick your teeth out.'

"While they had this kid they also had a kid named William in another section in E Dorm. He had his pants off and he was bent over and they were taking turns on him. This was Horse, Cheyenne, and about seven other colored fellows. Two of the seven were brothers.

"Horse came back and stated, 'Boy, I got two virgins in one night. Maybe I should make it three.' At this time he was standing over me. I stated, 'What are you looking at?' and he said 'We'll save him for tomorrow night.' "

Julius Brown, 18 years old:

"Brown stated that he has been in Holmesburg since March 29, 1968, and that about a week and a half ago,

A Note on This Report

This article is based on the results of a three-month investigation conducted jointly by the Philadelphia District Attorney's office and the Police Department, under the supervision of the author. It culminated in a 103-page report submitted to Judge Alexander F. Barbieri and the public on Sept. 11, 1968. More than half of the report contains detailed recommendations for controlling sexual assaults and for the general reform of the Philadelphia prison system. Many of these recommendations are now being implemented by the city administration. This article relates only to those portions of the report analyzing sexual assaults and comparing the physical and psychological characteristics of the victims and aggressors.

on Thursday, he was in I block; his cell was number 926. On this date, in the morning after breakfast, James Williams called him into his cell; he went into William's cell. Donald Reese was in there also. Further that he had owed Williams four cartons of cigarettes. Williams said to him that he would have to give the cigarettes back right now or he would have to give them something else. He [Brown] then started to walk out of the cell and Williams pushed him down. Williams picked up the window pole, Reese picked up a bench and stood blocking the door. Reese told him that if he goes to the guard they are going to get him anyway; there were other men outside the cell.

"Further that he walked out of the cell, they were all around him and walked to cell 971, and they pushed him inside. He went over and sat on the toilet seat. Twin [Roger Jones] came into the cell, they made him lay down on the floor, and Twin pulled his [Brown's] pants down and made him lay face down. Twin pushed his [Brown's] legs apart and Twin put his penis into his [Brown's] rectum. He was on him until he discharged. When he got through, Brown saw that he was bleeding from the rectum. Then Twin, Williams, Reese, and McDuffy told him that if he went to the guard their boys would get him to D block, and he was scared then to tell the guard. Further that he did cry out when Twin did this to him, but the guard wouldn't be able to hear him because the block is long.

"Brown went on to say that the next day after chow [breakfast] James Williams, McDuffy, Ike (Isaiah Franklin), and Leftenant got him in cell 972 [Roger Jones's cell]. They told him that everything is cool now as long as he doesn't tell. Further that he had never been in jail before and he was too scared to tell anybody. Then four of them did it to him—they put their penises into his rectum, James first, Ike second, Leftenant third, McDuffy fourth. Twin did not bother him that time. That after they did this he was bleeding and got sick.

"That night, Roach [Thomas Roach] came into his cell and changed with his partner. Roach told him that he would have to do it. When the guard came to check the cells, Roach turned over so he wouldn't be recognized. After the guard counted and left, Roach got on top of him, put his penis into his [Brown's] rectum, and discharged."

Nineteen-Year-Old Is Beaten

Charles Williams, 19 years old:

"On Tuesday morning, the first week of June at about 9:30 A.M., I was in my cell 412 on D block and I had started to clean up. A tall, heavy-set fella came into the cell and asked for a mirror and shaving brush and a comb, and that my cell partner said he could borrow.

"He then said that he heard something about me concerning homosexual acts. I told him what he had heard was not true. He then started to threaten me and if I didn't submit to him. Then I hit him with my fist in his face before he could hit me. Then about three more men came into the cell, and they started to beat me up, too. I fought back the best I could and then I fell on the floor and I got kicked in the ribs. Three guys were holding me while the other one tore my pants off; I continued to fight until one of the guys knocked me out. One of the guys was holding me on the floor and had my arm pinned to the floor. And about seven or eight guys came into the cell and they took turns sticking their penis up my ass. When they finished they left my cell, and I was still laying on the floor."

Clarence Garlick, 26 years old:

"Back in April this year, about 10:30 A.M. I was in my cell 455 on block D when Joe Lovett came into my cell. I was laying on my bed. When he came in I jumped up. He told me to get greased up. I told him I wasn't going to do nothing. He told me, 'You're going to do something.' He started punching me. I had backed up into a corner of the cell. He seen some mineral-oil grease I had on the table and he reached over and handed it to me saying, 'Put this on.' I put some on and layed down on the bed. He took out his penis and got on top of me. After he did what he wanted to do he got up and got some toilet paper and wiped himself off and went out of the cell."

"This is the second incident. He came to me on July 18, 1968, in the morning about 10 o'clock. I was standing up in the doorway of my cell, 455. He told me to 'Get it fixed.' I told him I wasn't going to do nothing, that today was my birthday. He walked on away."

"The next day, on the 19th, he came to me again. I was in my cell, this was about the same time. He stated, 'Today isn't your birthday, you're going to do something.' I told him I wasn't going to do anything. He started punching me again. I told him I was going to call the guard. He stated, 'Go ahead and call, you'll only call him one time and I'll knock you out.' He got the grease from off the table and handed it to me, told me to put some on, which I did. I laid down on the bed, he took out his penis and got on top. A friend he walks with, Kincaid, was standing out by the door, he was laughing. Joe got up after he got through, got toilet paper and wiped himself off. He then walked out of the cell."

During the 26-month period, we found, there had been 156 sexual assaults that could be documented and substantiated—through institutional records, polygraph examinations, or other corroboration. Seven of the assaults took place in the sheriff's vans, 149 in the prisons. Of the sexual assaults, 82 consisted of buggery; 19 of fellatio; and 55 of attempts and coercive solicitations to commit sexual acts. There were assaults on at least 97 different victims by at least 176 different aggressors. With unidentified victims and aggressors, there were 109 different victims and 276 different aggressors.

For various reasons, these figures represent only the top of the iceberg.

■ Our investigators, as mentioned, interviewed only a twentieth of the inmates who passed through the prison system. We discovered 94 assaults—excluding those reported in institutional records. This suggests that if all 60,000 inmates had been interviewed, 20 times 94—or 1880—additional assaults would have come to light.

■ Almost all of the victims still in prison were so terrified of retaliation by other prisoners that they were very reluctant to cooperate with us.

■ Many guards discouraged complaints by indicating that they did not want to be bothered. One victim screamed for over an hour while he was being gang-raped in his cell; the block guard ignored the screams and laughed at the victim when the rape was over. The inmates who reported this passed a polygraph examination. The guard who had been named refused to take the test.

Then too, some guards put pressure on victims not to complain—such complaints, after all, would indicate that the guards were failing in their duty. We found many cases where victims, after filing complaints, had "voluntarily" refused to prosecute, and a number of them told us that guards urged them to rely on prison discipline rather than to bring the facts out into the open. Very often, these guards asked the victim if he wanted his parents and friends to find out about his humiliation.

■ Without prompting from the prison guards, many victims and their families wanted to avoid the shame and dishonor they believed would follow such a complaint.

■ Inmates have little faith in the ability of a guard to protect them from retaliation should they complain. Their fears are justified by the lack of supervision by guards, and the inadequate facilities to provide security for complainants.

■ Inmates who complain are themselves punished by the prison system. It is usual procedure to place a victim of a sexual assault on "lock-in feed-in," obstensibly for his own protection. This means that after a complaint is made, and especially if it is pressed, the complainant is locked in his cell all day, fed in his cell, and not permitted recreation, television, or exercise until it is determined that he is safe from retaliation. Many victims consider this "solitary confinement" worse than a homosexual relationship with one aggressor.

■ Sometimes very little comes of a complaint. Some compaints are just not acted upon; action, when taken,

Steel vans like this one, which are neither heated in winter nor ventilated in summer, are used to transport prisoners. Despite crowding, sexual assaults often occur on the rides between courthouse and prison.

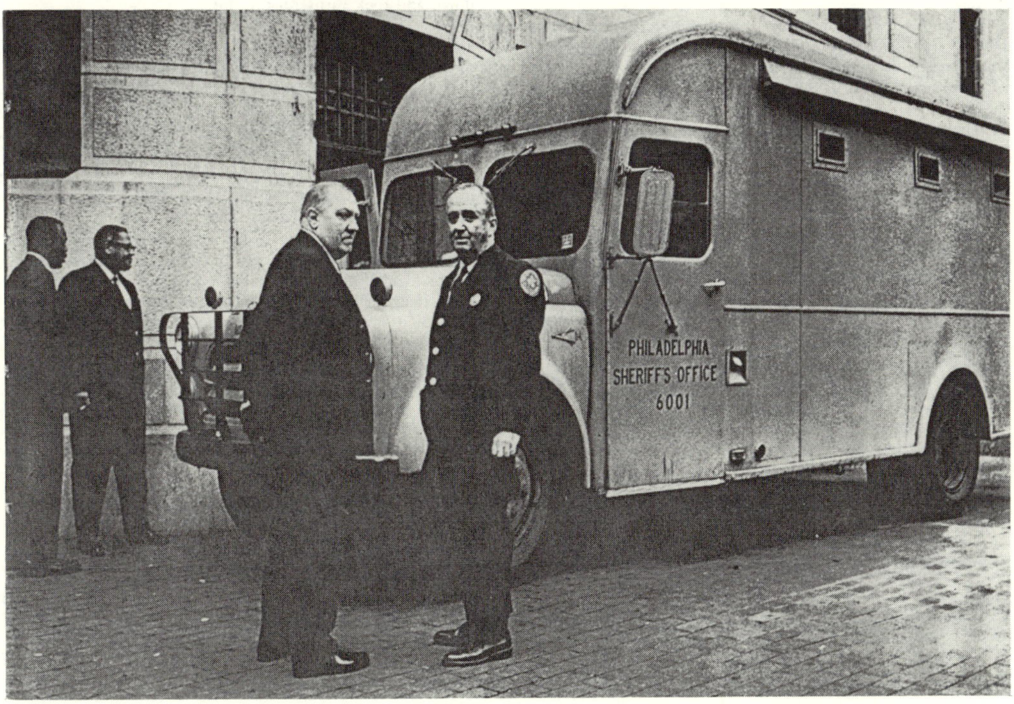

The Sheriff's Vans

The sheriff of Philadelphia County is responsible for transporting prisoners between the courts and the various county and state prisons. For this purpose, there are five sheriff's vans and seven station wagons. Only five inmates can be carried in each station wagon. Some 35 to 40 inmates are crammed into each van. Since hundreds of prisoners must be transported back and forth each day, the vans do most of the work.

Investigators are in complete accord with the following essay written by one articulate inmate who had traveled on the vans some 50 times:

"Prisoners confined in Philadelphia's three prisons commute from their institutions to the courts by way of a prison van. The van is a truck externally resembling the sort of refrigerated delivery truck that delivers meat to food stores. The body of the truck has no windows. At the very top of the truck there is a tiny row of slots purportedly for ventilating purposes.

"Winter—The van is parked overnight in the House of Correction. At eight o'clock in the morning the van driver picks it up and drives it to the Detention Center. There, some 40 prisoners, who have been waiting since six o'clock (packed like sardines in a steel-barred can), are loaded into the van. It has only seating capacity for 15 people. The rest must make themselves 'comfortable' as best they can. There are no handholds. There is no heat. It is freezing with an intensity so great that some prisoners relinquish their seats: The pain of frozen iron pressed against their backsides is unendurable. Packed into the mass of men they may find a little warmth jammed together. The trip from northeast Philadelphia is an hour of grinding stops and bumping halts. The standing men are tossed about inside the van. There is no light in the vehicle and the darkness is punctured by the grunts and groans.

"Summer—The prison van is a sweltering cauldron of red-hot cast iron. The packed bodies of men stink. Prisoners who were arrested in winter are still in their heavy clothes. The sun winks occasionally through the narrow slits on top, but the outside air remains aloof, not wishing to contaminate itself with this Dante's Inferno on wheels.

"Some Interesting Highlights—Riding in the prison van is virtually the only time in a prisoner's detention that he is completely unsupervised, and some strange things do occur. If anyone is homosexually inclined, and it is summer, a stinking sex orgy may take place in the dim confines of the van. Sometimes this is with mutual consent, sometimes by coercion. All the time it is done with utter disregard for the feelings of the other men in the van, who cannot even avert their faces. Sometimes a prisoner who is going to be a [state] witness is accidentally thrown into the company of the very people he is going to testify against. Threats and even violence break out. The van drivers roll merrily on their way, blissfully unaware of what is taking place.

"The prisoners are alone in their walled-up cage, alone with their dry bologna sandwiches that must serve as sustenance for the next 24 hours. No cooked meal awaits them at the Detention Center when they return from court at night, only the same bologna sandwich. On the return trip from court, the van drops prisoners off at Holmesburg, the Detention Center, and the House of Correction, in that order. At Holmesburg the van drives into a walled-off enclosure that is barred by two massive solid doors and topped by solid concrete and steel. Believe me, it's a very snug fit. It generally takes between 15 to 20 minutes of paperwork until the van is allowed to proceed, and during this time the already high temperature rises sharply, the atmosphere becomes completely stagnant, and the waiting becomes interminable and finally unbearable. The prisoners scream and bang on the sides of the van but there is no relief. The time never gets any shorter, sometimes it gets longer.

"It is difficult to comprehend how the city justifies the van as treatment for untried, unconvicted, unsentenced men, who are the bulk of its passengers.

"I know, as a matter of fact, that the Interstate Commerce Commission requires that certain minimum space be provided for each individual hog shipped in commerce. Couldn't untried prisoners get the same that a pig gets?

"I have written these few words not out of bitterness, but out of the experience of 50 trips.

"I was there, Charlie."

Dennis Cujdik, a 17-year-old charged only with being a runaway from home, describes his ride on the van:

"I was at 1801 Vine in a cell when four Negro boys started bothering me for not having underwear on. Then when we got on the sheriff's van and started moving they told everyone that I didn't have on underwear. As the van was moving they started getting close to me. One of them touched me and I told them to please stop.

"All of a sudden a coat was thrown over my face and when I tried to pull it off I was viciously punched in the face for around ten minutes. I fell to the floor and they kicked me all over my body, including my head and my privates. They ripped my pants from me and five or six of them held me down and took turns fucking me.

"My insides feel sore and my body hurts, my head hurts, and I feel sick in the stomach. Each time they stopped I tried to call for help, but they put their hands over my mouth so that I couldn't make a sound. While they held me, they burned my leg with a cigarette. When the van stopped at the prison, they wiped the blood from me with my shirt. They threatened my life and said they would get me in D1 if I told anyone what happened. They said that if they didn't get me in D1 they'd get me in the van again. When the door opened they pushed me to the back so they could get out first. At first, I told the guard I tripped and fell, but then I thought I'd better tell the truth. I pointed out those who beat me up. A doctor looked at me and said I'd have to go to the hospital. They took pictures of the bruises on my body, and I could just about breathe because my nose and jaw seemed to be broken in many different places. I was asked by the lieutenant to write down what happened, and this is exactly what happened."

Why has this situation been allowed to continue for so long, despite the fact that it was brought to the attention of public officials at least two years ago? The answer is simple: The responsible city officials have blatantly neglected their duty.

usually consists of putting the aggressor in the "hole" for 30 days or less. Meanwhile, the victim also is usually locked in, and looks forward—when released—to terror from the aggressor's friends, and from the aggressor himself when he is let out of the "hole." Finally,

■ Many of the victims themselves distrust and are hostile to constituted authority, and could not bring themselves to cooperate by filing a complaint.

Taking all of these facts into consideration, we conservatively estimate that the true number of assaults in the 26-month period was about 2000. Indeed, one guard put the number at 250 a year in the Detention Center alone.

Of the estimated 2000 assaults that occurred, 156 of which were documented, the inmates reported only 96 to prison authorities. Of this 96, only 64 were mentioned in the prison records. Of these 64, only 40 resulted in internal discipline against the aggressors; and only 26 incidents were reported to the police for prosecution.

Consensual Homosexuality Excluded

Now, in our study of sexual assaults we excluded any that were cases of truly "consensual" homosexuality. Nonetheless, it was hard to separate consensual homosexuality from rape, since many continuing and isolated homosexual liaisons originated from a gang rape, or from the ever-present threat of gang rape. Similarly, many individual homosexual acts were possible only because of the fear-charged atmosphere. Thus, a threat of rape, expressed or implied, would prompt an already fearful young man to submit. Prison officials are too quick to label such activities "consensual."

At the opposite end of the spectrum from innocent victims of homosexual rape are the male prostitutes. These homosexuals—known as "sissys," "freaks," or "girls"—were supposed to be segregated from the general prison population, yet they were readily available. We learned of repeated instances where homosexual "security" cells were left unguarded by a staff that was too small or too indifferent, or who turned their backs so that certain favored inmates could have sexual relations.

Many of these male prostitutes were created not only by force and the threat of force, but by bribery. The fact is that a person with economic advantage in prison often uses it to gain sexual advantage. Typically, an experienced inmate will give cigarettes, candy, sedatives, stainless-steel blades, or extra food pilfered from the kitchen to an inexperienced inmate, and after a few days the veteran will demand sexual repayment. It is also typical for a veteran to entice a young man into gambling, have him roll up large debts, and then tell the youth to "pay or fuck." An initial sexual act stamps the victim as a "punk boy," and he is pressed into prostitution for the remainder of his imprisonment.

Despite the important role that economic advantage plays in the creation of homosexuality, it is virtually impossible to obliterate economic distinctions between inmates. Even a small accumulation of money or luxuries gives an inmate substantial economic advantage: In the prison economy, a shopworker earns 15 to 25 cents a day; half of the inmates have no prison jobs at all, and most inmates get little or no material help from friends or relatives outside the prison.

It is the duty of prison officials to reduce the economic power that any inmate might exercise over another inmate. Yet we discovered one area in which Philadelphia prison officials, either through neglect or indifference, disregarded this duty. As a result, at least one inmate became so powerful economically that he was able to choose, as cellmates, a series of young men he found attractive, and then use bribery to sexually subvert each one.

The University of Pennsylvania and a private concern operate a large laboratory on H block of Holmesburg Prison, where they test inmates' reactions to new medicines and to experimental commercial products like soaps, shaving creams, suntan lotions, and toilet tissue. The prisoners are excellent "human guinea pigs" (1) because they live under controlled conditions, and (2) because they will submit to tests for a fraction of the fee that a free individual would demand. Prison officials—because there is very little other activity for the prisoners, and because the laboratory pays 20 percent of the inmates' wages to the prison system—have allowed the project to expand to the extent that it constitutes a separate government within the prison system.

All the inmates at Holmesburg wanted to "get on the tests" because, by prison standards, they can earn a fortune. Just by wearing a chemical patch on his back, for example, a prisoner can earn $10 to $15 a week. By participating in some tests that last longer, a prisoner—for doing almost nothing—will receive over $100. Altogether, the Holmesburg inmates earn more than $250,000 a year from the project. A few prisoners end up with bodies crazyquilted with motley scars and skin

Alan J. Davis is an associate with the firm of Wolf, Block, Schorr and Solis-Cohen in Philadelphia. In his law practice he specializes in civil and criminal trial work. After his training at Harvard Law School, where he edited the *Harvard Law Review*, he was Clerk to the Honorable John Biggs, Jr., Chief Judge of the United States Court of Appeals for the Third Circuit.

patches, but to these men, in the context of a prison economy, it seems well worth it.

To save money another way, the operators of the project also use inmates as laboratory assistants. An experienced assistant, working an eight-hour day, will get $100 a month—in the prison economy, the equivalent of a millionaire's income. Even a few prison guards are employed in the project, after their regular hours, and they work side by side with the prisoners.

University of Pennsylvania Project Disastrous

Generally, the "U. of P." project has had a disastrous effect upon the operations of Holmesburg Prison; it is one of the reasons why morale of the employees is at the lowest in that institution. The disproportionate wealth and power in the hands of a few inmates leads to favoritism, bribery and jealousy among the guards, resulting in disrespect for supervisory authority and prison regulations. What is more, the project contributed to homosexuality in the prison.

Stanley Randall, a 38-year-old con man serving a four- to eleven-year sentence, was employed in laboratory cell 806, H block, as an assistant. Although prison and laboratory officials at first denied it, Randall had the power to decide which inmates would serve as subjects on various tests. Since the 806 cell disbursed $10,000 to $20,000 a year, Randall's power was considerable.

Randall's special taste was newly admitted young inmates. Through his influence with the guard staff he had his pick of these young men assigned to him as cellmates—and for as long as he wished. When his victims moved in, Randall solicited them to engage in sexual acts in return for his giving them a steady stream of luxuries and for "getting them on the tests." At least half a dozen of these inmates submitted, and went on to profit handsomely from the University of Pennsylvania project.

Although top prison officials assured us that no inmate was permitted to earn more than $1200 a year, and that $400 was unusually high, in six months Randall's present cellmate had earned over $800. The record was held by a prior cellmate of Randall's, who had earned $1740 in just 11 months. When we asked university project managers about these high incomes, they told us they had never heard of any $1200-a-year-limit. The prison's accounting office had apparently never heard of this $1200-a-year limit either, because that office had credited these high amounts to the accounts of Randall's cellmates.

How had Randall managed to get his choice of cellmates? One guard told us that H-block guards had been instructed by "higher ups" not to interfere in the affairs of inmates working for the U. of P. Another guard reported he had received such instructions, and said they had come from the guard lieutenant. The lieutenant denied this, and agreed to take a lie-detector test. Later he reversed his position and refused. Randall admitted he had often given cigars to this lieutenant.

Other inmates besides Randall exploited their powerful positions. One inmate worker, for example, forged test results and fee vouchers, and got fees for inmates who had not actually been test subjects. It also seems that at least a few guards were also corrupted.

As a result of our investigation, prison officials have relieved the powerful inmate workers of their positions with the U. of P. project. They are also considering phasing out the project entirely.

How did sexual aggressors in the prisons differ from their victims? On the average, aggressors tended to be older, heavier, taller, and more serious offenders. Data on hundreds of victims and aggressors yielded the following comparisons:

	Victims	Aggressors
Average Age	20.75	23.67
Average Height	5'8¼"	5'9"
Average Weight	140.9	157.2

Both victims and aggressors tended to be younger than the average inmate, as comparison with the following table shows:

	Average Age of Prisoners (July 31, 1968)
Detention Center	27.9
Holmesburg	29.3
House of Correction	28.9
All Prisons	28.8

Yet although aggressors on the average are older and larger than victims, these differences are rather slight. In many cases, there may be no differences, and in others they are reversed. Still, after having observed hundreds of victims and aggressors we believe that there are other, more subjective, physical criteria which can be used to differentiate between aggressors and victims:

- Victims tend to look young for their age.
- Victims tend to look less athletic, and less physically coordinated.
- Victims tend to be better-looking.

A comparison of 164 aggressors and 103 victims showed that 68 percent of the former and only 38 percent of the latter had been charged with serious felonies. Among aggressors, violent assaultive felonies were particularly common. Thus, 14 aggressors had been charged with rape, but only three victims; six aggressors had been charged with weapons offenses, and no victims; 34 aggressors with robbery and aggravated robbery, but only eight victims; and seven aggressors with assault with intent to kill, but only one victim.

As many victims as aggressors, however, had been charged with homicide. On the other hand, many more victims than aggressors were charged with relatively less serious offenses, such as the larceny of a car, going AWOL from the armed forces, violating parole, and delinquency.

We also made a study of the 129 documented assaults in which the races of both aggressors and victims had been ascertained, and found that a disproportionate number involved Negro aggressors and white victims:

Type of Incident	Number of Incidents	Percentage
White Aggressors & White Victims	20	15%
Negro Aggressors & Negro Victims	37	29%
White Aggressors & Negro Victims	0	0%
Negro Aggressors & White Victims	72	56%
Total	129	100%

These statistics in part reflect the fact that 80 percent of the inmates are Negro—it is safer for a member of a majority group to single out for attack a member of a minority group. Then too, Negro victims seemed more reluctant than white victims to disclose assaults by Negro aggressors. But it also seems true that current racial tensions and hostilities in the outside community are aggravated in a criminal population.

Now, we are not professionally qualified to offer a scientific theory to explain the sexual aggression in the Philadelphia prison system. We have, however, reached certain conclusions that should be recorded for possible use by psychiatrists, psychologists, and social scientists. The conclusions and the analysis set forth are based upon our observations, upon pertinent literature, and upon discussions with a psychiatrist and a psychologist who are experts in forensic psychology.

- We were struck by the fact that the typical sexual aggressor does not consider himself to be a homosexual, or even to have engaged in homosexual acts. This seems to be based upon his startlingly primitive view of sexual relationships, one that defines as male whichever partner is aggressive and as homosexual whichever partner is passive.
- It appears that need for sexual release is not the primary motive of a sexual aggressor. After all, in a sexually segregated population, autoeroticism would seem a much easier and more "normal" method of release than homosexual rape. As recent studies have shown (Masters and Johnson, *Human Sexual Response*, 1966), autoerotic stimulation yields a measure of physical release and pleasure similar to that yielded by sexual intercourse.
- A primary goal of the sexual aggressor, it is clear, is the conquest and degradation of his victim. We re-

peatedly found that aggressors used such language as "Fight or fuck," "We're going to take your manhood," "You'll have to give up some face," and "We're gonna make a girl out of you." Some of the assaults were reminiscent of the custom in some ancient societies of castrating or buggering a defeated enemy.

■ Another primary goal of many of the aggressors, it appears, is to retain membership in the groups led by militant sexual aggressors. This is particularly true of some of the participants in gang rapes. Lacking identification with such groups, as many of the aggressors know, they themselves would become victims. And finally,

■ Most of the aggressors seem to be members of a subculture that has found most nonsexual avenues of asserting their masculinity closed to them. To them, job success, raising a family, and achieving the respect of other men socially have been largely beyond reach. Only sexual and physical prowess stands between them and a feeling of emasculation. When the fact of imprisonment, and the emptiness of prison life, knock from under them whatever props to their masculinity they may have had, they became almost totally dependent for self-esteem upon an assertion of their sexual and physical potency.

In sum, sexual assaults, as opposed to consensual homosexuality, are not primarily caused by sexual deprivation. They are expressions of anger and aggression prompted by the same basic frustrations that exist in the community, and which very probably were significant factors in producing the rapes, robberies, and other violent offenses for which the bulk of the aggressors were convicted. These frustrations can be summarized as an inability to achieve masculine identification and pride through avenues other than sex. When these frustrations are intensified by imprisonment, and superimposed upon hostility between the races and a simplistic view of all sex as an act of aggression and subjugation, then the result is assaults on members of the same sex.

Assuming that this analysis is valid, then the principal psychological causes of sexual assaults in the Philadelphia prison system are deeply rooted in the community—in that millions of American men, throughout their lives, are deprived of any effective way of achieving masculine self-identification through avenues other than physical aggression and sex. They belong to a class of men who rarely have meaningful work, successful families, or opportunities for constructive emotional expression and individual creativity. Therefore, although sexual assaults within a prison system may be controlled by intensive supervision and effective programing, the pathology at the root of sexual assaults will not be eliminated until fundamental changes are made in the outside community.

SOCIAL ROLES IN A PRISON FOR WOMEN

ROSE GIALLOMBARDO
New York University

A neglected area in deviance studies of the adult prison setting concerns female forms of deviation. The study of deviance in the prison setting has typically been concerned with male forms of deviation. Indeed, with the exception of Harper's analysis of the "fringer" role[1] and the recently reported study of a women's prison by Ward and Kassebaum[2] which describes the homosexual adaptation of female inmates, scientific description and analysis of the informal organization of the adult female prison have been overlooked.[3] In the present paper, in-

The complete study is reported in *Society of Women: A Study of a Women's Prison*, New York: John Wiley and Sons, forthcoming. The writer is indebted to Richard D. Schwartz and Paul J. Bohannan for their critical reading and comments of an earlier version of this paper. Acknowledgment is also made to Eliot Freidson for his constructive criticism and invaluable suggestions.

1 Ida Harper, "The Role of the 'Fringer' in a State Prison for Women," *Social Forces*, 31 (October, 1952), pp. 53-60.

2 David A. Ward and Gene G. Kassebaum, "Lesbian Liaisons," *Transaction*, 1 (January, 1964), pp. 28-32. Also David A. Ward and Gene G. Kassebaum, "Homosexuality: A Mode of Adaptation in a Prison for Women," *Social Problems*, 12 (Fall, 1964), pp. 159-177. In this institution, the authors found little evidence of the differentiated social types or of inmate solidarity that is typical of the male prison.

3 In this connection, it should be pointed out that in addition to the aforementioned studies of the adult women's prison, there are several reports of institutions for juvenile girls which reveal homosexual practices and/or the presence of "family" groups among the delinquent girls. These reports are unsystematic investigations and impressionistic reports. See, for example, Charles A. Ford, "Homosexual Practices of Institutionalized Females," *Journal of Abnormal and Social Psychology*, 23 (January-March, 1929), pp. 442-444; Margaret Otis, "A Perversion Not Commonly Noted," *Journal of Abnormal Psychology*, 8 (June-July, 1913), pp. 112-114; Lowell S. Selling, "The Pseudo Family," *The American Journal of Sociology*, 37 (September,

mate social roles and social organization in a women's prison will be described in some detail; comparisons of this informal social structure will be made with relevant literature on the social roles assumed by male prisoners; and the social structure inside the prison setting will be viewed in relation to the external environment.

Previous accounts of the male prison have taken the view that the most important features of the inmate culture emerge as a response to the conditions of imprisonment. The features of this system are well-known and need not be repeated here.[4] The point to be stressed, however, is that the functional interpretation which is made for the emergence of the inmate system typically views the culture that forms within the prison as a response to the problems found in the internal world of the prison and the crucial ways in which it differs from the external world. It is argued that while the prisoner cannot completely eliminate the pains of imprisonment, a cohesive inmate system which has group allegiance as its dominant value provides the inmate with a meaningful reference group that may reinstate the inmate's self image, or in some sense neutralize the deleterious effects of its loss. This formulation derives from case studies of single institutions, and, therefore, it is extremely difficult to ascertain the validity of the conclusions drawn as previous writers have not explored systematically the interaction of the external culture with the conditions for survival faced by the prison aggregate. Nor has anyone assessed several adult prisons simultaneously so that a comparative analysis could be made.[5] I think we are just beginning to understand the variability of one prison from another as they are affected by organizational goals, the composition of staff and inmates. Indeed, recent systematic studies of socialization in the male prison by Wheeler and Garabedian call into question the solidary opposition model

1931), pp. 247-253; Seymour L. Halleck and Marvin Hersko, "Homosexual Behavior in a Correctional Institution for Adolescent Girls," *American Journal of Orthopsychiatry,* 32 (October, 1962), pp. 911-917; Sidney Kosofsky and Albert Ellis, "Illegal Communication Among Institutionalized Female Delinquents," *The Journal of Social Psychology,* 48 (August, 1958), pp. 155-160; Romolo Toigo, "Illegitimate and Legitimate Cultures in a Training School for Girls," *Proceedings of the Rip Van Winkle Clinic,* 13 (Summer, 1962), pp. 3-29. Ward and Kassebaum, however, reported that there were no indications of family groups in the prison they studied; *Social Problems, op. cit.*

4 See esp. Gresham M. Sykes and Sheldon L. Messinger, "The Inmate Social System" in *Theoretical Studies in Social Organization of the Prison,* New York: Social Science Research Council, March, 1960, pp. 5-19; Gresham M. Sykes, *The Society of Captives,* Princeton, New Jersey: Princeton University Press, 1958; Erving Goffman, "On the Characteristics of Total Institutions: Staff-Inmate Relations," in Donald R. Cressey (ed.), *The Prison: Studies in Institutional Organization and Change,* New York: Holt, Rinehart and Winston, 1961, chs. 1 and 2; Richard A. Cloward, "Social Control in the Prison," *Theoretical Studies in the Social Organization of the Prison, op. cit.,* pp. 20-48. See also Donald Clemmer, *The Prison Community,* New York: Holt, Rinehart and Winston, 1958 (reissue of the 1940 edition); Morris G. Caldwell, "Group Dynamics in the Prison Community," *Journal of Criminal Law, Criminology and Police Science,* 46 (January-February, 1956), pp. 648-657; Norman S. Hayner, "Washington State Correctional Institutions as Communities," *Social Forces,* 21 (1943), pp. 316-322; Norman S. Hayner and Ellis Ash, "The Prison as a Community," *American Sociological Review,* 5 (August, 1940), pp. 577-583; Hans Reimer, "Socialization in the Prison Community," *Proceedings of the American Prison Association,* 1937, pp. 151-155.

5 It is interesting that an analysis of variations in organizational goals and an examination of data on the inmates of several juvenile correctional institutions for boys call into question the "solidary opposition" model of the inmate group. See David Street, "The Inmate Group in Custodial and Treatment Settings," *American Sociological Review,* 30 (February, 1965), pp. 40-55.

of inmate culture even within single institutions, as these scholars found that prisoners varied in their support of the inmate culture over time and according to type of prisoner.[6]

Moreover, Irwin and Cressey have advanced the thesis that there are three subcultures in the prison which they maintain reflect the presence of different types of prisoners. These differences presumably are a reflection of the values and attitudes particular inmates bring into the prison and are related to latent identities.[7] Similarly, Schrag attempts to account for inmate deviants with respect to internalization of inmate culture and support of the inmate code in terms of their preprison characteristics and identities.[8] Thus, the developing theoretical considerations tend to emphasize values and attitudes learned by inmates prior to entering the prison.

The present findings from a case study of a women's prison bear on this matter. In the adult female prison which the writer studied, it was found that in order to cope with the major problems of institutional living, the female inmates have also labeled the reactions of prisoners according to the mode of response exhibited by the inmate to the prison situation and the quality of the inmate's interaction with other inmates and staff. However, although the deprivations of imprisonment were present and felt keenly by the female prisoners, the female argot roles differ in structural form and in the sentiment attached to them from the roles assumed by male prisoners. In addition, it should be pointed out that homosexual dyads cast into marriage alliances, family groups, and other kinship ties formed by the inmates integrate the inmates into a meaningful social system and represent an attempt to create a substitute universe within the prison.[9]

The empirical evidence to be presented supports the thesis that differences in the informal social structure in male and female prison communities can be understood in terms of the differential cultural definitions ascribed to male and female roles in American society. More specifically, it is suggested that the prison structure incorporates and reflects the *total* external social structure in that the differential cultural definitions ascribed to male and female roles in the external world influence the definitions made within the prison, and function to determine the direction and focus of the inmate cultural system.

Cultural Expectations of Male and Female Roles

Are sex roles so sharply differentiated in American society that we would expect wide variations in behavior patterns to be found in the two prison communities? There are a number of areas in which American society differentiates male and female roles. In the main, it may be said that in contrast to the male, who is expected to prepare for an occupational role,

---

[6] Stanton Wheeler, "Socialization in Correctional Communities," *American Sociological Review,* 26 (October, 1961), pp. 696-712; Peter C. Garabedian, "Social Roles and Processes of Socialization in the Prison Community," *Social Problems,* 11 (Fall, 1963), pp. 139-152.

[7] John Irwin and Donald R. Cressey, "Thieves, Convicts, and the Inmate Culture," *Social Problems,* 10 (Fall, 1962), pp. 142-155.

[8] Clarence Schrag, "Some Foundations for a Theory of Correction," in Donald R. Cressey (ed.), *The Prison: Studies in Institutional Organization and Change,* New York: Holt, Rinehart and Winston, 1961, pp. 309-357.

[9] Marriage, family, and kinship in the female prison will be discussed in a forthcoming paper. However, in this context it might be worthwhile pointing out that the differentiation of sex roles is crucial as it structures at the outset many other roles which the inmate may legitimately play. Once an inmate has adopted a sex role, it automatically closes off some family roles, while at the same time it opens up legitimate avenues for other roles.

and whose prestige rank is established by the nature of his life work, the female's life goal is achieved through marriage and child-rearing. Although the "career woman" is an important social type,[10] the percentage of women who pursue uninterrupted careers is very small in our society. So long as women bear children, there must be some social arrangement to ensure that the functions of nurturing and training during the period of dependency are fulfilled.

And we may point to other areas in which American culture tends further to differentiate male and female roles. It does not discourage and accepts a public display of affection between two women such as the use of terms of endearment, embracing, holding hands, and kissing. Such behavior on the part of the male, however, would immediately be defined as homosexual. Moreover, women are said to be more dependent, emotional, less aggressive, and less prone to violence than men. It is said that women generally show less initiative in openly defying authority, whereas men have been defined as independent, violent, and aggressive.[11] This *generalized popular culture* persists for women on another level—the woman-to-woman popular culture. In this vein, the mass media perpetuate the stereotype that a "woman's worst enemy is another woman." Because of the female's orientation to the marriage market, it is argued that she tends to see other women as rivals.[12] This view finds its significance and signature underscored in the highly stylized type of the best friend "betrayed." A similar theme is operative when we find that working women state preferences for male supervisors rather than female supervisors.

To the extent that this generalized popular culture persists in the prison setting, a situation of calculated solidarity may be said to obtain between the female inmates. Calculated solidarity is defined as a social unity based not upon automatic conformity to a set of common norms perceived to be morally binding, but, rather, a unity which is subject to constant interpretation by the inmate as she perceives each situation from the point of view of her own interests. Common responsibility in any particular situation, then, exists only to the extent that the individual perceives her own interests to be served.[13] Unless the formal organization can supply the inmates with all of their wants, then perforce inmates must turn to one another for the satisfaction of those needs which are attractive and agreeable to them, and which cannot be fulfilled by the formal

[10] Robin M. Williams, Jr., *American Society* (rev. ed.), New York: Alfred A. Knopf, 1960, pp. 64-65. Although many married women at one time or another do some kind of work outside the home for which they earn a salary, marriage and family are the primary goals for most American women. Indeed, despite the marked increase in the number of married women in the labor market, the worker role of women continues to be regarded by society as secondary to the traditional role of women as mothers and homemakers.

[11] Indeed, the architecture of the male prison has been historically oriented upon the general belief that the male criminal is aggressive and dangerous.

[12] Simone de Beauvoir, *The Second Sex,* trans. and ed. by H. M. Parshley, New York: Bantam Books, 1961, p. 514. She argues that the marriage market from one age period to another is very unstable for the female. Consequently, the process of acquiring a husband becomes an urgent matter, and this concern is often destructive of feminine friendships, for the young girl sees rivals rather than allies in her companions. In this connection, Jules Henry has stated that the self-orientation of the female begins at an early age; see *Culture Against Man,* New York: Random House, 1963, pp. 150-155.

[13] As Malinowski has cogently pointed out, however, automatic conformity does not exist empirically. But we may conceive of automatic conformity and lawlessness as ideal types with the prison approximating calculated solidarity. See Bronislaw Malinowski, *Crime and Custom in Savage Society,* New York: Harcourt, Brace, 1932, esp. chs. 3, 4, and 5.

organization. Clemmer's finding is relevant here. In response to questionnaire items, seventy per cent of his subjects concluded that "friendships in prison result from the mutual help man can give man rather than because of some admired trait."[14] However, if the popular culture on the woman-to-woman level is imported into the prison environment, then we would expect that violations of much tabooed behavior may not be severely punished, or may be overlooked, as the very nature of the case implies that expectations of behavior cannot be consistent. Possible latent dysfunctions of the popular culture, then, would be to neutralize deviant acts.

Method of Study

I was fortunate to have the opportunity to undertake field work for a period of one year in a large women's prison in a correctional system generally regarded as one of the most progressive. Data were gathered by personal observation of the inmates as they participated in formally scheduled inmate activities: work assignments, vocational and avocational classes, group counseling sessions, academic educational classes, recreational and religious activities. At all inmate functions, the observer sat with the inmates. Other sources of data were obtained by personal observation of informal interaction patterns in the cottage units and on the grounds. During the year it was possible to get to know all the inmates who were at the prison when the study began, approximately 650, and, also, many of the inmates who were committed during the course of the year as well. Interviews of one hour to three hours in length were held with these inmates. These interviews provided basic information on the nature and meaning of the cultural experiences and activities of the group, as well as the social values attached to them. The sociological characteristics of the inmate population were obtained by an examination of the record files of 653 inmates who were confined at the same time.

Other data were obtained by attendance at classification and subclassification meetings; the disciplinary court; meetings of the lieutenants and correctional officers; and other scheduled staff meetings. Informal interviews with correctional officers, prison administrators, and other staff members provided additional data. During the last week of the study, an anonymous questionnaire was administered to all the correctional officers to obtain data on the sociological characteristics of the correctional officers and perceptions of their role function.

The Deprivations of Imprisonment

Sykes has noted in his study of the Trenton prison that the pains of imprisonment for the modern prisoner are not rooted in physical brutality, but rather may be seen as attacks on the psychological level.[15] The "residue of apparently less acute hurts," he argues, such as the deprivation of liberty, goods and services, heterosexual relations, autonomy and security, "may indeed be the acceptable or unavoidable implications of imprisonment, but we must recognize the fact that they can be just as painful as the physical maltreatment which they have replaced."[16]

What would constitute deprivations for women? Interview data revealed that although the perception of the female inmates vary from one another in this regard depending upon the stage of the inmate's prison career, one's former commitment history,[17]

---

14 Donald Clemmer, *The Prison Community, op. cit.*, p. 123.

15 Gresham M. Sykes, *The Society of Captives, op. cit.*, p. 64.

16 *Ibid.*, p. 64.

17 On a selected day the records revealed that 52.1 per cent had been previously jailed or imprisoned. The commitment age

and/or the relative ease with which the individual may adjust to the inmate social system, there is nevertheless a "hard core of consensus" among the female prisoners that prison life *is* depriving and frustrating.

In the female institution studied, it is quite true that in some areas the deprivations of imprisonment are less harsh. The physical surroundings are certainly more pleasant; the cottages although starkly simple are clean and provide the inmate with adequate physical living conditions; with some ingenuity and mutual aid, the inmates enjoy limited opportunity for variety in the matter of dress.[18] The list could doubtless be expanded.

In spite of the mitigation of the pains of imprisonment, however, the differences cited are merely peripheral to the major concerns of prison life. The problems to be solved by the female inmate in this institution are the same conditions for survival as those which the male prisoner has found it necessary to provide solutions in order to survive psychically in the prison environment. These problems have their basis in the disorientation resulting from the abrupt termination of the individual's freedom: the lack of opportunity for heterosexual relations—the fracturing of every influence favorable to the cultivation of emotional reciprocity as a result of being cut off from family and friends; withholding of material goods; attacks on the self through the humiliating experiences incidental to a prison commitment; the loss of autonomy and responsibility to which life in a prison inevitably leads; and the lack of security, and privacy.

The loss of liberty and autonomy are among the most uniformly felt deprivations of imprisonment among the female inmates. Restraints on the inmate's freedom are keenly felt, and the transition from liberty to rigidly restricted movement is a matter with which the female must come to terms in order to survive psychically in the prison world.

Whatever the material circumstances may have been for the individual inmate in civil society, the punishing aspect of denying the inmate ownership of personal goods in prison is that it removes the last resource the inmate possesses to express individuality, and, therefore, the abrupt removal of personal effects tends to destroy the inmate's self-image. The stripping and mortifying process[19] occurs immediately after the inmate's entrance into the prison; the personal clothing and other possessions of the inmate are replaced by the prison issue which is fairly uniform, certain to have been worn by generations of prisoners, and to be either sizes too large or sizes too small. When one recalls that it is always open season on women's fashions, it is not surprising to learn that the attack on the individual's self-image with reference to clothing is particularly acute for the female inmate. The strategies employed by some of the inmates in the admission and

---

of the inmates ranged from fifteen to sixty-seven years, with a mean of 32.2 and a median of 30.5. Fifty-six per cent of the inmate population were white and forty-four per cent were Negro. The marital status of the inmates indicated that 27.1 per cent were single; 31.5 per cent were married; 20.7 per cent were separated; 16.4 per cent were divorced and slightly over 4 per cent were widows.

18 Yarn may be purchased at the commissary store. Knitted items such as socks and sweaters provide another means by which the loss of goods may be mitigated.

19 Stripping and mortifying practices are discussed in Erving Goffman, *Asylums*, New York: Doubleday, 1961; see esp. pp. 14-25. In the prison, no clothing may be kept by the inmates except girdles (if they are not the panty type), brassieres and shoes of simple (relatively low-heeled) closed styles. Medals, simple style earrings and wedding rings which are not studded with precious or semi-precious stones may be kept by the inmate, as well as wrist watches which are valued under fifteen dollars.

orientation unit to individualize the prison issue by monograms, embroidery, or the strategic placement of pleats on a surplus WAC jacket in an attempt to make them "more like free world clothes" are all evidence of the subtlety of deprivation.

For the male prisoner, it has been pointed out that lack of heterosexual intercourse is frustrating and depriving, and the evidence indicates that the same holds true for the great majority of the female inmates. Most inmates have enjoyed the company of men outside, and sex constitutes a major problem of adjustment for almost every inmate. Women do not choose to live their lives entirely apart from men, and the necessity of doing so in prison is frustrating for the individual.[20] Indeed the situation for the imprisoned female may, perhaps, be seen to be more serious than for the male. "[American] culture," writes Jules Henry, "gives women no firm role except an erotic one."[21] In this regard, Parsons has discussed three broad categories of adjustment for the American female: 1) the "good companion" role; 2) the "glamor girl" role; and 3) the "domestic" role.[22] Thus, with the closing of the prison gate, the female prisoner finds herself cut off from the structure of American society conducive to the cultivation of a female role which is the avenue through which she achieves self-respect and status.

The evidence, however, suggests that the other major deprivation suffered by the male prisoner, namely, the loss of security,[23] occurs on another level of experience for the female inmate, which is consistent with the popular culture. In the words of the inmates: "The hardest part of living in a prison is to live with other *women*." Commonly expressed attitudes of the nature of women are: "You can't trust another woman"; "Every woman is a sneaking lying bitch." Hence, it is not so much the constant fear of violence or sexual exploitation such as is the case for the male prisoner which creates a hardship for the female inmates, but, rather, the strain involved in being in the forced company of women who are believed to be untrustworthy, capable of predatory tactics. Thus, the female inmate is apt to fear the consequences of aroused jealousy transformed into vitriolic verbal attacks;[24] and she suffers acute insecurity in confronting and handling the frequent attacks of *penitentiary darby*—gossip which takes place at all times and on all sides within the

[20] The obvious exceptions to this, of course, are the homosexuals who have practiced homosexuality in the free community. Approximately 5 per cent of the inmate population falls into this category. For this group, it cannot be said that this aspect of imprisonment is depriving. In a sense, the imprisonment of the homosexual—whether male or female—is ironical, for the loss of liberty, except in a few countries, is always accompanied by the denial of contact with the opposite sex so as to increase the burden of punishment. The homosexual in prison, however, is actually in a favored position, because the competition of the opposite sex has been excluded.

[21] Jules Henry, *op. cit.*, p. 61; also cf. Margaret Park Redfield, "The American Family: Consensus and Freedom," *The American Journal of Sociology*, 52 (November, 1946), p. 182. "Beyond the roles of glamor girl and nursemaid, the part to be played by women is but vaguely defined in our society."

[22] Talcott Parsons, "Age and Sex in the Social Structure of the United States," *American Sociological Review*, 7 (October, 1942), pp. 610-613.

[23] Sykes, *op. cit.*, p. 78.

[24] This is not to say, however, that there are no fights which take place among the inmates, but the real violence that occurs in the prison, however, tends to be in connection with a homosexual triangle. And in this connection the great fear is not so much for one's life, as the fear of *disfigurement*—the fear that an inmate "out to get" another will use razor or scissors to disfigure one's face. It is worthwhile noting that the prison officials issue scissors to each inmate; the blades are fairly blunt, but, nevertheless, this indicates the widely held belief of women as nonaggressive types.

prison. Moreover, there is enough differentiation among the inmates so that some women experience insecurity in adjusting to living in the forced company of others whom they consider to be socially inferior; some of the white women, for example, find living in close proximity with Negroes to be distasteful; others feel repulsion at having to associate with prostitutes, women who are untidy in their personal habits, or who use vulgar language.[25]

As does the male prisoner, the female prisoner soon discovers that escape routes in prison are few. Psychological and physical withdrawal are not significant modes of adaptation to mitigate the pains of imprisonment for the inmates in this institution. What follows now is a description of the informal social structure which provides a complex of clearly defined social roles for the female prisoners and sets the limits of mutual accommodation.

The Social Roles

Snitchers and Inmate Cops or Lieutenants

Communication across caste lines is strictly forbidden in the female prison studied except for matters of urgent business, and all such interaction is expected to be handled with swift dispatch. Indeed, to violate the ban placed on legitimate communication flowing from inmates and staff is considered to be a very serious matter. The female inmates argue that no inmate should jeopardize the successful execution of activities based upon the common interests of the inmates in connection with the performance of illegal functions to relieve the pains of imprisonment; and secondly, supplying information to officials may result in the withdrawal of privileges or other forms of punishment, thereby adding to the pains of imprisonment for the inmate.

In the female prison, the role of the *snitcher* is the female counterpart to the "rat" in the male prison. To accuse an inmate of snitching is the most serious accusation which one inmate may hurl at another because it clearly signifies the division of loyalty between the staff and the inmates. The importance placed upon the "no snitching" norm is apparent as it covers every range of behavior and is put in the imperative to the new inmate or the deviant: "See and see nothing! Hear and hear nothing!"

Although the female prisoners agree that inmates should never give any information concerning an inmate to the staff, any prisoner according to the female inmates may occasionally engage in snitching when it is believed to serve the individual's interest. Moreover, the female's self-orientation and the tendency to see one another as rivals both function to decrease general expectations of rigid alliance from one another. Consequently, the female inmate rarely expresses any surprise when she suspects another inmate of deviating from the norm prohibiting communication of inmate affairs across caste lines—only a kind of bitterness that the status of inmate is not sufficient to bind and solidify the inmates completely into a cohesive group. The popular culture, then, in connection with the extent to which any female may be trusted, functions to neutralize many deviant acts in the prison. As a result, many deviant acts are overlooked, or are not severely punished; in contrast to the situation in the male prison, we find that violation of the "no snitching" norm does not often result in violence. In the words of one prisoner: "A lot is said about what will be done if you catch a snitch, but you know women! They talk loud, draw a crowd, and that's as far as it goes. When it comes to a showdown,

[25] Types of contaminative exposures have been discussed by Erving Goffman in *Asylums, op. cit.*, pp. 25-35.

they chicken out." This does not mean, however, that negative sanctions are not imposed. Panning and signifying are common modes of punishment to control behavior in the female inmate community.

Panning is general derogatory gossip about an inmate when the inmate is not physically present. *Signifying,* on the other hand, is a more compelling negative sanction because the offending inmate is physically present. A group of inmates will discuss a deviant act in considerable detail with biting sarcasm, scorn, and mimicry; the inmate's name is not at any time mentioned, but little doubt is left as to the inmate's identity. Both panning and signifying are extremely effective modes of social control. But sanctions need not always be so obvious to be effective. The fact that the prison is isolated,[26] of course, makes the prisoners extremely dependent upon one another for emotional reciprocity, and this in itself serves to check much continued deviant behavior. In the words of an inmate: "It's rough when the group ignores you." Inflection in one's voice, then, pretense that one has not seen another, and turning the head to avoid a greeting, can be exquisite punishment in the prison community, and can often be quite as devastating as the more pointed panning and signifying.

Inmates who violate the ban on communication are watched closely and pertinent information concerning their activities is circulated quickly to other inmates. The snitcher, in short, is *persona non grata* in the prison community, and any common cause with an inmate assuming this role would in all certainty hurt one's reputation and close off interaction with the great majority of inmates. The snitcher is condemned by the female inmates because she denies the cohesion of the inmate community and jeopardizes the successful execution of the many illegal activities that take place in the prison to mitigate the pains of imprisonment. And the fact that the snitcher is disloyal to the inmate group adds to the burden of imprisonment.

The behavior subsumed under "center man" in the male prison finds expression in the role of *inmate cop* or *lieutenant.* The inmate cop is a prisoner who is in a position of authority over other inmates, and in the process of executing her work function will issue orders to other inmates or report infractions of rules in connection with work. The prison experience is considered to be the "great equalizer"[27] and inmates resent taking orders from other inmates. As one prisoner said contemptuously: "She tries to act just like an officer. She forgets that she came through that gate and she's got five numbers across her chest just like the rest of us. She's an officer without a uniform, and she tries to tell another inmate what to do. They're always in the officer's face. . . ." The inmate cop or lieutenant in effect takes the role of the officer and thereby violates an important tenet of the inmate code: she denies the egalitarian ethos of the inmates.

The inmate cop's disloyalty is despised not only because it is open to view, but also because it is often flaunted in the face of other inmates. Here is an open and shut case of identification with staff values, and the inmate cop's actions deny the solidarity of the inmate body and weaken the bonds of interdependence which bind them together. Moreover, the inmate

26 Most women, as a matter of fact, serve their entire sentence without a visit from the outside world. In the year 1962, for example, an examination of the records revealed that 79 inmates or about twelve per cent of the inmate population received visits during the entire year.

27 Cf. Judge M. Murtagh and Sara Harris, *Cast the First Stone,* New York: Cardinal, 1958, p. 244.

cop is apt to rationalize her actions in terms of noncriminal values which according to the inmate code have no place in the prison. Unless this inmate can be persuaded to "see the light" through socialization into the inmate culture, she cannot be reasoned with or bought. In this sense she poses a real threat to the inmate community, because the inmate cop is an added bulwark to the staff's forces, and the fact that an inmate is adding to the pains of imprisonment by joining forces with the staff makes her doubly despised.

Squares and Jive Bitches

Along with the snitchers and the inmate cops, the *squares* are truly the pariahs of the inmate community. "Square" is a derisive label pinned on inmates who are considered to be accidental criminals. The behavior of the square in the prison community clearly betrays her alien status, as she is oriented to the prison administration and tends to possess "anti-criminal" loyalties. Degrees of "squareness" are recognized by the female inmates ranging from the inmate who is said to be "so square that she's a cube" to the inmate designated as a "hip square." The "cube square" is very definitely oriented to societal values and the prison administration, whereas the "hip square" tends to sympathize with the inmate code and adheres to some of its principles, sometimes going so far as to *pin*—act as a lookout—for other inmates. Her sympathy tends to take the form of stated tolerance for inmate activities. The distinguishing characteristic of the "hip square," however, is that she does not engage in homosexual activity, as well as the fact that she is oriented to the administration and societal values. In the female prison studied, it should be pointed out that anyone who does not engage in homosexual activities in the prison in one form or another is automatically labeled a square.

Not only are *squares* outside the main stream of inmate activities—excluded and ostracized by the inmate population—but more important for the inmate social system, squares are pitied. It is said that squares "don't know any better," and, further, it is widely believed that the square is not "woman enough" to commit a crime. "They're suckers and fools—gullible without even knowing it." And herein lies the key to understanding the threat that the square poses for the inmate community. Like the inmate cop or lieutenant, the square tends to identify with the institutional officials. In the case of squares, however, association is considered to be doubly hazardous, for in their presumed gullibility squares may unwittingly divulge information to the officials. It is for this reason that squares are apt to be "fed with a long-handled spoon," that is, information concerning inmate activities is carefully sifted and censored.

While the deviance of the square is often the consequence of an artless simplicity—and presumably leaves open the possibility that induction into the inmate culture may remedy the situation (Indeed, the pressures applied are so great that this frequently does occur.)—the deviance of the *jive bitch,* on the other hand, is a deliberate, calculated strategy to cause conflict. In short, the *jive bitch* is a troublemaker whose strategy often involves a distortion of the facts, as in the case, for example, when she is interested in breaking up an established homosexual relationship: she will often volunteer information about *kites* (prison letters) and illicit rendezvous to the injured party who, in many cases, would prefer not to be the recipient of such information—as it will mean that ignorance is no longer bliss—and who may be goaded into terminating an affair, which although perceived not to be perfect may be felt to be better than none.

Moreover, the jive bitch can't be

trusted to keep her word when she gives it, indicating her disloyalty to the inmate group. Although female inmates claim that women are not trustworthy, it is normatively demanded that once you give your word to a prisoner, you should keep it—particularly in connection with matters concerning mutual aid. An example of a jive bitch supplied by an inmate follows:

> You're out of cigarettes, and you go to a girl and say, "Look, I'm out of cigarettes, and I won't have any money until next week. When you go to Commissary, would you buy me a carton, and I'll pay you back next week?" She says, "Sure, baby, sure. I'll get them for you on Friday." When Friday comes, you go to her house to get the cigarettes and when you say, "Did you get the cigarettes?" she opens her mouth like she's surprised and maybe slaps her cheek and she looks at you and says, "Oh, baby, I forgot all about it. I'm sorry, baby, honest!" That's a jive bitch 'cause she had no intention of getting you those cigarettes in the first place.

The jive bitch, in short, is an example *par excellence* of the woman-to-woman popular culture translated into role behavior. And the fact that she cannot be depended upon weakens even the bonds of calculated solidarity which exist among the female inmates.

Rap Buddies and Homeys

While no inmate trusts another woman completely—"You pick your people and even then you only go so far."—within the limitations imposed by this definition of the situation, an inmate may single out another prisoner as a special friend. She is one with whom an inmate can converse easily, and, further, assume reasonably that the conversation will be mutually binding as secret. Any two people who find one another compatible in this way may become *rap buddies* to one another. This relationship is dissolved if the expectations concerning the relationship are not honored by either of the incumbents of the rap buddy role; or if the relationship develops into a homosexual relationship, the inmates become a "couple" and assume the obligations relevant to a homosexual relationship.

The *homey* role is probably as close to "blood" relationship that one comes to in the female prison, and the relationship holds a special place in the lexicon of the inmates. Technically speaking, even if conflict ensues between homeys, the relationship still holds. The homey is the inmate who is from another inmate's home town or nearby community. Homeys may or may not have known one another before incarceration; but whatever the case, within the prison these inmates become homeys to one another. Contact is made as soon as the presence of a homey becomes known; information is usually obtained from inmate orientation helpers or inmate office workers. Inquiries as to whether a homey's needs in the orientation unit have been met are immediately made: cigarettes, soap, toothpaste, facial tissues, and any other commissary items which she needs will somehow be routed to her. The special bond of reciprocity which is established between homeys is of a vastly different degree of intensity than that between rap buddies, and is expected to cover a wide range of behavior; homeys have the right to turn to one another when material need arises, and the further expectation exists that if economically possible, the merchandise is to be returned at a later date.

Although superficially the rap buddy and homey roles may appear to be quite similar, the basis for the allocation of these roles and functions is quite different. What is the basis for allocation of functions with respect to the homey role? While there is a special relationship that exists between homeys, significantly the homey relationship excludes homosexuality. Indeed, an inmate will express great indignation if the suggestion—however lightly veiled—is made that a homosexual relationship exists between her and a homey. "That's my homey. I wouldn't do that to her," certainly suggests the exploitative evaluation many inmates have of the homosexual relationship. But when we examine other aspects of the role this explanation adds little to our understanding of the function the role plays in the lives of the female inmates.

A significant aspect of the homey relationship lies in the fact that inmates sharing this status address and refer to one another by the term "homey," emphasizing to the incumbents of the role and the inmate community alike the nature of the special relationship involved. Indeed, a novitiate who calls a homey by her given name is promptly corrected by other inmates. One is quite reasonably led to ask why it is that mutual aid and mode of address are patterned between homeys and not, for example, between rap buddies. Does the answer lie in the fact that they are from the same geographical area? Given the self-orientation of the female, it is not very likely that this would seem to be a plausible explanation. Actually the occupants of the homey role are, as it were, buying insurance for the future. The extension of mutual cooperation between homeys insures both role occupants that the possibility will not arise that a homey will "read" her—that is, speak derogatively of her behavior in prison to anyone in civil society. Presumably, the inmate who resides in the same geographical area would most likely be in a favored position to do so.

The homey relationship is a splendid example of the refinement in social roles which takes place in the female community to solve the special problems of the inmates stemming from the cultural definition females have of one another.

Connects and Boosters

The fifteen dollars which inmates are permitted to spend per month at the commissary store is not a large sum when one takes into account that it covers almost all purchases, including cigarettes.[28] Furthermore, even this modest sum is beyond the reach of most inmates. Few legitimate channels are open to the female inmates to improve their economic lot in the prison. Like the male prisoners, the female inmates also find it necessary to exploit the environment in order to improve their material circumstances. Here it takes the form of stealing from institutional supplies. Significantly, a role based upon aggressive physical tactics such as the "gorilla" reported by Sykes who takes what he wants from other inmates by force does not emerge in the female inmate community. By contrast, in the female prison the *connect* is any inmate with a "good job" who will cooperate in the procurement of scarce goods and/or information. Connects are also those inmates who are in a position to negotiate with other inmates to obtain information or goods, that is, acting both as middleman and distributor. Thus, this role includes the procurement of both goods and services.

In this connection, the inmates draw a sharp line between the connect who often takes a dual role, and the *booster* whose exploitation of the environment consists solely of stealing from official stores and carries on a successful business enterprise. Of course, it should be made clear that stealing from the officials is universal at the prison. Even inmates designated by sister inmates as squares and inmate cops declare they will sometimes take a pot of coffee out of the dining room "on principle." Inmates, however, make a clear distinction between the petty

[28] It is possible to make special withdrawals for yarn purchases.

boosting which is engaged in by all the inmates—say a few teaspoonfuls of sugar placed in a napkin, a sandwich, and the like, while in the dining room —and the stealing engaged in by the booster. The difference lies mainly in the source of supply, the regularity with which the goods may be procured, and the purpose for which the items are stolen. Items stolen sporadically for individual consumption tend to be classified under the category petty boosting. The booster is the inmate who is in a position to steal desired objects regularly and in fairly large quantities.

Now in the male prison, regardless of the source of supply, giving and sharing is normatively demanded by the inmate code—especially if the materials have been stolen from the officials. The "pedlar" or "merchant" has been described as "a man so alienated from other prisoners, so selfish in his pursuit of material advantage, that he is willing to thrive on the misery of his companions. He places his own well-being above the well-being of the inmates as a whole. He does not share the goods in short supply but exploits, instead, the needs of others."[29] Interestingly, the same behavior for which the "merchant" is despised in the male prison is that which receives words of praise from female inmates. To "get a good thing going," that is, to engage in a successful enterprise is to draw forth admiration from the inmates. It is held: "If you can get a little racket going, more power to you." And yet at the same time inmates rationalize many of their actions by saying, "If I don't get there first, someone else will," which clearly indicates the self-orientation of the inmates. In a real sense, boosters are inmates who have "gotten there first," and for this feat there is admiration—albeit tinged with not a little envy. In addition, inmates tend to feel gratitude to the booster, for it is recognized that the booster's role involves a certain amount of risk. Whatever recompense is necessary to enjoy the pleasure of making a cup of coffee at odd hours of the day is thought to be well worth the price. The inmates will gladly exchange a carton of cigarettes for a pound of coffee,[30] and if this transaction can be made a weekly matter, prison life is made more tolerable.

In contrast to the male prisoner, no sharp line is made by the female inmates between selling and giving, except between *homeys,* inmates participating in a homosexual marriage, and other "family" members. Who are the inmates that become the clients for the supply of illicit goods? All prisoners do not have an opportunity to enjoy these luxury items, regardless of their financial situation. Low caste inmates, such as snitchers, squares, and inmate cops or lieutenants, of course, lie outside the boundary of legitimate giving, as these inmates have deviated from the inmate code and, therefore, have roped themselves off from the privilege of sharing in the scarce goods that circulate about the prison. They are in the same boat as "rats," "center men," "weaklings," and "fish" in the male prison. Apart from the pariahs in the female prison, mutual aid is greater near the locus of high intensity of emotional reciprocity. As intensity of emotional reciprocity decreases, mutual aid decreases proportionately.

Pinners

Since complete elimination of detection is never possible in the performance of many illicit activities, the female inmates find it necessary to minimize the risk of being detected by the prison officials. For this reason, the role of *pinner* is very crucial in the prison.

The pinner in the female prison is a

[29] Sykes, *op. cit.,* p. 94.

[30] Cigarettes are the most important nexus of exchange among the inmates.

lookout, stationed as a sentry to prevent a surprise attack upon inmates engaging in illicit activities from all unauthorized persons—whether they be staff or inmates. With discovery always imminent and punishment a certainty, the pinner's role is not one to allocate to amateurs or to inmates whose loyalty is in doubt. The pinner must be an inmate who can be trusted, stand up under pressure, and she must be "in the know." Depending upon the task at hand, sometimes the female inmates find it necessary to mobilize a team of pinners—each of whom must share the responsibility that the task at hand be carried out successfully. The interdependence of the inmates requires the cooperation of other inmates in order to carry out their activities successfully. In the words of an inmate:

> Even if you wanted to go it alone, it's almost impossible to do. The situation is such that you need the help of other inmates. For example, if you're makin' it with someone, you need a pinner. This means initiating the aid of a third party—maybe more. And you might be called up to help two other people in the same situation. . . . The way pinning works is this—maybe I've got two friends who are involved with each other. O.K., well, I'll go into the office and keep the officer busy for an hour talking about a problem I have or I make one up. She can't be in two places at one time, so usually this is a safe procedure. Or a girl will stand at the foot of the stairs with a tin can in her hands. If the officer or a person known to be a snitcher goes up the stairs, she drops the can, or she whistles loudly. These signals are understood.

Now while it is important to the female inmates that the pains of imprisonment be mitigated, it is also imperative that in the process of doing so their deviant actions do not result in disciplinary action which will increase the burden of punishment. The pinner, therefore, is a valued individual, as she imparts a measure of reasonable security to the inmates that their deviant performances will not result in loss of days or other forms of punishment.

The Homosexual Cluster: Penitentiary Turnouts, Lesbians, Femmes, Stud Broads, Tricks, Commissary Hustlers, Chippies, Kick Partners, Cherries, Punks, and Turnabouts

The problems and concerns of the female inmates in adjusting to deprivation of heterosexual relationships are revealed by the number of roles channeled into homosexual behavior. Moreover, the female inmate's *role refinement* with respect to the categories of homosexual activity illustrates its function as both a motivating force in the lives of the inmates and as an organizing principle of social organization.

The inmates apply a number of labels to homosexual behavior in the prison depending upon the specific role assumed, the adeptness with which the assumed role is played, or the motivation for the behavior. Broadly speaking, the inmates differentiate between penitentiary turnouts and lesbians. The *penitentiary turnout* is the prisoner who resorts to homosexuality in the prison because heterosexual relationships are not available; in contrast, the *lesbian prefers* homosexual relations in the free community. In this respect she resembles the "fag" in the male prison. The *lesbian* is labeled as a sick person by the inmates because it is argued that the preference and selection of homosexual relations in a situation where choice is possible clearly constitute a true perversion. It is only in the penitentiary world where men are unavailable that the values and norms regarding homosexual behavior are redefined by the inmates and—within the limits imposed by this definition—accepted as a temporary substitute for heterosexual relations.

Stylized symbolic devices make it possible for the female inmates to attach new meanings to a culturally defined sex *role* representation seen as a variation of a sex *type* based upon biological attributes. The institutionalized character of the differential sex roles orders the behavior of the inmates and defines the limits of permissible behavior and regulates the interaction between the inmates.

The *femme*[31] or *mommy* is the inmate who plays the female role in a homosexual relationship. The femme role is a highly sought-after role in the prison because most of the inmates want to continue to play the feminine role in a meaningful way in the prison. Cast in the context of a "marital" relationship, the femme continues to act out many of the functions assigned to the role of wife in civil society. The complementary role to the femme is the *stud broad*[32] or *daddy* who assumes the male role. The stud broad is accorded much prestige by other inmates for these reasons: first, the stud is said to provide the prison with the male image; secondly, the role is considered to be a more difficult one for an inmate to assume and sustain over a period of time, because it is thought to be "unnatural" for a female to assume the guises of the male. Moreover, the role is considered to be difficult because studs not only assume certain external symbols of sex differentiation, but in addition are expected to incorporate into role behavior the many social expectations of the male role.

As far as homosexual relations are concerned, the evidence is consistent with that reported by Ward and Kassebaum; that is, homosexual relations are established voluntarily between the principals involved. No physical coercion is applied in obtaining a homosexual partner.[33] In seeking a solution to the problem engendered by the lack of heterosexual relations, interpersonal relations in connection with homosexuality play a major part in the lives of the female inmates. Cast in the context of a "marital" relationship, the homosexual dyad is viewed by the inmates as a meaningful personal and social relationship. From the mass of interview data it is clear, however, that this mode of adjustment (with the exception of homosexuals who practice homosexuality in the free community) would be repugnant for most prisoners, but the uniqueness of the prison situation compels the inmate to redefine and attach new meanings to this behavior within the prison structure.[34]

The inmates are not able to resolve their sense of isolation within the formal organization, and, therefore, develop relationships and behavior patterns within an informal structure. For the vast majority of the inmates, adjustment to the prison world is made by establishing a homosexual alliance with a compatible partner as a marriage unit. Although we cannot discuss the dynamics of mate selection, courtship, and marriage in this paper, it should be pointed out that when a stud and femme have established a homosexual alliance, they are said to be "makin' it" or to be "tight"; that is to say, they are socially recognized as constituting a legitimate married pair.

31 This role is also reported in Ward and Kassebaum, *op. cit.*, p. 169.

32 Cf. the role of the butch in Ward and Kassebaum, *ibid.*, pp. 168-169.

33 Ward and Kassebaum, *ibid.*, p. 171.

34 Estimates of the number of inmates who are involved in homosexuality vary. Inmates who are very much involved in this phase of inmate culture place the figure at ninety or ninety-five per cent. The Associate Warden (treatment) estimated that eighty per cent of the inmates were involved in homosexual relations. Correctional officers tended to set the figure at fifty or seventy-five per cent which agrees with the usual estimates I obtained from squares. Some officers and other staff members set the figure at one hundred per cent. At one point in the study, I made a cottage count of inmates assuming the male role, and the studs totaled 215 inmates. The number of "males" in the prison tends to vary slightly from day to day depending upon inmate releases and individual role choice. And the same is equally true of the inmates playing the femme role. At this time, there were 336 femmes out of a total of 639 inmates. At any rate, it is apparent that femmes are competing for a scarce commodity.

Since one of the important goals in establishing a homosexual marriage alliance is to strive for what is referred to as a "sincere" relationship, which is translated to mean a stable relationship and one based upon romantic love, the *trick* is held in low esteem by the inmates because she allows herself to be exploited, rather than to develop a relationship that is sincere. And the trick permits exploitation in a variety of ways—usually economically and as a source of labor. Any individual who allows herself to be exploited in this manner is considered "weak." Moreover, tricks are regarded as "suckers" and "fools" because they may be kept dangling with promises.

Who are the inmates who utilize exploitative tactics? The *commissary hustler* is so labeled as an individual who establishes a single homosexual alliance with an inmate who lives in the same cottage, but in addition establishes relationships with one or more inmates in other cottages for economic purposes. This is called "mating for commissary reasons," and any femme other than the inmate who lives in the stud's cottage is labeled as a trick in the relationship. The commissary hustler presents a commissary list to the tricks scattered throughout the prison, and they, in turn, supply the commissary hustler with needed material items. The function of all the tricks in this "polygynous" system is an economic one. The "wife" in the cottage takes precedence over all others. She shares in the bounty and usually knows of the existence of other femmes, i.e., tricks. Indeed, if the "couple" is in serious economic difficulty, she may suggest to her stud that this role be assumed. Or the stud may consult the femme in arriving at a decision to "work a few tricks."

So long as the "wife" shares the same household as the stud, the existence of other femmes (tricks) in the relationship is tolerable. As the inmates put it: "The nearest is the dearest, and the closest gets the mostest." In addition, it should be pointed out that the "wife" who lives in the same household as the stud also derives security from the public recognition of the relationship as legitimate. They are recognized as a "couple." The additional wife (or wives) merely serves an economic function. One would be well advised to ask why an inmate enters into a trick role. The stud population is outnumbered by the femme population, and competition for studs is very keen. Actually, each trick in this situation anticipates and plans for the day when the relationship will become a permanent one; each trick anticipates displacing the cottage "wife" in the affections of the stud. And since the trick is, after all, an inmate with a commissary account, the possibility that this might occur is a good one. While it is more or less understood that she wait for an invitation to move to the stud's cottage, sometimes a trick may lose patience and forego prison etiquette. Such cottage moves present complicating triangular situations, often leading to violence.

The role of commissary hustler is one which requires a certain amount of adroitness to carry out successfully. The inmates argue that in the free community, the commissary hustler would tend to exploit men, but since there are no men in prison, they exploit women. Although there may be individual personality factors involved, there are structural features in the prison which precipitate this role. Every inmate is not compensated for work performed in the prison, and the role of commissary hustler provides an avenue whereby an inmate may solve her economic needs.

The dyad configuration cast into the framework of a marital relationship covers a wide range of behavioral expectations. The commissary hustler, although in some respects exploitative, nevertheless does maintain a stable and sincere relationship with the femme who shares the same cottage. However, when the individual exploits *each* situation with a partner for its unique possibilities, whether it be sexual gratification or material, the inmate is said to occupy a *chippie* role. This role differs from the commissary hustler in a very important way. Although the commissary hustler actually establishes one sincere relationship and exploits other inmates in order to provide for the femme in the relationship, the chippie establishes no single relationship of this type. Chippies are said to be "makin' it," but not to be "in love" with any individual. The chippie, in the inmates' eyes, is the prison prostitute. The inmate who "chippies from one bed to another"—i.e., terminates affairs too quickly—is held in scorn by the inmates, as her behavior is held to be promiscuous. This behavior draws forth words of scorn from the inmates because the ideal cultural pattern in the prison is to establish a permanent relationship. The chippie clearly deviates from the ideal pattern, as the affairs of this inmate are characterized by their striking temporary quality.

The female inmates distinguish clearly between homosexual activity that is considered to be promiscuous and that which is engaged in solely for sexual gratification. Although *kick partners* are also not involved as "lovers," there is, nevertheless, a predictable permanence in the relationships maintained between kick partners, but the motivation for entering into the partnership is clearly understood to be solely for physical gratification. There is usually no economic exchange in this relationship, and the inmates exhibit no jealousy. An inmate is apt to enter such a relationship when she does not wish to assume the responsibilities that a more permanent tie would entail. The object of this relationship is to release sexual tension. Kick partners sometimes consist of a group of several women among whom partners are exchanged and friendly relations exist between all members concerned. To the extent that kick partners are "discreet," the behavior is not looked down upon by the inmates.

Every society has a reserve of members from which potential mates may be obtained. When resources are limited, or because of cultural prescriptions, mates may be drawn from other groups. In the female prison, the kick partner is an individual who may be drawn into a permanent tie. And there is also the possibility that the square will in time come to "see the light" and enter into the inmate social organization. But there is one category of inmates in prison, namely, those labeled *cherries,* who constitute an uncommitted sizeable reserve for potential mates, as they are the inmates who have never been "turned out"—initiated into homosexual practices. Cherries, however, are not squares. Often they are young and first offenders, and they are usually initiated by older women. Cherries in this context are "hep" individuals, i.e., know what the score is from the point of view of the prisoners, but for one reason or another have not engaged in homosexuality. Sometimes a short sentence may be the deciding factor; a preference not to become emotionally involved; or it may be that the individual decides that this mode of adjustment may not be desirable.

One who assumes a false part or assumes a character other than the real is despised for his hypocrisy both within and without the prison gates. Within the female prison, the *punk* is despised for pretense and deceit. In the male prison, it will be recalled that the "punk" is an inmate who plays the submissive part in a homosexual relationship because he is coerced into doing so. In this respect it is said that "punks" differ and may be distinguished from "fags," who it is said are "born" not "made." In a sense, "fags" resemble the lesbians for it is said by the inmates that they are "born that way," or "something happened to them in their childhood."

The punk in the female prison, on the other hand, is the inmate so designated because she acts like a female, that is, takes on the coquettish mannerisms of a woman when the expected behavior is that of the male. The behavior of the punk elicits a combination of anger and ridicule from the inmates. The tendency is to heap blame upon the punk, because the punk's "impotence" is not a constitutional failure, but, rather, is due to incomplete role learning. Responsibility, therefore, is placed upon the individual. Punks are, as it were, self-proclaimed studs without substance—unconvincing sexual deviates. The punk is despised and ridiculed by the inmates.

While the punk is guilty of incomplete role learning, the *turnabout,* on the other hand, claims expertise at playing both male and female roles. As a matter of fact, she not only describes herself glowingly in terms of her versatility, that is, "good either way," but stands ready to put her boasted skill to the test. Such protean versatility, however, is viewed with amused contempt by the inmates. As a prisoner put it, "There's a lot of talk, but not the right kind of talk. She should know what she is and stay that way. And we tell them, 'Get yourself together and find out what you are!' "

The female inmates prefer a structured situation in their prison world, and inmates playing male roles one day and female roles the next confuse the issue greatly, especially for the inmate who may be planning a strategy of conquest. In addition, anything which tends to decrease the "male" population in the prison is apt to be alarming to the inmates. It is not surprising, therefore, that the turnabout is held in low esteem.

Conclusion

The social roles as distinguished and labeled by the female inmates constitute the basic structure of social relationships formed by the inmates in response to the problems of a prison commitment. While it is apparent from the previous discussion that some argot roles are mutually exclusive, other roles clearly are not. Furthermore, an inmate may assume one role soon after commitment, for example, such as square, but may assume many other roles at a later point in time if drawn into the inmate social organization.

In addition to the comparisons with the male prison community that have already been made, there are other important differences that may be pointed out at this time. Consistent with the cultural definition of the female as nonaggressive, the roles of violence that emerge in the male prison, namely, those of "wolf," "tough," "gorilla," "hipster," and "ball buster," are notably absent among the female inmates. Also significant is the fact that a role resembling the structure of the "right guy" who is such a dominant figure in the male prison does not emerge in the female prison. Concepts such as "fair play," "courage," and the like—which are consistent with the concepts of endurance, loyalty, and dignity associated with the "right guy" —are not meaningful to the female. Although it is true that the norm of inmate loyalty exists in the prison world, the popular culture of women as untrustworthy is imported into the prison world and serves both to neutralize many deviant acts and to furnish the rationale for their commitment.

The need to assert or defend one's femininity, in the same way that the male inmate must prove his masculinity in the group if his manhood is called into question, clearly does not arise for the female inmate. This is a reflection of the self-orientation of the female, and the fact that the female validates her femininity by proving she can attract men. In other words, it appears that general features of American society in connection with the cultural definitions ascribed to male and female roles are imported into the prison and are reflected in the structure of social relationships formed by the inmates. Nowhere is this more dramatically revealed than in the extraordinary function of the homey role with its extended implications for the reentry of the inmate into civil society. From the same vantage point, we saw that the function of the pinner's role serves to control the physical distance between inmates engaging in illicit activities on the one hand, and the snitcher on the other, in order to make it possible for the female inmates to avoid discovery and punishment.

The number of roles clustered about homosexual behavior clearly reveals the problems and concerns of the female inmates in connection with adjustment to deprivation of heterosexual relationships. Moreover, the distinctions made by the inmates as to motivation, role assumed, adeptness with which the assumed role is played, and so on, indicate the values and expectations of the inmates with respect to this behavior. But the rights and obligations attached to a legitimate "marital" relationship automatically close off much interaction among the inmates, as inmates assuming this type of relationship must account for all of their contacts with members of the "opposite sex." As the inmates move closer to legitimate relationships in the prison, then, the refinement of roles becomes necessary in order to control and to account for the behavior of every inmate in the system.

The cultural orientation of males, however, precludes legitimate marriage and family groupings as a feasible alternative solution for the male prisoners, as the serious adoption of a female role is contrary to the definition of the male role as masculine. Hence, family groups do not emerge in the male prison. It is noteworthy that in the male prison the "fags" and "punks" are both held in derision by the vast majority of male inmates as it is felt that they have sacrificed their manhood, but the homosexuality of "wolves" is looked upon as a temporary adjustment to sexual tensions generated by the prison setting. The absence of sentiment and the aggressive behavior of the "wolf" is consistent with the cultural definition of the *masculine* role, and thus homosexuality loses the taint of femininity in the prison that male homosexuality tends to carry in civil society. In addition, the cultural orientation of the male role with respect to demonstrations of affection toward another member of the same sex clearly precludes the adoption of legitimate feminine roles by male inmates in informal kinship groupings such as those found among the female inmates. The ease with which women may demonstrate acts of affection, both verbally and physically, toward members of the same sex, perhaps may provide a *predisposition* to widespread homosexuality and its ready acceptance under the extreme conditions of isolation in the prison setting. This fact alone, however, is not enough to account for the emergence of the female inmate social system.

Why do these remarkable differences in inmate culture emerge in the two prison communities? Two theoretical positions have already been posed. The first of these is the typical structural-functional analysis of total institutions which asserts that behavior systems of various types of inmates are a result of the conditions of imprisonment. However, when we consider that the deprivations of imprisonment were found to be present in the female prison studied and keenly felt by the female prisoners—yet the typical cultural system which emerges in the adult male prison is not present—we must conclude that the differences in structural form found in the two prison communities are inadequately explained by current functional analysis *solely* as a response to the deprivations of imprisonment. The deprivations may provide necessary conditions for the emergence of an inmate system, but they are not in themselves sufficient to account for the structural *form* that the inmate social system assumes in the male and female prison communities.

The second interpretation views inmate culture as somehow imported into the prison world from the external world by the inmates who compose that culture, through the particular attitudes and values which inmates learned prior to entering the prison. This position has been most forcibly suggested by Schrag, Irwin, and Cressey, and calls our attention to the thesis that the behavior patterning of inmates is influenced by pre-prison experiences, social identities, and cultural background. Simply stated, the behavior patterns in the prison are the result of the inmates' relations in the external world; however, the external world is important only in providing the particular cultural elements that the inmates learn. Inasmuch as the individuals who enter the prison world are not a random sample of the population, the values and attitudes brought into the prison do not comprise a random sample of elements of outside culture; hence, prison culture differs—especially by the presence of increased hostility, violence, and traffic in illicit goods. The three sub-culture groups (thief, convict, and legitimate) in Irwin and Cressey's typology presumably demonstrate this thesis,[35] as these authors maintain that their three sub-culture groups share learned behaviors which are common and peculiar to them in or out of prison. Elsewhere, it has been cogently pointed out that Irwin and Cressey do not demonstrate that this is so.[36] Nevertheless, they have called attention to the important thesis that the behavior patterning of inmates may be influenced by social identities and cultural backgrounds.

We suggest, rather, that the culture that forms within the prison by males and females can be understood in these terms: the prison inmate social system is not an intrinsic response to the deprivations of imprisonment, although the deprivations of imprisonment may be important in precipitating inmate culture; nor can inmate culture be viewed as a mere reflection of the values and attitudes inmates bring into the prison world. The evidence presented here suggests that the male and female inmate cultures *are* a response to the deprivations of prison life, but the nature of the response in both prison communities in influenced by the differential participation of males and females in the external culture. The culture that emerges within the prison structure may be seen to incorporate and reflect the total external social structure; that is, the way in which roles are defined in the external world influence the definitions made within the prison. General features of

---

[35] Irwin and Cressey, *op. cit.*, esp. pp. 148-153.

[36] Julian Roebuck, "A Critique of 'Thieves, Convicts, and the Inmate Culture,'" *Social Problems,* 11 (Fall, 1963), pp. 193-200. It should be pointed out that Schrag's analysis also remains unclear, for at one point he comments: "Juxtaposed with the official organization of the prison is an unofficial social system originating within the institution and regulating inmate conduct with respect to focal issues, such as length of sentence, relations among prisoners, contacts with staff members and other civilians, food, sex, and health, among other things." This suggests that all inmates face a number of common problems of adjustment as a result of incarceration and that social organization develops to provide solutions. See Clarence Schrag, "Some Foundations for a Theory of Correction," in Cressey (ed.), *The Prison, op. cit.*, p. 342.

American society with respect to the cultural definitions and content of male and female roles are brought into the prison setting and they function to determine the direction and focus of the inmate cultural system. These general features I have suggested are those concerned with the orientation of life goals for males and females; second, cultural definitions with respect to dimensions of passivity and aggression; third, acceptability of public expression of affection displayed toward a member of the same sex; and, finally, perception of the same sex with respect to what I have called the popular culture.

It is the *system* of roles and statuses that is imported into the prison setting, and not merely the values and attitudes of the individuals who enter the prison world. It is in these terms that the importance attached to the female role, marriage ties, and family groups can be understood as salient elements of prison culture in the female prison community, but not in the male prison community. It would seem, then, that there is greater unity between the inner and outer worlds than has heretofore been thought. Accordingly, greater understanding of the prison communities may be accomplished by focusing our attention on the relationship of the external and internal cultures rather than trying to understand the prison as an institution isolated from the larger society.

THE HOMOSEXUAL IN PRISON*

This paper should be prefaced by at least 50 photographs of those whom society chooses to stigmatize as homosexual. The pictures would reveal that such men are all racial colors, that there is a wide range of physical build and intellectual achievement, and that they come from all walks of life. Homosexuals do not fit into any kind of specific categorization except that they are sexually orientated in a way different from others. And even in that difference the range of sexuality is extremely wide. This paper is concerned with these men and how they move and function in prison. The observations, based upon almost three years' first hand experience in a maximum security prison, were made by the author who was living in the same environment and milieu. It has been estimated that about 20% of the prison population is homosexual. My personal estimate is that it is nearer 33 1/3%. The following discussion will indicate why.

The thesis posited here is that the homosexual in prison fills a slightly different role from those outside. In prison the homosexual role is that of female replacement. The matriarchal society, in effect, is transferred into the prison subculture by the presence of the female counterpart, i.e. the homosexual. Therefore the role of the homosexual is more important and has a far greater meaning and social significance. The subculture resembles the total culture and makes internal adjustments to secure its own identity.

PRISON ECOLOGY AND HOMOSEXUAL MEMBERSHIP

The major portion of this paper is concerned with the conditions and patterns inside a maximum security prison in California. However in order to arrive at San Quentin, all felons must be processed at one of the California Reception and Guidance Centers, the largest being in the Medical Facility at Vacaville. This correctional facility (a polite term for a medium security prison) is divided into two parts: one housing those who are in transit to other prisons; and the other, those who are resident at the medical facility. Those who are transient, wear green; those who stay, wear blue. The 'blue' side has a distinguished company of felons who are purportedly under medical programs, i.e. care and treatment; a large proportion are classified as neurotic, psychotic, or otherwise mentally unstable. However, this center is also one of the easiest places in the prison system to serve time because the guard-inmate relationship is softened by the doctor-client relationship. Thus those who can manipulate the State machine, stay at Vacaville. This center has a high proportion of those who are wealthy, those who have influence, and those who have peer support from middle and upper class levels. The center has a large staff of psychologists, sociologists, psychiatrists, doctors, and other qualified personnel. These pleasant benefits and amenities decrease rapidly as one progresses to maximum security of State Prison where, as custody takes control, the iron fist is taken out of the velvet glove and prison reality sets in.

But what is unique at Vacaville is the alphabetizing of the corridors: A Wing, B Wing, etc. W Wing is for maximum security; X Corridor is for medical and psychological check-ups. It was inevitable therefore that as groups were segregated into neat compartments, all the homosexuals, for the sake of convenience, would be put in one area. This became known as "Queen's Row."

The "queens" were allowed a great deal of freedom and were virtually outside of police control. Since they were regarded as people with a problem they became the object of medical rehabilitation. This whole approach, instituted by Dr. Keating around 1955, merely reinforced the styles of homosexuals in prison. To many first termers arriving at Vacaville, this was their first acquaintance with "queers" in large numbers. They were literally all over the place, having little regard for the guards whom they openly solicited. As time went on (1964-1968) they became an accepted part of the population both on the blue side and the green. It was not uncommon to see overt homosexuality in a so-called rehabilitation center. While this may not be objectionable to some, it must be remembered that this was the *only* form of sexual outlet available to prisoners. The prisoner either masturbated, became homosexual, or literally repressed the fact that he existed as a man by sublimating his sexual urges in work, study, or a ritual of both. Considering the fact that most of these men were in prison for at least three years, the show put on at Vacaville had a great deal of meaning.

As time progressed into the late 60's fewer and fewer actual homosexual arrests were made. But nevertheless the homosexual population of the prisons remained about constant. What was apparent was that homosexuals came from all walks of life and committed all sorts of crimes. The heterosexual committed crimes along the same spectrum. Thus, although no actual research has been done along this line, I am sure that types of crimes committed by homosexuals are very similar to those committed by heterosexuals. I would venture to say that the percentage would correspond. But what happens when they both meet in prison is another matter entirely.

While Vacaville specialized in the overt homosexual, this was not true of maximum security. Here there are all kinds. But once again, far from actually recruiting for companions, they are themselves the target of the hunt. Being as they are, they are able to train and educate others to a socially acceptable norm of criminal society.

While homosexuality is classified as deviant in Californian society, very few homosexuals are sent to prison for that specific offense. The great majority of homosexuals in prison commit other crimes; they are sentenced for crimes ranging all through the Penal Code. During the initial sentencing and conviction, the homosexual is unidentifiable, and often is discreetly heterosexual until his arrival in prison. A comparable situation is the illiterate who claims a grade 7 or 11 education until testing proves otherwise.

The advantage for the homosexual is that if he is immediately identified, he may be kept at Vacaville where he is in competition with all the other "queers" and will be so named and subject to homosexual peer group norms prevailing on "Queen's Row." This may be quite repugnant to many homosexuals who prefer to operate discreetly within a society that will not stigmatize them. An advantage with sexual anonymity is that once in prison, the homosexual will be assigned to a two-man cell with a person of similar criminal background (similar religion and race and within five years of his own age). If he is detected, he will be segregated particularly if there is a suspicion of trouble, e.g. a young attractive homosexual with too many suitors. This type of situation may and often does lead to murder.

That prisons shall have a homosexual environment is determined by the State. The male prisoners are deprived of all normal sexual intercourse for a median period of three years (or up to life). The male prisoner is forced to sleep in the same cell with another male adult. He is forced to bathe with males and defecate with them publicly. He may be stripped in front of his peers at any time and searched in a humiliating and degredating ritual. For the rest of his prison life, except for rare visits from family, his whole life is predicated on homosexualized group contact. Is it any wonder, then, that prisons are breeding grounds for homosexual membership?

SOCIAL ORGANIZATION AND THE MATRIARCHAL SOCIETY

It is precisely because the prison sub-culture is isolated, enclosed, and homosexual that internal forces are created to correct the existing social inbalance. In a society without women, the natural drive of men will subordinate the more effeminate, literally creating a class of substitute women. *These "women" will be given all the status and privilege according to the customs and mores of outside society.* In other words, the society set up inside prison walls will in all points resemble the society from whence it came. It will have the same institutions, the same customs and, more or less, the same laws. It has one different aspect of great importance. It is a deviant society, balanced between administrative norms and peer group norms. There will be a shell culture and a core culture—a shell anomie and a core anomie. Thus the inmate society will adapt social institutions to its own use and orient them towards its own social preservation and survival. What is acceptable in the inmate world may be completely unacceptable in the total community, but the social structure will be the same; only the function is different. Homosexual marriage is unacceptable in contemporary society, whereas it is totally acceptable in the inmate society. The institution is the same, the function is different, though the difference is minimal in many respects. The major difference is in the non-existent family and kin patterns.

Because no kinship patterns exist, the inmate marriage cannot survive; but its function does serve to release sexual and emotional frustrations. It also serves to create a social pattern of simulated normalcy. It can be seen at this point that the homosexual has a very important role in prison sub-culture. *Not only does he assume the role of the "female," but also that of "wife" and "mother."* The power and status of these roles is transferred into prison styles of life. *Prison society becomes a matriarchal society* with the same social roles filled with accepted and designated members. In order that these roles may be maintained, the institutions into which they fit must also be maintained to preserve the interactional nature of social behaviour. Simply stated, without the homosexual in prison sub-culture, an imitative social system could not be established. What would be substituted in its place is hard to conceive. Certainly it would be beyond any acceptable standards and probably terminate in rabid insanity. *Thus, the homosexual, in the prison sub-society acts as catalyst through which the social system is transferred and at the same time preserves the sanity of the prison system.* The paradoxical view expressed here perhaps for the first time is that sanity is preserved through a socially deviant norm.

That the *homosexual functions therapeutically* in a prison situation suggests that such a role is not necessary in normal society. Again the ready acceptance of the homosexual in prison implies that there may well be a hidden preference for homosexuality, if there has been prior ego fragmentation from heterosexual experience.

HOMOSEXUAL ARRANGEMENTS AND CONTACTS

Meeting a homosexual in prison was almost inevitable. Knowing how to conduct oneself without becoming involved or causing offense was an art of diplomacy. Contact could be made in several ways. The first is approaching a known homosexual and arranging a meeting. This would be consummated in the maximum prison by "buying" a cell move so that partners could be together, by meeting in the showers, at games on the week-end, in the gym, or one of the many places known where there was privacy from the guards. This initial meeting was literally a "date" in every sense of the word. It fulfilled the same function. The aggressive male would buy candy or some favor as an introductory present. The idea was to show "class." The finesse of "class" may well be relevant to inmate class structure, i.e. doing things in style.

In a "no-class" association, the first contact was strictly a financial deal. Goods were passed in return for services rendered. It was as cold blooded as that. In a "class" relationship, the romance was likely to ripen into a *marriage*. This would be a significant event within the in-group. Only prominent people would be invited; gifts were expected in much the same way as any other similar social occasion; and the union would be legalized, complete with certificate. Following the ceremony, there would be a honeymoon, which culminated the process that was easily as important as any outside event for those who "counted." As on the outside, the marriage demonstrated stability within the inmate society.

SOME IMPLICATIONS OF "SETTING UP HOUSE"

Wedding invitations (embossed in gold) were secretly printed in the prison and circulated. The marriage certificate usually stated that the two people involved would agree to the terms of a homosexual contract. Such a contract defined the masculine-feminine roles of the relationship. Usually it implied a class (status) relationship. That is, the more sophisticated the formalities, the greater the responsibilities; and the more that society expected, the greater the number of rules to be adherred to. A husband was expected to provide the comforts of life for his homosexual wife who, in turn, assumed the housekeeping duties and other wifely responsibilities. Such an arrangement meant that the partners would "set up house." The "pad" would be decorated with carpets and curtains. There would be paintings, colored lights, perfume–the makings of a whole boudoir scene which is, of course, strictly contraband under correctional rules, but is obliquely tolerated in order to keep the peace. In any case the officers were somewhat afraid of the power of the "women." Given enough incentive, such as a raid on the cells where the guards would "rip off" the contraband (stealing some for their own use), the "broads" would club together in a way resembling a homosexual P.T.A. They would then proceed to make life miserable for the guards until they got their own way. If one thinks this is impossible, one should stand in the bottom tier during a raid (usually for dope) and witness the mass of contraband thrown out—and it always gets back. Indeed, as it is thrown out, certain inmates are allocated by consent to gather up the more valuable items and to return them to the owners. Inmates stealing such items had best beware of penalties from the owners if they were caught.

Thus the homosexual housekeeping arrangements also established property lines and permissible infringements of the administrative rules. Such infringements became universally adopted by others and almost become common usage, to the extent that the guards are cautious about who is raided. Homosexual wives are notorious carriers for illicit and dangerous contraband, i.e. drugs and weapons. A reason for this is that guards are loathe to shake down a "woman." It not only embarasses them, but it is also against their own accepted tradition.

So well has the inmate culture created the concept of "broad" that it is accepted as if it were real (in the sense that women are there). The concept is created by role-playing, reciprocal interaction, status giving and status acceptance, terminology and chiromenic communication. It is more than a theatrical performance, it is an actual life situation. It may well be seen as a response to acute sensory deprivation and superimposed mental patterning. The fact is that the homosexual is an established and essential part of the prison system. *The prisons breed homosexuals and intensify the nature of the homosexual propensity of men deprived of normal sexuality.* While many are not participants, no one is unaffected.

Prison populations are divided into three main types. The participants (those who do), the observers (those who don't and watch), and participant observers (those who watch and also occasionally participate). About 30% of the *long term inmates* are participants, and another 20% are participant/observers. As to the rest, they either are not interested, do not serve enough time, or have sufficient heterosexual activities (visits or the nature of assigned jobs) to avoid homosexual implications. I would venture to suggest that under sufficiently severe long term incarceration, with acute deprivation and patterning, that these percentages would rise considerably. Under such an observation, one could hardly call prisonization an effective sexual rehabilitation.

PARTIAL FAVOR ARRANGEMENTS

A second form of approach in prison is that made by the homosexual toward a prospect. This consists of passing gifts to the prospect or of discreetly laying them upon the subject's bed. In due course an inquiry is made to find out "if the gifts have been received and accepted." Unless the prospect is incredibly naive, the answer is affirmative or the gifts are returned. Upon an acceptance, the arrangements are then put on a continuing basis. This method is also used to effect in securing partial favors, rather than the establish the more durable arrangements discussed above. It is also used to gain favor with a married type who is susceptible to gifts. Partial favors indicate that what is wanted is a temporary and often freakish arrangement. In this paper I shall not discuss prison pornography or bizarre sexual acts.

In a true homosexual relationship, the favors secured are those of intercourse and substitute marriage. The male-female relationship is played to the hilt. The course of events is such that while there is no sexual restriction, *there is no loss of masculine aggressiveness and feminine submissiveness.* The "female" never exceeds the proper sexual role. Such females often dress the part and respond in all ways with feminine gestures. It should be pointed out here that many sophisticated "female" homosexuals are not offensive and indeed have as much sense of propriety as any woman. The males likewise are not offensive and do not conduct themselves any differently from most other men.

Nevertheless, as in heterosexual relationships, there are "freak-outs" and bizarre happenings. In fact all the observable deviance of heterosexual relationships is manifest in homosexual relationships. This is one more way in which the inmate sub-culture reflects the total social image. Intellectually, the capacities of both males and females apparently range over the whole spectrum, from I.Q.'s of illiterates to near genius (135 or better).

In many ways homosexuality is discreet and in many ways it is not. It is with the indiscreet aspects of homosexuality that I shall deal next. This phase of homosexuality is most offensive, but in the same way that heterosexuality may be offensive in its indiscretion. The total deviance to accepted normality creates problems and sanctions, and yet, at the same time, provides services desired by a section of the community.

INDISCREET HOMOSEXUALITY AND SOME IMPLICATIONS

By 'indiscreet,' I mean the type of homosexuality that is practiced blatantly and publicly. I am not prepared to moralize upon this issue as it also has its counterpart in heterosexual relationships. Perhaps the most offensive "freaking" that occurs is the "gang-bang" of a young homosexual. This is sometimes voluntary, sometimes involuntary. It occurs usually during shower times. The guard is diverted and men are set up to "point," i.e. to direct other inmates away from the scene and to permit uninterrupted pleasure to proceed. The "point" also warns of police approach. During the "gang-bang" (which has several variations) the homosexual is subjected to or submits to intercourse from several men. In a voluntary situation, the homosexual is paid; in an involuntary situation, it may be payment for a debt, or rape by force.

I would like to comment here on the phrase "rape by force." *There is absolutely no protection in society for the homosexual who is raped by force.* It is the same as far as the prison administration is concerned: "A faggot deserves all he gets and he gets what he deserves!" Such a comment demonstrates the attitude of officials toward the problem. However, it should be noted here that among the inmates who do not participate, there is a strong sanction against homosexual rape. The penalty is death. In any case involving an in-group inmate who is threatened with rape (by virtue of age or attractiveness), the aggressor is politely warned that his life is forfeit. In the core code regulating relations between inmates, the penalty of death is not lightly invoked. Thus the seriousness of such an offense as homosexual rape by force merits attention.

There is, in the first place, no counterpart in total society of homosexual rape. Recognizing a unique offense—the rape of one man by another—the inmate code reinforces the concept of "woman" in prison society. A very famous criminal decision—one which changed California law—was based on the inmate penalty for just this offense. The killer received life. Had the real facts come out as to code pressure, he should have been exonerated. As it was, he was saved by over-zealousness of the police. What is important here is that when a potential aggressor is told he will be killed if he violates another person's body, under the inmate code, he does not challenge the statement or proceed. Usually the message is conveyed by a "committee" of the inmate's friends; this reinforces the code. But in spite of the code, rape does occur in prison, just as it occurs outside prison. Unless the inmate is a core-inmate, he has no protection. Thus the very young and the very new are susceptible prey. As in normal society, there is no protection against homosexual rape for these men. And once raped they are classified as homosexual!

Rape by force of a known homosexual, on the other hand, results in a substantial violation of moral codes and is revenged by the male partner. The code is so strong in this respect that the inmate must revenge the rape or face social exclusion. In prison, this would mean social isolation that would place sufficient pressure on an inmate to affect his mind.

As for the indiscreet nature of the "gang-bang," it was pointed out above that variations do exist. In some cases the white homosexual is serviced by several blacks; or the situation is reversed; or there is a "mixed party." As far as race lines go, the homosexual world is somewhat democratic.[1] Even inter-racial marriage occurs. Again in the case of the gang situation, in a variation of "straight" intercourse, there may be oral as well as anal with adaptations depending on the number of members in the "gang-bang." In the event that there is more than one homosexual (submissive) available, the party soon becomes a "freak-out." Although no one becomes pregnant as a result of such prison orgies, gonorrhea is known to have been spread by homosexuals.

It is interesting how such parties are set up and how the officials remain in "complete ignorance" of what is going on. They are in fact diverted, paid-off, and given reciprocal favors. Or they owe a reciprocal favor and stay away from the "action." Occasionally they are homosexuals themselves and secretly indulge. Certainly, homosexuals are patronized, and do have connections within the administrative system as well as within the inmate culture. Certain officials permit the movement of homosexuals into cells occupied by other homosexuals; that is, two men are allowed to cell together with consent of officials. Other times, when homosexuals occupy key positions in the administrative hierarchy (clerks, accountants, stenos, etc.) favors permitting activity are given for smooth operation of the prison. These favors consist of permitting inmates to shower together on night details when there is minimal or no supervision at all. Or inmates are permitted in certain rooms together without supervision. In a prison that has an educational and an industrial complex, there are plenty of places where supervision is minimal or deliberately overlooked. Such inmates also keep secrets of what goes on when the officials are involved in deviant practices (such as participating homosexuality, narcotics traffic, theft, fraud, etc.).

Thus advertently or inadvertently, *the homosexual is a key figure in the corruption of officials and part of the deviant sub-culture.* While seldom a core figure, the homosexual is both peripheral and necessary. The homosexual may not only "pack" goods, but may also "get the goods" on officials and thus aid in their blackmail. This kind of "blackmail" may be described as operational consent, i.e. a favor for a favor; nevertheless, it is corruption, and its effects result in damaging consequences. Such an official may be used to pack weapons, narcotics, or other desired contraband into the prison. He may also be used to cover up crime and corruptly exert influence. Obviously, such an official will not announce his own deviance; in fact he will probably "scream bloody murder" if he is denounced, but it does happen and will continue to happen as long as the prison system retains its own peculiar emphasis on homosexual isolation. As was stated earlier, homosexuality knows no race lines, class lines, or status barriers.

OTHER FORMS OF CONTACT AND VARIANT STYLES

If there is one thing that is in demand in prison it is the masculine style; i.e. the inmate who adjusts to prison, is "cool" (does not get involved unnecessarily, but when he does always comes out on top), and has acquired wealth (demonstrated in a "bonnaru" style of life, with pressed clothes, new shoes, and ample funds for canteen, commissary, or influence). He might be described as the "man about prison." Such a person should also have a reputation. Usually a status inmate like this is approached directly by submissives (female) and told that they are desirable as partners on almost any terms.

Disengagement from such an offer requires diplomacy. A direct rebuff causes an affront, because the offer is made in the sincerest terms and actually represents a token of high prison flattery. The offer means that the inmate has "arrived." Moreover, at face value, the offer boosts the male ego: obviously if the individual is attractive to men, he must also be attractive to women. Therefore refusal is made in terms of courtesy. The way of inmate etiquette requires that the party so approached state that he is already committed and is sorry to turn down such an attractive offer. Such a reply causes no offense and actually returns the compliment, thereby making a friend instead of an enemy. A direct rebuff, or a moral refusal, (such as "Get off my back, you punk!") could result in retaliation and reprisal, thereby lowering the status of the inmate from "cool" to that of a "no-good bastard."

The argot here has particular significance. While homosexuals are referred to as 'fags,' 'punks,' 'bitches,' 'broads,' 'whores,' etc., the word 'fag' is seldom used; the word 'punk' signifies a younger homosexual in a slave category (and was good for blood if used indiscriminately). The more usual definition was 'broad' or 'bitch' or even 'old lady.' The term 'girl' was reserved for the younger more nearly virgin, flirtacious, fun-loving type of younger homosexual. What is important here is the sub-societal definition of a homosexual. As the designation of a homosexual was feminine, the male aggressive was never self-defined or societally defined as homosexual.[2]

Regardless of what dictionaries or psychiatrists say of both members of a homosexual act, *in prison the male partner was never normally defined as homosexual.* Therefore *masculinity was preserved and defined by homosexuals* in the deviant sub-culture. As was stated previously, one of the greatest forms of flattery was to be in demand by homosexual "women." This could cause embarrassment as other inmates would concern themselves as to what "that s.o.b. has that I haven't got." Nevertheless it was a mark of status to be singled out for "female" attention. In accordance with one's "core" status, it was a mark of distinction to be able to travel freely without creating offense. In the in-group the celibate was admired for his skill. Abstinency, like virginity was "no big thing." An inmate's personal life was his own affair.

Because the inmate culture is faithful to the outside community, the styles of homosexuals are similarly related. There are those who operate alone, those who have a pimp and those who are "on call." This stresses the demand for feminine services in prison and the way in which those services are defined by the homosexual.

One service that is generally touted along the tiers is that of "a head job for two packs." This means that an act of oral coition is offered for two packs of cigarettes. Cigarettes are the main token of currency in prison. The service is offered "over the bars" in the maximum sections and in comfort in the honor blocks. Once a service is contracted for (usually through a tier tender or block worker), at a convenient time when a guard is diverted, the copulator will press himself against the cell bars as to be as nearly hidden as possible. The copulatee will then place his penis in the other inmate's mouth until ejaculation is effected. Some "broads" pride themselves on the success of their methods, and they certainly are in demand. In the honor blocks, where the status inmates live, the act is performed in a more comfortable surrounding. There is privacy. The frequency with which this happens, and those who participate have led me to conclude that this more nearly establishes a male-female relationship. It is clear that the secrecy of the honor blocks has covered many such acts by high status members.

For reasons that I am unable to explain (or so far, apparently, anyone else), the act of oral copulation is viewed as more deviant than an act of anal homosexuality. In the inmate-inmate relationship, both acts are normative; in the inmate-administration relationship, oral acts are "sexual perversion" as defined by the California Penal Code. I would suggest here that the femininity of oral acts, accepted by the inmates, violates the administration definition of homosexual deprivation. A famous story is told of two inmates who were caught red-handed (and red-faced) in such an act. They were in the same cell. They appeared before the captain who is now in another state. The seriousness of such an offense was that both could be subject to isolation, adjustment, loss of parole consideration, etc. To explain the event, one inmate explained that he was having a sexual dream; during the dream he fell out of his top bunk, and as he did his erect organ landed squarely in the mouth of his partner in the bottom bunk, and it was in this position that he was caught. The captain laughingly dismissed this pair with the remark, "Well, I can't convict you anyway, it appears you have swallowed the evidence."

It is well to comment here that the most serious injury that can be inflicted upon such homosexuals is a blow in the mouth. Such an injury may be interpreted in the Freudian sense as a desire for physical contact. During fights, an injury to the mouth takes on the aspect of a mortal wound. Again, it is common practice for status inmates to have their own cups. The reason for this is that should anyone use someone else's cup, he is told, "I wouldn't use that cup if I were you; you'll be a cocksucker by proxy." Strangely enough this comment is not directed at the homosexual, but at the preservation of prison hygiene. Status inmates are a remarkably clean group. They do not take the risk of infection lightly. It is also sport to pull an exchange of cups on an unsuspecting inmate, especially if he is a moralizing self-righteous type. The subsequent look of horror upon the inmate's face is compensation for pseudomorality.

It is in this type of humor that we see yet another function of the homosexual in prison. Such humor tends to preserve the stability of prison sub-culture and gives support to the role of the homosexual. In essence, *the homosexual provides a basis for humor*—an indispensable relief for the severity of prison deprivation. Perhaps the maturity (or irony) of the situation is that the homosexuals themselves participate in this type of humor. In the honor blocks, the service usually costs more. And it is not unknown that such services continue on a retainer basis. I was unaware of this practice until a close friend revealed that he had been paying for legal services out of his retainer. Should prices go up, he would demand a greater retainer. In this case, the inmate was heterosexual, was the male, and was serviced regularly by an older man. The usual relationship was for an older man to retain "a kid," "*his* kid" as defined by property rights.

LIFE STYLES OF SUBMISSIVES

The word 'submissive' is used to designate the "female" of the male-female homosexual relationship. The "broads,"[5] as they are usually referred to, always keep this feminine designation, as 'she,' 'her,' 'hers.' Because they assume the female role, and because they are designated as females, they meet group expectation of role requirements. They are seldom referred to as "fruit." This word is usually reserved for the type who "flip-flops;" that is one who goes either way as male or female or who "freaks" out. This type is also known as 'pitcher-catcher.' The expression here means that "today's pitcher is tomorrow's catcher." A person given to this disorientation of roles acquires the name of 'fruit' (in the sense of over-ripeness). As for the true submissives, it must be noted that the *mental* patterning, induced by society, results in a feminine *physical* style. The "girls" behave in the showers in a feminine way. They wear shower caps, they are quite different in their washing procedures; they wrap their towels differently. When they go to the washrooms together, they carry "douche-bags" with their toiletries packed within. They use make-up, cosmetics, perfume, any and everything that simulates the outside feminine world. On occasions when the contraband situation is just right, they wear stockings, panties, bra, and any other item of female apparel. The conversation is feminine. They refer to each other by girl's names (and are generally known by feminine names; this can be disconcerting if one does not know who the person is). They refer to "tarts" and "bitches" of their own kind who break accepted rules. They discuss marriage, divorce, affairs and sexual qualities of their lovers. In this instant, the argot of prison asserts itself when they discuss men. The sexual organ is referred to as a 'bone.' This is taken apparently from the domino cult of the "Big Yard." Here the dominoes are referred to as bones; the game itself is called 'slapping big six' (the method of opening the game). In cosmetic habits, the "broads" shave their legs and bodies; they wear tight pants; they do anything to accentuate sexual appeal. Their hair-dos are specially catered to. Negro "girls" have a real problem in this respect. Yet in a maximum security prison this is what actually takes place right under the noses of the officials and often with their sub-rosa consent.

For long term inmates the submissive style becomes sophisticated; and, in the case of a stable marriage, serious problems can arise upon release of one partner and not the other. Inmates may commit crimes to stay in, even murder to avoid separation, or in despair they may attempt suicide. It has been known that paroles have been refused because of the homosexual institutionalization of inmates, who have literally established a home in prison. There is a strong homosexual security feeling in prison life styles.

Here then, we see that *the homosexual functions to defeat rehabilitation and to actually create security within prison walls.* Recidivism may well be related to homosexual propensities. No studies have been done in this area. But it has been clear to my own observations that the homosexual is more secure in prison than outside. Within prison, the homosexual has *ascribed status.* Indeed, he can achieve higher status along with the recognition he would not receive on the outside, especially if it is known that he is a homosexual.

Moreover, homosexuals tend to settle in jobs that appeal to them, tending to manipulate job situations until they can get what they want. In prison, jobs can be bought or sold for favors as anywhere else. Thus they will congregate in groups. The clothing industry attracts large numbers, and many will end up as stenos to officials. They are allowed to work with women as they are a safe risk. They are permitted outside. (It would be impossible to "drive some of them off with a stick," as long as their partners are inside.) But in groups, they behave quite differently. Towards people they know and trust, they make female gestures, little girlish waves, obvious male compliments—the sort of pleasantries reserved in offices for status people. They feel safe. Towards someone they confide in and who protects them the "girls" reciprocate in terms of protection. Other favors are available, but neutrality is respected and admired.

Homosexuals also attend church. Although it has been said that church has been used as a meeting place, I doubt it. Homosexuals have not frightened Christians out of church, rather the opposite is true. Although homosexuality is incompatible with the Christian religion, one cannot imagine that any one has the right to deny beliefs to any person. As in outside churches, where the preponderance of the congregations are women, and the workers are women, it appears that in the inmate sub-culture, the same life styles will be practiced. Thus when the homosexual takes the female role, church attendance is merely one more factor of that role rather than religion *per se.* This applies to all other institutions that are reflected in the sub-culture. In the prison homosexual society, a vacuum is created that demands filling.

In short, once more, with the complete deprivation of women and sexuality, the homosexual is an essential part of inmate society. In a life situation that demands the interaction between the sexes, the prison community will adopt a model or a reasonable facsimile that approximates the normal social structure. With two basic groups, male and female, in society, the prison will also divide into basic divisions. As long as it "takes two to tango," the partners will have to be drawn from opposite groups. Where society institutes closure and isolation, the contained group will modify and adjust to resemble the structures of the former society.

CONCLUSION

Homosexuality, possibly with the exception of organic displacement, is learned behaviour. In a normal society, the homosexual is seen as socially and sexually disoriented, as somewhat schizoid. But in a prison society, constituting a sub-culture of adult males, persons exhibiting this type of social-sexual deviancy are essential to the function of the prison community. Thus in an abnormal inmate culture, deviancy to social norms is now acceptable as approximating social needs. The homosexual, schizophrenic in normal society, is adjusted and normal in the maladjusted prison sub-culture. His partial role as male or female is fulfilled in prison, whereas on the outside it was incomplete. In consequence, the homosexual is absolutely essential to the function of the adult male prison.

In summary, the homosexual meets the social need of an all male society in the following ways:

1 He assumes the role of female, wife, mother in various orders and styles.

2 He acts as a catalyst through which the image of matriarchal society is transferred (by institutions).

3 His deviancy acts to preserve the social sanity of the prison sub-system, thus acting as a therapeutic.

4 The homosexual by his role defines male-female status and preserves the hierarchical order (role-status-class).

5 The homosexual creates stability in prison by establishing property lines (marriage-contact-home).

6 The homosexual provides a basis for humor.

7 The homosexual adopts and preserves life styles of normal society.

In contrast to the essential function of the homosexual, there is also a built-in dysfunction. The homosexual:

1 acts as a key figure in the corruption of officials;

2 sets deviant norms and sanctions for inmate anomie; and

3 defeats the rehabilitation process by establishing strong security feelings within prison walls.

In conclusion, therefore, it can be seen that the homosexual is not only essential to the function of prison society, but is also a product in that prison intensifies and perpetuates homosexuality. Such deviant behaviour is carried and transmitted into normal society upon the release of inmates. Because of the security of homosexuals in prison, the more natural act of the homosexual is to return to prison where his status is assured.

By isolating women from their husbands and men friends, the prison administration gives silent consent to the extension and propagation of homosexuality. In any case, no prisoner can remain unaffected from the impact of such overt practice; thus rehabilitation is token and actually more directed at homosexual education than heterosexual adjustment. The younger the inmate, the longer the term, the greater the deprivation—the more likely the inmate is to become homosexual or become socially deviant by State direction. The State of California punishes crime by making offenders more prone to deviance, by making deviants more so, and by punishing (indirectly) the families of those in prison.

The problem is not a happy one but then, without exception, neither were any of the homosexuals I knew.

Edwin Johnson
Sacramento, California

NOTES

* The writer spent three years as an inmate in a California maximum security prison (San Quentin) on the basis of an allegation for which he was later exonerated. During this time he was teacher, aide to a supervisor, and legal counselor to many inmates. Because he was not involved, and remained neutral, he was trusted and confided in without fear of reprisal. Details disclosed here are true and verifiable.

1 Ned Polsky, *Hustlers, Beats and Others* (Chicago: Aldine Publishing Co., 1967), p. 87. A. Cohen, *Deviance and Control* (New York: Prentice-Hall, 1966), p. 87.

2 Cf., A. Reiss, "The Social Integration of Peers and Queers," in *The Other Side*, ed. by Howard S. Becker (New York: The Free Press, 1964), pp. 181-210.

3 L. Hinsie and R. Campbell, *Psychiatric Dictionary* (Oxford: Oxford University Press, 1960).

4 See note 2.

5 Homosexual prostitutes (tramps) are rare and are not discussed here. See: Edwin Schurr, "The Homosexual Prostitute," in *Crimes Without Victims* (New York: Prentice-Hall, 1965), p. 89ff.

Prison Homosexuality and Its Effect on Post-Prison Sexual Behavior

Edward Sagarin

ALTHOUGH THERE HAS grown up a considerable literature on sex experiences in prison, little has been written on the post-prison behavioral patterns of those who, voluntarily or involuntarily, become initiated into homosexuality while incarcerated. In the light of the considerable number of prisoners and ex-prisoners in the original Kinsey sample, it is possible that the Institute for Sex Research might have in its files material that would shed light on this problem. To date, nothing has been forthcoming. In one of the few references to the subject, Kirkham (1972, p. 42) suggests that sexual experiences in prison may have permanent effects on the lives of some of the participants: "Can such men return to conventional heterosexual lives after release, or has the experience of being forced into acts of passive homosexuality been so traumatic as to preclude the resumption of sexual relations with members of the opposite sex?" In a search for an answer to his question, the present paper studies ex-prisoners whose initiation into homosexuality occurred during prison.

The Nature and Incidence of the Experience

Opposition to prison homosexuality has usually come from one of two sources. For some, it is a matter of immorality and degradation; for others, homosexuality in male prisons has been associated with violence. However, a third consideration, the effect of such experiences on the prisoner's life following release, has generally been ignored, and to my knowledge never researched, although it may be highly significant in the evaluation of this phenomenon.

It is widely stated that for a considerable number of prisoners, homosexual contact takes place for the first time in their lives during confinement. Buffum reviews the various estimates of the incidence of prison homosexuality among males, noting that it clusters in the range between 30 to 45 percent, although Irwin makes a lower estimate (around 15 percent). Buffum then goes on to state: "Working on the assumption that 40 to 50 percent of a penal population will have homosexual experience in prison, Gagnon has estimated that 5 to 10 percent will have had no prior homosexual experience, 25 to 30 percent will have had casual or intermittent prior experience, and 5 to 10 percent will have had extensive or nearly exclusive homosexual commitment in the free community" (p. 13).

It is difficult to translate these percentages into absolute numbers. While there are approximately a quarter of a million

Dr. Sagarin (PhD New York Univ. 66) is Professor of Sociology at City College of New York and Past President of American Society of Criminology.

The writer is indebted to Harry Allen, Simon Dinitz, and Robert J. Kelly, all of whom read earlier versions of this paper, and offered many suggestions and insights.

inmates (mostly males) in federal and state prisons at any one time in the United States, this figure becomes much larger when the inmates of local lockups and city and county jails are included. On the one hand, the incidence of homosexuality may be larger in these local jails, with their inferior security, poor recreational facilities, and other difficulties; on the other, some of the local lockup residents are present for such a short time, perhaps overnight while making bail, that they could go in and out before having an opportunity to become a victimizer or to be exposed to the latter's assaults. Nevertheless, using Gagnon's figures, one could estimate that there are probably 25,000 males (a very rough estimate, indeed) at present in jails or prisons, whose initial homosexual experience took place during incarceration, and at least that number, and perhaps more, of ex-convicts who can be placed into the same category. Further, it is the contention of Akers and his colleagues that there is considerably more homosexuality (as well as use of drugs) in custodial-type than in treatment-type institutions. The implications from this work would appear to be that prison homosexuality is indeed related to violence. The custodial institutions are more deprivational, punitive, and repressive; the treatment types are more open, nonpunitive, and imbued with some humanitarian concerns for inmates, and utilize the rhetoric, if not the means, of correction. It is not only the amount of homosexuality that differs in the two types, but the content, with brutality, rape, and gang sodomy found in the custodial institutions.

Working in the California prison system, Kirkham (1971) found that there were three categories that prisoners themselves used to describe inmates involved in homosexual relations. In the vernacular of the prison, these are called "fairies," "punks," or "jocks" (or "jockers"), with numerous synonyms available for each word. To avoid the pejorative terminology, I am going to refer to the three as "effeminates," "involuntary recruits," and "voluntary aggressors," respectively.

The effeminates are males with obviously recognizable traits and mannerisms; all of these inmates have had a considerable history of homosexuality before incarceration, make a homosexual identification, and usually seek to take advantage of their availability for sexual purposes while in prison. Although there is a prison population of males who have been convicted of homosexual offenses against adults, minors, or children, as described by Gebhard and his colleagues, it is probably the case that most effeminate prisoners have not been incarcerated for sex-related crimes.

The involuntary recruits have come into prison with a self-image of themselves as heterosexual, and are raped, cajoled, threatened, or in some other way made into the passive (or insertee) partner.[1] Once raped or seduced, these persons become known as "jailhouse turnouts" or JTOs, a term that is used even when the event takes place in a prison rather than a jail.

The voluntary participants here described as aggressors use the effeminates or the involuntary recruits for homosexual acts (anal intercourse or fellatio), and are (or claim to be) the insertors.

These categories do not exhaust the possibilities for types of prisoners involved in homosexual conduct. According to a considerable amount of popular and even scientific literature, the majority of people following an exclusive or near-exclusive homosexual pattern are not effeminate. Any such persons who find their way into prison do not fit into any of the three categories. Their relationships would be voluntary and nonaggressive, and once it becomes known, or even suspected, in the inmate community that they participate in such acts, they become classified with and treated like the effeminates and the JTOs.

There is a special type of aggressive jocker, described to me in a letter from a young white prisoner who is a nonparticipant heterosexual, and who has spent most of his adult life behind bars. There is, he writes,

---

[1] See Kelly for a description of one way in which such a new inmate is recruited.

what is sometimes referred to as a "Folsom jocker." To best explain it, I'll tell the usual joke that describes him perfectly. Two men are celling together—one is the prison bully, the other a poor, meek, young-looking kid who has just come in and was thrown into the cell with this bully. The guy is beating up the kid, yelling at him, threatening him, and screaming, "Look, kid, you better do this or I'm gonna . . . ," and the poor kid is protesting, "But I DON'T KNOW HOW!" And the bully replies, "Well, dammit, I'll show you one more time!"[3]

Finally, there is the question of whether there are people in a sex-segregated institution who make sexual alliances of a more voluntary and affectionate nature, even if such persons had no previous homosexual history. Instead of rape and threat, or the promiscuity so often associated with homosexuality, might there not be stable homosexual couples, similar to those described by Ward and Kassebaum in female prisons? There is little indication that there are such couples in male institutions. This may be merely a reflection of the lesser stability of all-male as compared with all-female couples in a marital-like situation, whether in prison or in the outside world. But toughness itself is a male prison value, and affection is its reverse, having an implication of softness. The male prison atmosphere not only is not conducive to affectionate homosexuality, but might be so hostile as to make its survival impossible. Reports of females who continue their relationships after prison, whatever may be the elements of truth or exaggeration in these stories, seldom have counterparts in the male world. Nevertheless, the prisoner mentioned above writes that he has encountered affectionate sexuality in a male prison.

For an inmate to escape stigmatization for his homosexual behavior, Kirkham suggests that he must fulfill two criteria:

(1) the homosexual act or acts must represent only a situational reaction to the deprivation of heterosexual intercourse, and (2) such behavior must involve a complete absence of emotionality and effeminacy—both of which are regarded as signs of 'weakness' and 'queerness.' An inmate who engages in homosexual activity must present a convincing façade of toughness and stereotypical 'manliness' in order to escape being defined as a homosexual. [1971, p. 331]

It is clear, then, that these conditions are not conducive to affectionate homosexual coupling.

Victims and Victimizers

Inasmuch as the present study is concerned with how prison homosexuality affects post-prison sexual adjustments and behavior, the effeminates are excluded from the sample. They had made a homosexual identification before prison, and if they continued these patterns after release (as one might conjecture), it is hardly reasonable to consider the period of confinement as a contribution to such a way of life.

The interest, then, is in the involuntary recruits and the voluntary aggressors. Kirkham (1971) notes that if the involuntary recruit has been in prison before, and had been "turned out" there, his reputation follows him, and any effort he might make to resist would be doomed from the start. He is usually among the youngest prison inmates, and after being subdued, is highly stigmatized; like the female who is a victim of rape, he has what Goffman calls a "spoiled identity."

The voluntary aggressors, on the other hand, are usually older. Sometimes they commit forcible rape and even gang rapes on others, as vividly described by Davis. They are physically bigger and stronger, and frequently part of the inmate power group, show no signs of effeminacy, and make a heterosexual identification, not only for their pre-prison life but for their incarcerated life. It is said that they sometimes work with the tacit consent or approval of corrections officers, a statement that is difficult to validate.

Although the literature on homosexuality has frequently downplayed the importance of whether one is an active or passive partner, or, more accurately, an insertor or insertee, this appears to be an important

[3] Personal communication, 1975.

element in the prison homosexual scene. The voluntary aggressors are invariably, or claim to be, the insertors (save for the Folsom jocker already described), and insertion is an act of masculinity, of dominance, of forcing another into submission. The adolescent hustlers described by Reiss likewise claimed to be exclusively insertors, although in their case the insertion was claimed to be oral-genital; their relationship, if their descriptions are believable and not viewed as self-serving, cannot be understood as one of dominance and submission, but perhaps as dominance and humiliation.

The involuntary recruits and the voluntary aggressors have relatively fixed statuses. They are not marked by social mobility, but have a permanence attached to them. Once recruited by force or threat, by cajolery or trickery, the recruit has little hope for escape. After a first experience, an involuntary recruit may stave off his subduers and prevent the repetition of the act, but having been defined as one who had been subdued, his chances for success in having himself redefined are minimal.

Bartollas and his colleagues, studying the homosexual scene in a juvenile institution, found a pattern in which older, tougher boys subdued, exploited, overcame, seduced, and forced into fellatio the younger and weaker youths. The latter were then defined as "scapegoats," an extremely low status inside the institution, similar to that of the involuntary recruit in adult prisons. The scapegoat status followed the individuals after release:

> The institutional subculture, including the informal power and status hierarchy of the inmates, enforced the "unclean" status assigned to the inmate by isolating him in the institution. Staff, in addition, reinforced his identity by providing him with little assistance in getting "off the bottom." The anomic state he is placed in, with his norms and values threatened, results in identity confusion and generally makes the time he is in this institution a living hell. Furthermore, his institutional "career" is likely to evolve into his community "occupation" as he continues to be a social outcast committing serious personal and property crimes. *He probably also will remain a sexual scapegoat in the community.* [Bartollas et al., p. 95; italics added]

Body build seems to be an important factor in determining whether one will be a successful aggressor or be successfully subdued. Davis writes that

> virtually every slightly-built young man committed by the courts is sexually approached within a day or two after his admission to prison [in Philadelphia]. . . . Only the tougher and the more hardened young men, and those few so obviously frail that they are immediately locked up for their own protection, escape homosexual rape. [pp. 108-109]

Working with Davis' figures, which were made in a lockup (not a state or federal prison) where 81 percent of the inmates were black, Scacco notes that 85 percent of the aggressors were black. The difference between the two figures is small, but when the data on the vctims are examined, one finds that 71 percent of the victims are white. This is due to the fact that 56 percent of the offenders were blacks who victimized whites, whereas the 15 percent of the offenders who were white chose only white victims. That white aggressors victimized only whites may have been due to their fear of reprisal by the larger and more powerful black inmate population. That blacks so often victimized whites may be due to the fact that the meaning of the act, as Gagnon and Simon have pointed out, may not be primarily sexual in character, but rather may be an expression of dominance needs. It is clear, as Scacco discusses in detail, that the atmosphere of racial oppression in America, particularly as seen by an inmate, would bring forth a need in blacks to lash out at whites and to express some dominance at a time of utter powerlessness. Nevertheless, Buffum suggests that some of the instances of interracial sex may not be rape, but may reflect "the desire of some overt white male homosexuals for Negro 'jockers'" (p. 23).

After Prison: Nine Subjects

For a long time, I have been deeply interested in what occurs to the voluntary aggressors and the involuntary recruits after release from prison. I have been able to locate only a few people—five aggressors and four recruits—and the small number must make the findings suspect. One must challenge deductions, and be constantly aware of the possibility of unrepresentativeness. Nevertheless, such work need not be discarded outright; a major question is whether the findings can be reconciled with other data and are capable of lending themselves to convincing and parsimonious explanation.

In addition to the small sample, other difficulties arose. I met the JTOs through social circles in which homosexually inclined persons were gathering. Thus, the sample of JTOs was confined to those who had made a post-prison identification with homosexuality. None of them had succeeded in resuming their previous heterosexual life (assuming that their pre-prison pattern had indeed been heterosexual), and with one exception, had made little effort to do so. Lost to such a sample were those whose resocialization with a girlfriend or a wife was sufficiently successful so that the homosexuality had been a temporary experience, to be remembered perhaps as no more than another unpleasant reason for not wanting to return to prison. As for the five voluntary aggressors, I met them only through parole and corrections officers, who assisted me in locating persons meeting the qualifications for this study and willing to submit to an interview on the subject.

A further difficulty was in the deliberate dissembling attempted by all those studied. For the aggressors, there was an insistence that there had been no homosexual experience, or very little, before incarceration; second, there was an effort to play down the unwillingness of the partner or partners to participate in the prison sexual experience, and an assertion that nothing more was ever used than persuasion; and third, a denial that there was any further homosexual experience following prison. The first and third of these contentions can be understood as efforts to project an image of self as heterosexual. The second—that no forcible rape had ever occurred—was more ambiguous. An important factor here was not only the projection of an image as a nonviolent person (the very reverse of the way a prisoner often wants to be seen by his convict-peers), but also the suspicion that anything said might find its way back to the parole officers. Further, if one were seeking sex with a male to the point of wanting to subdue him and force oneself upon him, this suggests the possibility of a homosexual component that an ex-prisoner might not like to make known to self or others.

In the involuntary recruits, there were two contentions that had to be accepted with caution. The first involved their pre-prison sexual lives. Were they really jailhouse turnouts, or had they been involved in voluntary homosexuality, without showing signs of effeminacy? Second, and related thereto, how unwilling had they been in their first prison homosexual experiences? Since they were now making open homosexual identifications, there did not seem to be any vested interest in claiming pre-prison heterosexuality, or prison victimization. But the possibilities for dissembling were there.

The five aggressors had been out of prison a relatively short time (averaging four months) at the time of the interviews. The four JTOs had been free a longer time (the average was more than two years, and the range was from four months to five years). Both groups were young while in prison; none of the nine had been over 25, and none had been under 18. The latter figure is particularly significant: (1) they had all had sexual experiences before prison, and (2) the events that they describe did not take place in a youth facility, as did those depicted by Bartollas and his colleagues. None had been convicted of political crimes, draft evasion, white-collar crimes, or sexual crimes. All their convictions had been for nonsexual crimes against persons or against property, including burglary, street robbery, and automobile theft. Eight of the nine had been out on suspended sentences at the time of their arrest. None had served more than one prison term, except for local lockups pending trial, at the time of the interview. The five aggressors consisted of three blacks, one Puerto Rican who made a white identification, and one white. The four recruits consisted of three whites and one Puerto Rican who could have made a white or black identification; when asked if he thought of himself as white or as black, the latter replied, "I'm Hispanic." There may be more blacks among the subdued recruits than this would indicate (29 percent of all the recruits, according to the Davis figures), but the homosexual social circles in which these persons were located were predominantly white. The narration of the events as they took place in prison was unverifiable, and must be seen essentially as how the narrator wanted the interviewer to know about such activities. This was also true of the pre-prison sexual history, in which there may have been a tendency to show less homosexuality than actually occurred, and it could also be true of the post-prison sexuality, although I did make some effort to confirm this part of the narration whenever possible.

The Stories of the Aggressors

The five aggressors were all tall, muscular, strong, and tough-looking; two of them might well have been culled from a photographic album of the stereotypical hard criminal. They admitted (or claimed) sexual experiences in prison, and in all instances insisted with tremendous verisimilitude that they had done all the inserting. They showed no affection for anyone with whom they had had sexual contact; in fact, in all instances they displayed so much contempt that it seemed to fortify the truth of their denial of any insertee role at any time (although one can also interpret their attitudes as an expression of a reaction formation). They talked of the recruits as homos, punks, fairies, fags, JTOs, cocksuckers, boy-girls, and in other terms that betrayed nothing but contumely.

The aggressors were particularly sensitive about the private nature of what they said. They had to be promised complete anonymity. They insisted that nothing that they said should be taped, and that there should be no hidden tape-recorders. The researcher made a commitment that no information would reach parole officers. Because the number of people was so small, it might have been possible to identify them nonetheless, but sufficient time has passed since the interviews so that this would by now be practically impossible, and, further, would have few, if any, adverse effects.

The aggressors, while denying violence, claimed to have been capable of having any boy-girl that they wanted, whenever they so desired, but at the same time they would never admit having forced themselves on "a kid." Davis gives a particularly vivid picture of a rape, but it was obtained from a victim; the victimizer tends to deny, conceal, or embellish the same occurrence. There was never an admission of a gang-bang in which one aggressor held down a victim, while another performed an act of sodomy (here defined as anal intercourse) or forced fellatio. Rather, they presented the homosexuality as having resulted from persuasion or sometimes from threat or a show of potential force; but in the narration of the aggressors, when the chips were down "the kid" gave in because he really wanted it. He was "really a queer" and just had not come out yet, one aggressor insisted, and if he hadn't wanted it, he would have fought to the end against it.

This is obviously an embellished version of what had occurred, and whenever something like this was said during a discussion (all interviews were separate from one another, and to my knowledge, none of the ex-convicts was acquainted with any of the others), I made known my skepticism, with the hope that it would not destroy whatever trust they had in me. When the question of force was raised, one former prisoner laughed and said that everybody knows that there's no real difference "between rapping and raping," that it's only a matter of the word you use and how you want to see it. The aggressors mentioned a variety of methods of advances used, in shower, recreation, and laundry rooms; some of these types of encounters are described in detail by Kirkham (1971). They claimed that with the connivance of both other inmates and corrections officers, they had arranged to be alone with the object of their interest at a particular time and place, a statement not unlike one made by a victim and reported by Sagarin and MacNamara. Three of the five aggressors volunteered the information that there was never a problem about time, place, or even privacy. One claimed that he used to ask a corrections officer to let the youth of his choice into his cell at night, to play a game of cards or checkers. It was all worked out with utmost simplicity and full cooperation. When a victim arrived, he knew what was expected of him and—according to the narration of the ex-convict—either accepted it as a matter of fate, or protested only meagerly.

The following conversation is reproduced from memory, written down soon after the interview:

RESEARCHER: If he had screamed, would anyone have come to his aid?

PAROLEE: Well, no, I guess not.

R: So he'd have screamed, and wouldn't give in, and nobody would come to help him. What would you have done? The next step would be up to you, wouldn't it?

P: Well, like I say, this did happen, this kid screamed, and I said to him that if he hollered again I'd have to hit him, and I told him that I didn't want to do that. You know, I wouldn't have wanted to hurt the kid.

R: So you told him that, and what happened then?

P: He just looked at me, and I told him to pull down his pants and lay down on my bed, and he said, "Take it easy, just don't hurt me," and that is what happened.

R: That's all?

P: Well, I told him I wouldn't hurt him, so I put on a lot of grease, and I just went in slow, and he didn't scream any more, so I figured he must have liked it.

R: You wouldn't say you were forcing him to do it?

P: No, I wouldn't call that forcing him. I sure as hell didn't rape him.

R: But you said to him that if he hollered again, you'd have to hit him. That's threatening him, isn't it? You're a pretty big and strong guy. Maybe he was just afraid that you'd kill him, or knock the shit out of him?

P: No, he didn't even try to fight with me. The first time that I told him to stop hollering, he just gave in. Like a girl—first she's got to say no, and then she says yes, or she just lets you without saying anything. So I figure he must have really liked it.

The interview went on to other matters, and about an hour later, without questioning or provocation, the parolee returned to the previous conversation.

P: You know this kid I was telling you about, the one who hollered and then I told him he better not do it again?

R: Sure, what about him?

P: You still think I forced him, because I told him he better not holler or I'd hit him? You think I forced him, don't you?

R: I'm not sure. If you say you didn't, then you didn't. Or at least that's your way of looking at it.

P: You know, I told you he liked it. Well, I had him two-three times a week, and then there was another kid I had my eyes on, and I just played it cool, and then nothing happened for a week or so. Then Sandy comes up to me in the yard, and he says, "What's the matter, Joe? I ain't heard from you for a while." So I says, "I thought you said you're not a fairy, that you didn't like it, so I figure I'd give you a break. If you don't want it, you don't have to have it." And he says, "Well, you get used to things, Joe. I'm not saying I like it, but it's better than having nothing."

R: Why are you telling me this, all of a sudden? We weren't even talking about it anymore.

P: Well, I just want you to know, nobody forces a punk. Maybe the first time you get him scared, and he thinks it's going to hurt, but if he didn't really want it, he'd fight like hell. This punk was like all the rest. You break them in, and the first thing you know they're dying for it. You give them up and you find somebody else, and if they can't get back with you, they start chasing every prick they can get. They're not innocent like you think. They want it, I tell you, they want it, but they just don't like to admit it at first. They got to come out, just like any other fairy.

R: I still want to know why you're telling me this.

P: Because I want you to know, I never raped, and I never knew anybody else who raped. We find a kid that's a nice piece of ass, and we just fool around and see if he's going to fight us off, and if he don't, then he wants it, even if he can't realize it himself yet.

The aggressors all said that at times they had had a single inmate as sex partner, using the same person over and over, and not permitting him to be touched by any other inmate. But these exclusive arrangements are short-lived. In one instance, an aggressor insisted that he was taking care of three younger inmates over the same period of time, that he did not allow any of them other experiences; but he appeared to be exaggerating, perhaps fantasizing with regard to power and sexual prowess. When there were new arrivals in prison, or someone tired of an old "lover," partners were frequently exchanged (sometimes without the prior consent or knowledge of the recruits), and new bedmates acquired. One aggressor claimed to have had a homosexual pimping operation going in the prison for a time, in which he was "renting out" to others a group that he called "his boys." Claims of this sort are not only unverifiable, but carry an air of braggadocio; despite the damaging nature of the admissions (but made to someone pledged to secrecy), they may indeed be false confessions. Yet, as such, they are not to be ignored, for they shed a great deal of light on those who make these apparently untrue statements.

The Stories of the Involuntary Recruits

The four subdued tell another story, which in large measure is complementary to that of their subduers. They insist that they were either physically raped, or so completely threatened that they were afraid to resist. They told of being slapped on the face, punched in the stomach, and given other brutal treatment until they were willing to be passive and accept sodomy, or be the receptor in fellatio. With their first experience of sodomy, they could recall the pain and the humiliation; with fellatio, a tremendous amount of disgust, retching, unwillingness or inability to pursue the sucking even when hit, and a meager attempt to perform. When the first such event was over, they were told by the subduers that they were punks, "which is worse than being a fairy, because it's a fairy that won't admit it." When they protested that they had been forced into the act, the aggressors laughed, saying, "That's an old story, nobody could force you if you really didn't want it," and said that the "punks" would learn to like it so much that they would be coming around begging for it. Reports of this sort are all the more remarkable because they are being recalled by people who later made a homosexual identification and who at the time of the interview found pleasurable something that they nevertheless were recalling with extreme disgust.

The predictions made by the aggressors about these men turned out to be true. Everyone thought of them as punks, and they began to suspect that that was what they were. The experience began to lose its displeasure, and they found themselves even liking it a little, especially if not accompanied by physical pain. They had all heard about latent homosexuals, and they began to suspect that that was their fate.

One may ask why there is no complaint from the victim, if indeed he is the unwilling recruit. Buffum writes:

> Today, if one who is the victim of a prison sexual attack has the temerity to complain, the likely result will be (1) retaliation by other prisoners, (2) segregation and attendant loss of privileges within the prison, (3) ridicule and embarrassment and (4) possible prosecution of

the offender, which in fact provides the prisoners with no tangible relief. [p. 33]

Further, Scacco emphasizes the role of the correction officer in not aiding the victim, whether because of a desire to keep the peace by not antagonizing the most powerful groups in the inmate society, or because of corruption. Gibbons puts the issue of staff involvement very strongly:

This kind of violence has usually been covertly encouraged by the institutional staff. It is not the work of disturbed youths, or mess-ups; instead, it must be seen as a basic feature of the social organization of correctional institutions. [p. 8]

It is a story of accommodation and of self-identification, in which one sees himself as he thinks he is seen by others. The recruits thought that they had no alternative but to submit—that this was the only path to survival, very much like the method of survival in concentration camps described by Bettelheim. They discovered that almost immediately after the first event, which became known throughout the prison with great rapidity, they were labeled, not as victims, but with the pejorative terms used for those who had sought and enjoyed the experience. Everyone looked upon them as homosexuals and talked about them as if they were, and they were approached as if they were open territory for anyone who wanted them, unless the consent of a specific aggressor was required. Two brief excerpts:

You get used to anything. You got to live. And I suppose getting used to it, you get to like it. Liking it is your way of getting used to it.

Maybe they were right. Maybe I was one of them all along. I don't know. But I came out in prison, I know that.

Sexual Patterns After Prison

What happens to men whose first homosexual experiences are as prisoners? What occurs to them upon release and resocialization into the two-sexed society?

The five aggressors all claimed, and with a great deal of convincing evidence, that they were living exclusively heterosexual lives—"normal" is the word that most of them used. They were in some instances with a girlfriend or a wife—in one case, the same wife as before prison. Two of them were "playing the field." In the words of one man, "You know sex ain't hard to get. I get as much as I want of it." All categorically denied any interest in males.

R: How about the kind of sex you had in prison?

P: Punks?

R: Boys, young men, kids.

P: Why would I want a fairy, when I can get a broad?

This last remark was expressed with such astonishment at the question, that to disbelieve the ex-convict was hardly possible. It is a spontaneous reply of this sort, with the quizzical look of someone who cannot understand why he has been asked something incredibly stupid, that imparts credibility to the answer of a respondent.

Inquiries with girlfriends and with a wife did elicit some verification that there is heterosexual activity, but with a new element: some sexual violence, some tendency toward brutality during and preceding sexuality, an overlording and demanding attitude that might be interpreted as a continuation of the violent sex of prison. Some would argue, as do Rosenberg and Bensman, that a good deal of lower-class nonmarital and even marital sex is accompanied by crudity and brusqueness, bordering on or deeply involved with violence. The problem of determining whether these people had become more violent in their sexual lives is complex, and an answer can only be conjectural; further, if the violent component of their sexuality had increased, was it prison itself that brutalized them, or was it the manner in which they obtained sex while in prison? I would not argue that the people I met had displayed a violence typical of lower-class persons; they seemed to me to represent the small proportion of the lower class that engages in violent crimes, and who are hence very likely to continue their violent patterns, criminal or noncriminal, following prison.

As for the four who had been the reluctant and subdued partners in prison, as I indicated, it is difficult to generalize on their post-prison homosexuality because they were encountered through homosexual social circles. Efforts to locate jailhouse turnouts who had returned to the heterosexual life, through legal circles, parole officers, counselors, therapists, and others, were unsuccessful, but this may not be because they do not exist (they probably do, in large numbers), but because those who have relinquished homosexuality seem to regard it as especially stigmatizing and seem to avoid admitting it.

Conclusions and Implications

If one were to take these nine persons as representative of the aggressors and their victims, the outcome of their lives is ironic, but the irony is not beyond explanation. Of those who had actively sought a homosexual experience and not only had willingly entered into it but also had inflicted it on others, all returned to heterosexuality. On the contrary, all of those who had been forced and subdued into homosexuality, who insisted that it had hurt and disgusted them and that they had entered it most unwillingly, continued the pattern and pursued it in their post-prison years.

For an explanation of the plausibility of the first finding, the work of Gagnon and Simon, both on prison homosexuality and on sexual conduct generally, is most valuable. For the actors, the manner in which they define an event is significant. The meaning that they impute to it and find in it, especially when reinforced by similar definitions by significant others, will influence the consequences of the event for their life patterns. For the aggressors, the subduing of another was not primarily a search for sexual outlet, affection, or even release from tension. It was a means for the reaffirmation of masculinity in a subculture in which few other methods were available for such expression; the fact that the same event, the sodomizing of another male, would have been defined in their own outside world as a flight from masculinity was irrelevant. In prison, sexuality was a means for the expression of dominance over another.

That the act itself was homosexual is indisputable from the viewpoint of a behavioral scientist. But this is not quite so clear to the participants. They were concerned not with the definition of the act, but only with the labeling of the actors, including themselves. They did not see themselves as homosexual, and this definition of self was reinforced by the acceptance of it by their peers. The boy-girl was the one who received the phallus, whether orally or anally, and a boy-girl was (for them) a punk, a fairy, a homosexual.

For themselves, the aggressors knew that the person with whom they were having sexual contact was a male, but they conceived of him as a substitute for a female (not the same as fantasizing that he was female, which might also have been the case). Hence, they saw the act as one that they were performing as normal or straight persons on another who was "queer."

During their stay in prison, there was no pressure to define themselves as homosexual. They placed temporal limits on the sodomistic acts, in much the same way that young males in a primitive society, as described by Money and Ehrhardt, become fellators for a short time and then mature into heterosexuality along lines of normative expectations and culturally approved socialization processes. For the aggressors, the prison homosexuality was a temporary expedient, and because they always thought of it in that fashion, they could emerge with their heterosexuality untouched, their masculinity undiminished, their normalcy unquestioned, their self-image untarnished. Similarly, Buffum refers to the active participants in a homosexual gang rape as defining it as a heterosexual experience.

When one understands inmate homosexuality as an expression of masculinity and of the need for dominance in a prison atmosphere in which dominance is almost completely crushed by the very fact of incarceration, one can grasp the reason for the interracial character of prison homosexual patterns. Many of the prisoners are black, and they see themselves in large measure as having been victimized by a white society, imprisoned by white judges, and kept in cages by white wardens and corrections officers. To subdue another is an affirmation of strength and power; when that other is a white man, and when he is humiliated by being reduced to the status of punk, the act may be particularly gratifying.

As for the subdued, it is unfortunate that many who note that people accommodate to the homosexual pattern interpret this as an indication of latent homosexuality (Kirkham, 1971). The concept of latent homosexuality is at best ambiguous, as pointed out by Salzman, and because it is applied ex post facto and with near-universality, I have contended elsewhere (1974) that it has little or no explanatory value. There is nothing in the previous life histories of people converted to homosexuality for the first time in prison, or in a sex-segregated school, that indicates that they had strong "tendencies" in that direction before such experiences. The connection of lack of resistance with latency is similar to the belief in the old saw that if a woman did not unconsciously want to be raped, she would be able to resist. The prison surrender can much more readily be explained by the size of the aggressor and his apparent strength, and by fear, degree of demoralization, nature of the institution, number of persons present, methods used by the aggressor, and other factors.

Assuming that there must be many of the subdued who do return to a life of heterosexuality, one is still confronted by the fact that others do not. Perhaps length of sentence, or anticipated length of incarceration, may have been a factor affecting the post-prison behavior. Nonetheless, it is true that some persons with a previous heterosexual history did become jailhouse turnouts, and then continued a homosexual pattern that they had entered reluctantly and under protest. For these persons, it appears that prison homosexuality was an experience to which they had to adjust if they were to survive. The choice was acceptance or suicide, and after the first painful experience with homosexual aggression, it is possible that even accommodation to prison may have been facilitated by acceptance of their new role, deeply denigrating but nonetheless offering some advantages. Acceptance of this role meant that they had to learn to struggle less, and success in it meant that they had to learn to enjoy it and to adjust to it as a form of sexuality. Surrounded by people who knew of their activities and who defined them as "queer," they might very well have found it easier to accept this pejorative appellation than to fight it. The belief in the concepts of latency and of coming out, and the language surrounding these reified ideas, perhaps served as self-fulfilling prophecies. Writing of those who take a passive role, Buffum calls attention to "the possibility of the distortion of their self-conceptions" (p. 28). A distortion (or a change, to use a more neutral term) in self-conception seems to take place in some instances.

All four of the involuntary recruits claim to have had regular pre-prison heterosexual experience. Two had wives (one was separated at the time of the arrest) and one had a girlfriend with whom he had had regular sexual relations at the time of arrest. The fourth was "playing the field." The man with the girlfriend made an unsuccessful effort to resume the relationship with her, and he drifted into homosexual circles, including some occasional "hustling" (male prostitution); the others made little effort to return to their former heterosexual lives. The man who had been married and living with his wife when arrested was bitter because the wife had disappeared, had never visited him, and had started divorce proceedings; he blamed his subsequent homosexuality as much on this as on the occurrences in prison.

The experiences of these four are congruent with what is often reported in the literature about adolescents. Humphreys describes a man who protested that he had disliked certain physical acts when he first participated in the homosexual scene:

> Well, I started off as the straight young thing. Everyone wanted to suck my cock. I wouldn't have been caught dead with one of the things in my mouth! . . . So, here I am at forty—with grown kids—and the biggest cocksucker in [the city]! [p. 109; ellipses and bracketed material in the original]

This, however, is by no means the same situation as that being described in this paper, since Humphreys is talking about someone who did participate in homosexual acts, but exclusively as an insertor until he changed his role and became an insertee. "Such preferences, however, are learned" (p. 109), he writes, referring to the preference for one type of physical act over another, "and sexual repertories tend to expand with time and experience." The experiences of these ex-prisoners would suggest that preferences for a same-sex or other-sex partner can also be learned, and that sexual repertories may contract with time and lack of experience, just as they can expand with time and experience.

Male prostitutes have frequently been interviewed, particularly on television, and one of the most common refrains is that they had engaged in their first homosexual experiences for financial gain or some other nonsexual reason, that they had initially reacted with apathy or even disgust, and that they had almost without exception learned to like the experiences. Again, this is true only of those who, in their late teens or early twenties, were still in prostitution; it does not include those who, after one or two experiences, recoiled from it, or after many more, relinquished it. In the novel *City of Night*, Rechy describes how male prostitutes adapt to and learn to enjoy the process, although in the early part of their career, they are emotionally uninvolved.

It would appear, then, from these few interviews, that homosexuality can be a learned way of life, but that the learning need not take the form that has so often been described in the literature of deviance. It may not be a matter of initiation into a form of conduct toward which one is relatively neutral and that one learns to enjoy through repetition. Rather, the learning may take place even under conditions of active unpleasantness. It takes place through adaptation and accommodation, through an effort to suppress fear and disgust in order to make the act less repugnant, and it is reinforced by the definitions of others and by the concepts of latency that are today widely known even in relatively less educated groups. Furthermore, the experience of going from heterosexual to homosexual identification and life pattern can take place after the onset of maturity; it need not be during adolescence, as has frequently been suggested.

The question of whether repeated homosexual experiences lead to fixed or exclusive homosexuality, or are time-limited in a one-sex setting, does not depend primarily on whether the experiences are actively sought, nor on the amount of sexual pleasure obtained, but on the meanings imputed to the experience by the actor.

The post-prison experiences of these nine persons, when compared with their pre-prison and prison sexual behavior, would suggest not a theory of latency, but a theory of the malleability of human sexual orientation.

Department of Sociology
City College of New York
New York, N.Y. 10031

REFERENCES

Akers, R. L., et al. "Homosexual and Drug Behavior in Different Types of Prisons," in E. Sagarin and D. E. J. MacNamara (Eds.), *Corrections: Problems of Punishment and Rehabilitation;* Praeger, 1973.

Bartollas, C., et al. "Becoming a Scapegoat: Study of a Deviant Career," *Sociol. Symposium* (1974) 11(Spring):84-97.

Bettelheim, B. "Individual and Mass Behavior in Extreme Situations," *J. Abnormal and Social Psychol.* (1943) 38:417-452.

BUFFUM, P. C. *Homosexuality in Prison*, U.S. Dept. of Justice, Law Enforcement Assistance Admin., Natl. Inst. Law Enforcement and Criminal Justice; Govt. Printing Office, 1972.

A. J. DAVIS. "Sexual Assaults in the Philadelphia Prison System," in J. H. Gagnon and W. Simon (Eds.), *The Sexual Scene;* Aldine, 1970.

GAGNON, J. H. Working paper presented to Conference on Prison Homosexuality, 1971; reported in Buffum, 1972.

GAGNON, J. H., and SIMON, W. *Sexual Conduct: The Social Sources of Human Sexuality*; Aldine, 1973.

GEBHARD, P. H., et al. *Sex Offenders: An Analysis of Types;* Harper & Row, 1965.

GIBBONS, D. C. "Violence in American Society: The Challenge to Corrections," *Amer. J. Correction*, March-April, 1969.

GOFFMAN, E. *Stigma: Notes on the Management of Spoiled Identity;* Prentice-Hall, 1963.

HUMPHREYS, L. *Tearoom Trade: Impersonal Sex in Public Places;* Aldine, 1970.

IRWIN, J. "Some Research Questions on Homosexuality in Jails and Prisons," working paper presented to Conference on Prison Homosexuality, 1971; reported in Buffum, 1972.

KELLY, R. J. "Commentary on Gene Kassebaum, 'Sex in Prison,'" *Sexual Behav*., Jan. 1972, p. 41.

KINSEY, A. C., et al. *Sexual Behavior in the Human Male;* Saunders, 1948.

KIRKHAM, G. L. "Homosexuality in Prison," in J. M. Henslin (Ed.), *Studies in the Sociology of Sex;* Appleton-Century-Crofts, 1971.

KIRKHAM, G. L. "Commentary on Gene Kassebaum, 'Sex in Prison,'" *Sexual Behav*., Jan. 1972, p. 42.

MONEY, J., and EHRHARDT, A. A. *Man and Woman, Boy and Girl;* Johns Hopkins Univ. Press, 1972.

RECHY, J. *City of Night;* Grove Press, 1963.

REISS, A. J., JR. "The Social Integration of Queers and Peers," *Soc. Problems* (1961) 9:102-120.

ROSENBERG, B., and BENSMAN, J. "Sexual Patterns in Three Ethnic Subcultures of an American Underclass," *Annals Amer. Acad. Polit. and Soc. Science* (1968) 376:61-75.

SAGARIN, E. "Homosexuality and the Homosexual: An Overview of the Former and a Denial of the Reality of the Latter," presented to Amer. Sociol. Assn. and Society for Study of Soc. Problems, Montreal, Aug. 26, 1974.

SAGARIN, E., and MACNAMARA, D. E. J. "The Homosexual as a Crime Victim," *Int. J. Criminol. and Penol.* (1975) 3:13-25.

SALZMAN, L. "The Concept of Latent Homosexuality," *Amer. J. Psychoanal.* (1957) 17:161-69.

SCACCO, A. M., JR. *Rape in Prison;* Charles C Thomas, 1975.

WARD, D., and KASSEBAUM, G. *Women's Prison: Sex and Social Structure;* Aldine, 1965.

HOMOSEXUALITY: A MODE OF ADAPTATION IN A PRISON FOR WOMEN

DAVID A. WARD
GENE G. KASSEBAUM
University of California, Los Angeles

The Problem

Compared to the sociological literature on men's prisons, little is known about the women's prison, and virtually no systematically collected empirical data have been published. Sociological investigations of prisons for men have in recent years been conducted from a theoretical perspective which views the behavior of inmates as a response to the material, social and psychological pains of imprisonment.[1] It has been consistently reported that one response of male prisoners to these deprivations is the establishment of a social system militating against the process of degradation, mortification of the self; depersonalization and anomie. In response to these deprivations and pains inmates come to play certain roles, and these roles come to constitute the inmate social system to which the new prisoner adapts. The rules and maxims covering these adaptations constitute the so-called inmate code. New inmates find information available from inmate *politicians* and scarce goods are available from *merchants.* Rationalizations are provided for criminal behavior; solutions for getting scarce goods and services are made known; and methods of dealing with the staff and for interacting with fellow inmates are detailed. The code provides a philosophy for doing time and the inmate social organization provides the mechanism for implementing the maxims of the code. It has, however, become increasingly apparent that prisoner behavior is rooted in more than just the conditions of confinement. In a number of studies the impact of the inmate culture and degree of support of the inmate code have been shown to vary over time and according to type of prisoner.[2]

This is a revised and expanded version of a paper read before the annual meeting of the American Sociological Association, Los Angeles, August, 1963. It is one of a series of reports of the California Study of Correctional Effectiveness, School of Public Health, University of California, Los Angeles. This research is supported by a grant from the National Institute of Mental Health (5-Rii-MH-00089). We are indebted to Western Data Processing Center, and the Health Sciences Computing Center, for access to electronic data processing equipment. The conclusions are not necessarily endorsed by the Department of Corrections or the National Institute of Mental Health. We wish to express our thanks to Mrs. Iverne R. Carter, for her encouragement and assistance in conducting this study. Renée Goldman assisted in the interviewing of inmates and in editing this paper and John Vincent did the computor work. The complete study is reported in *Women's Prison: Sex and Social Structure*, Chicago: Aldine Publishing Co., forthcoming.

[1] See Gresham M. Sykes and Sheldon L. Messinger, "The Inmate Social System" in *Theoretical Studies in Social Organization of the Prison* New York: Social Science Research Council, Pamphlet 15 (March 1960), pp. 5-19; Erving Goffman, "On the Characteristics of Total Institutions," in Donald R. Cressey, editor, *The Prison*, New York: Holt, Rinehart and Winston, Inc., 1961, Chapters 1 and 2; and Richard A. Cloward, "Social Control in the Prison," *Theoretical Studies in Social Organization of the Prison, op. cit.*, pp. 20-48.

[2] See Stanton Wheeler, "Socialization in Correctional Communities," *American Soci-*

These studies have prompted consideration of other factors in accounting for prisoner behavior. One theory which has been advanced to explain discrepancies in support of the inmate code and internalization of inmate culture focuses on the pre-prison characteristics and experiences of inmates.[3] Irwin and Cressey have recently argued that there are a number of subcultures in the prison community, reflecting the presence of different types of prisoners.[4] Salient factors related to past experience seem to be the history of involvement in criminal activity, the extent of experience in "doing time" and the influence of latent culture and latent identities which inmates bring to prison with them.[5]

The bases for prisoner behavior are now seen to be the kinds of deprivations, limitations and hardships posed by confinement, coupled with the pre-prison backgrounds of the inmates. For any prison the content and degree of support given to an inmate code (or the number of inmates making adaptations of various kinds) should provide clues as to the kinds of needs which are being denied to that population.

From this perspective we shall describe a mode of adaptation to the pains of confinement utilized by many of the inmates in the largest prison for women in the United States. Specifically, we shall direct attention to the question of whether the behavior of female prisoners is similar to, or different from, that of male prisoners. If differences are found, to what extent are they due to differential sex roles in the free society or to dissimilarities in the physical, legal and social deprivations of prison experienced by women when compared with prisons for men?

During the study various sources of information were utilized. Demographic and background data were obtained through analysis of the record files of 832 inmates, not all of whom were confined at the same time. Over a period of sixteen months repeated interviews were conducted with 45 inmates. These individual interviews provided basic information necessary to conceptualize the process and varieties of adaptive behavior. An anonymous 69-item questionnaire was administered to 293 inmates (a 45 percent random sample of the population).

---

ological Review, 26 (October, 1961), pp. 706-711; Daniel Glaser and John R. Stratton, "Measuring Inmate Change in Prison," in Donald R. Cressey, editor, *The Prison, op. cit.*, pp. 388-390; Peter G. Garabedian, "Social Roles and Processes of Socialization in the Prison Community," *Social Problems*, 11 (Fall, 1963), pp. 139-152; and Gresham M. Sykes, "Men, Merchants, and Toughs," *Social Problems*, 4 (October, 1956), p. 134.

[3] This emphasis may be found in the work of Clarence Schrag, "Some Foundations for a Theory of Correction," in Donald R. Cressey, editor, *The Prison, op. cit.*, pp. 346-357; and Donald L. Garrity, "The Prison as a Rehabilitation Agency," in Donald R. Cressey, editor, *The Prison, op. cit.*, pp. 358-380.

[4] Donald R. Cressey and John Irwin, "Thieves, Convicts, and Inmate Culture," *Social Problems*, 10 (Fall, 1962), pp. 142-155; see also Lloyd W. McCorkle and Richard R. Korn, "Resocialization Within Walls," *The Annals*, 293 (May, 1954), pp. 88-89.

[5] The concept of latent culture is described by Howard S. Becker and Blanche Geer, "Latent Culture: A Note on the Theory of Latent Social Roles," *Administrative Science Quarterly*, 5 (September, 1960), pp. 304-313; see also Alvin W. Gouldner, "Cosmopolitans and Locals: Toward an Analysis of Latent Social Roles I," *Administrative Science Quarterly*, 2 (December, 1957), pp. 281-306.

Toward the end of the study an anonymous questionnaire was administered to all staff members who had sustained and direct contact with inmates. Throughout this period we also attended meetings of the disciplinary committee and held private discussions with staff members.

Impact of the Total Institution

It is a trait of Western culture to be more protective toward females and consequently to manifest a general reluctance to submit them to measures deemed appropriate for their allegedly more aggressive and dangerous male counterparts. Women are far less often arrested, tried, convicted and sentenced to prison than are men.[6] The impact of imprisonment is, we believe, more severe for females than for males because it is more unusual. Female inmates generally have not come up through the "sandlots of crime," in that they are not as likely as men to have had experience in training schools or reformatories. Statistics on the prior commitment records of male and female prisoners in the state in 1963 indicate that 31 percent of the females had had no prior commitments compared to 11 percent for males. In our own data we found that of the 293 inmates who filled out our questionnaire, only 15 percent had been committed to a juvenile training school and 65 percent had never had a prior adult commitment to prison. While jail terms, especially for prostitution and petty theft, are fairly frequent, there are many for whom long-term confinement in an institution for felons represents a completely new experience.

During their first weeks in the institution most inmates report two major emotions: surprise and fear. Most of the women are pleasantly surprised at the physical appearance of the institution and the demeanor of the staff and other inmates:

> It's less difficult than I assumed, it's not like home but it's going to be easy compared to how I thought it would be. It's neater, cleaner, you got combs, towels, etc. If you just have patience. I got time. The girls as a whole are not rough or tough, they've got more heart than the people I associated with on the outside. We can talk to each other, knowing it will only go that far. I'll tell you what scared me—that rolled wire. I said, "Take one last look" [at the outside], but the inside looked better than the parks in the city.

Being frightened is also characteristic of most new arrivals: they fear being mistreated by staff or other inmates, the rigors of prison life, and suffer from uncertain expectations, including not knowing how long they will be locked up and how their families and friends will react to their imprisonment. In addition, there is another concern that becomes particularly serious for a woman in prison—the severing of ties with her children.[7] The male prisoner can serve time with the knowledge that, although the family may experience great difficulty while he is not the breadwinner, the wife can care for the children. The confined mother,

[6] Women account for only 3.6 percent of imprisoned adult felons in state institutions and 3.8 percent of federal prisoners. "Prisoners in State and Federal Institutions 1961," *National Prisoner Statistics*, No. 30 (August, 1962).

[7] Sixty-eight percent of the inmates are mothers; more than half have minor children. *Women Prisoners and Their Families*. Serapio R. Zalba, Department of Welfare and of Corrections, State of California (in press), pp. 27-32.

however, loses her ability to fill what is, in our society, her most important role. Her concern is not only with separation from her children but also with how they will be cared for while the husband works; moreover, she fears that the children may be taken under official care or the husband may look for another female to take over the maternal role. The impact of separation from family is evident in response to a question asking about the aspects of prison life to which the women found it most difficult to adjust.[8] The frustration does not appreciably lessen over time, as may be seen in Table I. It is in regard to coping with these fears and deprivations that women are especially ill-prepared. Many of them have played the generally dependent role characteristic of women in our society and the removal of emotional support which has been provided by parents, husbands or lovers is a shattering experience. Upon arrival at the prison many inmates immediately turn to the staff for information as well as material goods.[9]

The reception program offered by the institution has, however, been

[8] Some respondents could not be coded because they marked more than one answer. Of the 44 who did this, 27 selected "absence of home and family," among their other choices.

[9] The women can bring in with them or have sent in: coats, jackets, raincoats (all with "no quilting, padding or fur"), sweaters ("no turtle neck, V-neck or tight slipover"), gowns or pajamas, bathrobes ("no quilting or padding"), shoes ("low heels, bedroom, thongs, tennis"), "simple costume jewelry—earrings, necklaces, scatter pins, bracelets," non-electric clocks, dark glasses, unopened packages of cigarettes, suitcases (no larger than 18" × 26"), unfinished knitting and light hand sewing material, tooth brush, hair rollers, etc. Thus the complete stripping of all personal possessions that occurs in prisons for men does not take place. The pains of the admission experience are perhaps mitigated slightly by permitting girls to have these items. Since all inmates can have these belongings, and because so many articles are permitted, there is no evidence that we know of which suggests any organized merchandising of these goods by inmates.

TABLE I

INMATE RESPONSES TO THE QUESTION, "WHAT IS THE MOST DIFFICULT ASPECT OF ADJUSTMENT," CORRELATED WITH TIME AT THE INSTITUTION (PER CENT)

Most Difficult Aspect of Adjustment	Less than 6 months	6 months to 1 year	1 year or more	Total
Rules and regulations	5	6	6	5
Other inmates	9	10	19	13
Lack of privacy	6	8	9	8
Custodial officials	2	3	4	3
Absence of home & family	43	42	38	42
Absence of social life and friends on the outside	11	7	6	8
Nothing, adjustment is easy	5	3	4	4
Other	4	3	6	4
More than one answer	16	17	8	13
	100%	100%	100%	
Total	29(82)	31(88)	40(108)	100(282)*

* No answer to one or the other question = 14 cases.
Chi-square = 61.9, significant at more than 99.95.

unable to meet the needs of new commitments. The social distance between staff and inmate and the severe limitations on the number of professional clinical personnel make it difficult for inmates to get from the staff the kinds of information, support and guidance they especially need during the initial confinement period. These inadequacies coupled with the need to deal with the pains of separation from family, the limitations on freedom of choice and activity, the stigma resulting from the process of status degradation, the apprehension about length of confinement due to indeterminate sentencing laws, and the lack of experience in doing "big time," are the pains of imprisonment to which the inmate must adjust. Male prisoners have adjusted in characteristic ways, and in the next section we shall discuss their adaptations and those of female prisoners.

Inmate Solidarity

In the institution we studied there is little evidence of the differentiated inmate types and degree of social solidarity reported in studies of prisons for men. In all interviews inmates reported that informing on other inmates was characteristic of almost the entire inmate population.[10]

TABLE II
Proportion of 293 Female Prisoners Approving Inmate Loyalty Items

Item	%	N
1. Two inmates, who are planning an escape, ask one of their close inmate friends, Brown, to distract the supervisor's attention so that they will have a chance to get out of her sight. Brown refuses, stating that she doesn't want to get involved.		
Agree with Brown	88	258
2. Inmates Brown and Henry are planning an escape. They threaten inmate Smith with a beating unless she steals some rope for them from the maintenance shop where she works. She thinks they mean business. While she is trying to smuggle the rope out, she is caught by a supervisor and is accused of trying to escape. She may have her parole date changed unless she describes the whole situation. Smith can avoid this by blaming Brown and Henry, but she keeps quiet and takes the punishment herself.		
Agree with Smith	39	116

In the questionnaire survey, descriptions of problematic situations, in which one alternative was an affirmation of inmate solidarity,[11] were endorsed in this manner by only 41 and 12 percent respectively.

---

[10] The prison "rat" has always been present in prisons for men, but efforts have been made by inmates to levy punitive sanctions against informers. In the women's prison the label of "snitch" was applied to almost the entire inmate population at one time or another. For some discussions of the "rat" role in prisons for men, see Elmer H. Johnson, "Sociology of Confinement: Assimilation and the Prison 'Rat,' " *Journal of Criminal Law, Criminology and Police Science*, 51 (January-February, 1961), pp. 528-533; S. Kirson Weinberg, "Aspects of the Prison's Social Structure," in *American Journal of Sociology*, 47 (March, 1942), pp. 217-226; and Gresham M. Sykes, *Society of Captives*, Princeton, New Jersey: Princeton University Press, 1958, pp. 87-90.

[11] These items were developed by Peter Garabedian in his study, *Western Penitentiary: A Study in Social Organization*, unpublished doctoral dissertation, University of Washington, 1959, pp. 51-52, and by

Of six items measuring elements of the "inmate code,"[12] only two were strongly endorsed, three were endorsed by about half of the inmates and one was agreed to by only a fifth of the sample. These six items formed a Guttman Scale indicating that the items were perceived as a dimension of response in a meaningful manner. The scale is shown in Table III.

When the scale scores were cross-tabulated with time in prison, time before release and number of prior commitments and offense, no significant correlations were obtained. In studies of prisons for men, Wheeler and Glaser and Stratton found that orientation to conventional norms was highest for those who had been in prison only a short time and for those near the end of their terms. We found no evidence of either a U-shaped curve of normative orientation or a linear progression of increasing support of criminal norms as length of

Stanton Wheeler, "Role Conflict in Correctional Communities," in Donald R. Cressey, editor, *The Prison, op. cit.*, p. 232. Wheeler found that 70 percent of the male inmates in his sample approved of the inmate keeping quiet.

12 The six items were based on descriptions of the inmate code by Gresham M. Sykes and Sheldon L. Messinger, "The Inmate Social System," *op. cit.*, pp. 5-19; Lloyd E. Ohlin, "The Theory of Individualization in Treatment and Institutional Practice" (mimeo) paper presented at the 11th Annual Institute of the Illinois Academy of Criminology, Chicago, Illinois (April, 1959); Peter Garabedian, *op. cit.*; and Richard R. Korn and Lloyd W. McCorkle, *Criminology and Penology*, New York: Henry Holt and Co., Inc., 1959, pp. 512-530.

TABLE III

PROPORTION OF 293 FEMALE PRISONERS ENDORSING INMATE CODE

Item	%	N
1. In her dealings with the staff the inmate should stick up for what she feels is right and not let the staff set her standards or morals for her. (Positive)	92	264
2. When the inmates stick together it is a lot easier to do time. (Positive)	77	213
3. The best way to do time is to grin and bear it and not let the staff know that anything is getting you down. (Positive)	61	173
4. In some situations, it is all right to inform on another inmate. (Negative endorsement)	57	163
5. In prison, a good rule to follow is to share any extra goods with your friends. (Positive)	56	157
6. There are basically just two kinds of people in the world, those in the know and those who are suckers. (Positive)	22	63

These items constitute a Guttman Scale with a coefficient of reproducibility of .88 and a marginal reproducibility of .68. The cutting points were established as follows:

	%	N
Strong rejection	15	(44)
Moderate rejection	32	(93)
Moderate endorsement	37	(108)
Strong Endorsement	16	(48)
	100	(293)

time served increases.[13] The most important factor related to degree of support of the code was, in fact, a variable which took into account experience outside of prison—age at first arrest. As can be seen in Table IV, women first arrested after the age of twenty-five less often endorsed the code than women whose first officially recorded contact with the police came earlier in life.

Length of involvement in criminal activity, as measured by age at first arrest, seems to be more important in accounting for the attitudes of these female prisoners than the experience of serving time in prison—what Clemmer has referred to as *prisonization.* The importance of pre-prison experiences evident here will also be noted in the sections dealing with inmate roles to follow. To complete this brief discussion of the contrast between male and female prison communities, it should be noted that, consistent with the lack of support for the inmate code, few inmates were found to play the roles of *merchants* or *politicians* characteristic of prisons for men. In addition, there were virtually no women who played the role of the *tough* or *gorilla.*

That female prisoners do not endorse more strongly norms which characterize the male prison community and, in particular, that they do not feel bound to maintain group solidarity by rules prohibiting informing, may, however, indicate more than just a low degree of cohesion in the female prison community and absence of resulting role types. Lack of support of these norms does not preclude the possibility of consensus on different norms. There may be little support of this code because such maxims are not as relevant for women. The components of the code may more accurately reflect male needs for status, independence, autonomy, and masculine self-image. (It should be noted that a number of sociologists, including the authors, are now questioning the assumption that most male prison communities are characterized by even a moderate degree of group solidarity.) The culture and social structure of prisons for men seems to reflect a wider variety of pains of im-

[13] For a discussion of the view that internalization of criminal norms is related to length of time served, see Donald Clemmer, "Imprisonment as a Source of Criminality," *Journal of Criminal Law, Criminology and Police Science*, 41 (September-October, 1950), pp. 311-319. For an opposing view see Garrity, *op. cit.*, pp. 358-380.

TABLE IV
DEGREE OF ENDORSEMENT OF INMATE CODE AND AGE AT FIRST ARREST
(PER CENT)

	Age at First Arrest		
	17 or younger	18 to 25	26 or older
Strong rejection	11	6	31
Moderate rejection	29	31	33
Moderate endorsement	39	46	24
Strong endorsement	21	17	12
	100	100	100
	(72)	(125)	(91)

Chi square = 30.25, significant at more than 99.95.

prisonment than is the case in the women's prison. There are homosexuals in male prisons and norms surrounding homosexuality, but there are other important concerns and these are articulated in the roles of *merchant*, *politician*, *tough*, *right guy*, and *square john*. Emotional deprivation and lack of experience in fending for oneself combine in the women's prison to promote one predominant compensatory response, that of homosexual involvement. Inmate roles in the female prison community are thus differentiated primarily along sexual lines. In the sections to follow we shall describe the process of *turning out*, the dynamics of prison love affairs, the principal homosexual roles and the extent to which this type of adaptation has been made.

THE PREVALENCE OF HOMOSEXUAL BEHAVIOR

Estimates of the prevalence of homosexuality in the prison vary widely. Official records identify 19 percent of the population as homosexual. In the survey of staff members, more than half of the respondents estimated between 30 and 70 percent of the inmates "have sexual affairs while in prison." Estimates were higher on the inmate questionnaire, with 69 percent of the respondents estimating that between 30 and 70 percent of the girls were having homosexual affairs and an additional 7 percent estimating as high as 90 percent or more. These data, with comparative estimates made by prisoners in a medium security prison for men located in the same state, can be seen in Table V.[14]

In the interviews with female inmates, guesses of the extent of homo-

[14] In addition to our own data estimating the incidence of homosexuality among male prisoners, Donald Clemmer's study of an institution for adult male felons indicated that ". . . 16 percent of the sampling admitted to homosexual activity during their present incarceration. Of these 38 men, only two were partners with each other in the abnormal acts, so it is suggested that since homosexuality cannot occur singly, that the actual percentage of men engaging in this practice is 32 percent." Donald Clemmer, "Some Aspects of Sexual Behavior in the Prison Community," *Proceedings of the Eighty-Eight Annual Congress of Correction of The American Correctional Association*, Detroit, Michigan, 1958, p. 383.

TABLE V

ESTIMATES OF PREVALENCE OF INSTITUTIONAL HOMOSEXUALITY (PER CENT)

Replies of women's prison staff and female and male inmates to the statement:

"A rough estimate of the number of women (men) who haxe sexual affairs at one time of another with other women (men) while in prison would be:"

Estimate of Homosexuality	Women's Prison Staff	Female Inmates	Male Inmates
5 percent or less	12	12	29
15 percent	31	12	25
30 percent	29	25	25
50 percent	14	22	12
70 percent	9	22	6
90 percent or more	5	7	3
	100(58)	100(263)	100(744)

Note: 6 staff members, 30 female inmates, and 127 male inmates refused or were unable to make an estimate.

sexuality were never less than 50 percent, with most estimating 60 to 75 percent. Individual conversations with staff members yielded similar estimates. Overall, it can be conservatively estimated that at least 50 percent of the inmates are sexually involved at least once during their prison terms. By sexually involved we mean kissing and fondling of the breasts, manual and oral stimulation of the clitoris and simulation of intercourse. Our definition of homosexuality does not include mere emotional arousal, or kissing, hand holding and embracing, when these activities are not followed by overt sexual behavior and are not seen as being sexual in intent by the participants.[15]

Reliable estimates of the extent of homosexual involvement of women in other institutional settings—the military, mental hospital, schools—are non-existent. However, in the outside community, data from the Kinsey Report indicate that, of their national sample, 13 percent experienced orgasm in homosexual relations, an additional 6 percent had had homosexual experience, and another 9 percent had experienced "psychological arousal" for a total of 28 percent of the population.[16] Comparatively, the incidence of overt homosexual behavior in this prison is high.

Homosexual Roles

In the prison setting the total number of women involved sexually with other inmates is less interesting sociologically than the sharp distinction between those referred to by the inmates as "true" homosexuals and those identified as "jailhouse turnouts."

The *jailhouse turnout* or *J.T.O.*, in contrast to the true homosexual, has her introduction to homosexuality in jail or prison. All inmates interviewed and 80 percent of the staff who filled out the questionnaire asserted that 90 percent or more of the homosexually involved women had their first affair in jail or prison. In addition, 84 percent of the inmates and 85 percent of the staff agreed on the questionnaires that most of the homosexually involved women return to heterosexual relationships when they leave prison.

The *true homosexual* is, as defined by the inmates, a woman who was homosexual before she arrived at the institution and will be after she leaves. Incidentally, a few of the true homosexuals remain faithful to lovers on the outside and do not become involved with other inmates. Such persons would not, therefore, be included in our estimate of institutional homosexuality.

[15] These figures may be compared with other data that have been gathered on homosexuality among girls in youth institutions. A study by Selling, published in 1931, estimated that two percent of the population of a girl's institution were involved in an overt homosexual existence and another 40 percent engaged in behavior which involved embracing, kissing and fondling of another inmate. Lowell S. Selling, "The Pseudo Family," *The American Journal of Sociology*, 37 (September, 1931), pp. 247-253. A more recent study by Halleck and Hersko indicates that 69 percent of the girls in a training school were homosexually involved. The majority of these cases did not, however, involve breast fondling, or direct genital contact. Seymour L. Halleck and Marvin Hersko, "Homosexual Behavior in a Correctional Institution for Adolescent Girls," *American Journal of Orthopsychiatry*, XXXII (October, 1962), pp. 911-917.

[16] Alfred C. Kinsey, Wardell B. Pomeroy, Clyde E. Martin, Paul H. Gebhard, *Sexual Behavior in the Human Female*, Philadelphia, Pa.: W. B. Saunders Co., 1953, pp. 452-454.

Those true homosexuals who are active in prison come to the relationship with a perspective based on experience. They believe the impact of a homosexual affair is never forgotten, and they feel that they enter such relationships more for the positive features they perceive than in reaction to the negative features of confinement. It is also likely that the labels of "criminal" and "prisoner" are less traumatic for people who already have a self-conception of being stigmatized by most of the general community. As a result of homosexual affairs many of these women appear to have made adjustments in their self-conceptions which make adjustment to the pains of imprisonment less difficult. Our data indicate that among those few inmates who can be classified as prison politicians and merchants, there are a large number of true homosexuals. Like the experienced male con, they are more concerned with alleviating the material deprivations of confinement, getting a good prison job and living quarters, and doing time without attracting attention. In the following remarks a young woman who is a true homosexual playing the masculine or *butch* role, speaks with disdain of the blatant and opportunistic behavior of the jailhouse turnouts:

> . . . They want companionship, they just want to play a little game with you, you know, and they LOVE you, oh, everybody loves you, God, they're in love with you. They've seen you once, but they're in love with you. They turn out right away because they need somebody to care, someone to look up to. They're afraid, and somehow a butch is sort of a protective symbol—"She'll take care of me so nobody will hurt me." They need somebody to talk to, they're lonesome. And they've been taken away from everything they love, and they sort of project all of this love into the butch. . . . But mostly, it's just a big game with them. They're lonesome, there's nothing else to do, and I'm the closest thing they can get to a man. . . . These other ones [butch turnouts] I can't see at all—the ones that come in here with long hair and all of a sudden they're big romp-stomping butches. . . . I can respect a person that's been that way all their life and knows what's happening, but these kids that just cut their hair and think they're really hitting on something, and then they can't wait to get out on the streets to get with a dude again—they make me sick. While they're in here you'd swear to God they'd been gay their whole life. There's nothing but women in this world for them—while they're in here. They have their hair short one week and then, God, they're just too lovely the next—I mean it. One week they're my brother and the next week they're hitting on me. They swagger and drop their belt and all of a sudden they're big stuff. When really they're not. They don't feel any of this inside, they don't go through any of the emotions that a butch [true homosexual] goes through, they're not involved in this and they're gonna forget it as soon as they're out of the institution.

Whether homosexuality is learned prior to imprisonment or is restricted to the prison experience, another distinction involves the roles played by homosexuals in their affairs. These roles are represented by a combination of appearance, behavior and personality characteristics, and are found among both true homosexuals and jailhouse turnouts. The most obvious is the *butch*, *stud broad*, or *drag butch*,[17] the aggressive, active sexual

[17] Neither staff nor inmates use the term *lesbian*. Staff members use the term homosexual because it is consistent with departmental directives, rule books and references to male prisoners. Inmates use more colloquial terms such as *playing*, *being together*, *making it*, and *turning out*. The term lesbian apparently suggests what staff and inmates agree is usually not the case

partner. Her hair is close-cropped or worn in pixie or "D.A." style; she wears no makeup; her legs are unshaven; she usually wears pedal pushers or, if a dress, the belt is worn low on the hips. Masculine gait, manner of smoking and other gestures are adopted. A variation of this is the woman who dresses femininely, but acts aggressively and plays the dominant role in her homosexual relationship. The transition to the role of butch is a dramatic manifestation of inversion of sexual role, representing such a change that a disproportionately small number of women in prison actually make it. Our personal observation is that many of the jailhouse turnouts who are butches are singularly unattractive, according to some of the criteria used to judge feminine attractiveness in our society. Many of these women are overweight or underweight, have skin disorders or appear unusually wiry or muscular.[18] Some of the severely unattractive women and the women possessing aggressive personality traits and inclined toward masculine habits and demeanor express themselves in the butch role when these predisposing factors are combined with the experience of imprisonment. In prison they have found that by emphasizing dissimilarity to the female role and appearance, they can attract attention from some members of their own sex. Here they can take the initiative in both social and sexual interaction and these women find in prison a functional role they did not find outside.[19] The role of the butch in the prison community seems to be an effort to solve a variety of problems and conflicts of which adjustment to imprisonment is one.

The complimentary role of the butch is the *femme*, who maintains a feminine appearance and ideally plays a more submissive, passive role. Of the two, the butch appears to have a greater commitment to homosexuality. The butch changes the love object and her behavior, thereby substituting a role. The femme changes only the love object. It is less difficult to describe and to understand the role of the femme because she often does in the homosexual affair what she did in heterosexual relationships. She continues to play the role often expected of women—to be relatively more submissive and passive in sexual relations, to be dependent, and to provide housekeeping services. The role of the femme provides relief from the need to fend for oneself in a strange and threatening environment. This role provides for the establish-

—a long-term definite commitment to homosexuality.

18 There is, however, no evidence of any unusual physiological or anatomical features which characterize these masculine-appearing women. Physicians at the prison reported that they had observed no constitutional differences in terms of distribution and abundance of body hair, size of the clitoris, muscle distribution or any other factor.

19 For a description of the butch role among female homosexuals living in the free world, see Jane McKinnon, "I am a Homosexual Woman," in A. M. Krich, editor, *The Homosexuals*, New York: The Citadel Press, 1954, pp. 4-5. The butch role played by call girls is described by Harold Greenwald in *The Call Girl*, New York: Ballantine Books, 1958, pp. 119-122. See also, Frank S. Caprio, *Female Homosexuality*, New York: Grove Press, Inc., 1954, pp. 16-18. While the author has a more general point to make, an excellent discussion of the "masculine protest" can be found in Simone De Beauvoir, *The Second Sex*, New York: Bantam Books, 1961, pp. 379-399.

ment of supportive relationships similar to those which characterized relationships with fathers, husbands or lovers. The femme does not have to make the radical transition to a new role that the butch has made. She often comes to view herself as bisexual and she expects to resume heterosexual relations upon release—both of which militate against homosexual self-definition.

While the butch can display her role in terms of dress, mannerisms and appearance, the femme emphasizes her role largely in behavior. She walks with her arms around the butch, embraces and kisses her in public, and allows the butch to speak in her behalf.[20] Recently the staff has attempted to reduce these public demonstrations of affection by making inmates liable for disciplinary action. Couples flaunting their relationship are often housed in separate cottages in an effort to prevent them from seeing one another. The staff has also required 48 butches to change their hair style to a less masculine coiffure and more effort has been devoted to preventing personal (bodily) contact on the institution grounds. While there has been less visible evidence of homosexuality, these efforts, to date, have not reduced the number of homosexual involvements.

THE DYNAMICS OF PRISON LOVE AFFAIRS

For many girls the pressure to *turn out* begins when they enter the receiving unit. Two types of women in particular are the object of concerted attention by the general population. The arrival of a *butch broad* causes a stir on the campus as the femmes vie for her affection. The rush is intense, and the femme makes it clear that she is available:

> It's just like the outside. I flirted, I got things for her, I did her clothes, I woke her in the morning, we went to dances —the same things you do for a man on the outside. Girls are approached in the same way a man approaches a woman. He . . . she . . . looks at her and the way she looks back gives him the clue as to further action. He . . . she . . . looks at you like she wants you, a look of desire.

The rushing process includes plying the butch with love notes, candy, coffee, cigarettes and other articles, referred to as *commissary.*

This adaptation by femmes of the usual tactics employed by males in heterosexual affairs was explained by our respondents as a matter of supply and demand because there are fewer butches then femmes in the population. (Our interviews and analysis of inmate file data indicate that about one-third of the jailhouse turnout population are butch, with a somewhat higher proportion of butches among the true homosexuals.) In addition, broken love affairs sustain a supply of femmes who express great interest in the relatively small number of new butches. A twenty-year-old true homosexual butch described her reception at the institution:

> When I came into the institution I didn't go after anybody. I had a bad experience on the street that was part of what got me here, and I didn't want anything to do with any more women. So I was very bitter. But I got here and all of a sudden I was getting all these kites [notes] and

[20] For descriptions of the butch role in a girl's school, see Halleck and Hersko, *op. cit.*, p. 912, and for the femme role see the description of the *soft mama* by Romolo Toigo, "Illegitimate and Legitimate Cultures in a Training School for Girls," *Proceedings of the Rip Van Winkle Clinic*, Vol. 13, No. 3 (Summer, 1962), pp. 9-11.

> I had all these girls come to me—I never went to them. They're real aggressive with a new butch, everybody wants to snatch her up before somebody else gets her. And so I looked around at some of the people I was getting messages from —I checked them out and there wasn't too much there that I wanted. But I played the field for about six weeks, and like I said, I'd get a message from a girl to please come over and see her and she'd give me cigarettes and, you know, give me everything I needed. So I'd walk her out to the field, or to the canteen, and then I dated a few girls, I took some of them to the show, but I never saw anybody that I wanted.

In other instances butches approach new arrivals, exert special attention on young, homosexually uninitiated and attractive girls, win them over and then exploit them for contraband, commissary items, and other services.

Once the butch has secured the affection of the femme, she may then exact tribute in the form of goods and services in exchange for her assurance that she will not play around with anyone else (as one woman paraphrased the song: "I love you for commissary reasons"). In each of these cases the butch role has the advantage of material gains in addition to sexual recompense. However, many of the homosexual pairs do not involve exploitation of one lover by the other and are not dissimilar to love affairs between males and females on the outside. Exploitation, when it does occur in these relationships, comes when one of the parties is tiring of the other. There was only one report that butch broads had stables (more than one femme of her own). This case, it is our impression, involved a transitional stage at which time a butch was getting over her affair with one femme and beginning another. There were no indications of homosexual families or clans.[21] Finally, in contrast to prisons for men, no inmate reported, nor was there any evidence of, any inmate using force to exact sexual favors from another.

The behavior of one partner often appears to be exploitative of the other in the actual sexual relationship. Interviews conducted with both homosexual and non-homosexual inmates indicated that in about one-third of the homosexual relationships at the institution the butch refuses to let the femme touch her or reciprocate sexually. Some butches remain completely clothed during sexual activity. This seems in part to facilitate maintaining the illusion of masculinity which would be exposed by the removal of her clothing. The role of the femme, in these cases, is one of complete passivity in which the butch *gives work* (also referred to as *giving some head*), i.e., engages in cunnilingus, manual manipulation of the

---

[21] The building of family constellations has been reported in studies of youth institutions for females by Sheriff in Michela Robbins, "The Inside Story of a Girl's Reformatory," *Colliers*, 132 (October 30, 1953,), p. 76; Sidney Kosofsky and Albert Ellis, "Illegal Communication Among Institutionalized Female Delinquents," *The Journal of Social Psychology*, 48 (August, 1958), pp. 155-160; see also Charles A. Ford, "Homosexual Practices of Institutionalized Females," *The Journal of Abnormal and Social Psychology*, XXIII (January-March, 1929), p. 446; by Selling, *op. cit.*, pp. 248-253 and by Toigo, *op. cit.*, pp. 3-29. It is not surprising to find young girls who are still oriented toward the consangual family establishing substitute *daddies, brothers* and *cousins*. The separation from parents, siblings and other relatives seems to be less a source of real stress for older women. Most of them have established their own families and the pain of separation comes from being away from conjugal rather than the consangual family.

clitoris, and breast fondling. While the butch gives work, the denial of sexual gratification for herself is called *giving up the work.* Such self-denial militates against becoming obligated to the femme and from developing emotional ties that would be painful to disturb or break. Participation in a relationship where only the butch gives work is functional for some femmes as well. They can receive sexual satisfaction and at the same time avoid viewing themselves as homosexual. For a number of women, homosexual self-definition only follows active participation in sexual activity.[22]

The following statement from a tape recorded interview describes the practice of giving up the work as seen by a femme jailhouse turnout:

> Giving up the work means who's gonna do who. I mean, which one of you is going to commit the sexual act on the other one. Usually the one that's the aggressor and doing the lovemaking is the one that's giving up the work. [Note the butch is *giving* work at the same time she is giving *up* reciprocal sexual interaction.] The other one isn't giving up anything, she's receiving. It usually refers to the stud broad and usually the stud broad will be very modest and strict about who knows if she's been receiving any work or not.
>
> I think it's that butches realize a woman is satisfied by a man, as a rule, this is the natural role, and that they want to satisfy you as much as a man would, if not more. They want to get this certain edge over you, this certain control over you. But being aware in the back of their minds that they're a woman too, they know that it's just as possible for you to get control over them, and I think that they fight this because in their minds their main goal is to satisfy and control you, and keep you.

The butch partner of the respondent quoted above reported her reason for wishing to have a relationship where only she gave work:

> In myself—the only desire I have is to make love and not have love made to me. I don't feel the need for it or the desire for it. The desire for it can be aroused and has been—I'm not saying that a girl hasn't made love to me—but it's very few and far between that I want somebody to make love to me. I want to do the work, and that's the way I get my pleasure, by making love to her, a woman. When I make love to a woman I like the power of being able to satisfy her. It gives me a good feeling to know that she responds to me and that I can satisfy her desires. And this is where I get my enjoyment.
>
> *Q.* When you talk about satisfaction for yourself, is this satisfaction in terms of orgasm, or is satisfaction in other terms?
>
> It's a satisfaction more or less mentally, and not really—it's a physical satisfaction but merely because I know I've done a good job, or I hope I have, and I'm satisfied with knowing that I've pleased her and I'm just relaxed through the whole act. Otherwise, no, I don't reach a climax. I have, but it's very seldom that I do. I don't lose myself that much, and I don't like to lose that much control. I like to keep my mind as clear as I can so I'm aware of exactly what I'm doing, and I'm aware of my timing, and I'm aware of the girl—if she's responsive at a certain time then I know that's what she likes, and then if she's not responding then I can do something else. Where, if I was just lost in passion I don't recognize any of these things, and I don't feel that I would satisfy her as fully as if I didn't lose myself all that much and kept concentrating on her, watching her—

---

[22] The attitude of the femme here is similar to that of the young male delinquents who permit male adults to perform fellatio on them but who do not think of themselves as homosexuals. The boys define themselves and each other not on the basis of homosexual behavior *per se*, but on the basis of non-participation in the role which is perceived as the homosexual role, that of the fellator. Albert J. Reiss, Jr., "The Social Integration of Queers and Peers," *Social Problems*, 9 (Fall, 1961), p. 118-119.

> that's what I do. And when the act is over I'm tired and that tiredness brings on a satisfaction in itself. And it gives me a form of release, the tension sort of release, after I've made love to somebody. But I don't reach a climax—not generally.

In practice, however, giving up the work seems to characterize the early stage of a homosexual relationship. Presuming that there is some mutual attraction to begin with, it seems to be difficult to have such intimate contact without, over time, developing more intense affectional ties. It often happens that the butch comes to ask for sexual reciprocity and that the femme is then ready to reciprocate. Hence, this behavior can, in some cases, be an effective means of total seduction in which the femme who is resistant or feeling guilty is brought along slowly. Stresses accompanying attempted transitions from giving up the work to reciprocal sexuality result in the failure of some sexual affairs that are carried on satisfactorily until the femme finally refuses to reciprocate. Such refusal is interpreted by the butch as lack of affection and low degree of commitment to the homosexual role.

There is an apparent parallel between a prostitute receiving the attentions of a customer and the femme receiving a butch who gives up the work, but there is a major difference implicit in the rationale for the latter. The male customer, while an active sex partner and to some degree the aggressor, is not viewed as being in danger of becoming emotionally involved with the prostitute. The action of the active and aggressive butch is specifically directed toward preventing herself from becoming more deeply attached to her partner. For many women who have assumed the butch role because they were unsuccessful in heterosexual affectional relationships, there is still the danger of being rejected again. For the butch then, the initial period during which the femme remains passive serves the important function of screening out femmes who are "chippying" (promiscuous). As one respondent said, "You check them out, to see if she's gonna stay." In addition, the period of giving up the work serves to more deeply involve the femme, as she may experience satisfaction with the relationship. Thus, after this trial period, the butch may ask for reciprocity if the femme has not indicated that she wants to play a more active sexual role. It is beyond this point that some femmes refuse to go, and this usually terminates the affair. Enough women stop here to confirm the fears of butches so that they must continue the same testing process.

The term jailhouse turnout indicates, and inmates confirm, that most prison love affairs are temporary and situational.[23] The insecurity and

---

[23] In the male homosexual community, Hooker reports that there is a constant searching for sexual partners, and that long-enduring relationships are rare, with change not stability the rule. Evelyn Hooker, "A Preliminary Analysis of Group Behavior of Homosexuals," *The Journal of Psychology*, 42 (October, 1956), pp. 223-224. Halleck and Hersko report that homosexual relationships among the girls in the youth institution they studied were usually short-lived and characterized by jealousy and unfaithfulness. Halleck and Hersko, *op. cit.*, p. 913. The shifting of homosexual roles among girls in the youth institution is also reported by Toigo, *op. cit.*, p. 10. The ability to play both roles—active and passive—is reported by Helene Deutsch, "On Female Homosexuality," in Robert Fliess, editor, *The Psychoanalytic Reader*, New York: International Universities Press, Inc., 1948, p. 243.

anxiety which is promoted by the movement of the population out of the institution results in the use of certain defense mechanisms to protect oneself from being hurt too badly. This is especially the case for butches who have made a more definite and dramatic commitment to homosexuality. They cannot count on holding the affection of the femme, not only because of separation by staff or parole, but also because femme jailhouse turnouts do not have a long-term commitment to the *gay life*. This is apparent in the high percentage of women whom the inmates believe will return to heterosexual affairs once they leave prison. The prison homosexuals who are expected to revert to heterosexuality are the femmes and not the butches.

In summary, the process of turning out seems to represent socialization of the new inmates into practices which provide support, guidance and emotional satisfactions during a period when these are lacking. This mechanism for coping with the stress of imprisonment is presented to the new inmate at a time when she is likely to be most responsive and when she is least aware of alternative courses of action. Turning out often involves a series of steps through which both partners initially seek to insulate themselves from strong involvement. Reciprocity of sexual behavior is often delayed until confidence in the stability of the union is felt. This is particularly true for those butches who have made more definite commitments to homosexuality. However, instability is not unknown for other butches who change from homosexual involvements to heterosexual involvements and back again as they are paroled, violate parole and are returned to prison. (This role alteration prompted one inmate to remark, "There's something hypocritical about a pregnant butch.")

Inmates believe that most homosexual involvement occurs early in imprisonment, that most affairs are situational, with heterosexual relationships to be resumed upon release, and that many are "once-only" affairs.[24] The folklore of the female prison community provides rationalizations for homosexuality by emphasizing that women involved in prison affairs are not homosexual but bisexual, by referring to those who do not play as "prudes," by emphasizing the alleviation of loneliness that such involvements can bring, by alleging greater satisfactions than can be found in heterosexual affairs and by repeating stories about the women who return to men upon release. While the intrinsic satisfactions are described it is made clear that one may return to heterosexual relationships without any damaging effects. Such a rationale helps make homosexual involvement a more likely adaptation

[24] In view of these characteristics of institutional homosexuality, Ford questions whether such involvements represent true sexual inversion. See Ford, *op. cit.*, p. 448. Deviant behavior in prison may be temporary because ties to significant others in the free world are not voluntarily severed. Their absence is forced and they remain significant others. Thus while escape into institutional deviance can be rationalized on the basis of "they aren't around" or "they won't know," long-term commitment is unlikely because it is to these others and not to those in prison that long-run loyalty is given. Loyalty to a homosexual partner in prison is fortuitous. For a discussion of deviant careers and of the important implications of membership in an organized deviant group see Howard S. Becker, *Outsiders*, New York: The Free Press of Glencoe, pp. 25-39.

than other mechanisms of adjustment. There can be a number of reactions to stress and each of these may assume a variety of forms. For some of the inmates psychological withdrawal and fantasy is one adaptation.[25] Other inmates actively rebel and become chronic rule violators (so-called troublemakers and malcontents) who fight with staff and fellow inmates. Our analysis of the files of 832 inmates, however, indicates that this is not a frequent reaction. Eighty-two percent (668) of the sample had never violated rules pertaining to staff authority.[26] Sixty-two percent had never been reported for any violation of prison rules and an additional 22 percent had received only one or two such reports.

There are some inmates who are continually in trouble, but it is our impression that they fall into two principal categories—severely emotionally disturbed individuals and young homosexuals who use the violation of institutional rules and abuse of authority to demonstrate their love for partners or to react to staff interventions in their affairs.

Another adaptation is what Goffman has called "colonization," the acceptance of institutional life as a satisfactory existence. These are inmates who are commonly referred to as "having found a home."[27] Generally, they do not want to bother or be bothered by staff or inmates or by institutional programs as they perform the ritual of doing time. A small number of women, in most cases older and serving long sentences for serious offenses such as homicide, used this mode of adjustment. Their age, a number of inmates reported, precluded these women from being sought as desirable homosexual partners. Not all inmates use one or more of these adaptations. Some women play a role referred to in prisons for men as "square johns"—persons who maintain a view toward criminality consistent with that of the larger community and who tend to be more receptive to staff efforts at rehabilitation. The worst feature of confinement for these inmates is the forced association with other inmates. These women tend to accept the pains of imprisonment as justified penalties for their behavior.

For the majority of women in the prison, however, we did not observe such accommodations to deprivations and limitations of confinement. The lack of experience in doing time, the lack of criminal sophistication and the absence of conventional sources of emotional support by husbands, lovers, or families combine to make many inmates receptive to homosexuality as a mode of adjustment when it is offered to them upon arrival at the prison. Our data clearly indicate that more inmates resort to homosexuality than to psychological withdrawal, rebellion, colonization or any other type of adaptation.

---

[25] This reaction is described by Gresham M. Sykes, *The Society of Captives, op. cit.*, p. 80. See also, Erving Goffman, *Asylums*, Garden City, New York: Anchor Books, 1961, pp. 61-62; and Terence and Pauline Morris, "The Experience of Imprisonment," *The British Journal of Criminology*, 2 (April, 1962), pp. 351-352.

[26] Included as rule violations were refusal to work, destruction of state property as a protest gesture, insolence, disrespect, disobedience to staff, assault (or attempted) on staff; escape (or attempted) and rioting.

[27] Goffman, *op. cit.*, pp. 62-63, and Terence and Pauline Morris, *op. cit.*, pp. 350-351.

CONCLUSIONS

Homosexuality exists because it serves a variety of functions for a large number of women, not because prison inmates are callous, unprincipled or basically amoral or because the institution staff is lax or "soft" on inmates. In fact, it has been suggested that the maladjustment of prison inmates may reflect demands on the behavior of the individual made by the special environment of the prison. These modes of behaving may be viewed as maladaptive outside of prison, but they are adaptive in the prison setting.[28]

Initially, this study considered sex-role differences in the free community, and features of male prisons, as a way of understanding the female prison. From a knowledge of differences in the backgrounds, experiences and identities of males and females in the outside world, we surmised that women prisoners would be less likely to actively rebel in prison. We did not expect and did not find elaborate operations for obtaining and distributing contraband or for conducting gambling operations. We expected and found that women require more emotional support than do male prisoners. This need, and others, are reflected in the culture of the female prison community which contains maxims dealing with the experiences and problems of women in prison and in the inmate social system composed of roles which are responses to the pains of imprisonment as women experience them. It is on these bases that male and female prison communities can be distinguished.

Finally, a conjecture about the post-prison effects of institutional involvements. Prison homosexuality is viewed, even by many of those involved, as temporary, with heterosexual relations to be resumed upon release. We cannot answer definitely whether this actually happens. Some information was gleaned from conversations with all women parole officers in the state. While the parole agents had little knowledge of the patterns of homosexual behavior at the institution, they agreed that most of the women they knew who had had homosexual experiences in prison returned to men upon release. The parole agents noted that the women who tended to continue playing a homosexual role were those who had made a greater commitment to homosexuality—the butches. However, the majority of the homosexual population are femme jailhouse turnouts who maintain a conception of themselves as bisexual. If we are correct that homosexual involvements begun in prison do not, in fact, usually persist on release, it is reasonable to raise the question of how problematic prison homosexuality is in terms of long-run rehabilitation goals of the institution.

Our study has focused attention on deviance in an institutional setting but our findings, however tentative, raise questions for research in the society at large. Unanswered questions involve delineation of the principal homosexual roles in the free community and the procedures by which women are induced to indulge in deviant sexual behavior outside the prison.

For example, it would be important to know whether initial deviant

[28] Patrick J. Driscoll, "Factors Related to the Institutional Adjustment of Prison Inmates," *The Journal of Abnormal and Social Psychology*, 47 (July, 1952), pp. 593-596.

involvement leads to membership in an organized deviant group. Any follow-up study of parolees would require knowledge of the gay life in the larger community, since it is not known whether there are short-lived homosexual periods in civilian life as there are in prison and whether or not true homosexuals in the community need to utilize protective mechanisms such as giving up the work. Adequate description of the sexual deviance of the female prisoner awaits further inquiry into deviant behavior of women in the world outside the prison.

Acknowledgments

Akers, Ronald L., Norman S. Hayner and Werner Gruninger. "Homosexual and Drug Behavior in Prison: A Test of the Functional and Importation Models of the Inmate System." *Social Problems* 21 (1974): 410–422. Reprinted with the permission of the University of California Press. Copyright 1974 by the Society for the Study of Social Problems. Courtesy of Yale University Sterling Memorial Library.

Branch, Taylor. "Closets of Power." *Harper's* 265 (1982): 34, 36–50. Copyright by *Harper's Magazine*. All rights reserved. Reprinted from the October issue by special permission. Courtesy of the *Harper's Magazine*.

Coggeshall, John M. "'Ladies' behind Bars: A Liminal Gender as Cultural Mirror." *Anthropology Today* 4 (1988): 6–8. Reprinted with the permission of the Royal Anthropological Institute of Great Britain and Ireland. Courtesy of Yale University Kline Science Library.

Cohan, A.S. "Obstacles to Equality: Government Responses to the Gay Rights Movement in the United States." *Political Studies* 30 (1982): 59–76. Reprinted with the permission of Basil Blackwell Ltd. Courtesy of Yale University Sterling Memorial Library.

Cook, Blanche Wiesen. "Female Support Networks and Political Activism: Lillian Wald, Crystal Eastman, Emma Goldman." *Chrysalis* 3 (1977): 43–61. Courtesy of Yale University Sterling Memorial Library.

Davis, Alan J. "Sexual Assaults in the Philadelphia Prison System and Sheriff's Vans." *Trans*-action 6 (1968): 8–16. Reprinted with the permission of Société Transaction. Courtesy of Yale University Sterling Memorial Library.

Davis, Jeffrey S. "Military Policy toward Homosexuals: Scientific, Historical, and Legal Perspectives." *Military Law Review* 27-100-131 (1991): 55–108. Courtesy of Yale University Law Library.

D'Emilio, John. "Making and Unmaking Minorities: The Tensions between Gay Politics and History." *Review of Law & Social Change* 14 (1986): 915–922. Reprinted with the permission of the *Review of Law & Social Change*. Courtesy of the *Review of Law & Social Change*.

Epstein, Steven. "Gay Politics, Ethnic Identity: The Limits of Social Constructionism." *Socialist Review* 93/94 (1987): 9–54. Reprinted with the permission of the Center for Social Research and Education. Courtesy of the *Socialist Review*.

Escoffier, Jeffrey. "Sexual Revolution and the Politics of Gay Identity." *Socialist Review* 82/83 (1985): 119–153. Reprinted with the permission of the Center for Social Research and Education. Courtesy of the *Socialist Review*.

Giallombardo, Rose. "Social Roles in a Prison for Women." *Social Problems* 13 (1966): 268–288. Reprinted with the permission of the University of California Press. Copyright 1966 by the Society for the Study of Social Problems. Courtesy of Yale University Sterling Memorial Library.

Gibson, James L. and Kent L. Tedin. "The Etiology of Intolerance of Homosexual Politics." *Social Science Quarterly* 69 (1988): 587–604. Reprinted from *Social Science Quarterly*, by permission of the authors and the University of Texas Press. Courtesy of Yale University Sterling Memorial Library.

Jernigan, David. "Why Gay Leaders Don't Last: The First Ten Years after Stonewall." *Out/Look* (1988): 33–49. Reprinted with the permission of *Out/Look*. Courtesy of Wayne R. Dynes.

Johansson, Warren. "Periods of the Movement." *Caucus of Lesbian and Gay History Newsletter* 4 (1990): 15–18. Reprinted with the permission of the *Caucus of Lesbian and Gay History Newsletter*. Courtesy of Wayne R. Dynes.

Johnson, Edwin. "The Homosexual in Prison." *Social Theory and Practice* 1 (1971): 83–95. Reprinted with the permission of *Social Theory and Practice*. Copyright 1971. Courtesy of the *Social Theory and Practice*.

Knopp, Lawrence. "Social Theory, Social Movements and Public Policy: Recent Accomplishments of the Gay and Lesbian Movements in Minneapolis, Minnesota." *International Journal of Urban and Regional Research* 11 (1987): 243–261. Reprinted with the permission of Basil Blackwell Ltd. Courtesy of Yale University Social Science Library.

Martin, Robert A. "Student Homophile League: *Founder's Retrospect.*" *Cabirion and Gay Books Bulletin* 9 (1983): 30–33. Reprinted with the permission of the Gay Academic Union, Inc. Courtesy of Wayne R. Dynes.

Sagarin, Edward. "Prison Homosexuality and Its Effect on Post-Prison Sexual Behavior." *Psychiatry* 39 (1976): 245–257. Reprinted with the permission of *Psychiatry*. Courtesy of Yale University Medical Library.

Tucker, Donald. "A Punk's Song: View from the Inside." In Anthony M. Scacco, Jr., ed., *Male Rape* (New York: AMS Press, 1982): 58–79. Reprinted with the permission of AMS Press Inc. Courtesy of AMS Press Inc.

Ward, David A. and Gene G. Kassebaum. "Homosexuality: A Mode of Adaptation in a Prison for Women." *Social Problems* 12 (1964): 159–177. Reprinted with the permission of the University of California Press. Copyright 1964 by the Society for the Study of Social Problems. Courtesy of Yale University Sterling Memorial Library.

Williams, Colin J. and Martin S. Weinberg. "Being Discovered: A Study of Homosexuals in the Military." *Social Problems* 18 (1970): 217–227. Reprinted with the permission of the University of California Press. Copyright 1971 by the Society for the Study of Social Problems. Courtesy of Yale University Sterling Memorial Library.

Wittman, Carl. "Refugees from Amerika: A Gay Manifesto." In Joseph A. McCaffrey, ed., *The Homosexual Dialectic* (Englewood Cliffs, NJ: Prentice-Hall, 1972): 157–171. Reprinted with the permission of Simon & Schuster, Inc. Courtesy of Yale University Cross Campus Library.

Index